THE ULTIMATE ENCYCLOPEDIA OF

SOCCER

Copyright © Carlton Books Ltd
1994, 1995, 1996, 1997, 1998, 1999

First published by Carlton Books Ltd,
1997

10 9 8 7 6 5 4 3 2 1

Sixth edition 1999

A CIP catalogue record for this book is
available from the British Library

ISBN 1 85868 848 5

Project editor: Martin Corteel
Project art direction: Russell Porter
Production: Sarah Schuman
Design: Stephen Cary

Printed and bound in Spain

Carlton Books Ltd
20 St Anne's Court
Wardour Street
London W1V 3AW

To Aidan, Lyndon, Noel and Christy

GENERAL EDITOR

KEIR RADNEDGE is the editor of
the magazine *World Soccer*, the
acknowledged authority on the international game. He has also worked
on the *Daily Mail* sports desk since
1975, and broadcasts regularly on
international football for BBC Radio.
He has scripted World Cup and many
other football videos, includes the
acclaimed *World Club Directory*
among previous publications and
was the 1990 British Sports Magazine
Writer of the Year.

OTHER CONTRIBUTORS

COLIN BENSON is well known
around the British game for his work
in myriad media activities, including
club programmes, soccer videos, local
radio commentaries and freelance
contributions to many magazines.

IAN CRUISE, a self-confessed
Luton Town fan, began his career in
journalism with Hayters Sports
Agency in London in 1986. Four
years later he moved on to *Shoot!* magazine where he spent seven years as
a feature writer and sub-editor.

KEN GOLDMAN, has been edi-
tor of *Soccer Coach Magazine* for 27
years and editor of *Normidian*, the
North Middlesex referee's magazine, for 13 years. He has held
coaching qualifications for 30 years
and has been a qualified referee
since 1971.

JAMES HOOLEY joined the *Daily
Mail* sports staff in London in 1976
and is now Chief Sub-Editor. He
also reports on Premier League
matches and basketball and has contributed to other soccer books,
including *The Official History of
Arsenal FC*.

MARK IRWIN is a past editor of
Shoot! magazine, who became, in
1993, a partner in the Teamwork
Sports Agency of London before
joining the *Daily Mirror*.

JOHN KELLY is a London-based
soccer writer, statistician and
researcher. He is a regular contrib-
utor to *World Soccer* magazine and
helps compile its comprehensive
results and tables service. He worked
as a consultant for one of the biggest
play-by-mail football games. He also
contributes to other soccer magazines around the world and claims
Portman Road as his spiritual home.

DAVID PROLE was a veteran of
what used to be known as Fleet Street
before retiring from his position as
a pools specialist on *The People*.
Born on Merseyside and later a graduate of the *Hampstead and Highgate
Express*, he is the author of seven
books on soccer, including *Football
in London* and *Come On The Reds*,
an original history of Liverpool FC.

GENERAL EDITOR'S ACKNOWLEDGEMENTS

Thanks are due to all those, seen
and unseen, who worked so hard
and with such enthusiasm to bring an
ambitious project to fruition. Particular thanks to all my fellow writers
for their contributions on the many
and varied aspects of football considered in these pages. Thanks also
to Steve Dobell, Peter Arnold and
David Ballheimer for their work on
the text; Sharon Hutton and Gina
Wardrop for picture research; to
special photographer Christine Don-
nier-Valetin; and to Nick Cooper
and John Lucas for their help with the
illustrations. To Ian Cook and Mark
Wylie, curators of the Arsenal and the
Manchester United Museums respectively, for their assistance with special
photography. Last, but not least, to
Martin Corteel, Executive Editor
of Carlton Books, for keeping the
show on the road from initial plan-
ning meeting to final print run.

OPPOSITE: PARTY TIME *The Manchester
United players celebrate their last-
gasp treble-clinching triumph as they
overcame Bayern Munich to add the
European Champions Cup to their
domestic and Premiership and FA Cup
double.* **OVERLEAF: DESCHAMPS** *France's
history-making captain holds the
World Cup aloft.*

THE ULTIMATE ENCYCLOPEDIA OF
SOCCER

The definitive illustrated guide to world soccer

Sixth Edition

General Editor: Keir Radnedge
Executive Editor of World Soccer magazine

Foreword by Gary Lineker

CARLTON

CONTENTS

COMPETITIONS *Madrid Champions Cup*

STADIUMS *Stadio Giuseppe Meazza*

PLAYERS *England's Alan Shearer*

7 FOREWORD BY GARY LINEKER

8 THE EARLY HISTORY OF FOOTBALL
Looks at the village contests that were the forerunners of Association Football; the codification of the game in the 19th century; and the expansion of the game world-wide.

14 THE MAJOR COMPETITIONS
Describes principal club competitions in Europe, the Americas and the rest of the world and leading international competitions, including the World Cup from 1930 to 1998.

50 THE COUNTRIES
Describes the great moments in the history of the main soccer nations, and lists the date of foundation and date of affiliation to FIFA of all the soccer playing nations of the world.

80 THE GREAT CLUBS
Profiles of 43 of the world's most prestigious teams from Ajax Amsterdam to Vasco da Gama, plus listing of principal honours.

103 LEGENDS
Pays tribute to 10 of soccer's all-time greats.

124 THE GREAT PLAYERS
Profiles 226 of the game's famous names from Florian Albert of Hungary to Andoni Zubizarreta of Spain, with a verdict on what made that player great.

168 THE GREAT MATCHES
Looks at 21 epic encounters, encompassing the 1923 "White Horse Cup Final" and the semi-final of the 1990 World Cup that reduced Gazza to tears.

178 THE STADIUMS
Provides a paean to soccer's shrines from the twin towers of Wembley to the high-tech splendour of the Stadio Giuseppe Meazza in Milan.

188 THE BUSINESS OF FOOTBALL
Reviews the operations of the soccer media, the wheeling and dealing in the boardrooms and the political manoeuvring in the game's administrative citadels.

196 THE LAWS AND TACTICS
Explains the laws of the game and outlines the history of soccer tactics, including team formations, attacking and defensive strategies and set-pieces.

206 EQUIPMENT
Showcases the boots and the balls, the shorts and the shirts that have been integral to the soccer scene from the turn of the century to the present day.

212 SOCCER CULTURE
Celebrates the fans who are the lifeblood of the game: the dancing and chanting, the face painting and the community singing.

220 SCANDALS & DISASTERS
Describes the Babylonian excesses of betting, bribery, drugs and drinking and the disasters that have befallen the game, such as air crashes and stadium accidents.

226 FOOTBALL IN GREAT BRITAIN AND IRELAND
Provides statistics on the principal league and cup competitions and the international playing record of the four home countries and the Republic of Ireland.

244 SOCCER CHRONOLOGY

246 MAJOR SOCCER AWARDS

248 INDEX

FOREWORD
BY GARY LINEKER

So far as I'm concerned, the best thing about football is playing it. But there are other pleasures to be had from football – and watching it, reading about it, talking about it and arguing about it are some of them. I suggest anybody who reads this encyclopedia will not only enjoy it for its own sake, but will be much better informed afterwards for those discussions and friendly arguments. What I like particularly about it is its international perspective.

My footballing career has been centred mainly on three English cities, Leicester, Liverpool and London, on a great Spanish city, Barcelona, and on Nagoya, a major port and key area for Japan's car industry.

At Leicester, my family were so keen on football they even moved house to ensure that I attended a football school rather than a rugby one. Nobody thought this odd, and nobody thought my first footballing move – from Filbert Street to Goodison Park – was odd either. Everton rivalled Liverpool as the strongest side in the country, and it certainly

was a good opportunity for me. Moving to Barcelona was different. Some shook their heads and said it was a mistake to leave "the strongest league in the world".

I don't agree with this assessment. It is the hardest league in the world, perhaps. But I think there are leagues where sharper, more skilful football is played. This is no reflection on British players. The game is more demanding than ever now, and with a 20-club Premier League and two Cup competitions, playing in England at the top level is very tiring. By comparison, the players in Serie A, the top Italian division, can more consistently produce their best form, and play better football, because they are fresher. There are fewer pressure games – this is true in Spain, too – and players can rise to the big occasion more readily. I hope the situation will improve in Britain as we go through the rigours of qualifying for the World Cup in 1998, especially since the Home nations missed out in 1994.

I undoubtedly enjoyed one of my best club footballing memories with Barcelona – winning the European

Cup-winners' Cup in 1989, an experience that compares with the two unforgettable games at Wembley in 1991 where Spurs beat Arsenal and then Forest to win the FA Cup.

I knew there was no danger that this book would take the blinkered view that many English soccer followers have in undervaluing overseas football compared to our domestic game. The general editor, Keir Radnedge, is not editor of the magazine *World Soccer* for nothing, and I recall talking to him when he was invited by the J-League to study the boom in Japan, where I finished my playing career. He shared my enthusiasm about the prospects there.

In fact, this book covers the world game in such depth, that I don't mind admitting that a number of the 200 or so international footballers in the Great Players section were relatively new to me. There's a great deal of new and fascinating information about equipment, stadiums, culture, and all aspects of football. For me, it certainly is the "ultimate" encyclopedia of football. I hope you get as much pleasure from it as I do.

THE EARLY HISTORY OF FOOTBALL

The precise origin of Association football is unknown. Its modern format of 11 players against 11 in a confined area can be attributed to the British in the nineteenth century, but there is evidence of a form of football being played in China long before Julius Caesar brought the Roman game of harpastum to Britain.

AN ANCIENT BALL GAME

China provides history's first football report, in the writings of the Han Dynasty 2000 years ago. Then Japan supported their bid to win hosting rights for the 2002 World Cup by noting 14-century-old records of a local game called kenatt. The rules may have changed down the centuries but the pursuit of what we term a football has remained one of man's most consistent entertainments.

It was just so for the Greeks and the Romans. Pollux describes the pastime of harpastum in the following terms: "The players divided themselves into two bands. The ball was thrown upon the line in the middle. At the two ends behind the places where the players were stationed there were two other lines (which would seem to be equivalent to modern goal-lines), beyond which they tried to carry it, a feat that could not be done without pushing one another backward and forward." This suggests that harpastum was the origin of both rugby football and association football.

Ball games in Britain seem to have started as annual events staged over Shrovetide. As a rule these contests began in the market-place and involved two teams of unlimited numbers trying to propel a ball into the opposite side's goal, which was usually some convenient spot not too remote from the centre of town.

It was very hostile, violent, and extremely dangerous. Householders had to barricade their lower windows as the mobs did battle along the streets. The hero was the lucky player who eventually grounded the ball in goal. Not that it was always a ball. The followers of the rebel leader Jack Cade kicked a pig's bladder in the streets of London. In Chester the object of the boot was a little more distasteful. There the game originated as a celebration of victory over the marauding Danes, and the head of one of the vanquished army was

AN ANCIENT SPORT *This early drawing confirms that a game similar to football was played in a confined area as early as the 16th century*

BLOWING UP THE BALL FOR PALLO *It is assumed that Pallo was a forerunner to football*

used as a football. Later generations were content to boot a leather ball at their Shrove Tuesday festivals.

There is a record of London schoolboys playing organized football before Lent in 1175, and so popular had the game become in the streets of London in the reign of Edward II that the merchants, fearing this most robust and violent activity was affecting their trade, petitioned the king to prohibit the game. On April 13, 1314, Edward II issued the following proclamation forbidding the practice as leading to a breach of the peace: "Forasmuch as there is great noise in the city caused by hustling over large balls, from which many evils may arise, which God forbid; we command and forbid on behalf of the King, on pain of imprisonment, such game to be used in the city in future."

This was just one of many attempts to stamp out this popular activity. In 1349 Edward III tried to put an end to football because he felt the young men of the day were spending more time playing football than practising archery or javelin throwing. He commanded his sheriffs to suppress "such idle practices". Similar orders were issued by Richard II, Henry IV and James III, without any lasting effect. One such Royal proclamation in 1491 forbade the people to participate in football and golf: it was to be an offence if "in a place of the realme ther be used futeball, golfe, or other sik unprofitable sports."

Despite these spoilsport measures the game flourished in the Tudor and Stuart epoch. It took Cromwell to effectively suppress the activity, after which the game did not come back into vogue until the Restoration. Samuel Pepys, writing a hundred years after the event, describes how, in the great freeze of January 1565, "the streets were full of footballs." There were still no rules, the game basically being an excuse for an uninhibited ruck. Sir Thomas Elyot, in a well-known book entitled *The Governour*, published in 1564, waxes wroth against football, which he dismisses as "beastlike furie and extreme violence deserving only to be put in per-

A SPLASH FROM THE PAST *The men of Ashbourne continue their tradition of the annual Shrove Tuesday game. The game dates back to the 16th century, but this encounter took place in 1952 with the rules almost entirely unchanged*

petual silence". But the lusty men of England were not to be denied their vigorous activity. During the reign of Elizabeth I football was played widely, and, in the absence of rules and referees, there were frequent and sometimes fatal accidents.

In the seventeenth century, football appears to have had various titles. In Cornwall it was termed "hurling", a name subsequently applied to hockey; while in Norfolk and parts of Suffolk it was known as "campynge" or "camping".

Carew, in his *Survey of Cornwall*, suggests that the Cornish were the first to adopt regular rules. He records that no one was permitted to "but or handfast under the girdle", which presumably meant that tripping, charging, or grabbing below the waist was prohibited. He goes on to state that it was also not allowed "to deal a foreball", which suggests that it was forbidden to pass forward, another similarity with Rugby football.

Such rules were obviously not in general use. Strutt, in his *Sports and Pastimes*, describes football thus: "When a match at Football is made, two parties, each containing an equal number of competitors, take the

field and stand between two goals, placed at the distance of eighty or one hundred yards the one from the other. The goal is usually made with two sticks driven into the ground about two or three feet apart. The ball, which is commonly made of blown bladder and cased with leather, is delivered in the midst of the ground, and the object of each party is to drive it through the goal of their antagonists, which being achieved, the game is won.

"The abilities of the performers are best displayed in attacking and defending the goals, and hence the pastime was more frequently called a goal at Football than a game at Football. When the exercise becomes exceeding violent, the players kick each other's shins without the least ceremony, and some of them are over-thrown at the hazard of their limbs."

It seems that "hacking" was as keenly relished in those days as it was when the game's modern renaissance began in the mid-19th century. By the end of the 20th century, of course, the very idea of "hacking" for its own sake would be considered with horror.

ROYAL DISPLEASURE *Football in the streets of London at the time of Edward II*

CODIFICATION OF ASSOCIATION FOOTBALL

Football's sometime image as the "working man's game" overlooks one salient piece of history: it was the public schools, and Oxford and Cambridge Universities in particular, which brought shape and order out of the almost aimless fury of multitudinous violence.

Nearly all the schools and numerous clubs which had mushroomed in the wake of the Industrial Revolution had their own sets of rules. Some catered for the ball to be handled, some did not; some limited the number of participants on each side, some did not. Some favoured hacking and tripping and grounding opponents by hand, while others barred these things.

The overall situation was chaotic

to say the least so, in 1846 the first serious attempts to unify a code of rules was instigated at Cambridge University by Messrs H. de Winton and J.C. Thring. They met representatives from the major public schools with a view to formulating a standardized set of rules.

Their deliberations took seven hours 55 minutes and were published as the Cambridge Rules. These were well accepted and years afterwards, with very few alterations made, became the Association Rules. Unfortunately there is no copy of the original regulations, and the earliest set of rules to which those of the Football Association may be traced are those issued by Mr Thring in 1862 when he was the Assistant

Rules

THE SIMPLEST GAME

1. A goal is scored whenever the ball is forced through the goal and under the bar, except it be thrown by hand.

2. Hands may be used only to stop a ball and place it on the ground before the feet.

3. Kicks must be aimed only at the ball.

4. A player may not kick the ball whilst in the air.

5. No tripping up or heel kicking allowed.

6. Whenever a ball is kicked beyond the side flags, it must be returned by the player who kicked it, from the spot it passed the flag line, in a straight line towards the middle of the ground.

7. When a ball is kicked behind the line of goal, it shall be kicked off from that line by one of the side whose goal it is.

8. No player may stand within six paces of the kicker when he is kicking off.

9. A player is "out of play" immediately he is in front of the ball, and must return behind the ball as soon as possible. If the ball is kicked by his own side past a player, he may not touch or kick it, or advance, until one of the other side has first kicked it, or one of his own side has been able to kick it on a level with, or in front of him.

10. No charging allowed when a player is out of play; that is, immediately the ball is behind him.

C.W. ALCOCK *One of football's first and best administrators*

Master at Uppingham. These were the rules for what he termed "The Simplest Game," and as they are so important to the development of Association football as we know it today they are worthy of reproduction (above).

The Football Association came into being in October 1863 following a meeting at the Freemasons' Tavern, Great Queen Street, London, "for the purpose of forming an Association with the object of establishing a definite code of rules for the regulation of the game".

Representatives of all the major clubs were present and they appointed Mr A. Pember as president and Mr E.C. Morley as honorary secretary. Mr Morley was asked to write to the captains of the leading schools inviting them to co-operate in the movement but at a second

meeting, held a few days later, it was revealed that replies from Harrow, Charterhouse and Westminster indicated they preferred to cling to their own rules.

At a third meeting a letter of acceptance was read from Mr Thring of Uppingham School and considerable progress was made with the laws, which were published on December 1, 1863. At the sixth meeting held that month the first committee of the Association was appointed.

It consisted of: Mr J.F. Alcock (Forest Club) — an elder brother of C.W. Alcock who came upon the scene later — Mr Warren (War Office); Mr Turner (Crystal Palace); Mr Steward (Crusaders) and the treasurer Mr Campbell (Blackheath); together with Pember and Morley.

It was at this meeting, however, that the "split" between the Rugby Unionists (as they were now termed) and the Associationists occurred. Blackheath withdrew their membership, though Campbell agreed to stay in office as treasurer.

Although there were no further major upsets it seems there was still some uneasiness about the way the game should be played.

At the Association's annual meeting in February, 1866, a representative of the No Names (from Kilburn, north London) complained that only Barnes and Crystal Palace were playing strictly to Association rules. All present, apart from the Lincoln club who withdrew, agreed that no member clubs should ever play under any other rules.

The Association and the game grew steadily in public favour following the introduction of the FA Cup and international fixtures but the comparatively peaceful progress enjoyed until 1880 was followed by a decade of drastic reforms.

The number of the rules of the Association had by now increased from 10 to 15. Scotland still refused to adopt the English throw-in, or the English understanding of the offside rule; apart from that the two Associations were on friendly terms with each other.

But there loomed another crisis which was to become as significant as that which separated the Associationists from the Rugby followers. It was the advent of the paid player — the first professionals.

By now the membership of the FA, including clubs and affiliated associations, amounted to 128, of which 80 belonged to the South of England, 41 to the North, six to Scotland and one to Australia.

Amid persistent rumours that many of the northern contingent were paying men to play for them the following new rule (No 16) was added in 1882: "That any member of a club receiving remuneration or consideration of any sort above his actual expenses and any wages actually lost by any such player taking part in any match, shall be debarred from taking part in either cup, inter Association, or International contests,

OPIUM OF THE PEOPLE *Hampton scores for Aston Villa in the 1905 FA Cup Final against Newcastle at Crystal Palace*

and any club employing such player shall be excluded from this Association."

The liberty to pay "wages lost" was extensively abused and this falling away from amateurism was seen by those in the south as a reflection of an unsportsmanlike spirit spreading through Northern and Midlands clubs.

Football had flourished with far greater rapidity in Scotland than in the rest of the UK and English clubs looked north of the border to strengthen their teams.

The FA at first turned a blind eye, but its hand was forced by the Sheffield, Lancashire, and Birmingham Associations, each of which held inquiries into charges of professionalism. In January 1883 an FA commission was appointed to look into the allegations. It consisted of: C.W. Alcock, N.L. Jackson, J.H. Cofield, T. Hindle and J.R. Harvey. They proved nothing. Yet the disquiet amongst the best amateur clubs continued and there was a veiled threat by some to boycott the

FA Cup at the commencement of the 1883–84 season.

The row came to a head early in 1884 when the Upton Park Club lodged a complaint against Preston North End on the grounds of professionalism. The case attracted wide publicity and when William Sudell, the president of the Preston club and in effect the manager, admitted that they did pay their players and that he could prove that nearly every other important club in Lancashire and the Midlands did likewise, the cat was out of the bag.

Preston were disqualified from that season's FA Cup but the frankness of Sudell's confession brought home to the FA councillors the need to face reality. At their next committee meeting C.W. Alcock proposed "that the time has come for the legalization of professionalism". This was seconded by Dr Morley but was by no means a unanimous decision and a concerted battle to repress the move raged until July 1885 when the football professional was at last legalized.

The amateur/professional dispute rumbled on for years and affected other countries as well. In Argentina in the late 1920s amateur and professional leagues existed briefly in competition and it was the growth of professionalism which helped lead to the foundation of the World Cup, while the amateur-based Olympic Games lost credibility as a representation of the true strengths of each nation.

Simultaneously, British opposition to broken-time payments — the practice of making up players' wages for pay lost while playing football — provoked the departure of the four Home Countries from FIFA. This cost them the right to participate in the first three World Cups, prior to the outbreak of World War II. And, as the Hungarians proved in 1953, it also hindered seriously the technical development of the British game.

Yet, only 13 years later, England were celebrating victory in the World Cup. The modern football had, apparently, rolled full circle.

FOOTBALL DIASPORA

The British were the original missionaries of modern, organised football. As communications and travel developed, so sailors, soldiers, merchants, engineers, teachers, students and other professional classes took their sports — cricket and football — around the world.

Local people joined in and football, consequently, gained universal popularity. Towards the end of the nineteenth century the game invaded Austria. There was a sizeable British colony in Vienna and their influence is manifest in the names of the two oldest clubs, the 1st Vienna FC and the Vienna Cricket and Football Club, from which FK Austria descended.

One of Vienna Cricket's keenest members was a little inside-forward named Hugo Meisl, who was to become an influential secretary of the Austrian Football Association. He recalled that the first ever game staged in Austria proper was between the Cricketers and Vienna on November 15, 1894. Cricketers won 4–0. In 1897 M.D. Nicholson was posted to the Vienna office of Thomas Cook and Sons and he became the most prominent English player in Austria's soccer history and the first president of the Austrian Football Union.

It was Meisl, though, who did most to spread the game on the continent. It was he who provided the driving force behind the launch of the Mitropa Cup — forerunner of today's European club events — and the Nations Cup competitions which popularized the game in central Europe.

Football has flourished in Hungary for longer than in almost any other European country. A young student returning from England imported the first football in the 1890s and two Englishmen, Arthur Yolland and Ashton, were included in the first Hungarian team. Before the First World War English teams had visited and impressed.

In Italy too the English played a great part in developing the game, as the names of some of the clubs reflect: Genoa Football and Cricket Club (founded by Englishmen in 1892) and Milan (not Milano). The game was introduced to Italy by a Turin businessman, Edoardo Bosio, in 1887, but Genoa were the first great club.

English boys at boarding school are claimed to have brought a rough type of football to Germany as early as 1865, though German football owes much to the enthusiasm of the two Schricker brothers. They actually borrowed money from their mother to help finance the first foreign tour ever made by a Football Association team, in 1899, which was a mixture of amateur and professional players. Steve Bloomer, the England and Derby County inside-right, went to Germany to coach and was interned during the First World War as was the highly influential coach, Jimmy Hogan.

Hogan was also to play a big part in the development of Dutch football. By 1908 Holland had 96 clubs and a competent national side under the direction of former England international Edgar Chadwick.

Football was introduced to Russia in 1887 by two Englishmen, the Charnock brothers, who ran a mill at Orekhovo near Moscow. They acquired equipment from England but had insufficient money for boots. Clement Charnock overcame the problem by getting a strap piercer at the mill to attach studs to the players' ordinary footwear. The Russians took to the game eagerly and by the late 1890s a Moscow League was in operation — the Charnocks' team, now called Morozovisti, winning the championship for the first five years.

The first continental country to master football was perhaps Denmark. Coached by English professionals the Danes were the outstanding continental side in Europe in the early part of the twentieth century and reached the Final of the Olympic Games in 1908, where they lost, unluckily, 2–0 to Great Britain.

It had all started when an English boy studying at Soro Akademi, a famous Danish public school, received a football from home. There were other links too. The English "Football Club" was formed in Copenhagen in 1879 and two Englishmen, Smart and Gibson, were instrumental in popularizing the game.

Football was exported to all four corners of the world. In Brazil, British sailors were the first to play on their shores in 1874, and in 1878 men from the ship *Crimea* allegedly put on an exhibition match for Princess Isabel. But Charles Miller, born in São Paulo, the son of English immigrants, who came to England to study and returned ten years later with kit and two new footballs after playing for Southampton, is acknowledged as the true inspiration of the game in Brazil. Miller encouraged the British workers in establishments such as the Gas Company, the London Bank and the São Paulo Railway and the founders of the São Paulo Athletic Club — which was then exclusively concerned with cricket — to form football teams. The first real match was staged in April 1894 with the Rail team beating the Gas team 4–2.

The first club comprising mainly Brazilians was established in 1898: the Associaciao Athletica Mackenzie College in São Paulo. Thus the game in South America is as old as it is on the European continent. The British influence is seen clearly in the names of some of the club sides: Corinthians in Brazil; Liverpool and Wanderers in Uruguay; and Everton and Rangers in Chile, while Argentina boasts Newell's Old Boys and River Plate.

In Argentina although football was begun in the last century by British residents of Buenos Aires, it was slow to catch on with the locals. The national side of 1911 was full of Englishmen, though one, Arnold Hutton, a star forward, declined to play in one match because he had agreed to play rugby for his club. But it was Italian immigrants who really triggered the game's popularity there, as indeed they did through much of Latin America.

In Africa not only the English but the French and, to a lesser extent, German and Portuguese colonial movements played predominant roles in introducing football. For Portugal, the investment paid off spectacularly: their outstanding team at the 1966 World Cup drew its finest players, Eusebio and Mario Coluna, from the colony of Mozambique.

Independence movements in Africa and Asia changed the balance of international football power. The traditionalist powers of Europe and South America now find themselves in a political minority within FIFA, the world governing body. Asia has 45 members and Africa 52 compared with Europe's 51 and South America's 10. Indeed, Europe has swollen in size in the early 1990s since the fragmentation of the former Soviet Union and Yugoslavia.

GOLD RUSH *Great Britain beat Denmark in the 1908 Olympic Games Final*

THE MAJOR COMPETITIONS

The international football programme has grown in piecemeal fashion since the first match between Scotland and England in November 1872. Some competitions, like the Mitropa Cup, faded and disappeared. But the strongest, like the World Cup for nations and the Copa Libertadores and the European club cups, flourished as a world-wide competitive structure developed.

First there was the British Home Championship, the South American Championship and the Mitropa Cup for continental Europe's top clubs, then the World Cup itself... by the start of the 1930s the foundations of today's international competitive structure had been laid. The 1950s brought a further expansion, with the success of the European club cups and the launch of the European Championship. Each developing geographical region copied the competitive structures of Europe.

Now the sheer weight of the international fixture list has led football's world governing body, FIFA, into designing a worldwide fixture schedule around which the game can organize into the next century.

To qualify for the World Cup, many nations play around a dozen matches. When the various club competitions are added, top players can face around 70 games year with very little let-up.

THE WORLD CUP

The World Cup was conceived by FIFA's founders, but the driving force behind its launch was Frenchman Jules Rimet, the president of both FIFA and the French federation in the 1920s. The British had shunned FIFA's first meeting in Paris in 1904, and by the time the inaugural World Cup tournament was introduced in 1930 they had both joined and then withdrawn from the world governing body over the question of broken time payments for amateurs.

Italy, Holland, Spain, Sweden and Uruguay all applied to stage the tournament, but the European countries withdrew after an impassioned plea from the Latin Americans, who in 1930 would be celebrating a hundred years of independence. Uruguay were to build a new stadium in Montevideo and would pay all travelling and hotel expenses for the competing nations. However, faced by a three-week boat trip each way, the Europeans were reluctant to participate, and two months before the competition not one European entry had been received. Meanwhile, Argentina, Brazil, Paraguay, Peru, Chile, Mexico and Bolivia had all accepted, as well as the United States.

The Latin American federations were bitter and threatened to withdraw from FIFA. Eventually France, Belgium, Yugoslavia and, under the influence of King Carol, Romania, all relented and travelled to Uruguay.

URUGUAY 1930
Triumph for ambitious party-throwers

Because of the limited response the 13 teams were split into four groups, with Uruguay, Argentina, Brazil and the USA the seeded nations.

On the afternoon of Sunday, July 13, France opened the tournament against Mexico, and in the 10th minute lost goalkeeper Alex Thepot, who was kicked on the jaw. Left-half Chantrel took over between the posts (there would be no substitutes

VIVE LA FRANCE *French coach Aime Jacquet shows off the World Cup trophy*

14

for another forty years), but even with 10 men the French proved too good. Goals by Laurent, Langiller and Maschinot gave them a 3–0 advantage before Carreno replied for Mexico. Maschinot then grabbed a second to complete a 4–1 victory for France.

Two days later France lost to Argentina through a goal scored by Monti, nine minutes from time. The game had ended in chaos when Brazilian referee Almeida Rego blew for time six minutes early as Langiller raced through for a possible equalizer. In their next match, against Mexico, Argentina brought in young Guillermo Stabile, known as "El Infiltrador". He scored three goals in Argentina's 6–3 victory – in a game of five penalties – and finished as the top scorer of the tournament.

Argentina topped Group 1, while from Group 2 Yugoslavia qualified with victories over Brazil and Bolivia. The USA were most impressive in Group 4, reaching the semi-final without conceding a goal. However, their hit-on-the-break tactics were no match for Argentina, who cruised into the Final 6–1. In the other semi-final Uruguay dispatched Yugoslavia by the same margin to set up a repeat of the 1928 Olympic Final.

On this occasion Pablo Dorado shot Uruguay into a 12th-minute lead but Peucelle equalized and Argentina forged ahead in the 35th minute with a disputed goal by Stabile – who the Urugayans claimed was offside! Excitement grew when Pedro Cea made it 2–2 just after the break. In the 65th minute outside-left Santos Iriarte made it 3–2 for Uruguay, who underlined their victory with a fourth goal, smashed into the net by Castro in the closing seconds.

ITALY 1934
Tetchy Europeans battle it out

RESPITE *Italy prepare for extra time*

Uruguay are the only World Cup winners in history who did not defend their title. Upset by the Europeans' reluctance to participate in 1930, and plagued by players' strikes, they stayed at home.

No fewer than 32 countries – 22 from Europe, eight from the Americas and one each from Asia and Africa – contested a qualifying series in which even hosts Italy had to take part, and before the competition proper got under way the USA beat Mexico in Rome, but then crashed 7–1 to Italy in Turin.

Of the 16 finalists, Italy and Hugo Meisl's "Wunderteam" were the clear favourites, though the Austrians, who were just past their peak, were taken to extra time by a spirited French side in the first knockout round. Belgium led Germany 2–1 at half-time, then crumbled as Conen, Germany's centre-forward, completed a hat-trick in a 5–2 win.

Brazil, beaten 3–1 by Spain, and Argentina, defeated 3–2 by Sweden, had travelled 8,000 miles to play one solitary game.

Spain forced Italy to a replay in the second round after a physical 1–1 draw was not resolved by extra time. In the replay, the following day, Meazza's 12th-minute header put Italy into the semi-finals. Austria, who led Hungary 2–0 after 51 minutes through Horwarth and Zischek, then found themselves in what Meisl described as "a brawl, not an exhibition of football". Sarosi replied for Hungary from the penalty spot, but the Magyars' comeback was spoiled when Markos foolishly got himself sent off.

Italy and Austria now faced each other in the semi-finals. A muddy pitch was not conducive to good football and Italy won when right-winger Guaita capitalized on a brilliant set-play routine, following a corner, to score in the 18th minute. Czechoslovakia, the conquerers of Romania and Switzerland joined Italy in the Final after a 3–1 victory over Germany, with two goals by Nejedly.

In the Final, Puc shot the Czechs into a deserved 70th-minute lead, Italian keeper Combi reacting late to the shot from 20 yards. Sobotka then squandered a fine opportunity and Svoboda rattled a post as the Czechs impressed with their short-passing precision. With eight minutes left the Slavs were still 1–0 ahead. Then left-winger Raimondo Orsi left Czech defenders in his wake as he dribbled through on goal. He shaped to shoot with his left but hit the ball with his right boot. The ball spun crazily goalwards, and though Planicka got his fingers to it, he could not prevent a goal. Schiavio grabbed the Italian winner seven minutes into extra time. Italy were World Champions.

FRANCE 1938
Italians make it two in a row

Europe was in turmoil, Argentina and Uruguay were absent but the tournament welcomed for the first time Cuba, Poland and Dutch East Indies.

1930	Pool 1							Pool 2									P	W	D	L	F	A	Pts	Semi-finals				
	France	4		Mexico	1			Yugoslavia	2		Brazil	1		Uruguay		2	2	0	0	5	0	4	Argentina	6	USA	1	ARGENTINA Botasso, Della Torre,
	Argentina	1		France	0			Yugoslavia	4		Bolivia	0		Romania		2	1	0	1	3	5	2	Uruguay	6	Yugoslavia	1	Paternoster, Evaristo J., Monti,
	Chile	3		Mexico	0			Brazil	4		Bolivia	0		Peru		2	0	0	2	1	4	0					Suarez, Peucelle, Varallo, Stabile,
	Chile	1		France	0				P	W	D	L	F	A	Pts	Pool 4												Ferreira (capt.), Evaristo M.
	Argentina	6		Mexico	3			Yugoslavia	2	2	0	0	6	1	4	USA	3		Belgium	0				Final				
	Argentina	3		Chile	1			Brazil	2	1	0	1	5	2	2	USA	3		Paraguay	0				Uruguay (1) 4		Argentina(2) 2		Leading scorers:
		P	W	D	L	F	A	Pts	Bolivia	2	0	0	2	0	8	0	Paraguay	1		Belgium	0			*Dorado, Cea,*		*Peucelle,*		8 Stabile (Argentina); 5 Cea
	Argentina	3	3	0	0	10	4	6	Pool 3								P	W	D	L	F	A	Pts	*Iriarte, Castro*		*Stabile*		(Uruguay).
	Chile	3	2	0	1	5	3	4	Romania	3		Peru	1		USA		2	2	0	0	6	0	4	URUGUAY Ballesteros, Nasazzi				
	France	3	1	0	2	4	3	2	Uruguay	1		Peru	0		Paraguay		2	1	0	1	1	3	2	(capt.), Mascheroni, Andrade,				
	Mexico	3	0	0	3	4	13	0	Uruguay	4		Romania	0		Belgium		2	0	0	2	0	4	0	Fernandez, Gestido, Dorado,				
																								Scarone, Castro, Cea, Iriarte.				

1934	First round				Second round				Semi-finals				Final				CZECHOSLOVAKIA Planicka (capt.),
	Italy	7	USA	1	Germany	2	Sweden	1	Czech.	3	Germany	1	Italy	(0) 2	Czech.	(0) 1*	Zenisek, Ctyroky, Kostalek,
	Czech.	2	Romania	1	Austria	2	Hungary	1	Italy	1	Austria	0	*Orsi, Schiavio*		*Puc*		Cambal, Kreil, Junek, Svoboda,
	Germany	5	Belgium	2	Italy	1	Spain	1*									Sobotka, Nejedly, Puc.
	Austria	3	France	2*	Italy	1	Spain	0®	Third place match				ITALY Combi (capt.), Monzeglio,				
	Spain	3	Brazil	1	Czech.	3	Switzerland	2	Germany	3	Austria	2	Allemandi, Ferraris IV, Monti,				Leading scorers:
	Switzerland	3	Holland	2									Bertolini, Guaita, Meazza, Schiavio,				4 Nejedly (Czechoslovakia),
	Sweden	3	Argentina	2									Ferrari, Orsi.				Schiavio (Italy), Conen (Germany).
	Hungary	4	Egypt	2													

*Notes: * After extra time ® Replay*

BACK TO BACK *Vittorio Pozzo brandishes the World Cup in Paris*

In the first round only Hungary, who eclipsed the Dutch East Indies 6–0, and France – 3–1 winners over Belgium – came through in 90 minutes, all the other ties going to extra time or replays. Defending champions Italy were saved by their goalkeeper Olivieri, who made a blinding save from Norwegian centre-forward Brunyldsen in the last minute of the game to earn extra time, and Piola struck to see them through.

Brazil emerged from the mud of Strasbourg after an 11-goal thriller. A Leonidas hat-trick gave the South Americans a 3–1 half-time lead, but the Poles ran riot after the break to force extra time. Willimowski netted four times but by then Leonidas had grabbed his fourth to help Brazil to a 6–5 win! The second round provided no shocks, though Brazil needed two games to eliminate Czechoslovakia and earn a semi-final joust with Italy, whose captain, Meazza, converted the winning penalty. In the other semi-final, Hungary beat Sweden, 5–1.

When Italy met Hungary in the final, Colaussi drilled Italy ahead in the sixth minute after a scintillating run almost the length of the field from Biavati, but Titkos equalized from close range within a minute. Then, with inside-forwards Meazza and Ferrari in dazzling form, Italy asserted themselves. Piola scored in the 15th minute, and Colaussi made it 3–1 in the 35th. In the 65th minute Sarosi forced the ball over the Italian line, but a magnificent back-heeled pass from Biavati set up Piola to smash in the decisive goal.

BRAZIL 1950
Hosts upstaged in final act

The first tournament after the war – for what was now known as the Jules Rimet Trophy – was to prove a thriller. Argentina refused to play in Brazil, and the Czechs and Scots declined to take their places, but England were there for the first time.

The competition was arranged, as in 1930, on a pool basis. Brazil won Pool 1 despite a 2–2 draw with Switzerland, and Uruguay topped two-team Pool 4, where they thrashed Bolivia 8–0. The shocks came in Pools 2 and 3. Italy started well enough, Riccardo Carapellese shooting them into a seventh-minute lead against Sweden. But by the break they were 2–1 down to goals from Jeppson and Sune Andersson. Jeppson grabbed another midway through the second half and, though Muccinelli replied and Carapellese hit the bar, this was Sweden's day. It was a setback the Italians were unable to overcome.

The greatest shock of all time, however, was to beset England. After a 2–0 victory over Chile, the game against the USA in Belo Horizonte seemed a formality. Instead it became a fiasco. England hit the bar and found goalkeeper Borghi unbeatable. Then in the 37th minute the impossible happened. Bahr shot from the left and Gaetjens got a touch with his head to divert the ball into the net. 1–0 to the USA!

There was no final in this competition, Brazil, Uruguay, Sweden and Spain qualifying for the Final Pool. The hosts were favourites as they faced Uruguay in the last game (a virtual final), a point ahead. A draw would make Brazil champions.

It proved a real thriller. Brazil's much-acclaimed inside-forward trio of Zizinho, Ademir and Jair, weaving gloriously through the Uruguayan defence, found goalkeeper Maspoli playing the game of his life. The giant Varela proved another stumbling block, as did Andrade. They cracked in the 47th minute, Friaca shooting past Maspoli. Uruguay's response was positive, and in the 65th minute Ghiggia's cross found Schiaffino unmarked – his thunderous shot gave Barbosa no hope. Brazil were shaken, the fizz went out of their game, and when Ghiggia ran in to shoot home in the 79th minute they were beaten. After 20 years the World Cup returned to Uruguay.

1938

First round

Switzerland	1	Germany	1*
Switzerland	4	Germany	2®
Cuba	3	Rumania	3*
Cuba	2	Rumania	1®
Hungary	6	Dutch E.Ind.	0
France	3	Belgium	1
Czech.	3	Holland	0*
Brazil	6	Poland	5*
Italy	2	Norway	1*

Second round

Sweden	8	Cuba	0
Hungary	2	Switzerland	0
Italy	3	France	1
Brazil	1	Czech.	1*
Brazil	2	Czech.	1®

Semi-finals

Italy	2	Brazil	1
Hungary	5	Sweden	1

Third place match

Brazil	4	Sweden	2

Final

Italy	(3) 4	Hungary (1) 2	
Colaussi (2),		*Titkos, Sarosi*	
Piola (2)			

ITALY Olivieri, Foni, Rava, Serantoni, Andreolo, Locatelli, Biavati, Meazza (capt.), Piola, Ferrari, Colaussi.

HUNGARY Szabo, Polgar, Biro, Szalay, Szucs, Lazar, Sas, Vincze, Sarosi (capt.), Szengeller, Titkos.

Leading scorers

8 Leonidas (Brazil); 7 Szengeller (Hungary); 5 Piola (Italy).

1950

First round Pool 1

Brazil	4	Mexico	0
Yugoslavia	3	Switzerland	0
Yugoslavia	4	Mexico	1
Brazil	2	Switzerland	2
Brazil	2	Yugoslavia	0
Switzerland	2	Mexico	1

	P	W	D	L	F	A	Pts
Brazil	3	2	1	0	8	2	5
Yugoslavia	3	2	0	1	7	3	4
Switzerland	3	1	1	1	4	6	3
Mexico	3	0	0	3	2	10	0

Pool 2

Spain	3	USA	1
England	2	Chile	0
USA	1	England	0
Spain	2	Chile	0
Spain	1	England	0
Chile	5	USA	2

	P	W	D	L	F	A	Pts
Spain	3	3	0	0	6	1	6
England	3	1	0	2	2	2	2
Chile	3	1	0	2	5	6	2
USA	3	1	0	2	4	8	2

Pool 3

Sweden	3	Italy	2
Sweden	2	Paraguay	2
Italy	2	Paraguay	0

	P	W	D	L	F	A	Pts
Sweden	2	1	1	0	5	4	3
Italy	2	1	0	1	4	3	2
Paraguay	2	0	1	1	2	4	1

Pool 4

Uruguay	8	Bolivia	0

	P	W	D	L	F	A	Pts
Uruguay	1	1	0	0	8	0	2
Bolivia	1	0	0	1	0	8	0

Final pool

Uruguay	2	Spain	2
Brazil	7	Sweden	1
Uruguay	3	Sweden	2
Brazil	6	Spain	1
Sweden	3	Spain	1
Uruguay	2	Brazil	1

	P	W	D	L	F	A	Pts
Uruguay	3	2	1	0	7	5	5
Brazil	3	2	0	1	14	4	4
Sweden	3	1	0	2	6	11	2
Spain	3	0	1	2	4	11	1

Deciding match

Uruguay	(0) 2	Brazil	(0) 1
Schiaffino,		*Friaca*	
Ghiggia			

URUGUAY Maspoli, Gonzales, M., Tejera, Gambetta, Varela, Andrade, Ghiggia, Perez, Miguez, Schiaffino, Moran.

BRAZIL Barbosa, Augusto, Juvenal, Bauer, Danilo, Bigode, Friaca, Ziziho, Ademir, Jair, Chico.

Leading scorers:

9 Ademir (Brazil); 6 Schiaffino (Uruguay); 5 Zarra (Spain).

*Notes: * After extra time ® Replay*

SWITZERLAND 1954
'Magic Magyars' found out by astute Germans

Hungary arrived in Zurich as the hottest ever World Cup favourites. The magic of Puskas, Hidegkuti and Kocsis had added a new dimension to the beautiful game and, what is more, had proved an unbeatable combination in the 1952 Olympic tournament.

No one was really surprised when the Magyars rattled in 17 goals in their opening pool matches against Korea and Germany. Kocsis scored four against the Germans but Hungary were left a significant legacy by their opponents, centre-half Werner Liebrich delivering a fateful kick on Puskas that caused him to retire from the match in the 30th minute. It was an injury from which he never fully recovered during the remainder

NOT SO FAST *Morlock gets one back*

of the tournament. Hungary of course cruised into the quarter-finals, where they dispatched Brazil 4–2, but Germany had to win a play-off with Turkey to earn the right to face Yugoslavia.

England began with a 4–4 draw with Belgium, yet secured a quarter-final place with a 2–0 win over Switzerland. The Scots were not so successful. They failed to score and were beaten by Austria and Uruguay,

neither of whom conceded a goal in their pool. Stanley Matthews and Schiaffino took the individual honours as Uruguay beat England 4–2, but the competition was sullied by a notorious clash between Brazil and Hungary, which was dubbed "The Battle of Berne". Three players were sent off, and a shameful fight ensued in the dressing-rooms afterwards. If that was infamous, then the Austria-Switzerland tie was incredible. The Swiss scored three in 20 minutes, and Austria replied with three in three minutes. In one seven-minute period, there were five goals! Eventually Austria came out 7–5 winners.

Puskas returned for the Final, but it was a mistake. Although he scored the opening goal in a devastating start which saw Hungary score twice in eight minutes, his ankle was not fully recovered. Morlock replied for Germany in the 11th minute and Rahn blasted in two fine goals – the last only seven minutes from time – to win it for Germany.

SWEDEN 1958
Brazil teach the world a football lesson

Brazil enthralled the world in this competition, which was notable for the emergence of 4–2–4 and the outstanding individual talents of stars such as Didi, Garrincha, Vava and the teenager Pele. France too were to perform with style, Just Fontaine and Raymond Kopa providing the magic, while hosts Sweden provided their share of surprises.

West Germany headed Pool 1, where Northern Ireland, who had eliminated Italy in the qualifying rounds, caused an upset by beating Czechoslovakia in a play-off to earn a quarter-final tie with France, who headed Pool 2 with Yugoslavia. Likewise Wales also made the quarter-finals, following a play-off with Hungary, and did themselves proud

---

1954

Pool 1

Yugoslavia	1	France	0
Brazil	5	Mexico	0
France	3	Mexico	2
Brazil	1	Yugoslavia	1

	P	W	D	L	F	A	Pts
Brazil	2	1	1	0	6	1	3
Yugoslavia	2	1	1	0	2	1	3
France	2	1	0	1	3	3	2
Mexico	2	0	0	2	2	8	0

Pool 2

Hungary	9	Korea	0
W. Germany	4	Turkey	1
Hungary	8	W. Germany	3
Turkey	7	Korea	0

	P	W	D	L	F	A	Pts
Hungary	2	2	0	0	17	3	4
W. Germany	2	1	0	1	7	9	2
Turkey	2	1	0	1	8	4	2
Korea	2	0	0	2	0	16	0

Play-off

W. Germany	7	Turkey	2

Pool 3

Austria	1	Scotland	0
Uruguay	2	Czech.	0
Austria	5	Czech.	0
Uruguay	7	Scotland	0

	P	W	D	L	F	A	Pts
Uruguay	2	2	0	0	9	0	4
Austria	2	2	0	0	6	0	4
Czech.	2	0	0	2	0	7	0
Scotland	2	0	0	2	0	8	0

Pool 4

England	4	Belgium	4
England	2	Switzerland	0
Switzerland	2	Italy	1
Italy	4	Belgium	1

	P	W	D	L	F	A	Pts
England	2	1	1	0	6	4	3
Italy	2	1	0	1	5	3	2
Switzerland	2	1	0	1	2	3	2
Belgium	2	0	1	1	5	8	1

Play-off

Switzerland	4	Italy	1

Quarter-finals

W. Germany	2	Yugoslavia	0
Hungary	4	Brazil	2
Austria	7	Switzerland	5
Uruguay	4	England	2

Semi-finals

W. Germany	6	Austria	1
Hungary	4	Uruguay	2

Third-place match

Austria	3	Uruguay	1

Final

W. Germany (2) 3		Hungary	(2) 2
Morlock,		Puskas, Czibor	
Rahn (2)			

WEST GERMANY: Turek, Posipal, Kohlmeyer, Eckel, Liebrich, Mai, Rahn, Morlock, Walter O., Walter F. (capt.), Schäfer.

HUNGARY: Grosics, Buzansky, Lantos, Bozsik, Lorant, Zakarias, Czibor, Kocsis, Hidegkuti, Puskas (capt.), Toth J.

Leading scorers
11 Kocsis (Hungary); 8 Morlock (W. Germany); 6 Probst (Austria), Hügi (Switzerland).

1958

Pool 1

W. Germany	3	Argentina	1
N. Ireland	1	Czech.	0
W.Germany	2	Czech.	2
Argentina	3	N. Ireland	1
W. Germany	2	N. Ireland	2
Czech.	6	Argentina	1

	P	W	D	L	F	A	Pts
W. Germany	3	1	2	0	7	5	4
Czech.	3	1	1	1	8	4	3
N. Ireland	3	1	1	1	4	5	3
Argentina	3	1	0	2	5	10	2

Play-off

N. Ireland	2	Czech.	1

Pool 2

France	7	Paraguay	3
Yugoslavia	1	Scotland	1
Yugoslavia	3	France	2
Paraguay	3	Scotland	2
France	2	Scotland	1
Yugoslavia	3	Paraguay	3

	P	W	D	L	F	A	Pts
France	3	2	0	1	11	7	4
Yugoslavia	3	1	2	0	7	6	4
Paraguay	3	1	1	1	9	12	3
Scotland	3	0	1	2	4	6	1

Pool 3

Sweden	3	Mexico	0
Hungary	1	Wales	1
Wales	1	Mexico	1
Sweden	2	Hungary	1
Sweden	0	Wales	0
Hungary	4	Mexico	0

	P	W	D	L	F	A	Pts
Sweden	3	2	1	0	5	1	5
Hungary	3	1	1	1	6	3	3
Wales	3	0	3	0	2	2	3
Mexico	3	0	1	2	1	8	1

Play-off

Wales	2	Hungary	1

Pool 4

England	2	Soviet Union	2
Brazil	3	Austria	0
England	0	Brazil	0
Soviet Union	2	Austria	0
Brazil	2	Soviet Union	0
England	2	Austria	2

	P	W	D	L	F	A	Pts
Brazil	3	2	1	0	5	0	5
England	3	0	3	0	4	4	3
Soviet Union	3	1	1	1	4	4	3
Austria	3	0	1	2	2	7	1

Play-off

Soviet Union	1	England	0

Quarter-finals

France	4	N. Ireland	0
W. Germany	1	Yugoslavia	0
Sweden	2	Soviet Union	0
Brazil	1	Wales	0

Semi-finals

Brazil	5	France	2
Sweden	3	W. Germany	1

Third place match

France	6	W. Germany	3

Final

Brazil	(2) 5	Sweden (1) 2	
Vava (2),		Liedholm	
Pele (2), Zagallo		Simonsson	

BRAZIL: Gilmar, Santos D., Santos N., Zito, Bellini (capt.), Orlando, Garrincha, Didi, Vava, Pele, Zagallo.

SWEDEN: Svensson, Bergmark, Axbom, Boerjesson, Gustavsson, Parling, Hamrin, Gren, Simonsson, Liedholm (capt.), Skoglund.

Leading scorers
13 Fontaine (France); 6 Pele (Brazil), Rahn (W. Germany); 5 Vava (Brazil), McParland (N..Ireland).

by limiting Brazil to one goal, inevitably scored by Pele. Brazil had comfortably emerged from Pool 4 without conceding a goal, but England were knocked out, when they lost 1–0 to Russia in another play-off.

The semi-finals pitted Sweden against West Germany and Brazil against France. Hans Schäfer blasted West Germany into the lead with a spectacular volley from 25 yards. Sweden's equalizer from Skoglund should not have been given – Liedholm blatantly controlling the ball with a hand before setting up the chance. Juskowiak was sent off in the 57th minute, and Sweden took full advantage to clinch their Final place with goals from Gren and Hamrin. Brazil took a second-minute lead against France thanks to a spectacular finish from Vava. Fontaine equalized within nine minutes, but Didi restored the lead for the South Americans, and in the second half young Pele ran riot with three more goals.

There was a sensational start to the Final, when Liedholm kept his poise and balance to shoot Sweden into a fourth-minute lead. It was the first time in the tournament that Brazil had been behind. Six minutes later it was 1–1. Garrincha exploded down the right, and cut the ball back for Vava to run on to and fire firmly past Svensson. This was proving a fascinating spectacle. Pele slammed a shot against a post, Zagallo headed out from beneath the bar. In the 32nd minute the Garrincha-Vava combination struck again, and when Pele made it 3–1 in the 55th minute with a touch of sheer magic, the game

LAP OF HONOUR *Brazil celebrate their first World Cup triumph in 1958*

was won. Bringing a dropping ball down on a thigh in a crowded penalty area, the youngster hooked it over his head, spun and volleyed thunderously into the net. Zagallo and Pele added further goals, either side of a dubious second Swedish goal from Agne Simonsson, who looked offside. There was no doubt that Brazil were the best in the world.

CHILE 1962
Brazil without Pele still can't be matched

Brazil retained their world crown as Garrincha took centre stage and 4–3–3 became the subtle change. But this was a World Cup marred by violence.

The Soviet Union and Yugoslavia comfortably overcame the Uruguayan and Colombian challenge in Group 1, while in Group 3 Brazil's only hiccup was a goalless draw with Czechoslovakia, who were to prove the surprise package of this tournament.

England got off to a bad start. Unable to break down the massed Hungarian defence after Springett was beaten by a thunderous long-range effort from Tichy, they equalized from a Ron Flowers penalty, but the impressive Albert clinched it for Hungary 18 minutes from time with a glorious individual goal. England did find some form to beat Argentina 3–1. Another Flowers penalty, a Bobby Charlton special and Jimmy Greaves clinched their first World Cup finals victory since 1954.

The Chile-Italy tie turned into a violent confrontation, with spitting, fighting, and two-footed tackles

intended to maim. That referee Ken Aston sent only two players off was amazing in a game that sullied the name of football. Brazil, however, continued to thrill, even without the injured Pele, who was to take no further part after the group match against Mexico. Garrincha mesmerized England to defeat, then took Chile apart in the semi-final, only to be sent off for retaliation.

In Vina del Mar a mere 5,000 watched Czechoslovakia earn their Final place at the expense of Yugoslavia, and the Czechs threatened to upset all the odds when Masopust cleverly gave them the lead over Brazil in the 16th minute. The equalizer, from Amarildo – Pele's replacement – was quickly registered but it was not until the 69th minute that Zito headed them into the lead. Vava made it 3–1 when goalkeeper Schroiff fumbled a lob.

SIMPLY THE BEST *Pele bides his time*

1962

Group 1

Uruguay	2	Colombia	1
Soviet Union	2	Yugoslavia	0
Yugoslavia	3	Uruguay	1
Soviet Union	4	Colombia	4
Soviet Union	2	Uruguay	1
Yugoslavia	5	Colombia	0

	P	W	D	L	F	A	Pts
Soviet Union	3	2	1	0	8	5	5
Yugoslavia	3	2	0	1	8	3	4
Uruguay	3	1	0	2	4	6	2
Colombia	3	0	1	2	5	11	1

Group 2

Chile	3	Switzerland	1
W. Germany	0	Italy	0

Chile	2	Italy	0
W. Germany	2	Switzerland	1
W. Germany	2	Chile	0
Italy	3	Switzerland	0

	P	W	D	L	F	A	Pts
W. Germany	3	2	1	0	4	1	5
Chile	3	2	0	1	5	3	4
Italy	3	1	1	1	3	2	3
Switzerland	3	0	0	3	2	8	0

Group 3

Brazil	2	Mexico	0
Czech.	1	Spain	0
Brazil	0	Czech.	0
Spain	1	Mexico	0
Brazil	2	Spain	1
Mexico	3	Czech.	1

	P	W	D	L	F	A	Pts
Brazil	3	2	1	0	4	1	5
Czech.	3	1	1	1	2	3	3
Mexico	3	1	0	2	3	2	2
Spain	3	1	0	2	2	3	2

Group 4

Argentina	1	Bulgaria	0
Hungary	2	England	1
England	3	Argentina	1
Hungary	6	Bulgaria	1
Argentina	0	Hungary	0
England	0	Bulgaria	0

	P	W	D	L	F	A	Pts
Hungary	3	2	1	0	8	2	5
England	3	1	1	1	4	3	3
Argentina	3	1	1	1	2	3	3
Bulgaria	3	0	1	2	1	7	1

Quarter-finals

Yugoslavia	1	W. Germany	0
Brazil	3	England	1
Chile	2	Soviet Union	1
Czech.	1	Hungary	0

Semi-finals

Brazil	4	Chile	2
Czech.	3	Yugoslavia	1

Third place match

Chile	1	Yugoslavia	0

Final

Brazil (1)3 Czech. (1)1
Amarildo, Zito, Vava   Masopust

BRAZIL: Gilmar, Santos D., Mauro (capt.), Zozimo, Santos N., Zito, Didi, Garrincha, Vava, Amarildo, Zagallo.

CZECHOSLOVAKIA: Schroiff, Tichy, Novak (capt.), Pluskal, Popluhar, Masopust, Pospichal, Scherer, Kvasniak, Kadraba, Jelinek.

Leading scorers
4 Garrincha (Brazil), Vava (Brazil), Sanchez L. (Chile), Jerkovic (Yugoslavia), Albert (Hungary), Ivanov V. (USSR); 3 Amarildo (Brazil), Scherer (Czechoslovakia), Galic (Yugoslavia), Tichy (Hungary).

ENGLAND 1966
Victory for Ramsey's wingless wonders

For the first time in 32 years the host nation was to win the title. This was a series that had everything – passion, controversy, some fine football, and one of the greatest upsets of all time when North Korea knocked Italy out at Ayresome Park!

The tournament got off to a slow start, with England held 0–0 by Uruguay, but in Group 2 West Germany quickly displayed their potential with a 5–0 win over Switzerland. Brazil, alas, disappointed. Having beaten Bulgaria 2–0, they lost a classic encounter with Hungary, for whom Albert was the dominating factor, then succumbed to Portugal, whose striker Eusebio was to be one of the stars of the competition. The Soviet Union, efficient and technically sound, cruised through to the quarter-finals without alarm. For Italy, however, there was a rude awakening. Having lost 1–0 to the Soviets, they had to beat North Korea to stay in the competition, but what seemed a formality turned into a nightmare. In the 42nd minute Pak Doo Ik dispossessed Rivera, advanced and crashed a searing shot past Albertosi. It was the only goal. Italy were eliminated.

At Goodison Park there was a sensational opening to Korea's quarter-final with Portugal. There was a goal in the opening minute, followed by a second and a third – and all for Korea. It was then that Eusebio proved his genius and, thanks to him and the towering Torres, the Portuguese clawed back the deficit to win a sensational game 5–3.

The England–Portugal semi-final produced an emotional classic, Bobby Charlton upstaging the mercurial Eusebio with what many felt was his greatest game for England. This, unlike the bad-tempered quarter-final shambles with Argentina, when Rattin was sent off and Geoff Hurst arrived as a new shooting star, was a wonderful advertisement for the game.

West Germany had edged out the Soviet Union, in a disappointing tie, to secure their place in the Final, and there they struck the first blow through Haller. Hurst equalized and his West Ham colleague Martin Peters gave England the lead. But a scrambled goal from Weber just before time forced the game into extra time. In the 100th minute controversy raged. Alan Ball crossed, and Hurst coming in on the near post, hammered his shot goalwards. It thumped against the underside of the bar and dropped – but which side of the line? Swiss referee Dienst was not sure, but the Soviet linesman Bakhramov was. 3–2 England! Any feeling of injustice felt by the Germans was quickly irrelevant. Bobby Moore swept a long ball upfield for Hurst to chase, and the big striker slammed his shot into the roof of Tilkowski's net to become the first player ever to score a hat-trick in a World Cup Final.

IT'S ALL OVER NOW *Bobby Moore celebrates with England their extra-time victory over West Germany at Wembley*

1966

Group 1

England	0	Uruguay	0
France	1	Mexico	1
Uruguay	2	France	1
England	2	Mexico	0
Uruguay	0	Mexico	0
England	2	France	0

	P	W	D	L	F	A	Pts
England	3	2	1	0	4	0	5
Uruguay	3	1	2	0	2	1	4
Mexico	3	0	2	1	1	3	2
France	3	0	1	2	2	5	1

Group 2

W. Germany	5	Switzerland	0
Argentina	2	Spain	1
Spain	2	Switzerland	1
Argentina	0	W. Germany	0
Argentina	2	Switzerland	0
W. Germany	2	Spain	1

	P	W	D	L	F	A	Pts
W. Germany	3	2	1	0	7	1	5
Argentina	3	2	1	0	4	1	5
Spain	3	1	0	2	4	5	2
Switzerland	3	0	0	3	1	9	0

Group 3

Brazil	2	Bulgaria	0
Portugal	3	Hungary	1
Hungary	3	Brazil	1
Portugal	3	Bulgaria	0
Portugal	3	Brazil	1
Hungary	3	Bulgaria	1

	P	W	D	L	F	A	Pts
Portugal	3	3	0	0	9	2	6
Hungary	3	2	0	1	7	5	4
Brazil	3	1	0	2	4	6	2
Bulgaria	3	0	0	3	1	8	0

Group 4

Soviet Union	3	North Korea	0
Italy	2	Chile	0
Chile	1	North Korea	1
Soviet Union	1	Italy	0
North Korea	1	Italy	0
Soviet Union	2	Chile	1

	P	W	D	L	F	A	Pts
Soviet Union	3	3	0	0	6	1	6
North Korea	3	1	1	1	2	4	3
Italy	3	1	0	2	2	2	2
Chile	3	0	1	2	2	5	1

Quarter-finals

England	1	Argentina	0
W. Germany	4	Uruguay	0
Portugal	5	North Korea	3
Soviet Union	2	Hungary	1

Semi-finals

W. Germany	2	Soviet Union	1
England	2	Portugal	1

Third place match

Portugal	2	Soviet Union	1

Final

England (1) 4   W. Germany (1) 2*
Hurst (3), Peters   Haller, Weber

ENGLAND: Banks, Cohen, Wilson, Stiles, Charlton J., Moore (capt.), Ball, Hurst, Hunt, Charlton R., Peters.

WEST GERMANY: Tilkowski, Höttges, Schülz, Weber, Schnellinger, Haller, Beckenbauer, Overath, Seeler (capt.), Held, Emmerich.

Leading scorers
9 Eusebio (Portugal); 5 Haller (West Germany); 4 Beckenbauer (West Germany), Hurst (England), Bene (Hungary), Porkujan (USSR).

*Note: * After extra time*

MEXICO 1970
Beautiful football secures the Jules Rimet trophy

Football triumphed again in Mexico, where the colourful free-flowing Brazilians delighted, overcoming the heat, the altitude and, in a dramatic Final, Italy – the masters of defensive caution.

There were no surprises in Groups 1 and 2 where the Soviet Union and Mexico and Italy and Uruguay qualified comfortably. The fixture between Brazil and England in Group 3 provided the outstanding tie of the series. In the 10th minute Jairzinho, a wonderful player of power and pace, delivered the perfect cross from the line. Pele timed his run and jump to perfection, and his header was hard and true, angled to bounce before passing just inside the left post. The shout of "Goal!" was already in the air when Gordon Banks, who had anticipated the ball going the other way, twisted athletically to pounce and incredibly push the wickedly bouncing ball over the bar. It was one of the greatest saves ever seen.

The only goal was scored in the second half by Jairzinho, who was to score in all of Brazil's six matches. England faltered in the quarter-final. Without Banks, because of an upset stomach, they squandered a two-goal lead to lose to West Germany in extra time.

The semi-final between Italy and

TOTAL FOOTBALL *But Johan Cruyff could not overcome West Germany in '74*

West Germany was dramatic. Having taken the lead through Boninsegna, Italy withdrew in the second half to protect their advantage. Given control of midfield, Germany took the initiative but did not equalize until the third minute of injury time through Schnellinger. In extra time, the goals came thick and fast: Müller for Germany, 1–2, Burgnich, then Riva for Italy, 3–2. Müller again, 3–3, before Rivera clinched it for Italy.

The Final proved a marvellous affirmation of attacking football. Pele opened the scoring and made two more after Boninsegna had made it 1–1, capitalizing on a dreadful error by Clodoaldo. Gerson drove in a powerful cross-shot in the 66th minute, and the match was sewn up with goals from Jairzinho and Carlos Alberto.

WEST GERMANY 1974
Pyrrhic victory for 'Total Football'

European teams dominated this series in which West Germany regained the World Cup after 20 years. It was another triumph for positive tactics, as Holland and Poland – who had surprisingly eliminated England – demonstrated to the full the attributes of skill and technique. The term "Total Football" crept into the football vocabulary, with Cruyff, Neeskens and Rep leading the Dutch masters who abandoned the rigidity of 4–2–4 and 4–3–3 to introduce the concept of "rotation" play.

Half of the 16 competing nations had been eliminated after the first series of group matches. The two Germanys qualified for the second phase comfortably, as did Holland and Sweden, and Poland from Group 4, where Argentina just pipped Italy on goal difference thanks to a 4–1 victory over Haiti, whom Italy had beaten 3–1.

Group 2 proved to be the most competitive. Brazil, now sadly without the retired Pele, could only draw 0–0 with Yugoslavia and Scotland. Zaïre were to be the key factor. Scotland defeated them 2–0, but Yugoslavia overwhelmed them 9–0 to clinch pole position on goal difference. As they went into the final round Scotland needed victory over Yugoslavia to win the group. They could only draw 1–1, and Brazil squeezed through, by virtue of one goal, thanks to a 3–0 win over Zaïre.

Holland looked impressive. They topped Group A to qualify for the Final without conceding a goal. Brazil, a shadow of their former selves, bowed out leaving us with one magic memory, their winning goal against East Germany. Jairzinho, standing on the end of the German wall facing a free-kick, ducked as Rivelino crashed his shot towards him, the ball swerving past the bewildered goalkeeper Croy.

West Germany's passage was a little more uncertain. It hinged on their clash with the impressive Poles in the final game of Group B. On a waterlogged pitch they made their physical strength pay. Tomaszewski saved a Hoeness penalty, but the German atoned for his miss when his shot was deflected to "The Bomber",

1970

Group 1			
Mexico	0	Soviet Union	0
Belgium	3	El Salvador	0
Soviet Union	4	Belgium	1
Mexico	4	El Salvador	0
Soviet Union	2	El Salvador	0
Mexico	1	Belgium	0

	P	W	D	L	F	A	Pts
Soviet Union	3	2	1	0	6	1	5
Mexico	3	2	1	0	5	0	5
Belgium	3	1	0	2	4	5	2
El Salvador	3	0	0	3	0	9	0

Group 2			
Uruguay	2	Israel	0
Italy	1	Sweden	0
Uruguay	0	Italy	0

Sweden	1	Israel	1
Sweden	1	Uruguay	0
Italy	0	Israel	0

	P	W	D	L	F	A	Pts
Italy	3	1	2	0	1	0	4
Uruguay	3	1	1	1	2	1	3
Sweden	3	1	1	1	2	2	3
Israel	3	0	2	1	1	3	2

Group 3			
England	1	Romania	0
Brazil	4	Czech.	1
Romania	2	Czech.	1
Brazil	1	England	0
Brazil	3	Romania	2
England	1	Czech.	0

	P	W	D	L	F	A	Pts
Brazil	3	3	0	0	8	3	6
England	3	2	0	1	2	1	4
Romania	3	1	0	2	4	5	2
Czech.	3	0	0	3	2	7	0

Group 4			
Peru	3	Bulgaria	2
W. Germany	2	Morocco	1
Peru	3	Morocco	0
W. Germany	5	Bulgaria	2
W. Germany	3	Peru	1
Morocco	1	Bulgaria	1

	P	W	D	L	F	A	Pts
W. Germany	3	3	0	0	10	4	6
Peru	3	2	0	1	7	5	4
Bulgaria	3	0	1	2	5	9	1
Morocco	3	0	1	2	2	6	1

Quarter-finals
W. Germany	3	England	2*
Brazil	4	Peru	2
Italy	4	Mexico	1
Uruguay	1	Soviet Union	0

Semi-finals
Italy	4	W. Germany	3*
Brazil	3	Uruguay	1

Third place match
W. Germany	1	Uruguay	0

Final
Brazil	4	Italy	1

Pele, Gerson, Jairzinho, Carlos Alberto — *Boninsegna*

BRAZIL: Felix, Carlos Alberto (capt.), Brito, Piazza, Everaldo, Clodoaldo, Gerson, Jairzinho, Tostao, Pele, Rivelino.

ITALY: Albertosi, Cera, Burgnich, Bertini (Juliano), Rosato, Facchetti (capt.), Domenghini, Mazzola, De Sisti, Boninsegna (Rivera), Riva.

Leading scorers
9 Müller (West Germany); 7 Jairzinho (Brazil); 4 Pele (Brazil), Cubillas (Peru), Byscevietz (USSR), Seeler (West Germany).

*Note: * After extra time*

1974

Group 1

W. Germany	1	Chile	0
E. Germany	2	Australia	0
W. Germany	3	Australia	0
E. Germany	1	Chile	1
E. Germany	1	W. Germany	0
Chile	0	Australia	0

	P	W	D	L	F	A	Pts
E. Germany	3	2	1	0	4	1	5
W. Germany	3	2	0	1	4	1	4
Chile	3	0	2	1	1	2	1
Australia	3	0	1	2	0	5	1

Group 2

Brazil	0	Yugoslavia	0
Scotland	2	Zaïre	0
Brazil	0	Scotland	0
Yugoslavia	9	Zaïre	0
Scotland	1	Yugoslavia	1
Brazil	3	Zaïre	0

Holland	2	Uruguay	0
Sweden	0	Bulgaria	0
Holland	0	Sweden	0
Bulgaria	1	Uruguay	1
Holland	4	Bulgaria	1
Sweden	3	Uruguay	0

Group 3

	P	W	D	L	F	A	Pts
Yugoslavia	3	1	2	0	10	1	4
Brazil	3	1	2	0	3	0	4
Scotland	3	1	2	0	3	1	4
Zaïre	3	0	0	3	0	14	0

	P	W	D	L	F	A	Pts
Holland	3	2	1	0	6	1	5
Sweden	3	1	2	0	3	0	4
Bulgaria	3	0	2	1	2	5	2
Uruguay	3	0	1	2	1	6	1

Group 4

Italy	3	Haiti	1
Poland	3	Argentina	2
Italy	1	Argentina	1
Poland	7	Haiti	0
Argentina	4	Haiti	1
Poland	2	Italy	1

	P	W	D	L	F	A	Pts
Poland	3	3	0	0	12	3	6
Argentina	3	1	1	1	7	5	3
Italy	3	1	1	1	5	4	3
Haiti	3	0	0	3	2	14	0

Group A

Brazil	1	E. Germany	0
Holland	4	Argentina	0
Holland	2	E. Germany	0
Brazil	2	Argentina	1
Holland	2	Brazil	0
Argentina	1	E. Germany	1

	P	W	D	L	F	A	Pts
Holland	3	3	0	0	8	0	6
Brazil	3	2	0	1	3	3	4
E. Germany	3	0	1	2	1	4	1
Argentina	3	0	1	2	2	7	1

Group B

Poland	1	Sweden	0
W. Germany	2	Yugoslavia	0
Poland	2	Yugoslavia	1
W. Germany	4	Sweden	2
Sweden	2	Yugoslavia	1
W. Germany	1	Poland	0

	P	W	D	L	F	A	Pts
W. Germany	3	3	0	0	7	2	6
Poland	3	2	0	1	3	2	4
Sweden	3	1	0	2	4	6	2
Yugoslavia	3	0	0	3	2	6	0

Third place match

Poland	1	Brazil	0

Final

W. Germany (2) 2 Holland (1) 1
Breitner (pen),   Neeskens (pen)
Müller

WEST GERMANY: Maier, Beckenbauer (capt.), Vogts, Schwarzenbeck, Breitner, Bonhof, Hoeness, Overath, Grabowski, Müller, Hölzenbein.

HOLLAND: Jongbloed, Suurbier, Rijsbergen (De Jong), Haan, Krol, Jansen, Neeskens, Van Hanegem, Rep, Cruyff (capt.), Rensenbrink (Van de Kerkhof, R.).

Leading scorers 7 Lato (Poland); 5 Neeskens (Holland), Szarmach (Poland); 4 Müller (West Germany), Rep (Holland), Edstroem (Sweden).

Gerd Müller, who booked the date with Holland.

The Dutch produced the most dramatic opening to a Final in the history of the competition. Right from the kick-off the ball was fluently played into the German area, where Cruyff was brought down by Hoeness. Neeskens calmly converted the first penalty awarded in a World Cup Final to record the fastest Final goal ever. And the Germans had yet to play the ball.

After being outplayed, West Germany got off the hook. Hölzenbein was homing in on goal when he was tripped by Jansen, and Breitner duly rammed in the resultant penalty himself to make it 1–1. A 43rd-minute goal from Gerd Müller – his 68th, last and most important for his country – won the World Cup.

CLINCHER *Bertoni scores for Argentina*

ARGENTINA 1978
Tickertape triumph for hyper hosts

Ecstasy and euphoria greeted Argentina's eventual triumph on home soil, yet for neutrals the failure of Holland, as in 1974, to claim their rightful crown as the best team in the world left a void.

The home nation, backed by fanatical support and animated tickertape adoration in the River Plate Stadium, staged a colourful and dramatic tournament. Yet their passage to the Final was not without controversy. Their opening game proved a torrid affair. Hungary took the lead in 12 minutes through Zombori only for Leopoldo Luque to equalize three minutes later. The Hungarians were to have two players sent off before Bertoni fired the winning goal. Italy and Argentina had already qualified for the second stage when they met to decide the final Group 1 places. The Italians played it tight and snatched the win through Bettega in the 67th minute.

In Group 2 Poland carried on where they left off in Germany, with slick precise play. The shock result featured Tunisia, who held West Germany to a goalless draw and could have won. Brazil once again failed to inspire, and only a fortunate 1–0 victory over Austria, who topped their group, squeezed them into the second phase. Scotland, the United Kingdom's only representatives, suffered humiliation. Rocked by a 3–1 defeat by Peru, they received a further blow to morale when Willie Johnston failed a drugs test and was ordered home. A 1–1 draw with Iran added to the troubles, but they went out in style against Holland.

While Italy and West Germany played not to lose, Holland thrilled with their adventurous attitude. The "reprise" of the 1974 Final between them and Germany provided one of the best games of this series. The final score was 2–2 and Holland were back in the Final. Meanwhile Brazil's

1978

Group 1

Argentina	2	Hungary	1
Italy	2	France	1
Argentina	2	France	1
Italy	3	Hungary	1
Italy	1	Argentina	0
France	3	Hungary	1

	P	W	D	L	F	A	Pts
Italy	3	3	0	0	6	2	6
Argentina	3	2	0	1	4	3	4
France	3	1	0	2	5	5	2
Hungary	3	0	0	3	3	8	0

Group 2

W.Germany	0	Poland	0
Tunisia	3	Mexico	1
Poland	1	Tunisia	0
W. Germany	6	Mexico	0
Poland	3	Mexico	1
W. Germany	0	Tunisia	0

	P	W	D	L	F	A	Pts
Poland	3	2	1	0	4	1	5
W.Germany	3	1	2	0	6	0	4
Tunisia	3	1	1	1	3	2	3
Mexico	3	0	0	3	2	12	0

Group 3

Austria	2	Spain	1
Sweden	1	Brazil	1
Austria	1	Sweden	0
Brazil	0	Spain	0
Spain	1	Sweden	0
Brazil	1	Austria	0

	P	W	D	L	F	A	Pts
Austria	3	2	0	1	3	2	4
Brazil	3	1	2	0	2	1	4
Spain	3	1	1	1	2	2	3
Sweden	3	0	1	2	1	3	1

Group 4

Peru	3	Scotland	1
Holland	3	Iran	0
Scotland	1	Iran	1
Holland	0	Peru	0
Peru	4	Iran	1
Scotland	3	Holland	2

	P	W	D	L	F	A	Pts
Peru	3	2	1	0	7	2	5
Holland	3	1	1	1	5	3	3
Scotland	3	1	1	1	5	6	3
Iran	3	0	1	2	2	8	1

Group A

Italy	0	W. Germany	0
Holland	5	Austria	1
Italy	1	Austria	0
Austria	3	W.Germany	2
Holland	2	Italy	1
Holland	2	W. Germany	2

	P	W	D	L	F	A	Pts
Holland	3	2	1	0	9	4	5
Italy	3	1	1	1	2	2	3
W. Germany	3	0	2	1	4	5	2
Austria	3	1	0	2	4	8	2

Group B

Argentina	2	Poland	0
Brazil	3	Peru	0
Argentina	0	Brazil	0
Poland	1	Peru	0
Brazil	3	Poland	1
Argentina	6	Peru	0

	P	W	D	L	F	A	Pts
Argentina	3	2	1	0	8	0	5
Brazil	3	2	1	0	6	1	5
Poland	3	1	0	2	2	5	2
Peru	3	0	0	3	0	10	0

Third place match

Brazil	2	Italy	1

Final

Argentina (1)3 Holland (0)1*
Kempes (2),   Nanninga
Bertoni

ARGENTINA: Fillol, Olguin, Galvan, Passarella (capt.), Tarantini, Ardiles (Larrosa), Gallego, Kempes, Bertoni, Luque, Ortiz (Houseman).
HOLLAND: Jongbloed, Krol (capt.), Poortvliet, Brandts, Jansen (Suurbier), Van de Kerkhof W., Neeskens, Haan, Rep (Nanninga), Rensenbrink, Van de Kerkhof R.

Leading scorers
6 Kempes (Argentina); 5 Rensenbrink (Holland), Cubillas (Peru).

*Note: * After extra time*

3–1 defeat of Poland left Argentina needing to beat Peru by at least four goals to make the Final. They beat them by six in a shambolic exercise that tarnished the image of the whole competition.

The Final, more dramatic than distinguished, saw Mario Kempes score twice as once more Holland fell at the final hurdle.

SPAIN 1982
Italy have the last laugh

Italy deservedly won the 1982 World Cup, after a slow start in which they drew all three games in Group 1 and qualified on the slenderest goal difference. West Germany, who were to finish runners-up, were on the wrong end of a shock 2–1 defeat in their opening tie against Algeria but, like Italy, got better as the tournament progressed.

England, in contrast, started with a bang then gradually eased up. Skipper Bryan Robson got them off to a dream start against France with a goal in 27 seconds, but although Ron Greenwood's team proved hard to beat, without the injured Keegan

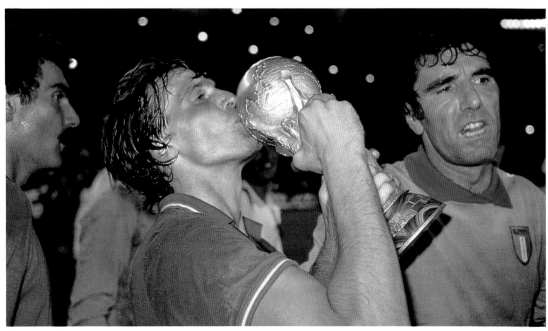

CIAO BELLA *Marco Tardelli kisses the cup alongside Dino Zoff after Italy's triumph over West Germany in 1982*

and Brooking they had little guile. The outstanding game was that between Italy and the favourites, Brazil. Three times Italy took the lead, twice Brazil came back to level the score in a classic that would not be matched for quality. Paolo Rossi, back after a two-year suspension, was the hero with a brilliant hat-trick.

In the semi-finals Rossi scored twice more to beat the impressive Poles, while West Germany and France, who had grown in stature and confidence following that initial setback against England, were involved in a pulsating thriller. With Platini, Tigana and Giresse at their teasing best, many fancied France as winners. In a tense 90 minutes they carved out the better chances but failed to make them count, then in extra-time fell victim on penalties after German keeper Toni Schumacher got away with an appalling foul on Battiston.

The less glamorous sides also had their moments. Algeria, Honduras and Kuwait caught the eye, and Northern Ireland – whose Norman Whiteside was, at 17, the youngest ever

1982

Group 1

Italy	0	Poland	0
Peru	0	Cameroon	0
Italy	1	Peru	1
Poland	0	Cameroon	0
Poland	5	Peru	1
Italy	1	Cameroon	1

	P	W	D	L	F	A	Pts
Poland	3	1	2	0	5	1	4
Italy	3	0	3	0	2	2	3
Cameroon	3	0	3	0	1	1	3
Peru	3	0	2	1	2	6	2

Group 2

Algeria	2	W. Germany	1
Austria	1	Chile	0
W. Germany	4	Chile	1
Austria	2	Algeria	1
Algeria	3	Chile	2
W. Germany	1	Austria	0

	P	W	D	L	F	A	Pts
W. Germany	3	2	0	1	6	3	4
Austria	3	2	0	1	3	1	4
Algeria	3	2	0	1	5	5	4
Chile	3	0	0	3	3	8	0

Group 3

Belgium	1	Argentina	0
Hungary	10	El Salvador	1

Argentina	4	Hungary	1
Belgium	1	El Salvador	0
Belgium	1	Hungary	1
Argentina	2	El Salvador	0

	P	W	D	L	F	A	Pts
Belgium	3	2	1	0	3	1	5
Argentina	3	2	0	1	6	2	4
Hungary	3	1	1	1	12	6	3
El Salvador	3	0	0	3	1	13	3

Group 4

England	3	France	1
Czech.	1	Kuwait	1
England	2	Czech.	0
France	4	Kuwait	1
France	1	Czech.	1
England	1	Kuwait	0

	P	W	D	L	F	A	Pts
England	3	3	0	0	6	1	6
France	3	1	1	1	6	5	3
Czech.	3	0	2	1	2	4	2
Kuwait	3	0	1	2	2	6	1

Group 5

Spain	1	Honduras	1
N. Ireland	0	Yugoslavia	0
Spain	2	Yugoslavia	1
N. Ireland	1	Honduras	1

Yugoslavia	1	Honduras	0
N. Ireland	1	Spain	0

	P	W	D	L	F	A	Pts
N. Ireland	3	1	2	0	2	1	4
Spain	3	1	1	1	3	3	3
Yugoslavia	3	1	1	1	2	2	3
Honduras	3	0	2	1	2	3	2

Group 6

Brazil	2	Soviet Union	1
Scotland	5	New Zealand	2
Brazil	4	Scotland	1
Soviet Union	3	New Zealand	0
Scotland	2	Soviet Union	2
Brazil	4	New Zealand	0

	P	W	D	L	F	A	Pts
Brazil	3	3	0	0	10	2	6
Soviet Union	3	1	1	1	6	4	3
Scotland	3	1	1	1	8	8	3
New Zealand	3	0	0	3	2	12	0

Group A

Poland	3	Belgium	0
Soviet Union	1	Belgium	0
Soviet Union	0	Poland	0

	P	W	D	L	F	A	Pts
Poland	2	1	1	0	3	0	3
Soviet Union	2	1	1	0	1	0	3
Belgium	2	0	0	2	0	4	0

Group B

W. Germany	0	England	0
W. Germany	2	Spain	1
England	0	Spain	0

	P	W	D	L	F	A	Pts
W. Germany	2	1	1	0	2	1	3
England	2	0	2	0	0	0	2
Spain	2	0	1	1	1	2	1

Group C

Italy	2	Argentina	1
Brazil	3	Argentina	1
Italy	3	Brazil	2

	P	W	D	L	F	A	Pts
Italy	2	2	0	0	5	3	4
Brazil	2	1	0	1	5	4	2
Argentina	2	0	0	2	2	5	0

Group D

France	1	Austria	0
N. Ireland	2	Austria	2
France	4	N. Ireland	1

	P	W	D	L	F	A	Pts
France	2	2	0	0	5	1	4
Austria	2	0	1	1	2	3	1
N. Ireland	2	0	1	1	3	6	1

Semi-finals

Italy	2	Poland	0
W. Germany	3	France	3*

(West Germany won 5–4 on pens)

Third place match

Poland	3	France	2

Final

Italy	(0) 3	W. Germany	(0) 1

Rossi, Tardelli *Breitner*
Altobelli

ITALY: Zoff (capt.), Bergomi, Cabrini, Collovati, Scirea, Gentile, Oriale, Tardelli, Conti, Graziani (Altobelli) (Causio), Rossi.

WEST GERMANY: Schumacher, Kaltz, Förster K., Stielike, Förster B., Breitner, Dremmler (Hrubesch), Littbarski, Briegel, Fischer (Müller, H.), Rummenigge (capt.).

Leading scorers

6 Rossi (Italy); 5 Rummenigge (West Germany); 4 Zico (Brazil), Boniek (Poland).

*Notes: * After extra time*

to play in the finals – distinguished themselves in a win over Spain.

The Final did not live up to its billing. There was not a shot on target in the opening 45 minutes including Cabrini's effort from a penalty. But in the second half the Germans paid, in fatigue, the price of their extra-time victory over France. Italy, inspired by the effort of Marco Tardelli and counter-attacking pace of Bruno Conti, were deserving winners – thus sealing a World Cup hat-trick.

MEXICO 1986
Divine intervention determines destiny of Cup

Mexico staged its second World Cup finals in the wake of a tragic earthquake, and set records all round with 52 matches played before 2,406,511 spectators.

THEY SHALL NOT PASS *Karl-Heinz Rummenigge is stopped by Argentina's Oscar Ruggeri during the Final in 1986*

West Germany continued their impressive World Cup record by reaching their fifth Final, once again eliminating France at the semi-final stage, while Argentina overcame the impressive Belgiums to make a third Final appearance. However, their 2-1 quarter-final victory over England had been soured by the infamous "hand of God" incident,

when Maradona knocked the ball past goalkeeper Peter Shilton with a hand to score the opening goal. There was no argument about Argentina's second goal, a brilliant solo run by the Argentinian ace taking him past three England defenders before he dispatched the ball into the back of the net.

Of the earlier games, the Soviet

Union's 6–0 demolition of Hungary and Belgium's thrilling 4–3 victory over the Soviets in the second round were the most memorable. England muddled through after a desperate start, Carlos Manuel's lone strike giving Portugal a 1–0 win. Bobby Robson's team were then held 0–0 by Morocco. A Gary Lineker hat-trick against Poland revived England's flag-

ging fortunes and earned them a place in the second round.

In a dramatic Final Argentina led 2–0 through Brown and Valdano before West Germany launched a remarkable recovery to equalize through Karl-Heinz Rummenigge and Völler. Burruchaga snatched the winner for Argentina's second World Cup title.

1986

Group A
Bulgaria	1	Italy	1
Argentina	3	South Korea	1
Italy	1	Argentina	1
Bulgaria	1	South Korea	1
Argentina	2	Bulgaria	0
Italy	3	South Korea	2

	P	W	D	L	F	A	Pts
Argentina	3	2	1	0	6	2	5
Italy	3	1	2	0	5	4	4
Bulgaria	3	0	2	1	2	4	2
South Korea	3	0	1	2	4	7	1

Group B
Mexico	2	Belgium	1
Paraguay	1	Iraq	0
Mexico	1	Paraguay	1
Belgium	2	Iraq	1
Paraguay	2	Belgium	2
Mexico	1	Iraq	0

	P	W	D	L	F	A	Pts
Mexico	3	2	1	0	4	2	5
Paraguay	3	1	2	0	4	3	4
Belgium	3	1	1	1	5	5	4
Iraq	3	0	0	3	1	4	0

Group C
Soviet Union	6	Hungary	0
France	1	Canada	0
Soviet Union	1	France	1
Hungary	2	Canada	0
France	3	Hungary	0
Soviet Union	2	Canada	0

	P	W	D	L	F	A	Pts
Soviet Union	3	2	1	0	9	1	5
France	3	2	1	0	5	1	5
Hungary	3	1	0	2	2	9	2
Canada	3	0	0	3	0	5	0

Group D
Brazil	1	Spain	0
N. Ireland	1	Algeria	1
Spain	2	N. Ireland	1
Brazil	1	Algeria	0
Spain	3	Algeria	0
Brazil	3	N. Ireland	0

	P	W	D	L	F	A	Pts
Brazil	3	3	0	0	5	0	6
Spain	3	2	0	1	5	2	4
N. Ireland	3	0	1	2	2	6	1
Algeria	3	0	1	2	1	5	1

Group E
W. Germany	1	Uruguay	1
Denmark	1	Scotland	0
Denmark	6	Uruguay	1
W. Germany	2	Scotland	1
Scotland	0	Uruguay	0
Denmark	2	W.Germany	0

	P	W	D	L	F	A	Pts
Denmark	3	3	0	0	9	1	6
W. Germany	3	1	1	1	3	4	3
Uruguay	3	0	2	1	2	7	2
Scotland	3	0	1	2	1	3	1

Group F
Morocco	0	Poland	0
Portugal	1	England	0
England	0	Morocco	0
Poland	1	Portugal	0
England	3	Poland	0
Morocco	3	Portugal	1

	P	W	D	L	F	A	Pts
Morocco	3	1	2	0	3	1	4
England	3	1	1	1	3	1	3
Poland	3	1	1	1	1	3	3
Portugal	3	1	0	2	2	4	2

Second round
Knock-out phase comprising the top two teams from each group plus the four best third-placed teams.

Mexico	2	Bulgaria	0
Belgium	4	Soviet Union	3*
Brazil	4	Poland	0
Argentina	1	Uruguay	0
France	2	Italy	0
W.Germany	1	Morocco	0
England	3	Paraguay	0
Spain	5	Denmark	1

Quarter-finals
France	1	Brazil	1*

(France won 4–3 on pens)

W.Germany	0	Mexico	0*

(W Germany won 4–1 on pens)

Argentina	2	England	1
Spain	1	Belgium	1*

(Belgium won 5–4 on pens)

Semi-finals
Argentina	2	Belgium	0
W.Germany	2	France	0

Third place match
France	4	Belgium	2

Final
Argentina (1) 3   W.Germany (0) 2
Brown, Valdano,   Rummenigge,
Burruchaga   Völler

ARGENTINA: Pumpido, Cuciuffo, Olarticoechea, Ruggeri, Brown, Giusti, Burruchaga (Trobbiani), Batista, Valdano, Maradona (capt.), Enrique.

WEST GERMANY: Schumacher, Berthold, Briegel, Jakobs, Förster, Eder, Brehme, Matthäus, Allofs (Völler), Magath (Hoeness, D.), Rummenigge (capt.).

Leading scorers
6 Lineker (England); 5 Butragueño (Spain), Careca (Brazil), Maradona (Argentina); 4 Altobelli (Italy), Belanov (USSR), Elkjaer (Denmark), Valdano (Argentina).

*Note: * After extra time*

24

TOP OF THE WORLD *West German captain Lothar Matthäus celebrates victory over Argentina after the Final in Rome*

ITALY 1990

Penalties decide in a tear-jerking anti-climax

The 14th World Cup finals did not live up to the setting. There was a miserly shortage of goals, but perhaps the saddest failure of all was on the part of the established stars who failed to enhance their reputations. The occasion was saved by the Italians themselves, for this was the People's World Cup.

It started dramatically with Cameroon beating the champions Argentina – Omam Biyik scoring the only goal. The Africans topped their group, with Argentina trailing in third place, and were later to frighten the life out of England when they took a 2–1 lead over them in the quarter-finals. "Toto" Schillaci's tense expressions were to reflect the Italian mood. He scored the winner against Austria and the first against the Czechs as Italy comfortably headed Group A. Scotland were humiliated by Costa Rica, bounced back against Sweden, then crashed out to Brazil after taking them all the way. Scotland's gloom contrasted with the Republic of Ireland's popular success, their shoot-out win over Romania earning them a tilt at the hosts in the quarter-finals. Belgium emerged as an impressive combination, but their journey ended when David Platt thumped home a brilliant volley to see England to the last eight.

The highlights included the drama in Milan, when Littbarski's goal seemed to have ended Colombia's dream before one of the great characters of the tournament, Carlos Valderrama, who had been carried off, returned to lay on an equalizer for Freddy Rincon. There was the reckless stupidity of Colombian goalkeeper René Higuita, the grace of Tomas Skuhravy, the Czech striker and the magic of Yugoslavia's Dragan Stojkovic. There was also the sheer theatre of West Germany blasting England in a penalty shoot-out, with Gascoigne sobbing.

But the lasting impression of Italia '90 was of the villain of the piece, Argentina, who ousted Brazil, and spoilt the script by beating Italy on penalties to reach a Final they were to sully with their dour tactics and flagrant abuse of the rules. Two Argentines were sent off, before, ironically, they were beaten by a penalty.

1990

Group A

Italy	1	Austria	0	
Czech.	5	USA	1	
Italy	1	USA	0	
Czech.	1	Austria	0	
Italy	2	Czech.	0	
Austria	2	USA	1	

	P	W	D	L	F	A	Pts
Italy	3	3	0	0	4	0	6
Czech.	3	2	0	1	6	3	4
Austria	3	1	0	2	2	3	2
USA	3	0	0	3	2	8	0

Group B

Cameroon	1	Argentina	0	
Romania	2	Soviet Union	0	
Argentina	2	Soviet Union	0	
Cameroon	2	Romania	1	
Argentina	1	Romania	1	
Soviet Union	4	Cameroon	0	

	P	W	D	L	F	A	Pts
Cameroon	3	2	0	1	3	5	4
Romania	3	1	1	1	4	3	3
Argentina	3	1	1	1	3	2	3
Soviet Union	3	1	0	2	4	4	2

Group C

Brazil	2	Sweden	1	
Costa Rica	1	Scotland	0	
Brazil	1	Costa Rica	0	
Scotland	2	Sweden	1	
Brazil	1	Scotland	0	
Costa Rica	2	Sweden	1	

	P	W	D	L	F	A	Pts
Brazil	3	3	0	0	4	1	6
Costa Rica	3	2	0	1	3	2	4
Scotland	3	1	0	2	2	3	2
Sweden	3	0	0	3	3	6	0

Group D

Colombia	2	UAE	0	
W. Germany	4	Yugoslavia	1	
Yugoslavia	1	Colombia	0	
W. Germany	5	UAE	1	
W. Germany	1	Colombia	1	
Yugoslavia	4	UAE	1	

	P	W	D	L	F	A	Pts
W. Germany	3	2	1	0	10	3	5
Yugoslavia	3	2	0	1	6	5	4
Colombia	3	1	1	1	3	2	3
UAE	3	0	0	3	2	11	0

Group E

Belgium	2	South Korea	0	
Uruguay	0	Spain	0	
Belgium	3	Uruguay	1	
Spain	3	South Korea	1	
Spain	2	Belgium	1	
Uruguay	1	South Korea	0	

	P	W	D	L	F	A	Pts
Spain	3	2	1	0	5	2	5
Belgium	3	2	0	1	6	3	4
Uruguay	3	1	1	1	2	3	3
South Korea	3	0	0	3	1	6	0

Group F

England	1	Rep of Ireland	1	
Holland	1	Egypt	1	
England	0	Holland	0	
Egypt	0	Rep of Ireland	0	
England	1	Egypt	0	
Holland	1	Rep of Ireland	1	

	P	W	D	L	F	A	Pts
England	3	1	2	0	2	1	4
Rep of Ireland	3	0	3	0	2	2	3
Holland	3	0	3	0	2	2	3
Egypt	3	0	2	1	1	2	2

Second phase

Knock-out phase comprising the top two teams from each group plus the four best third-placed teams

Cameroon	2	Colombia	1*	
Czech.	4	Costa Rica	1	
Argentina	1	Brazil	0	
W. Germany	2	Holland	1	
Rep of Ireland	0	Rumania	0*	

(Rep. of Ireland won 5–4 on pens)

Italy	2	Uruguay	0	
Yugoslavia	2	Spain	1*	
England	1	Belgium	0*	

Quarter-finals

Argentina	0	Yugoslavia	0*	

(Argentina won 3–2 on pens)

Italy	1	Rep of Ireland	0	
W. Germany	1	Czech.	0	
England	3	Cameroon	2*	

Semi-finals

Argentina	1	Italy	1*	

(Argentina won 4–3 on pens)

W. Germany	1	England	1*	

(West Germany won 4–3 on pens)

Third place match

Italy	2	England	1

Final

W.Germany (0) 1 Argentina (0) 0
Brehme (pen)

WEST GERMANY: Illgner, Berthold (Reuter), Kohler, Augenthaler, Buchwald, Brehme, Littbarski, Hässler, Matthäus (capt.), Völler, Klinsmann.

ARGENTINA: Goycochea, Lorenzo, Serrizuela, Sensini, Ruggeri (Monzon), Simon, Basualdo, Burruchaga (Calderon), Maradona (capt.), Troglio, Dezotti.

Leading scorers

6 Schillaci (Italy); 5 Skuhravy (Czechoslovakia); 4 Michel (Spain), Milla (Cameroon), Matthäus (West Germany), Lineker (England).

*Note: * After extra time*

USA 1994
Brazil's glory in Final shoot-out

History was made twice over at the 1994 World Cup finals. Brazil secured a fourth title to add to their triumphs in 1958, 1962 and 1970. But to do so they needed to win the first-ever penalty shoot-out at the end of extra time after a goalless Final against Italy in the Rose Bowl in Pasadena.

FIFA introduced four radical measures in an attempt to improve the quality of the action: three points for a win instead of two in the first round group matches; a relaxation over the offside law by which play was to be stopped only if an attacking player was interfering with play; a crackdown on the tackle from behind in particular – for which a red card would be automatic – and violent conduct in general; and finally, injured players would be taken off the field immediately for treatment.

In simple statistical terms these changes added up to 15 sendings off and a record 235 bookings. But, on the positive side, they also computed to 141 goals in 52 matches, a match average of 2.71 and an improvement on Italia '90.

More Than a Game

The biggest shadow over the finals was cast by the death of Andres Escobar, the Colombian defender, who was shot dead a few days after returning back home to Medellin. The exact reason for his murder is not known – gambling losses, probably involving drug barons, is thought to be the cause – but what was certain was that the centre-back had, inadvertently, scored an own goal against the United States in Colombia's 2–1 defeat.

That victory for the US was probably the most significant single result in the finals because it virtually ensured the hosts a place in the second round. This success struck a chord with the domestic audience which helped carry the World Cup along on a wave of excitement and enthusiasm which surprised even the most optimistic of American soccer people.

However, the team of Group A were undoubtedly Romania, inspired by their attacking general Gheorghe Hagi. The well-organized Swiss team qualified in second place, but Colombia – among the pre-tournament favourites – played without conviction or pattern and were eliminated.

Group B offered clear favourites in Brazil and they did not disappoint their colourful, noisy and musical supporters. Brazil's strength was the striking partnership of Romario and Bebeto. Romario either scored or had a creative hand in 10 of Brazil's 11 goals. Brazil topped the group with Sweden second.

FIVE GOALS IN ONE MATCH *Russia's Oleg Salenko set an individual goalscoring record for the World Cup finals*

Group C included the formal Opening Match in which holders Germany beat Bolivia 1–0. The Germans appeared laboured, and Stefan Effenberg was expelled from the squad at the end of the first round for making a rude gesture towards jeering German fans in the narrow 3–2 win over South Korea. This was the other group which provided only two, rather than three, second round qualifiers. Germany finished top followed by Spain.

Maradona's Misery

In Group D Argentina's Diego Maradona was his team's attacking inspiration in the opening 4–0 win over Greece and in the 2–1 follow-up defeat of Nigeria, but it was after this game that he failed a dope test which showed traces of the banned stimulant ephedrine. The tourna-ment was over for Maradona and Argentina lost their next game, without him, 2–0 to Bulgaria. The Bulgarians thus qualified for the second round despite having crashed 3–0 to the entertaining World Cup newcomers Nigeria in the group's opening match.

Ten Men Fight Back

The tightest division was Group E, featuring Italy, the Republic of Ireland, Mexico and Norway, and the six matches produced only eight goals.

Ireland shocked Italy with a 1–0 victory in their opening match, and Norway appeared on the verge of inflicting a second defeat on the group favourites when goalkeeper Gianluca Pagliuca was sent off. Remarkably, however, Italy fought back to win, 1–0, when defeat would have resulted in almost certain elimination. Wasting that numerical superiority cost Norway dear. All four teams ended up on four points and zero goal difference, but Norway finished bottom of the group on goals scored and were thus eliminated.

Another favoured team who struggled in the first round were Holland. They beat Saudi Arabia only 2–1 in their first match then lost an exciting duel 1–0 to Belgium next time out and escaped early elimination by defeating Morocco 2–1 in their final match, to qualify along with Belgium and World Cup newcomers Saudi Arabia – who beat Belgium 1–0 along the way.

The opening match of the second round saw Germany, as on the opening day, playing in Chicago. This time they defeated Belgium 3–2 in an exciting game which marked the successful two-goal return of veteran World Cup-winner Rudi Völler.

The Republic of Ireland committed defensive suicide against Holland, losing 2–0 on mistakes by full-back Terry Phelan and goalkeeper Packie Bonner. Spain had an easy time in beating Switzerland 3–0 and Sweden saw off Saudi Arabia 3–1. Brazil also spoiled the Americans' Independence Day holiday by defeating the hosts more easily than the 1–0 scoreline suggests. The other three second-round games were even more dramatic. Bulgaria defeated Mexico 3–1 on penalties – the first shoot-out of the finals – after an entertaining 1–1 draw, marred by two contentious sendings-off.

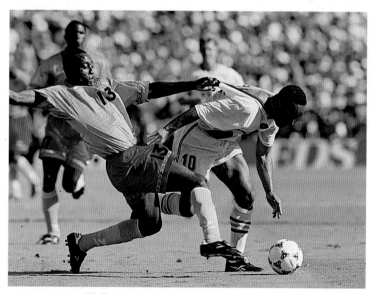

AFRICAN CHALLENGE *Kalla Nkongo of Cameroon tussles with Dahlin of Sweden*

A TANGO NOT A SAMBA *Romario and Baresi battle for supremacy in the Final at the Rose Bowl*

Hagi's Army March On

In Pasadena, Romania's Ilie Dumitrescu played the game of his life scoring twice and creating a third for Hagi in a 3–2 defeat of Argentina. Italy dramatically defeated Nigeria; with two minutes remaining the Italians were 1–0 down and had again been reduced to ten men by the dismissal, this time, of midfield substitute Gianfranco Zola. Roberto Baggio snatched an equaliser and as the Nigerians sagged in extra time, he scored again, from the penalty spot.

In the quarter-finals, Sweden, themselves down to 10 men after Stefan Schwarz was sent off, defeated Romania on penalties after a 2–2 draw.

Roberto Baggio confirmed his star rating with Italy's late second goal in their 2–1 victory over Spain. Another tight game saw Brazil defeat Holland 3–2, the first time an opposing team had put Brazil's defence under serious sustained pressure.

Completing the semi-final line-up were rank outsiders Bulgaria. Germany went ahead through a Lothar Matthäus penalty. But the holders conceded two last-gasp goals, from Hristo Stoichkov and Iordan Lechkov. It was Germany's earliest elimination since their quarter-final failure in 1962 and Bulgaria, who had played 16 matches at the finals without winning one before this tournament, were into the semi-finals.

That was to prove the end of the road. The two-goal brilliance of Roberto Baggio lifted Italy into their fifth Final while, in the other semi-final, Brazil encountered few difficulties in defeating a lacklustre and leg-weary Sweden 1-0.

Penalties in Pasadena

Italy gambled twice over, in playing superstar striker Roberto Baggio despite a hamstring strain and in recalling veteran sweeper Franco Baresi for his first appearance after a cartilage operation following his injury against Norway in the first round.

In fact, Baresi was Italy's man of the match. The game saw Brazil employing their technical brilliance to try to outflank Italy's defensive discipline while the Italians sat back and waited for the right moment to unleash their rapid counter-attacks.

It was a game of few chances, most of which fell to Brazil. Romario misplaced a first-half header and Mazinho couldn't quite capitalize on a half-chance when Pagliuca spilled a Branco free-kick. In the 75th minute Pagliuca also allowed a long-range Mauro Silva effort to slip through his hands, but the ball bounced off the post and back into his arms. Pagliuca kissed the post in gratitude. Italy's best chance ended with Taffarel saving from Massaro.

Roberto Baggio went close with one effort in each half of extra time while Brazil should again have taken the lead in the 109th minute when the industrious Cafu crossed to the far post and Romario put the ball fractionally the wrong side of the post from four yards out just beyond the far post.

In the penalty shoot-out, Taffarel benefited immediately when Baresi shot over. Baresi sank to his knees in despair. Pagliuca then saved from Marcio Santos and Italy went briefly ahead as Albertini scored from kick No 2. Romario squared for Brazil, Evani netted for Italy and Branco for Brazil. This was the point at which it fell apart for Italy as Taffarel saved from Massaro and Dunga shot what proved the vital Brazilian kick. Baggio needed to score with Italy's last kick of the five to keep his country alive. Instead, he scooped the ball over the bar. Brazil were back on top of the world.

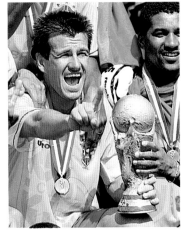

WE ARE THE CHAMPIONS *Dunga with the World Cup trophy*

1994	Group A			Group C			Group E			Second phase			Final		
	USA	1 Switzerland	1	Germany	1 Bolivia	0	Italy	0 Rep of Ireland	1	Germany	3 Belgium	2	Brazil	0 Italy	0*
	Colombia	1 Romania	3	Spain	2 South Korea	2	Norway	1 Mexico	0	Spain	3 Switzerland	0	(*Brazil won 3–2 on pens*)		
	USA	2 Colombia	1	Germany	1 Spain	1	Italy	1 Norway	0	Saudi Arabia	1 Sweden	3			
	Romania	1 Switzerland	4	South Korea	0 Bolivia	0	Mexico	2 Rep of Ireland	1	Romania	3 Argentina	2	BRAZIL: Taffarel, Jorginho		
	USA	0 Romania	1	Bolivia	1 Spain	3	Rep of Ireland	0 Norway	0	Holland	2 Rep of Ireland	0	(Cafu 20), Aldair, Marcio Santos,		
	Switzerland	0 Colombia	2	Germany	3 South Korea	2	Italy	1 Mexico	1	Brazil	1 USA	0	Branco, Mazinho (Viola 106),		
										Nigeria	1 Italy	2*	Dunga (capt.), Mauro Silva, Zinho,		
		P W D L F A Pts			P W D L F A Pts			P W D L F A Pts			Mexico	1 Bulgaria	1*	Romario, Bebeto.		
	Romania	3 2 0 1 5 5 6		Germany	3 2 1 0 5 3 7		Mexico	3 1 1 1 3 3 4		(*Bulgaria won 3–1 on pens*)					
	Switzerland	3 1 1 1 5 4 4		Spain	3 1 2 0 6 4 5		Rep of Ireland	3 1 1 1 2 2 4					ITALY: Pagliuca, Mussi (Apolloni		
	USA	3 1 1 1 3 3 4		South Korea	3 0 2 1 4 5 2		Italy	3 1 1 1 2 2 4		Quarter-finals			34), Maldini, Baresi (capt.),		
	Colombia	3 1 0 2 4 5 3		Bolivia	3 0 1 2 1 4 1		Norway	3 1 1 1 1 1 4		Italy	2 Spain	1	Benarrivo, Berti, Albertini, D.		
										Holland	2 Brazil	3	Baggio (Evani 94), Donadoni, R.		
	Group B			Group D			Group F			Germany	1 Bulgaria	2	Baggio, Massaro.		
	Cameroon	2 Sweden	2	Argentina	4 Greece	0	Belgium	1 Morocco	0	Sweden	2 Romania	2*			
	Brazil	2 Russia	0	Nigeria	3 Bulgaria	0	Holland	2 Saudi Arabia	1	(*Sweden won 5–4 on pens*)			Leading scorers		
	Brazil	3 Cameroon	0	Argentina	2 Nigeria	1	Belgium	1 Holland	0				6 Salenko (Russia), Stoichkov		
	Sweden	3 Russia	1	Bulgaria	4 Greece	0	Saudi Arabia	2 Morocco	1	Semi-finals			(Bulgaria);		
	Russia	6 Cameroon	1	Greece	0 Nigeria	2	Morocco	1 Holland	2	Brazil	1 Sweden	0	5 K. Andersson (Sweden),		
	Brazil	1 Sweden	1	Argentina	0 Bulgaria	2	Belgium	0 Saudi Arabia	1	Italy	2 Bulgaria	1	R. Baggio (Italy), Klinsmann		
													(Germany), Romario (Brazil)		
		P W D L F A Pts			P W D L F A Pts			P W D L F A Pts		Third place match			4 Batistuta (Argentina), Dahlin		
	Brazil	3 2 1 0 6 1 7		Nigeria	3 2 0 1 6 2 6		Holland	3 2 0 1 4 3 6		Sweden	4 Bulgaria	0	(Sweden), Raducioiu (Romania)		
	Sweden	3 1 2 0 6 4 5		Bulgaria	3 2 0 1 6 3 6		Saudi Arabia	3 2 0 1 4 3 6							
	Russia	3 1 0 2 7 6 3		Argentina	3 2 0 1 6 3 6		Belgium	3 2 0 1 2 1 6							
	Cameroon	3 0 1 2 3 11 1		Greece	3 0 0 3 0 10 1		Morocco	3 0 0 3 2 5 0							

Note: * After extra time

FRANCE 1998
After 68 years, the French triumph

FRANCE, the nation which invented the World Cup, finally won it in 1998 with a spectacular 3–0 victory over Brazil on home soil.

It was Frenchman Jules Rimet who first introduced the idea of a worldwide tournament of nations in 1930. And he would no doubt have been delighted that 68 years on, France should host the finals and be crowned world champions.

Even before it began, France '98 was billed as the biggest and most glamourous World Cup of all time – not least because it featured 32 teams instead of the usual 24. And due to the ever-increasing popularity of football, and the ever-expanding sponsorship and media circus which surrounds it, it was virtually impossible to escape the tournament wherever you lived in the world.

The line-up included four nations, Jamaica, Japan, South Africa and Croatia, making their debut in a World Cup finals – and that only served to add to the anticipation – with many pundits predicting upsets.

In fact, although Croatia proved to be the fairytale side of the finals, France '98 really only confirmed the status quo, with European and South American countries dominating as usual and the African and Asian nations failing to make an impact.

Brazil get off to a flyer

The opening game saw champions Brazil win 2–1 against the Tartan Army of Scotland, thanks to an unfortunate own goal from Tom Boyd. And when the Samba stars went on to crush Morocco 3–0, they became the first team to qualify for round two.

But there was still plenty of drama to come in the group. Scotland (having held Norway to a draw) faced Morocco in the final fixture, with each team believing that the winner would go through – providing Norway didn't do the unthinkable and beat Brazil.

The Moroccans were already partying after they went 3–0 up – only to find that Norway had turned the tables by winning 2–1. The pictures of Moroccan celebrations turning to tears were some of the most haunting of the World Cup.

In Group B, Italy came back to draw 2–2 with Chile when Roberto Baggio, who missed a penalty in the 1994 World Cup final shoot-out, bravely volunteered to take a spot-kick when his side were 2–1 down – and duly converted.

The Azzuri went on to crush Cameroon and beat Austria to reach the second round, with striker Christian Vieri helping himself to four goals. Chile, led by three-goal striker Marcelo Salas, were second.

French prove they can score goals

Hosts France defied criticism that they would struggle to hit the net by beating South Africa 3–0, Saudi Arabia 4–0 (despite Zinedine Zidane being sent off) and Denmark 2–1 in Group C. And the Danes, with the inspirational Laudrup brothers Michael and Brian, also qualified.

Nigeria won Group D by winning their opening two games, and ended up as the only African nation in the second round. The key to their progress was a stunning 3–2 victory over Spain, in which they twice came from behind. But it was an awful mistake from experienced Spanish keeper Zubizarreta, credited as an own goal, which turned the game.

There was more misery to come for Spain, who had to beat Bulgaria to go through in the final group game. They romped to a thrilling 6–1 victory – only to find that Paraguay (without a goal up to that point) had unexpectedly beaten a weakened Nigeria side 3–1 to snatch second place.

In Group E, Holland posted a fine 5–0 win against South Korea and drew 2–2 with Mexico in a thriller.

The Mexicans won many fans with their never-say-die attitude, twice coming from 2–0 down to secure draws. Striker Cuauhtemoc Blanco also provided one of the light-hearted moments of the tournament with his 'bunny-hop' trick that bamboozled opposition defenders!

Group F saw German captain Jürgen Klinsmann, playing his farewell tournament, turn back the years by firing goals against the United States and Iran to send his side comfortably into round two.

Peace breaks out at Iran vs USA

Perhaps the most memorable match of Group F, and the first round, was the politically sensitive clash between the USA and Iran. Both sets of players exchanged gifts before the kick-off and posed for a joint team picture, arms around each other, to prove that politics has no place on the football field. Iran won the battle, 2–1.

Group G saw England, tipped to be one of the big guns of France '98, open with a comfortable 2–0 win over Tunisia. But they then crashed to a 2–1 defeat against Romania when Dan Petrescu, based in England with Chelsea, rolled home the winner.

The one consolation for England was that teenage substitute Michael Owen looked lively, scoring once and hitting a post in the last minute. Not surprisingly, he started England's crucial third game against Colombia, and helped them to a comfortable 2–0 victory, sealed by a stunning David Beckham free-kick.

Group H was rather more clear-cut. Argentina dominated, winning all three of their games including a 5–0 thrashing of Jamaica in which Gabriel Batistuta hit a hat-trick. Croatia took second spot and Jamaica scored their first victory in a World Cup finals, beating a disappointing Japan side 2–1.

The tension increased in round two, where Vieri handed Italy a narrow win over Norway and the Klinsmann-Bierhoff combination sent

"All the players showed they wanted the French flag flying high. France now knows it has a great team..."

Aime Jacquet, coach of champions France

Germany through against Mexico.

A Davor Suker penalty saw Croatia scrape past Romania; Brazil cruised home against South American rivals Chile with Ronaldo and Cesar Sempaio scoring twice each in a 4–1 win, and Denmark easily disposed of Nigeria by the same score.

The Dutch, though, needed a dramatic 90th minute strike from Edgar Davids to beat Yugoslavia, while France relied on a "Golden Goal" from defender Laurent Blanc to see off a stoic challenge from Paraguay.

The England vs Argentina clash, as expected, proved to be the tie of the round. A penalty for each side, both converted, made for an exciting opening and then Owen ran all the way from the half-way line to score the goal of the tournament.

The Argentinians hit back with a cleverly-worked free-kick and must have expected to win after England's Beckham was controversially sent off for petulantly kicking out at Diego

BRAZILIAN DESPAIR *Inconsolable Brazil players after their 3-0 final defeat*

ZIDANE THE HERO *French star Zinedine Zidane thunders home a header from a corner in the 3–0 win over Brazil*

was a red card for Laurent Blanc (the 15th of the finals) after some terrible play-acting from Slaven Bilic.

Suker, of course, scored for Croatia and he did so again in a 2–1 third-place play-off win against Holland to clinch the Golden Boot with six goals.

Ronaldo drama in final

The final, between hosts France and champions Brazil, proved to be dramatic, controversial and disappointing all at the same time.

The drama began when Brazil handed in their teamsheet – with Ronaldo left out of the side. But 15 minutes later they sent out a correction – with the striker back in.

It later transpired that Ronaldo had suffered a convulsive fit on the morning of the match, and was only passed fit to play at the last minute.

The whole affair clearly affected Brazil, who looked deflated right from the start. But in contrast, France were magnificent. Two headed goals from the inspirational Zinedine Zidane, both from corners, put them in control and then Emmanuel Petit rounded things off in a 3–0 win.

The celebrations in Paris were remarkable, with millions packing the streets for three days.

Simeone. But the English showed their bulldog spirit by surviving with 10 men all the way to the end of extra-time, before losing 4–3 on penalties (David Batty missing the last one).

Surprise package Croatia

In the quarter-finals, Croatia confirmed their reputation as the surprise of the tournament by crushing Germany (who had defender Christian Wörns sent off) 3–0 with goals from Jarni, Vlaovic and that man Suker. Holland beat Argentina 2–1 thanks to a glorious goal from Dennis Bergkamp in the very last minute, while France needed a penalty shootout to beat Italy following a 0–0 draw.

The match of the round was undoubtedly Brazil's exciting 3–2 win over Denmark, with two-goal Rivaldo breaking Danish hearts.

In the semi-finals, Holland more than matched Brazil and Patrick Kluivert sent the game into extra-time by equalising a Ronaldo strike in the 87th minute. But the Dutch cruelly lost on penalties. In contrast, France, cannily coached by Aime Jacquet, send the home fans wild with a 2–1 victory over Croatia.

As usual, the French struggled up front but found an unexpected hero in the shape of right-back Lilian Thuram, who scored twice. The only blot

---

1998

Round 1

Group A

Brazil	2	Scotland	1
Morocco	2	Norway	2
Brazil	3	Morocco	0
Scotland	1	Norway	1
Brazil	1	Norway	2
Scotland	0	Morocco	3

	P	W	D	L	F	A	Pts
Brazil	3	2	0	1	6	3	6
Norway	3	1	2	0	5	4	5
Morocco	3	1	1	1	5	5	4
Scotland	3	0	1	2	2	6	1

Group B

Italy	2	Chile	2
Austria	1	Cameroon	1
Chile	1	Austria	1
Italy	3	Cameroon	0
Chile	1	Cameroon	1
Italy	2	Austria	1

	P	W	D	L	F	A	Pts
Italy	3	2	1	0	7	3	7
Chile	3	0	3	0	4	4	3
Austria	3	0	2	1	3	4	2
Cameroon	3	0	2	1	2	5	2

Group C

Saudi Arabia	0	Denmark	1
France	3	South Africa	0
France	4	Saudi Arabia	0
South Africa	1	Denmark	1
France	2	Denmark	1
South Africa	2	Saudi Arabia	2

	P	W	D	L	F	A	Pts
France	3	3	0	0	9	1	9
Denmark	3	1	1	1	3	3	4
S Africa	3	0	2	1	3	6	2
S Arabia	3	0	1	2	2	7	1

Group D

Paraguay	0	Bulgaria	0
Spain	2	Nigeria	3
Nigeria	1	Bulgaria	0
Spain	0	Paraguay	0
Nigeria	1	Paraguay	3
Spain	6	Bulgaria	1

	P	W	D	L	F	A	Pts
Nigeria	3	2	0	1	5	5	6
Paraguay	3	1	2	0	3	1	5
Spain	3	1	1	1	8	4	4
Bulgaria	3	0	1	2	1	7	1

Group E

South Korea	1	Mexico	3
Holland	0	Belgium	0
Belgium	2	Mexico	2
Holland	5	South Korea	0
Belgium	1	South Korea	1
Holland	2	Mexico	2

	P	W	D	L	F	A	Pts
Holland	3	1	2	0	7	2	5
Mexico	3	1	2	0	7	5	5
Belgium	3	0	3	0	3	3	3
S Korea	3	0	1	2	2	9	1

Group F

Germany	2	USA	0
Yugoslavia	1	Iran	0
Germany	2	Yugoslavia	2
USA	1	Iran	2
Germany	2	Iran	0
USA	0	Yugoslavia	1

	P	W	D	L	F	A	Pts
Germany	3	2	1	0	6	2	7
Yugoslavia	3	2	1	0	4	2	7
Iran	3	1	0	2	2	4	3
USA	3	0	0	3	1	5	0

Group G

England	2	Tunisia	0
Romania	1	Colombia	0
Colombia	1	Tunisia	0
Romania	2	England	1
Romania	1	Tunisia	1
Colombia	0	England	2

	P	W	D	L	F	A	Pts
Romania	3	2	1	0	4	2	7
England	3	2	0	1	5	2	6
Colombia	3	1	0	2	1	3	3
Tunisia	3	0	1	2	1	4	1

Group H

Argentina	1	Japan	0
Jamaica	1	Croatia	3
Japan	0	Croatia	1
Argentina	5	Jamaica	0
Argentina	1	Croatia	0
Japan	1	Jamaica	2

	P	W	D	L	F	A	Pts
Argentina	3	3	0	0	7	0	9
Croatia	3	2	0	1	4	2	6
Jamaica	3	1	0	2	3	9	3
Japan	3	0	0	3	1	5	0

Second phase

Italy	1	Norway	0
Brazil	4	Chile	1
France	1	Paraguay	0

(golden goal, after extra time)

Nigeria	1	Denmark	4
Germany	2	Mexico	1
Holland	2	Yugoslavia	1
Romania	0	Croatia	1
Argentina	2	England	2

(Argentina won 4–3 on pens)

Quarter-finals

Italy	0	France	0

(France won 4–3 on pens)

Brazil	3	Denmark	2
Holland	2	Argentina	1
Germany	0	Croatia	3

Semi-finals

Brazil	1	Holland	1

(Brazil won 4–2 on pens)

France	2	Croatia	1

Third place match

Holland	1	Croatia	2

Final

Brazil	0	France	3

BRAZIL: Taffarel, Cafu, Junior Baiano, Aldair, Roberto Carlos, Dunga, Cesar Sempaio (Edmundo 75), Leonardo (Denilson 45), Rivaldo, Bebeto, Ronaldo

FRANCE: Barthez, Thuram, Leboeuf, Desailly, Lizarazu, Petit, Deschamps, Karembeu (Boghossian 58), Zidane, Guivarc'h (Dugarry 66), Djorkaeff (Viera 76)

Leading scorers
6 Suker (Croatia)
5 Vieri (Italy), Batistuta (Argentina)
4 Salas (Chile), Hernandez (Mexico), Ronaldo (Brazil)
3 Sampaio, Rivaldo (both Brazil), Henry (France), Klinsmann, Bierhoff (Germany), Bergkamp (Holland)

INTERNATIONAL COMPETITIONS

FIFA UNDER-17 WORLD CHAMPIONSHIP

FIFA have made no secret of their desire to encourage football at the grass roots level, and the Under-17 (Junior) and Under-20 (Youth) World Championships are crucial elements of that process. The Under-17 World Championship in particular has shown that skilful football is not confined to Europe and South America. Of the seven tournaments held so far, Africa has won four times and Asia once.

FIFA Under-17 World Championship Finals	
1985	Nigeria 2, West Germany 0.
1987	Soviet Union 1, Nigeria 1.
	Soviet Union won 4–2 on penalties.
1989	Saudi Arabia 2, Scotland 2.
	Saudi Arabia won 5–4 on penalties.
1991	Ghana 1, Spain 0.
1993	Nigeria 2, Ghana 1.
1995	Ghana 3, Brazil 2
1997	Brazil 2, Ghana 1

FIFA UNDER-20 WORLD CHAMPIONSHIP

The World Youth Championship, as the Under-20 event is often known, reflects the gap between Europe and South America and the rest of the world which exists from this level up. The reasons for this are too numerous to list, but socio-economic problems and the strong club base in Europe and South America are important factors. After 12 tournaments, Africa and Asia have yet to win, although Qatar, Ghana, Nigeria and Japan have been runners-up.

FIFA Under-20 World Championship Finals	
1977	Soviet Union 2, Mexico 2
	Soviet Union won 9–8 on penalties.
1979	Argentina 3, Soviet Union 1
1981	West Germany 4, Qatar 0
1983	Brazil 1, Argentina 0
1985	Brazil 1, Spain 0
1987	Yugoslavia 1, West Germany 1
	Yugoslavia won 5–4 on penalties.
1989	Portugal 2, Nigeria 0
1991	Portugal 0, Brazil 0
	Portugal won 4–2 on penalties.
1993	Brazil 2, Ghana 1
1995	Argentina 2, Brazil 0
1997	Argentina 2, Uruguay 1
1999	Spain 4, Japan 0

NORWAY'S JOY *1995's World Champions*

WOMEN'S WORLD CHAMPIONSHIP

Introduced in 1991, the Women's World Cup has massive potential, with over half the world's population to cater for. FIFA are giving great encouragement to women's football and the first finals took place in China in 1991. Norway lost 2-1 to the United States in the Final in Guangzhou, but won the title two years later in Sweden. Their inspiration was Helge Riise, successor to American Michelle Akers-Stahl as the world's top woman player.

Women's World Championship Finals	
1991	USA 2, Norway 1.
1995	Norway 2, Germany 0

OLYMPIC GAMES

Football has been part of the Olympic Games since 1908, but until the Olympic "revolution" of Juan Antonio Samaranch, the amateur ethos of the Olympics seemed at odds with senior football, which had long been predominantly professional. Trouble erupted as far back as the 1920s, when the four British Associations withdrew from FIFA in a row over broken time payments to players to compensate for loss of income from their regular jobs while they were away playing football.

Football was first played at the Olympics in 1896, when a scratch tournament involving select teams from Denmark, Athens and Izmir was organized. (The only recorded result was a 15–0 victory for the Danish XI against the Izmir XI.) In Paris in 1900, football was again included as a demonstration sport, with Upton Park FC, representing England, beating France 4–0 in the only game played. In 1904 in St Louis, three North American teams entered a demonstration event which was won by Galt FC from Ontario representing Canada.

Football finally arrived as an accepted Olympic sport with the 1908 Games in London. The England amateur team (not a United Kingdom team), containing many of the best players in the country, won the title, beating Denmark 2–0 in the Final at the White City Stadium. Vivian Woodward, one of the outstanding players of the day, scored the second goal at the White City, and led the England side four years later in Stockholm. Denmark, the best amateur side on the continent, were again England's Final opponents, and again they ended up with the silver medal. Berry, Walden and Hoare (twice) scored for England in a 4–2 win against a Danish side which contained Nils Middelboe, later to play for Chelsea – one of Woodward's clubs.

The 1920 Games in Antwerp are remembered for the bad-tempered Final between Belgium and Czechoslovakia. Trailing by two goals, the Czechs felt the referee was favouring the home side and walked off the pitch before the game had ended. They were duly disqualified by FIFA, and a tournament had to be quickly arranged to decide the silver and bronze medals. Spain, having won the consolation tournament, beat Holland 3–1 to claim the silver medal.

In 1924 the Games returned to Paris and a South American nation, Uruguay, appeared for the first time. The Uruguayans brought with them dazzling ball skills which most Europeans had never seen before. They fielded a side containing some of the greats of Uruguayan football: Nasazzi, Andrade, Vidal, Scarone, Petrone, Cea and Romano, and

GOLD GETTERS *France's 1984 Olympic-winning side*

TIGHT SQUEEZE *Spain's Albert Ferrar between Poles Dariusz Gestar (left) and Andrzej Kobylanski in the 1992 Final*

Switzerland were beaten 3–0.

Four years later the Uruguayans returned, along with their great rivals Argentina, to take part in the 1928 Amsterdam Games. They met in the Final and Uruguay won after a replay 2–1 to retain the title.

Uruguay's success in 1924 and 1928 confirmed the emergence of South America as a major footballing continent, and undoubtedly led to the idea of the World Cup. From 1930, the Olympic title assumed a less important role for the major players from Western Europe and South America. Italy were the next Olympic champions, when they beat Austria 2–1 in the 1936 Final – there was no tournament in 1932.

In London in 1948, the title went to Sweden. The Swedes, featuring the famous "Grenoli" trio forward line of Gunnar Gren, Gunnar Nordahl and Nils Liedholm (all of whom later joined Milan), beat Yugoslavia 3–1 at Wembley, with Gren scoring twice. Yugoslavia reached the Final again in Helsinki in 1952, but they came up against Hungary's "Magic Magyars". Ferenc Puskas and Zoltan Czibor scored in Hungary's 2–0 win – only major title.

The period from 1952 to 1976 was dominated by the "state amateurs" from the East where all players, officially "state amateurs" but indirectly professional, were allowed to compete; in the West, players were openly professional and thus ineligible.

A qualifying series was introduced for the 1956 Melbourne Games. Lev Yashin's Soviet Union won the gold medal, beating Yugoslavia 1–0 in the Final in front of an amazing 120,000 crowd at the Melbourne Cricket Ground.

Yugoslavia made it fourth time lucky in Rome, beating the Danes, 3–1, in the Final. Hungary clinched a hat-trick of titles when they beat Czechoslovakia in 1964 in Tokyo and Bulgaria in 1968 in Mexico City; Poland ended the Hungarians' run by beating them 2–1 in the Final in Munich in 1972; and East Germany made it seven in a row for Eastern Europe when they defeated Poland 3–1 in Montreal in 1976.

FIFA changed the rules for the 1980 tournament, preventing any European or South American who had played in a World Cup qualifier from taking part. Eastern European countries had a last hurrah in Moscow, where Czechoslovakia beat East Germany 1–0. But the new eligibility ruling, even if only an unsatisfactory compromise, did break the monopoly in 1984, when France won gold in Los Angeles.

The 1988 tournament in Seoul featured a host of top professional players and many emerging youngsters yet to play in the World Cup. Ironically, the Soviet Union again struck gold, beating Brazil 2–1 in the Final. The tournament also produced one of the biggest shocks in football history; Zambia beat Italy 4–0.

For 1992, the UEFA under-21 Championship became a qualifying competition. Hosts Spain won a splendid final, beating Poland 3–2 with goals from Kiko (two) and Abelardo. They were unable to hang on to their medals, however, four years later at the Atlanta Olympics.

Yet none of the football matches were played in Atlanta itself – a discourtesy which grated with FIFA, particularly after the world body had bent the rules again to permit each nation to field three over-age players. The hope was that this would encourage mainstream nations to send a handful of star names whose presence would contribute promotional support to US soccer.

In fact, it was not a mainstream nation who carried off gold at all but Nigeria who thus made history as first African winners of the Olympic title. No-one could say they did not deserve it. Relying on the experienced nucleus of their 1994 World Cup squad, the Nigerians beat favourites Brazil 4–3 in the semi-final and then Argentina 3–2 in the final.

Winners

Olympic Games Finals

1908 *London:* England 2 (Chapman, Woodward), Denmark 0
1912 *Stockholm:* England 4 (Berry, Walden, Hoare 2), Denmark 2 (Olsen 2)
1920 *Antwerp:* Belgium 2 (Coppee, Larnoe), Czechoslovakia 0
1924 *Paris:* Uruguay 3 (Petrone, Cea, Romano), Switzerland 0. Att: 41,000

1928 *Amsterdam:* Uruguay 1 (Ferreira), Argentina 1 (Petrone) – *Amsterdam* (replay): Uruguay 2 (Figueroa, Scarone H.), Argentina 1 (Monti)
1936 *Berlin:* Italy 2 (Frossi 2), Austria 1 (Kainberger, K.). Att: 90,000
1948 *London:* Sweden 3 (Gren 2, Nordahl G.), Yugoslavia 1 (Bobek). Att: 60,000
1952 *Helsinki:* Hungary 2 (Puskas,

Czibor), Yugoslavia 0. Att: 60,000
1956 *Melbourne:* Soviet Union 1 (Ilyin), Yugoslavia 0. Att: 120,000
1960 *Rome:* Yugoslavia 3 (Galic, Matus, Kostic), Denmark 1 (Nielsen, F.). Att: 40,000
1964 *Tokyo:* Hungary 2 (o.g., Bene), Czechoslovakia 1 (Brumovsky)
1968 *Mexico City:* Hungary 4 (Menczel 2, Dunai A. 2),

Bulgaria 1 (Dimitrov)
1972 *Munich:* Poland 2 (Deyna 2), Hungary 1 (Varadi). Att: 50,000
1976 *Montreal:* East Germany 3 (Schade, Hoffmann, Hafner), Poland 1 (Lato). Att: 71,000
1980 *Moscow:* Czechoslovakia 1 (Svoboda), East Germany 0. Att: 70,000
1984 *Los Angeles:* France 2 (Brisson, Xuereb), Brazil 0. Att: 101,000

1988 *Seoul:* Soviet Union 2 (Dobrovolski, Savichev), Brazil 1 (Romario) aet. Att: 73,000
1992 *Barcelona:* Spain 3 (Abelardo, Quico 2), Poland 2 (Kowalczyk, Staniek). Att: 95,000
1996 *Athens, Georgia:* Nigeria 3 (Babayaro, Amokachi, Amunike), Argentina 2 (C Lopez, Crespo). Att: 45,000

COPA AMERICA (SOUTH AMERICAN CHAMPIONSHIP)

The South American Championship is the oldest running international competition in the world. The Copa America, as the competition has been known since 1975, is contested by the 10 members of CONMEBOL, the South American Confederation, and is 50 years older than its European equivalent.

The first tournament, in 1910, was not an official championship ("extra-ordinario"). Argentinia decided to arrange a tournament involving themselves, Uruguay, Brazil and Chile. Brazil withdrew before the tournament began, but on May 29, 1910, Uruguay and Chile contested the very first South American Championship match at in Buenos Aires.

Penarol's José Piendibene scored the first goal in the Copa America as Uruguay ran out 3–0 winners. Seven days later Argentina had an even easier 5–1 victory over Chile.

Almost 40,000 crowded into the Gimnasia ground to see the great rivals, Argentina and Uruguay, battle it out for the inaugural title, but they were to be disappointed. The fans burned one stand and the match was abandoned before it started. A day later a rearranged match was staged at Racing Club's ground, where only 8,000 saw Argentina win 4–1. The second tournament, in 1916, was also unofficial, organized to celebrate

NO PLACE LIKE HOME *When Uruguay host the Copa America they usually win it*

Argentina's centenary as an independent country. Argentina and Uruguay again clashed in the "decider", with Uruguay avenging their defeat of six years previously.

Between 1916 and 1959 the tournament was held, on average, every two years in one country. Uruguay won six of the first 11 tournaments.

Argentina then gained the upper hand winning 11 of the 18 tournaments from the 1920s to the 1950s. Brazil's four victories have all been on home soil but it was unlucky that, when they were at their peak, in the 1960s, only two tournaments were staged. Successes for the rest of the South American nations have

been few and far between. Peru won their titles in 1939 and 1975, Paraguay triumphed in 1953 and 1979. Most remarkably of all, Bolivia won in 1963 when they were hosts.

There is credence to the belief that the tournament had been held in disdain by some countries. Some countries entered weak or "B" teams or even youth sides. Indeed, 1975 was the first occasion on which all 10 CONMEBOL countries played.

Argentina has played host nine times, Chile seven, Uruguay six, Peru five and the indifferent Brazilians only four. The 1987 tournament was played in Argentina and won by Uruguay, repeating their 1983 triumph. Brazil hosted the 1989 event and won their first title in 40 years, while Argentina won in 1991.

In 1993, in Ecuador, the tournament underwent another face-lift. Mexico and the United States were invited to take part as guests, and three first round groups produced eight quarter-finalists. One of the invited guests, Mexico, almost spoiled the party by reaching the Final, where they lost 2–1 to Argentina. Mexico and the USA were invited again in 1995 in Uruguay and this time it was the US turn to embarrass their hosts, reaching the semi-finals before losing 1–0 to Brazil. But Brazil lost in the Final to hosts Uruguay, 5–3 in a penalty shoot-out, after a 1–1 draw.

Brazil made up for lost time in 1997, beating Bolivia at altitude by 3–1 in the final at La Paz with a new hero, Ronaldo, among the goals.

Winners

South American Championship

1910 *Buenos Aires*: 1st Argentina, 2nd Uruguay*
1916 *Buenos Aires*: 1st Uruguay, 2nd Argentina*
1917 *Montevideo*: 1st Uruguay, 2nd Argentina
1919 *Rio de Janeiro* (play-off): Brazil 1 (Friedenreich), Uruguay 0. Att: 28,000
1920 *Vina del Mar*: 1st Uruguay, 2nd Argentina
1921 *Buenos Aires*: 1st Argentina, 2nd Brazil
1922 *Rio de Janeiro* (play-off): Brazil 3 (Formiga 2, Neco), Paraguay 1 (Rivas G.). Att: 20,000
1923 *Montevideo*: 1st Uruguay, 2nd Argentina
1924 *Montevideo*: 1st Uruguay, 2nd Argentina

1925 *Buenos Aires*: 1st Argentina, 2nd Brazil
1926 *Santiago*: 1st Uruguay, 2nd Argentina
1927 *Lima*: 1st Argentina, 2nd Uruguay
1929 *Buenos Aires*: 1st Argentina, 2nd Paraguay
1935 *Lima*: 1st Uruguay, 2nd Argentina*
1937 *Buenos Aires* (play-off): Argentina 2 (De la Mata 2), Brazil 0. Att: 80,000
1939 *Lima*: 1st Peru, 2nd Uruguay.
1941 *Santiago*: 1st Argentina, 2nd Uruguay*
1942 *Montevideo*: 1st Uruguay, 2nd Argentina
1945 *Santiago*: 1st Argentina, 2nd Brazil*
1946 *Buenos Aires*: 1st Argentina, 2nd Brazil*

1947 *Guayaquil*: 1st Argentina, 2nd Paraguay
1949 *Rio de Janeiro* (play-off): Brazil 7 (Ademir Menezes 3, Tesourinha 2, Jair R. Pinto 2), Paraguay 0. Att: 55,000
1953 *Lima* (play-off): Paraguay 3 (Lopez A., Gavilan, Fernandez R.), Brazil 2 (Baltazar 2). Att: 35,000
1955 *Santiago*: 1st Argentina, 2nd Chile
1956 *Montevideo*: 1st Uruguay, 2nd Chile*
1957 *Lima*: 1st Argentina, 2nd Brazil
1959 *Buenos Aires*: 1st Argentina, 2nd Brazil*
1959 *Guayaquil*: 1st Uruguay, 2nd Argentina
1963 *Bolivia*: 1st Bolivia, 2nd Paraguay
1967 *Montevideo*: 1st Uruguay,

2nd Argentina
1975 *Bogota* (1st leg): Colombia 1 (Castro P.), Peru 0. Att: 50,000
Lima (2nd leg): Peru 2 (Oblitas, Ramirez O.), Colombia 0. Att: 50,000
Caracas (play-off): Peru 1 (Sotil), Colombia 0. Att: 30,000
1979 *Asuncion* (1st leg): Paraguay 3 (Romero C. 2, Morel M.), Chile 0.
Santiago (2nd leg): Chile 1 (Rivas), Paraguay 0. Att: 55,000
Buenos Aires (play-off): Paraguay 0, Chile 0. Att: 6,000 (*Paraguay won on goal difference*)
1983 *Montevideo* (1st leg): Uruguay 2 (Francescoli, Diogo), Brazil 0. Att: 65,000
Salvador (2nd leg): Brazil 1 (Jorginho), Uruguay 1 (Aguilera). Att: 95,000
1987 *Buenos Aires*: Uruguay 1 (Bengochea), Chile 0. Att: 35,000

1989 *Brazil*: 1st Brazil, 2nd Uruguay
1991 *Chile*: 1st Argentina, 2nd Brazil
1993 *Guayaquil*: Argentina 2 (Batistuta 2), Mexico 1 (Galindo pen.). Att: 40,000
1995 *Montevideo*: Uruguay 1 (Bengoechea 48), Brazil 1 (Tulio 30). (*Uruguay 5-3 on pens*). Att: 58,000
1997 *La Paz*: Brazil 3 (Edmundo 37, Ronaldo 79, Ze Roberto 90), Bolivia 1 (Irwin Sanchez 45). Att: 45,000

Notes: Details of finals or championship play-offs have been given where applicable. For all other tournaments, played on a league basis, only the first and second have been listed
* unofficial "extraordinarios" tournaments

EUROPEAN CHAMPIONSHIP

The European Championship, surprisingly, was the last of the continental tournaments to get under way, and was yet another French innovation. Proposed in the mid-1950s by Henri Delaunay, secretary of the French football federation, the European Nations Cup, as the event was previously known, was designed to bring together the various regional tournaments such as the British Home International Championship, the Nordic Cup and the Central European Championship for the Dr Gero Cup.

Delaunay, sadly, died before the tournament got under way, but the trophy still bears his name, and his idea has grown into the second most important international competition after the World Cup.

The first tournament was held in 1959–60, and was played on a straightforward home and away knock-out basis. A four-team final series followed, though the hosts for the final matches were not decided until the semi-finalists were known. The very first European Championship match took place in Moscow on September 28, 1958, when the Soviet Union beat Hungary 3–1 in a first round, first leg tie. Soviet winger Anatoly Ilyin scored the first ever European Championship goal after four minutes. There were many absentees from the tournament, including Sweden, Italy, West Germany, Switzerland, Holland and the four British nations.

The Eastern Bloc occupied three of the four semi-final slots in the 1960 finals, which France hosted. In the Final, Yugoslavia's all-out attack threatened to overrun the Soviets, but Lev Yashin responded with a string of fine saves. The Yugoslavs did take the lead, but the Soviets equalized almost immediately and made their superior physical strength count in extra time to win 2–1.

The 1964 finals tournament took place in Spain, where the hosts made good use of home advantage to win the trophy beating the Soviet Union in Madrid, 2–1.

The qualifying tournament was expanded to eight groups for the 1968 event. Hosts Italy beat the Soviet Union in the first semi-final, but only by the rather dubious method of tossing a coin. World champions England also reached the semi-finals, but were beaten 1–0 by Yugoslavia. The final went to a replay, where goals by Riva and Anastasi were too much for the exhausted Yugoslav players, who again had to be content with runners-up medals.

The Soviets reached their third final out of four in 1972, but were no match for the West Germans. The incomparable Gerd Müller was at his peak, and two goals by him in the Final set up a 3–0 victory, and confirmed the Germans as favourites for the World Cup to be held two years later on their home soil

The 1976 tournament threw up surprises from start to finish. England, Italy and France were eliminated in the qualifying round, and the semi-final line-up comprised surprising Czechoslovakia, 1974 World Cup winners West Germany and runners-up Holland and hosts Yugoslavia. Both semi-finals went to extra-time, the Czechs beating the Dutch 3–1 and the West Germans defeating the Yugoslavs 4–2, with a hat-trick from substitute Dieter Müller.

The Germans were clear favourites, but the Czechs had other ideas. Goals by Svehlik and Dobias gave them a 2–0 lead inside half an hour, but West Germany fought back, Holzenbein snatching an equalizer in the 89th minute. Extra time failed to separate the teams, and in the penalty shoot-out, Antonin Panenka chipped his penalty past Sepp Maier to win the trophy.

In 1980 the format for the final stages of the competition changed. The quarter-finals were abolished and the seven qualifying group winners proceeded straight to the finals along with the hosts, Italy, who received a bye direct to the final stage. The eight teams were divided into two groups of four, with the winners meeting in the final.

The Soviets failed to qualify for their "favourite" tournament, and the Yugoslavs also missed out, but there was a first-ever finals appearance for Greece. Belgium proved the surprise package of the tournament, reaching the final after conquering England, Spain and Italy in the group matches. West Germany won the other group with a little to spare and became the only nation to win the trophy twice when they beat the Belgians 2–1 with two goals from Horst Hrubesch – one early in the game, the other two minutes from time.

The 1984 tournament was the best to date, with the flamboyant French hosts in unstoppable form. They had Michel Platini to thank for their success. His nine goals in five games was a superb achievement as the French swept aside Denmark, Belgium and Yugoslavia in the group matches. Unfancied Spain clinched the other group and then squeezed past the impressive Danes on penalties after a 1–1 draw in the re-introduced semi-finals. The Final was more conclusive. Platini and Bellone scored the goals as the host country won for the third time in seven events.

The 1988 finals in West Germany included all Europe's big names, bar the French, plus one new one: the Republic of Ireland. The Irish shocked lacklustre England in their first game and almost qualified for the semi-finals, but lost 1–0 to a late Dutch goal from Wim Kieft, a miscued header which spun past Pat Bonner into the Irish net.

The Soviet Union qualified with Holland to reach the semi-finals, where they met – and beat – Italy and West Germany respectively. With Rinus Michels in charge, the Dutch played irresistible football, beating the hosts 2–1 in the semi-final with a splendidly taken goal by Marco Van Basten two minutes from time. Van Basten did even better in the Final against the Soviet Union, crashing home a volley from an almost impossible angle to seal a 2–0 victory following Ruud Gullit's first-half opener.

Sweden hosted the 1992 finals. They and Scotland were making their debut in the finals and the now former Soviet Union played under the banner of Commonwealth of Independent States, but the biggest surprises were Denmark, last-minute replacements for the suspended Yugoslavia. They arrived with little time to prepare and walked off with the trophy after beating Holland in penalties in the semi-finals and then a shocked Germany by 2–0 in the final in Gothenburg. Midfielders John Jensen and Kim Vilfort were their goal-scoring heroes with Peter Schmeichel a rock in goal.

The 1996 finals took the European Championship to a new plane. Entry doubled to 16 finalists in four groups in the most exciting football extravanza in England since the 1966 World Cup. England started slowly with a 1–1 draw against Switzerland and steadily improved. Alan Shearer was the tournament's top scorer with an impressive five goals. But in the semi-finals Germany once again proved the masters of the penalty shoot-out at the hosts expense. Despite a horrendous injury list, Berti Vogt's men went on to beat the Czech Republic 2–1 in the final. Substitute Oliver Bierhoff made history, scoring both German goals including the first top-level golden goal decider.

Finals

European Championship Finals

1960 *Paris:* Soviet Union 2 (Metreveli, Ponedelnik), Yugoslavia 1 (Galic). Att: 18,000

1964 *Madrid:* Spain 2 (Pereda, Marcelino), Soviet Union 1 (Khusainov). Att: 105,000

1968 *Rome:* Italy 1 (Domenghini), Yugoslavia 1 (Dzajic). Att: 85,000. Replay – *Rome:* Italy 2 (Riva, Anastasi), Yugoslavia 0. Att: 85,000

1972 *Brussels:* West Germany 3 (Müller G. 2, Wimmer), Soviet Union 0. Att: 65,000

1976 *Belgrade:* Czechoslovakia 2 (Svehlik, Dobias), West Germany 2 (Müller D., Holzenbein) (aet). Czechoslovakia won 5–4 on penalties. Att: 45,000

1980 *Rome:* West Germany 2 (Hrubesch 2), Belgium 1 (Vandereycken). Att: 48,000

1984 *Paris:* France 2 (Platini, Bellone), Spain 0. Att: 47,000

1988 *Munich:* Holland 2 (Gullit, Van Basten), Soviet Union 0. Att: 72,000

1992 *Stockholm:* Denmark 2 (Jensen, Vilfort), Germany 0. Att: 37,000

1996 *Wembley:* Germany 2 (Bierhoff 72, 94 golden goal), Czech Republic 1 (Berger 59pen). Att: 73,611

EUROPEAN UNDER-21 CHAMPIONSHIP

Started in 1978, this is Europe's top competition for up-and-coming players. The event now doubles up as the European qualifying tournament for the Olympic Games.

European Under-21 Championship Winners	
1978 Yugoslavia	**1990** Soviet Union
1980 Soviet Union	**1992** Italy
1982 England	**1994** Portugal
1984 England	**1996** Italy
1986 Spain	**1998** Spain
1988 France	

EUROPEAN YOUTH CHAMPIONSHIP

This tournament began life, in 1948, as the European Junior Championship for Under-18s. It was renamed the European Youth Championship in 1981. England have the best overall record with nine victories, including a hat-trick of titles between 1971 and 1973, and were winners in 1993.

European Youth Championship Winners	
1948 England	**1972** England
1949 France	**1973** England
1950 Austria	**1974** Bulgaria
1951 Yugoslavia	**1975** England
1952 Spain	**1976** Soviet Union
1953 Hungary	**1977** Belgium
1954 Spain	**1978** Soviet Union
1957 Austria	**1979** Yugoslavia
1958 Italy	**1980** England
1959 Bulgaria	**1981** W. Germany
1960 Hungary	**1982** Scotland
1961 Portugal	**1983** France
1962 Romania	**1984** Hungary
1963 England	**1986** E. Germany
1964 England	**1988** Soviet Union
1965 E. Germany	**1990** Soviet Union
1966 Soviet U/Italy	**1992** Turkey
1967 Soviet Union	**1993** England
1968 Czechoslovakia	**1994** Portugal
1969 Bulgaria	**1995** Spain
1970 E. Germany	**1996** France
1971 England	**1997** France

AFRICAN NATIONS CUP

The African Nations Cup is the blue ribbon event of African football, and the tournament is as old as the Confederation of African Football itself. Held every two years in a nominated country, the tournament has grown from humble beginnings to embrace the whole continent.

The first finals took place in Khartoum in 1957 and involved only Sudan, Egypt and Ethiopia. South Africa were initially due to take part, and were scheduled to play Ethiopia in the semi-final, but would only send either an all-black team or an all-white team. The CAF insisted on a multi-racial team, South Africa refused and withdrew, and, until readmitted to the CAF in 1992, they took no further part in African or international football.

Egypt won the first tournament, with El Diba scoring all four goals in the 4–0 win over Ethiopia in the Final. The same three nations took part in the second, which Egypt hosted in 1959. The tournament was played on a league basis, and Egypt retained the trophy by beating Ethiopia 4–0, with Gohri scoring a hat-trick, and Sudan 2–1. Ethiopia hosted the third tournament in 1962, where Tunisia and Uganda took part for the first time. This time round the Ethiopians prevented the Egyptians completing a hat-trick of consecutive titles by beating them 4–2 in a Final which went to extra time.

Ghana and Nigeria joined the fray for the 1963 tournament, held in Ghana, with two groups of three producing the two finalists – Ghana and Sudan. The hosts won 3–0 and went on to become the dominant force in African football during the decade, twice winning and twice finishing as runners-up.

Two years later, in Tunisia, the Ghanaians won again, this time beating the hosts 3–2 after extra time. A new rule allowing each country to field only two overseas-based players was also introduced in 1965, to encourage development of the game in Africa.

The tournament had by now grown from its original three to 18 entrants, and a qualifying tournament was introduced to produce eight finalists, with the hosts and holders qualifying for the final round automatically. Congo Kinshasa, as Zaïre was known, duly faced reigning champions Ghana in the 1968 Final in Addis Ababa, and pulled off something of a shock by winning 1–0 with a goal by Kalala. Ghana returned for the 1970 Final in Khartoum, but lost 1–0 to the hosts Sudan.

In 1972, in Yaounde, Zaïre's neighbours Congo won the title, beating Mali 3–2 in the Final. But Zaïre returned in 1974 to face Zambia in the Final. A 2–2 draw in the first game was followed by a 2–0 win for Zaïre, who travelled to the World Cup finals a few months later as reigning African champions and the first African side to reach the finals of the world's premier event. Here Zaïre striker Ndaye scored twice in the first match and repeated the trick in the second – the first time that the African Nations Cup had required a replay.

Guinea won numerous club honours during the 1970s, but these triumphs were never reflected at national level. They went closest to winning the African title in 1976 in Ethiopia. A final round group replaced the semi-finals and Final, and Guinea needed a win in their final match against Morocco to take the title. Cherif gave them the lead after 33 minutes, but an equalizer by Baba four minutes from time gave Morocco a 1–1 draw and the title by a point.

Morocco, like their North African neighbours, have not done particularly well in the African Nations Cup. Despite qualifying for the World Cup finals on three occasions, 1976 remains Morocco's only African title. Given the success of North African clubs in continental competitions, it is curious that the national sides have not matched them.

Nigeria won their first African Nations Cup title on home soil in 1980. The semi-finals featured the hosts, Algeria, Egypt and Morocco, but again the North Africans revealed a dislike for travelling. Paired with Algeria in the Final, and spurred on by a crowd of 80,000 in Lagos, the Nigerians won 3–0 with goals by Odegbami (two) and Lawal.

The 1982 tournament in Libya saw the return of Ghana to the African throne. The two-overseas-players rule, which had become impractical with so many of them earning a living in Europe, was abolished, and nations could choose their best line-ups once again. In the opening game of the tournament Libya beat Ghana 2–0, but both countries progressed to the Final. This time round the Ghanaians made their greater experience count as they fought out a 1–1 draw before taking the trophy for a record fourth time with a 7–6 penalty shoot-out victory.

Cameroon emerged for their only victory in the 1984 finals in the Ivory Coast. Having squeezed past Algeria in the semi-finals, on penalties, they beat Nigeria 3–1 in the Final. Their side contained many who had performed so well at the 1982 World Cup finals in Spain, including the incomparable Roger Milla.

In 1986 Egypt hosted the tournament, which was marked by incidents on and off the field. A week before the tournament began, secu-

Winners

African Nations Cup Finals				
1957 *Khartoum:* Egypt 4, Ethiopia 0.	**1968** *Addis Ababa:* Congo Kinshasa (Zaïre) 1, Ghana 0.	**1978** *Accra:* Ghana 2, Uganda 0. Att: 40,000.	**1986** *Cairo:* Egypt 0, Cameroon 0 (aet). (*Egypt won 5–4 on penalties.*) Att: 100,000.	**1994** *Tunis:* Nigeria 2, Zambia 1 (Litana). Att: 25,000
1959 *Cairo:* 1st Egypt, 2nd Sudan.	**1970** *Khartoum:* Sudan 1, Ghana 0. Att: 12,000.	**1980** *Lagos:* Nigeria 3, Algeria 0. Att: 80,000.	**1988** *Casablanca:* Cameroon 1, Nigeria 0. Att: 50,000.	**1996** *Johannesburg:* South Africa 2 (Williams 2), Tunisia 0. Att: 80,000
1962 *Addis Ababa:* Ethiopia 4, Egypt 2 (aet).	**1972** *Yaounde:* Congo 3, Mali 2.	**1982** *Tripoli:* Ghana 1, Libya 1 (aet). (*Ghana won 7–6 on penalties.*) Att: 50,000	**1990** *Algiers:* Algeria 1, Nigeria 0. Att: 80,000.	**1998** *Ougadougou (Burkina Faso):* Egypt 2, South Africa 0. Att: 40,000
1963 *Accra:* Ghana 3, Sudan 0.	**1974** *Cairo:* Zaïre 2, Zambia 2 (aet). *Cairo* (replay): Zaïre 2, Zambia 0. Att: 1,000.	**1984** *Abidjan:* Cameroon 3, Nigeria 0. Att: 50,000.	**1992** *Dakar:* Ivory Coast 0, Ghana 0 (aet). (*Ghana won 11–10 on penalties.*) Att: 60,000.	
1965 *Tunis:* Ghana 3, Tunisia 2 (aet).	**1976** *Addis Ababa:* 1st Morocco, 2nd Guinea.			

BAFANA BAFANA *The rallying call by African champions South Africa in 1996*

rity police conscripts in Egypt rioted. A curfew was imposed and there was the very real threat that the finals would have to be cancelled. Thankfully the curfew was lifted so that the tournament could take place, but tanks and armoured cars still surrounded the stadiums to prevent further trouble.

On the pitch many of the teams complained about the standard of refereeing, and there were several angry outbursts from players and managers. Morocco manager José Faria was even prompted to describe one match as being rougher than the England vs. France Rugby Union international which was staged at about the same time! Defending champions Cameroon again reached the Final, where they met the hosts Egypt. The tournament as a whole had been laden with defensive play, and the Final was no exception. After a very dull 0–0 draw the hosts won the Cup, 5–4 on penalties, to the delight of the 100,000 crowd at Cairo's International Stadium.

Cameroon recovered from this disappointment by winning the 1988 title in Morocco. In the semi-finals, they beat the hosts by a single goal while Nigeria needed penalties to get past Algeria. A crowd of 50,000

in Casablanca saw Cameroon win 1–0 with a goal by Emmanuel Kunde after 55 minutes.

Two years later, in Algiers, the Nigerians again reached the Final. Unfortunately for them, they met the hosts and were again beaten by a single goal, from Oudjani after 38 minutes, in front of 80,000 fans. For the poor Nigerians, it was their third final defeat in four tournaments.

In 1992 a new name was added to the list of winners: the Ivory Coast. The tournament, held in Senegal for the first time, was expanded to 12 teams in the final round because of the ever-increasing number of countries taking part – even tiny nations such as Burkina Faso, Swaziland and the Seychelles now consider the African Nations Cup a worthwhile exercise. The Ivory Coast and their western neighbours Ghana reached the Final, although the Ivorians needed penalties to overcome Cameroon in the semi-finals. The Final finished goalless and, in one of the most amazing penalty shoot-outs ever seen, the Ivory Coast won 11–10.

Zambia suffered a catastrophe in April 1993, when the plane carrying their squad to a World Cup match in Senegal crashed into the sea off Gabon, en route from a nations cup

qualifier in Mauritius. All 30 people on board, including 18 players, died. But several European-based players were not on the flight, and the Zambians rebuilt their team around them, completed their qualifying programme and duly qualified for the 1994 finals in Tunisia. Neutrals must have been hoping that Zambia would win, but they fell to Nigeria who, in their fourth final in 10 years, finally triumphed

The tournament has come a long way since 1957 with the expanded 1996 finals, up to 16 teams from 12. Much of this has to do with the late switch to South Africa as host venue after Kenya withdrew through lack of funds.

With the home fans still celebrating their success in winning rugby union's World Cup in 1995, South Africa surprised the continent by proving too strong for everybody and with a number of players now based in northern Europe, they won the trophy. Their task was made easier by Nigeria's decision to pull out of the tournament a few days before the opening ceremony.

South Africa were again finalists in 1998. Ajax forward Benni McCarthy was voted star player and was joint top-scorer with seven goals. But he failed to score in the final and South Africa lost 2–0 to Egypt.

ASIAN CUP

The Asian Cup, for national teams started in 1956 and, until the 1980 tournament, was dominated by South Korea and Iran. Since then Kuwait and Saudi Arabia have enjoyed success, reflecting the shift of power in Asian football towards the Arab states, although Japan won in 1992 and appear to be getting stronger.

Asian Cup Finals
1956	South Korea 2, Israel 1
1960	South Korea 3, Israel 0
1964	Israel 2, India 0
1968	Iran 3, Burma 1
1972	Iran 2, South Korea 1
1976	Iran 1, Kuwait 0
1980	Kuwait 3, South Korea 0
1984	Saudi Arabia 2, China 0
1988	Saudi Arabia 0, South Korea 0
	(Saudia Arabia won 4–3 on penalties)
1992	Japan 1, Saudi Arabia 0
1996	Saudi Arabia 0, United Arab Emirates 0
	(Saudia Arabia won 4–2 on penalties)

ASIAN GAMES

The first Asian games were organized by India in 1951, and six countries brought teams for the football tournament. Since then the Asian Games football tournament has expanded to include most of the continent, and is effectively the region's second continental championship.

Asian Games Finals
1951	India 1, Iran 0
1954	Taiwan 5, South Korea 2
1958	Taiwan 3, South Korea 2
1962	India 2, South Korea 1
1966	Burma 1, Iran 0
1970	Burma 0, South Korea 0
1974	Iran 1, Israel 0
1978	North Korea 0, South Korea 0
1982	Iraq 1, Kuwait 0
1986	South Korea 2, Saudi Arabia 0
1990	Iran 0, North Korea 0
	(Iran won 4–1 on penalties)
1994	Uzbekistan 4, China 2

Note: The trophy was shared in 1970 and 1978

CONCACAF CHAMPIONSHIP

The Central American Championship has been contested, under various formats and with varying numbers of participants, since 1941. Costa Rica has the most outstanding record, with 10 victories, including three in a row between 1960 and 1963. In 1991 Mexico and the United States became involved in what was now upgraded as the CONCACAF Gold Cup. The Americans beat Honduras on penalties in that final but Mexico dominated the rest of the 1990s. In 1996 they beat invited guests Brazil and then completed the hat-trick by defeating the United States in front of a crowd of 91,000 in Los Angeles in 1998.

CONCACAF Championship Winners
1941	Costa Rica	**1967**	Guatemala
1943	El Salvador	**1969**	Costa Rica
1946	Costa Rica	**1971**	Mexico
1948	Costa Rica	**1973**	Haiti
1951	Panama	**1977**	Mexico
1953	Costa Rica	**1981**	Honduras
1955	Costa Rica	**1985**	Canada
1957	Haiti	**1989**	Costa Rica
1960	Costa Rica	**1991**	USA
1961	Costa Rica	**1993**	Mexico
1963	Costa Rica	**1996**	Mexico
1965	Mexico	**1998**	Mexico

CLUB COMPETITIONS

WORLD CLUB CUP

The World Club Cup is not, as its name suggests, open to every side in the world. In reality it is a challenge match between the champions of Europe and the champions of South America. Asia, Africa and the rest of the world do not get a look in …yet. FIFA is now considering plans to expand the tournament to include the best sides from each of the continental confederations in an end-of-season event in years in between World Cups and European Championships. The idea is still in its infancy and may never come to fruition.

Henri Delaunay, UEFA general secretary, first suggested the idea of a challenge match between the champions of Europe and South America in a letter to CONMEBOL, the South American Confederation, in 1958. His idea provided the impetus for them to get the Copa Libertadores (the South American Club Cup) up and running because, at that stage, South America had no continental championship for its clubs, even though an event for national sides had been taking place since 1910.

Before 1980, matches in the World Club Cup, or Intercontinental Cup as it is sometimes known, were played on a home and away basis, and up until 1968 the result was decided by points, not the aggregate score. This meant that if the clubs won one match each or both were drawn, a decider had to be played. Until 1964 this decider had, for reasons never fully explained, to take place on the ground of the team who played at home in the second leg, giving them a massive advantage. Then for another four years the decider at least had to be played on that club's continent.

Despite these tortuous rules, the competition got off to a flying start in 1960, when Real Madrid met Penarol of Uruguay. Madrid had just won their fifth European Cup in a row, with a 7–3 demolition of Ein-tracht Frankfurt, while Penarol had become the first winners of the Copa Libertadores. The first leg, in Montevideo, produced a 0–0 draw, but in the return two months later Real Madrid pounded the Uruguayans 5–1. The Real forward line was one of the best ever, and contained Del Sol, Di Stefano, Gento and Puskas, who scored twice. A combined attendance of 200,000 saw the matches.

In 1961 it was Penarol's turn to chalk up five goals, this time against the emerging Portuguese eagles, Benfica. However, a solitary Coluna goal in the first leg meant a decider was necessary, and Penarol only just managed to win 2–1 at home against a Benfica side bolstered by a young Eusebio, who was specially flown in.

Benfica represented Europe again in 1962, but this time they ran head-long into Brazil's Santos …and Pele. The "Black Pearl" scored twice in Rio as Santos narrowly won 3–2, and then scored a breathtaking hat-trick in Lisbon as Benfica crashed to a 5–2 home defeat. Santos became one of only four sides to retain the trophy when they beat Milan in 1963. Both teams won 4–2 at home, but the decider provided a nasty taste of things to come, with a player from each side sent off and a penalty deciding the outcome, in favour of the Brazilians, who were without Pele for the second and third games.

The next two editions were contested by Internazionale of Italy and Independiente of Argentina, with Inter winning on both occasions. A goal by Corso in a decider in Madrid was enough in 1964, and the following year Inter drew 0–0 away and won the home leg 3–0 to retain the trophy. Among the famous names in the Inter line-up were Suarez, Mazzola and Fachetti.

In 1966 Penarol returned to win for the third time, beating Real Madrid 2–0 in both legs, with Spencer scoring three of the Uruguayans' goals. From this encouraging start, the World Club Cup ran into severe problems in the late 1960s and early 1970s, largely owing to different styles of play and behaviour.

The 1967 series paired Argentina's Racing Club with Scotland's Celtic. Feelings in Argentina were still running high over their 1966 World Cup quarter-final elimination by England, and the matches degenerated into a bad-tempered farce. After a 1–0 Celtic win in Glasgow, the return in Buenos Aires was chaotic. Celtic goalkeeper Ronnie Simpson was struck by a missile from the crowd before the kick-off, and could not play. Racing won 2–1 to set up a decider, in Montevideo, which was doomed before it began. Celtic lost their composure under extreme provocation and had four men sent off after Basile had spat at Lennox. Racing also had

WORLD'S BEST *Barcelona's Dane Michael Laudrup takes the ball away from São Paulo's Rai in Tokyo in 1992*

two men sent off but won 1–0.

It was extremely unfortunate, therefore, that the next team to represent South America – for three years running – were Estudiantes de la Plata of Argentina, a team who were solely interested in winning, and would stop at nothing to do it. At home in 1968 they battered Manchester United, who had Nobby Stiles sent off for a gesture to a linesman and Bobby Charlton taken off with a shin injury caused by a kick from Pachame. In the return at Old Trafford, Medina and Best were sent off for fighting as, under the competition's revised rules, the Argentinians completed a 2–1 aggregate win.

The following year, 1969, Milan came off even worse than United. After winning 3–0 at home, Milan were savaged in Buenos Aires, where Combin had his nose broken and Prati was kicked in the back while receiving treatment, but managed to hold on for a 4–2 aggregate victory. Three Estudiantes players were imprisoned after the game for their outrageous behaviour and were given severe suspensions at the request of the Argentinian president.

Sadly, Estudiantes did not learn their lesson, and things were as bad in 1970 when they played Feyenoord, who came out on top after drawing the drawing the first leg in Buenos Aires. In the return in Rotterdam, Feyenoord's bespectacled Van Deale had his glasses smashed early in the game but still scored the winner. Feyenoord made it known that they would not have taken part in a decider if it had been needed, and the following year their countrymen, Ajax, went a step further by refusing to play against Nacional of Uruguay. Panathinaikos, beaten finalists in the European Cup, were appointed by UEFA to replace Ajax, and put up a brave performance before losing 3–2 on aggregate.

After such violent clashes, the value of the competition came into question, and it looked as if the World Club Cup would fade into history. Ajax did restore some credibility with a fine 4–1 aggregate win over Independiente in 1972, despite some rough treatment for Johan Cruyff, but the trend they started the year before continued throughout the 1970s.

Rather than risk their valuable players being mangled by the South Americans, Ajax, Liverpool, Bayern Munich and Nottingham Forest refused to take part, reducing the competition to a side-show. On all bar two occasions, 1975 and 1978 (when the competition was not held), the beaten European Cup finalists substituted for the real champions – Atletico Madrid even managing a victory in 1974 against Independiente, who were making the fourth of their six appearances in the event. Clearly this situation could not continue and it is, ironically, Japan we have to thank for the event's survival.

In 1980 the format of the World Club Cup was changed. The two-legged tie was replaced by a single game at the National Stadium in Tokyo. The car manufacturer Toyota sponsored the competition.

The tournament has now regained much of its credibility, and since 1980 the European and South American champions have consistently taken part. The South Americans won the first five matches played in Tokyo, with the Europeans enjoying more success in the second half of the decade. In 1991 Red Star Belgrade became the first Eastern European side to win when they beat Chile's Colo Colo 3–0, with two goals from midfielder Vladimir Jugovic – whose European Cup-winning penalty in 1996 would earn Juventus another crack at the crown.

In the meantime, Barcelona and Milan (twice), however highly-rated in Europe, were successively dismissed by São Paulo (twice) and Argentina's Velez Sarsfield. While European commentators called Milan the world's best, their duel with São Paulo suggested otherwise.

Not until 1995 did Europe regain the trophy and then they clung on to it. First Ajax needed a penalty shoot-out to defeat yet another contestant from Brazil in Gremio. Then Juventus, having succeeded the Dutch as European champions, took over their world mantle with a 1–0 win over River Plate.

Winners

World Club Cup Finals

1960 Montevideo: Penarol 0, Real Madrid 0. Att: 75,000
Madrid: Real Madrid 5 (Puskas 2, Di Stefano, Herrera, Gento), Penarol 1 (Borges). Att: 125,000
1961 Lisbon: Benfica 1 (Coluna), Penarol 0. Att: 50,000
Montevideo: Penarol 5 (Sasia, Joya 2, Spencer 2), Benfica 0. Att: 56,000
Montevideo (play-off): Penarol 2 (Sasia 2), Benfica 1 (Eusebio). Att: 62,000
1962 Rio de Janeiro: Santos 3 (Pele 2, Coutinho), Benfica 2 (Santana 2). Att: 90,000
Lisbon: Benfica 2 (Eusebio, Santana), Santos 5 (Pele 3, Coutinho, Pepe). Att: 75,000
1963 Milan: Milan 4 (Trapattoni, Amarildo 2, Mora), Santos 2 (Pele 2). Att: 80,000
Rio de Janeiro: Santos 4 (Pepe 2, Almir, Lima), Milan 2 (Altafini, Mora). Att: 150,000
Rio de Janeiro (play-off): Santos 1 (Dalmo), Milan 0. Att: 121,000
1964 Avellaneda: Independiente 1 (Rodriguez), Internazionale 0. Att: 70,000
Milan: Internazionale 2 (Mazzola, Corso), Independiente 0. Att: 70,000
Milan (play-off): Internazionale 1 (Corso), Independiente 0 (aet). Att: 45,000
1965 Milan: Internazionale 3 (Peiro, Mazzola 2), Independiente 0. Att: 70,000
Avellaneda: Independiente 0, Internazionale 0. Att: 70,000
1966 Montevideo: Penarol 2 (Spencer 2), Real Madrid 0. Att: 70,000
Madrid: Real Madrid 0, Penarol 2 (Rocha, Spencer). Att: 70,000
1967 Glasgow: Celtic 1 (McNeill), Racing Club 0. Att: 103,000
Avellaneda: Racing Club 2 (Raffo, Cardenas), Celtic 1 (Gemmell). Att: 80,000
Montevideo (play-off): Racing Club 1 (Cardenas), Celtic 0. Att: 65,000
1968 Buenos Aires: Estudiantes 1 (Conigliaro), Manchester United 0. Att: 65,000
Manchester: Manchester United 1 (Morgan), Estudiantes 1 (Veron). Att: 60,000
1969 Milan: Milan 3 (Sormani 2, Combin), Estudiantes 0. Att: 80,000
Buenos Aires: Estudiantes 2 (Conigliaro, Aguirre-Suarez), Milan 1 (Rivera). Att: 65,000. Milan won 4–2 on aggregate
1970 Buenos Aires: Estudiantes 2 (Echecopar, Veron), Feyenoord 2 (Kindvall, Van Hanegem). Att: 65,000

Rotterdam: Feyenoord 1 (Van Deale), Estudiantes 0. Att: 70,000. Feyenoord won 3–2 on aggregate.
1971 Athens: Panathinaikos 1 (Filakouris), Nacional (Uru) 1 (Artime). Att: 60,000
Montevideo: Nacional 2 (Artime 2), Panathinaikos 1 (Filakouris). Att: 70,000. Nacional won 3–2 on aggregate
1972 Avellaneda: Independiente 1 (Sa), Ajax 1 (Cruyff). Att: 65,000.
Amsterdam: Ajax 3 (Neeskens, Rep 2), Independiente 0. Att: 60,000. Ajax won 4–1 on aggregate
1973 Rome (single match): Independiente 1 (Bochini 40), Juventus 0. Att: 35,000.
1974 Buenos Aires: Independiente 1 (Balbuena 33), Atletico Madrid 0. Att: 60,000
Madrid: Atletico Madrid 2 (Irureta 21, Ayala 86), Independiente 0. Att: 45,000. Atletico won 2–1 on aggregate
1975 not played.
1976 Munich: Bayern Munich 2 (Müller, Kapellmann), Cruzeiro 0. Att: 22,000
Belo Horizonte: Cruzeiro 0, Bayern Munich 0. Att: 114,000. Bayern won 2–0 on aggregate
1977 Buenos Aires: Boca Juniors 2 (Mastrangelo, Ribolzi), Borussia Monchengladbach 2 (Hannes,

Bonhof). Att: 50,000.
Karlsruhe: Borussia Mönchengladbach 0, Boca Juniors 3 (Zanabria, Mastrangelo, Salinas). Att: 21,000. Boca Juniors won 5–2 on aggregate
1978 not played.
1979 Malmö: Malmö 0, Olimpia 1 (Isasi). Att: 4,000
Asuncion: Olimpia 2 (Solalinde, Michelagnoli), Malmö 1 (Earlandson). Att: 35,000. Olimpia won 3–1 on aggregate
1980 Tokyo: Nacional (Uru) 1 (Victorino), Nottingham Forest 0. Att: 62,000
1981 Tokyo: Flamengo 3 (Nunes 2, Adilio), Liverpool 0. Att: 62,000
1982 Tokyo: Penarol 2 (Jair, Charrua), Aston Villa 0. Att: 62,000
1983 Tokyo: Gremio 2 (Renato 2), Hamburg SV 1 (Schroder). Att: 62,000
1984 Tokyo: Independiente 1 (Percudiani), Liverpool 0. Att: 62,000
1985 Tokyo: Juventus 2 (Platini, Laudrup M.), Argentinos Juniors 2 (Ereros, Castro) (aet). Att: 62,000 (Juventus won 4–2 on penalties)
1986 Tokyo: River Plate 1 (Alzamendi), Steaua Bucharest 0. Att: 62,000
1987 Tokyo: FC Porto 2 (Gomes, Madjer), Penarol 1 (Viera) (aet). Att: 45,000
1988 Tokyo: Nacional (Uru) 2

(Ostolaza 2), PSV Eindhoven 2 (Romario, Koeman R.) (aet). Att: 62,000 (Nacional won 7–6 on penalties)
1989 Tokyo: Milan 1 (Evani), Nacional (Col) 0 (aet). Att: 62,000
1990 Tokyo: Milan 3 (Rijkaard 2, Stroppa), Olimpia 0. Att: 60,000
1991 Tokyo: Red Star Belgrade 3 (Jugovic 2, Pancev), Colo Colo 0. Att: 60,000
1992 Tokyo: São Paulo 2 (Rai 2), Barcelona 1 (Stoichkov). Att: 80,000
1993 Tokyo: São Paulo 3 (Palinha, Cerezo, Müller), Milan 2 (Massaro, Papin). Att: 52,000
1994 Tokyo: Velez Sarsfield 2 (Trott, Abad), Milan 0. Att: 65,000
1995 Tokyo: Ajax 0, Gremio 0 (aet). Att: 62,000 (Ajax won 4–3 on penalties)
1996 Tokyo: Juventus 1 (Del Piero), River Place 0. Att: 55,000
1997 Tokyo: Borussia Dortmund 2 (Zorc, Herrlich), Cruzeiro 0. Att: 60,000
1998 Tokyo: Real Madrid 2 (Naza og, Raul), Vasco da Gama 1 (Juninho). Att: 51,514
Notes:
From 1960 to 1979 the World Club Cup was decided on points, not goal difference. Since 1980 it has been a one-off match in Tokyo.

WORLD'S SECOND BEST *Liverpool lost to Independiente in 1984*

Cruzeiro returned in 1997 for the first time since their 1976 defeat by Bayern Munich, but lost once more to German opposition in Borussia Dortmund.

COPA LIBERTADORES (SOUTH AMERICAN CLUB CUP)

The Copa Libertadores is undoubtedly South America's premier club event, but has had a long history of problems both on and off the pitch.

The competition was started in 1960 after a proposition from UEFA that the champions of South America should play against the European champions for the world title. A South American Champion Clubs Cup had been organized by Chile's Colo Colo as early as 1948, but the competition, won by Brazil's Vasco da Gama, was a financial disaster and was not staged again. But UEFA's success with the European Cup prompted CONMEBOL to consider giving the competition another chance, and the lucrative carrot of the World Club Cup swayed the balance in favour of trying again.

The first series was held in 1960, with seven of the continent's champions playing home and away matches on a knock-out basis, including the Final. This has always been played over two legs, with games won, not goal difference, deciding the winners. Goal difference only came into the equation if the play-off failed to produce a winner, and is no longer rel-

evant, since recently penalties have replaced the play-off.

The first two competitions were won by Penarol, and almost passed unnoticed. Alberto Spencer scored in both those victories, against Olimpia and Palmeiras, and he remains top scorer in the Copa Libertadores with over 50 goals.

In the following year, 1962, the format of the competition changed as more teams entered. The home-and-away knock-out method was replaced by groups, played for points, up until the Final. Penarol again appeared in the Final, against Santos, and the first of many unsavoury incidents which have scarred the Copa Libertadores occurred.

The first leg, in Montevideo, passed peacefully with a 2–1 win for Santos, but the second leg took three and a half hours to complete! The game was suspended shortly after half-time, with Penarol leading 3–2, because the Chilean referee, Carlos Robles, had been hit by a stone and knocked unconscious. After discussions lasting 80 minutes he agreed to continue the game, but there was more trouble to follow.

Santos equalized just as a linesman, raising his flag, was knocked out by another stone from the terraces, prompting Robles to suspend the game once more. At a disciplinary hearing later, Robles claimed that the match had officially been suspended when Penarol were 3–2 up, and that he had only concluded the match to ensure his own safety! So, the game was duly logged as a 3–2 win for Penarol, forcing a play-off which

Santos won easily, 3–0.

Santos retained their trophy a year later, beating Boca Juniors home and away, but had been helped by the rule which gave the holders a bye into the semi-finals. With Pele in the Santos side, the Copa Libertadores received the image boost it needed. Interest in the competition increased dramatically, and by 1964 every CONMEBOL country entered.

Boca's run to the Final was another important factor, as it encouraged the other Argentinian clubs to take the competition more seriously. Independiente became champions in 1964, and retained the trophy in 1965. That year, a Uruguayan proposal to include league runners-up almost killed the tournament. The Brazilians refused to enter in 1966, as more matches would make it even less financially rewarding.

The 1966 tournament involved no fewer than 95 games – without the Brazilians – Penarol, the winners, playing 17 games to win the title. Here again, controversy occurred. A play-off with River Plate was needed in the Final, and, having led 2–0 at half-time, River Plate eventually lost 4–2 after extra time. River had two former Penarol players in their side, Matosas and Cubilla, who both played badly and were accused of "selling" the game.

The 1967 Final, between Argentina's Racing Club and Uruguay's Nacional, witnessed the birth of the South American clubs' win-at-all-costs approach to the competition, especially the Argentinians. The three-game final series was peppered with gamesmanship and rough play, a familiar sight in Copa Libertadores and World Club Cup finals to come.

Racing's win marked the beginning of a period of Argentinian dominance, especially by the small-town club Estudiantes de La Plata, who won the Copa Libertadores three years running (1968–70) on the back of a single Argentine championship in 1967. Estudiantes were the worst offenders when it came to gamesmanship. Every conceivable method was employed to distract opponents, from verbal harassment and time-wasting to spitting and even pricking opponents with pins when out of the

referee's view! Estudiantes made few friends and very little money. Indeed, their hat-trick of titles earned them a net loss of $1,600,000. As a result, their president committed suicide, the board resigned and their replacements were forced to sell the players at knock-down prices.

The second leg of their third Final, against Penarol, ended in a free-for-all between both sets of players and reserves in the middle of the pitch. The disciplinary committee were extremely lenient, and then came down heavily on Boca Juniors a year later, after a battle between the players in a first-round tie against Peru's Sporting Cristal in Buenos Aires, which resulted in all of them being locked up in prison!

Top-level diplomatic negotiations earned the players' release the following day, and they were all promptly suspended by the clubs. Then, inexplicably, CONMEBOL punished Boca by closing their stadium for cup games, a strange move given that the fans were generally well-behaved on the day. Boca refused to accept this and duly turned up at their stadium for their next match, against Universitario of Peru, who did not – on the express orders of CONMEBOL's Peruvian president Salinas Fuller. Universitario were awarded the points and Boca were expelled from the competition... just another strange tale in the history of the Copa Libertadores.

With the ever-increasing disruption caused to domestic championships, Argentina joined Brazil in a boycott in 1969, prompting CONMEBOL to streamline the competition slightly by reducing the number of group matches. Argentina's Independiente then embarked on an unprecedented sequence of victories, winning the trophy four times in succession from 1972 to 1975.

The Brazilians, who returned in 1970, also began to enjoy some success, with Cruzeiro, Flamengo and Gremio winning between 1976 and 1983. Overall, however, Brazil's record in the tournament was disappointing until the 1990s.

Boca Juniors won the trophy for Argentina in 1977 and again in 1978, but in 1979 Olimpia of Paraguay broke the Argentina-Uruguay-Brazil domination of the competition. Olimpia's breakthrough marked a new era for the competition, which became more even and more open. Argentinian clubs still enjoyed success – Independiente, Argentinos Juniors and River Plate all tasted victory – but the "smaller" nations were starting to make an impression. Chilean champions Cobreloa reached two successive finals in 1981 and 1982, and were followed by Colombia's America Cali, who lost three successive finals from 1985.

Uruguay came back into contention with wins by Nacional (1980 and 1988) and by Penarol (1982 and 1987), but no Argentinian or Uruguayan club has won the Copa Libertadores since 1988.

In 1989 Nacional of Medellin won the trophy for Colombia for the first time, beating Olimpia 5–4 on penalties after a 2–2 aggregate draw. Olimpia returned the following year to win for the second time, beating Barcelona of Ecuador in the Final, and made it a hat-trick of Final appearances in 1991 when they lost to Chile's Colo Colo.

In 1992 São Paulo beat Newell's Old Boys, of Argentina, to win Brazil's first Copa Libertadores for almost a decade. The São Paulo side, containing many Brazil internationals such as Rai, Cafu, Palinha and Muller, won again in 1993, beating Chile's Universidad Catolica 5–3 on aggregate, to become the first club to retain the trophy since 1978.

The Copa Libertadores is now a respectable, clean competition which attracts all the continent's leading clubs. There are still moments of controversy and high drama, but that is all part and parcel of South American football. Such is the excitmentement generated that it is worth putting up with the constantly changing format which, at present, involves five first-round groups, playing 60 matches to eliminate just five teams!

The holders still receive a bye into the second round, which is a huge help, because any team progressing from the first round to ultimate victory will have to play a gruelling 14 games on the way.

São Paulo almost made it a hat-trick in 1994 – reaching the Final for a third straight year – but lost on penalties to Velez Sarsfield. A year later, Gremio took Brazilian revenge, beating Nacional of Colombia in the Final. The 1996 Final saw a repeat of 1986, with River Plate again beating America. Cruzeiro and Vasco da Gama then re-emphasised the Brazilian club revival in 1997 and 1998.

Winners

Copa Libertadores Finals

1960 *Montevideo*: Penarol 1 (Spencer), Olimpia 0
Asuncion: Olimpia 1 (Recalde), Penarol 1 (Cubilla).

1961 *Montevideo*: Penarol 1 (Spencer), Palmeiras 0. *São Paulo*: Palmeiras 1 (Nardo), Penarol 1 (Sasia).

1962 *Montevideo*: Penarol 1 (Spencer), Santos 2 (Coutinho 2). *Santos* Santos 2 (Dorval, Mengalvio), Penarol 3 (Spencer, Sasia 2) *Buenos Aires* (play-off): Santos 3 (Coutinho, Pele 2), Penarol 0.

1963 *Rio de Janeiro*: Santos 3 (Coutinho 2, Lima), Boca Juniors 2 (Sanfilippo 2).
Buenos Aires: Boca Juniors 1 (Sanfilippo), Santos 2 (Coutinho, Pele).

1964 *Montevideo*: Nacional (Uru) 0, Independiente 0
Avellaneda: Independiente 1 (Rodriguez), Nacional (Uru) 0

1965 *Avellaneda*: Independiente 1 (Bernao), Penarol 0
Montevideo: Penarol 3 (Goncalvez, Reznik, Rocha), Independiente 1 (De la Mata)
Santiago (play-off): Independiente 4 (Acevedo, Bernao, Avallay, Mura), Penarol 1 (Joya)

1966 *Montevideo*: Penarol 2 (Abbadie, Joya), River Plate 0.
Buenos Aires: River Plate 3 (Onega E., Onega D., Sarnari), Penarol 2 (Rocha, Spencer).
Santiago (play-off): Penarol 4 (Spencer 2, Rocha, Abbadie), River Plate 2 (Onega D., Solari).

1967 *Avellaneda*: Racing Club 0,

Nacional (Uru) 0.
Montevideo: Nacional (Uru) 0, Racing Club 0.
Santiago (play-off): Racing Club 2 (Cardozo, Raffo), Nacional (Uru) 1 (Esparrago).

1968 *La Plata*: Estudiantes 2 (Veron, Flores), Palmeiras 1 (Servillio)
São Paulo: Palmeiras 3 (Tupazinho 2, Reinaldo), Estudiantes 1 (Veron)
Montevideo (play-off): Estudiantes 2 (Ribaudo, Veron), Palmeiras 0

1969 *Montevideo*: Nacional (Uru) 0, Estudiantes 1 (Flores).
La Plata: Estudiantes 2 (Flores, Conigliaro), Nacional (Uru) 0.

1970 *La Plata*: Estudiantes 1 (Togneri), Penarol 0.
Montevideo: Penarol 0, Estudiantes 0.

1971 *La Plata*: Estudiantes 1 (Romeo), Nacional (Uru) 0.
Montevideo: Nacional (Uru) 1 (Masnik), Estudiantes 0.
Lima (play-off): Nacional (Uru) 2 (Esparrago, Artime), Estudiantes 0.

1972 *Lima*: Universitario 0, Independiente 0.
Avellaneda: Independiente 2 (Maglioni 2), Universitario 1 (Rojas).

1973 *Avellaneda*: Independiente 1 (Mendoza), Colo Colo 1 (o.g.).
Santiago: Colo Colo 0, Independiente 0.
Montevideo (play-off): Independiente 2 (Mendoza, Giachello), Colo Colo 1 (Caszely).

1974 *São Paulo*: São Paulo 2 (Rocha, Mirandinha), Independiente 1 (Saggioratto).
Avellaneda: Independiente 2 (Bochini, Balbuena), São Paulo 0.
Santiago (play-off): Independiente 1 (Pavoni), São Paulo 0.

1975 *Santiago*: Union Espanola 1 (Ahumada), Independiente 0.
Avellaneda: Independiente 3 (Rojas, Pavoni, Bertoni), Union Espanola 1 (Las Heras).
Asuncion (play-off): Independiente 2 (Ruiz Moreno, Bertoni), Union Espanola 0.

1976 *Belo Horizonte*: Cruzeiro 4 (Nelinho, Palinha 2, Waldo), River Plate 1 (Mas).
Buenos Aires: River Plate 2 (Lopez, J., Gonzalez), Cruzeiro 1 (Palinha).
Santiago (play-off): Cruzeiro 3 (Nelinho, Ronaldo, Joazinho), River Plate 2 (Mas, Urquiza).

1977 *Buenos Aires*: Boca Juniors 1 (Veglio), Cruzeiro 0.
Belo Horizonte: Cruzeiro 1 (Nelinho), Boca Juniors 0.
Montevideo (play-off): Boca Juniors 0, Cruzeiro 0.

1978 *Cali*: Deportivo Cali 0, Boca Juniors 0
Buenos Aires: Boca Juniors 4 (Perotti 2, Mastrangelo, Salinas), Deportivo Cali 0

1979 *Asuncion*: Olimpia 2 (Aquino, Piazza), Boca Juniors 0.
Buenos Aires: Boca Juniors 0, Olimpia 0.

1980 *Porto Alegre*: Internacional PA 0, Nacional (Uru) 0.
Montevideo: Nacional (Uru) 1 (Victorino), Internacional PA 0.

1981 *Rio de Janeiro*: Flamengo 2 (Zico 2), Cobreloa 1 (Merello).
Santiago: Cobreloa 1 (Merello), Flamengo 0.
Montevideo (play-off): Flamengo 2 (Zico 2), Cobreloa 0.

1982 *Montevideo*: Penarol 0, Cobreloa 0. *Santiago*: Cobreloa 0, Penarol 1 (Morena).

1983 *Montevideo*: Penarol 1 (Morena), Gremio 1 (Tita).
Porto Alegre: Gremio 2 (Caio, Cesar), Penarol 1 (Morena).

1984 *Porto Alegre*: Gremio 0, Independiente 1 (Burruchaga).
Avellaneda: Independiente 0, Gremio 0.

1985 *Buenos Aires*: Argentinos Juniors 1 (Comisso), America Cali 0.
Cali: America Cali 1 (Ortiz), Argentinos Juniors 0.
Asuncion (play-off): Argentinos Juniors 1 (Comizzo), America Cali 1 (Gareca). (*Argentinos Juniors won 5–4 on penalties*).

1986 *Cali*: America Cali 1 (Cabanas), River Plate 2 (Funes, Alonso).
Buenos Aires: River Plate 1 (Funes), America Cali 0.

1987 *Cali*: America Cali 2 (Bataglia, Cabanas), Penarol 0.
Montevideo: Penarol 2 (Aguirre, Villar), America Cali 1 (Cabanas).
Santiago (play-off): Penarol 1 (Aguirre), America Cali 0.

1988 *Rosario*: Newell's Old Boys 1 (Gabrich), Nacional (Uru) 0.
Montevideo: Nacional (Uru) 3 (Vargas, Ostolaza , De Leon), Newell's Old Boys 0.

1989 *Asuncion*: Olimpia 2 (Bobadilla, Sanabria), Atletico Nacional 0. *Bogota*: Atletico Nacional 2 (o.g., Usurriaga), Olimpia 0. (*Atletico Nacional won 5–4 on penalties*).

1990 *Asuncion*: Olimpia 2 (Amarilla, Samaniego), Barcelona 0.
Guayaquil: Barcelona 1 (Trobbiani), Olimpia 1 (Amarilla).

1991 *Asuncion*: Olimpia 0, Colo Colo 0.
Santiago: Colo Colo 3 (Perez 2, Herrera), Olimpia 0.

1992 *Rosario*: Newell's Old Boys 1 (Berizzo), São Paulo 0.
São Paulo: São Paulo 1 (Rai), Newell's Old Boys 0. (*São Paulo won 3–2 on penalties*).

1993 *São Paulo*: São Paulo 5 (o.g., Dinho, Gilmar, Rai, Muller), Universidad Catolica 1 (Almada).
Santiago: Universidad Catolica 2 (Lunari, Almada), São Paulo 0. São Paulo won 5–3 on aggregate.

1994 *Buenos Aires*: Velez Sarsfield 1 (Asad), São Paulo 0 Att:48,000
São Paulo: São Paulo 1 (Muller), Velez Sarsfield 0. (*Velez Sarsfield won 5–3 on penalties*)

1995 *Porto Alegre*: Gremio 3 (Marulanda og, Jardel, Paulo Nunes), Nacional Medellin 1 (Angel).
Medellin: Nacional 1 (Aristizabal), Gremio 1 (Dinho pen). Gremio won 4–2 on agg.

1996 *Cali*: America 1 (De Avila), River Plate 0.
Buenos Aires: River Plate 2 (Crespo 2), America 0. River Plate won 2–1 on agg.

1997 *Lima*: Sporting Cristal 0, Cruzeiro 0.
Belo Horizonte: Cruzeiro 1 (Elivelton), Sporting Cristal 0. Cruzeiro won 1–0 on agg.

1998 *Rio de Janeiro*: Vasco da Gama 2 (Donizette. Luizao), Barcelona Guayaquil 0.
Guayaquil: Barcelona Guayaquil 1 (De Avila), Vasco da Gama 2 (Donizette. Luizao).
Vasco da Gama won 4–1 on agg.

SOUTH AMERICAN RECOPA

The Recopa is basically a play-off between the winners of the Libertadores Cup and the Super Cup, and is thus South America's answer to the European Super Cup. Curiously, in 1990 Paraguay's Olimpia won the Recopa without having to play a match, because they also won the Libertadores and Super Cups. Japanese sponsorship means it is always staged in ... Tokyo.

South American Recopa Winners			
1988	Nacional	**1993**	São Paulo
1989	Boca Juniors	**1994**	São Paulo
1990	Olimpia	**1995**	Independiente
1991	Colo Colo	**1996**	Gremio
1992	São Paulo	**1997**	Velez Sarsfield

SOUTH AMERICAN SUPER CUP

Introduced in 1988, the South American Super Cup, or Trofeo Havelange as it is known, is a competition for previous winners of the Libertadores Cup. The event, dismissed to start with as just another unnecessary tournament, is gaining in popularity and has the advantage of involving only the continent's top sides. Played at present on a knock-out basis, the competition may eventually change to a league format, which would effectively create a South American Super League.

South American Super Cup Winners			
1988	Racing Club	**1994**	Independiente
1989	Boca Juniors	**1995**	Independiente
1990	Olimpia	**1996**	Velez Sarsfield
1991	Cruzeiro	**1997**	River Plate
1992	Cruzeiro	**1998**	*Not contested*
1993	Botafogo		

CONMEBOL CUP

In 1993, the South American club scene was further complicated by the creation of the Copa CONMEBOL, which like the UEFA Cup featured the two next-best clubs in the domestic championships who had not qualified for the top event.

EUROPEAN CUP

Originally the European Champion Clubs Cup, what is now the UEFA Champions League is not only the most lucrative club event in the world but has become, since its inception in 1956, also the most prized trophy in world club football. Reputations have been made and broken over the four decades since the competition began, and it has always had an aura of romance and glamour about it, some say even more so than international competition.

The idea for the competition came, typically, from the French. Gabriel Hanot, a former international and then editor of the French daily sports paper *L'Equipe*, was angered by English newspaper claims that Wolverhampton Wanderers were the champions of Europe because they had beaten Honved and Moscow Spartak in friendlies.

Hanot decided to launch a competition to find the real champions of Europe and, in 1955, invited representatives of 20 leading clubs to Paris to discuss the idea. The meeting was attended by 15 clubs and it was agreed that the competition should begin in the 1955–56 season. FIFA supported the idea and consequently UEFA approved the tournament and took over its administration.

The clubs, restricted to the champions of each country plus the holders after the first series, play home and away on a knock-out basis, and the result is decided by the aggregate score – except in the Final, which has always been a one-off match played at a neutral venue. Drawn ties used a play-off to produce a winner until 1967, when a new method was introduced, whereby the team scoring most away goals progressed. In the event of a draw even on away goals, a toss of a coin decided the winner until 1971, when penalty kicks were introduced.

Sixteen teams entered the first tournament, though several were not really champions, merely replacements for teams who could not, or would not, take part. Chelsea, the English champions, stayed away on the short-sighted advice of the notoriously aloof Football League, while Hibernian, who had finished fifth, represented Scotland.

By a fortunate coincidence, just as the competition was launched, Real Madrid were blossoming into one of the greatest club sides the world has ever seen. In the Final, fittingly played in Paris, Real faced a Stade de Reims side containing the legendary Raymond Kopa, who joined Real the following season. Despite leading twice, Reims could not cope with Real's deadly forwards, Alfredo Di Stefano, Hector Rial and Paco Gento, and lost 4–3.

Real went on to win the Cup for the next four years running, a feat which is unlikely to be matched in the modern game. Fiorentina (1957), Milan (1958), Reims again (1959) and Eintracht Frankfurt (1960) were all beaten in successive finals, with the match against Frankfurt being arguably the best final ever. In front of 135,000 fans at Hampden Park in Glasgow, Real thrashed the West German champions 7–3, with Ferenc Puskas, the "galloping major" of the great Hungarian team of the 1950s, scoring four goals and Di Stefano getting a hat-trick.

Real's run came to an end the following season in the second round, beaten by deadly rivals Barcelona, who went on to contest the Final with Portugal's Benfica – the newly emerging kings of Europe. Benfica contained the bulk of the Portuguese national side and would go on to play in five Finals during the 1960s, winning two of them. The first, against Barcelona, was won without Eusebio, the Mozambique-born striker.

Eusebio was in the line-up the following year, though, when Benfica faced Real Madrid, and he scored twice as Benfica won 5–3 despite Puskas scoring another hat-trick for Real. In 1963, the Lisbon Eagles appeared in their third consecutive Final, but lost 2–1 to Italy's Milan.

Milan's victory was the first of three for the city of Milan in the mid-1960s, as their city rivals Internazionale emerged to win the trophy in 1964 and 1965. Coached by the legendary Helenio Herrera, Inter fielded a host of international stars including Sarti, Burgnich, Facchetti, Jair from Brazil, Mazzola and the Spaniard Suarez. Their Final victims were Real Madrid and Benfica.

Real returned to claim "their" crown in 1966 with a 2–1 win over Partizan Belgrade in Brussels. Of the 1950s attack all bar Gento had gone, but Amancio and Serena proved worthy successors as both scored in the Final. Real's sixth triumph marked the end of an era in the European Cup. For the first 11 years of its existence, the Cup had only been won by clubs from Latin countries – Spain, Portugal and Italy – and of the first 22 finalists, 18 were from these three countries. Now the power-base of European club football shifted from the Mediterranean to northern Europe – Britain, Holland and Germany to be precise. The 1967 Final paired Inter with Scotland's Celtic. The Scots, under the

PARIS MATCH *Bayern Munich players celebrate victory in 1975*

NOT THIS TIME *Real Madrid's Dominguez saves during his team's 7–3 win over Eintracht Frankfurt in 1960*

guiding hand of the great Jock Stein, won every competition open to them that season, rounding off with a fine 2–1 win over the Italians in Lisbon. The breakthrough had been made, and Manchester United consolidated the position by becoming England's first winners the following season. Benfica were again the unfortunate losers in the Final, at Wembley, where Matt Busby's side won 4–1 after extra time with goals by Bobby Charlton, George Best and a young Brian Kidd.

Milan regained the trophy in 1969, with a 4–1 demolition of Ajax in Madrid, but it was the last Latin success in the Cup for 17 years as Holland, Germany and then England dominated the trophy during the 1970s and early 1980s.

Feyenoord of Rotterdam were the first Dutch winners, in 1970, when they narrowly defeated Celtic 2–1 after extra time in Milan. Feyenoord's great rivals, Ajax, maintained Holland's position the following season when they beat Panathinaikos of Greece 2–0 at Wembley. It was the first of three consecutive titles for the Amsterdam club, which contained the bulk of the thrilling Dutch "total football" side of the 1970s. Johan Cruyff was the star of the show, but his impressive supporting cast includ-

ed Johan Neeskens, Barrie Hulshoff, Wim Suurbier, Arie Haan, Rudi Krol and Piet Keizer.

Ajax's second victory was an impressive 2–0 win over Inter in Rotterdam, where Cruyff scored twice. The following year, 1973, Ajax beat Juventus in Belgrade with a solitary goal by the mercurial Johnny Rep. In the quarter-finals, Ajax had beaten Bayern Munich, and it was the West German champions who would dom-

AT LAST *Matt Busby in 1968*

inate the Cup for the next three years.

Udo Lattek moulded Bayern into a highly effective unit, and players such as Franz Beckenbauer, Sepp Maier, Gerd Müller, Paul Breitner, Georg Schwarzenbeck and Uli Hoeness went on to form the core of the West German side which won the European Championship in 1972 and the World Cup in 1974. Bayern needed a replay to dispose of Atletico Madrid in the first of their three wins, Hoeness and Müller scoring two each in a 4–0 win after a 1–1 draw in Brussels. In 1975 they beat Leeds United 2–0 in a hotly-disputed match in Paris, after which distraught Leeds supporters trashed the stadium. Bayern's hat-trick came with a 1–0 win over France's Saint-Etienne in Glasgow.

Then, in 1977, Liverpool clinched the first of six consecutive English victories with a 3–1 win over Germany's Borussia Mönchengladbach, veteran defender Tommy Smith scoring the decisive second goal. Liverpool, under Bob Paisley, retained the trophy at Wembley the following year by beating Belgium's Club Brugge. Kenny Dalglish, signed from Celtic to replace the Hamburg-bound Kevin Keegan, scored the only goal.

In 1979 a cruel twist of fate drew Liverpool with Brian Clough's Nottingham Forest in the first round.

Forest had come up from the Second Division to win the title in successive seasons, and they out-fought Liverpool to win 2–0 on aggregate. In the Final, against Swedish rank outsiders Malmö, Britain's first million-pound footballer, Trevor Francis, scored the only goal in a very tight game. Forest retained the Cup in 1980, ironically against Hamburg, who included Keegan in their side. On the night, the player who had twice been European Footballer of the Year was completely shackled by Forest's uncompromising Scottish centre-back Kenny Burns, and a single goal by winger John Robertson was enough for victory.

Liverpool returned for their third triumph the following season with a 1–0 win over Real Madrid in Paris, and Aston Villa became the fourth English winners in 1982, when they beat Bayern Munich 1–0 in Rotterdam. Hamburg broke the English monopoly in 1983 by beating Juventus 1–0, but it was only a brief respite. Liverpool, the most successful side in the history of English football, returned for the 1984 Final and, against all the odds, beat AS Roma in Rome. After a 1–1 draw, Liverpool won 4–2 on penalties.

The period of English dominance was about to end, however, and the 1985 Final at the Heysel Stadium in Brussels will always be remembered, not for the football, but for the appalling loss of life. Before the game, against Juventus, a group of English hooligans charged at the Italian fans behind one of the goals. A safety wall collapsed and 39 people, mostly Italian, lost their lives in the crush. Two weeks previously, 53 supporters had died in a fire at Bradford City's Valley Parade ground, leaving the image of English football at its lowest point ever.

Juventus won a meaningless game 1–0 with a Michel Platini penalty. More significantly, Liverpool were banned from European competitions indefinitely, while all English clubs were banned for five years. The ban took some of the gloss off the Cup because, without the English clubs, who had such a fine record in the competition, winning it was less satisfactory. Meanwhile the hooligan problem still remained.

In 1986 Romania's Steaua Bucharest became the first Eastern European side to win the Cup, beating Barcelona – coached by Terry Venables – in Seville. The Final, however, was one of the worst in the tournament's history; still goalless after extra time, the penalty shoot-out produced only two successful kicks – both for the Romanian army club.

Portugal's FC Porto won in 1987 in Vienna with a fine 2–1 win over the favourites Bayern Munich, having been a goal down. PSV Eindhoven became Holland's third European champions when they beat poor old Benfica in 1988. A dull 0–0 draw in Stuttgart was followed by a 6–5 penalty win for the Dutch team.

Milan then returned to reclaim the trophy. Free from the restrictions on importing foreign players, and backed by media magnate Silvio Berlusconi's money, Milan bought the best and beat the rest. Their Dutch axis of Frank Rijkaard, Ruud Gullit and Marco Van Basten steered them to a crushing 4–0 victory over Steaua in 1989, Gullit and Van Basten both scoring twice, while a single goal from Rijkaard was enough to beat the perennial bridesmaids Benfica in 1990.

BACK ON TOP *Karlheinz Riedle celebrates his second goal in the 1997 Cup Final*

In 1991 English clubs were back in the running, but it was Yugoslavia's Red Star Belgrade and Marseille who met in the Final in Bari.

France, originators of the European Cup, were still hoping for a first ever victory ... but the wait had to go on. Red Star abandoned their free-flowing, attacking style of play in favour of a blanket defence approach designed to stifle president Bernard Tapie's expensively assembled French champions. The plan worked. Red Star took the game to penalties and won the shoot-out 5–3, to become the second side from the East to be crowned European champions.

The format of the competition was radically changed in 1992, after direct pressure from Europe's bigger clubs who have made no secret of their desire to see a European Super League formed. The quarter-finals and semi-finals were replaced with two groups of four, playing home and away, to produce the two finalists. Johan Cruyff's Barcelona took the Cup for the first time – completing a hat-trick of European trophies – by beating Italy's Sampdoria 1–0 at Wembley with a rocket free-kick by Ronald Koeman.

Then, in 1993, came the biggest scandal the competition has ever witnessed. After 37 long years, the French drought in the European Cup seemed to have ended. Marseille beat Milan 1–0 in Munich, with a goal by centre-back Basile Boli, but the celebrations were cut short when it emerged that Marseille officials had allegedly paid three Valenciennes players to "take it easy" in a league game shortly before the Final. Chaos ensued, but in the end, Marseille were banned from Europe stripped of their French title and the right to play São Paulo in the World Club Cup. Marseille's outspoken owner – socialist, millionaire and politician Tapie – was ultimately punished with a jail term.

The format changed slightly again for the 1994 tournament, with the re-introduction of semi-finals for the winners and runners-up of the two Champions League groups. But nothing could stop Milan, their 4–0 defeat of Barcelona was a stunning display.

Yet more tinkering with the format followed in 1994–95 as UEFA sought a compromise with the bigger clubs' desire for a TV-bankrolled European League.

The holders and top seeded teams went through directly to the

Champions Cup Finals

1956 *Paris*: Real Madrid 4 (Di Stefano, Rial 2, Marquitos), Stade de Reims 3 (Leblond, Templin, Hidalgo). Att: 38,000

1957 *Madrid*: Real Madrid 2 (Di Stefano, Gento), Fiorentina 0. Att: 124,000

1958 *Brussels*: Real Madrid 3 (Di Stefano, Rial, Gento), Milan 2 (Schiaffino, Grillo) (aet). Att: 67,000

1959 *Stuttgart*: Real Madrid 2 (Mateos, Di Stefano), Stade de Reims 0. Att: 80,000

1960 *Glasgow*: Real Madrid 7 (Di Stefano 3, Puskas 4), Eintracht Frankfurt 3 (Kress, Stein 2). Att: 127,621

1961 *Berne*: Benfica 3 (Aguas, o.g., Coluna), Barcelona 2 (Kocsis, Czibor). Att: 33,000

1962 *Amsterdam*: Benfica 5 (Aguas, Cavem, Coluna, Eusebio 2), Real Madrid 3 (Puskas 3). Att: 68,000

1963 *Wembley*: Milan 2 (Altafini 2), Benfica 1 (Eusebio). Att: 45,000

1964 *Vienna*: Internazionale 3 (Mazzola 2, Milani), Real Madrid 1 (Felo). Att: 72,000

1965 *Milan*: Internazionale 1 (Jair), Benfica 0. Att: 80,000

1966 *Brussels*: Real Madrid 2 (Amancio, Serena), Partizan Belgrade 1 (Vasovic). Att: 55,000

1967 *Lisbon*: Celtic 2 (Gemmell, Chalmers), Internazionale 1 (Mazzola). Att: 55,000

1968 *Wembley*: Manchester United 4 (Charlton 2, Best, Kidd), Benfica 1 (Graca) (aet). Att: 100,000

1969 *Madrid*: Milan 4 (Prati 3, Sormani), Ajax 1 (Vasovic). Att: 50,000

1970 *Milan*: Feyenoord 2 (Israel, Kindvall), Celtic 1 (Gemmell) (aet). Att: 53,187

1971 *Wembley*: Ajax 2 (Van Dijk, o.g.), Panathinaikos 0. Att: 90,000

1972 *Rotterdam*: Ajax 2 (Cruyff 2), Internazionale 0. Att: 61,000

1973 *Belgrade*: Ajax 1 (Rep), Juventus 0. Att: 93,500

1974 *Brussels*: Bayern Munich 1 (Schwartzenbeck), Atletico Madrid 1 (Luis) (aet). Att: 65,000
Brussels (replay): Bayern Munich 4 (Hoeness 2, Müller 2), Atletico Madrid 0. Att: 23,000

1975 *Paris*: Bayern Munich 2 (Roth, Müller), Leeds United 0. Att: 48,000

1976 *Glasgow*: Bayern Munich 1 (Roth), St Etienne 0. Att: 54,684

1977 *Rome*: Liverpool 3 (McDermott, Smith, Neal), Borussia Mönchengladbach 1 (Simonsen). Att: 57,000

1978 *Wembley*: Liverpool 1 (Dalglish), Club Brugge 0. Att: 92,000

1979 *Munich*: Nottingham Forest 1 (Francis), Malmö 0. Att: 57,500

1980 *Madrid*: Nottingham Forest 1 (Robertson), Hamburg 0.Att: 51,000

1981 *Paris*: Liverpool 1 (Kennedy A.), Real Madrid 0. Att: 48,360

1982 *Rotterdam*: Aston Villa 1 (Withe), Bayern Munich 0. Att: 46,000

1983 *Athens*: Hamburg 1 (Magath), Juventus 0. Att: 80,000

1984 *Rome*: Liverpool 1 (Neal), AS Roma 1 (Pruzzo) (aet). (*Liverpool won 4–2 on penalties*). Att: 69,693

1985 *Brussels*: Juventus 1 (Platini), Liverpool 0. Att: 58,000

1986 *Seville*: Steaua Bucharest 0, Barcelona 0 (aet). (*Steaua won 2–0 on penalties*). Att: 70,000

1987 *Vienna*: FC Porto 2 (Madjer, Juary), Bayern Munich 1 (Kogl). Att: 56,000

1988 *Stuttgart*: PSV Eindhoven 0, Benfica 0 (aet). (*PSV won 6–5 on penalties*). Att: 55,000

1989 *Barcelona*: Milan 4 (Gullit 2, Van Basten 2), Steaua Bucharest 0. Att: 97,000

1990 *Vienna*: Milan 1 (Rijkaard), Benfica 0. Att: 56,000

1991 *Bari*: Red Star Belgrade 0, Marseille 0 (aet). (*Red Star won 5–3 on penalties*). Att: 50,000

1992 *Wembley*: Barcelona 1 (Koeman R.), Sampdoria 0 (aet). Att: 74,000

1993 *Munich*: Marseille 1 (Boli), Milan 0. Att: 72,300 (*Marseille were later stripped of their title for alleged match fixing*)

1994 *Athens*: Milan 4 (Massaro 2, Savicevic, Desailly), Barcelona 0. Att: 76,000

1995 *Vienna*: Ajax 1 (Kluivert), Milan 0. Att 49,000

1996 *Rome*: Juventus 1 (Ravanelli), Ajax 1 (Litmanen) (aet). (*Juventus won 4–2 on penalties*). Att: 67,000.

1997 *Munich*: Borussia Dortmund 3 (Riedle 2, Ricken), Juventus 1 (Del Piero). Att: 55,000

1998 *Amsterdam*: Real Madrid 1 (Mijatovic), Juventus 0. Att: 47,000

1999 *Barcelona*: Manchester United 2 (Sheringham, Solskjaer), Bayern Munich 1 (Basler). Att: 85,000

Champions League, which was expanded to 16 teams in four groups of four; the eight other teams came from a preliminary round involving the teams ranked eight to 23 in the seeding list. All the other "minnow" national champions were off-loaded into an expanded UEFA Cup as the price of progress.

The first redeveloped Champions League Cup Final – as it was clumsily repackaged – was won by Ajax of Amsterdam, who defeated Milan 1–0 in the Final in Vienna.

Ajax's success generated enormous interest in the Dutch club's youth development system. But big money spoke louder in 1996 when they lost in a penalty shoot-out to Juventus in Rome. The Italian club, just for good measure, thrashed Ajax in the 1997 semi-finals but were then themselves beaten, surprisingly decisively by 3–1, by Borussia Dortmund. Two goals from Karlheinz Riedle and

another by Lars Ricken, within 20 seconds of his appearance as a second-half substitute, shook Juventus out of their pretty patterns. History repeated itself in 1998 when Juventus returned to the final as favourites and were again beaten. The underdogs, oddly considering the tournament's history, were Real Madrid. But the Spaniards laid the ghost of history by claiming their record seventh Cup thanks to a brilliant piece of six-yard-box opportunism from Yugoslav striker Mijatovic. As if to prove the staying power of traditional giants, Manchester United succeded Madrid in 1999 with an appropriately sensational victory to mark the end of the century. Two goals in injury time from substitutes Teddy Sheringham and Ole Gunnar Solskjaer turned an apparent 1–0 defeat by Bayern Munich into a win. United became the first English club to achieve the treble of European Cup, domestic league and F.A. Cup.

UEFA CUP

The UEFA Cup started life in 1955, and, unusually, was not a French idea. When UEFA was formed in 1954, FIFA vice-president Ernst Thommen, of Switzerland, thought up the idea of a European competition to give a competitive edge to friendly matches between cities holding trade fairs.

This rather dubious reason for a competition was no deterrent, as officials from 12 cities holding trade fairs approved Thommen's plans in April 1955, and the International Inter-Cities Fairs Cup, as it was originally named, was under way. The competition was to be held over two seasons to avoid disrupting domestic fixtures, but because the original entrants represented cities holding trade fairs, and wherever possible fixtures were designed to coincide with the fairs, the first tournament over-

ran into a third year.

The Fairs Cup, as it was commonly known, was designed for representative sides, but it soon became clear that it was a competition that the clubs would dominate. In the first tournament, which ran from 1955 to 1958, 12 cities were represented by select teams. But the composition of the sides was a matter of individual choice. Thus while London chose its team from the 11 professional sides in the city, Barcelona was represented by CF Barcelona, with one token Español player, and Birmingham was represented by the entire Birmingham City side. This discrepancy clearly favoured the more coherent clubs, and it was almost inevitable that two would meet in the Final.

The 12 teams were organized into four groups of three, with each side to play the other two in its group at home and away. The group winners then went on to the semi-finals and

MONEY MOVE *Ronaldo, at the time the world's most expensive player, with the UEFA Cup in 1998.*

ultimately the Final, which, unlike Europe's other competitions, was to be over two legs on an aggregate basis. However, the first tournament was disrupted by the withdrawals of Vienna and Cologne, leaving just two teams in Groups 1 and 3. Barcelona were too good for Copenhagen in Group 1, but things were much tighter in Group 3. Leipzig's 6–3 win over Lausanne in the first leg in Germany seemed conclusive, but the Swiss pulled off a 7–3 win in the return to go through on goal average.

Switzerland's other entrants, Basle, played a key role in Group 4, where their shock 6–2 victory against Eintracht Frankfurt allowed the London XI to qualify. England's second entrants, Birmingham, also made it to the semi-finals, beating Zagreb home and away to set up a decider with Internazionale. After a hard-fought 0–0 draw in Milan, the

TOP MAN *Maradona for Napoli*

English side won 2–1 at St Andrews to join London in the semi-finals.

Birmingham met Barcelona in a thrilling encounter that needed a third match to separate them. After Birmingham had won 4–1 at home, a late goal by Kubala in the return sent

the tie to a third game. Kubala duly repeated his late-scoring trick to send Barcelona through to the Final, where they met the London XI, who beat Lausanne 3–2 on aggregate.

Almost three years after the first ball had been kicked in the tournament, London and Barcelona fought out a 2–2 draw at Stamford Bridge in the first leg of the Final, only for the Spaniards to win the return 6–0 – Suarez and Evaristo each scoring twice. Barcelona's win was the first of six in a row by Latin clubs in the competition, in keeping with the European Cup, which was also dominated by Latin sides in the early years of its existence.

The second tournament, 1958–60, drew 16 entrants, mostly club sides, and was played on a straight home-and-away knock-out basis. Barcelona, strengthened by the arrivals of Hungary's Sandor Kocsis and Zoltan Czibor, retained the tro-

phy without losing a match. Their opponents were again English, but this time it was Birmingham and not London who made it to the Final. A 0–0 draw on a terrible pitch in Birmingham set Barcelona up for the 4–1 return win, with goals by Martinez, Czibor (two) and Coll.

Barcelona's attempt to win a hat-trick of Fairs Cups ended in the second round of the 1960–61 tournament, at the unlikely hands of Scotland's Hibernian. The Edinburgh side only took part because Chelsea withdrew but, having beaten Lausanne in the first round, they surprised everybody by beating the holders in the next round. Birmingham again made it the Final, where they faced Italy's Roma, who needed a third match to beat Hibs in the semi-finals. This extended semi-final meant that the Final itself was held over until the following season, by

---

Winners

Fairs Cup Finals

1958 *London*: London Select XI 2 (Greaves, Langley), Barcelona 2 (Tejada, Martinez). Att: 45,000
Barcelona: Barcelona 6 (Suarez 2, Evaristo 2, Martinez, Verges), London Select XI 0. Att: 62,000
1960 *Birmingham*: Birmingham City 0, Barcelona 0. Att: 40,000
Barcelona: Barcelona 4 (Martinez, Czibor 2, Coll), Birmingham City 1 (Hooper). Att: 70,000
1961 *Birmingham*: Birmingham City 2 (Hellawell, Orritt), Roma 2 (Manfredini). Att:21,000
Rome: Roma 2 (o.g., Pestrin), Birmingham City 0. Att: 60,000
1962 *Valencia*: Valencia 6 (Yosu 2, Guillot 3, Nunez), Barcelona 2 (Kocsis 2). Att: 65,000
Barcelona: Barcelona 1 (Kocsis), Valencia 1 (Guillot). Att: 60,000
1963 *Zagreb*: Dinamo Zagreb 1 (Zambata), Valencia 2 (Waldo, Urtiaga). Att: 40,000
Valencia: Valencia 2 (Manio, Nunez), Dinamo Zagreb 0. Att: 55,000
1964 *Barcelona*: Real Zaragoza 2 (Villa , Marcelino), Valencia 1 (Urtiaga). Att: 50,000
1965 *Turin*: Ferencvaros 1 (Fenyvesi), Juventus 0. Att: 25,000.
1966 *Barcelona*: Barcelona 0, Real Zaragoza 1 (Canario). Att: 35,000
Zaragoza Real Zaragoza 2, (Marcellino 2), Barcelona 4 (Pujol 3, Zaballa) . Att: 29,000
1967 *Zagreb*: Dinamo Zagreb 2 (Cercek 2), Leeds 0. Att: 40,000.
Leeds: Leeds 0, Dinamo Zagreb 0. Att: 35,000
1968 *Leeds*: Leeds 1 (Jones), Ferencvaros 0. Att: 25,000

Budapest: Ferencvaros 0, Leeds 0. Att: 76,000
1969 *Newcastle*: Newcastle 3 (Moncur 2, Scott), Ujpest Dozsa 0. Att: 60,000
Budapest: Ujpest Dozsa 2 (Bene, Gorocs), Newcastle 3 (Moncur, Arentoft, Foggon). Att: 37,000
1970 *Brussels*: Anderlecht 3 (Devrindt, Mulder 2), Arsenal 1 (Kennedy). Att: 37,000
London: Arsenal 3 (Kelly, Radford, Sammels), Anderlecht 0. Att: 51,000
1971 *Turin*: Juventus 2 (Bettega, Capello), Leeds 2 (Madeley, Bates). Att: 65,000
Leeds: Leeds 1 (Clark), Juventus 1 (Anastasi). Att: 42,000. (*Leeds won on away goals*)

UEFA Cup Finals

1972 *Wolverhampton*: Wolverhampton 1 (McCalliog), Tottenham Hotspur 2 (Chivers 2). Att: 38,000
London: Tottenham Hotspur 1 (Mullery), Wolverhampton 1 (Wagstaffe). Att: 54,000
1973 *Liverpool*: Liverpool 3 (Keegan 2, Lloyd), Borussia Mönchengladbach 0. Att: 41,000
Mönchengladbach: Borussia Mönchengladbach 2 (Heynckes 2), Liverpool 0. Att: 35,000
1974 *London*: Tottenham Hotspur 2 (England, o.g.), Feyenoord 2 (Van Hanegem, De Jong). Att: 46,000.
Rotterdam: Feyenoord 2 (Rijsbergen, Ressel), Tottenham Hotspur 0. Att: 59,000
1975 *Düsseldorf*: Borussia Mönchengladbach 0, Twente Enschede 0. Att: 42,000
Enschede: Twente Enschede 1

(Drost), Borussia Mönchengladbach 5 (Simonsen 2, Heynckes 3). Att: 21,000
1976 *Liverpool*: Liverpool 3 (Kennedy, Case, Keegan), Club Brugge 2 (Lambert, Cools). Att: 49,000
Bruges: Club Brugge 1 (Lambert), Liverpool 1 (Keegan). Att: 32,000
1977 *Turin*: Juventus 1 (Tardelli), Athletic Bilbao 0. Att: 75,000
Bilbao: Athletic Bilbao 2 (Churruca, Carlos), Juventus 1 (Bettega). Att: 43,000. (*Juventus won on away goals*.)
1978 *Corsica*: Bastia 0, PSV Eindhoven 0. Att: 15,000
Eindhoven: PSV Eindhoven 3 (Van der Kerkhof W., Deijkers, Van der Kuijlen), Bastia 0. Att: 27,000
1979 *Belgrade*: Red Star Belgrade 1 (Sestic), Borussia Mönchengladbach 1 (o.g.). Att: 87,000
Düsseldorf: Borussia Mönchengladbach 1 (Simonsen), Red Star Belgrade 0. Att: 45,000
1980 *Mönchengladbach*: Borussia Mönchengladbach 3 (Kulik 2, Matthäus), Eintracht Frankfurt 2 (Karger, Holzenbein). Att: 25,000
Frankfurt: Eintracht Frankfurt 1 (Schaub), Borussia Mönchengladbach 0. Att: 59,000. (*Eintracht won on away goals*.)
1981 *Ipswich*: Ipswich 3 (Wark, Thijssen, Mariner), AZ 67 Alkmaar 0. Att: 27,000
Amsterdam: AZ 67 Alkmaar 4 (Welzl, Metgod, Tol, Jonker), Ipswich 2 (Thijssen, Wark). Att: 28,000
1982 *Gothenburg*: IFK Gothenburg 1 (Tord Holmgren), Hamburg SV 0. Att: 42,000
Hamburg: Hamburg SV 0, IFK Gothenburg 3 (Corneliusson,

Nilsson, Fredriksson). Att: 60,000
1983 *Brussels*: Anderlecht 1 (Brylle), Benfica 0. Att: 55,000
Lisbon: Benfica 1 (Sheu), Anderlecht 1 (Lozano). Att: 80,000
1984 *Brussels*: Anderlecht 1 (Olsen), Tottenham Hotspur 1 (Miller). Att: 35,000
London: Tottenham Hotspur 1 (Roberts), Anderlecht 1 (Czerniatynski) (aet). (*Tottenham won 4–3 on penalties*). Att: 46,000
1985 *Szekesfehervar*: Videoton 0, Real Madrid 3 (Michel, Santilana, Valdano). Att: 30,000
Madrid: Real Madrid 0, Videoton 1 (Majer). Att: 90,000
1986 *Madrid*: Real Madrid 5 (Sanchez, Gordillo, Valdano 2, Santilana), Köln 1 (Allofs). Att: t: 85,000
Berlin: Köln 2 (Bein, Geilenkirchen), Real Madrid 0. Att: 15,000
1987 *Gothenburg*: IFK Gothenburg 1 (Pettersson), Dundee United 0. Att: 50,000
Dundee: Dundee United 1 (Clark), IFK Gothenburg 1 (Nilsson L.). Att: 21,000
1988 *Barcelona*: Español 3 (Losada 2, Soler), Bayer Leverkusen 0. Att: 42,000
Leverkusen: Bayer Leverkusen 3 (Tita, Gotz, Cha-Bum-Kun), Español 0 (aet). (*Leverkusen won 3–2 on penalties*). Att: 22,000
1989 *Naples*: Napoli 2 (Maradona, Careca), Stuttgart 1 (Gaudino). Att: 83,000
Stuttgart: Stuttgart 3 (Klinsmann, o.g., Schmaler O.), Napoli 3 (Alemao, Ferrera, Careca). Att: 67,000
1990 *Turin*: Juventus 3 (Galia, Casiraghi, De Agostini), Fiorentina

1 (Buso). Att: 45,000
Avellino: Fiorentina 0, Juventus 0. Att: 32,000
1991 *Milan*: Internazionale 2 (Matthäus, Berti), Roma 0. Att: 75,000
Rome: Roma 1 (Rizzitelli), Internazionale 0. Att: 71,000
1992 *Turin*: Torino 2 (Casagrande 2), Ajax 2 (Jonk, Pettersson). Att: 65,000
Amsterdam: Ajax 0, Torino 0. Att: 42,000. (*Ajax won on away goals*)
1993 *Dortmund*: Borussia Dortmund 1 (Rummenigge), Juventus 3 (Baggio D., Baggio R. 2). Att: 37,000
Turin: Juventus 3 (Baggio D. 2, Möller), Borussia Dortmund 0. Att: 60,000
1994 *Vienna*: Salzburg 0, Internazionale 1 (Berti). Att: 43,500
Milan: Internazionale 1 (Vonk), Salzburg 0. Att: 80,326
1995 *Parma*: Parma 1(D. Baggio), Juventus 0. Att: 26,350
Milan: Juventus 1 (Vialli) , Parma 1 (D. Baggio). Att: 80.750
1996 *Munich*: Bayern Munich 2 (Helmer, Scholl), Bordeaux 0. Att: 62,500
Bordeaux: Bordeaux 1 (Dutuel), Bayern Munich 3 (Scholl, Kostadinov, Klinsmann). Att: 36,000
1997 *Gelsenkirchen*: Schalke 1 (Wilmots), Internazionale 0. Att: 56,824
Milan: Internazionale 1 (Zamorano), Schalke 0 (Schalke won 4–1 on penalties). Att: 81,675
1998 *Paris*: Internazionale 3 (Zamorano, Zanetti, Ronaldo), Lazio 0. Att: 45,000
1999 *Villa Park, Birmingham*: Lazio 2 (Vieri, Nedved), Mallorca 1 (Dani).

which time Roma had added to an already impressive line-up. Birmingham did well to force a 2–2 draw at home, but were beaten 2–0 in Rome in the return . . . their second successive defeat in the Final.

The organizers had decided to allow three teams per country to enter the 1961–62 tournament, which had an entry of 28, and now the Spanish showed their dominance. Barcelona and Valencia reached the Final, with Valencia powering to a 7–3 aggregate victory over their countrymen. Valencia held on to the trophy the following season, beating Dinamo Zagreb 4–1 on aggregate in the Final, but were thwarted in their hat-trick bid by another Spanish side, Real Zaragoza. The 1964 Final was played as a one-off match in Barcelona, where goals by Villa and Marcelino secured a 2–1 win for Zaragoza.

The 1965 competition attracted 48 entries, and for the first time the Cup left Latin Europe, and headed east. Hungary's Ferencvaros fought their way through from the first round, with victories over Spartak Brno, Wiener Sport-Club, Roma, Athletic Bilbao and Manchester United, to face Juventus in the Final. The Italians, having safely negotiated the two opening rounds, were given a bye in the quarter-finals as the organizers sought to balance the numbers. This, coupled with the fact that the Final (again a one-off match) was in Turin, seemed to give Juve a definite advantage. But Ferencvaros produced a defensive formation that surpassed even the Italians' catenaccio, and a single goal by Fenyvesi after 74 minutes was enough.

The 1966 tournament returned to the two-game format for the Final, but the earlier rounds were marked by violence. Chelsea were pelted with rubbish in Rome, Leeds and Valencia fought a battle which resulted in three dismissals, and Leeds then had Johnny Giles sent off in the semi-final against Real Zaragoza. The Spanish again emerged triumphant, as Barcelona and Real Zaragoza met in the Final. A goal by Canario in the first leg at the Nou Camp gave Zaragoza the edge, but a hat-trick by the teenager Pujol in the return sealed a 4–2 victory for the

UEFA CUP SHUT-OUT *Schalke foiled Internazionale in the 1997 final*

Catalans, who won the trophy for the third time on a 4–3 aggregate.

The tournament was now moving into an era of English dominance. Leeds reached the 1967 Final, where they lost to Dinamo Zagreb, but they made amends the following season by beating Ferencvaros 1–0 on aggregate in the Final, after going unbeaten in previous rounds. This was the first of six consecutive victories by English clubs during the late 1960s and early 1970s.

In 1971 the Cup returned to Leeds, who beat Juventus. The first leg of the Final, in Turin, was abandoned at 0–0 because of rain, and in the rearranged fixture Leeds forced an excellent 2–2 draw. Juve were more threatening in the return, but could only manage a 1–1 draw, which meant Leeds won on away goals. Both sides were unbeaten in the tournament, and it was most unfortunate for the Italians to play 12 matches, without defeat, and still not win the Cup!

The competition name changed in 1972, and the first UEFA Cup Final was between two English clubs – Tottenham and Wolverhampton Wanderers. Tottenham won 3–2 on aggregate, and Liverpool won the next tournament, beating Borussia Mönchengladbach in the Final, to

complete a double hat-trick for English clubs in the tournament. Tottenham returned for the 1974 Final, but could not cope with Holland's Feyenoord – European champions in 1970 – who won 4–2 on aggregate. The Final, however, was marred by violence as both sets of supporters fought running battles with each other and the police.

Another Dutch club, Twente Enschede, reached the Final in 1975, but they were outclassed by Borussia Mönchengladbach of West Germany. After a surprising 0–0 draw, Borussia turned on the power in the return to win 5–1, with Jupp Heynckes scoring a hat-trick, and Allan Simonsen two. Liverpool won again in 1976, beating Club Brugge 4–3 on aggregate in the Final. It was ironic, therefore, that this emerging Liverpool side should then go on to win two successive European Cups, 1977 and 1978, beating Borussia and Brugge respectively in the Finals.

Italy and Spain contested the 1977 UEFA Cup Final, represented by Juventus and Athletic Bilbao, with the Italians winning on away goals after a 2–2 aggregate draw. In 1978 PSV Eindhoven won the Cup for Holland again, beating France's Bas-

tia 3–0 at home after a 0–0 draw in Corsica – the only time a European Final has been played on an island outside the British Isles.

Borussia Mönchengladbach got to their third Final in 1979, and made it two wins out of three by beating Red Star Belgrade 2–1 on aggregate, although they needed an own goal and a Simonsen penalty to do it. Borussia reached the Final again the following year, and faced fellow West Germans Eintracht Frankfurt in the Final. After winning the home leg 3–2, Borussia went down 1–0 in the return, giving Eintracht the victory on the away goals rule. In 1981 Ipswich Town brought the Cup back to England with a splendid 5–4 aggregate victory over the little-known Dutch side AZ 67 Alkmaar. Ipswich's John Wark scored in both legs of the Final to bring his total in that season's competition to 14 – equalling the all-time record set by Milan's José Altafini in the 1963 European Cup.

IFK Gothenburg became the first Swedish winners of a European trophy when they beat Hamburg in 1982, and they went on to win again in 1987, beating Dundee United. Between those two victories, Anderlecht and Real Madrid dominated the competition. Anderlecht beat Benfica 2–1 on aggregate to win the 1983 competition, and they returned to the Final the following year against Tottenham. Both legs produced 1–1 draws, and after extra time produced no winner, Tottenham took the Cup on penalties, reserve goalkeeper Tony Parks saving the decisive kick.

Tottenham's defence of the trophy in 1985 ended in the quarter-finals, where they were narrowly and unluckily beaten 1–0 on aggregate by Real Madrid. The Spaniards, aided by the German Uli Stielike and the Argentinian Jorge Valdano, went on to beat Hungary's Videoton 3–1 in the Final. Real retained the trophy the following season with a far more impressive demolition of West Germany's Köln. A 5–1 win in Madrid was followed by a 2–0 defeat in Germany, but Real kept the trophy with a 5–3 aggregate margin.

Following Gothenburg's second success in 1987, the Cup was won on penalties for the second time when

Bayer Leverkusen and Español contested the Final. Español won the first leg 3–0 at home and looked all set for Spain's ninth victory, but Bayer levelled the aggregate score in the second leg, and then won 3–2 on penalties.

Since then the UEFA Cup has been dominated by Italian clubs. In the seven Finals up to 1995, 10 finalists have been Italian, three have been all-Italian affairs, and Serie A clubs have won six. In 1989 Napoli, led by Diego Maradona, beat VfB Stuttgart; Juventus and Fiorentina contested an all-Italian Final in 1990, with Juventus winning 3–1 at home and on aggregate; in 1991 Internazionale narrowly beat Roma 2–1; in 1992 Torino lost to Ajax – who were completing a hat-trick of European trophy wins – but only on away goals after 2–2 and 0–0 draws; and in 1993 Juventus won the Cup again, proving themselves to be far too good for Borussia Dortmund.

Internazionale overcame Austrians Salzburg to win in 1994, 1–0 in both games. In 1994–95, Juventus and Parma were first and second for most of the Serie A season, and reached both the UEFA and domestic Cup finals.

In the UEFA Cup it was the newcomers who prevailed 2–1 on aggregate, with ex-Juventus player Dino Baggio scoring both goals.

The system of entry into the UEFA Cup, based on past performances, ensures that the more successful countries, such as Italy, Spain, Germany and England, get four entrants. However, as more countries enter UEFA, more clubs are entering the tournament, and UEFA had to expand the tournament with a preliminary round in mid-July.

The rebuilt UEFA-Intertoto Cup was used as a qualifying event for 1995–96. French club Bordeaux entered through that route went all the way to the final – beating Milan in a shock quarter-final, reversing a 2–0 first leg deficit – before losing with honour to Bayern Munich. Jürgen Klinsmann scored 15 goals in the tournament, a record for a European club competition.

The Cup stayed in Germany in 1997 when historic Schalke from the Ruhr, appearing in a European final for the first time, defeated Internazionale on penalties in Milan.

Inter bounced back a year later to beat their fellow Italians of Lazio 3–0 in the Parc des Princes in Paris. UEFA's decision to abandon the two-leg format in favour of a single-match final was vindicated by a superb display from Inter while Parma maintained Italy's pre-eminence in 1999.

EUROPEAN CUP-WINNERS' CUP

When Lazio held aloft the Cup-Winners' Cup after beating Mallorca at Villa Park, Birmingham in May 1999 they were also celebrating the end of an era – UEFA having decided that the tournament should be scrapped to make way for its expansion of the Champions League and the UEFA Cup. Yet the Cup-Winners' Cup had earned a distinguished place in the history of the game since its launch in the 1960–61 season. Following the success of the European Cup, it seemed a logical step to introduce a competition for the winners of national knock-out competitions. However, many European countries did not have a knock-out competition and it

was only in Britain, where the Cup dates back further than the League, that cup competitions fired the imagination of both the clubs and the public. Consequently, in many countries, new competitions were introduced, or old ones were revived.

Run along the same lines as the European Cup – home and away knock-out up to the Final, which was initially a two-leg, but is now a one-off match – the first Cup-winners' Cup attracted entrants from 10 countries. Vorwärts Berlin, Red Star Brno, Ferencvaros and Rangers contested the qualifying round to decide the quarter-final line-up. Rangers, having disposed of Ferencvaros, demolished West Germany's Borussia Mönchengladbach 11–0 on aggregate in the quarter-finals, before overcoming Wolverhampton Wanderers in an all-British semi-final. Italy's Fiorentina – European Cup finalists four years previously – beat FC Luzern 9–2 in the quarter-finals, before beating Dinamo Zagreb 4–2 on aggregate in the semi-finals.

The Final, played over two legs for the first and only time, saw Fiorentina at their best – defending solidly

MARKED MAN *Manchester United's Hughes in action during the 1991 final. The Welsh international scored both of United's goals.*

while always retaining the ability to break quickly, led by Swedish winger Kurt Hamrin. In the first leg, in Glasgow, Fiorentina frustrated the Rangers forwards, while Hamrin twice led the charge for Milani to score. In the return Hamrin again proved the match-winner, setting up Milani for the first and scoring the winner after Scott had equalized.

The success of the first tournament encouraged more clubs to get involved, and 23 entered the second in 1961–62. Swansea Town and Floriana of Malta were among them, clearly attracted by the prospect of money-spinning ties with some of Europe's biggest clubs and by the outside possibility of a "giant-killing". It was not to be, though, as both went out in the preliminary round – Swansea beaten 7–3 on aggregate by Motor Jena, Floriana trounced 15–4 by Ujpest Dozsa.

Fiorentina's impressive defence took them all the way again in 1962, where they met Atletico Madrid in the Final, now played as a one-off. The match, in Glasgow, produced a disappointing 1–1 draw, and when the replay took place – four months later – Atletico won the Cup with a straightforward 3–0 win.

In the 1963 competition the holders again reached the Final, and again they lost. Atletico faced Tottenham in Rotterdam and could not contain Bill Nicholson's international-packed side, who had won

REAL GOOD WIN *Zaragoza's Nayim celebrates victory in 1995*

the FA Cup in successive seasons. Jimmy Greaves and Terry Dyson both scored twice as Tottenham won 5–1 to become the first English winners of a European trophy.

Tottenham's reign ended in the second round in 1964, when they were unfortunate to be drawn against Manchester United, who won 4–2 on aggregate. United fell in the quarter-finals to Portugal's Sporting Lisbon, who went on to win the Cup against MTK Budapest, although they needed a 1–0 replay win after a 3–3 draw in Belgium.

The Cup-winners' Cup had now established itself on the European scene, and 30 clubs entered the 1965 tournament. West Ham United, essentially novices at the European game, emulated Tottenham's success by beating TSV Munich 1860 in

front of a full house at Wembley. The match was fast and open, but two goals in two minutes by reserve winger Tony Sealey won the Cup for the Londoners.

The following year, 1966, featured another England-West Germany Final, this time involving Liverpool and Borussia Dortmund. On a rain-lashed night in Glasgow, the Germans were slightly fortunate to win in extra time when a mis-hit lob by Libuda was deflected in by Yeats. Rangers returned for the 1967 Final, also against a German club, Bayern Munich – and were strangely out of sorts. Gerd Müller was well shackled but in the 18th minute of extra time Roth fired home the winner to keep the Cup in Germany. Another German club, Hamburg, contested the 1968 Final, but were no match for

Milan, for whom Hamrin scored twice to win his second medal.

In 1969 the original draw was abandoned after Soviet troops entered Czechoslovakia, and a new draw, keeping East and West apart, was made. Most Eastern countries were against the idea and withdrew, but the Czechs remained . . . and with sweet irony Slovan Bratislava collected the trophy, beating the favourites Barcelona 3–2 in Basle.

For the following three years the Cup stayed in Britain as Manchester City, Chelsea and, at the third attempt, Rangers all won. Manchester City beat Poland's Gornik Zabrze 2–1 in front of a poor crowd of 8,000 in Vienna in 1970; Chelsea needed a replay the next year in Athens to overcome Real Madrid, and Rangers finally won the trophy with a 3–2 victory over Moscow Dynamo in 1972.

The Rangers victory, however, was marred by ugly scenes in and around the Nou Camp stadium in Barcelona. The lunatic fringe of their supporters invaded the pitch before, during and after the match, and charged riot police outside the stadium, leaving one dead and scores injured. Rangers, having done so well to hang on for their victory, were banned for a year and were consequently unable to defend their title.

Leeds United almost made it four in a row for Britain in 1973 when they faced Milan in the Final in Salonika. Milan scored after five

Winners

European Cup-winners' Cup Finals

1961 *Glasgow*: Rangers 0, Fiorentina 2 (Milani 2).
Florence: Fiorentina 2 (Milani, Hamrin), Rangers 1 (Scott). Fiorentina won 4–1 on aggregate.

1962 *Glasgow*: Atletico Madrid 1 (Peiro), Fiorentina 1 (Hamrin) (aet). *Stuttgart*: Atletico Madrid 3 (Jones, Mendonca, Peiro), Fiorentina 0.

1963 *Rotterdam*: Tottenham Hotspur 5 (Greaves 2, White, Dyson 2), Atletico Madrid 1 (Collar).

1964 *Brussels*: Sporting Lisbon 3 (Mascaranha, Figueiredo 2), MTK Budapest 3 (Sandor 2, Kuti) (aet). *Antwerp* (replay): Sporting Lisbon 1 (Morais), MTK Budapest 0.

1965 *Wembley*: West Ham United 2 (Sealey 2), TSV Munich 1860 0.

1966 *Glasgow*: Borussia Dortmund

2 (Held, Libuda), Liverpool 1 (Hunt) (aet).

1967 *Nuremberg*: Bayern Munich 1 (Roth), Rangers 0 (aet).

1968 *Rotterdam*: Milan 2 (Hamrin 2), Hamburg SV 0.

1969 *Basle*: Slovan Bratislava 3 (Cvetler, Hrivnak, Jan Capkovic), Barcelona 2 (Zaldua, Rexach).

1970 *Vienna*: Manchester City 2 (Young, Lee), Gornik Zabrze 1 (Oslizlo).

1971 *Athens*: Chelsea 1 (Osgood), Real Madrid 1 (Zoco) (aet). *Athens* (replay): Chelsea 2 (Dempsey, Osgood), Real Madrid 1 (Fleitas).

1972 *Barcelona*: Rangers 3 (Stein, Johnston 2), Moscow Dynamo 2 (Estrekov, Makovikov).

1973 *Salonika*: Milan 1 (Chiarugi), Leeds United 0.

1974 *Rotterdam*: FC Magdeburg 2 (o.g., Seguin), Milan 0.

1975 *Basle*: Kiev Dynamo 3 (Onischenko 2, Blokhin), Ferencvaros 0.

1976 *Brussels*: Anderlecht 4 (Rensenbrink 2, Van der Elst 2), West Ham United 2 (Holland, Robson).

1977 *Amsterdam*: Hamburg SV 2 (Volkert, Magath), Anderlecht 0.

1978 *Paris*: Anderlecht 4 (Rensenbrink 2, Van Binst 2), FK Austria 0.

1979 *Basle*: Barcelona 4 (Sanchez, Asensi, Rexach, Krankl), Fortuna Düsseldorf 3 (Allofs K., Seel 2) (aet).

1980 *Brussels*: Valencia 0, Arsenal 0 (aet). (*Valencia* won 5–4 on pens.)

1981 *Düsseldorf*: Dynamo Tbilisi 2 (Gutsayev, Daraselia), Carl Zeiss

Jena 1 (Hoppe).

1982 *Barcelona*: Barcelona 2 (Simonsen, Quini), Standard Liège 1 (Vandermissen).

1983 *Gothenburg*: Aberdeen 2 (Black, Hewitt), Real Madrid 1 (Juanito) (aet).

1984 *Basle*: Juventus 2 (Vignola, Boniek), FC Porto 1 (Sousa).

1985 *Rotterdam*: Everton 3 (Gray, Steven, Sheedy), Rapid Vienna 1 (Krankl).

1986 *Lyons*: Kiev Dynamo 3 (Zavarov, Blokhin, Yevtushenko), Atletico Madrid 0.

1987 *Athens*: Ajax 1 (Van Basten), Lokomotive Leipzig 0.

1988 *Strasbourg*: Mechelen 1 (De Boer), Ajax 0.

1989 *Berne*: Barcelona 2 (Salinas, Recarte), Sampdoria 0.

1990 *Gothenburg*: Sampdoria 2

(Vialli 2), Anderlecht 0 (aet).

1991 *Rotterdam*: Manchester United 2 (Hughes 2), Barcelona 1 (Koeman).

1992 *Lisbon*: Werder Bremen 2 (Allofs K., Rufer), Monaco 0.

1993 *Wembley*: Parma 3 (Minotti, Melli, Cuoghi), Antwerp 1 (Severeyns).

1994 *Copenhagen*: Arsenal 1 (Smith), Parma 0.

1995 *Paris*: Real Zaragoza 2 (Esnaider, Nayim), Arsenal 1 (Hartson).

1996 *Brussels*: Paris St Germain 1 (N'Gotty), Rapid Vienna 0.

1997 *Rotterdam*: Barcelona 1 (Ronaldo), Paris St Germain 0.

1998 *Stockholm*: Chelsea 1 (Zola), Stuttgart 0.

1999 *Moscow*: Parma 3 (Crespo, Vanoli, Chiesa), Marseille 0.

minutes through Chiarugi and promptly began using spoiling tactics, which were not appreciated by the Greek crowd. Leeds' frustration finally boiled over two minutes from the end, when Hunter and Sogliano were sent off for fighting.

Milan reached the Final again the following year, but lost to FC Magdeburg, who became the only East German winners of a European trophy. A paltry crowd of 4,000 in Rotterdam, the smallest for a Final in the competition's history, saw an own goal by Lanzi just before half-time set the East Germans on their way to a 2–0 victory

Kiev Dynamo kept the trophy behind the Iron Curtain with their first win, by beating Ferencvaros 3–0 in Basle in 1975. Belgium's Anderlecht then emerged as the competition's specialists with three successive appearances in the Final – of which they won the first and the third. In 1976 they beat West Ham 4–2 in Brussels, then lost 2–0 to Hamburg in 1977, before beating FK Austria 4–0 in Paris. Dutch striker Rob Rensenbrink scored two in each of the wins.

The 1979 tournament produced the highest-scoring Final in the competition's history as Barcelona beat Fortuna Düsseldorf 4–3 in Basle. Level at 2–2 after 90 minutes, Austrian striker Hans Krankl scored the clincher for the Spanish in extra time – after Rexach had made it 3–2 and Seel had equalized. Valencia retained the Cup for Spain the following season in the first European Final to be decided on penalties. A disappointing 0–0 draw in Brussels was decided when Graham Rix missed Arsenal's fifth penalty in the shootout, giving Valencia a 5–4 victory.

In the 1981 competition, Welsh Cup winners Newport County, then in the English Fourth Division, caused a sensation by knocking out the holders Valencia in the second round. Newport then narrowly lost in the quarter-finals to East Germany's Carl Zeiss Jena, who went on to contest an all-Eastern Final with Dynamo Tbilisi, who had destroyed West Ham in the quarter-finals. Tbilisi, with several internationals in the side, won 2–1 to clinch the Soviet Union's second Cup.

MAKING IT A BLUE DAY *Steve Clarke and Dennis Wise in 1998.*

Barcelona won for the second time in four years in 1982, when they beat Belgium's Standard Liège 2–1 at the Nou Camp. Real Madrid spurned the chance to match their Catalan rivals the next year, when they lost to Aberdeen. . Juventus became the third Italian side to win the Cup when they beat FC Porto 2–1 in 1984. Everton won it for England the following season by outplaying Rapid Vienna in Rotterdam to complete a League Championship and Cup-winners' Cup double.

In 1986 Kiev Dynamo won their second title with an outstanding 3–0 win over Atletico Madrid. Kiev, at the time, were one of the top clubs in Europe and supplied the bulk of the Soviet Union's national squad, including the great Oleg Blokhin, who scored in Kiev's 1975 triumph and again against Atletico.

Ajax of Amsterdam appeared in the next two finals. In 1987 they beat Lokomotive Leipzig 1–0 in Lyon, with Marco Van Basten scoring the winner in his last game for the club before his move to Milan. The following season Ajax were expected to retain the trophy against European debutants Mechelen, but the Belgians pulled off a shock 1–0 win.

Barcelona collected their third Cup-winners' Cup in 1989, beating Italy's emerging Sampdoria 2–0 in Bern. The Italians, though, made amends the following year, beating Anderlecht 2–0, with Gianluca Vialli scoring twice in extra time.

Barcelona were back for 1991, and so were the English clubs. Manchester United went all the way to the Final and then won 2–1. The match provided Welsh striker Mark Hughes – dumped by Barcelona three years before – with sweet revenge as he scored both United's goals.

In 1992 Werder Bremen beat Monaco, veteran striker Klaus Allofs putting the German club on the way with the opening goal in a 2–0 win. Then Parma completed a remarkable 10-year transition from the Italian Third Division to European trophy-winners in 1993, when they beat Antwerp 3–1 at Wembley.

In both 1994 and 1995 the defending champions lost in the Final to extend the record of no holder retaining the Cup. Arsenal beat Parma 1–0 in 1994, but lost 2–1 to a freak 120th minute goal to Spain's Zaragoza.

Zarargoza's attempt to become the first club to retain the cup faltered in their 1996 quarter-finals against compatriots La Coruña, who fell to Paris Saint-Germain at the next stage. PSG became only the second French club to win a European trophy when they beat Rapid Vienna 1–0 in the final – the first in Brussels since 1985. The unwritten law which prevents holders from retaining the cup was again evident in 1997, when PSG fell 1–0 to Barcelona in Rotterdam. A penalty from Ronaldo was all that separated the teams on paper though Barcelona were far superior on the day. The same could not be said of Chelsea when they beat Stuttgart the following year in Stockholm. Vialli was back in his new role as Chelsea player-manager, but it was Gianfranco Zola who scored a superb winner.

Chelsea continued the odd tradition of failing to hold onto the trophy, defeated by European newcomers Mallorca who were themselves duly despatched by Lazio, winning their first European trophy.

EUROPEAN SUPER CUP

The European Super Cup is played annually between the winners of the European Cup and the European Cup-Winners Cup. Its status is being upgraded with a switch to a neutral, single-venue final.

European Super Cup Winners		
1972 Ajax	**1987** FC Porto	
1973 Ajax	**1988** Mechelen	
1975 Kiev Dynamo	**1989** Milan	
1976 Anderlecht	**1990** Milan	
1977 Liverpool	**1991** Manchester	
1978 Anderlecht	United	
1979 Nottingham	**1992** Barcelona	
Forest	**1993** Parma	
1980 Valencia	**1994** Milan	
1982 Aston Villa	**1995** Ajax	
1983 Aberdeen	**1996** Juventus	
1984 Juventus	**1997** Barcelona	
1986 Steaua	**1998** Chelsea	
Bucharest		

MITROPA CUP

The Mitropa Cup was an important competition in the inter-war period, and was the forerunner of the European Cup. Created by Hugo Meisĺ, the Mitropa Cup (shortened form of Mittel Europa) was restricted to clubs from Austria, Italy, Hungary,

Czechoslovakia, Switzerland, Romania and Yugoslavia.

The competition involved the champions of each country, and was suspended between 1939 and 1950 and lost much of its status once the European Cup got under way in 1955. From 1980 entry was restricted to the Second Division champions of each country, and was eventually suspended in 1992.

Mitropa Cup Winners			
1927	Sparta Prague	1968	Red Star
1928	Ferencvaros		Belgrade
1929	Ujpest Dozsa	1969	TJ Internacional
1930	Rapid Vienna	1970	Vasas Budapest
1931	First Vienna	1971	Celik Zenica
1932	Bologna	1972	Celik Zenica
1933	FK Austria	1973	Tatabanya
1934	Bologna	1974	Tatabanya
1935	Sparta Prague	1975	Wacker
1936	FK Austria		Innsbrück
1937	Ferencvaros	1976	Wacker
1938	Slavia Prague		Innsbrück
1939	Ujpest Dozsa	1977	Vojvodina
1951	Rapid Vienna	1978	Partizan
1955	Voros Lobogo		Belgrade
1956	Vasas Budapest	1980	Udinese
1957	Vasas Budapest	1981	Tatran Presov
1959	Honved	1982	Milan
1960	VasasBudapest	1983	Vasas Budapest
1961	Bologna	1984	SC Eisenstadt
1962	Vasas Budapest	1985	Iskra Bugojno
1963	MTK Budapest	1986	Pisa
1964	Spartak	1987	Ascoli
	Sokolovo	1988	Pisa
1965	Vasas Budapest	1989	Banik Ostrava
1966	Fiorentina.	1990	Bari
1967	Spartak Trnava	1991	Torino

INTERTOTO CUP

The event, dating back to the 1960s for summer football pools purposes, was relaunched in 1995. The offer to semi-finalists of places in the UEFA Cup failed to attract the best efforts of some nations, such as Italy, Spain and England, but Bordeaux went all the way to the UEFA Cup Final.

LATIN CUP

The Latin Cup was Europe's top post-war club event. Played between the champions of France, Spain, Italy and Portugal, it ended in 1957.

Latin Cup Winners			
1949	Barcelona	1953	Stade de Reims
1950	Benfica	1955	Real Madrid
1951	Milan	1956	Milan
1952	Barcelona	1957	Real Madrid

CONCACAF CHAMPIONS CUP

The premier club competition for teams from the Central American and Caribbean regions has been contested since 1962, and is now known as the American Airlines Cup.

CONCACAF Champions Cup Winners	
1962	Guadalajara CD (Mexico)
1963	Racing Club (Haiti)
1964	Not completed.
1965	Not completed.
1966	Not held
1967	Alianza (El Salvador)
1968	Toluca (Mexico)
1969	Cruz Azul (Mexico)
1970	Cruz Azul (North), Deportivo Saprissa (Central), Transvaal (Caribbean)
1971	Cruz Azul (Mexico)
1972	Olimpia (Honduras)
1973	Transvaal (Surinam)
1974	Municipal (Guatemala)
1975	Atletico Espanol (Mexico)
1976	Aguila (El Salvador)
1977	America (Mexico)
1978	Univ Guadalajara (North), Comunica- ciones (Central), Defence Force (Carib.).
1979	Deportivo FAS (El Salvador)
1980	UNAM (Mexico)
1981	Transvaal (Surinam)
1982	UNAM (Mexico)
1983	Atlante (Mexico)
1984	Violette (Haiti)
1985	Defence Force (Trinidad and Tobago)
1986	LD Alajuelense (Costa Rica)
1987	America (Mexico)
1988	Olimpia (Honduras)
1989	UNAM (Mexico)
1990	America (Mexico)
1991	Puebla (Mexico)
1992	America (Mexico)
1993	Deportivo Saprissa (Costa Rica)
1994	Cartagines (Costa Rica)
1995	Deportivo Saprissa (Costa Rica)
1996	Not completed
1997	Cruz Azul (Costa Rica)
1998	DC United (USA)

INTER-AMERICAN CUP

The Inter-American Cup pits the club champions of CONCACAF and South America against each other. Played over two legs, the Cup has only been won by CONCACAF clubs on three occasions, and all three were Mexican clubs.

No less than five different clubs from Argentina have won the Inter-American Cup, including Independiente three successive occasions. America of Mexico is the only other team to have won the trophy on more than one occasion, although Chilean clubs were successful twice in the 1990s.

Inter-American Cup Winners	
1968	Estudiantes.(Argentina)
1971	Nacional (Uruguay)
1973	Independiente (Argentina)
1975	Independiente (Argentina)
1976	Independiente (Argentina)
1977	America (Mexico)
1979	Olimpia (Paraguay)
1980	UNAM (Mexico)
1985	Argentinos Juniors (Argentina)
1986	River Plate (Argentina)
1988	Nacional (Uruguay)
1989	Atletico Nacional (Colombia)
1990	America (Mexico)
1992	Colo Colo (Chile)
1993	Univ Catolica (Chile)
1994	Velez Sarsfield (Argentina)

AFRICAN CHAMPIONS CUP

The African Champions Cup is run along similar lines to its European equivalent, with the champions of each country plus the defending champions playing on a home-and-away knock-out basis. The early years of the competition were dominated by West and Central African clubs; by Cameroon and Ghana in the 1970s and by North African clubs since the 1980s.

African Champions Cup Winners	
1964	Oryx Douala (Cameroon)
1965	Not held
1966	Stade Abidjan (Ivory Coast)
1967	TP Englebert (Zaïre)
1968	TP Englebert (Zaïre)
1969	Al Ismaili (Egypt)
1970	Asante Kotoko (Ghana)
1971	Canon Yaounde (Cameroon)
1972	Hafia Conakry (Ghana)
1973	AS Vita Kinshasa (Zaïre)
1974	CARA Brazzaville (Congo)
1975	Hafia Conakry (Ghana)
1976	MC Algiers (Algeria)
1977	Hafia Conakry (Ghana)
1978	Canon Yaounde (Cameroon)
1979	Union Douala (Cameroon)
1980	Canon Yaounde (Cameroon)
1981	JE Tizi-Ouzou (Algeria)
1982	Al Ahly (Egypt)
1983	Asant Kotoko (Ghana)
1984	Zamalek (Egypt)
1985	FAR Rabat (Morocco)
1986	Zamalek (Egypt)
1987	Al Ahly (Egypt)
1988	EP Setif (Algeria)
1989	Raja Casablanca (Morocco)
1990	JS Kabylie (Algeria)
1991	Club Africain (Tunisia)
1992	Wydad Casablanca (Morocco)
1993	Zamalek (Egypt)
1994	Esperance (Tunisia)
1995	Orlando Pirates (South Africa)
1996	Zamalek (Egypt)
1997	Raja Casablanca (Morocco)
1998	ASEC Abidjan (Ivory Coast)

AFRICAN CUP-WINNERS' CUP

Encouraged by the success of the African Champions Cup, the CAF decided to launch a competition for each nation's Cup-winners in 1975. Again, the new event mirrored its European counterpart, and has been dominated by clubs from North and West Africa. Egyptian clubs have done especially well, with five victories including a hat-trick for Cairo's Al Ahly between 1984 and 1986. Clubs from the Cameroon and from Nigeria have also done well over the years.

African Cup-Winners Cup Winners	
1975	Tonnerre Yaounde (Cameroon)
1976	Shooting Stars (Nigeria)
1977	Enugu Rangers (Nigeria)
1978	Horoya Conakry (Guinea)
1979	Canon Yaounde (Cameroon)
1980	TP Mazembe (Zaire)
1981	Union Douala (Cameroon)
1982	Al Mokaoulum (Egypt)
1983	Al Mokaoulum (Egypt)
1984	Al Ahly (Egypt)
1985	Al Ahly (Egypt)
1986	Al Ahly (Egypt)
1987	Gor Mahia (Kenya)
1988	CA Bizerte (Tunisia)
1989	Al Merreikh (Sudan)
1990	BCC Lions (Nigeria)
1991	Power Dynamos (Zambia)
1992	Africa Sports (Ivory Coast)
1993	Al Ahly (Egypt)
1994	Daring Club (Zaire)
1995	J.S Kabylie (Algeria)
1996	Arab Contractors (Egypt)
1997	Etoile Sahel (Tunisia)
1998	Esperance (Turkey)

CAF CUP

The CAF Cup began in the light of the success of the other two continental competitions and the CAF introduced it in 1992. The CAF is Africa's answer to the UEFA Cup, involving the best clubs not involved in the other two competitions . The first winners of the Cup were Nigeria's Shooting Stars – appropriately because the gold-plated trophy was donated to the CAF by a Nigerian businessman.

CAF Cup Winners	
1992	Shooting Stars (Nigeria)
1993	Stella Abidjan (Ivory Coast)
1994	Bendel Insurance (Nigeria)
1995	Etoile Sahel (Tunisia)
1996	Kawkab (Morocco)
1997	Esperance Sportive (Tunisia)
1998	Club Sportif Sfax (Tunisia)

THE COUNTRIES

The world governing body of Association Football boasts more than 200 members. They are grouped into six regional confederations – Europe (UEFA), South America (CONMEBOL), Central and North America (CONCACAF), Africa, Asia and Oceania. All have an equal role to play in football's international democracy, every member country having a single vote in the FIFA Congress.

EUROPE

Austria and Hungary in 1902 played the first international match outside Britain. In the 1920s it was central Europeans who launched the Mitropa Cup, the predecessor of today's hugely successful European club competitions. France were leaders in founding FIFA and bringing the vision of a World Cup to reality and, later, launching the European competitive structures which are so familiar, and so avidly followed, today.

Professionalism swept through western Europe in the late 1920s, engulfing Spain, Italy, France and Portugal. Big clubs in those countries imported star foreigners from the turn of the 1930s. It was not until the mid-1950s that Belgium, Holland and Germany caught up with full-time professionalism. When they did, the balance of the European game changed yet again. Great nations spawned great clubs – Juventus, Real Madrid, Ajax Amsterdam, Bayern Munich and Anderlecht. But the foundation remained Europe's framework of mixed nationalities. By the end of 1996, UEFA, the European federation, boasted 51 members.

Many of those nations are too new to offer a note to history. They do deserve a statistical starting point here for the international record.

ALBANIA

Federata Shqiptare Futbollit
Founded: 1930
FIFA: 1954

Football in Albania started at the beginning of the twentieth century, but progress was hampered by, first, the ruling Turks and, second, Mussolini's annexation in 1939. The Communist take-over in 1944, under Enver Hoxha, promised a new dawn – but it was a short-lived period of hope for Albanian soccer. Throughout the 1950s, Albania was in isolation, and between 1954 and 1963 they played only one international – against East Germany. Some progress was made in the 1960s, with Albania gaining entry to both the World Cup and the European Championship. But the isolationist cloak which shrouded the country for so long has ensured that its footballing prospects remain as poor as those of its economy.

ANDORRA

Federacio Andorrana de Futbol
Founded: 1996
FIFA: 1996

ARMENIA

Football Federation of Armenia
Founded: 1922
FIFA: 1992

AUSTRIA

Österreichischer Fussball-Bund
Founded: 1904
FIFA: 1905

Vienna arguably was the focal point of continental European football in the first half of the twentieth century, a situation which lasted until the 1960s. Britons living in Vienna provided Austrian football's early impetus and, in 1902, Austria beat Hungary 5–0 at the Prater in what has become the world's second oldest regular international fixture after England vs. Scotland.

The inter-war period was Austria's most successful era, when the

CAPTAIN FANTASTIC *Germany's Klinsmann*

Great Coaches

HUGO MEISL

Austria manager and general secretary 1906–37; born November 16, 1881; died February 17, 1937

Meisl was the errant son of a Viennese banking family who was too infatuated with football in Central Europe in the early years of the century to want to enter the business. Meisl was playing inside-forward for FK Austria when he met the English coach, Jimmy Hogan, whom he persuaded to come and work in Vienna. Later Meisl became involved with neighbours Admira and then became secretary of the Austrian federation. Simultaneously he was also national manager, and his partnership with Hogan led to the rise of the legendary Austrian "Wunderteam" of the 1920s and early 1930s. Meisl and Vittorio Pozzo were the two dominant figures in pre-war continental football.

"Wunderteam" – led by Matthias Sindelar – swept all before them. In 30 matches from 1931 to 1934, the "Wunderteam" scored 101 goals, and the 1934 World Cup seemed to be at their mercy. But defeat in the semi-final by hosts Italy ended their hopes. Austria's chances in the 1938 event were destroyed by the German occupation, and from March 1938 "Austrian" football ceased to exist.

A new side came together in the 1950s, led by Ernst Ocwirck and Gerhard Hanappi, which looked set for World Cup success in 1954. But the Germans again spoiled the plan, winning the semi-final, 6–1. A poor showing in 1958 in Sweden was followed by an inexorable decline, and the low point was reached on September 12, 1991 when the Faroe Islands – playing their first ever competitive match – won 1–0 in a European Championship qualifier.

Austria did qualify for France 98, but won few friends with a negative approach, and not even two last-minute equalisers in group-stage games against Cameroon and Chile could clinch a second-round place.

AZERBAIJAN

Association of Azerbaijan Football Federations
Founded: 1993
FIFA: 1994

The Azeris made their independent international debut in the 1996 European Championship but were forced, because of civil war, to play home games in Turkey. Not surprisingly, they lost nine of their 10 matches.

BELARUS

Belarus Football Association
Founded: 1992
FIFA: 1992

BELGIUM

Union Royale Belge des Sociétés de Football-Association
Founded: 1895
FIFA: 1904

Belgian football has taken a long time to develop. With an association formed in 1895 and the second-oldest league outside Great Britain, it was natural for the Belgians to be a driving force behind the formation of FIFA and one of only four European sides to go to Uruguay for the first World Cup in 1930. But the strictly amateur nature of the domestic game severely hindered progress.

The yoke of amateurism was discarded in 1972, with the introduction of professionalism, and the national side immediately improved. From 1972 to 1984 Belgium reached the last eight of four successive European Championships, and in 1980 they appeared in the final, losing to West Germany. The class of 1980 represented Belgium for almost a decade and contained many of their most celebrated players, including goalkeeper Jean-Marie Pfaff, full-back Eric Gerets and 96-cap striker Jan Ceulemans.

Their finest hour came at the 1986 World Cup finals, where they lost to Argentina in the semi-finals, with Enzo Scifo the star.

But at the 1998 finals, despite the presence of world-class striker Luc Nilis, Belgium lacked inspiration and failed to win a single game. In the end a 1–1 draw against lowly South Korea ended their hopes of reaching the second round.

BOSNIA-HERZEGOVINA

Bosnia and Herzegovina Football Federation
Founded: 1991
FIFA: 1992

Bosnia made history, on eventual admittance following independence, as UEFA's 50th member nation.

BULGARIA

Bulgarski Futbolen Solus
Founded: 1923
FIFA: 1924

WORLD'S NO. 1 *Belgium's Michel Preud'homme was voted top 'keeper at USA '94*

STILL TRYING *Bulgaria in Mexico 1986*

Bulgarian football is facing a mini-crisis after a disastrous 1998 World Cup finals in France.

The team finished bottom of their group, scored only one goal in the tournament and ended with a crushing 6-1 defeat against Spain.

It was a disappointing exit for an ageing side which differed very little to the team which had charmed the world by finishing fourth at USA '94, knocking out Germany on the way. But now the Bulgarians face a major rebuilding exercise as they try and replace their veterans with younger plaers.

History shows they should be able to do it. Like many Eastern Bloc countries Bulgaria made little impact in international football until the Communists had taken over in 1944 – and completely reorganized the domestic game.

A rigid style of passing play was imposed on the national side, and the results were significant, making Bulgaria very difficult opponents and one of Europe's top sides during the 1960s and 1970s. But this system discouraged individual flair and flexibility – a point illustrated by Bulgaria's astonishingly poor record in the World Cup finals. They qualified for five finals between 1962 and 1990, playing 16 matches... and did not win any of them! But this period did produce one of Bulgaria's greatest players, Georgi Asparoukhov, who scored 19 goals in 50 games before dying, with teammate Nikola Kotkov, in a 1971 car crash. This marked the end of an era and the start of a period of transition.

Bulgaria progressed beyond the group round of a World Cup for the first time in Mexico in 1986. They failed to do themselves justice, but went on to take the 1997 World Cup by storm.

Bulgaria qualified with a last-gasp 2–1 victory over France, then eliminated defending Cup-holders Germany 2–1 in the quarters on their way to finishing fourth.

Hristo Stoichkov, a Champions Cup-winning hero with Barcelona, emerged as one of the world's finest players, with fellow striker Emil Kostadinov and midfielders Yordan Lechkov and Krasimir Balakov not far behind.

But, four years on and four years older, the same players failed to make an impact in France and, having also lost in the first round of Euro '96, the Bulgarians face some major re-building work.

CROATIA

Croatian Football Federation
Founded: 1991
FIFA: 1992
Croatian foootball is on a high, having seen the team finish third in the 1998 World Cup finals - just seven years after independence.

Until 1991 Crotia didn't even exist as a country, and they weren't recognised by FIFA until a year later. But since then their impact on the world stage has been huge.

They reached the quarter-finals of Euro '96, beating Italy on the way, and then stormed to third place in France with a classy brand of football, which confirmed that players such as Zvonimir Boban, Davor Suker and Robert Prosinecki (all World Youth Cup-winners with Yugoslavia in 1987) are some of the most technically gifted in the game.

Suker, in particular, proved himself in France by scoring six goals to win the Golden Boot. He scored in every round, including the semi-final which Croatia lost 2–1 to France, and the third-place play-off in

PRIDE OF PLACE *Davor Suker, who won the Golden Boot at France '98 by scoring six goals in Croatia's march to third place*

which they beat Holland 2–1.

The only low point was Slaven Bilic's over-reaction to a shove by Laurent Blanc which led to the Frenchman being sent off and to Bilic being vilified by both fans and the media.

CYPRUS

Cyprus Football Association
Founded: 1934
FIFA: 1948
Cypriot football developed in the 1930s thanks to British colonial encouragement. Independent FIFA membership came in 1948 but Cyprus remain one of Europe's minnows. Their 2–0 win over the Faroe Islands in 1992 was their first in competition for nearly 20 years.

CZECH REPUBLIC

Cesko Moravsky Fotbalovy Svaz
Founded: 1993
FIFA: 1994
European Championship: 1976
Olympics: 1980 (as Czechoslovakia)
When the 1994 World Cup ended and Czechoslovakia ceased to exist as a football nation, the Czech Republic and Slovakia went their separate ways, each setting up a new association, league and national team. From the time Czechoslovakia came into existence in 1918, the Czechs were at the forefront of European football. They were runners-up in both the 1920 and 1964 Olympic Games, before finally winning the tournament in 1980, in Moscow. They were finalists at the 1934 World Cup with a side containing Antonin Puc, Frantisek Planicka, the finest pre-war goalkeeper, and Oldrich Nejedly. The Communist take-over after the war led to the usual reorganization of the domestic game, which hindered rather than helped as clubs like Sparta and Slavia Prague had been doing very well as professional sides. The army team Dukla

Prague rose to prominence and provided the basis of the 1960s Czech side which was among the best in the world. Josef Masopust, Czechoslovakia's most famous player, led the side to third place in the inaugural European Championship in 1960, and to the 1962 World Cup Final, which was lost to Brazil.

Czechoslovakia's biggest success came at the 1976 European Championship when, with stars such as goalkeeper Ivo Viktor, defender Anton Ondrus, Antonin Panenka, in midfield, and Zdenek Nehoda, in attack, they beat West Germany on penalties in the final.

The political split in 1994 affected Slovakia more than the Czech Republic, who qualified for Euro 96 and proved to be the most spirited of dark horses – beating Italy, Portugal and France and drawing with Russia *en route* to the final where they lost 2–1 to Germany by a "Golden Goal" scored in extra time.

DENMARK

Dansk Boldspil-Union
Founded: 1889
FIFA: 1904
European Championship: 1992
Olympics: 1906
Denmark was one of the first countries in continental Europe to take up football and has some of the oldest clubs in the world. But their rigid adherence to the principle of amateurism meant that Denmark was left behind when most of the rest of Europe adopted professionalism.

As a strong "amateur" nation, Denmark has perhaps inevitably enjoyed its greatest success at the Olympics. Winners in 1906 and runners-up in 1908 and 1912, the Danes were a force to be reckoned with at this level and produced some outstanding players – notably Nils Middelboe, who played with great distinction for Chelsea .

A period of decline occurred during the inter-war years, but qualification for the 1948 and 1960 Olympics sparked hopes of a revival. But the amateur nature of the domestic game, together with a rule which barred foreign-based players from the national side, stifled progress. The 1970s prompted great chances for Danish soccer, though, as a flood of players – led by 1977 European Footballer of The Year Allan Simonsen – left Denmark to join clubs in Western Europe. The rule barring "exported" players such as Michael Laudrup, Preben Elkjaer, Jesper Olsen, Morten Olsen and Soren Lerby from the national side was lifted in 1976 and undoubtedly helped the national side develop. These players formed the nucleus of the 1980s "Dinamite" side which

TREBLE TOP *Geoff Hurst scores his third goal in the 1966 World Cup Final*

reached the 1984 European Championship semi-finals and the 1986 World Cup second round.

In the late 1980s the league was restructured, and a new generation of players – including Michael Laudrup's brother, Brian – emerged to propel Denmark to the dizzying heights of European Champions in 1992. That unexpected success in Sweden was all the more remarkable as they were eleventh-hour replacements for the expelled Yugoslavs.

The Danes were also impressive in France '98, reaching the quarter-finals before going out to Brazil. But with both Laudrup brothers deciding to quit international football after the World Cup, they now need to find new heroes.

ENGLAND

The Football Association
Founded: 1863
FIFA: 1905–1920, 1924–1928, 1946
World Cup: 1966
Olympics: 1908, 1912 (as Great Britain)
England, as every schoolboy enthusiast knows, gave soccer to the world. Developed on the playing fields of England's great public schools in the middle of the nineteenth century, the game was first codified and organized in the 1860s, when the Football Association was formed – hence the name Association Football, and the nickname "soccer", to distinguish it from Rugby Football, or "rugger". The FA Cup was introduced in 1871, both the first and now the oldest surviving tournament in the world, and was fundamental in the development of the game – pitting the established amateur sides of the south against the burgeoning professional outfits of the north.

A year later, the very first international match was played, between England and Scotland in Glasgow, and in 1888 the Football League was formed – to organize what was, by now, a largely professional game based mostly in the industrial north.

As the century closed, the British Championship, played between England, Scotland, Wales and Ireland, was the zenith of world football. Before the First World War, England and Scotland were well above the rest of the world and, as Great Britain, won Olympic gold in 1908 and 1912.

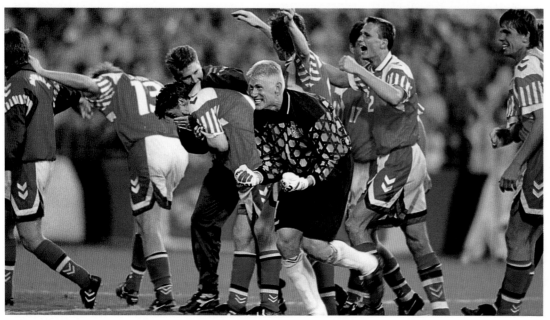

DANISH DYNAMITE *Denmark's players celebrate their shock European Championship win in 1992*

The inter-war period was a period of increasing isolation, though, as the rest of the world warmed to the game. The FA, which joined FIFA in 1905, always took a disdainful attitude to it and withdrew in 1920 and 1928.

Even an ignominious 1–0 defeat by the United States in the 1950 World Cup (which was dismissed as a fluke) didn't change England's superiority complex. However in 1953, Hungary's "Magic Magyars" came to Wembley, and destroyed English arrogance forever with a 6-3 victory.

And further defeats at the 1954, 1958 and 1962 World Cup finals confirmed the rest of the world had caught up.

The challenges presented by the new order were spectacularly answered in 1966, however, when England's "wingless wonders" won the World Cup on home soil. Alf Ramsey moulded his side around the outstanding talents of goalkeeper Gordon Banks, captain Bobby Moore, and the Charlton brothers Bobby and Jack. He created a system which worked with the players at his disposal, and instilled a team spirit and an understanding which has proved difficult to match.

The 1966 success was the springboard from which English club sides launched an unprecedented assault on the three European competitions, winning trophy after trophy between 1964 and 1985. Conversely, as the clubs prospered the national side suffered. A defeat by West Germany in the quarter-final of the 1970 World Cup in Mexico marked the beginning of the end of the Ramsey era, and failure to qualify for the 1974 and 1978 finals confirmed England's slump.

Following dismal performances at the 1988 and 1992 European Championship finals and, worse, the failure to qualify for the 1994 World Cup finals, the structure of the English game came under scrutiny. Changes forced by the appalling loss of life at Bradford (1985) and Hillsborough (1989) led to a modernization of stadia, assisted by the influx of cash from a lucrative Sky TV contract - and a boom in attendances.

The popularity of football in England is now at an all-time high, and the national team's performances

have also improved, although they still appeared to be dogged by bad luck.

They went out of the 1986 World Cup finals in Mexico after Diego Maradona's infamous 'Hand of God' goal, and lost to Germany on penalties in the semi-final of Italia '90 and in the last four of Euro '96 - which was held in England and created football fever throughout the country.

The same bad luck struck again at France '98, when England (now managed by Glenn Hoddle) reached the second round but lost on penalties to old foes Argentina.

Not only that, but England had to survive almost the entire second half and the whole of extra-time with only 10 men after David Beckham was sent off for petulant retaliation. However, a glorious individual goal from Liverpool teenager Michael Owen offered hope for the future – as did the subsequent managerial accession of Kevin Keegan.

ALF RAMSEY

England manager 1963–74; born January 22, 1920; died April 30, 1999

Ramsey earned a knighthood for managing England to World Cup victory over West Germany at Wembley in 1966, the peak of a double international career as both player and administrator. As a player, Ramsey was a creative and intelligent right-back with Southampton and Tottenham and an integral member of Spurs' push-and-run team which won the Second and First Division titles in successive seasons in 1950 and 1951. On retiring in 1955, Ramsey became manager of Ipswich and his success in taking the East Anglian club from the Third Division to the First Division title in just seven years earned his appointment in 1963 as England's first "proper" manager with sole responsibility for team selection. He was dismissed after the World Cup qualifying failure against Poland a decade later.

ESTONIA

Estonian Football Federation
Founded: 1921
FIFA: 1923

Estonia, like Baltic neighbours Lithuania and Latvia, ceased to exist after 1940 when the Soviet Union took over. However, Estonia never withdrew from FIFA, their membership was merely put on ice, and in 1992 they came back into the fold. The hand-to-mouth survival of the game was illustrated in 1996 when Estonia became embroiled in controversy over the suitability of hired floodlights for a World Cup-tie against Scotland. The Scots turned up for the FIFA-adjusted kick-off in Tallinn, but the Estonians stayed away. The match was initially awarded to Scotland by default but then FIFA had second thoughts, and ordered a replay on neutral territory – in Monaco – which finished 0–0.

FAROE ISLANDS

Fotboltssamband Foroya
Founded: 1979
FIFA: 1988

Football has been played on these tiny islands since before the Second World War, with a league starting in 1942 and a cup competition in 1967. But owing to the Faroes' remoteness and lack of grass pitches, competitive matches against overseas opponents were few and far between.

The Faroes' entry into the 1992 European Championship, however, was spectacular. A 1–0 win over Austria in their first competitive match made headlines across Europe and stimulated development of the domestic game. Funds were found for a grass pitch in Toftir, so that matches could be played at home, and now the clubs, too, enter European competitions.

FINLAND

Suomen Palloliito Finlands Bollofoerbund
Founded: 1907
FIFA: 1908

Football in the land of lakes and long winters lags well behind ice hockey, athletics, winter sports and motor

rallying in terms of popularity, and that situation seems unlikely to change. Prior to the 1970s, national team outings were confined to other Nordic countries, and even though, since then, Finland have regularly entered the World Cup and European Championship, success has been scarce. However, the Finns did almost qualify for the 1980 European Championship finals and from time to time have given one of their rivals a severe fright.

FRANCE

Fédération Française de Football
Founded: 1918
FIFA: 1904
World Cup: 1998
European Championship: 1984
Olympics: 1984

As England gave the game to the world, so the French organized it into a structured sport – and now, finally, they have their reward after becoming world champions.

Their incredible 3–0 victory over Brazil in the 1998 World Cup final, on

ALLEZ FRANCE *The 1986 World Cup side*

home soil, has been long-awaited.

The French were prime movers behind the creation of FIFA, UEFA, the World Cup, the European Championship and the European club cups. Yet until that Brazil clash, the 1984 European Championship and an Olympic title were all they had to show for their skills in innovation and organization.

In fact, the first three World Cups were disasters for the French, and it was not until the 1950s, when Stade de Reims twice reached the European Cup Finals, losing to Real Madrid, that things improved.

The impressive Stade de Reims side contained Raymond Kopa and Just Fontaine – two truly great players and both key members of the national side which finished third in the 1958 World Cup (Fontaine's 13 goals in those finals remain a record).

International club success proved elusive until May 1993, when Marseille beat Milan 1–0 to win the Champions Cup. France went wild. But only briefly. Within a month Marseille had been engulfed by a match-fixing scandal which prevented them defending the Cup, prompted their relegation and brought suspensions and legal action against the players and officials involved, including president Bernard Tapie.

On the international front, Michel Platini arrived in the 1970s and transformed France into the most attractive side Europe had seen.

Platini, a midfielder with immense skill, vision and grace, inspired France to reach the final stages of three World Cups (1978, 1982 and 1986), reaching the semi-finals in Spain in 1982 before losing to West Germany on penalties.

Platini's two finest hours have come on French soil. Firstly in 1984 when his nine goals in five games earned France the European Championship and him the title as the world's most accomplished player. And secondly, not as player or manager, but as organiser of France '98.

He worked tirelessly to make the event a success, and he was rewarded when Aime Jacquet's French side took the tournament by storm, winning all their group games and then beating Paraguay, Italy and Croatia on the way to the final.

The greatest day in French football then saw Les Bleus crush Brazil 3–0 with two goals from man-of-the-tournament Zinedine Zidane and one from Emmanuel Petit. The celebrations in Paris afterwards were described as the most emotional since the French revolution.

GEORGIA

Football Federation of Georgia
Founded: 1992
FIFA: 1992

Georgia seceded, in football terms, from the old Soviet Union, in the late 1980s. Their latent strength was quickly underlined when Georgia

GERMAN BITE *The German national team had much to do in the late 1990s*

thrashed Wales 5–0 in a Euro 96 qualifier. Their inspiration was darting schemer Georgi Kinkladze.

GERMANY

Deutscher Fussball-Bund
Founded: 1900
FIFA: 1904–1946, 1950
World Cup: 1954, 1974, 1990
European Championship: 1972, 1980, 1996
Olympics: 1976 (East Germany)

Since the Second World War, Germany have enjoyed a record of success unparalleled in the history of the game. Yet Germany's pre-war record was quite poor, with third place at the 1934 World Cup the peak of their achievement. The war brought division and in 1948 East Germany, under the Soviets, formed its own association, league and national side. The East Germans, though, with their state-sponsored emphasis on individual rather than team sports, never matched the suc-

cess of their countrymen on the other side of the Berlin Wall. In fact, half a century of East German football only produced two successes of note: Olympic gold in Montreal in 1976 and a 1–0 victory over West Germany, in the only match ever played between the two, at the 1974 World Cup finals.

But while the East floundered, the West flourished. Banished from FIFA in 1946, they were readmitted in 1950 as West Germany . . . and won the World Cup just over four years later. That victory, engineered by coach Sepp Herberger, was all the more amazing because their Final opponents were the "Magic Magyars", whose 3–2 defeat was their second loss in five years!

From then on the Germans grew in stature. In the World Cup, they were semi-finalists in 1958, quarter-finalists in 1962 and runners-up in 1966.

And the 1970s seemed to belong to Bayern Munich and West Germany. Bayern, won a hat-trick of European Cups in 1974, 1975 and 1976, and provided the nucleus of the national side which won the European Championship in 1972, the World Cup in 1974, and after finishing second in 1976, the European Championship again in 1980.

Franz Beckenbauer single-handedly revolutionized the sweeper's role into one of attack as well as defence, and Gerd Müller was the closest thing to a scoring machine yet seen. In 62 internationals, he scored an incredible 68 goals.

The 1970s sides were replaced by new stars of the world game: Karl-Heinz Rummenigge, Lothar Matthäus, Rudi Völler, Jürgen Klinsmann, Thomas Hässler and Matthias Sammer. Following the World Cup success and German reunification in 1990, they capitalized on their new-found resources by securing victory in Euro '96 with a 2–1 defeat of the Czech Republic.

But there is now some re-building work to do after the team crashed out of the 1998 World Cup finals in France following a 3–0 quarter-final defeat against Croatia – a reverse which left the German public in shock. And with captain Jürgen Klinsmann officially retiring from international football, the Germans will be looking to a new breed to come forward and take his place.

Great Coaches

JOSEF "SEPP" HERBERGER

Germany manager 1936–63; born March 28, 1897; died April 28, 1977
Herberger was the founder of a German management dynasty. An inside-forward who played three times for Germany between 1921 and 1925, he became assistant national manager to Dr Otto Nerz in 1932 and then succeeded him after the disastrous defeat by Norway at the 1936 Berlin Olympics. Herberger travelled widely to keep abreast of the world game and astutely managed his players and tactics to maximum effect, above all at the 1954 World Cup. There he took the bold step of fielding his reserves for a first-round match against Hungary. He was unfazed by the 8–3 defeat, knowing that his fresh "first team" could still reach the later stages and go on, as they did, to beat Hungary 3–2 in the Final.

HELMUT SCHÖN

West Germany manager 1963–78; born September 15, 1915; died February 23, 1996
Schön scored 17 goals in 16 internationals for Germany between 1937 and 1941 when he was a star inside-forward with the famous Dresden SC. After the war he played on in Berlin for a while and then became national coach to the briefly independent federation of the Saar. In 1955 Schön was appointed No. 2 to Sepp Herberger as manager of West Germany and succeeded him, with enormous success, in 1963. Schön took West Germany to World Cup runners-up spot in 1966, third place in 1970 and finally to victory in 1974. Under Schön, Germany were also European Champions in 1972 and runners-up in 1976.

GREECE

Fédération Hellénique de Football
Founded: 1926
FIFA: 1927
Greek football's development in the first half of the twentieth century was severely hampered by civil war and the unstable political climate in the Balkans. These factors, linked to the "Olympian" adherence to the amateur spirit of the game, meant that a national league was formed only in 1960, and full professionalism arrived as late as 1979. Consequently, success for Greek sides at national and club level has been rare.

The clubs, centred on Athens and Salonica, have spent vast amounts on players, but have so far failed to win a single European trophy. Panathinaikos went closest to breaking that duck when they reached the 1971 European Cup Final, where they lost to Ajax. Similarly, the national side has consistently failed to make an impression. Qualification for the 1980 European Championship was the first time the Greeks had qualified for any finals tournament, and it was to be another 13 years before they tasted success again. Coach Alketas Panagoulias – the man behind the 1980 success – returned to guide Greece through to the 1994 World Cup finals for the first time in their history.

In the United States, Greece paid a heavy price for attacking weakness and lost all three games. Unfortunately, the league's leading marksman was a Pole, Krzyzstof Warzycha. His impressive opportunism led Panathinaikos to the semi-finals of the 1996 UEFA Champions League and a famous, though

HERO RETURNS *Greece's Panagoulias*

TAKE OFF *Holland's Rep beats Argentina's Passarella and Gallego in 1978*

ultimately vain, first-leg victory away to Ajax Amsterdam.

HOLLAND

Koninklijke Nederland Voetbalbond (KNVB)
Founded: 1889
FIFA: 1904
European Championship: 1988
The Dutch were early devotees of football, partly owing to the country's close proximity to Britain, and were among the continent's leading amateur sides in the early 1900s. Indeed they reached the semi-finals of four consecutive Olympic Games from 1908 to 1924... but lost them all. Third place in 1908 and 1912 was their best. The 1920s marked a move away from amateurism in other countries, and Dutch football entered a decline which lasted until the 1960s. Up until that decade, internationals were mostly played against European neighbours, especially Belgium, and first-round defeats in the 1934 and 1938 World Cups did little to encourage them to venture further afield.

The low point came just after the Second World War, when a dismal sequence of results, with just one victory in over five years, prompted

modernization of the domestic game. So, in 1957, a national league was created and professionalism was introduced in an attempt to staunch the flow of Dutch players going abroad. The main beneficiaries of the reorganization were Ajax of Amsterdam, Feyenoord of Rotterdam and PSV Eindhoven – the "big three" who have dominated Dutch football ever since. The big breakthrough came in 1970, when Feyenoord won the European Cup. It was the beginning of a golden era for Dutch football, in which Ajax won a hat-trick of European Cups (1971, 1972, 1973), Feyenoord and PSV both won the UEFA Cup, and Holland reached two consecutive World Cup Finals.

The generation of Dutch players which emerged in the 1970s was among the finest the modern game has seen. Ajax led the way, providing the backbone of the national side, with hugely talented players such as Johan Neeskens, Arie Haan, Ruud Krol, Wim Suurbier and, of course, Johan Cruyff, arguably the best player of his day. Along with the Feyenoord duo of Wim Van Hanegem and Wim Jansen, they formed the nucleus of a side which was unfortunate to lose the 1974 and 1978 World Cup Finals

to the host nations, West Germany and Argentina respectively. Coach Rinus Michels was the architect of the success with his "total football" system, which involved moulding highly skilled players into a team unit, with the emphasis on interchangeability and with every player totally comfortable in possession.

As the "total football" side broke up, the Dutch slipped into a malaise, failing to qualify for the 1982 and 1986 World Cup finals. But a revival was soon to follow, spearheaded by a new generation of players at Ajax and PSV.

PSV won the European Cup in 1986, while Ajax won the European Cup-winners' Cup in 1987 , the UEFA Cup in 1992 (making them only the third side to complete a treble of all three European trophies) and the Champions Cup again in 1995 - remaining unbeaten in all 11 games.

To add to that, Ruud Gullit, Frank Rijkaard, Marco Van Basten and Ronald Koeman, once again under Rinus Michels' guidance, triumphed in the 1988 European Championship.

That remains Holland's only international triumph. But recent performances suggest that further glory may not be far away – and the Dutch were back to their best at France '98, where they finished fourth.

Many described them as the most technically gifted team of the tournament, and there is no question they were unlucky to lose their semi-final to Brazil – only going out on penalties after a 1–1 draw .

Earlier, a glorious goal from Dennis Bergkamp beat Argentina in the quarter-finals, while Frank and Ronald De Boer, Edgar Davids, Patrick Kluivert and Marc Overmars proved they are world-class players.

HUNGARY

Magyar Labdarugo Szovetseg
Founded: 1901
FIFA: 1906
Olympics: 1952, 1964, 1968
Just as Austria will always be renowned for the "Wunderteam" of the 1930s, so Hungary will be for the "Magic Magyars" side of the 1950s. This side was the finest the world had ever seen and had lost only one

MAGIC MAGYARS *Hidegkuti scores Hungary's sixth goal at Wembley in 1953*

international in five years before, heartbreakingly, they failed in the 1954 World Cup Final. The forward line of Zoltan Czibor, Jozsef Toth, Nandor Hidegkuti, Sandor Kocsis and Ferenc Puskas – the greatest player of his era and still regarded as one of the best ever – terrorized opposition defences and scored 173 goals in this spell. In 1953, they became the first non-British side to beat England at home, winning 6–3.

Yet this was not the first outstanding side Hungary had produced. Hungarian clubs, notably MTK Budapest, who won 10 consecutive titles (1914–25), dominated European football in the inter-war period, winning five Mitropa Cups in the 1930s. The national side reached the World Cup Final in 1938, where they were beaten by the Italians. The 1930s side contained such fine players as Gyorgy Sarosi and Gyula Zsengeller.

The Hungarian uprising of 1958 broke up the "Magic Magyars" side, but by the 1960s another had emerged. The new stars were Florian Albert and Ferenc Bene, who led Hungary to the 1962 and 1966 World Cup quarter-finals and Olympic gold in 1964 and 1968. The 1970s marked the beginning of an insipid decline for the national side, despite some notable successes for the clubs, particularly Ujpest who won nine titles in eleven years. Failure to qualify for the 1970, 1974, 1990 and 1994 World Cup finals was matched by poor performances at the 1978, 1982, and 1986 tournaments, especially in Mexico in 1986 when they lost 6–0 to the Soviet Union.

The lowest point came, however, in a World Cup qualifier in June 1992 when Hungary lost 2–1 to Iceland … in Budapest!

ICELAND

Knattspyrnusamband Island
Founded: 1947
FIFA: 1929
Iceland, although definitely one of Europe's "minnow" nations, are often capable of upsetting Europe's bigger fish. In the 1994 World Cup qual-

ifiers they beat Hungary home and away and finished five points above them in the group! They played their first international in 1946, against Denmark, and have only entered the World Cup and European Championship regularly since the 1970s.

Iceland has produced several outstanding players in recent years, notably Asgeir Sirgurvinsson and Petur Petursson. In the spring of 1996 they also made history when a father and son, Arnor and Eidur-Smari Gudjohnsen, both played in a friendly against Estonia.

ISRAEL

Hitachdut Lekaduregel Beisrael
Founded: 1928
FIFA: 1929
Asian Championship: 1964
Although the state of Israel was not founded until 1948, a football association was formed, in the former Palestine, some 20 years earlier. Palestine played only a handful of international matches before the national side was revived, in 1949, as Israel.

At first only World Cup matches or friendlies were played, as Israel found itself surrounded by hostile Arab nations. All of them being members of the Asian Federation, this situation was to lead to problems as the Arab states refused to play the Israelis. In the 1958 World Cup, for instance, Israel's opponents all withdrew, forcing FIFA to order them to play-off against Wales for a finals place. Similar withdrawals disrupted the Asian Championships, which Israel hosted and won in 1964 – their only honour.

In 1976, Israel were thrown out of the Asian Confederation because it was felt their presence was disrupting the development of the game. They led a nomadic existence, as associate members of Oceania, until they were formally accepted into UEFA in 1991.

The national side and clubs now take part in European competitions, and to the benefit of the Israeli game. In 1993, Maccabi Haifa knocked Moscow Torpedo out of the European Cup-winners' Cup, and in a World Cup qualifier in Paris the national side pulled off a remarkable 3–2 win against France.

ITALY

Federazione Italiana Giuoco Calcio
Founded: 1898
FIFA: 1903
World Cup: 1934, 1938, 1982
European Championship: 1968
Olympics: 1936
The first 30 years of Italian football were chaotic and complicated, with various regional leagues and the industrial cities of the north – Milan and Turin – competing for power. But the Association finally settled in Rome, in 1929, and a national league was formed in 1930, providing the boost the game needed and leading Italy to unmatched success in the 1930s.

Under legendary coach Vittorio Pozzo, Italy lost only seven games during the decade, winning the World Cup in 1934 and 1938 and the 1936 Olympic title in between to confirm their superiority. The 1930s also saw the beginnings of a trend for Italian clubs to import foreign players to

AVANTI AZZURRI *Italy's hero Rossi (left) in the 1982 World Cup Final*

gain an advantage in the league. The best-known stars of this era were Luisito Monti and Giuseppe Meazza.

After the war Torino were the dominant side, winning four consecutive titles, and providing virtually all of the national team. But, returning from Lisbon, their plane crashed into the Superga Hill outside Turin killing all on board, including ten internationals. Hardly surprisingly, this led to a decline for both Torino and Italy during the 1950s.

Many blamed the failure on the lnumber of foreign imports in the Italian game, – led by Milan with their Swedish trio of Gunnar Gren, Gunnar Nordahl and Nils Liedholm. Consequently, the importation of foreigners was banned in 1964. This hampered the clubs, who were making headway in Europe, but allowed a new generation of Italian players to develop, and they won the 1968 European Championship.

The 1970s, though, witnessed the rise of *catenaccio*, defensive, sterile football, reflecting the attitude that not losing was more important than winning.

For the clubs it was a lean time in Europe, but the national side did better, reaching the 1970 World Cup Final. The import ban was lifted in the early 1980s, and it was to be a decade of great successes for the clubs, who made full use of their foreign quota. Juventus, with French midfield genius Michel Platini, dominated the first half of the decade, while the national side, skippered by 40-year-old Dino Zoff, swept to victory at the 1982 World Cup in Spain. Then Milan – with a Dutch axis of Gullit-Rijkaard-Van Basten – dominated the second half, when Napoli, Internazionale and Sampdoria also tasted European success.

Now Italy has the best league in the world, with the biggest stars, huge attendances and regular success in Europe. Arrigo Sacchi's attacking Milan side of the late 1980s and early 1990s has smashed *catenaccio*.

The national side failed both to win the 1990 World Cup, in Italy, and to qualify for the 1992 European Championship. But a rebuilding programme halted the slide and, with Roberto Baggio leading the way,

Italy reached the 1994 World Cup Final, where they lost on penalties to Brazil.

However, disappointments at Euro '96 (where they went out in the first round) and France '98 (where they lost to the hosts on penalties in the quarter-finals) mean the Italian public are not happy.

Italy only qualified for France after a play-off against Russia, and star man Alessandro Del Piero, not always picked, failed to make an impact. The post mortem will go on for some time.

LATVIA

Football Association of Latvia
Founded: 1921
FIFA: 1923

Latvia were the strongest of the Baltic sides before the Second World War, but still represented easy pickings for European opponents, as when France hammered them 7–0 at the 1924 Olympics. Despite this, Latvia only failed narrowly to qualify for the 1938 World Cup finals.

Occupied, and wiped off the political map of Europe by the Soviet Union in 1940, Latvia continued playing full internationals until 1949. Their return to competitive competition came on August 12, 1993, when they lost a World Cup qualifier to Lithuania. That was followed by a 0–0 draw with Denmark, and further draws in games with Spain and Lithuania and in both games against Albania. Latvia are proving to be awkward opponents.

LIECHTENSTEIN

Liechtensteiner Fussball-Verband
Founded: 1933
FIFA: 1974

With a population of just 27,000, it is remarkable that Liechtenstein has a national side at all. An association was formed in 1933, and they joined FIFA and UEFA in 1974, but few matches have been played. Liechtenstein made unsuccessful attempts to qualify for the 1988 and 1992 Olympic Games, before entering the competitive mainstream in the 1996 European Championship qualifying round. Liechtenstein's few teams compete in regional Swiss leagues.

LITHUANIA

Lithuanian Football Association
Founded: 1921
FIFA: 1923

Lithuania were FIFA members between 1923 and 1940, at a time when the Baltic nations were among the weakest in Europe. Their first international was in June 1923, when they lost 5–0 at home to Estonia, and they made an unsuccessful bid to qualify for the 1924 Olympic tournament. The Soviets took over in 1940, but Lithuania continued playing until 1949, by which time they were the strongest of the Baltic states. Lithuania played their first World Cup match since 1937 in April, 1992, a 2–2 draw with Northern Ireland in Belfast. Lithuania now has its own national league, and a pattern has yet to emerge, but while under the Soviets, Zalgiris Vilnius made the biggest impact, reaching the Supreme Division in 1982. Lithuania's most successful players are Arminas Narbekovas and Valdas Ivanauskas, who have played with some success in both Austria and Germany.

LUXEMBOURG

Fédération Luxembourgeoise de Football
Founded: 1908
FIFA: 1910

Luxembourg have yet to finish better than bottom in any of their 14 World Cup qualifying groups! It is a similar story in the European Championship, except in 1964, when they were shock quarter-finalists, and 1996 when Malta were eight points below them. Luxembourg's clubs have been equally unsuccessful in Europe. Jeunesse Esch are the only Luxembourg side to have reached the second round of the European Cup, in 1964. A few players have made the grade in France and Belgium, notably Guy Hellers, who was a regular for Standard Liège.

MACEDONIA
(FORMER YUGOSLAV REPUBLIC OF)

Football Association of the Former Yugoslav Republic of Macedonia
Founded: 1908
FIFA: 1994

MALTA

Malta Football Association

Founded: 1900

FIFA: 1959

Malta, as a British colony, took up football early. The Malta FA was affiliated to the Football Association in London until 1959, when they decided to go their own way and join FIFA. They entered the 1960 Olympic qualifiers, in the African section, but made no headway. Indeed, Malta have never qualified for the World Cup or the European Championship finals. Maltese clubs have been regulars in European competitions since the 1960s, but consistently heavy losers. Curiously, the league has no home and away games. Since the opening of the Ta'Qali national stadium in 1980, all Premier League matches have been played there.

MOLDOVA

Moldavian Football Federation

Founded: 1993

FIFA: 1994

Moldova marked their competitive "arrival", after the collapse of the Soviet Union, by defeating Wales 3–2 in a Euro 96 qualifying tie in the capital, Chisinau (formerly Kissinev).

NORTHERN IRELAND

Irish Football Association

Founded: 1880

FIFA: 1911–20, 1924–28, 1946

Northern Ireland have the fourth oldest association and the third oldest league in the world, and have been playing internationals for 111 years. But it was not until 1951, when France visited Belfast, that non-British sides were engaged. They qualified for the 1958 World Cup finals, led by Tottenham's Danny Blanchflower, and fared better than England and Scotland, reaching the quarter-finals. In the 1960s and 1970s, despite having George Best in the side, the Irish were at a low ebb, but they revived in the 1980s. Managed by Billy Bingham, a player in 1958, Ireland reached the second round of the 1982 World Cup, and qualified again in 1986.

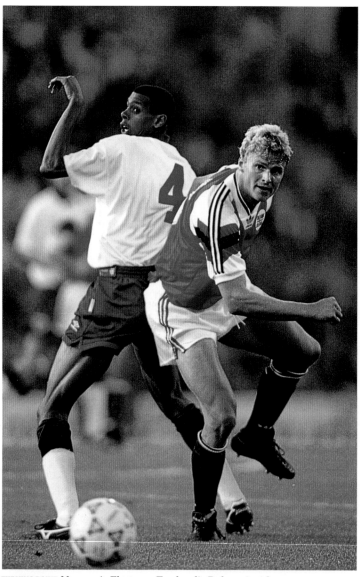

TURNING POINT *Norway's Flo turns England's Palmer inside out*

Those two sides contained Pat Jennings, one of the greatest goalkeepers of all time and a fine ambassador for a country riven by conflict for 25 years.

NORWAY

Norges Fotballforbun

Founded: 1902

FIFA: 1908

Norway, traditionally a European football minnow, upset the form book in the 1994 World Cup qualifiers, easily winning their group ahead of Holland, England and Poland - and they have continued to progress ever since.

They also made the 1998 finals in France – and beat Brazil 2–1 in a group-stage match before losing to Italy in the second round.

It was the second time the Norwegians had beaten the mighty Brazil, having also won 3–1 in a friendly in Olso.

It has been an incredible rise up the national rankings for the Scandinavian side, thanks largely to the fact that so many of their players are now based abroad. Most of them are in England (such as Chelsea's Tore Andre Flo, Manchester United's Ole Gunnar Solskjaer and Henning Berg and Liverpool's Oyvind Leonhardsen) – and the Norwegians could field an entire English Premiership XI if they wanted to.

The nation's only previous heydays came in the 1930s. Having won the 1929–32 Scandinavian Championship, they finished third at the 1936 Berlin Olympics.

POLAND

Polski Zwlazek Pilki Noznej

Founded: 1919

FIFA: 1923

Olympics: 1972

Poland's history has been turbulent to say the least, with numerous boundary changes, and between 1874 and 1918 – when continental football was just developing – it did not even exist! The Polish state was created in 1921, and Poland made their debut in 1921 against Hungary. Despite reaching the 1938 World Cup finals, the pre-war record was poor, but the post-war Communist take-over brought great change. Clubs became attached to government bodies and new ones were formed – notably Gornik Zabrze, who reached the European Cup-Winners' Cup Final in 1969.

In the 1970s Poland embarked on a 15-year reign of achievement which started in 1972 with the gold medal at the Munich Olympics. This side contained Wlodzimierz Lubanski, their top scorer, Kazimierz Deyna, capped 102 times, and Robert Gadocha. For the 1974 World Cup finals, this trio was joined by Gregorz Lato, Poland's most capped player (104 times), with Jan Tomaszewski in goal. Poland finished third and this team stayed together for most of the decade, reaching the World Cup finals again in 1978.

There was more success at the 1982 finals when, with Zbigniew Boniek outstanding, Poland reached the semi-finals. They also reached the second round in 1986, but since then, the collapse of Communism has led to the withdrawal of state subsidies, forcing clubs to sell star players.

Legia did manage to reach the quarter-finals of the 1996 UEFA Champions League but Poland disappointed in the World Cup qualifiers and failed to reach France '98.

PORTUGAL

Federacao Portuguesa De Futbol

Founded: 1914

FIFA: 1926

The Portuguese Football Association was founded in 1914 as the result of a merger between the associations of Lisbon and Oporto – the two cities

IN FLIGHT *Portugal's Augusto*

which have utterly dominated domestic football. The Lisbon duo of Benfica and Sporting Lisbon, along with their rivals FC Porto from Oporto, are among the most famous names in world club football. The League Championship, set up in 1935, has only ever been won by these three, except in 1948 when Belenenses broke the monopoly.

Portugal's greatest era was in the 1960s, when Benfica won the European Cup twice (1961 and 1962) and reached a further three finals. The bulk of this Benfica side formed the nucleus of the national team which was then at its peak. The most famous of them was Eusebio, a strong, Mozambique-born striker who was arguably the best player of the 1966 World Cup. Fellow Mozambican Mario Coluna and Angola-born José Aguas were other "adopted" players who augmented an impressive side which also included the Benfica quartet Costa Pereira, in goal, Germano, in defence, and Cavem and José Augusto raiding down the wings.

In those 1966 finals Eusebio scored nine goals, including four in a remarkable 5–3 quarter-final victory over North Korea – Portugal were three down after 22 minutes – as the Portuguese finished third. The national side has never again scaled such heights.

Portuguese clubs, though, staged a revival in the 1980s. Benfica reached the UEFA Cup Final in 1983, and in 1987 FC Porto became the third club side to win in Europe – Sporting had won the Cup-winners' Cup in 1964 – when they won the European Cup. Benfica also lost in European Cup finals in 1988 and 1990, while Portugal's youngsters won the World Youth Cup in 1989 and 1991 and provided the nucleus of the side who reached the European Championship quarter-finals in 1996.

REPUBLIC OF IRELAND

The Football Association of Ireland
Founded: 1921
FIFA: 1923

Since their first international in 1924, an Olympic qualifier against Bulgaria, the Republic of Ireland have always been on the verge of great things. With virtually all the top players earning their living in England and Scotland, the domestic league has always been weak, while the national side often had gifted individuals, but never a team strong enough to qualify for the big tournaments.

All that changed in 1986 when Jack Charlton, a World Cup winner with England in 1966, was appointed manager. He utilized the Republic's physical strength, determination and skills perfected in the English League, to give the side belief in itself. In 1988 they qualified for the European Championship finals, but unfortunately Liam Brady, perhaps the greatest Republic player in history, missed the tournament and thus never displayed his exquisite passes on the big stage.

Having made the initial breakthrough, the Republic made progress and qualified for the 1990 World Cup finals in Italy. No matter that Italy beat them in the quarter-finals, the Republic had arrived.

They narrowly missed out on a place in the 1992 European Championship finals in Sweden, but succeeded, where England, Scotland, Wales and Northern Ireland all failed, in appearing at the 1994 World Cup Finals. Failure to reach Euro 96 – Ireland lost 2–0 to Holland in a play-off in Liverpool – led to the departure of Charlton. Mick McCarthy was appointed to undertake the challenge of redeveloping the house that Jack built.

ROMANIA

Federatia Romana de Fotbal
Founded: 1908
FIFA: 1930

Romania embraced football before most of her Balkan neighbours, mainly owing to the influence of the country's sovereign, King Carol, who was a soccer fanatic. He instigated the formation of a federation in 1908 and, having returned to power in 1930 after an abdication, he was determined that Romania should enter the first World Cup.

Romania duly made the long trip to Uruguay, but were beaten by the hosts in the first round. They also entered the 1934 and 1938 tournaments, but could not progress beyond the first round, despite the presence of Iuliu Bodola, their top scorer to this day.

The Communists took over in 1944 and, as usual, reorganized the domestic game. Two of the clubs created in Bucharest, Steaua, the army team, and Dinamo, the police team, have dominated Romanian soccer ever since - and in 1986 Steaua became the first team from behind the Iron Curtain to win the European Cup.

On the international front, the Romania enjoyed a brief upsurge with qualification for the 1970 World Cup finals, and a quarter-final finish in the 1977 European Championship. But, despite Anghel Iordanescu, one of the greats of Romanian football, it was not until 1984 that they qualified for the finals of a major tournament again, the European Championship in France.

Since then, however, they have been to three World Cups in a row and qualified for the Euro '96 finals, too.

The only disappointment has been that despite the midfield inspiration of Gheorghe Hagi, they haven't had the best of luck.

In 1990 and 1994 Romania were eliminated after a penalty shoot-out, losing to the Republic of Ireland in the second round in Italy then to Sweden in the quarter-finals in the USA.

In 1998, in France, they finished top of their group (above England) in the first round, and showed their togetherness when every single member of the team dyed his hair yellow to celebrate! But the party didn't last, because the team lost 1–0 to Croatia in the second round.

SHOOT-OUT SHUT-OUT *Ireland's Pat Bonner saves the decisive penalty against Romania in the 1990 World Cup*

RUSSIA

Russian Football Federation

Founded: 1922 (as Soviet Union)
FIFA: 1922 (as Soviet Union)
European Championship: 1960 (as Soviet Union)
Olympics: 1956, 1988 (as Soviet Union)

Russia's footballing history is inextricably entwined with that of the former Soviet Union, and it is under the banner of the latter that her greatest achievements have occurred. By the early years of the twentieth century, leagues had been formed in most of the cities of the Russian empire, notably in what was then the capital, St Petersburg.

In 1912, an all-Russian football union was created and a championship was introduced. In the same year "Tsarist Russia" entered the Stockholm Olympics but were beaten in the first round, by Finland, and by Germany in the consolation tournament that followed – by 16 goals to nil! The First World War ended Russia's brief international career and, after the Revolution, Russia took on the guise of the Soviet Union.

The Communists reorganized football from top to bottom, with the emphasis on teamwork rather than individual flair. Moscow, now the Soviet capital, became the main football centre with five great workers' clubs: Dynamo (electrical trades), Spartak (producers' co-operatives), Torpedo (car manufacturers), Lokomitive (railways) and CSKA (the army). The development of these clubs, and many more throughout the Union, promoted the formation of a pan-Union league in 1936, which Moscow dominated until the 1960s.

In the 1950s the national side, which had previously played few matches, began to venture out. They won a poorly-attended 1956 Olympic Games and reached the quarter-finals of the 1958 World Cup at their first attempt. This side contained some of Soviet football's greatest names, including Igor Netto, Valentin Ivanov, Nikita Simonyan and the great goalkeeper Lev Yashin.

In 1960 they entered and won the very first European Championship, beating Yugoslavia 2–1 in the final in Paris. This, however, remains the only major triumph that either the Soviet Union or Russia has ever had.

In the 1960s, the Soviets promised much, but delivered little. They

NEW BREED
Winger Andre Kanchelskis in action for the CIS in Sweden, 1992

lost in the final of the European Championship in 1964 and 1972, and reached the semi-finals in 1968.

In the World Cup, they reached the quarter-finals in 1962 and went a stage further in 1966 in England. This gave rise, justifiably, to the notion that the Soviet

"method" would always produce good sides, but never great ones.

In the 1970s Oleg Blokhin emerged as the Soviet Union's greatest-ever player at a time when the national side was in decline, failing to qualify for the 1974 and 1978 World Cup tournaments. An upturn occurred with qualification for the 1982 and 1986 finals, but on neither occasion could they progress beyond the second round. In 1988 they reached the European Championship Final.

The Soviet sides of 1986 and 1988 were arguably the best since the 1960s, but were composed of mainly Kiev Dynamo players. Indeed, it is a curious fact that, despite Moscow's, and therefore Russia's, dominance of Soviet football, the only Soviet sides to win European club competitions were not Russian. Kiev, in the Ukraine, won the European Cup-winners' Cup in 1975 and 1986, and Tbilisi Dynamo, from Georgia, won the same tournament in 1981.

In September 1991, the Soviet Union began to disintegrate. The three Baltic states achieved independence and went their own way, quickly followed by the other 12 republics. The Soviets had qualified for the 1992 European Championship finals and took part under a "flag of convenience" name, the Commonwealth of Independent States. Soon afterwards the Soviet Union was swept away completely and the 15 former republics began organizing themselves into new and separate footballing nations. This poses great problems for FIFA, and more so for UEFA, who have, somehow, to incorporate these new states into their competition structures. Some will join the Asian Confederation, but the bulk will have to be accommodated in Europe. Russia, picking up where the Soviet Union left off, entered the 1994 World Cup qualifying competition and qualified, with what proved misleading ease, from a very poor group. In the finals, Oleg Salenko scored a record five goals in a game against Cameroon, but they lost the other two games. They will undoubtedly emerge as the most powerful of the states once the initial teething problems, particularly at club level, have been overcome.

TARTAN TERRIERS *Scotland's Billy Bremner and Jimmy Johnstone celebrate victory over the old enemy, England*

SAN MARINO

Federazione Sammarinese Giuoco Calcio
Founded: 1931
FIFA: 1988
Located entirely within Italy, the Most Serene Republic of San Marino, to give the state its full title, is one of the smallest nations ever to enter the international arena. Its population is just 24,000.

SCOTLAND

Scottish Football Association
Founded: 1873
FIFA: 1910–20, 1924–28, 1946
Scotland boasts a proud footballing heritage and, for such a small country, it has been a remarkable story. Founded in 1873, the Scottish FA still retains a permanent seat on the international board.

Scotland was also the venue for the world's first international match when, on November 30, 1872, Scotland and England drew 0–0. The Scotland vs. England rivalry has continued ever since, sharpened by the fact that many of England's most

successful club sides have contained or been managed by Scots: Bill Shankly at Liverpool, Matt Busby at Manchester United, Alex Ferguson also at United and George Graham at Arsenal have been outstanding, while the players include Hughie Gallacher (Newcastle), Alex James (Arsenal), Denis Law (Manchester United), Billy Bremner (Leeds) and Kenny Dalglish (Liverpool).

This continual draining of manpower would have withered many countries. But the Scottish League survives, thanks mainly to the two great Glasgow clubs, Celtic and Rangers. These two have dominated the domestic scene unlike any other country in Europe. Scottish club football was at its peak in the 1960s, with Celtic winning the European Cup in 1967 – the first British side to do so – and reaching the final again in 1970.

The Glasgow monopoly was briefly threatened by Aberdeen (European Cup-winners' Cup winners in 1983) and Dundee United (UEFA finalists in 1987), but the Old Firm, with Celtic breaking Rangers' hold on the championship in 1998, still rule the roost.

As for the national side, having entered the World Cup for the first time in 1950 they qualified for the finals in 1970, 1974, 1978, 1982, 1986, 1990 and 1998 - a remarkable record. And they also reached the European finals in 1992 and 1996.

Only one thing holds the Scots back, however: they seem incapable of making it past the first round in a major finals.

In seven World Cups they have always got the plane home after the opening stage – and it was no different at France '98. Having performed heroically against Brazil in the opening game (only losing 2–1 after a heart-breaking own goal) they failed to beat Norway and then lost embarrassingly 3–0 to Morocco. So, for now, the jinx continues.

SLOVAKIA

Slovak Football Association
Founded: 1993
FIFA: 1994
Slovakia were always poor relations in football terms before the split from the Czech Republic though Slovan Bratislava did once win the Euro-

pean Cup-winners' Cup in the 1960s. Slovakia made their international competitive debut in the 1996 European Championship and finished third in a tough group behind Romania and France.

SLOVENIA

Nogometna Zveza Slovenije
Founded: 1991
FIFA: 1992
Slovenia, the first state to break free of the former Yugoslavia, finished a disappointing fifth – out of six – in their 1996 European Championship qualifying group on their competitive debut.

SPAIN

Real Federacion Española de Futbol
Founded: 1913
FIFA: 1904
European Championship: 1964
Olympics: 1992
Spain's reputation as a world power in football is based largely on the exploits of her clubs, particularly Real Madrid and Barcelona, and the successes of the national side in the 1950s and 1960s. Football first got a foothold in the Basque country of Northern Spain, through migrant British workers, in the 1890s. Indeed, Spain's oldest club, Athletic Bilbao, still retain their English title. The game spread rapidly and was soon popular in Madrid, Barcelona and Valencia. The various regional organizations were brought together in 1913, when the Real Federacion Española de Futbol was formed. In 1920 the national side made its debut, with a 1–0 win over Denmark, and until the Civil War Spain's record was quite good. They reached the quarter-finals of the 1928 Olympics, and the 1934 World Cup finals – losing to

TRADITIONAL GIANTS *Amavisca of Spain*

Italy both times. Star of the side was goalkeeper Ricardo Zamora.

The Civil War and the Second World War halted internationals for almost a decade. But the domestic league grew stronger as the rivalry between Real Madrid, the "Royal" club, and Barcelona, the Catalan people's club, intensified. Barcelona had been a centre of resistance to Franco's fascists, and for the defeated and emasculated Catalan people, became their standard-bearers. This rivalry intensified in the 1950s, as both clubs began importing foreign talent. Real had Alfredo Di Stefano and Ferenc Puskas, while Barca had the Hungarian trio of Kubala, Kocsis and Czibor. Real Madrid won the first five European Cups (1956–60), heralding the 1960s as a decade of huge success at club and national level. Barcelona won the Fairs Cup, the former name of the UEFA Cup, in 1959, 1960 and again in 1966; Valencia won it in 1962 and 1963, Real Zaragoza in 1964. Meanwhile Atletico Madrid won the European Cup-winners' Cup in 1962, and Real Madrid won the European Cup again in 1966.

The national side qualified for the 1962 and 1966 World Cup finals and won the European Championship in 1964. A side containing Luis Suarez, possibly the greatest Spanish footballer ever, and one of the few Spaniards to play in Italy (with Internazionale), beat the Soviet Union 2–1 in Madrid to clinch Spain's first major trophy.

The 1970s, however, marked a decline. A ban on foreign imports, imposed in 1963, was lifted in 1973 in order to improve the national side. But it had the reverse effect. Spain failed to reach the 1970 and 1974 World Cup finals and, after Real's 1966 European Cup success, it was not until 1979 that European success returned, when Barcelona won the European Cup-winners' Cup. Spain hosted the 1982 World Cup, but failed miserably. They qualified again in 1986 and 1990 but could do no better than the quarter-finals in Mexico.

When the national side failed to qualify for the 1992 European Championship finals, the question of banning foreign imports was raised again.

When the import ban was lifted in the early 1970s, many of the world's top stars moved to Spain, including Cruyff, Neeskens, Breitner, Netzer and Rep. This influx coincided with a decline in the fortunes of the national team. Similarly, the 1980s saw the arrivals of Diego Maradona, Gary Lineker, Hugo Sanchez and Ronald Koeman, while the national team stuttered.

Spanish clubs benefitted, though. Real won two UEFA Cups in the 1980s, while Barcelona won the European Cup-winners' Cup in 1982 and 1989 and completed a hat-trick of European trophies by winning the European Cup in 1992.

Spain hoped the national side would follow suit and were boosted by the success of the Under-23s at the 1992 Barcelona Olympics. But although several of the youngsters were integrated into the full national side, which reached the quarter-finals of both the 1994 World Cup and the 1996 European Championship, it all fell apart at at France '98 – where they went out in the first round despite being one of the favourites.

A disastrous 3–2 defeat against Nigeria cost Spain dear and even though they recovered to crush Bulgaria 6–1, the biggest win of the finals, they were edged out by Paraguay.

SWEDEN

Svensk Fotbollforblundet
Founded: 1904
FIFA: 1904
Olympics: 1948
Sweden have, since the 1920s, been Scandinavia's top national side and have a deserved reputation for producing quality players. An Association was formed in 1904 and joined FIFA the same year.

Gothenburg was, and still is, the centre of Swedish domestic football and the National League, instituted in 1925, has been dominated by Gothenburg's clubs, Orgryte, IFK and GAIS, along with AIK and Djurgardens of Stockholm. Sweden's national side made their debut in 1908 and entered the first four Olympic tournaments – with mixed

IN TRIM *Liedholm (left) and Svensson*

success. This era, however, produced the country's greatest striker, Sven Rydell, who scored 49 goals in 43 games. Sweden were at their best in the late 1940s when they boasted one of the most famous forward lines in history. Gunnar Gren, Gunnar Nordahl and Nils Liedholm – the "Gre-No-Li" trio – sparked Sweden to Olympic gold in 1948 and were promptly signed up by Milan, where they enjoyed great success. Swedes were regularly bought by European clubs but were then barred from the national side by the strictly-amateur rules of the association. Despite this handicap, Sweden finished third in the 1950 World Cup, with Nacka Skoglund the new star.

The import ban was lifted in time for the 1958 World Cup finals, which Sweden hosted, and with all their players available they reached the Final. A decline followed in the 1960s, but Sweden qualified for all three World Cup finals in the 1970s, with Bjorn Nordqvist clocking up a record 115 appearances between 1963 and 1978.

The clubs too began to make an impact, and Malmo reached the

European Cup Final in 1979. IFK Gothenburg enjoyed the greatest success, though, winning the UEFA Cup in 1982 and 1989 – as part-timers, because Sweden has not yet introduced full professionalism. Until it does, its top stars will continue to move abroad in droves.

Sweden's first appearance in the European Championship finals came in 1992, by virtue of being hosts, but they were beaten in the semi-finals by Germany. They followed up by finishing third in the 1994 World Cup and toppling Denmark as top dogs in Scandinavia.

SWITZERLAND

Schweizerischer Fussballverband
Founded: 1895
FIFA: 1904
Switzerland have always been at the forefront of world football without ever actually winning anything, because both FIFA and UEFA are based in the country.

The British helped develop the game in Switzerland in the late 1800s, and this can clearly be seen in the names of two of her top clubs: Grasshopper (Zurich) and Young Boys (Bern). They, along with Servette (Geneva), have dominated Swiss football without prospering in European competition.

The national side, however, have fared slightly better, particularly in the 1920s and 1930s when they were runners-up in the 1924 Olympics and quarter-finalists at both the 1934 and 1938 World Cups. The most

HODGSON'S CHOICE *The Swiss celebrate a Chapuisat goal against Italy*

BACK IN ACTION *Sinisa Mihajlovic starred for Yugoslavia on both sides of his country's international suspension*

TURKEY

Turkiye Futbol Federasyono
Founded: 1923
FIFA: 1933

How Turkey have failed to develop into a top European football nation is a mystery. With a population of 55 million, a fiercely competitive and well-attended league and plenty of talented players, one World Cup finals appearance in 1954 is a pretty sorry return. The British brought football to Turkey in the 1890s, and by 1910 the country's top clubs – Besiktas, Galatasaray and Fenerbahce – had been founded. The clubs attract fanatical support and have done better than the national side, with Gala reaching the semi-finals of the European Cup in 1989 and dismissing Manchester United from the same competition in 1993. The international authorities may need to think again about Turkey's traditional minnow rating after the manner in which they reached the finals of the 1996 European Championship. Centre-forward Hakan Sukur was their goalscoring hero.

UKRAINE

Football Federation of Ukraine
Founded: 1992
FIFA: 1992

Considering that Kiev Dynamo were one of Europe's top clubs, Ukraine's international competitive debut after the Soviet collapse was disappointing. They offered little threat to Croatia and Italy in the Euro 96 qualifying tournament. At club level mafia infiltration and bribery problems have added to the difficulties.

WALES

Football Association of Wales
Founded: 1876
FIFA: 1910–20, 1924–28, 1946

Football has always come second behind Rugby Union in Wales, but the tide may be turning. In 1992, for the first time, the Welsh FA set up a National League, with a place in the Europe as an incentive for the "exile" clubs playing in England to join. Simultaneously, the national side is at its best since the inter-war period, when Billy Meredith led them to six British Championships, and the 1950s when Wales reached the 1958 World Cup quarter-finals with a side containing the legendary John Charles.

Welsh hopes of a 1994 World Cup finals appearance rested on the stunning forward line of Ian Rush, the country's top scorer, Mark Hughes, Dean Saunders and the "wonder boy" Ryan Giggs. They went very close but it was not to be. Further disappointment followed in the Euro 96 qualifiers when Wales changed manager three times in less than two years. Bobby Gould finally took on the challenge of building a new team which can no longer rely on the now-veteran skills of Rush, Hughes and Neville Southall.

YUGOSLAVIA

Fudbalski Savez Jugoslavije
Founded: 1919
FIFA: 1919
Olympic Games: 1960

Yugoslavia confirmed their return to international football by reaching the second round of France '98 - having been banned from the 1992 and 1996 European Championships and the 1994 World Cup.

In the 1980s, the Yugoslavs were often called the "Argentina of Europe" for the way in which they exported hundreds of fine players and coaches all over the world.

This was the Yugoslavia who were World Cup semi-finalists in 1930 and again in 1962, and won the Olympic title in 1960.

In 1991, however, the old nationalist tensions which have plagued the area for centuries erupted, and Yugoslavia violently disintegrated into several independent states.

Their match against Holland in the spring of 1992 was their last for two years (with Denmark taking their place in the European Championship finals) and then they played only friendlies until being allowed to take part in the qualifiers for France '98.

Just reaching the finals this time was a milestone. But with Dejan Savicevic, Predrag Mijatovic and Sinisa Mihajlovic on form they reached the second round – beating Iran and America and drawing with Germany – before going out 1–0 to Holland.

famous names of this era were the Abegglen brothers, Max and André, who scored over 60 goals between them.

The man responsible for this success was Karl Rappan – the father of Swiss football. He devised the "Swiss Bolt" system, which involved using a free man at the back as a sort of *libero*, and under Rappan the Swiss reached the finals of four of the first five World Cups played after the war. Their best performance was in 1954 when, as hosts, they reached the quarter-finals.

After 1966 the national side suffered a reversal of fortunes and failed to qualify for six consecutive World Cups and seven European Championships. But under English coach Roy Hodgson, they staged a come-back. They narrowly missed qualifying for the 1992 European Championship finals, but claimed a place at the 1994 World Cup finals after a fine qualifying programme that included a 1–0 win over Italy. They followed up by reaching the finals of the 1996 European Championship, where they drew 1–1 with hosts England in the Opening Match, but fell away, losing their other two games.

SOUTH AMERICA

Wanderers and Liverpool in Uruguay, Rangers and Everton in Chile, Newells Old Boys in Argentina, Corinthians in Brazil . . . are all names which provide proof of the debt that football around South America owes to British soccer missionaries.

But the British were not alone in taking the round ball west. So did the French (namely Racing Club of Argentina), Italians (Boca Juniors of Argentina and Penarol of Uruguay), Spanish (Barcelona of Ecuador), and Portuguese (Vasco da Gama of Brazil).

The success of these missions is clear to see on the international stage. Uruguay won the Olympic Games in 1924 and '28, then the same nation hosted the inaugural World Cup in 1930, and won that too. The 1950s opened with Uruguay winning the World Cup in Brazil and ended with the Brazilians becoming the first South American nation to win the World Cup in Europe when they beat hosts Sweden in 1958. The star of that team was the legendary Pele, and he was at the heart of outstanding team of 1970. The 1970s and 80s belonged to Argentina, winners of two World Cups, in 1978 and '86 and to another footballing genius, Diego Maradona.

South American clubs have also dominated the World Club Cup, where success over European clubs has been at the rate of three to two since 1960.

ARGENTINA

Asociacion del Futbol Argentino
Founded: 1893
FIFA: 1912
World Cup: 1978, 1986
South American Championship: 1910, 1921, 1925, 1927, 1929, 1937, 1941, 1945, 1946, 1947, 1955, 1957, 1991, 1993
Of all South American nations, Argentina are the most consistently successful.

Football was brought to Argentina by the British in the 1860s, and although, at first, it was exclusive to the British residents in Buenos Aires, by the turn of the century numerous clubs had been formed.

The Argentine Football Association was founded in 1891 by an Englishman, Alexander Hutton, and a league was formed the same year. Although the championship was not a truly national competition, as it contained only clubs from Buenos Aires, La Plata, Rosario and Santa Fé, the intense rivalry of the clubs in Buenos Aires ensured that Argentina had a vibrant domestic scene from the outset.

The national side also made an early start, and in 1901 a representative side played neighbouring Uruguay, in the first international match to be staged outside Great Britain. The seeds were sown for a rivalry which has grown into one of the most enduring and intense derby matches in the world.

Professionalism was adopted in 1931, and River Plate and Boca Juniors soon emerged as dominant forces. River's side of the 1940s was the greatest of them all, containing a forward line of Muñoz, Moreno, Pedernera, Labruna and Loustau which became known as *La Maquina* – the machine.

The national side were runners-up, to Uruguay, in the 1928 Olympics and met their deadly rivals again two years later in the 1930 World Cup Final. Although they lost 4–2 the impressive Argentine side was plundered by Italian agents – starting a draining process which continues today. To avoid a repeat, a third-rate side went to the 1934 tournament, and Argentina did not make a serious attempt on the World Cup again until the 1950s.

Indeed, the 1950s saw the birth of an exceptional side, with another famous forward line of Corbatta, Maschio, Angelillo, Sivori and Cruz.

Little progress was made in the 1960s and 1970s, despite Independiente and Estudiantes dominating the Libertadores Cup, and Argentina had to wait until 1978 for her first success in the World Cup. On home soil, and with a side containing only one overseas-based player, Mario Kempes, Argentina deservedly won the tournament.

They did so again in Mexico in 1986, when the side was led by Diego Maradona – who ranks as one of the greatest players the world has ever seen despite his drug abuse problems. In fact, Argentina featured in the final of three of the four World Cups from 1978 to 1990, they won the first two South American Championships of the 1990s, and they continue to produce extremely gifted footballers.

The captain of the 1978 World Cup winning team, Daniel Passarella, became national coach in 1995 and led them to the France '98 finals, where (with Ariel Ortega being hailed as the new Maradona) they beat England on penalties in the second round before losing to Holland in the last eight.

BOLIVIA

Federacion Boliviana de Futbol
Founded: 1925
FIFA: 1926
South American Championship: 1963
Since their first international outing in 1926, Bolivia have been the perennial whipping boys of South American football – until now. In the 1994 World Cup qualifiers the Bolivians finished a close second in Group B to qualify for the finals for the first time in forty years, recording a notable 2–0 victory over Brazil along the way and knocking out Uruguay and Ecuador in the process. Prior to that, apart from World Cup qualification in 1930 and 1950, the 1963 South American Championship victory, played at home, was the only success of note.

BRAZIL

Confederacao Brasileira de Futbol
Founded: 1914
FIFA: 1923
World Cup: 1958, 1962, 1970, 1994
South American Championship: 1919, 1922, 1949, 1989
Brazilian football has a romantic air about it that sets it apart from other nations. Between 1958 and 1970 they won the World Cup three times, with a team packed full of star players, including arguably the greatest in history – Pele. Brazil remains the only country to have played in every World Cup finals tournament and the only four-time winner.

Brazilian football developed at the end of the nineteenth century, prompted by migrant British workers, and leagues were established in Rio de Janeiro and São Paulo by the turn of the century. The vast size of Brazil meant that a national league was impractical and until the 1970s these leagues dominated domestic football. The "classic" Rio derbies between Flamengo, Fluminense, Botafogo and Vasco da Gama regularly attracted massive crowds to the 200,000-capacity Maracana Stadium.

The national team were a little slower out of the blocks, and their first real international was not played until 1914 with a visit to Buenos Aires. In 1916 Brazil entered the South American

ARGENTINE ACES *The 1986 World Cup-winning side*

the national side again scaled such heights by winning the 1994 World Cup – albeit thanks to a penalty shoot-out. Their best showing along the way was in the 1982 World Cup, when a side containing Zico, Socrates, Junior and Falcao lost to the eventual winners Italy.

Ironically, in 1994's qualifiers, Brazil lost to Bolivia, their first defeat ever in a World Cup qualifier, and scrambled through in an unconvincing fashion. But, having won the title, they set about building a new, more attractive, side under coach Mario Zagallo.

The emergence of young genius Ronaldo, who was an unused substitute in the 1994 final, together with the flair of Rivaldo, Roberto Carlos and Cafu ensured they were favourites to win at France '98. The team came very close to fulfilling that promise, reaching the final by beating Chile, Denmark and Holland in the knock-out stages. But the final itself proved a major disappointment, and could well put Brazilian football back years.

Ronaldo was included in the side even though he had suffered a convulsive fit hours before the kick-off. He barely touched the ball, and his teammates looked disillusioned and devoid of ideas as they crashed 3–0 to hosts France in a one-sided game.

CHILE

Federacion de Futbol de Chile
Founded: 1895
FIFA: 1912
Until Colo Colo's Libertadores Cup triumph in 1991, no Chilean side had ever won a major honour, and Chile have often been seen as the "nearly-men" of South American football. But they came of age in the 1998 World Cup finals in France.

Led by multi-million pound striker Marcelo Salas (who scored four goals) they reached the second round (holding Italy to a draw on the way) before going out to Brazil.

Chile qualified for five of the 11 post-war World Cups, but have only once before progressed beyond the first round, in 1962, when they reached the semi-finals on home soil. Their best performances in the South American Championship came in 1979 and 1987, when they were runners-up.

ALL SQUARE *Aldair clashes with Italy's Nicola Berti in the 1994 World Cup Final at the Rose Bowl in Pasadena*

Championship, but this event has not been a rewarding one for the Brazilians, who have won it only four times .

The World Cup, however, is another matter. The first attempt on the trophy was made in 1930, when they went out in the first round. The 1934 campaign was equally bad, despite the presence of such fine players as Leonidas da Silva and Artur Friedenreich. In 1938, however, they showed the first signs of what was to come by reaching the semi-finals, where they lost to Italy.

The golden age of Brazilian football was between 1950 and 1970, and it is the sides of this era that stick in the memory. In 1950 they were runners-up

as Uruguay pipped them for the title in the deciding match. In 1954, with Nilton and Djalma Santos established at the back and Didi running the midfield, they reached the quarter-finals in Switzerland, losing to Hungary.

In 1958 Brazil finally won the honour the nation's fans craved. With a forward line consisting of Garrincha, Vava, Zagalo and the 17-year-old Pele, they stormed to victory in Sweden, beating the hosts 5–2 in the Final. In Chile in 1962, an almost identical team – minus the injured Pele – triumphed again, beating Czechoslovakia 3–1.

In 1966, in England, the side was being rebuilt and Brazil fell in the first

round. But the newcomers Tostao, Gerson and Jairzinho were present in Mexico four years later when Brazil clinched a hat-trick of World Cups, earning them the right to keep the Jules Rimet Trophy in perpetuity.

The 1970 side has been described as the best ever seen, and with some justification. The defence, marshalled by Carlos Alberto, was not all that strong, but this did not matter as the Brazilian approach was all-out attack. This was football with a flourish and the global TV audience loved it. In attack, Pele was back to his best, superbly assisted by Jairzinho, Rivelinho and Tostao.

After 1970, it was 24 years before—

SANTIAGO STRUGGLE *Chile vs. Switzerland in the first round of the 1962 World Cup, which the South Americans won 3–1*

COLOMBIA

Federacion Colombiana de Futbol
Founded: 1924
FIFA: 1936

Colombia's history has been dominated by years of internal disputes, disruptions and turbulence. The most notorious came in 1950, shortly after professionalism was introduced, when a break-away league outside FIFA jurisdiction, the DiMayor, was formed and Colombian sides began importing players from all over South America and from Britain. The huge salaries on offer led to the four years of its existence being known as the "El Dorado" period. The bubble burst in 1954, when Colombia were readmitted to FIFA and the league collapsed.

The national side made its debut as late as 1938, and results at first were poor. Between 1949 and 1957 no internationals were played at all, and thereafter outings were infrequent. It was a huge surprise, then, when Colombia qualified for the 1962 World Cup in Chile.

In 1965 another breakaway federation was formed and confusion reigned once more. FIFA had to intervene and effectively ran Colombian football up until 1971, when the present administration was installed. A new league structure was introduced in 1968, careful controls on the number of foreign imports were implemented, and the national side soon benefited.

In 1989 Nacional Medellin won the Libertadores Cup, the country's only victory, and a year later the national

side, coached by Francisco Maturana, qualified for the 1990 World Cup finals.

But the best – and worst – followed. In the 1994 World Cup qualifiers, Argentina were thrashed 5–0 in Buenos Aires and consigned to a play-off. This performance led a number of people to consider the Colombians a good bet to win the whole competition.

But at USA '94, Colombia's efforts foundered on poor morale, not helped by death threats against players and coach Maturana. Worst of all came after their surprise first-round elimination. Defender Andres Escobar – who had scored an own goal in the shock 2–1 defeat by the USA – was shot to death in Medellin. Drug and gambling cartels – believed to be behind the unsolved murder – still threaten to undermine all the good work achieved by outstanding players such as Carlos Valderrama.

The veteran was again running midfield at France '98, but his side lost to England and Romania and crashed out at the first hurdle. Once again there was controversy, with star striker Faustino Asprilla sent home during the tournament for breaking a team curfew and questioning tactics.

ECUADOR

Asociacion Ecuatoriana de Futbol
Founded: 1925
FIFA: 1926

Ecuador are one of South America's weakest nations, and they have yet to qualify for any major tournament. The closest they have gone to reach-

SPEED MERCHANT *Few players in world football can keep up with Colombia's striker Faustino Asprilla when he is in full flight*

ing the World Cup finals was in 1966, when they lost a play-off to Chile. Between 1938 and 1975 the national side managed only eight wins, but there are signs of improvement. In 1990, Barcelona of Guayaquil were runners-up in the Libertadores Cup.

PARAGUAY

Liga Paraguaya de Futbol
Founded: 1906
FIFA: 1921
South American Championship:
1953, 1979

Paraguay's heroic performances at France '98 have given the country a boost. Led by charasmatic goal-

keeper Jose Chilavert (who likes to take penalties and free-kicks) they reached the second round with a shock 3–1 over Nigeria and draws against Spain and Bulgaria.

Only a Golden Goal by France's Laurent Blanc denied them a quarter-final place, a fine achievement for such a smal country.

On the club front, Olimpia are Paraguay's most successful side and have won the Libertadores Cup twice, in 1979 and 1990, and have been runners-up three times.

The national side won the South American Championship in 1953 and 1979 and have now qualified for five World Cup finals.

PERU

Federacion Peruana de Futbol
Founded: 1922
FIFA: 1924
South American Championship:
1939, 1975.

Football in Peru has always been dominated by Lima, and the national association was founded there in 1922.

The local Lima League was the strongest in the country and, until a national championship was introduced in 1966, the winners were considered national champions. Lima's clubs, Alianza, Universitario and Sporting Cristal, have dominated at home, but none have achieved success in the Libertadores Cup. Sadly, the eyes of the world were focused on Peru in 1964, when 300 spectators died in a riot, and in 1988, when the Alianza team was wiped out in a plane crash.

Peru's international debut came in the South American Championship of 1927, and they won the event at home in 1939. The World Cup record was poor, however, until the 1970s, when a generation of notable players came together and made the decade the country's most successful ever.

Stars of the 1970s side were the highly eccentric and entertaining goalkeeper Ramon "El Loco" Quiroga, Hector Chumpitaz and midfield maestro Teofilo Cubillas, the greatest Peruvian player of all time. Coached by Brazilian World Cup winner Didi, this side reached the quarter-finals of the 1970 World Cup, won the 1975 South American Championship, and qualified for the 1978 World Cup, where they fell in the second round.

Peru qualified for the World Cup again in 1982, but the side was past its best and went out in the first round. Since then, Peru have slipped back into their familiar role of the "middle-men" of South American football. Political problems in the country have not helped.

URUGUAY

Asociacion Uruguaya de Futbol
Founded: 1900
FIFA: 1923
World Cup: 1930, 1950
South American Championship:
1916, 1917, 1920, 1923, 1924, 1926, 1935, 1942, 1956, 1959, 1967, 1983, 1987, 1995.
Olympics: 1924, 1928
Before the Second World War, Uruguay were undoubtedly the best team in the world, effectively winning three World Championships. Today they are no longer a world power, but they have a proud history and can still be dangerous opponents. Montevideo dominates the domestic scene and, as it is located just across the River Plate estuary from Buenos Aires, the two cities can rightly claim to be the centre of South American football. Montevideo's two great clubs, Penarol and Nacional, have dominated Uruguayan football, winning more than 80 championships between them. The clubs are fierce rivals and have both enjoyed great success in the Libertadores Cup; Penarol winning it five times, Nacional three. Both clubs have also won the World Club Cup.

The national side dominated world football in the first half of this century, but has faded since the 1950s. Early successes in the South American Championship were followed by victory in the 1924 Olympics in Amsterdam, at a time when the Olympic winners could justifiably claim to be world champions. Having amazed Europe with their skill at the 1924 Olympics, Uruguay repeated the trick in 1928 and two years later, as the host nation, swept to victory in the first World Cup.

The side of the 1920s and 1930s contained many of Uruguay's all-time greats: skipper Jose Nasazzi, the midfield "Iron Curtain" of Jose Andrade, Lorenzo Fernandez and Alvarez Gestido, and outstanding forwards Hector Castro, Pedro Cea and Hector Scarone.

In 1950 Uruguay pulled off one of the biggest World Cup finals shocks in history, coming from a goal down to beat Brazil 2–1 in the deciding match … in Brazil. The side contained strikers Juan Schiaffino, Uruguay's greatest player, and Omar Miguez, Victor Andrade, nephew of Jose, Roque Maspoli in goal and Obdulio Varela in defence. In Switzerland in 1954, the defence of their crown ended with a 4–2 semi-final defeat by Hungary in one of the best World Cup games ever.

Since then, Uruguay have enjoyed regular success in the South American Championship, but in the World Cup they have failed to matched their feats of the 1930s and 1950s. They finished fourth in the 1970, but elimination by Bolivia in the 1994 qualifiers showed just how far they had slipped.

Uruguay still produces outstanding players, like Enzo Francescoli and Carlos Aguilera, but they often go to Europe to further their careers. With so many foreign-based players, Uruguay developed a schizophrenic approach to the World Cup and South American Championship, often entering wildly different teams for tournaments staged less than a year apart. This unpredictability was shown in 1995, when Uruguay won the Copa America, beating 1994 World Cup winners Brazil after a penalty shoot-out in the Final.

VENEZUELA

Federacion Venezolana de Futbol
Founded: 1926
FIFA: 1952
Venezuela are the weakest of the 10 South American countries, but this is hardly surprising because the national sport is baseball. Originally members of CONCACAF, they made their international debut in 1938 and switched to CONMEBOL in 1958. The national record is awful, with just one match won in the South American Championship and only a handful more in World Cup qualifiers, even though they have entered both regularly.

The clubs are weak too, and three Libertadores Cup semi-finals are the best they have managed. A professional league was finally set up in 1956, but Venezuela have a long way to go if they are even to catch up with the other South American minnows.

MIDFIELD MAESTRO *Teofilo Cubillas, Peru's greatest ever player*

NORTH & CENTRAL AMERICA

Many central American nations may appear little more than a statistical dot in the world game's atlas. But CONCACAF (North and Central American confederation) is very quickly learning how to capitalize on the commercial value of football. The income is being used profitably for coaching schemes and administrative improvements. "American" soccer is much more now than merely those nations which have done well in the World Cup: Mexico's double staging of the World Cup finals in 1970 and 1986 proves the point. So, of course, did USA '94 ...

ANTIGUA AND BARBUDA

Antigua Football Association
Founded: 1928
FIFA: 1970

ARUBA

Arubaanse Voetbal Bond
Founded: 1932
FIFA: 1988

BAHAMAS

Bahamas Football Association
Founded: 1967
FIFA: 1968

BARBADOS

Barbados Football Association
Founded: 1910
FIFA: 1968

BELIZE

Belize National Football Association
Founded: 1980
FIFA: 1986

BERMUDA

Bermuda Football Association
Founded: 1928
FIFA: 1962

CANADA

Canadian Soccer Association
Founded: 1912
FIFA: 1912
Olympics: 1904 (Galt FC of Ontario)
Football in Canada has struggled to establish itself for two main reasons. First, the enormous size of the country makes a coherent structure difficult to implement and consequently a true, national league was only set up in 1987. Second, the sport trails badly in popularity behind ice hockey, baseball, gridiron and basketball – the big North American sports.

Football took hold in Canada at the turn of the century, and in 1904 Galt FC from Ontario entered the St Louis Olympic Games. Soccer was only a demonstration sport, but Galt won the event, still Canada's only major honour. The national side made a few outings in the 1920s, but went into hibernation until the 1950s when they entered the 1958 World Cup – their first attempt. Success eluded them, however, and even when Montreal hosted the 1976 Olympics, they were eliminated in the first round.

In the 1970s, three Canadian clubs, from Vancouver, Toronto and Edmonton, played in the North American Soccer League – as many of Canada's ice hockey and baseball clubs do. In 1976, Toronto won the NASL Soccer Bowl, as did Vancouver in 1979, and many of the Canadians playing in the NASL formed the backbone of the national side which reached the 1986 World Cup finals, their only appearance to date.

In the 1994 qualifiers Canada, with five British-based professionals in the side, reached a play-off with Oceania winners Australia, but lost on penalties. The side was coached by Bobby Lenarduzzi, who had been a member of the 1986 side.

BRIEF ENCOUNTER *Canada at Mexico '86, their only World Cup appearance*

CAYMAN ISLANDS

Cayman Islands Football Association
Founded: 1992
FIFA: 1992

COSTA RICA

Federacion Costarricense de Futbol
Founded: 1921
FIFA: 1921
CONCACAF Championship: 1941, 1946, 1948, 1953, 1955, 1960, 1961, 1963, 1969, 1989
Costa Rica are one of the better teams from Central America, and between 1940 and 1970 they won an impressive nine CONCACAF Championships. Despite this, Costa Rica struggled to make an impact in the World Cup – El Salvador and Honduras both qualified before them – but in 1990 the breakthrough came. Under coach Bora Milutinovic, they not only qualified for the finals, but also defeated Scotland and Sweden to progress into the second round. Costa Rica has a very healthy domestic scene too, and two clubs, Deportivo Saprissa and LD Alajeulense, have both won the CONCACAF Club Championship.

CUBA

Asociacion de Futbol de Cuba
Founded: 1924
FIFA: 1932

DOMINICA

Dominica Football Association
Founded:
FIFA:

DOMINICAN REPUBLIC

Federacion Dominicana de Futbol
Founded: 1953
FIFA: 1958

EL SALVADOR

Federacion Salvadorena de Futbol
Founded: 1935
FIFA: 1938
CONCACAF Championship: 1943

El Salvador's biggest claim to soccer fame is the 1969 "Football War" with Central American neighbours Honduras. The countries met in a World Cup qualifying group and rioting followed both matches, especially after the second game when El Salvador forced a play-off. El Salvador won it and, as tension mounted, the army invaded Honduras on the pretext of protecting expatriate Salvadorean citizens. The World Cup match was more an excuse than a cause for the war, but the conflict cost 3,000 lives before it was settled.

El Salvador have qualified for the World Cup finals twice, losing all three games in 1970 and again in 1982 – which included a 10–1 thrashing by Hungary.

GRENADA

Grenada Football Association
Founded: 1924
FIFA: 1976

GUATEMALA

Federacion Nacional de Futbol de Guatemala
Founded: 1926
FIFA: 1933
CONCACAF Championship: 1967

GUYANA

Guyana Football Association
Founded: 1904
FIFA: 1968

HAITI

Fédération Haitienne de Football
Founded: 1904
FIFA: 1933
CONCACAF Championship: 1957, 1973

HONDURAS

Federacion Nacional Automana de Futbol
Founded: 1935
FIFA: 1946
CONCACAF Championship: 1981
Honduras, like neighbouring El Salvador, is a country which has been plagued by insurgency and guerrilla warfare. Indeed, the two went to war in 1969, over the outcome of a foot-

ball match, as described in the entry for El Salvador. Honduras made their sole appearance in the World Cup finals in 1982, when they drew 1–1 with hosts, Spain, and Northern Ireland, before losing 1–0 to Yugoslavia and going out of the tournament.

Honduran clubs have enjoyed some success in the CONCACAF Club Championship, notably Olimpia, who won the event in 1972 and 1988, and were runners-up in 1985.

JAMAICA

Jamaica Football Federation
Founded: 1910
FIFA: 1962
Jamaica have made incredible strides in recent years. Having qualified for their first-ever World Cup finals under Brazilian coach Rene Simoes, the Reggae Boyz went on a world tour and found they had fans all over the world – and especially in England. It's a carnival wherever they play, and although they went out in the first round of France '98, they did beat Japan to record their first ever victory in the finals.

MEXICO

Federacion Mexicana de Futbol Asociacion
Founded: 1927
FIFA: 1929
CONCACAF Championship: 1963, 1971, 1977, 1993
Mexico utterly dominate their Central American region, but this has hindered rather than helped their game. With no decent, local opposition for the national side or the clubs, Mexico have enjoyed their greatest moments in the World Cup.

The y entered their first World Cup in 1930 and nd have qualified for 11 of the 16 finals tournaments, a record which includes 1990, when they were barred by FIFA for breaches of age regulations in a youth tournament. Mexico's best World Cups were in 1970 and 1986, when they were hosts. They reached the quarter-finals of both and in 1986, when Hugo Sanchez became a world star, were unlucky to lose on penalties to West Germany.

Famous for his exuberant, cart-

wheeling celebrations when he scored, Sanchez was regarded as Mexico's greatest player since Antonio Carbajal, the goalkeeper who created a record by playing in all five World Cup finals tournaments from 1950 to 1966.

Mexico, who have won the CONCACAF Championship four times, also reached the final of the 1993 South American Championships after being invited to take part, and then reached the 1994 World Cup finals, where they lost to Bulgaria on penalties in the second round.

They also made it to France '98, this time losing in the second round to Germany. But the tournament threw up two new stars in the shape of Luis Hernandez and Cuauhtemoc Blanco, whose 'bunny-hop' trick proved to be one of the highlights of the first round!

NETHERLANDS ANTILLES

Nederlands Antiliaanse Voetbal Unie
Founded: 1921
FIFA: 1932

NICARAGUA

Federacion Nicaraguense de Futbol
Founded: 1931
FIFA: 1950

PANAMA

Federacion Nacional de Futbol de Panama
Founded: 1937
FIFA: 1938
CONCACAF Championship: 1951

PUERTO RICO

Federacion Puertorriquena de Futbol
Founded: 1940
FIFA: 1960

SAINT KITTS AND NEVIS

St Kitts and Nevis Football Association
Founded: 1992
FIFA: 1992

SAINT LUCIA

St Lucia National Football Association
Founded: 1988
FIFA: 1988

SAINT VINCENT & THE GRENADINES

St Vincent and the Grenadines Football Federation
Founded: 1988
FIFA: 1988

SURINAM

Surinaamse Voetbal Bond
Founded: 1920
FIFA: 1929

TRINIDAD AND TOBAGO

Trinidad and Tobago Football Association
Founded: 1906
FIFA: 1963

UNITED STATES

United States Soccer Federation
Founded: 1913
FIFA: 1913
CONCACAF Championship: 1991
The United States is viewed by many as a non-football country, yet US football has a long and interesting history. For example, the Oneida club of Boston was founded in 1862, making it the oldest outside England.

The national side entered the 1924 and 1928 Olympics and then travelled to Uruguay for the first World Cup in 1930 – where they reached the semi-finals. Four years later they were represented at the finals again, but lost to hosts Italy in the first round. In 1950 the US caused one of the biggest World Cup shocks ever when they beat England 1–0, with Haiti-born Joe Gaetjens scoring the winning goal. It would be 40 years before the US qualified for the World Cup finals again.

Apart from the victory over England, US soccer was long famed for one other reason – the North American Soccer League. Founded in 1967, the NASL featured corporate-backed teams which enabled the clubs to pay huge wages and attract top foreign stars. such as Pele, Franz Beckenbauer, Johan Cruyff and George Best, but the NASL collapsed in the late 1980s.

With Mexico suspended, the US qualified for the 1990 World Cup finals, but their international naivety was clearly shown, losing all three matches.

FIFA, bidding to promote the game world-wide, selected the US to host the 1994 finals,. and the team surprised many critics.

Under coach Bora Milutinovic they won the 1991 CONCACAF Championship – their only honour to date. Then the team, containing a number of players with experience of club football in Europe, produced one of the

shocks of the 1994 World Cup when they defeated dark horses Colombia in the group stage and lost only 1–0 to Brazil in the second round.

The 1995 Copa America, under new coach Steve Sampson, proved this success was not a fluke, as the US reached the semi-finals. But Sampson resigned after his team failed to make an impact at France '98. They qualified well, but then lost all three of their group matches in the finals, scoring only once and suffering an embarrassing reverse against Iran.

The main hope for the US is that the Major League Soccer, started in 1996, will provide some new home-grown talent in the near future.

OVER THE TOP *American Alexi Lalas tackles Colombian Ivan Valenciano*

OCEANIA

Oceania took a major step forward in 1996 when it was accepted by FIFA as a fully-fledged regional confederation. But that was still not enough to earn a guaranteed place for at least one of its nations at the World Cup finals. The best Oceania nation was still condemned to a qualifying play-off against one of the Asian nations.

AMERICAN SAMOA

American Samoa Football Association
Founded: 1975
FIFA: Associate member

AUSTRALIA

Australia Soccer Federation
Founded: 1961
FIFA: 1963
Soccer has struggled to gain a foothold in Australia, where cricket, Aussie Rules football and rugby are the most popular sports. The domestic league formed in 1977, has many ethnically linked clubs such as South Melbourne Hellas and Adelaide City Juventus

Australia's only World Cup finals appearance, in 1974, proved a disappointment. More upsetting still was their failure to qualify in 1994 and 1998 when they lost last-match play-offs to Argentina and Iran.

COOK ISLANDS

Cook Islands Football Federation
Founded: 1971
FIFA: 1994

FIJI

Fiji Football Association
Founded: 1938
FIFA: 1963

NEW CALEDONIA

Federation Neo-Caledonienne de Football
Founded: 1960
FIFA: Associate member

NEW ZEALAND

New Zealand Football Association
Founded: 1938
FIFA: 1963
New Zealand's only World Cup finals appearance was in 1982, when they were eliminated in the first round. Wynton Rufer was a member of that side, and won a German Championship medal with Werder Bremen in 1992–93 to establish himself as New Zealand's greatest-ever player.

PAPUA NEW GUINEA

Papua New Guinea Football Association
Founded: 1962
FIFA: 1963

SOLOMON ISLANDS

Solomon Islands Football Federation
Founded: 1988
FIFA: 1988

TAHITI

Fédération Tahitienne de Football
Founded: 1938
FIFA: 1990

TONGA

Tonga Football Association
Founded:
FIFA:

VANUATU

Vanuatu Football Federation
Founded: 1934
FIFA: 1988

WESTERN SAMOA

Western Samoa Football Association
Founded: 1968
FIFA: 1986

AFRICA

MOVING AHEAD *Algeria's Assad leaves a Chilean defender trailing*

FIFA has grown from the seven original members of 1904 through 73 in 1950 to more than 200 nations (including associate members). Africa is the largest of the regional confederations with 51 full members and one associate member state.

In the past 20 years FIFA has concentrated millions of dollars in educational programmes for coaches, referees, administrators and players in the developing world. Progress has been measured by World Cup finals entry: three African nations were present, for the first time, at USA '94, thanks to the feats of her entrants in 1990; the next World Cup, in France in 1998, will see expanded representation for the developing countries thanks to the enlargement of the event from 24 to 32 teams.

ALGERIA

Fédération Algérienne de Football
Founded: 1962
FIFA: 1963
African Nations Cup: 1990
The French brought football to Algeria in the late 1900s, and by the 1930s several Muslim Algerian clubs had been formed. The earliest was Mouloudia Challia (1920), and they won the African Champions Cup in 1976 at the first attempt.

Algeria gained independence in 1962, and since then the national side has improved considerably. In 1980 they reached the final of the African Nations Cup, where they lost 3–0 to hosts Nigeria, and two years later qualified for the World Cup finals in Spain. At the 1982 finals the Algerians pulled off one of the biggest World Cup shocks when they beat West Germany 2–1, and had it not been for a contrived result between the Germans and Austria, Algeria would have reached the second round. Rabah Madjer and Lakhdar Belloumi were the goalscorers against West Germany and they remain Algeria's greatest players. Madjer won a European Cup-winners' Cup medal with FC Porto in 1987, when he was also voted African Footballer of the Year.

Algeria were semi-finalists in the African Nations Cup in 1984 and 1988, and in between qualified for the 1986 World Cup finals. Then, in 1990 they won the African Nations Cup for the first time. In 1993 they qualified for the African Nations Cup finals, but were expelled for fielding an ineligible player in a qualifying game.

Algerian clubs have done well in African competitions, with MC Algiers (1976), J.S Kabylie (1981 and 1990) and ES Setif (1988), all winning the African Champions Cup.

ANGOLA

Federacao Angolana de Futebol
Founded: 1977
FIFA: 1980

BENIN

Fédération Beninoise de Football
Founded: 1968
FIFA: 1969

BOTSWANA

Botswana Football Association
Founded: 1970
FIFA: 1976

BURKINA FASO

Fédération Burkinabe de Football
Founded: 1960
FIFA: 1964

BURUNDI

Fédération de Football du Burundi
Founded: 1948
FIFA: 1972

CAMEROON

Fédération Camerounaise de Football
Founded: 1960
FIFA: 1962
African Nations Cup: 1984, 1988.
Of all the African nations to have reached the World Cup finals, Cameroon have made by far the biggest impact - so their first-round exit at France '98 was painful.

In 1982, in Spain, they drew all three of their first round games – against Italy (eventual winners), Poland (third) and Peru – but went out at that stage. They qualified again in 1990, beat reigning champions Argentina in the opening match and reached the quarter-finals, losing narrowly to England. As a result of these performances FIFA agreed to grant Africa a third berth at the 1994 finals. This time, the "Indomitable Lions" were a major disappointment, torn apart by internal strife.

Many hoped they would make up for that in France four years later. But instead, the decline continued as they finished bottom of their group, failing to win a single game.

Cameroon's greatest player is undoubtedly striker Roger Milla, who played in the 1982, 1990 and 1994 World Cup teams. He was voted African Footballer of the Year in 1976 and again in 1990.

Other Cameroon players to have won the award include Theophile Abega (1984), Thomas N'Kono (1979 and 1982) and Jean Onguene (1980).

Cameroon also won the African Nations Cup twice to confirm their status as the top side of the 1980s. Cameroon clubs have also enjoyed success in African competitions: with five wins in the Champions Cup and three in the Cup Winners' Cup.

CAPE VERDE

Federacao Cabo-Verdiana de Futebol
Founded: 1982
FIFA: 1986

CENTRAL AFRICAN REPUBLIC

Fédération Centrafricaine de Football
Founded: 1937
FIFA: 1963

CHAD

Fédération Tchadienne de Football
Founded: 1962
FIFA: 1988

CONGO

Fédération Congolaise de Football
Founded: 1962
FIFA: 1962
African Nations Cup: 1972

DJIBOUTI

Federation Djiboutienne de Football
Founded: 1977
FIFA: 1994

EGYPT

All Ettihad el Masri Li Korat el Kadam
Founded: 1921
FIFA: 1923
African Nations Cup: 1957, 59, 86, 98

Egypt were one of the four founder members of the Confédération Africaine de Football and were the first Africans to join FIFA, in 1923. Given this 20-year start on most of her neighbours, it is no surprise that Egypt became one of the great African powers , winning the first two Nations Cups in 1957 and 1959.

Egypt finished fourth in the 1928 Olympics and entered the World Cup in 1934. Having beaten Palestine in a qualifying play-off, they lost 4–2 to Hungary in the first round. Olympic semi-finalists again in 1964, Egypt entered only one of the World Cups played between 1938 and 1970.

A revival in the 1970s saw them finish third in the African Nations Cup in 1970 and 1974, fourth in 1976 and reach the Olympic quarter-finals in 1984. Two years later, as hosts, they won the African Nations Cup for the third time, and then qualified for the 1990 World Cup finals, where they did well to hold Holland and the Republic of Ireland to draws.

Allied to this success at national level, Egyptian clubs are among the most powerful in Africa. Well organized, wealthy and well supported, Egypt's clubs have won the African Champions Cup and the African Cup Winners' Cup ten times. Al Ahly, the most successful, have won the former twice and the latter thrice – in consecutive years from 1984 to 1986.

Al-Titsh, who played for Al Ahly in the 1920s, was one of Egypt's finest players, and Ahly's stadium still bears his name. Other great Egyptian players include Mahmoud Al Khatib, Ibrahim Youssef and Abu Zeid, Egypt's best striker during the 1980s.

EQUATORIAL GUINEA

Federacion Equatoguineana de Futbol
Founded: 1976
FIFA: 1986

ETHIOPIA

Yeithiopia Football Federechin
Founded: 1943
FIFA: 1953
African Nations Cup: 1962

DOWN AND OUT *Ireland's Moran is left grounded by Egypt's El Kass*

GABON

Fédération Gabonaise de Football
Founded: 1962
FIFA: 1963

GAMBIA

Gambia Football Association
Founded: 1952
FIFA: 1966

GHANA

Ghana Football Association
Founded: 1957
FIFA: 1958
African Nations Cup: 1963, 1965, 1978, 1982

Ghana achieved independence in 1957 and the "Black Stars" quickly established themselves as a powerful force in African football. They won the African Nations Cup in 1963, at their first attempt, retained the trophy two years later and in the following two events, 1968 and 1970, were beaten finalists. Ghana is the only nation to win the trophy four times.

In club football, Asante Kotoko have won the African Champions Cup twice and Ghana have produced some outstanding players. Mohamed Ahmed Polo and Adolf Armah were stars in the 1970s; Ibrahim Sunday, African footballer of the year in 1971, played for Werder Bremen in the German League; Abedi Pele won many trophies with Marseille in the 1980s; and Nii Lamptey, of PSV Eindhoven, led Ghana to victory in the 1991 World Youth Championship. Nevertheless, Ghana have yet to qualify for the World Cup finals.

GUINEA

Fédération Guinéenne de Football
Founded: 1959
FIFA: 1961

GUINEA-BISSAU

Federacao de Football da Guinea-Bissau
Founded: 1974
FIFA: 1986

IVORY COAST

Fédération Ivoirienne de Football
Founded: 1960
FIFA: 1960
African Nations Cup: 1992

The Ivory Coast are one of Africa's great footballing enigmas. Of the field, they have a stable government and a healthy economy; on it the Ivory Coast has a well-organized league – advantages which many African countries do not enjoy – and yet success at international level eluded them until 1992. In that year "The Elephants" won the African Nations Cup in Senegal, defeating Ghana on penalties in the final. They had previously been semi-finalists three times without going further.

The 1992 success confirmed the Ivorians as favourites to qualify for the 1994 World Cup finals for the first time ever, but they faded badly in the final round and finished second behind Nigeria.

KENYA

Kenya Football Federation
Founded: 1932
FIFA: 1960

LESOTHO

Lesotho Sports Council
Founded: 1932
FIFA: 1964

LIBERIA

Liberia Football Association
Founded: 1936
FIFA: 1962

LIBYA

Libyan Arab Jamahiriya Football Federation
Founded: 1962
FIFA: 1963

MADAGASCAR

Fédération Malagasy de Football
Founded: 1961
FIFA: 1962

MALAWI

Football Association of Malawi
Founded: 1966
FIFA: 1967

MALI

Fédération Malienne de Football
Founded: 1960
FIFA: 1962

MAURITANIA

Fédération de Football de la République de Mauritanie
Founded: 1961
FIFA: 1964

MAURITIUS

Mauritius Football Association
Founded: 1952
FIFA: 1962

MOROCCO

Fédération Royale Marocaine de Football
Founded: 1955
FIFA: 1956
African Nations Cup: 1976
Morocco can justifiably claim to be the unluckiest side at the 1998 World Cup finals in France. The Africans thought they had qualified for the second stage after a tremendous 3–0 victory over Scotland. But as the players celebrated on the pitch they were unaware that the unthinkable had happened and Norway had beaten Brazil to snatch second spot in the group.

SWERVING *Morocco's Lamriss*

Despite that, Morocco, with Mustapha Hadji outstanding, did plenty to confirm their emergence as a world force. They first qualified for the World Cup finals in 1970 – the first African side to do so – and have made progress since, even applying to host the finals in 1984 and 1998. In 1970 they held Bulgaria to a draw and gave West Germany a fright before losing 2–1. They qualified again in 1986 and won their first round group ahead of England, Poland and Portugal, before losing to the Germans again.

In 1976 they won the African Nations Cup for the only time and in 1994 reached the World Cup finals once more. Moroccan domestic clubs have also been successful. FAR Rabat won the Champions Cup in 1985, Raja Casablanca repeated the trick in 1989, followed by Wydad Casablanca in 1992.

Morocco has also provided several stars of French football, including Larbi Ben Barek, the "Black Pearl", who won 17 French caps, and. Just Fontaine, whose 13 goals in the 1958 World Cup finals remains a record.

MOZAMBIQUE

Federacao Moçambicana de Futebol
Founded: 1975
FIFA: 1978

NAMIBIA

Namibia Football Federation
Founded: 1992
FIFA: 1992

NIGER

Fédération Nigérienne de Football
Founded: 1967
FIFA: 1967

NIGERIA

Nigeria Football Association
Founded: 1945
FIFA: 1959
Olympic Games: 1996
African Nations Cup: 1980, 1994
Nigeria, with a huge population and over 500 registered clubs, has emerged at last in the 1990s as one of the most powerful nations in Africa – and was the only African nation to reach the second stage of France '98.

It's about time the seniors caught up, because Nigeria's youth teams have been leading the way for years.

In 1985 Nigeria won the World Under-17 Championship, becoming the first African side to win a FIFA world tournament at any level, beating West Germany 2–0 in the final; in 1989, Nigeria were runners-up in the World Under-20 Youth Championship; and in 1993 the "Green Eaglets" won their second Under-17 title in only the event's fifth staging.

A World Cup breakthrough came in 1994 when Nigeria nearly sprang one of the greatest of all upsets. They topped their first-round group – ahead of Argentina, Bulgaria and Greece – and came within a couple of minutes of eliminating eventual finalists Italy in the second round.

In 1997 they became the first African nation to win the Olympic tournament, beating favourites Brazil in the semi-final and Argentina in the final. Not surprisingly, there was plenty of expectation when Nigeria qualified for France '98, and there were even suggestions, fuelled by Pele no less, that they could win it.

They did reach the second round, topping their group and beating Spain and Bulgaria. But the dream ended in the second round when they were comprehensively beaten 4–1 by Denmark. Complacency and over-confidence were Nigeria's downfall, although in dazzling striker Jay-Jay Okocha they had one of the men of the tournament.

REUNION

Ligue de la Réunion
Founded: 1985
FIFA: Associate member

RWANDA

Fédération Rwandaise de Football Amateur
Founded: 1972
FIFA: 1976

SAO TOME AND PRINCIPE

Federacion Santomense de Futebol
Founded: 1975
FIFA: 1986

SO NEAR *Emmanuel Amunike's goal almost knocked Italy out of the World Cup*

SENEGAL

Fédération Sénégalaise de Football
Founded: 1960
FIFA: 1962

SEYCHELLES

Seychelles Football Federation
Founded: 1976
FIFA: 1986

SIERRA LEONE

Sierra Leone Amateur Football Association
Founded: 1923
FIFA: 1967

SOMALIA

Somalia Football Federation
Founded: 1951
FIFA: 1961

SOUTH AFRICA

South African Football Association
Founded: 1892
FIFA: 1952 (suspended 1964–76), 1992
African Nations Cup: 1996
Football has always been the sport of the masses in South Africa, with clubs such as the Kaiser Chiefs and Orlando Pirates hugely popular. But it is only since the end of apartheid that the national team has been able to prove its worth, winning the 1996 African Nations Cup on home soil and reaching the World Cup finals for the first time. South Africa were rather disappointing at France '98, however, going out in the first round after two draws and a defeat.

SUDAN

Sudan Football Federation
Founded: 1936
FIFA: 1948
African Nations Cup: 1970

SWAZILAND

National Football Association of Swaziland
Founded: 1964
FIFA: 1976

TANZANIA

Football Association of Tanzania
Founded: 1930
FIFA: 1964

TOGO

Fédération Togolaise de Football
Founded: 1960   *FIFA:* 1962

TUNISIA

Fédération Tunisienne de Football
Founded: 1956
FIFA: 1960
Tunisia reached their first ever World Cup finals by qualifying for France '98. The highlight was holding group winners Romania to a 1–1 draw, but they lost to England and Colombia and scored only once.

UGANDA

Federation of Uganda Football Associations
Founded: 1924
FIFA: 1959

ZAIRE

Fédération Zaïreoise de Football-Association
Founded: 1919
FIFA: 1964
African Nations Cup: 1968, 1974
Zaïre won their second African Nations Cup in 1974, the year in which they also became the first black African side to qualify for the World Cup finals. Since then, their best performances have been in the African Nations Cup.

ZAMBIA

Football Association of Zambia
Founded: 1929
FIFA: 1964
Zambia's national side have been semi-finalists in the African Nations Cup three times since 1974, and pulled off a remarkable victory over Italy in the 1988 Olympics in Seoul. The star was Kalusha Bwalya, who became a top professional with PSV in Holland.

Sadly, Zambia will always now be remembered for the plane crash in April 1993 which wiped out the entire national squad – bar the five overseas-based professionals who were not travelling with the rest to a World Cup qualifier in Senegal. Astonishingly, the Zambians rebuilt their squad around their five exports, and went on to reach the 1994 African Nations Cup Final. They only missed out on the World Cup finals after losing their last qualifying game 1–0 in Morocco. On the club front, Nkana Red Devils were runners-up in the 1990 Champions Cup, and Power Dynamos won the 1991 Cup-winners' Cup.

ZIMBABWE

Zimbabwe Football Association
Founded: 1950
FIFA: 1965
Zimbabwe won independence as recently as 1983 and have been making steady progress. They went within one game of reaching the 1994 World Cup finals, but lost the last group match 3–1 in Cameroon. English-based Bruce Grobbelaar and Peter Ndlovu were the key men.

HARARE'S HERO *Goalkeeper Bruce Grobbelaar savours victory, but Zimbabwe just missed World Cup qualification*

ASIA

Sheer geography makes Asia the most awkward of FIFA's regional confederations. The varied time zones and climates between Lebanon in the west, the former Soviet republics in the north, Japan in the east and India in the south long hindered the development of credible international tournaments.

A signal that Asian football has come of age was evident when FIFA awarded Japan and South Korean rights to – uniquely – co-host the 2002 World Cup finals. It will be the first time the game's top event has been staged in Asia.

Although it is probably many years away, the time will come when an Asian nation – whether it is a current power such as South Korea or Saudi Arabia, or a new force such as Japan or China – wins the World Cup.

AFGHANISTAN

The Football Federation of the National Olympic Committee
Founded: 1922
FIFA: 1948

BAHRAIN

Bahrain Football Association
Founded: 1951
FIFA: 1966

BANGLADESH

Bangladesh Football Federation
Founded: 1972
FIFA: 1974

BHUTAN

Bhutan Football Federation
Founded: 1960
FIFA: Associate member

BRUNEI

Brunei Amateur Football Association
Founded: 1959
FIFA: 1969

CAMBODIA

Federation Khmere De Football Association
Founded: 1933
FIFA: 1953

CHINA

Football Association of the People's Republic of China
Founded: 1924
FIFA: 1931–58, 1979
China took part in the first international match played on Asian soil, when they met the Philippines, in Manila, in February 1913, in the Far Eastern Games. But progress was thwarted because of the Taiwan issue. A side containing only Hong Kong players took part in the 1954 Asian Games, calling themselves China. The Chinese Association protested that they were the controlling body and subsequently withdrew from FIFA in 1958.

Despite being the most populous country on earth, success has utterly eluded China. Their greatest achievement to date is a runners-up spot in the 1984 Asian Cup.

Efforts to improve the game are now being made, with the launch of a professional league backed by multi-national sponsorship, but China are still some way short of their Asian rivals – as a disappointing first-round exit in the 1994 World Cup qualifiers illustrates. FIFA's desire to spread the game globally may give the Chinese an advantage here, and staging the game's premier event would provide a massive boost.

GUAM

Guam Soccer Association
Founded: 1975
FIFA: Associate member

HONG KONG

Hong Kong Football Association
Founded: 1914
FIFA: 1954
Football has been played in Hong Kong since the 1880s. The Hong Kong Shield – an early knock-out competition – was launched in 1896, a football association was founded in

1913 and affiliated to the Football Association in London a year later.

The sport reached its peak in the colony in the 1970s. The league's top clubs became fully professional and imported a string of veteran players from England and continental Europe. South China were one of the last clubs to turn pro, by which time sponsorship had arrived with powerful teams organized by the Seiko and Bulova corporations.

The national team competed regularly in international events over the past 20 years – having first entered the World Cup in vain in 1974 – and football independence was maintained even after the colony was handed back to China in 1997.

INDIA

All India Football Federation
Founded: 1937
FIFA: 1948
India's only successes at international level have come in the Asian Games, which they won in 1951 and 1962. They finished third at the 1956 Olympics, but since then the national side's record has been poor, despite massive enthusiasm for football in this huge heavily-populated country.

The annual Nehru Cup tournament, featuring guest European and South American national sides or selections, is a popular event, though India have never won it. The Calcutta League – the best in the country – is dominated by India's most famous clubs, Mohammedan Sporting, East Bengal and Mohun Bagan. Originally brought to India by the British in the late 1800s (the Gloucestershire Regiment were the first Calcutta champions), football is now rapidly gaining popularity in a country where cricket has always been the top sport.

INDONESIA

All Indonesia Football Federation
Founded: 1930
FIFA: 1952

IRAN

Football Federation of the Islamic Republic of Iran
Founded: 1920
FIFA: 1948
Asian Cup: 1968, 1972, 1976
Iran emerged as a major Asian power in the 1960s, and in the 1970s they were the continent's most successful side. They took a hat-trick of Asian Championships, in 1968, 1972 and 1976 (winning every game they played in the tournament over an eight-year period). won the gold medal at the 1974 Asian Games and qualified for the 1978 World Cup finals in Argentina, holding Scotland to a shock 1-1 draw.

They just missed out on qualification for USA '94, but set a new World Cup record by beating Maldives 17–0 in a qualifying match in June 1997 and ultimately made it to the finals in France. A 2-1 victory there in the politically-sensitive match against the USA was undoubtedly the highlight, along with the performances of impressive mid-

COMPETITIVE NEIGHBOURS *Iran (red shirts) and Iraq in World Cup action*

fielder Mehdi Mahdavikia.

Iranian teams have twice won the Asian Champions Cup – Taj Club in 1970 and Esteghlal SC in 1990.

IRAQ

Iraqi Football Association
Founded: 1948
FIFA: 1951

The 1970s witnessed a shift in the balance of power in Asian football towards the Arab states, and Iraq have been at the forefront of this movement. They won the Asian Games gold medal in 1982 and four years later qualified for the World Cup finals in Mexico, where they put up creditable performances.

Iraq have huge resources at their disposal, and this should ensure that the national side will remain strong for many years to come. Iraq were thrown out of FIFA and suspended from international football in 1991 because of the invasion of Kuwait, but have since been re-admitted to the international fold. They almost qualified for the 1994 World Cup finals. Iraq's most noted player was striker Ahmed Radhi.

JAPAN

The Football Association of Japan
Founded: 1921
FIFA: 1929–45, 1950
Asian Cup: 1992

Japan, who host the 2002 World Cup finals jointly with South Korea, were shaken by their team's poor performances at France '98.

The team has made incredible strides in recent years and has fanatical support. But three straight defeats and only one goal scored in the 1998 World Cup finals showed there is still some way to go before they can mix it with the world's top footballing nations.

Despite that, Japanese football is certainly growing. In 1993 the Japanese authorities launched an ambitious programme designed to put the country firmly on the international football map. The most spectacular "weapon" was a high-profile professional championship, the J League. Corporate-backed teams have used their wealth to attract

JAPANESE EXPORT *Kazu Miura starred in both the J. League and Serie A*

numerous star veterans, including England's Gary Lineker, Brazil's Zico, Italy's Toto Schillaci and Germany's Pierre Littbarski. The league has proved to be very successful with many teams drawing huge and fanatical crowds, and there is no doubt that Japan has the facilities to host a World Cup.

Whether they are good enough to make a challenge is a different matter. Japan almost qualified for the 1994 World Cup finals, only missing out when in the last minute of the match against Iraq, they conceded a soft equaliser. And, of course, they made it to France. But they will need to improve to make an impact in 2002.

JORDAN

Jordan Football Association
Founded: 1949
FIFA: 1958

KAZAKHSTAN

Football Association of the Republic of Kazakhstan
Founded: 1914
FIFA: 1994

KUWAIT

Kuwait Football Association
Founded: 1952
FIFA: 1962
Asian Cup: 1980

KYRGYZSTAN

Football Association of Kyrgyzstan
Founded: 1992
FIFA: 1994

LAOS

Fédération de Foot-Ball Lao
Founded: 1951
FIFA: 1952

LEBANON

Fédération Libanaise de Football
Founded: 1933
FIFA: 1935

MACAO

Associacao de Futebol de Macau
Founded: 1939
FIFA: 1976

MALAYSIA

Persuatuan Bolasepak Malaysia
Founded: 1933
FIFA: 1956

MALDIVES

Football Association of Maldives
Founded: 1983
FIFA: 1986

MYANMAR

Myanmar Football Federation
Founded: 1947
FIFA: 1947

NEPAL

All Nepal Football Association
Founded: 1951
FIFA: 1970

NORTH KOREA

Football Association of the Democratic People's Republic of Korea
Founded: 1945
FIFA: 1958

North Korea's national side has consistently lived in the shadow of more successful neighbours from the South, but in 1966 the North made headlines around the world. At the 1966 World Cup finals in England, the North Koreans stunned Italy in the first round, winning 1–0. Pak Do Ik will be remembered for ever as the man who scored the most famous goal in North Korean football history.

Then, in an incredible quarter-final against Portugal, the Koreans went 3–0 ahead after 22 minutes. But the dream faded almost as dramatically, as Portugal won 5–3.

North Korea has failed to qualify for the World Cup since then.

OMAN

Oman Football Association
Founded: 1978
FIFA: 1980

PAKISTAN

Pakistan Football Federation
Founded: 1948
FIFA: 1948

PALESTINE

Palestinian Football Federation
Founded: 1994
FIFA: 1995 (provisional member)

PHILIPPINES

Philippine Football Federation
Founded: 1907
FIFA: 1928

QATAR

Qatar Football Association
Founded: 1960
FIFA: 1970

SAUDI ARABIA

Saudi Arabian Football Federation
Founded: 1959
FIFA: 1959
Asian Cup: 1984, 1988, 1996
Saudi Arabia are one of the emergent nations of Asian football, and with untold oil-based wealth at their disposal, they could come to dominate the region's football as the Koreans and the Iranians have. Saudi's first honours came in the 1980s, when they won the 1984 and 1988 Asian Championships. The work continued with progress to the second round of the 1994 World Cup finals.

The Saudi Arabians are also developing their infrastructure and organization. Many foreign coaches have been employed and the magnificent King Fahd stadium in Riyadh is one of the best in the world.

They were the first hosts of the Intercontinental Cup in 1993 (a competition for the five continental champions), and the event is to become a regular event. They reached the 1998 World Cup finals, but finished bottom of their group, picking up only one point by drawing 2-2 with South Africa.

SINGAPORE

Football Association of Singapore
Founded: 1892
FIFA: 1952

SOUTH KOREA

Korea Football Association
Founded: 1928
FIFA: 1948
Asian Cup: 1956, 1960
South Korea has always been the strongest nation in Asian football, and they won the first two Asian Championship tournaments, in 1956 and 1960. Their World Cup record is also the best in Asia, with qualification comingt first in 1954 and then for the four most recent tournaments: 1986, 1990, 1994 and 1998.

In America they scored two late goals to snatch a draw with Spain in Dallas, then held Bolivia to a goal-less draw and almost embarrassed defending champions Germany before losing 3-2.

More recently, in France, they were disappointing, drawing with a poor Belgium side but being thrashed 5-0 by Holland and 3-1 by Mexico as they tumbled out in the first round.

Cha Bum Kun is probably South Korea's best-known player, having enjoyed a lengthy career in Germany's Bundesliga. In 1988 he helped Bayer Leverkusen win the UEFA Cup, scoring the crucial aggregate-levelling goal in the second leg of the final against Spain's Español.

In 1993, South Korea, decided to challenge front-runners Japan for the honour of becoming the first Asian hosts for the World Cup. Their competitive pedigree, plus positive memories of Seoul's staging of the 1988 Olympic Games, duly earned the Koreans joint hosting rights, with Japan in 2002.

SRI LANKA

Football Federation of Sri Lanka
Founded: 1939
FIFA: 1950

SYRIA

Association Arabe Syrienne de Football
Founded: 1936
FIFA: 1937

TAIWAN

Chinese Taipei Football Association
Founded: 1936
FIFA: 1954

TAJIKISTAN

Football Federation of Tajikistan
Founded: 1991
FIFA: 1994

THAILAND

Football Association of Thailand
Founded: 1916
FIFA: 1925

TURKMENISTAN

Football Federation of Turkmenistan
Founded: 1992
FIFA: 1994

UNITED ARAB EMIRATES

United Arab Emirates Football Association
Founded: 1971
FIFA: 1972
With only 25 registered clubs and 3,400 players, the United Arab Emirates caused a big surprise when they qualified for the 1990 World Cup finals. Brazilian coach Mario Zagalo led them in qualifying, but he was surprisingly sacked just prior to the tournament, and a Pole, Bernard Blaut, took over in Italy. The UAE were somewhat out of their depth in Italy and were beaten in all three of their first-round matches.

UZBEKISTAN

Football Federation of Uzbekistan
Founded: 1946
FIFA: 1994
Uzbekistan gained independence after the collapse of the Soviet Union. The federation gained immediate admittance into the Asian confederation which they stey stunned by winning the Asian Games title on their debut.

VIETNAM

Association de Football de la République du Vietnam
Founded: 1962
FIFA: 1964

YEMEN

Republic of Yemen Football Association
Founded: 1962
FIFA: 1980

ASIAN POWER *South Korea's 1986 World Cup finals team*

THE GREAT CLUBS

Professionalism swept through Britain in the 1880s and western Europe in the late 1920s. The big clubs of Spain, Italy, France and Portugal were importing star foreigners by the turn of the 1930s, but it was not until the mid-1950s that Belgium, Holland and then Germany caught up with full-time professionalism. When they did, the balance of the European game changed yet again.

The great traditions of football are kept alive, week in, week out, by the clubs. From Ajax in Holland to Vasco da Gama in Brazil, from Barcelona in Spain to Liverpool in England, they provide the first call of loyalty on the public. People who may never have attended a match in years still look out for the result of "their" club each week. Evidence of the depths of loyalty which certain clubs can inspire is widely available – from the way Real Madrid's fans came up with the money to fund the building of the Estadio Bernabeu in the 1940s to the proud boast from Portugal's Benfica of 122,000 members. Every club has its tales of the great days and great players, great managers and great victories. Some, like Manchester United, have been touched by tragedy, others, like Marseille, with controversy. The greatest, clearly, are those who have repeatedly proved their power and strength by lifting the continental club competitions in Europe and South America. Some of them are described here.

AJAX AMSTERDAM
HOLLAND

Founded: 1900
Stadium: Arena (50,000)
Colours: Red and white broad stripes/white
League: 26
Cup: 13
World Club Cup: 1972, 1995
European Cup: 1971, 1972, 1973, 1995
European Cup-winners' Cup: 1987
UEFA Cup: 1992
Supercup: 1972, 1973, 1995

Ajax, on beating Torino in the 1992 UEFA Cup Final, became only the second team after Italy's Juventus to have won all three European trophies and a full house of all seven titles on offer to clubs. The achievement was a popular one, bearing in mind the entertainment and style the Amsterdam club had consistently provided. The first hints of glory to come were in evidence in 1966–67 when, under former Dutch international Rinus Michels, Ajax thrashed Liverpool 5–1 in a European Cup tie. Two years later Ajax became the first Dutch side to reach the European Cup Final, though they lost 4–1 to Milan. In 1971 Ajax were back as winners, beating Panathinaikos 2–0 at Wembley. In the next two Finals, they beat Internazionale 2–0, then Juventus 1–0. Johan Cruyff was their inspiration.

Ajax's trademark was the "total football" system, which involved taking full advantage of a generation of skilled all-rounders whose versatility and football intelligence allowed bewildering changes of position. It was "The Whirl", as envisaged early in the 1950s by that football prophet, Willi Meisl. After the sale of Cruyff to Barcelona in 1973, Ajax fell away and it took his return, a decade later, as technical director, to propel them back to the peaks of the European game. Under Cruyff, the new Ajax generation won the

FINNISHED ARTICLE *Ajax's Jari Litmanen*

Great Managers

Marinus "Rinus" Michels

Coach of Ajax Amsterdam (Holland), Barcelona (Spain), Los Angeles Aztecs (US), Bayer Leverkusen (Germany); also Holland national team (born February 9, 1928)

Michels, a Dutch international centre-forward in the early 1950s, led a revolution in the late 1960s when he developed the "total football" philosophy at Ajax. Much of Michels's coaching career with Ajax was linked with the presence, as leader on the pitch, of Johan Cruyff. Michels went to Barcelona after winning the European Cup with Ajax in 1971, went back to Ajax to sign Cruyff and the pair were partners again when Holland finished runners-up at the 1974 World Cup. "Iron Rinus" was never afraid to take tactical risks, such as when he guided Holland to European Championship success in 1988 by using Ruud Gullit as a static, right-side attacker. Nor was Michels ever afraid of stating his opinions, however blunt.

Cup-winners' Cup in 1987 – his friend and pupil Marco Van Basten scoring the goal which beat Lokomotive Leipzig in the Final in Athens. Cruyff's successor Louis Van Gaal then secured the UEFA Cup five years later. Despite continuing to sell many of their best players, Ajax's 1994–95 squad was statistically their best ever; the team won the League championship without losing a game, and the European Cup for the fourth time. Injury problems foiled their bid for a fifth Cup the following season when Ajax lost on penalties to Juventus after a 1–1 draw in Rome.

ANDERLECHT
BRUSSELS, BELGIUM

Founded: 1908
Stadium: Constant Vanden Stock/Parc Astrid (28,063)
Colours: White with mauve/white
League: 23
Cup: 7
European Cup-winners' Cup: 1976, 1978
UEFA Cup: 1983
Supercup: 1976, 1978

Anderlecht's international debut was not a happy one: they crashed 10–0 and 12–0 on aggregate to Manchester United in an early European Cup. Since then, however, the Royal Sporting Club have earned respect far and wide for their domestic domination and an international outlook which has brought success in both the European Cup-winners' Cup and the UEFA Cup. Much credit reflects on the coaching work of Englishman Bill Gormlie, a former Blackburn goalkeeper, who helped lay the foundations for success in the late 1940s and early 1950s. Equally important was the financial power of the millionaire brewer, Constant Vanden Stock. Before his take-over Anderlecht relied mainly on homegrown talent like Paul Van Himst, the greatest Belgian footballer of all time. As Anderlecht's prestige grew, particularly thanks to the European Cup competitions, they were able to compete in the international transfer market. A significant coaching influence, in the early 1960s, was Frenchman Pierre Sinibaldi, who perfected a tactical formation which relied on a flat back four, the offside trap, and possession football in midfield. It worked well against almost all opposition except British clubs, whose more direct style constantly caught the defenders on the turn. Thus, the first time Anderlecht reached a European final – in the Fairs Cup in 1970 – they were beaten by Arsenal. European success, in the Cup-winners' Cup in 1976 and 1978, had to await the more pragmatic coaching approach of Dutchman Wiel Corver and Belgian Raymond Goethals. Later, with Van Himst having returned as coach, Anderlecht won the UEFA Cup and in Enzo Scifo produced the finest Belgian player since Van Himst himself.

ENZO SCIFO *Anderlecht discovery, and the finest Belgian player of recent years*

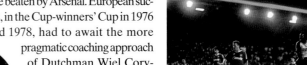

ARSENAL
LONDON, ENGLAND

Founded: 1886
Stadium: Highbury (38,500)
Colours: Red/white
League: 10
Cup: 6
European Cup-winners's Cup: 1994
Fairs Cup: 1970

Arsenal, today a North London club, had their origins south of the Thames, at the Woolwich Arsenal. The club turned professional in 1891 and entered the Football League a year later, reaching the First Division in 1904 and the FA Cup semi-finals in 1906. After the First World War they moved to Highbury, and appointed the legendary Herbert Chapman as manager in 1925.

Chapman had a flair for publicity, an innovative approach to tactics and a talent for motivation. He spent heavily but wisely on the likes of first Charlie Buchan and Alex James, introduced the stopper centre-half and created the all-conquering outfit which won the League five times in the 1930s and the FA Cup twice. Arsenal won the League twice more and the FA Cup once in the eight years after the war. A 17-year hiatus then followed before the Gunners ended their longest trophy drought by winning the Fairs Cup.

A year later, manager Bertie Mee celebrated a historic league and cup "double". Classy midfielder George Graham later returned as manager, master-minding a string of successes in the League, FA Cup, League Cup and Cup-winners' Cup, but his reign ended abruptly in 1995 amid controversy over transfer "bungs".

French manager Arsene Wenger arrived from Japan and turned the Gunners into a multi-national attacking side with flair, winning the "double" in his first full season.

ATLETICO MADRID
SPAIN

Founded: 1903
Stadium: Vicente Calderon/Manzanares (62,000)
Colours: Red and white stripes/blue
League: 9
Cup: 9
World Club Cup: 1974
European Cup-winners' Cup: 1962

Atletico Madrid have always existed in the shadow of neighbours Real, but they still rank among the Big Three of Spanish football and boast a proud record at international level. Not that life has always been easy. In the late 1930s, after the Spanish Civil War, it took a merger with the Air Force club to keep Atletico in business; in 1959, they just failed to reach the European Cup Final when Real beat them in a semi-final play-off; in the early 1960s they had to share Real's Estadio Bernabeu, because Atletico's Metropolitano had been sold to developers before the club's new stadium could be completed. European glory did come to Atletico in the shape of the Cup-winners' Cup in 1962 and was a well-deserved prize for players such as inside-left Joaquin Peiro and his wing partner Enrique Collar. But it was not until the early 1970s that Atletico put together a comparable team, thanks to the purchases of Argentines Ruben Hugo Ayala and Ramon Heredia. In 1974, Atletico secured that elusive place in the European Cup Final. But, after taking the lead against Bayern Munich in extra time, Atletico conceded a last-kick equalizer.

Consolation for their 4–0 defeat in the replay came with the opportunity to substitute for reluctant Bayern in the World Club Cup against Independiente of Argentina. By the time the tie came around Atletico had appointed as coach Luis Aragones, the midfielder who had scored their goal in the European Cup Final against Bayern. Atletico duly beat Independiente 1–0 and were, for a year at least, on top of the world. In the late 1980s the club was taken over by the extrovert builder Jesus Gil. He pumped millions of pounds into the club but generated more bad publicity than good, hiring and

KINGMAKER *Atletico Madrid's president Jesus Gil finally enjoyed success in 1996*

firing coaches at a breathtaking rate. It all came together in dramatic fashion when Atletico won the league and cup "double" in the spring of 1996.

ATLETICO NACIONAL
MEDELLIN, COLOMBIA

Founded: 1938
Stadium: Atanasio Giradot (35,000)
Colours: Green and white stripes/white
League: 5
South American Club Cup: 1989
Inter-American Cup: 1989

Atletico Nacional of Medellin are not the most famous club to come out of Colombia. That honour will always belong to Millonarios, who led the professional, pirate revolution in the early 1950s. But Nacional earned a place in history by becoming the first club to take the Copa Libertadores, the South American Club Cup, across the Andes to the western side of the continent. Nacional, who provided the base of the Colombian World Cup team in 1990, were in 1954 the first champions of Colombia after the rapprochement with FIFA. Yet it was not until 1971 that they made their debut in the South American Club Cup under Argentine coach Osvaldo Zubeldia. He had earned a fearsome reputation as boss of the rugged Estudiantes de La Plata team which had dominated Argentine and South American club football in the late 1960s. However, without resorting to the cynicism which made Estudiantes hated, he turned Nacional into Colombian champions three times in the mid-1970s and early 1980s. Zubeldia was followed by Luis Cubilla, at

whose suggestion, in 1986, Nacional appointed a former stalwart central defender, Francisco Maturana, as boss. In 1987 and 1988 they finished championship runners-up and then, in 1989, seized the South American club crown. Unfortunately, their preparations for the world club showdown with Milan were wrecked when the government halted the league season because of the increasing violence being engendered on the fringes of the game by the drug and betting cartels. Nacional did not emerge with their reputation unscathed. It was not only that Medellin was the centre of the drugs trade; several Nacional players were friends of the notorious drugs baron Pablo Escobar. Indeed, when Escobar was eventually killed in 1993 by security forces, at his funeral the coffin was draped in a Nacional flag.

BARCELONA
SPAIN

Founded: 1899
Stadium: Nou Camp (115,000)
Colours: Blue and red stripes/blue
League: 16
Cup: 24
European Cup: 1992
European Cup-winners' Cup: 1979, 1982, 1989, 1997
Fairs Cup: 1958, 1960, 1966
Supercup: 1992

Barcelona finally ended a duel with destiny when, in 1992, they beat Sampdoria 1–0 at Wembley to win the European Cup. It was a case of third time lucky, for the greatest prize in the European club game had twice eluded them at the final hurdle. Barcelona had been the first winners of the Inter-Cities Fairs Cup and had won the Cup-winners' Cup three times. But their European Cup campaigns seemed to have been jinxed. First, in 1961, when Barcelona had apparently achieved the hard part by eliminating the title-holders and their bitter rivals Real Madrid, they lost to Benfica in the Final in Berne. Barcelona hit the woodwork three times, yet lost 3–2 against the run of play. Great players such as Luis Suarez, Ladislav Kubala, Sandor Kocsis and Zoltan Czibor had everything on their side except luck.

Great Managers

HELENIO HERRERA

Coach of Red Star Paris, Stade Francais (France), Atletico Madrid, Valladolid, Sevilla (Spain), Belenenses (Portugal), Barcelona (Spain), Internazionale and Roma (Italy); also Spanish and Italian national teams (born April 17, 1916)

One of the world's most innovative and single-minded coaches. Herrera, born in Argentina, brought up in Morocco and a player in France, experimented at Barcelona in the 1950s by using inside-forwards at wing-half to turn "easy" matches into goal sprees. His attacking tactics proved ineffective at Inter so Herrera developed, instead, the most ruthlessly disciplined catenaccio. Herrera demanded total obedience, insisting that his players place their hands on the ball and swear loyalty to each other before going out for a match. Stars who baulked at such rituals were sold, however popular or successful. Inter won the World and European Cups twice each before Herrera's career went into decline at Roma.

NO LOVE LOST *Jürgen Klinsmann (right) shoots for goal in Bayern Munich's UEFA Cup semi-final victory over Spain's Barcelona – one year earlier, the beaten defender, Gica Popescu, had been Klinsmann's team-mate at Tottenham*

IMPORT DUTY *Portugal's Luis Figo was one of the more recent of Barcelona's foreign acquisitions*

History repeated itself in even more galling circumstances in 1986. Barcelona, coached by Terry Venables and gambling on the fitness of long-time injured Steve Archibald, faced Steaua Bucharest in Seville. Barcelona lost in a penalty shoot-out after a goal-less draw.

It took the return of 1970s inspiration Johan Cruyff, this time as coach, to steer a new generation of international stars – including Ronald Koeman, Hristo Stoichkov and Michael Laudrup – to victory long overdue for one of the world's biggest clubs. Barcelona's 1994 league title was their fourth in a row, the last three of them achieved in the closing moments of the final day, twice at the expense of great rivals Real Madrid.

Failure to win a trophy in 1995 or 1996, however, resulted in Cruyff's dismissal after eight years in charge. He was replaced by Bobby Robson.

BAYERN MUNICH
GERMANY

Founded: 1900
Stadium: Olimpiastadion (69,261)
Colours: All red
League: 15
Cup: 8
World Club Cup: 1976
European Cup: 1974, 1975, 1976
European Cup-winners' Cup: 1967
UEFA Cup: 1996

Bayern are Germany's most glamorous club, even though high tax rates mean they have never been able to hold stars tempted by the rich pickings of Italy. In the 1980s Bayern became almost an Italian nursery as they lost Karl-Heinz Rummenigge, Andy Brehme and Lothar Matthäus to Internazionale and Stefan Reuter and Jurgen Kohler to Juventus. All this transfer activity underlined the fact that the Bayern success story is – with the exception of one championship in 1932 and one cup in 1957 – a relatively recent affair. The identities of the men who secured all the glittering titles read like a Who's Who of the world game: Franz Beckenbauer, Gerd Müller, Sepp Maier, Paul Breitner, Rummenigge and Matthäus. The German championship was originally organized in regional leagues, with the winners playing off at the end of each season for the title: only once in the pre-war years did Bayern win all the way through. That was in 1932, when they defeated Eintracht Frankfurt 2–0. Not until 1957, and a 1–0 win over Fortuna Düsseldorf in the cup final, did Bayern have anything more to celebrate. Indeed their record was so mediocre that they were not included in the inaugural Bundesliga in 1963–64. But, a year later, Bayern won promotion; in 1966 they won the cup, and in 1967 they secured the European Cup-winners' Cup, thanks to an extra-time victory over Rangers. That was the team led and inspired by Beckenbauer in the role of attacking sweeper, with Maier in goal and Müller up front. All three stars shone even more brightly as Bayern landed a European Cup hat-trick in the mid-1970s. In the 1980s Bayern were twice European Cup runners-up, but complacency set in and it was not until Beckenbauer returned – first as vice-president, then coach, then president – that Bayern regained their pre-eminence. Their 1996 UEFA Cup triumph made Bayern the fourth club to win all three European trophies.

BENFICA
LISBON, PORTUGAL

Founded: 1904
Stadium: Estadio do Benfica/Da Luz (92,385)
Colours: Red/white
League: 29
Cup: 26
European Cup: 1961, 1962

Benfica are a national institution with their huge stadium – rated as 130,000 before recent security constraints – and 122,000 membership. Living up to the standards of history is what Benfica believe they owe Cosme Damiao who, on February 28, 1904, organized the first recorded local game of futebol on a patch of Lisbon wasteland. The next day he formed his "team" into a club named Sport Lisboa and, two years later was instrumental in arranging a merger with neighbours Sport Clube de Benfica. In the early years it was cycling which brought the club its first prizes. From the launch of a unified Portuguese championship in the late 1920s, Benfica lorded it over Portuguese sport. In due course, Benfica set their sights on international glory and, in 1950, won the Latin Cup – a forerunner of the European Cup. English manager Ted Smith laid the foundations of a team which would dominate not only Portugal but then Europe.

In 1954 Benfica followed the example being set in Spain and built a vast new stadium. An exiled Hungarian named Bela Guttman became coach, and his team filled the new stadium as Benfica twice swept to success in the European Cup in 1961 and 1962. First they beat Barcelona, amid intense drama, by 3–2 in Berne, then Real Madrid 5–3 in Amsterdam. On both occasions Benfica were captained by their veteran centre-forward, José Aguas. They also introduced one of the most famous Portuguese footballers of all time in Eusebio, greatest of the many fine players Benfica had discovered in the Portuguese colonies of Angola and Mozambique. Benfica's boast of only "Portuguese" (including colonial) players was scrapped in the mid-1970s, when the African colonies were cast adrift. Now they hunt Brazilians, Slavs and Danes with the rest.

BOCA JUNIORS
BUENOS AIRES, ARGENTINA

Founded: 1905
Stadium: Bombonera (58,740)
Colours: Blue with yellow hoop/blue
League: 19
World Club Cup: 1977
South American Club Cup: 1977, 1978
South American Supercup: 1989
Inter-American Cup: 1989

Boca are one of the two great clubs in the Argentine capital of Buenos Aires, along with old rivals River Plate. They were founded by an Irishman named Patrick MacCarthy and a group of newly-arrived Italian immigrants. They joined the league in 1913 and were immediately caught up in a domestic football "war" which saw two championships being organized for most of the 1920s and early 1930s. Boca bestrode the two eras. They won the last Argentine amateur championship in 1930 and the first unified professional one the following year. Two more titles followed in the next four years, thanks to some fine players, including the great Brazilian defender, Domingos da Guia. In the 1940s and 1950s Boca slipped into River Plate's shadow, re-emerging in 1963 when a team fired by the goals of José Sanfilippo reached the Final of the South American Club Cup.

Winning the title, however, would have to wait until the late 1970s. Then they reached the Final three years in a row – beating Brazil's Cruzeiro in 1977 and Deportivo Cali of Colombia in 1978 before losing to Olimpia of Paraguay in 1979. Boca's rugged style, under Juan Carlos Lorenzo, proved controversial. Not one Boca player figured in the squad which won the 1978 World Cup. But Boca had already secured their own world crown, beating West Germany's Borussia Mönchengladbach in the World Club Cup in 1977. Boca rebuilt their team around Diego Maradona in 1981, but had added few prizes to their trophy room when he rejoined them in 1995.

CELTIC
GLASGOW, SCOTLAND

Founded: 1888
Stadium: Celtic Park (51,709)
Colours: Green and white hoops/white
League: 35
Cup: 30
European Cup: 1967

SCANDINAVIAN STYLE *Henrik Larsson has brought a touch of flair to Celtic Park*

Celtic and old rivals Rangers are Scottish football's greatest clubs, but it was Celtic who first extended that hunger for success into Europe when, in 1967, they became the first British club to win the European Cup. It was a measure of the way they swept all before them that season that they won every domestic competition as well: the League, the Cup and League Cup. No other team in Europe had, until then, ended the season with a 100 per cent record in four major competitions. In winning the European Cup Celtic refuted accusations – mostly from England – that their Scottish honours owed more to a lack of solid opposition than their own abilities. Celtic's 1967 team was shrewdly put together by manager Jock Stein, a former Celtic player. As well as new Scottish stars he included veterans such as goal-keeper Ronnie Simpson and scheming inside-left Bertie Auld. In the Lisbon Final they beat former holders Internazionale 2–1 with goals from full-back Gemmell and centre-forward Chalmers.

Sadly, Celtic's golden touch did not survive long. A few months later they were beaten by Kiev Dynamo right at the start of their European Cup defence, and were then dragged down to defeat and fisticuffs in the infamous World Club Cup battle with Racing of Argentina. In 1970 Celtic returned to the European Cup Final, only to lose to Feyenoord in Milan; and, two years later, they lost only on penalties after two goal-less draws in the semi-finals against Inter. More trouble lay ahead as Celtic proved unable to match Rangers' commercial and playing example in the late 1980s and slipped to the brink of bankruptcy before turning the corner after a boardroom revolution.

COLO COLO
SANTIAGO, CHILE

Founded: 1925
Stadium: Colo Colo (50,000)
Colours: White/black
League: 19
South American Recopa: 1991

Colo Colo, Chilean nickname for a wildcat, were founded by five angry members of the old Magallanes FC. Even though Chilean football is gen-erally held to lag far behind that of traditional giants Brazil, Argentina and Uruguay, Colo Colo have an enviable reputation throughout the continent. The club's vision has always stretched beyond the Andes. Such a tradition was laid down by David Orellano. He was a founder member of Colo Colo and one of the five Magallanes rebels who dis-agreed over the choice of a new club captain. The choice of the five fell upon Orellano and, within two years of Colo Colo's foundation, they had sent a team off to tour Spain and Portugal. In 1933 Colo Colo were among the founders of a professional league; in 1941 they set another pio-neering trend by introducing a for-

eign coach in the Hungarian, Fer-enc Platko; and in 1948 they orga-nized a South American club tournament which can now be seen as a fore-runner of the Copa Lib-ertadores, the official South American Club Cup launched in 1960. Record league winners in Chile and the supreme transfer destination for most domestic players, Colo Colo's greatest achievement was in reaching the 1973 South American Club Cup Final. The teams drew 1–1 in Avellaneda and 0–0 in Santiago, and thus went on to a play-off in Mon-tevideo, which Independiente won 2–1 in extra time. Colo Colo's con-solation goal was scored by their most famous and popular player of the modern era, Carlos Caszely.

EINTRACHT FRANKFURT
GERMANY

Founded: 1899
Stadium: Waldstadion (61,146)
Colours: Black and red stripes/black
League: 1
Cup: 4
UEFA Cup: 1980

Eintracht Frankfurt occupy a very spe-cial place in football legend as the team Real Madrid beat in the European Cup Final at Hampden back in 1960. The score was 7–3 to Madrid, but Frankfurt were far from crushed and had proved their class by putting six goals past Glasgow Rangers – both home and away – in the semi-finals. Frankfurt's team was built on the midfield strength of Dieter Stinka and Jurgen Lindner, plus the creative talents of veteran inside-left Alfred Pfaff and right-winger Richard Kress. It may sound odd to suggest that everything after a defeat was an anti-climax, but though Frankfurt were founder members of the West Ger-man Bundesliga in 1963, they have

achieved comparatively little.

Boardroom problems in the mid-1980s dogged the club until the busi-nessman Matthias Ohms took over and appointed Bernd Holzenbein, a World Cup winner in 1974 and an old Frankfurt favourite, as his execu-tive vice-president. Holzenbein put Frankfurt back on a sound financial footing and bought stars such as mid-fielder Andy Möller (later sold to Juventus) and the brilliant Ghanaian striker, Anthony Yeboah. In 1992–93 they were pipped for the league title after the controversial mid-season departure of charismatic Yugoslav coach, Dragoslav Stepanovic. His successor Jupp Heynckes did not last long either, after falling out with Yeboah who was allowed to depart for English club Leeds, leaving Frankfurt to sink towards a first-ever relegation.

Frankfurt's one European suc-cess over the years was in winning the UEFA Cup in 1980. Frankfurt beat their fellow Germans, Borussia Mönchengladbach, on the away goals rule in the Final, losing 3–2 away and then winning 1–0 back in the Waldstadion. Holzenbein had him-self scored the all-important second away goal in the first leg.

FEYENOORD
ROTTERDAM, HOLLAND

Founded: 1908
Stadium: De Kuyp (52,000)
Colours: Red and white halves/black
League: 14
Cup: 10
World Club Cup: 1970
European Cup: 1970
UEFA Cup: 1974

Feyenoord were founded by min-ing entrepreneur C. R. J. Kieboom. Their star player in the successful pre-war years was left-half Puck Van Heel, who appeared in the final tour-naments of both the 1934 and 1938 World Cups and set what was for many years a Dutch record of 64 international appearances. The post-war years were bleak until after the introduction of professionalism in the late 1950s. Then Feyenoord entered their most glorious domes-tic era, winning the league title six times in 13 years. Indeed, their 1965 and 1969 successes brought them league and cup "doubles". Stars included goalkeeper Eddie Pieters-Graafland, a then record £20,000 signing from Ajax, half-backs Reinier Kreyermaat, Hans Kraay and Jan Klaasens and, above all, outside-left Coen Mouljin. He was still a key fig-ure when they won the European Cup in 1970, along with Swedish striker Ove Kindvall and burly mid-field general Wim Van Hanegem. Feyenoord's coach, for their extra time victory over Celtic in Milan, was Ernst Happel, the former Austrian international. Feyenoord – and not Ajax – were thus the first Dutch club to break through to European suc-cess, and they went on to defeat Estudiantes de La Plata of Argenti-na in the World Club Cup Final.

In 1974, with Van Hanegem pulling the strings in midfield, Feyenoord added the UEFA Cup to their trophy room. But, as time went on, they lost their grip on the Dutch game. Star players had to be sold to balance the books, among them Ruud Gullit, whom Feyenoord had discovered with Haarlem. He was sold to PSV Eindhoven and, later, of course, moved on to Milan. Not until the arrival as general manager of

Wim Jansen, a former Feyenoord star who starred with Holland at the 1974 World Cup, did Feyenoord pull themselves back together and regain the league title in 1993.

FK AUSTRIA
VIENNA, AUSTRIA

Founded: 1911
Stadium: Horr (10,500) / Prater (62,270)
Colours: White with mauve/white
League: 21
Cup: 21

The history of the Fussball Klub Austria-Memphis began with a game of cricket. Just as the English exported their industrial know-how and educational skills around the world in the latter half of the nineteenth century, they also took with them their newly codified games and sports. Thus the Vienna Cricket and Football Club was founded by the expatriate community in the 1890s. Cricket did not gain universal acceptance, but football was another matter, and November 15, 1894 saw the first proper football match ever staged in Austria. The Vienna Cricket and Football Club beat 1st Vienna FC by 4–0 – and they have been winning matches and titles ever since.

Changing their name in 1925, FKA notched up many domestic honours in a list which includes runners-up spot in the European Cup-winners' Cup in 1978, when a team inspired by midfield general Herbert Prohaska became the first Austrian side to reach a modern-day European final. That was long overdue since, in the late 1920s, FK Austria were one of the pioneers of European international club soccer when the Mitropa Cup drew clubs from Austria, Czechoslovakia, Hungary, Yugoslavia, Switzerland and Italy. FK Austria were triumphant in 1933 and 1936, inspired by the legendary centre-forward Matthias Sindelar. Their delicate style of play, known as the "Vienna School", was modelled on the old Scottish close-passing game and had been taught them by Englishman Jimmy Hogan. His coaching genius contributed mightily to the development of the so-called "Wunderteam" which lost unluckily to England, by 4–3, at

GIVING CHASE *Gaston Taument (right, behind Vitesse Arnhem's Philip Cocu) is one of Feyenoord's rising young stars*

Stamford Bridge in 1932 and then reached the semi-finals of the 1934 World Cup. The backbone of the Wunderteam was provided by FK Austria. That tradition has been maintained ever since. Thus no fewer than six FKA stars travelled with the national squad to the 1990 World Cup Finals in Italy.

FLAMENGO
RIO DE JANEIRO, BRAZIL

Founded: 1895 as sailing club; 1911 as football club
Stadium: Gavea (20,000) and Maracana (130,000)
Colours: Black and red hoops/white
Rio state league: 22
Brazil championship (incl. Torneo Rio-São Paulo): 5
World Club Cup: 1981
South American Club Cup: 1981

Flamengo are the most popular club in Brazil, having been formed by dissident members of the Fluminense club but under the umbrella of the Flamengo sailing club – which now boasts more than 70,000 members. They first competed in the Rio league in 1912, winning the title two years later. In 1915 they regained the crown without having lost a game. A string of great names have graced the red-and-black hoops over the years, among them defenders Domingos Da Guia and the legendary centre-forward Leonidas da Silva. Known as the "Black Diamond", Leonidas played for Flamengo from 1936 to 1942, inspiring two state championship triumphs and earning a worldwide reputation through his brilliance in the 1938 World Cup finals in France.

Flamengo ran up a Rio state hat-trick in the mid-1950s with their team nicknamed the "Steamroller", but had to wait until 1981 for their greatest success. Then, riding high on the goals of a new hero, Zico – the so-called "White Pele" – they won both the South American and World Club Cups. The South American Club Cup campaign was one of the most hostile in memory. Flamengo won a first round play-off against Atletico Mineiro after their rival Brazilians had five players sent off, provoking referee José Roberto Wright to aban-

don the game. In the Final, Flamengo beat Cobreloa of Chile in a play-off in Montevideo which saw the expulsion of five players. Fears about the outcome of Flamengo's world showdown against Liverpool proved unfounded. Zico was in a class of his own. Liverpool could not touch him as he created all of Flamengo's goals in a 3–0 win. The players dedicated the success to the memory of Claudio Coutinho, a former coach who had died in a skin-diving accident. In the mid-1990s, Flamengo sought to revive the glory days by signing World Cup-winning striker Romario from Spain's Barcelona.

FLUMINENSE
RIO DE JANEIRO, BRAZIL

Founded: 1902
Stadium: Laranjeira (20,000) and Maracana (130,000)
Colours: Red, green and white stripes/white
Rio state league: 27
Brazil championship (incl. Torneo Rio-São Paulo): 4

Fluminense have yet to win an international trophy, but that does not alter their status as one of South America's great clubs. "Flu" were founded in 1902 by an Englishman named Arthur Cox, and many of their first players were British residents. The club's wealth and upper-class clientele resulted in the nickname "Po de Arroz" ("Face Powder", after the fashion of the time at the turn of the century). Today the club's fans wear white powder on their faces as a sign of loyalty. In 1905 Flu were founder members of the Rio de Janeiro league and of the Brazilian confederation; they won the first four Rio (Carioca) championships in 1906–09; and, in 1932, Flu became the first Brazilian club to go professional.

By this time the "Flu-Fla" derby (against Flamengo) had been flourishing for 20 years, the first meeting between the clubs having taken place in 1912. In 1963 their clash drew an official crowd of 177,656 to the Maracana stadium in Rio, which remains a world record for a club game. By 1930 Flu's stadium was the home of the national team and the club had launched a weekly newspaper, among other schemes. A few years later and Flu were ruling the roost with five Rio titles between 1936 and 1941. Star players were forwards Romeu, Carreiro and Tim – who coached Peru at the 1978 World Cup finals. In the early 1950s Fluminense's star was the World Cup winning midfield general Didi.

In the late 1960s and early 1970s the key player was another World Cup winner, Brazil's 1970 captain and right-back, Carlos Alberto Torres. In the 1980s the mantle of inspiration-in-chief passed to the Paraguayan Romerito (Julio César Romero). Fluminense won a hat-trick of Rio titles in 1983, 1984 and 1985 with Romero their guiding light. He was rewarded by being nominated as South American Footballer of the Year in 1985 and later starred at the 1986 World Cup finals.

HAMBURG
GERMANY

Founded: 1887
Stadium: Volksparkstadion (61,234)
Colours: White/red
League: 6
Cup: 3
European Cup: 1983
European Cup-winners' Cup: 1977

Hamburg can be considered by many to be the oldest league club in Germany, if one takes as their foundation date that of SC Germania, the oldest of three clubs which later amalgamated. The other two were Hamburger FC (1888) and FC Falke (1905). Hamburg's tradition, from that day to this, has been one of attacking football. The first major trophy

ROMERITO *Fluminense's midfield general scoring for Paraguay against Chile in a World Cup qualifying tie in Santiago*

KEVIN KEEGAN *European Footballer of the Year with Hamburg in 1978 and 1979*

could have been theirs in 1922. But when the championship play-off was abandoned because injury-hit Nürnberg had only seven men left on the pitch, Hamburg sportingly declined to accept the title. A year later Hamburg did win the championship, and again in 1928.

They did not win it again until 1960, by which time they were being led by the greatest footballer in the club's history. Centre-forward Uwe Seeler, son of a former Hamburg player, was four times Hamburg's top scorer in the old regional league system, and after the creation of the Bundesliga was on one occasion the country's leading marksman. He also spearheaded Hamburg's thrilling 1960–61 European Cup campaign, in which they lost to Barcelona only in a play-off in the semi-finals. Seeler went on to captain West Germany in their brave World Cup efforts of 1966 and 1970, but he had retired by the time Hamburg achieved a European breakthrough and won the Cup-winners' Cup in 1977. Hamburg beat defending cup-holders Anderlecht of Belgium 2–0 in a final which was the big-occasion debuts of two long-serving internationals, defender Manni Kaltz and midfield general Felix Magath.

Both were stalwarts of the side beaten by Nottingham Forest in the 1980 European Cup Final, when Englishman Kevin Keegan tried in vain to stimulate the Hamburg attack. Keegan had returned to England by the time Hamburg beat Juventus in Athens three years later.

After a decade in the doldrums Uwe Seeler returned as president and Hamburg ended the 1995–96 German season in fifth position, their best placing for six years.

INDEPENDIENTE
AVELLANEDA, ARGENTINA

Founded: 1904
Stadium: Cordero (55,000)
Colours: Red/blue
League: 11
World Club Cup: 1973, 1984
South American Club Cup: 1964, 1965, 1972, 1973, 1974, 1975, 1984
Inter-American Cup: 1973, 1974, 1976

Independiente are perhaps the least familiar of international club football's great achievers, outside Argentina at least. This is because, despite two lengthy periods of command in South American club football, they won the world title only twice in five attempts, and that at a time when the competition's image was tarnished.

Also, Independiente have always relied on team football rather than superstar inspiration. One outstanding player who made his name with the club, however, was Raimundo Orsi. He was the left-winger who played for Argentina in the 1928 Olympics, signed for Juventus, and then scored Italy's vital equalizer on their way to victory over Czechoslovakia in the 1934 World Cup Final. Later, the Independiente fans had the great Paraguayan centre-forward, Arsenio Erico, to idolize. Erico had been the boyhood hero of Alfredo Di Stefano and, in 1937, set an Argentine First Division goalscoring

record of 37 in a season.

Independiente did not regain prominence until the early 1960s, when coach Manuel Giudice imported an Italian-style catenaccio defence which secured the South American Club Cup in both 1964 and 1965. Independiente were the first Argentine team to win the continent's top club prize. But in the World Club Cup Final they fell both years to the high priests of catenaccio, Internazionale of Italy.

In the 1970s Independiente's Red Devils won the South American Club Cup four times in a row and collected the World Club Cup. It was an odd victory: European champions Hamburg declined to compete, so runners-up Juventus took their place – on condition that the Final was a one-off match in Italy. Independiente not only agreed, they won it with a single goal from midfield general Ricardo Bochini.

INTERNAZIONALE
MILAN, ITALY

Founded: 1908
Stadium: Meazza (85,443)
Colours: Blue and black stripes/black
League: 13
Cup: 3
World Club Cup: 1964, 1965
European Cup: 1964, 1965
UEFA Cup: 1991, 1994

Internazionale were founded out of an argument within the Milan club in the early years of the century. Some 45 members, led by committee man Giovanni Paramithiotti, broke away in protest at the authoritarian way the powerful Camperio brothers were running the club. That was not the end of the politics, however. In the 1930s, fascist laws forced Internazionale into a name change to rid the club of the foreign associations of their title. So they took the name of the city of Milan's patron saint and became Ambrosiana. Under this title they led the way in continental club competition – being one of the leading lights in the pre-war Mitropa Cup.

After the war, the club reverted to the Internazionale name and pioneered a tactical revolution. First manager Alfredo Foni, who had been a World Cup-winning full-back before the war, won the league title twice by withdrawing outside-right Gino Armani into midfield; then Helenio Herrera conquered Italy, Europe and the world with catenaccio. Goalkeeper Giuliano Sarti, sweeper Armando Picchi and man-marking backs Tarcisio Burgnich, Aristide Guarneri and Giacinto Facchetti were as near watertight as possible. They were

MATTHÄUS *Internazionale's driving force and Germany's World Cup captain in 1990*

the foundation on which Spanish general Luis Suarez constructed the counter-attacking raids carried forward by Brazil's Jair da Costa, Spain's Joaquim Peiro and Italy's own Sandro Mazzola. Inter won the European and World Club Cups in both 1964 and 1965 – beating Real Madrid and Benfica in Europe, and Argentina's Independiente twice for the world crown. But even they could not soak up pressure indefinitely. In 1966 Real Madrid toppled Inter in the European Cup semi-finals, Celtic repeated the trick a year later in a memorable Lisbon final, and Herrera was lured away to Roma. Not until the late 1980s could Inter recapture their international and domestic allure, when West German midfielder Lothar Matthäus drove them to the 1989 league title, following up with success in the 1991 UEFA Cup.

JUVENTUS
TURIN, ITALY

Founded: 1897
Stadium: Delle Alpi (71,012)
Colours: Black and white stripes/white
League: 24
Cup: 10
World Club Cup: 1985, 1996
European Cup: 1985, 1996
European Cup-winners' Cup: 1984
UEFA Cup: 1977, 1990, 1993
Supercup: 1984, 1996

Juventus were founded by a group of Italian students who decided to adopt red as the colour for their shirts. In 1903, however, when the club was six years old, one of the committee members was so impressed on a trip to England by Notts County's black-and-white stripes that he bought a set of shirts to take home to Turin. In the 1930s Juventus laid the foundations for their legend, winning the Italian league championship five times in a row. Simultaneously they also reached the semi-finals of the Mitropa Cup on four occasions and supplied Italy's World Cup-winning teams with five players in 1934 and three in 1938. Goalkeeper Gianpiero Combi, from Juventus, was Italy's victorious captain in 1934, just as another Juventus goal-

GIOVANNI TRAPATTONI

Coach of Milan, Juventus, Internazionale, Bayern Munich, Cagliari, Bayern Munich (born March 17, 1939)

Trapattoni was a sure tackling wing-half in the 1950s and 1960s. He earned a reputation as the only man who could play Pele out of a game fairly. After winning two European Cups with Milan, Trapattoni retired and joined the coaching staff. He became first-team caretaker before moving to Juventus where he became the most successful club coach of all time. In eight years, Trapattoni took Juve to the World Club Cup, European Cup, European Cup-winners' Cup, UEFA Cup, European Supercup, seven Italian championships and two national cups. Nothing in his career, either at Internazionale or after returning to Juventus, matched that spell. But he proved that his coaching talent could transcend cultural and linguistic obstacles when he guided Bayern Munich to the 1997 German league title.

keeper, Dino Zoff, would be in 1982.

After the war, the Zebras (after the colours of their shirts) scoured the world for talent to match their imported rivals. First came the Danes, John and Karl Hansen, then the Argentine favourite Omar Sivori and the Gentle Giant from Wales, John Charles, followed by Spanish inside-forward Luis Del Sol and French inspiration Michel Platini. In 1971 they lost the Fairs Cup Final to Leeds on the away goals rule but in 1977 they beat Bilbao in the UEFA Cup Final on the same regulation.

In 1982 no fewer than six Juventus players featured in Italy's World Cup winning line-up, and Cabrini, Tardelli, Scirea, Gentile and Paolo Rossi helped Juve win the 1984 European Cup-winners' Cup and the 1985 European Cup. Seeking new magic in the 1990s, Juventus paid huge fees for Roberto Baggio and Gianluca Vialli. Both shared in the 1995 league and cup double triumph but Baggio then left for Milan on the eve of a season which saw Vialli captain Juventus to victory in the European Champions Cup Final over Ajax in Rome.

IGOR BELANOV *Kiev's European Footballer of the Year in 1986*

KIEV DYNAMO
UKRAINE

Founded: 1927
Stadium: Republic (100,100)
Colours: White/blue
League: 7 Ukraine, 13 Soviet
Cup: 3 Ukraine, 9 Soviet
European Cup-winners' Cup: 1975, 1986
Supercup: 1975

Kiev were founder members of the Soviet top division, yet had to wait until 1961 before they became the first club outside Moscow to land the title. Soon they were dominating the Soviet scene. They achieved the league and cup "double" five years later and went on to a record-equalling hat-trick of league titles. Key players were midfielders Iosif Sabo and Viktor Serebryanikov and forwards Valeri Porkuyan and Anatoli Bishovets. Porkuyan starred at the 1966 World Cup finals in England, and Bishovets four years later in Mexico.

In 1975 Kiev became the first Soviet team to win a European trophy when they beat Ferencvaros of Hungary by 3–0 in the Cup-winners' Cup. Later that year they clinched the league title for the seventh time in 14 seasons. It was then that the Soviet federation grew too demanding, saddling the Ukraine club en bloc with all the national team fixtures and, when the Olympic qualifying team began to falter, with their schedule as well. It all proved too much. But that did not deter Kiev coach Valeri Lobanovsky from going back to square one and painstakingly developing another formidable team around record goal-scorer Oleg Blokhin. In 1985, the renewed Kiev stormed to another league and cup "double". A year later, Kiev charmed their way to the European Cup-winners' Cup as well, defeating Atletico Madrid 3–0 in the Final. Igor Belanov was named European Footballer of the Year. Kiev were the richest and most powerful club in the Ukraine upon the collapse of the Soviet Union, but they failed to translanfluence into European success and were expelled from the 1995–96 Champions League after club officials were accused of trying to bribe a referee. A three-year ban was quashed by UEFA on compassionate grounds.

LIVERPOOL
ENGLAND

Founded: 1892
Stadium: Anfield (41,000)
Colours: All red
League: 18
FA Cup: 5
League Cup: 4
European Cup: 1977, 1978, 1981, 1984
UEFA Cup: 1973, 1976
Supercup: 1977

Liverpool: a name which says so much, in pop music, in sport – specifically, in soccer. The Beatles may have moved on, split up, become part of the memorabilia of a major industrial centre in the north-west of England. But the football club goes on, purveyor of dreams not only for the thousands who fill the seats and the condemned terracing but for the millions on Merseyside who achieved international acclaim through their footballers.

For years the proud boast of English football's hierarchy had been that such was the depth of talent that no one club would ever dominate the championship in the manner of Juventus in Italy, Real Madrid in Spain or Benfica in Portugal. Then, along came Bill Shankly. He was appointed manager of shabby, run-down, half-forgotten Liverpool FC in December, 1959. In two-and-a-half years he won promotion; the purchases of left-half Billy Stevenson and outside-left Peter Thompson, for a combined total of just £60,000, secured the League Championship in 1964; and a year later they had won the FA Cup. Those years and the succeeding 20 brought success on the greatest scale at home and abroad.

The secret was continuity. Shankly was succeeded in the manager's tracksuit by two of his former assistant coaches, Bob Paisley and Joe Fagan. A new player would be bought young and cheap, consigned to the reserves for a year to learn "the Liverpool way", then slotted in to replace one of the fading heroes whose game had lost its edge. Thus the generation of Emlyn Hughes, Ian St John, Roger Hunt and Ron Yeats gave way to the likes of Kevin Keegan and John Toshack, who were followed in turn by Alan Hansen, Kenny Dalglish and Graeme Souness, the last two of whom also later succeeded to Anfield managership. Under Dalglish Liverpool became in 1986 only the third English club to achieve the League and Cup "double" this century – a wonderful achievement on the pitch which was tarnished by the disasters off it, first at the Heysel stadium in 1985 and then at Hillsborough in 1989.

MANCHESTER UNITED
ENGLAND

Founded: 1878
Stadium: Old Trafford (55,000)
Colours: Red/white
League: 12
FA Cup: 10
League Cup: 1
European Cup: 1968, 1999
European Cup-winners' Cup: 1991
Supercup: 1991

Manchester United were appropriate leaders of English re-entry into Europe in 1990, after the five-year

TREBLE CLINCHER *Ole Gunnar Solskjaer secures United's historic treble*

Heysel disaster ban, since United had been the first English club to play in Europe in the mid-1950s when they reached the semi-finals of the European Cup in both 1957 (losing to eventual winners Real Madrid) and in 1958. On the latter occasion they lost to Milan with a somewhat makeshift side which had been hastily pulled together in the wake of the Munich air disaster in which eight players, including skipper Roger Byrne and the inspirational young Duncan Edwards, had been killed.

It took United ten years to recover, in international terms. Thus it was in May 1968 that manager Matt Busby's European quest was rewarded as United defeated Benfica 4–1 in extra time at Wembley. Bobby Charlton, a Munich survivor along with defender Bill Foulkes and manager Busby, scored twice to secure the club's most emotional triumph. Busby had been a Scotland international wing-half with Manchester

City in the 1930s and took over United when war damage to Old Trafford meant playing home games at Maine Road. Yet within three years Busby had constructed a side who scored a superb FA Cup Final victory over Blackpool and created the entertaining, attacking style which has been mandatory for the club ever since. In the 1960s United boasted not only Charlton but great crowd-pullers such as Scotland's Denis Law and Northern Ireland's George Best. Later came England's long-serving skipper Bryan Robson, who was still in harness in the 1990s when United, under Alex Ferguson, regained the English League title for the first time in 26 years and made history by winning the domestic double three times. Over and above all that, United wrote their name deeper into football legend by becoming, in 1999, the first English club to achieve the fabulous treble - adding the Champions League, in sensational style, to their domestic crown.

Great Managers
Bill Shankly

Manager of Carlisle, Grimsby, Workington, Huddersfield and Liverpool (born September 2, 1913; died September 29, 1981)

Shankly played for Carlisle, Preston and Scotland in the 1930s and returned to Carlisle to begin his managerial career. He took over a faded Liverpool in the Second Division in December, 1959, and there was no stopping either him or the club once promotion had been achieved in 1962. Shankly's dry humour struck a chord with Anfield fans. He brought them League, FA Cup and League successes in consecutive seasons, signed some of the club's greatest servants and laid foundations for further success both on and off the pitch. Shankly had an eye for youthful talent — which he squirrelled away in the reserves until they were ready — and for managerial expertise. Later managers Bob Paisley, Joe Fagan and Roy Evans came out of Shankly's fabled "boot room".

Great Managers
Matt Busby

Manager of Manchester United (born May 26, 1909; died January 20, 1994)

Busby was a Scottish international wing-half who played before the Second World War for Liverpool and Manchester City and took over as manager at Manchester United in 1945 when air raid damage had reduced Old Trafford to near-rubble. Such was his gift for management that, within three years, he had created the first of three memorable teams. His 1948 side won the FA Cup, his Busby Babes of the mid-1950s went twice to the European Cup semi-finals before being wrecked by the Munich air disaster, and his third team completed the European quest with victory over Benfica in 1968's European Cup Final. Busby's love of entertaining football inspired some of British football's greatest talents and set a standard which was emulated by his protege, Alex Ferguson.

DOOMED *Marseille's Basile Boli, scorer of the only goal, robs Milan's Marco Van Basten in the French club's ill-fated 1993 European Cup Final triumph*

MARSEILLE
FRANCE

Founded: 1898
Stadium: Vélodrome (46,000)
Colours: All white
League: 9 (1993 title revoked)
Cup: 10
European Cup: 1993

No French club had ever won the European Cup before Marseille; and no one will ever forget what happened when they did. Millionaire entrepreneur Bernard Tapie, the club's high-profile president, had invested millions of pounds in pursuit of European glory. Unfortunately, some of the money had been used to try to fix matches along the road – if not in Europe then in the French championship. Barely had Marseille finished celebrating their Cup-winning 1–0 victory over Milan in Munich in May, 1993, than it emerged that midfielder Jean-Jacques Eydelie had passed cash to

three players from Valenciennes to "go easy" on Marseille in a league fixture a week earlier. Marseille were duly banned from their European defence in 1993–94, the French federation revoked their league championship title and they were subsequently further penalised with enforced relegation. Bankruptcy, inevitably, followed

Marseille's first championship had been celebrated back in 1929. Personalities in those days included Emmanuel Aznar (scorer of eight goals in a 20–2 league win over Avignon) and three English managers in Peter Farmer, Victor Gibson and Charlie Bell. After the war Marseille soon won the championship in 1948, but heavy expenditure on big-name foreigners such as Yugoslavia's Josip Skoblar, Sweden's Roger Magnusson and Brazil's Jairzinho and Paulo César drew only sporadic rewards, and Marseille had slipped into the Second Division by the time

ambitious businessman-turned-politician Tapie took over the helm in 1985. Marseille immediately gained promotion and then, thanks to the attacking genius of Jean-Pierre Papin and Chris Waddle, swept to four league titles in a row. They also suffered a penalty shoot-out defeat by Red Star Belgrade in the 1991 European Cup Final.

MILAN
ITALY

Founded: 1899
Stadium: Meazza (85,443)
Colours: Red and black stripes/white
League: 16
Cup: 4
World Club Cup: 1969, 1989, 1990
European Cup: 1963, 1969, 1989, 1990, 1994
European Cup-winners' Cup: 1968, 1973
Supercup: 1989, 1990

Milan's domination of the European club game in the late 1980s and the early 1990s was achieved on a unique stage

which would appear to represent the pattern of the future for a sport increasingly controlled by the intertwined commercial interests and demands of big business and television. In Milan's case, all these strands were in the hands of a puppet-master supreme in media magnate and then Prime Minister of Italy, Silvio Berlusconi. He had come to the rescue in 1986, investing £20 million to save Milan from bankruptcy and turn the club into a key player in his commercial empire. Milan had been one of the founders of the Italian championship back in 1898, but until the Second World War they tended to be in the shadow of neighbours Inter. After the war Milan achieved spectacular success, largely thanks to the Swedish inside-forward trio of Gunnar Gren, Gunnar Nordahl and Nils Liedholm. They also paid a then world record fee of £72,000 for Uruguay's Juan Schiaffino. They were dangerous rivals to Real Madrid in the new European Cup – losing narrowly to the Spanish

SAFETY FIRST *Milan's Alessandro Costacurta (right) clears his lines in the 1993 European Cup Final*

club in the semi-finals in 1956 and then only in extra time in the Final of 1958. That was the year Milan's scouts first saw the teenage "Golden Boy" Gianni Rivera, whose cultured inside-forward play and partnership with José Altafini inspired Milan to a European Cup victory in 1963 over Benfica. Rivera was Milan's figurehead as they won the European Cup again in 1969 and the European Cup-winners' Cup in 1968 and 1973. But even his charisma could not save the club from the scandals and financial disasters inflicted by a string of disastrous presidents. That was where Berlusconi came in, providing the money and the men – among them Holland's Ruud Gullit and Marco Van Basten, Liberia's George Weah and Yugoslavia's Dejan Savicevic – who turned Milan into a millionaires' club.

MILLONARIOS
BOGOTA, COLOMBIA

Founded: 1938
Stadium: El Campin – Estadio Distrital Nemesio Camacho (57,000)
Colours: Blue/white
League: 13

Millonarios remain a legendary

name, if only because of the manner in which they led Colombia's fledgeling professional clubs into the El Dorado rebellion which lured star players from all over the world in the late 1940s and the early 1950s. Many famous names in the game made their reputations there. The then club president, Alfonso Senior, later became president of the Colombian federation and a highly-respected FIFA delegate. Star player Alfredo Di Stefano used Millonarios as a springboard to greatness with Real Madrid.

Taking massive advantage of an Argentine players' strike, Millonarios led the flight from FIFA and the chase for great players – not only Di Stefano but the acrobatic goalkeeper Julio Cozzi, attacking centre-half Nestor Rossi and attacking general Adolfo Pedernera. Nicknamed the "Blue Ballet", they dominated the pirate league and, when an amnesty was negotiated with FIFA, made lucrative "farewell" tours in Europe. Credit for the club's name goes to a journalist, Camacho Montayo. The club had been founded as an amateur side, Deportivo Municipal, in 1938. But as they pushed for a professional league, so Montayo wrote: "The

Municipalistas have become the Millonarios." The name stuck. Millonarios remain a leading club but, despite appearing frequently in the South American Club Cup, the glory days have never been repeated.

MOSCOW DYNAMO
RUSSIA

Founded: 1923
Stadium: Dynamo (51,000)
Colours: White/blue
League: 11 Soviet
Cup: 6 Soviet

Dynamo are probably the most famous of all Russian clubs, having been the first Soviet side to venture out beyond the Iron Curtain in the 1940s and 1950s. Also, they were fortunate enough to possess, in goalkeeper Lev Yashin, one of the greatest personalities in the modern game – a show-stopper wherever he went.

Dynamo's origins go back to the start of soccer in Russia, introduced by the Charnock brothers at their cotton mills towards the end of the last century. The team won successive Moscow championships under the name Morozovsti and, after the Russian Revolution, were taken over first by the electrical trades union

and then by the police. Thus the 1923 date marks the formal setting-up of Moscow Dynamo rather than the foundation of the original club. Immediately after the end of the Second World War, Dynamo became a legend as a result of a four-match British tour in the winter of 1945. They drew 3–3 with Chelsea and 2–2 with Rangers, thrashed Cardiff 10–1 and beat a reinforced Arsenal 4–3 in thick fog. Inside-forward Constantin Beskov later became national manager, but it was goalkeeper Alexei "Tiger" Khomich whose reputation lasted long after he had retired to become a sports press photographer. He was succeeded in the team by an even greater goalkeeper in Yashin, who was to become the first Soviet player to be nominated as European Footballer of the Year. Given Dynamo's leadership, it was appropriate that, in 1972, they became the first Soviet side to reach a European final. But their 3–2 defeat by Rangers in Barcelona also stands as the high point of their modern achievement. Back home, Dynamo were pushed back down the ranks by neighbours Moscow Spartak.

MOSCOW SPARTAK
RUSSIA

Founded: 1922
Stadium: Olympic-Lenin/Luzhniki (102,000)
Colours: Red and white/white
League: 5 Russia; 12 Soviet
Cup: 10 Soviet

Moscow Spartak, champions of Russia for both the first two seasons after the collapse of the Soviet Union, face an enormous challenge in the years ahead. Spartak were a power in the land under the old system, but those were the days when players were not allowed to move abroad. Now Spartak must maintain their domestic command and compete effectively in Europe in an "open" transfer society. This is all the more challenging because Spartak had, for years, represented the Party line. They play their home matches in what was known as the Lenin stadium in the Luzhniki suburb, and their past heroes included such officially-approved characters as 1950s' top scorer Nikita Simonian (a club record-holder with 133 goals) and left-half Igor Netto (another club record-holder with 367 appearances). Spartak's best season in European competitions was 1990–91, when they beat both Napoli and Real Madrid to reach the semi-finals of the European Cup, before falling 5–1 on aggregate to Marseille.

For years the club had been ruled by the most respected members of the managerial old guard in veteran administrator Nikolai Starostin and former national coach Constantin Beskov. Starostin, a Spartak player in the club's early days, stayed on after the political upheaval, but Beskov handed over the coaching mantle to his former pupil and international full-back, Oleg Romantsev. Despite the loss of sweeper Vasili Kulkov and mid-fielders Igor Shalimov and Alexander Mostovoi, Romantsev kept Spartak on top of the table. New heroes were left-back and skipper Viktor Onopko, versatile Igor Lediakhov and the young forward Mikhail Beschastnikh. Not only did Spartak win the 1992, 1993, 1994 and 1996 Russian league titles; they also won – in both 1993 and 1994 – the pre-season CIS Cup, contested by the champions of all the former Soviet states.

NACIONAL
MONTEVIDEO, URUGUAY

Founded: 1899
Stadium: Parque Central (20,000) and Centenario (73,609)
Colours: White/blue
League: 36
World Club Cup: 1971, 1980, 1988
South American Club Cup: 1971, 1980, 1988
South American Recopa: 1988
Inter-American Cup: 1971

Nacional and Penarol are the two great clubs of Uruguay and bitter rivals on both the domestic and international stages. Nacional were formed from a merger of the Montevideo Football Club and the Uruguay Athletic Club, and in 1903 were chosen to line up as Uruguay's national team against Argentina in Buenos Aires. Nacional won 3–2

and have enjoyed the international limelight ever since.

Penarol won the first South American Club Cup in 1960, but Nacional soon set about catching up: runners-up three times in the 1960s, they first won the cup by defeating Estudiantes de La Plata in 1971. That led Nacional on to the World Club Cup, where they beat Panathinaikos of Greece (European title-holders Ajax having refused to compete). The two decisive goals in Montevideo were scored by Nacional's former Argentine World Cup spearhead, Luis Artime. It was nine years before Nacional regained those crowds. This time they had a new centre-forward in Waldemar Victorino, who scored the only goal in the 1980 South

American Club Cup triumph over Internacional of Brazil, and then the lone strike which decided the world final against Nottingham Forest in Tokyo. By the time Nacional regained the crown in 1988 Victorino had left for Italy, just as so many Uruguayan stars before and since.

Back in the 1930s Nacional sold centre-half Michele Andreolo to Italy, with whom he won the 1938 World Cup. But Nacional quickly replaced him and, from 1939 to 1943, achieved what is nostalgically recalled as their Quinquenio de Oro: their golden five years. Nacional won the league in each of those seasons with a legendary forward line built around the prolific Argentine marksman Atilio Garcia. He was Uruguay's top scorer eight times and ended his career with a record of 464 goals in 435 games. Under Scottish manager William Reasdale, Nacional also celebrated an 8–0 thrashing of the old enemy from Penarol.

PENAROL
MONTEVIDEO, URUGUAY

Founded: 1891
Stadium: Las Acacias (15,000) and Centenario (73,609)
Colours: Black and yellow stripes/black
League: 43
World Club Cup: 1961, 1966, 1982
South American Club Cup: 1960, 1961, 1966, 1982, 1987
Inter-American Cup: 1969

Penarol were the first club to win the World Club Cup three times, but their success is no modern phenomenon. Penarol have been the pre-eminent power in Uruguayan football since its earliest days, providing a host of outstanding players for Uruguay's 1930 and 1950 World Cup-winning teams. Their own international awakening came in 1960, when Penarol won the inaugural South American Club Cup (the Copa Libertadores). They were thrashed by Real Madrid in the World Club Cup, but made amends the next year with victory over Benfica. It was no less than the talents of players such as William Martinez, centre-half Nestor Goncalves and striker Alberto Spencer deserved.

Penarol regained the world club crown in 1966, at the expense of Real Madrid, and then again in 1982 when they beat Aston Villa in Tokyo. By now Penarol had unearthed an other superstar in centre-forward Fernando Morena. He was the latest in a long line of great players, which included the nucleus of the Uruguayan national team who shocked Brazil by winning the 1950 World Cup. Goalkeeper Roque Maspoli – later World Club Cup-winning coach in 1966 – captain and centre-half Obdulio Varela, right-winger Alcide Ghiggia, centre-forward Oscar Miguez, right-half Rodriguez Andrade and inside-right Juan Schiaffino all came from Penarol. Schiaffino was the greatest of all.

Penarol had been founded as the Central Uruguayan Railway Cricket Club in 1891, and changed their name in 1913 as the British influence waned. The railways sidings and offices were near the Italian Pignarolo district – named after the landowner Pedro Pignarolo – and so the Spanish style of the name was adopted for the club.

FC PORTO
OPORTO, PORTUGAL

Founded: 1893
Stadium: Das Antas (76,000)
Colours: Blue and white stripes/white
League: 17
Cup: 11
World Club Cup: 1987
European Cup: 1987
Supercup: 1987

Porto were always considered to be No. 3 in the Portuguese football hierarchy until their thrilling European Cup victory over Bayern Munich in Vienna in 1987. Events then and since have ensured that, while their trophy count may not yet match those of Benfica and Sporting, Porto are clearly seen as an alternative centre of power in the domestic game. Porto beat Bayern with the Polish goalkeeper Mlynarczyk, Brazil-

EX COACH *Porto's Bobby Robson*

ians Celso and Juary, and Algerian winger Rabah Madjer supporting Portugal's own wonderboy, Paulo Futre. But that was entirely appropriate since, in the early 1930s, Porto had been pioneers in the international transfer market.

They began by bringing in two Yugoslavs, and that ambition was reflected in Porto's initial championship successes in 1938 and 1939. In those days Porto's home was the old, rundown Campo da Constituciao. Now, as befits a club with European Cup-winning pedigree, home is the impressive, 76,000-capacity Estadio das Antas.

Not only have Porto won the Champions' Cup; they also finished runners-up to Juventus in the European Cup-winners' Cup in 1984. The creative force behind the club's progress in the 1980s was the late José Maria Pedroto. He led Porto to the cup in 1977 and league title in 1978 and 1979.

His work would be carried on by his pupil, former national team centre-forward Artur Jorge, who coached Porto to their 1987 European title and later took over the national side. Later, under Brazilian Carlos Alberto da Silva, duly succeeded by Bobby Robson, Porto enhanced their standing as members of the European establishment when they reached the semi-finals of the Champions League in 1994 and the quarter-finals in 1997. Robson left Porto in 1996 after building a team which won a hat-trick of league titles.

PHILIPS SV
EINDHOVEN, HOLLAND

Founded: 1913
Stadium: Philips (30,000)
Colours: Red and white stripes/white
League: 14
Cup: 7
European Cup: 1988
UEFA Cup: 1978

PSV equalled the achievements of Celtic (in 1967) and Ajax Amsterdam (in 1972) when they defeated Benfica in a penalty shoot-out to win the 1988 European Cup. Only those other two clubs had previously secured the treble of European Cup and domestic league and cup all in the same season. Remarkably, PSV achieved all they did despite having sold their finest player, Ruud Gullit, to Milan at the start of the season for a world record £5.7 million. The money was, however, invested wisely to secure the best players from Holland, Denmark and Belgium.

Such success was the reward for a long wait since PSV had been one of the invited entrants in the inaugural European Cup in 1955–56, when they crashed 1–0, 1–6 to Rapid Vienna in the first round. Surprisingly, considering PSV's position as the sports club of the giant Philips electrics corporation, they were long outshone by Ajax and Feyenoord. For years the Philips company took comparatively little interest in PSV, even though an estimated 40,000 of the 200,000 urban population of Eindhoven work directly or indirectly for Philips. Only in the past decade have Philips become seriously involved with club policy and finance.

PSV had won the 1976 UEFA Cup without much fanfare. But ten years later, realising the potential to be reaped from soccer sponsorship, the company came up with the funds, and were duly rewarded two years later with the European Cup. In 1992, taking the process a stage further, the club changed its name in order to promote itself outside Holland as Philips SV (while domestic sponsorship regulations required it to stick with the PSV abbreviation in Holland).

RANGERS
GLASGOW, SCOTLAND

Founded: 1873
Stadium: Ibrox Park (50,471)
Colours: Blue/white
League: 48
Cup: 28
League cup: 19
European Cup-winners' Cup: 1972

Rangers are one half of the "Old Firm" – their rivalry with Celtic having dominated Scottish football for a century. Yet Rangers have never extended that power into Europe, their only prize from virtual non-stop international competition being the 1972 Cup-winners' Cup Final win over Moscow Dynamo. Not that Rangers' history is short on proud moments. One particularly glorious era was the 1920s, when Rangers' heroes included the legendary "Wee Blue Devil", Alan Morton.

In the 1960s, Rangers endured heavy European defeats at the hands of Eintracht Frankfurt, Tottenham and Real Madrid. The start of the 1970s was a time of mixed emotions: 1971 saw the Ibrox disaster, when 66 fans died in a stairway crush at the end of a game against Celtic. Then, a year later, Rangers' European Cup-winners' Cup triumph was immediately followed by a European ban because of the way their celebrating fans ran amok in Barcelona. The upturn began in November, 1985, when Lawrence Marlboro bought control of the club. He brought in Graeme Souness as player-manager. In 1988 David Murray bought Rangers, and Souness revolutionized their image by buying 18 English players and smashing the club's Protestants-only ethic with his £1.5 million capture of Catholic Mo Johnston. Subsequent signings such as Brian Laudrup and Paul Gascoigne enabled Rangers to maintain their league title dominance for a remarkable eight years in a row. Striker Ally McCoist smashed the club record of 233 goals set 60 years earlier by legendary Bob McPhail and in 1999 'Gers secured the domestic treble.

BRIAN LAUDRUP *The Dane is a double Scottish Footballer of the Year*

mered a free-kick through the defensive wall. Binder ended a great career with 1,006 goals and later became club coach.

Many of Rapid's old heroes returned as coaches, among them Karl Rappan (who developed the Swiss Bolt system), Edi Fruhwirth and Karl Decker. Great players in the post-war years included wing-half Gerhard Hanappi – an architect by profession, who laid out the designs for the club stadium – tough-tackling defender Ernst Happel and another prolific goal-scoring centre-forward in Hans Krankl. He led Rapid's attack in 1985 in the first of their two defeats in the European Cup-winners' Cup Final, but had long retired when they fell to Paris Saint-Germain in 1996.

REAL MADRID
SPAIN

Founded: 1902
Stadium: Santiago Bernabeu (105,000)
Colours: All white
League: 28
Cup: 17
World Club Cup: 1966, 1998
European Cup: 1956, 1957, 1958, 1959, 1960, 1966, 1998
UEFA Cup: 1985, 1986

What else is there left to say about Real Madrid? Six times champions of Europe, 27 times champions of Spain – both record achievements. They have also won the World Club Cup, two UEFA Cups and 16 Spanish cups, which add up to a football honours degree for the club founded by students as Madrid FC. (The Real prefix, meaning Royal, was a title bestowed on the club later by King Alfonso XIII.) Madrid were not only among the founders of the Spanish cup and league competitions: it was also the Madrid president, Carlos Padros, who attended on Spain's behalf the inaugural meeting of FIFA in Paris in 1904. In the late 1920s Madrid launched a policy of buying big. They paid a then Spanish record fee of £2,000 for Ricardo Zamora, still revered as the greatest Spanish goalkeeper of all time.

The Spanish Civil War left Madrid's Chamartin stadium in ruins. At the time the club had no money, but boasted one of the greatest visionaries in European football

CROWN PRINCE *Raul Gonzalez is the latest sensation to grace the Bernabeu Stadium at "royal" Real Madrid*

RAPID VIENNA
AUSTRIA

Founded: 1899
Stadium: Hanappi (19,600)
Colours: Green and white/green
League: 29
Cup: 13

Rapid were founded as the 1st Arbeiter-Fussballklub (First Workers Football Club) but, on changing their name, also set about refining the short-passing style of the "Vienna School" to such good effect that they won the championship eight times between 1912 and 1923. The success story did not end there. In 1930 Rapid became the first Austrian club to win the Mitropa Cup, defeating powerful Sparta Prague 2–0, 2–3 in the Final. Several of Rapid's key players were members of the "Wunderteam", the national side who finished fourth in the 1934 World Cup under the captaincy of Rapid centre-half Pepe Smistik.

Four years later Austria was swallowed up into Greater Germany, and the Austrian league was incorporated into the Greater German championship. To the mischievous delight of their fans, Rapid not only won the German Cup in 1938 (3–2 against FSV Frankfurt in the Final) but also the German championship in 1941. On a day which has entered football legend Rapid hit back from 3–0 down to defeat an outstanding Schalke side 4–3 before a 90,000 crowd in the Olympic stadium in Berlin. Their hero was centre-forward Franz "Bimbo" Binder, whose hat-trick was crowned by the winning goal when he ham-

history. He was Santiago Bernabeu, a lawyer who had been, in turn, player, team manager and secretary, and was now club president. Bernabeu launched an audacious public appeal which raised the cash to build the wonderful stadium which now bears his name. The huge crowds which flocked in provided the cash to build the team who dominated the first five years of the European Cup. Argentine-born centre-forward Alfredo Di Stefano was the star of stars, though Bernabeu surrounded him with illustrious team-mates such as Hungary's Ferenc Puskas, France's Ramond Kopa, Uruguay's José Santamaria and Brazil's Didi. They set impossibly high standards for all the players and teams who followed. Madrid won the European Cup again in 1966 and the UEFA Cup twice in the 1980s, but even later superstars such as Pirri, Santillana, Juanito, Hugo Sanchez and Emilio Butragueño would occasionally complain that nothing they achieved would ever be quite enough. The 1960 team had been, if anything, too good.

RED STAR BELGRADE
YUGOSLAVIA

Founded: 1945
Stadium: Crvena Zvezda (Red Star) (97,422)
Colours: Red and white stripes/white
League: 20
Cup: 15
World Club Cup: 1991
European Cup: 1991

This may be the most schizophrenic club in the world. In Germany they are known as Roter Stern; in France as Etoile Rouge; in Spain as Estrella Roja; in Italy as Stella Rossa; in Serbo-Croat it's Fudbalski Klub Crvena Zvezda; in English, of course, Red Star Belgrade. Under whichever name, the 1991 European and world club champions stood revered as one of the pillars of the worldwide establishment until civil strife in the former Yugoslavia led to international suspension for both country and clubs. The consequences for Red Star were almost disastrous, since millions of pounds paid in

transfer fees for their star players were suddenly frozen in banks around Europe.

But Red Star are no strangers to disaster, having been the last team to play Manchester United's "Busby Babes" before the Munich air disaster. Red Star fought back from 3–0 down to draw 3–3, but lost on aggregate despite all the efforts of balletic goalkeeper Vladimir Beara, gypsy midfielder Dragoslav Sekularac and dynamic striker Bora Kostic (scorer of a club record 157 goals in 256 league games). All three men later moved abroad, members of an ongoing exodus of more than 40 players including stars like Dragan Dzajic (to Bastia), Dragan Stojkovic (to Marseille), Robert Prosinecki (to Real Madrid) and Darko Pancev (to Internazionale). This explains, perhaps, why Red Star, for all their talent, boast only one victory in the European Cup (the 1991 penalty shoot-out victory over Marseille in Bari) and one runners-up spot in the UEFA Cup (beaten on away goals by Borussia Mönchengladbach in 1979).

Red Star were formally set up by students of Belgrade University after the war. They play their home matches in the so-called "Marakana", which was the first stadium in eastern Europe to host a mainstream European final, when Ajax beat Juventus in the 1973 European Cup.

ROBERT PROSINECKI *Outstanding graduate of the Red Star football "university"*

RIVER PLATE
BUENOS AIRES, ARGENTINA

Founded: 1901
Stadium: Antonio Liberti/Monumental (76,000)
Colours: White with red sash/black
League: 24
World Club Cup: 1986
South American Club Cup: 1986, 1996
Inter-American Cup: 1986

River Plate are one of the two giants of Argentine football, Boca Juniors being the other. Traditionally the club from the rich side of Buenos Aires, River were founder members of the first division in 1908, then took a leading role in the "war" which accompanied the introduction of professional football in the 1920s. Over the years River have fielded some wonderful teams. In the 1930s they boasted Bernabe Ferreyra, a legendary figure in Argentine football; in the late 1940s their high-scoring forward line was so feared and admired they were nicknamed "La Maquina" (The Machine). The names of Muñoz, Moreno, Pedernera, Labruna and Loustau mean little outside Argentina today, but there they inspire awe like Real Madrid in Europe.

Later River produced more great players: Alfredo Di Stefano, who would one day turn Real Madrid into possibly the greatest team of all time; Omar Sivori, who would form a wonderful partnership with John Charles after joining Juventus; and then 1978 World Cup winners Ubaldo Fillol, Daniel Passarella, Leopoldo Luque and Mario Kempes. In 1986 they were joined in River's Hall of Fame by the likes of goalkeeper Nery Pumpido, centre-back Oscar Ruggeri and schemer Norberto Alonso, after victory in the South American Club Cup provided River with formal confirmation of their lofty status. River really should have succeeded to the crown years earlier, but were unlucky runners-up in 1966 to Penarol of Uruguay and in 1976 to Cruzeiro of Brazil. In 1986 they made no mistake, beating America of Colombia, then adding the World Club Cup by defeating Steaua of Romania 1–0 in Tokyo.

SANTOS
SÃO PAULO, BRAZIL

Founded: 1912
Stadium: Vila Belmiro (20,000)
Colours: All white
São Paulo state league: 15
Brazil championship (incl. Torneo Rio-São Paulo): 5
World Club Cup: 1962, 1963
South American Club Cup: 1962, 1963

The name of Santos will always be synonymous with that of Pele, who played all his mainstream career with the club and returned as a director at the end of 1993 to try to help lift his old club out of the depths of a severe financial and administrative crisis.

Santos had been founded by three members of the Americano club, who stayed home in the port of Santos when their club moved to São Paulo. Santos joined the São Paulo state championship in 1916, became only the second Brazilian club to embrace professionalism in 1933, but did not hit the headlines until the mid-1950s. Then, to organize a host of talented youngsters, they signed the 1950 World Cup veteran, Jair da Rosa Pinto, and discovered the 15-year-old Pele.

To say that Santos were a one-man team, as it often appeared from the publicity, would be unfair. Santos harvested millions of pounds from whistle-stop friendly match tours around the world and reinvested heavily in surrounding Pele with fine players: World Cup winners in goalkeeper Gilmar, centre-back Mauro and wing-half Zito; an outside-left with a ferocious shot in Pepe; and the precocious young talents of right-winger Dorval, schemer Mengalvio and centre-forward Coutinho, Pele's so-called "twin" with whom he established an almost telepathic relationship on the pitch. Santos were more than a football team; they were a touring circus.

Sadly, the constant touring and playing burned out many young players before they had a chance to establish their talent. But not before Santos had scaled the competitive heights as

PELE *The man who "made" Santos*

Pele inspired their victories in the South American Club Cup and the World Club Cup in both 1962 and 1963.

One more year and it was all over. Independiente beat Santos in the 1964 South American Club Cup semi-finals, and the spell had been broken. Santos went on touring and raking in cash, capitalizing on Pele's name, for as long as they could. Pele returned, briefly, as a director in the 1990s, but without inspiring the sort of success Santos had achieved when he was a player.

SÃO PAULO
BRAZIL

Founded: 1935
Stadium: Morumbi (150,000)
Colours: White with a red and black hoop/white
São Paulo state league: 17
Brazil championship (incl. Torneo Rio-São Paulo): 4
World Club Cup: 1992, 1993
South American Club Cup: 1992, 1993

São Paulo's victories over Barcelona and Milan in the 1992 and 1993 World Club Cups in Tokyo left no doubt about which was the finest club side in the world – for all the European hype which had surrounded the Italian champions. Those victories also underlined the depth of talent available to São Paulo, since their key midfielder, Rai (younger brother of 1986 World Cup star Socrates), had been sold to French club Paris Saint-Germain in the summer of 1993. Dual success also enhanced the reputation of coach Tele Santana, Brazil's World Cup manager in 1982 and 1986 and one of the most eloquent

and down-to-earth of football coaches and analysts.

São Paulo are, even so, comparative newcomers – having been founded in 1935, at a time when the likes of River Plate, Penarol and the rest were already well-established powers in their own lands. The club was formed from a merger between CA Paulistano and AA Palmeiras. A leading light was Paulo Machado de Carvalho, who would later, as a senior administrator, contribute behind the scenes to Brazil's World Cup hat-trick.

Within a decade of being founded, São Paulo developed into the strongest team in the country, winning the state title five times in the 1940s. They imported Argentine inside-forward Antonio Sastre, and the continuing pressure of success led to the construction of the 150,000-capacity Morumbi stadium – the world's largest club-owned sports arena.

In the 1960s São Paulo had to take a back seat to Santos. In 1974 they reached their first South American Club Cup Final (losing to Argentina's Independiente), but it was not until the arrival of Santana, in the late 1980s, that São Paulo emerged from the doldrums. Despite the continuing sale of star players – key defender Ricardo Rocha went to Real Madrid – São Paulo secured three state league titles in four years, used the cash to strengthen their squad and were duly rewarded at the highest level.

São Paulo's World Club Cup victory over the highly rated European giants Milan in Tokyo in 1993 was very impressive, with Cafu and Massaro the outstanding players. São Paulo became the first side to register consecutive wins in the Tokyo final.

JAN STEJSKAL *Maintaining Sparta's great traditions*

SPARTA PRAGUE
CZECH REPUBLIC

Founded: 1893
Stadium: Letna (36,000)
Colours: All red
League: 23
Cup: 9

Sparta are the most popular club in what is now the Czech Republic, as well as one of the oldest. They were founded as King's Vineyard in 1893, and took the name of Sparta, from one of the states of Ancient Greece, a year later. They were one Europe's great sides preceding the Second World War, winning the Mitropa Cup in the inaugural final in 1927 against Rapid Vienna. Victory over Ferencvaros of Hungary followed in 1935, and they were runners-up in 1936. Sparta's team then included the great inside-left, Oldrich Nejedly.

He was a star in the 1934 World Cup, when Czechoslovakia finished runners-up. Again in 1962, when the Czechs next reached the World Cup Final, there were key places in the team for Sparta men such as right-winger Tomas Pospichal and schemer Andrzej Kvasnak.

Sparta suffered after the last war, and were forced to alter their name to Sparta Bratrstvi and then Spartak Sokolovo. But their loyal fans never called them anything but Sparta, and reality was recognized when the club's present title was adopted in 1965. That same year they celebrated their first league title in more than a decade. Memories of the glory days of the Mitropa Cup were revived by the club's run to the European Cup-winners' Cup semi-finals in 1973 and by the impressive 1983–84 UEFA Cup campaign, during which they scored notable victories over Real Madrid and Widzew Lodz. Sparta's continuing domination of the domestic game in the early 1990s was remarkable because, immediately after the World Cup finals, they lost a string of senior internationals, such as goalkeeper Jan Stejskal, defenders Julius Bielik and Michal Bilek, midfield general Ivan Hasek and striker Tomas Skuhravy, the second-top scorer at Italia '90 with five goals.

SPORTING CLUBE
LISBON, PORTUGAL

Founded: 1906
Stadium: José Alvalade (70,000)
Colours: Green and white hoops/white
League: 16
Cup: 16
European Cup-winners' Cup: 1964

Sporting Clube do Portugal last reached a European final back in 1964, when they won the Cup-winners' Cup. Now Benfica's deadly rivals – the grounds are barely a mile apart – dream of the day when they can bring those old heroes out of retirement obscurity to celebrate a European revival. The late 1980s and early 1990s brought Sporting the worst era in their history, an empty decade following the heady 1981–82 season in which they won the league and cup "double" under Englishman Malcolm Allison.

In 1992 the new president, José Sousa Cintra, brought in ex-England manager Bobby Robson to try to recapture the Allison magic. Robson was given only 18 months, however, before former Portugal national coach Carlos Queiros, instead, was given the task of reviving the glories of the 1950s, when Sporting rivalled Benfica as the country's top club and took the championship seven times in eight years.

En route to Sporting's sole European trophy, they beat APOEL Nicosia in the second round first leg by a European record 16–1. In the Final against MTK Budapest, an entertaining match saw Sporting go 1–0 down, recover to lead 2–1 then go 3–2 behind before securing a 3–3 draw and a replay. In Antwerp a single 20th-minute goal from winger Morais, direct from a corner, was enough to win the cup. Their back four

of Morais, Batista, José Carlos and Hilario starred in the Portugal team which finished third in the 1966 World Cup finals in England.

The nearest Sporting have since gone to European success was in 1990–91, when they reached the UEFA Cup semi-final before falling 0–0, 0–2 to eventual winners Internazionale.

STEAUA
BUCHAREST, ROMANIA

Founded: 1947
Stadium: Steaua (30,000)
Colours: Red/blue
League: 18
Cup: 17
European Cup: 1986

Steaua – the word means 'Star' – were one of the army clubs created in eastern Europe after the Communist takeovers of political power. Originally Steaua were known as CCA Bucharest, under which title they won the championship three times in a row in the early 1950s. Later, renamed Steaua, they won the cup five times in six seasons in the late 1960s and early 1970s.

In 1986 Steaua became the first eastern European team to win the European Cup when they beat Barcelona on penalties in Seville. Their penalty stopping hero in the climactic minutes was Helmut Ducadam, whose career ended prematurely by illness soon after. Steaua's power – including the right to sign any player they liked from

any other Romanian club – was significantly reduced after the overthrow of the Communist dicatorship of the Ceausescu family.

VASCO DA GAMA
RIO DE JANEIRO, BRAZIL

Founded: 1898 as sailing club, 1915 as football club
Stadium: São Januario (50,000) and Maracana (130,000)
Colours: All white with black sash
South American Cup: 1
Brazil championship (incl. Torneo Rio-São Paulo): 4

Like Flamengo, one of their long-time Rio de Janeiro rivals, Vasco grew from a sailing club – the impetus for football coming from former members of a club called Luzitania FC, who had been refused entry to the early Rio de Janeiro state championship because of their "Portuguese-only" policy. Transformed into Vasco da Gama, however, they were elected to the championship in 1915 and had progressed to the top flight by 1923. Support, both vocal and financial, has come to the club over the years from the city's Portuguese community. In spite of their original policies, Vasco quickly became noted for their inclusion of mixed-race players at a time, early in Brazilian football's development, when the game was riven by race and class divisions. Vasco led the way, too, by creating the São Januario stadium, which was the first national stadium in Brazil and hosted all major club and national team matches before the building of the Maracana in 1950.

In 1958 Vasco supplied Brazil's World Cup-winning team with centre-back Luiz Bellini, the captain, and centre-forward Vava. They earned a long-awaited consolation for events eight years earlier when no fewer than eight Vasco players had figured in the Brazilian squad which was pipped to the World Cup by Uruguay. In the 1960s and 1970s Vasco figured, as ever, among the most powerful of challengers to Fluminense and Flamengo – from whom they controversially signed the popular striker, Bebeto.

LEGENDS

In football, as in other sports, the word "great" is over-used and devalued, having been applied to almost any and every fleeting moment of drama or high skill. Thousands of players have been described in terms of ultimate praise. But at the highest echelon of the game there is a small elite group acknowledged by millions of fans as the truly great.

BECKENBAUER
WEST GERMANY

"Kaiser Franz" can boast that he has lifted the World Cup as both captain, in 1974, and manager, in 1990. But his achievements are not the only measure of his true greatness. Beckenbauer's innovative strength was through the revolutionary role of attacking sweeper which, with majestic calm and precision, he introduced in the late 1960s.

CHARLTON
ENGLAND

Bobby Charlton, throughout the world, is probably the most famous English footballer who has ever thrilled a crowd. He won 106 caps, and his name is synonymous with some of the greatest moments of the modern English game, but also with the highest traditions of sportsmanship, modesty and integrity.

CRUYFF
HOLLAND

Johan Cruyff stands out as not merely the greatest Dutch footballer but one of the greatest play-ers of all time. He made his first-team debut at 17, his goal-scoring international debut at 19 and went on to inspire Ajax and Holland through most of their golden 1970s.

DI STEFANO
SPAIN

Alfredo Di Stefano is reckoned by many to be the greatest footballer of all. Although Pele's admirers may consider that sacrilege, the millions who wondered at Di Stefano's awesome majesty as he dominated European football in the 1950s and early 1960s will happily concur.

EUSEBIO
PORTUGAL

Eusebio, the greatest Portuguese footballer in history, did not come from Portugal at all. Born and brought up in Mozambique, then still one of Portugal's African colonies, Eusebio was the first African footballer to earn a worldwide reputation. Fans around the world took Eusebio to their hearts not only for his ability but for the sportsmanlike way he played.

MARADONA
ARGENTINA

Diego Maradona was not only the world's greatest footballer throughout the 1980s and early 1990s. He was also the most controversial and the most enigmatic player, unable to appear in public or on a football pitch without arousing the most contrasting of emotions.

MATTHEWS
ENGLAND

Stanley Matthews was the first great footballer of the modern era. There will be cases made for Billy Wright, Bobby Charlton, Bobby Moore and others but none dominated his particular era as long as the barber's son from Hanley in the Potteries area of the English Midlands.

PELE
BRAZIL

Pele remains one of those great examples and inspirations of world sport: a poor boy taking the world stage at 17, whose talent lifted him to the peaks of achievement, fame and fortune ... yet who, amidst all that, retained his innate sense of sportsmanship, his love of his calling, the desire to entertain fans and the respect of fellow players.

PUSKAS
HUNGARY

Ferenc Puskas remains one of the greatest players of all time – a symbol of the legendary "Magical Magyars" who dominated European football in the early 1950s and stand as perhaps the greatest team never to have won the World Cup. He very rarely used his right foot (except to stand on, as they say) but his left was so lethal that he hardly ever needed it.

YASHIN
USSR

In South America they called Lev Yashin the "Black Spider"; in Europe the "Black Panther". Eusebio described him as "the peerless goalkeeper of the century". Yashin's fame spread throughout the world, not merely for his ability as a goalkeeper to stop shots that no one else could reach, but as a great sportsman and ambassador for the game.

BECKENBAUER

"KAISER FRANZ" AND A UNIQUE DOUBLE

Franz Beckenbauer has always been accompanied by the sort of luck which only a player of his genius deserves.

The smile of fate was on him through an illustrious playing career and on into management when – in his first appointment at any level – he took West Germany to the Final of the World Cup in Mexico in 1986 and four years later went one better with victory in Italy.

Thus only "Kaiser Franz" can boast that he has lifted the World Cup as both captain, in 1974, and manager, in 1990.

No other footballer has ever had a career which reached such tangible heights. He was the first German to reach a century of international appearances before leaving Bayern Munich for spells with New York Cosmos and then with Hamburg, where he wound down his playing career.

His honours include the World Cup in 1974 (runner-up in 1966), the European Championship in 1972 (runner-up 1976), the World Club Cup (1976), the European Cup (1974, 1975, 1976), the European Cup-winners' Cup (1967), as well as the West German league and cup. He was also a runner-up in the UEFA Cup with Hamburg and a runner-up in the SuperCup with Bayern. With New York Cosmos, Beckenbauer also won the NASL Soccer Bowl in 1977, 1978 and 1980.

But achievement is not the only measure of true greatness. Beckenbauer's innovative strength was through the revolutionary role of attacking sweeper which, with the encouragement of Bayern Munich coach Tschik Cajkovski, he introduced in the late 1960s.

The boy Beckenbauer took his first steps on the football ladder with local club Munich 1906, before

BECKENBAUER *Attacking sweeper*

he switched to Bayern and was first recognized by West Germany at youth level. Within a year of making his league debut with Bayern, as an outside-left, Beckenbauer was promoted into the senior national team.

The occasion was one to test the nerve of the most experienced player, never mind a fledgeling newcomer: West Germany were away to Sweden in a decisive qualifier for the 1966 World Cup. The odds were against them. Yet they won 2–1. West Germany's place in the World Cup finals was all but secured as was Beckenbauer's place in the national team for almost a decade.

In due course he was voted German Footballer of the Year and European Footballer of the Year. Out on the pitch he was grace and elegance personified, combining an athlete's physique with a computer-like brain for the game which saw

> ❝ He's converted football into an art form. ❞
>
> *Willi Schulz, 1966 World Cup team-mate*

gaps before they had opened and goal opportunities – for himself and his team-mates – for which the opposing defence had not prepared.

The Elegant Manipulator

Beckenbauer spent almost all his senior career with Bayern Munich as attacking sweeper. Many critics said he was wasting his talent. But Beckenbauer, in an increasingly crowded modern game, found that the sweeper role provided him with time and space in which to work his magical influence on a match. He was the puppet master, standing back and pulling the strings which earned West Germany and Bayern Munich every major prize.

Not that Beckenbauer shied away from the attacking opportunity when it presented itself. He scored the goal which inspired West Germany's revival against England in the 1970 World Cup quarter-final.

During his four years with Cosmos Beckenbauer made many friends and admirers in the United States and was expected to take a central role in their 1994 World Cup build-up before other interests distracted him.

On retiring, Beckenbauer was much in demand as a newspaper and television columnist. Then he was invited to put his words into deeds when offered the post of national manager in succession to Jupp Derwall after the disappointing 1984 European Championship.

The Germans had always promoted managers from within their system. Beckenbauer was an outsider with no coaching experience: his appointment represented a huge gamble. It paid off. Such was Beckenbauer's Midas touch that "his" West Germany were crowned world champions in Rome and he earned his unique place in history.

CHARLTON

ENGLAND'S AMBASSADOR

THUNDERBOLT SHOOTING *Charlton on target against West Ham*

Bobby Charlton, throughout the world, is probably the most famous English footballer who has ever thrilled a crowd. His name is synonymous with some of the greatest moments of the English game, but also with the highest traditions of sportsmanship and integrity.

Long after he had finished playing Charlton's reputation worked wonders in breaking down the tightest security at World Cups and European Championships. It only needed a player or manager to glance out and see Charlton arriving for barred doors and gates to be flung open. Today's heroes may possess a string of fan clubs and millions in Swiss banks, but they still recognize magic.

The delight which much of the English public took in Manchester United's success in the inaugural Premier League in 1992–93 may be partly explained by the respect in which Bobby Charlton is held for reasons which transcend "mere" football.

Football was always in the blood. The Charltons – Bobby and World Cup-winning brother Jackie – were nephews of that great Newcastle United hero of the 1950s, Jackie Milburn. They began in the back streets of Ash-ington in the north-east of England, and Charlton fulfilled every schoolboy's dream when, at 17, he was signed by Manchester United.

Busby Babe and United Captain

Matt Busby had invested more time and determination than any other manager in seeking out the finest young talents in the country. Not only Charlton, but Duncan Edwards, Eddie Colman, David Pegg and many more had been singled out for the Old Trafford treatment: turned from boys into young footballing men under the tutelage of assistant Jimmy Murphy, and then released to explode into the League.

This was the philosophy behind the Busby Babes, the team of youngsters who took the League by storm in the mid-1950s and brought a breath of optimistic fresh air into an austere post-war England. The sense of that spirit of a new generation being lost added to the nation's grief when United's plane crashed in the snow and ice at the end of a runway in Munich on their way home from a European Cup quarter-final in Belgrade in February 1958.

Charlton had established

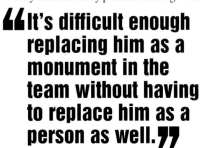

> **❝It's difficult enough replacing him as a monument in the team without having to replace him as a person as well.❞**
>
> *Tommy Docherty, then Manchester United manager, after Charlton's retirement*

his first-team potential the previous season. He was initially an inside-right, later switched to outside-left with England, and finally settled as a deep-lying centre-forward, using his pace out of midfield and thunderous shot to score some of the most spectacular goals English football has ever seen. One such goal marked his England debut against Scotland, another broke the deadlock against Mexico in the 1966 World Cup finals, and dozens of them inspired Manchester United's post-Munich revival.

The European Cup victory at Wembley in 1968, when he captained United and scored twice, was a highly emotional moment.

Then, as now, the newly-ennobled Sir Bobby has been a perfect ambassador for the game.

CRUYFF

CLOSE CONTROL *Cruyff tantalizes Argentine defender Pedro Sa at the 1974 World Cup*

THE TOTAL FOOTBALLER

Johan Cruyff stands out as not merely the greatest Dutch footballer but one of the greatest players of all time, a status which owes much to the persistence of his mother.

She worked as a cleaner in the offices of the Ajax club and persuaded the club coaching staff to take Johan into their youth sections when he was still only 12 years old. The rest is history and a virtually unbroken 25-year succession of trophies and awards on the highest plane as first player and then coach.

Cruyff made his first-team debut at 17, his goal-scoring international debut at 19 and went on to inspire Ajax and Holland through most of their golden 1970s. This was the era of "total football", a concept of the game first described as "The Whirl" in the early 1950s by the Austrian expert Willy Meisl. He saw the day when every player in a team would possess comparable technical and physical ability and would be able to interchange roles at will.

Cruyff was The Whirl in action. Nominally he played centre-forward. But Cruyff's perception of centre-forward was as orthodox as the squad No. 14 he wore on his back for most of his career with Ajax.

" Johan's secret is that he loves football, seeking out new ways of trying to achieve perfection. "

Stefan Kovacs, former Ajax coach

FINAL SHOWDOWN *Cruyff's face-to-face with Berti Vogts*

Cruyff did turn up at the apex of the attack: but he was also to be found meandering through midfield and out on the wings, using his nimble, coltish pace to unhinge defences from a variety of angles and positions.

Single-handed he not only pulled Internazionale of Italy apart in the 1972 European Cup final but scored both goals in Ajax's 2–0 win. The next year, in Belgrade, he inspired one of the greatest 20-minute spells of football ever seen as Ajax overcame another strong Italian outfit, Juventus.

Already the vultures were gathering. Spain had reopened their borders to foreign players and Cruyff was an obvious target. Eventually Barcelona won the transfer race – but after the close of the Spanish federation's autumn deadline. However, such was the magnitude of the transfer that the federation bent their own regulations so that Cruyff could play immediately.

When Cruyff arrived in Barcelona, the Catalans were struggling down the table. By the season's end they were champions, Cruyff's triumphant progress having included a spectacular 5–0 victory away to deadly rivals Real Madrid. Surprisingly, apart from that league title, Barcelona won little else, though Cruyff himself completed the first ever hat-trick of European Footballer of the Year awards.

RED ALERT *Cruyff created panic when he had the ball.*

It was at the end of his first season with Barcelona that Cruyff's career reached its international zenith. At the 1974 World Cup finals Holland took their total football through round after round. No one could withstand them. Above all, no one could handle the mercurial Cruyff, who inspired victories over Uruguay and Bulgaria in the first round, then provided two goals to lead the way against Argentina in the second. The last group match – in effect the semi-final – was against Brazil: the old masters against the new. Cruyff scored Holland's decisive second goal in a 2–0 victory which signalled a new era.

The Final, of course, ended in defeat at the hands of West Germany and, though Holland reached the Final again in 1978, Cruyff, by then, had retired from the national team and was about to head west.

First he joined the Los Angeles Aztecs in the NASL. He won the Most Valuable Player award that year, moved to the Washington Diplomats in 1980 and, late in 1981, returned to Holland to win the Championship twice more with Ajax and once, mischievously, with old rivals Feyenoord.

Retracing his steps as a Manager

Cruyff's move into management, typically, aroused new controversy as he had never obtained the necessary examination qualifications. Not that it mattered. He guided Ajax to the European Cup-winners' Cup in 1987, and repeated the trick in 1989 after retracing his steps to Barcelona. His innovations now cause as much fuss as the total football of his playing days.

Thus Cruyff ranks not only among the game's greatest players and personalities but among its greatest innovators as well.

1947 *Born on April 25 in Amsterdam*

1959 *Enrolled by his mother in the Ajax youth section*

1963 *Signed his first Ajax contract at 16 on the recommendation of English coach Vic Buckingham, then marked his debut with a goal*

1966 *Made his debut for Holland in a 2–2 draw against Hungary and scored a last-minute equalizer in the first of his 48 internationals*

1969 *Made his first European Cup final appearance with Ajax, but Milan won 4–1 in Madrid*

1971 *Won the first of three successive European Cups, helping Ajax defeat Panathinaikos of Greece at Wembley. He was also voted European Footballer of the Year, the first of three such accolades*

1973 *Sold by Ajax to Barcelona for a world record transfer fee of £922,000*

1974 *Captained and inspired Holland to reach the 1974 World Cup Final in Munich, where they lost 2–1 to hosts West Germany*

1978 *Retired from the national team before the World Cup finals in Argentina, and left Barcelona to play in America with Los Angeles Aztecs and Washington Diplomats*

1981 *Returned to Europe to play for minor club Levante in Spain, then to Holland with Ajax and, finally, Feyenoord*

1984 *Went back to Ajax, this time as technical director*

1987 *Guided Ajax to victory in the European Cup-winners' Cup as a parting gift before being appointed coach to Barcelona*

1992 *Managed Barcelona to their long awaited victory in the European Cup Final, where they beat Sampdoria 1–0 at Wembley*

1996 *Left Barcelona after a record seven years in charge including four consecutive league championships*

DI STEFANO

FIFA'S AMBASSADOR *Di Stefano leads the rest of the world by example against England at Wembley in 1963*

WORLD-CLASS ALL-ROUNDER

Alfredo Di Stefano is reckoned by many to be the greatest footballer of all. While Pele's admirers consider it sacrilege, the millions who wondered at Di Stefano's majestic domination of European football in the 1950s and early 1960s may concur.

Di Stefano's greatness lay not only in his achievement in leading Madrid to victory in the first five con-secutive European Cup Finals – and inspiring a great breakthrough in international football – but also because no other footballer so effec-tively combined individual expertise with an all-embracing ability to orga-nize a team to play to his command.

Today he is a wealthy elder statesman of soccer. Yet he was born in Barracas, a poor suburb of the Argentine capital of Buenos Aires, and learned his football first in the tough streets of the city, then out on the family farm. This was where he built up the stamina which would become legendary across the world in later years.

Di Stefano's grandfather had emigrated to Argentina from Capri. His father had played for the lead-ing Buenos Aires club, River Plate, but abruptly ended his career when professionalism was introduced. To Di Stefano senior football was a recreation, not a means to earn a liv-ing. Thus he was not particularly pleased when his sons Alfredo and Tulio launched their own teenage careers with local teams.

Eventually, he relented and young Alfredo – nicknamed "El Aleman" (the German), because of his blond hair – made his River Plate debut on August 18, 1944, at outside-right.

Plate left on Shelf

Di Stefano's hero had been Independiente's free-scoring Paraguayan centre-forward, Arsenio Erico. Di Stefano wanted to be a centre-forward himself. He learned his trade while on loan to Huracan, then returned to River Plate to replace the great Adolfo Pedernera.

River's forward line was nicknamed *La Maquina* (the Machine), for the remorseless consistency with which they took opposing defences apart. Di Stefano transferred his attacking prowess into the Argentine national team with equal success when they won the 1947 South American Championship.

In 1949 Argentine players went on strike. The clubs locked them out and completed their fixtures with amateur players. Meanwhile, the star professionals were lured away to play in the pirate league which had been set up, outside FIFA's jurisdiction, in Colombia.

Di Stefano was the star of stars there, playing for Millonarios of Bogota, the so-called "Blue Ballet". When Colombia was reintegrated in FIFA, Millonarios went on one last world tour . . . where Di Stefano was spotted by Real Madrid after starring in the Spanish club's fiftieth anniversary tournament.

Madrid agreed a fee with Millonarios and thus nearly outflanked rivals Barcelona, who had sealed a deal with Di Stefano's old club, River Plate. A Spanish soccer court ruled that Di Stefano should play one season for Madrid, one season for Barcelona. But after he made a quiet start to the season, Barcelona, unimpressed, sold out their share in Di Stefano to Madrid.

Four days later he scored a hat-trick in a 5–0 win against . . . Barcelona. A legend had been born.

"Two Players in every Position"

Madrid were Spanish champions in Di Stefano's first two seasons and European Cup winners in his next five. He scored in each of Madrid's European Cup Finals, including a hat-trick against Frankfurt in 1960 in a 90-minute spectacular which has become one of the most-admired football matches of all time.

Di Stefano was "total football" personified before the term had been invented. One moment he was defending in his own penalty area, the next organizing his midfield, the next scoring from the edge of the opponents' six-yard box. As Miguel Muñoz, long-time Madrid colleague as player and then coach, once said: "The greatness of Di Stefano was that, with him in your side, you had two players in every position."

THE BLOND ARROW
of Real Madrid and Spain

> **"Di Stefano is the greatest player I have ever seen. The things he does in a match will never be equalled."**
>
> *Luis Del Sol, 1960 European Cup-winning team-mate*

Career facts

1926 Born Alfredo Stefano Di Stefano Lauhle on July 4 in Barracas, a poor suburb of Buenos Aires, Argentina

1940 Hinted at things to come by scoring a hat-trick in 20 minutes for his first youth team, Los Cardales

1942 Left Los Cardales after a row with the coach, to join his father's old club, River Plate

1943 Made his debut for River Plate, playing as a right-winger, aged 17, against Buenos Aires rivals San Lorenzo

1944 Transferred on loan to Huracan, for whom he scored the winner in a league game against River Plate

1946 Returned to River Plate to succeed the great Adolfo Pedernera at centre-forward in an attack nicknamed La Maquina (the Machine)

1947 Already an international, won the South American Championship with Argentina

1949 Lured away, during the famous Argentine players' strike, to play in a pirate league outside of FIFA's jurisdiction in Colombia for Millonarios of Bogota

1953 Moved to Spain where he joined Real Madrid

1956 Inspired Madrid to the first of five successive European Cup victories and made his national team debut for Spain

1960 Scored a hat-trick in Real's legendary 7–3 victory over Eintracht Frankfurt in the European Cup final at Hampden Park, Glasgow

1963 Kidnapped – and later released unharmed – by urban guerrillas while on tour with Real Madrid in Venezuela

1964 Left Madrid for one last season as a player with Espanol of Barcelona, before becoming a coach in both Argentina and Spain

EUSEBIO

FRIENDLY INTENT *Eusebio outpaces Arsenal's admiring George Graham at Highbury*

HIS MAJESTY KING SOCCER

Eusebio, the greatest Portuguese footballer in history, did not, in fact, come from Portugal at all. Born and brought up in Mozambique, then still one of Portugal's African colonies, Eusebio was the first African footballer to earn a world-wide reputation.

The big Portuguese clubs such as Benfica, Sporting and Porto financed nursery teams in Mozambique and Angola and unearthed a wealth of talent which they then transported into not only Portuguese football but the Portuguese national team.

The young Eusebio, ironically, was a nursery product not of Benfica but of their great Lisbon rivals, Sporting. But when Sporting summoned him to Lisbon for a trial in 1961, he was virtually kidnapped off the aeroplane by Benfica officials and hidden away until the fuss had died down and Sporting, having all but forgotten about him, lost interest.

Hijacked by Benfica

Bela Guttmann, a veteran Hungarian, was coach of Benfica at the time. He had a high regard for the potential offered by Mozambique and Angola. The nucleus of the Benfica team which Guttmann had guided to European Cup victory over Barcelona that year came from Africa: goalkeeper Costa Pereira, centre-forward and captain Jose Aguas, and the two inside-forwards

terdam. In 13 seasons he helped Benfica win the League seven times and the Cup twice; he was European Footballer of the Year in 1965; top scorer with nine goals in the 1966 World Cup finals; scorer of 38 goals in 46 internationals and the league's leading scorer seven times before knee trouble forced a halt at 32.

But football was Eusebio's life. When the fledgeling North American Soccer League offered him the chance of a lucrative extension to his career, he flew west to play for the Boston Minutemen (alongside old Benfica team-mate Antonio Simoes), then for the Toronto Metros-Croatia, and then for the Las Vegas Quicksilver.

Benfica's faithful had mixed feelings about his self-imposed exile in North America. But controversy was soon forgotten when he returned to Lisbon to take up various appointments as television analyst, as assistant coach and as the most honoured public face of Benfica.

A Majestic Sportsman

Fans around the world took Eusebio to their hearts not only because of his ability but because of the sportsmanlike way he played the people's game. At Wembley in 1968 Eusebio very nearly won the European Cup Final for Benfica against Manchester United in the closing minutes of normal time, being foiled only by the intuition of Alex Stepney. Eusebio's reaction? He patted Step-

UNSTOPPABLE *against Milan*

ney on the back, applauding a worthy opponent.

Wembley Stadium played a major role in Eusebio's career. It was at Wembley, in a 2–0 World Cup qualifying defeat by England in 1961, that his youthful power first made the international game sit up; it was at Wembley, in 1963, that he scored one of his finest individual goals as consolation in a 2–1 European Cup Final defeat by Milan; and it was at Wembley again, in 1966, that Eusebio led Portugal to their best-ever third place in the World Cup. The semi-final, in which Portugal lost 2–1 to England, will long be remembered as as exemplary exhibition of sportsmanship under pressure.

Appropriately, a statue of Eusebio in action now dominates the entrance to the Estadio da Luz. Appropriately, also, a film made about his life was subtitled *Sua Majestade o Rei ...* His Majesty the King.

Career facts

1942 *Born Eusebio Da Silva Ferreira on January 25 in Lourenço Marques, Mozambique*

1952 *Joined the youth teams of Sporting (Lourenço Marques), a nursery team for the Portuguese giants of the same name*

1961 *Sporting tried to bring Eusebio to Lisbon, but he was "kidnapped" on arrival by Benfica. In the autumn, with barely a dozen league games to his name, he made his debut for Portugal*

1962 *Scored two thundering goals as Benfica beat Real Madrid 5–3 in a classic European Cup Final in Amsterdam*

1965 *Voted European Footballer of the Year*

1966 *Crowned top scorer with nine goals as Portugal finished third in the World Cup finals in England, where he was nicknamed the "new Pele" and the "Black Panther"*

1969 *Won Portuguese championship medal for the seventh and last time with Benfica before winding down his career in Mexico and Canada*

1992 *A statue in his honour was unveiled at the entrance to Benfica's Estadio da Luz in Lisbon*

Joaquim Santana and Mario Coluna. But Eusebio would prove the greatest of all.

Guttmann introduced him to the first team at the end of the 1960–61 season. He was a reserve when Benfica went to France to face Santos of Brazil – inspired by Pele – in the famous Paris Tournament. At half-time Benfica were losing 3–0. Guttmann, with nothing to lose, sent on Eusebio. Benfica still lost, but Eusebio scored a spectacular hat-trick and outshone even Pele. He was still only 19.

A year later Eusebio scored two cannonball goals in the 5–3 victory Benfica ran up against Real Madrid in the European Cup Final in Ams-

> ## " Everywhere I go, Eusebio is the name people mention. "
>
> *Mario Soares, President of Portugal*

HOLD-UP *Yashin foils Eusebio in the 1966 World Cup third place game*

MARADONA

IDOL OF TWO CONTINENTS

CROWD-PULLER, CROWD-PLEASER *Maradona, the inspiration of Napoli*

Diego Maradona was not only the world's greatest footballer throughout the 1980s and early 1990s. He was also the most controversial and the most enigmatic.

His admirers in Argentina, where he knew the early glory days with Argentinos Juniors and Boca Juniors, considered him little less than a god, and the *tifosi* in Italy, where he triumphed with Napoli, worshipped his bootlaces. So did all of Argentina after Maradona reached the zenith of his career, captaining his country to victory in the 1986 World Cup finals in Mexico.

English fans still rage over his "Hand of God" goal in the quarter-final in Mexico City. But Argentine fans remember most clearly his other goal in that game when he collected the ball inside his own half and outwitted five defenders and goalkeeper Peter Shilton before gliding home one of the greatest goals in the history of the World Cup. Maradona provided a repeat against Belgium in the semi-finals: another brilliant slalom through the defence but from the left, not the right. Then, in the Final against West Germany, his slide-rule pass sent Jorge Burruchaga away to score the dramatic winner.

Maradona's great ability made his subsequent fall all the greater. His love affair with Italian football went sour after the 1990 World Cup, when Maradona's Argentina defeated their hosts on penalties in the semi-final in Maradona's adopted home of Naples. The following spring a dope test showed cocaine traces. He was banned from Italian and then world football for 15 months, returned to Argentina and was arrested there for cocaine possession.

Released on probation, he sought to revive his playing career in Spain, but half a season at Sevilla proved a disaster. Even his 1994 World Cup comeback ended in the shameful ignominy of dope-test failure and a new 15-month international playing ban. He turned briefly to coaching with Deportivo Mandiyu, then with Racing Avellaneda before undertaking yet another playing comeback with his old love, Boca Juniors.

A Roller-Coaster Career

It all began in the working-class Fiorito suburb of Lanus in the province of Buenos Aires where Maradona began playing for a kids' team named Estrella Roja (Red Star) at the age of nine. Later he and his friends founded a team known as Los Cebollitas (The Little Onions) who were so promising that the team was signed up en bloc by Argentinos Juniors as one of the club's youth sides.

On October 20, 1976, Maradona (wearing No. 16) made his league debut as a 15-year-old substitute against Talleres of Cordoba, and a week later he played his first full match against Newells Old Boys from Rosario. In February 1977 he made his international debut. It appeared odds-on that Maradona would be a member of the squad with which manager Cesar Luis Menotti planned to win the World Cup for Argentina for the first time in front of their own fanatical fans in 1978, but he was one of the three players dropped on the eve of the finals. It was months before he would speak to Menotti again, but their eventual peace talk paved the way for the first international success of Maradona's career at the 1979 World Youth Cup in Japan.

Boca Juniors bought him for a world record £1 million and resold him two years later to Barcelona for £3 million, another record. Before joining the Catalans he succumbed to the pressures of the World Cup, in Spain in 1982, where he was sent off for an awful lunge at Batista of Brazil. It was the recurring theme of his career: a unique talent for football shadowed by a similarly unique aptitude for arousing controversy.

It says much for the magical technique of his left foot that, despite all the negative vibes, Maradona continued to entrance the game. In 1984 Napoli paid another world record, this time

> **❝Pele was the supreme player of his era; Maradona is the pre-eminent player of his time. You cannot compare them. Such greatness does not submit to comparison. ❞**
> *Cesar Luis Menotti, former manager of Argentina*

£5 million, to end Maradona's injury-battered two-year stay with Barcelona. Within weeks Napoli sold a staggering 70,000 season tickets. Two Italian League championships and one UEFA Cup success were the reward for the fans.

Seven glorious, roller-coaster years went by before the partnership was dissolved. Football in Naples will never be the same again.

Career facts

1960 *Born on October 30 in Lanus, Buenos Aires*
1976 *Made his league debut at 15 for Argentinos Juniors*
1977 *Made his international debut at 16 for Argentina in a friendly against Hungary*
1980 *Sold to Boca Juniors for £1 million, a record for a teenager*
1982 *Sold to Barcelona for another world record £3 million, then out of the game for four months after a reckless tackle by Bilbao's notorious defender Andoni Goicochea*
1984 *Sold to Napoli for a third world record, now £5 million*
1986 *Inspired Argentina to victory at the World Cup finals in Mexico: was unanimous choice as Player of the Tournament*
1987 *Led Napoli to their first-ever Italian league title plus victory in the Italian cup*
1988 *Won his only European prize as Napoli beat Stuttgart in the UEFA Cup Final*
1990 *Despite a collection of injuries, Maradona led Argentina back to the World Cup Final, where they were defeated 1–0 by West Germany*
1991 *Failed a dope test and was banned for 15 months*
1992 *Made a disappointing comeback with Sevilla in Spain*
1993 *Sacked by Sevilla, Maradona began a second comeback in Argentina with Newells Old Boys*
1994 *Banned again, for 15 months, after a positive drugs test during the World Cup*
1995 *Returns to playing with Boca Juniors after coaching stints with Deportivo Mandiyu and Racing Avellaneda*

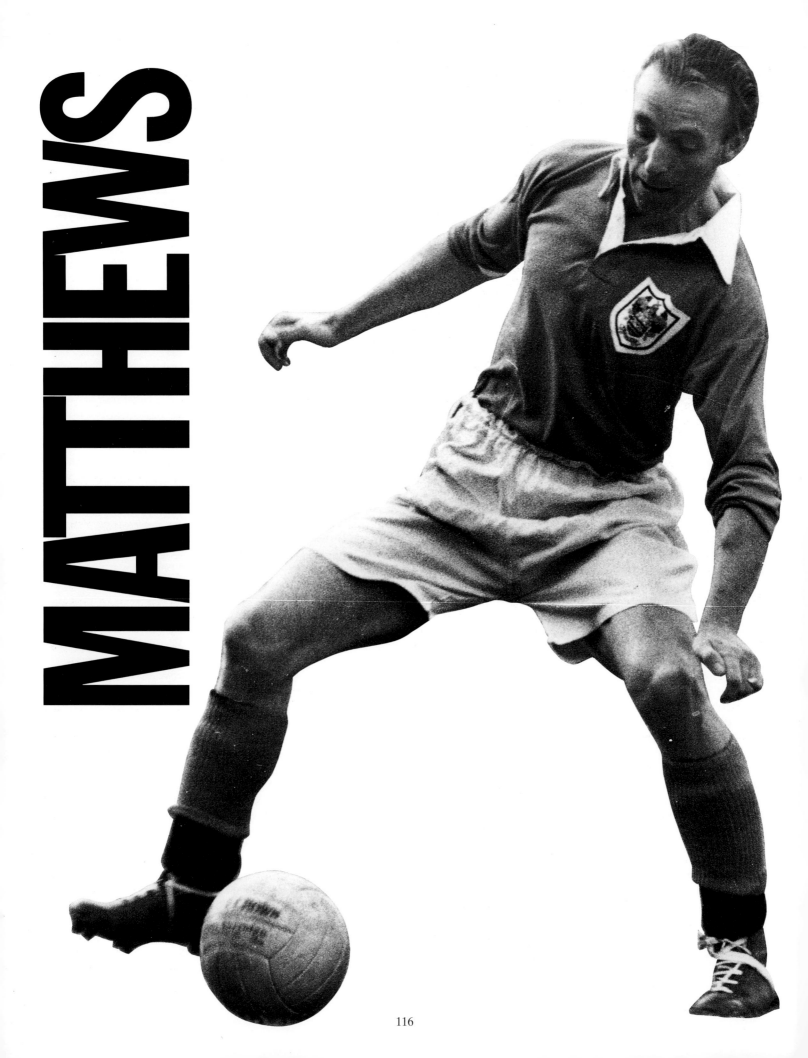

MATTHEWS

A LEFT-BACK'S NIGHTMARE

CHEERS! *Matthews is chaired off by his Cup-winning team-mates in 1953*

Stanley Matthews was the first great footballer of the modern era. There will be cases made for Billy Wright, Bobby Charlton, Bobby Moore and others but none dominated his particular era as long as the barber's son from Hanley in the Potteries area of the English Midlands.

Matthews was nicknamed the Wizard of Dribble and the magic of his talent and reputation survived right through to the closing days of his career when he returned to his original club, Stoke City, and inspired them to win promotion out of the Second Division doldrums. That achieved, at the climax of the longest first-class career of any player, he decided to retire, at the age of 50. Later, however, Matthews insisted that he could – and should – have played for several more years.

Matthews went out in a style befitting one of the legends of the game. Among the other great players who turned out for his testimonial match at Stoke were Di Stefano, Puskas and Yashin. Always keen to put back into football as much, if not more, than he had taken out in terms of fame and glory, Matthews became general manager of another Potter-

> **❝ The greatest tribute to Stanley Matthews is that he can go to any ground and make a monkey of a full-back and still be loved by the crowd. ❞**
>
> *Leslie Edwards,*
> Liverpool Echo

ies club, Port Vale. But the role was too restrictive for a man who had painted his football on a grand canvas, and Matthews left after 18 months to take coaching and exhibition courses around the world, in particular to Africa. Later he lived for many years in Malta before returning to settle again in England.

In the 1930s and 1940s Matthews was without rival as the greatest outside-right in the world. Opposing left-backs feared their duels with him as Matthews brought the ball towards them, feinted one way and accelerated clear another. His adoring public desperately wanted to see him crown his career with an FA Cup winners' medal. That dream was denied by Manchester United in 1948 and Newcastle in 1951. But in 1953 – a remarkable year for English sport with England reclaiming cricket's "Ashes" trophy from Australia and the veteran jockey Sir Gordon Richards winning the Derby – the 38-year-old Matthews tried again.

When Blackpool were 3–1 down to Bolton with time running out, it seemed Matthews was destined never to claim that elusive prize. But Matthews took over, ripping the Bolton defence to shreds and providing not only the inspiration for Blackpool's climb back to equality, but also the cross from which Bill Perry shot the winning goal. Blackpool scored twice in the last three minutes.

An Artist and a Gentleman

Like any footballer, Matthews knew his share of defeats. One of the most remarkable was England's 1–0 upset by the United States at the 1950 World Cup finals in Belo Horizonte, Brazil, when he had to watch in embarrassment after being omitted from the team. But England might have found more consistency if controversy had not been raised now and again over whether Matthews or Preston's Tom Finney was the more effective right-winger. Eventually the problem was solved by switching the versatile Finney to outside-left.

Matthews, by contrast, was always and only an outside-right, demonstrating supreme artistry in a posi-

tion which was later declared redundant when work-rate mechanics took over the game in the mid-1960s. Only much later, when coaches suddenly understood the value of breaking down massed defences by going down the wings, was old-fashioned wing play revived.

But Matthews was, like many of the game's greatest players, a personality and an inspiring example for all youngsters. His knighthood was appropriate recognition for a 33-year career, completed without a single booking, in which he had graced the game as the First Gentleman of Football.

Career facts

1915 Born on February 1 in Hanley, Stoke-on-Trent.

1932 Turned professional with local club Stoke City

1934 Made his debut for England in a 4–0 win over Wales in Cardiff

1946 Sold to Blackpool for £11,500

1948 Played a key role in one of England's greatest victories, by 4–0 over Italy in Turin, and was voted Footballer of the Year

1953 Sealed his place among football's legends by inspiring Blackpool's FA Cup Final comeback against Bolton

1955 One of his many summer exhibition tours took him to Mozambique, where among the ball boys mesmerized at a match in Lourenço Marques was Eusebio

1957 Played the last of 84 games for England (including wartime internationals) in a 4–1 World Cup qualifying victory over Denmark in Copenhagen

1961 Returned to Stoke for a mere £2,800 and, despite his 46 years, inspired their successful campaign to get back into the First Division

1965 Retired after a star-spangled Farewell Match at Stoke's Victoria Ground featuring the likes of Di Stefano, Puskas and Yashin

PELE

THE MASTER SHOWMAN

Pele remains one of those great examples and inspirations of world sport: a poor boy whose talent lifted him to the peaks of achievement, fame and fortune ... yet who, amidst all that, retained his innate sense of sportsmanship, his love of his calling and the respect of team-mates and opponents alike.

His father Dondinho had been a useful footballer in the 1940s, but his career had been ended prematurely by injury. He was his son's first coach and his first supporter.

Most Brazilian footballers are known by nicknames. Pele does not know the origin of his own tag. He recalled only that he did not like it and was in trouble at school for fighting with class-mates who called him Pele. Later, of course, it became the most familiar name in world sport.

World Cup Triumph

Pele's teenage exploits as a player with his local club, Bauru, earned him a transfer to Santos at the age of 15. Rapidly he earned national and then international recognition. At 16 he was playing for Brazil; at 17 he was winning the World Cup. Yet it took pressure from his team-mates to persuade national manager Vicente Feola to throw him into the action in Sweden in 1958.

Santos were not slow to recognize the potential offered their club by Pele. The directors created a sort of circus, touring the world, playing two

> ❝ Pele is to Brazilian football what Shakespeare is to English literature. ❞
>
> *Joao Saldanha, former manager of Brazil*

and three times a week for lucrative match fees. The income from this gave the club the financial leverage to buy a supporting cast which helped turn Santos into World Club Champions in 1962 and 1963.

Mexico Makes up for Everything

The pressure on Pele was reflected in injuries, one of which restricted him to only a peripheral role at the 1962 World Cup finals. He scored a marvellous solo goal against Mexico in the first round, but pulled a muscle and missed the rest of the tournament. Brazil, even without him, went on to retain the Jules Rimet Trophy.

In 1966 Pele led Brazil in England. But referees were unprepared to give players of skill and creativity the necessary protection. One of the saddest images of the tournament was Pele, a raincoat around his shoulders, leaving the pitch after being kicked out of the tournament by Portugal. Brazil, this time, did not possess the same strength in depth as in 1962, and crashed out.

Four years later Pele took his revenge in the most glorious way. As long as the game is played, the 1970 World Cup finals will be revered as the apotheosis of a great player, not only at his very best, but achieving the rewards his talent deserved.

As a 17-year-old Pele had scored one of the unforgettable World Cup goals in the Final

MUTUAL RESPECT *With Bobby Moore*

O REI *Pele, king of Brazilian football from the late 1950s to the early 1970s*

Career facts

1940 Born Edson Arantes do Nascimento on October 21 in Tres Coracoes

1950 Began playing with local club Bauru, where his father was a coach

1956 Transferred to big-city club Santos and made his league debut at 15

1957 Made his debut for Brazil, at 16, against Argentina

1958 Became the youngest-ever World Cup winner, scoring two goals in the Final as Brazil beat Sweden 5–2

1962 Missed the 1962 World Cup win because of injury in the first round ... but compensated by winning the World Club Cup with Santos

1970 Inspired Brazil to complete their historic World Cup hat-trick in Mexico

1975 Ended an 18-month retirement to play for Cosmos of New York in the dramatic, short-lived North American Soccer League

1977 Retired again after lifting Cosmos to their third NASL championship

1982 Presented with FIFA's Gold Medal Award for outstanding service to the worldwide game

1994 Appointed Brazil's Minister for Sport

against Sweden – in 1970 he twice nearly surpassed it. First, against Czechoslovakia, he just missed scoring with a shot from his own half of the field, and against Uruguay he sold an outrageous dummy to the goalkeeper and just missed again.

It says everything about Pele's transcending genius that he was the one man able to set light to soccer in the United States in the 1970s. Although the North American Soccer League eventually collapsed amid financial confusion, soccer was by that stage firmly established as a grass-roots American sport. Without Pele's original allure that could never have happened and the capture of host rights for the 1994 finals would never have been possible.

PUSKAS

THE MAGICAL LEFT FOOT

Ferenc Puskas remains one of the greatest players of all time – a symbol of the legendary "Magic Magyars" who dominated European football in the early 1950s and stand as perhaps the greatest team never to have won the World Cup.

Puskas's father was a player and later coach with the local club, Kispest. At 16 Ferenc was a regular at inside-left, terrorizing opposing goalkeepers with the power of his shooting. He rarely used his right foot but then his left was so lethal that he seldom needed it.

At 18 he was in the national team, too. His brilliance had much to do with the decision to convert Kispest into a new army sports club named Honved, that formed the basis of the national side.

For four years Hungary, built around goalkeeper Gyula Grosics, right-half Jozsef Bozsik and the inside-forward trio of Sandor Kocsis, Nandor Hidegkuti and Puskas, crushed all opposition. They also introduced a new tactical concept. The inside-forwards, Kocsis and Puskas, formed the spearhead of the attack, with Hidegkuti a revolutionary deep-lying centre-forward. Hungary won the 1952 Olympic title before ending England's record of invincibility against continental opposition with a stunning 6–3 triumph at Wembley.

Early the following year, Hun-gary thrashed England again, 7–1 in Budapest. No wonder they were overwhelming favourites to win the 1954 World Cup in Switzerland. But Puskas presented a problem. He had been injured in an early round game against West Germany and was a hobbling spectator at training before the Final, against these same West Germans, in Berne. Could his great left foot withstand the strain? Puskas thought so and decided to play, thus taking one of the most controversial gambles in the game's history. After only 12 minutes the gamble appeared to be paying off when Hungary led 2–0. However, they lost 3–2, their dominance finally ended in the one match which mattered most.

The Toast of Spain

It was eight long years before Puskas would return to the World Cup finals. Then, in Chile in 1962, his trusty left foot was doing duty for Spain, because Puskas had, in the meantime, defected to the West, joining Real Madrid. Honved had been abroad when the Hungarian Revolution of 1956 erupted. Puskas and several team-mates decided to stay in the West. He made an attempt to sign for several Italian clubs, but they thought him too old. How wrong they were was underlined when Puskas developed, at Madrid, a new career to emulate his first in brilliance.

Four times Puskas was the Spanish league's top scorer and his partnership with the Argentine centre-forward, Alfredo Di Stefano, was one of the greatest of all time. They hit perfection together on the famous night when Madrid thrashed Eintracht Frankfurt 7–3 in the European Cup Final before a record 135,000 crowd at Hampden.

Di Stefano scored three goals, Puskas four. The Spanish fans loved him. In his Hungarian army club days at Honved, Puskas had been known as the Galloping Major. Now they called him *Cañoncito* – the little cannon.

In 1966 he finally retired. His future was secure, thanks to business investments which included a sausage factory near Madrid. He tried his hand at coaching without a great deal of success – save for the remarkable 1970–71 season when he took Panathinaikos of Athens to the European Cup Final.

In the course of time he was able to visit his native Hungary, where he was celebrated once more as a national hero. Hardly surprising. After all, how many can boast 83 goals in 84 games for their country?

> ## " His was a name fit for any sporting hall of fame, worthy of any and every superlative. "
> *Billy Wright,*
> *England captain against*
> *Hungary in 1953*

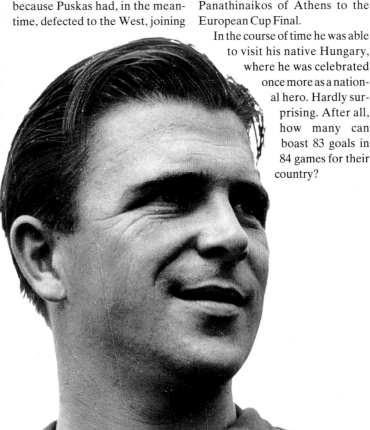

Career facts

1927 *Born on April 2 in Budapest*

1943 *Made his debut for his father's old club, Kispest*

1945 *Played his first international for Hungary against Austria*

1948 *Transferred with the entire Kispest playing staff to the new army club, Honved, and top-scored with 50 goals in the League championship*

1952 *Captained Hungary to victory over Yugoslavia in the final of the Olympic Games soccer tournament in Helsinki*

1953 *Earned a place in history by inspiring Hungary's historic 6–3 victory over England at Wembley*

1954 *Played despite injury, amid controversy, in the World Cup Final which Hungary lost 3–2 to West Germany in Berne – their first defeat for four years*

1956 *Stayed in western Europe when the Hungarian Revolution broke out while Honved were abroad to play a European Cup tie against Bilbao*

1958 *Signed for Real Madrid by his old manager at Honved, Emil Oestreicher*

1960 *Scored four goals for Madrid in their famous 7–3 demolition of Eintracht Frankfurt in the European Cup Final at Hampden Park, Glasgow*

1962 *Played in the World Cup finals in Chile, this time for his adopted country of Spain*

1966 *Retired and turned to coaching*

1971 *Achieved his greatest success as a trainer, guiding outsiders Panathinaikos of Athens to the European Cup Final (they lost 2–0 to Ajax at Wembley)*

1993 *Appointed, briefly, as caretaker-manager of Hungary during the 1994 World Cup qualifiers*

YASHIN

INTUITION PERSONIFIED *Yashin in action in his last active World Cup finals in 1966*

"BLACK PANTHER" WAS THE SUPREME SOVIET

In South America they called Lev Yashin the "Black Spider"; in Europe the "Black Panther". Portugal's Eusebio described him as "the peerless goalkeeper of the century". It says everything about his ability and his personality that the likes of Pele, Eusebio and Franz Beckenbauer made the journey to Moscow for his farewell match.

Yet Yashin very nearly gave up soccer altogether in favour of ice hockey. That was in 1953. He was tiring of standing in as reserve at Moscow Dynamo to the legendary Alexei "Tiger" Khomich. He was 23, after all, and Dynamo's ice hockey coaches were begging him to commit himself to their cause.

Then Khomich was injured. Dynamo coach Arkady Chereny-

"Yashin was the peerless goalkeeper of the century."

Eusebio

internationals, ending his career with a then Soviet record 78 caps to his name. For Dynamo, Yashin played 326 Supreme League matches and won the league title six times and the Soviet cup twice. On his death in 1990, the official news agency, Tass, described him as "the most famous Soviet sportsman ever".

First Goalkeeper and First Soviet

Yashin's fame had quickly spread throughout the world, not merely for his ability as a goalkeeper, to stop shots that no-one else could reach, but as an outstanding sportsman and ambassador for the game. Appropriately, in 1963 he became the first Soviet player to be nominated as European Footballer of the Year by the French magazine, *France Football*. To this day, he remains the only goalkeeper to have received the award. In South America, when the magazine *El Grafico* ran a readers' poll to determine the Greatest Team of All Time, Yashin was virtually unchallenged as goalkeeper.

The World Cups of 1958, 1962 and 1966 saw Yashin at work, and he was also in Mexico in 1970 though only as a reserve because of the value of his experience behind the scenes and in the dressing-rooms. In 1965, Yashin was outstanding in the Stanley

Matthews Retirement Match at Stoke when a British XI lost narrowly to a World XI featuring not only Yashin but Di Stefano, Puskas, the other great exiled Hungarian Ladislav Kubala, and Yashin's immediate predecessor as European Footballer of the Year, Czechoslovakia's Josef Masopust.

One of Yashin's saves that night – diving full length across the face of his goal to grip a shot from Jimmy Greaves which few goalkeepers would even have got a finger to – will live for ever in the memory of those who were present.

Yashin was said to have saved more than 150 penalties during his career. One of the few which got past him was struck by Eusebio in the third place play-off at the 1966 World Cup finals at Wembley. The Soviets finished fourth, but that remains their best finish in the game's greatest competition.

Grand Testimonial

When Yashin retired in 1970, a testimonial match was arranged and stars from all over the world turned out in honour of the great sportsman. The match at Lenin stadium, before 100,000 fans, was an unforgettable event in Soviet soccer history.

Yashin remained in sport after his retirement, not as a coach or trainer but as head of the Ministry of Sport's football department and then as a vice-president of the national association. His film archive, compiled from shots he had taken all round the world, was an object of admiration, as was his

modern jazz record collection. Towards the end of his career, Yashin was honoured by the Soviet government with its ultimate honour, the Order of Lenin. In recent years Lenin's reputation has gone into steep decline: something that could never be said of Lev Yashin.

Career facts

1929 Born Lev Ivanovich Yashin on October 22 in Moscow

1946 Joined Moscow Dynamo as an ice hockey goaltender

1951 Made his first-team debut for Moscow Dynamo

1953 Finally took over as Dynamo's first-choice keeper

1954 Made his debut for the Soviet Union in a 3–2 win over Sweden

1956 Won Olympic gold with the Soviet Union at the Melbourne Games

1958 Appeared in his first World Cup and helped the Soviet Union reach the quarter-finals

1960 Won the first European Championship with the Soviet Union against Yugoslavia in Paris

1963 Voted European Footballer of the Year and played for FIFA's World XI at Wembley in a match to mark the centenary of the Football Association

1968 Awarded the Order of Lenin by the Soviet government

shev called on the impatient reserve, and Yashin took over to such outstanding effect that, a year later, he was making his debut for the Soviet Union in a 3–2 win over Sweden. Two years later, in 1956, Yashin kept goal for the Soviet side who won the Olympic title in Melbourne, Australia. In 1960 he was goalkeeper for the Soviet side who won the inaugural European Championship, then called the Nations Cup.

After that first summons in 1953, Yashin had never looked back. In the first seven years after his debut for the Soviet Union he missed only two

SEMI-FINALISTS *The Soviet Union's 1966 World Cup side*

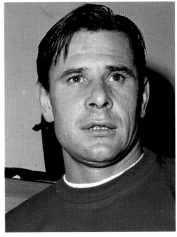

YASHIN *The "Black Panther"*

THE GREAT PLAYERS

Every country produces great players. These are the men who have delighted fans over the years not merely with their achievements but with their personalities. They drew spectators who may have had no previous attachment to their clubs but who were simply attracted by their skills. The advent of TV has widened their fame.

A

Andre "Trello" Abegglen

Born: March 7, 1909, Switzerland.
Clubs: Etoile Rouge, Cantonal, Grasshoppers (Swz), Sochaux (Fr), Servette, La Chaux-de-Fonds (Swz).

Abegglen was the first great Swiss player to make his mark on the world stage. He and brother Max, nicknamed Xam, were inside-forward stalwarts together at the Grasshoppers club of Zurich. Trello scored 30 goals in 52 internationals for Switzerland between 1927 and 1943. He starred at the 1934 and 1938 World Cup finals and won three Swiss championships, two while with Grasshoppers and one after moving on to Servette of Geneva. Brother Max played 68 times for Switzerland and was top scorer at the 1924 Olympic Games.

Ademir Marques de Menezes

Born: November 8, 1922, Brazil.
Clubs: FC Recife, Vasco da Gama, Fluminense, Vasco da Gama.

Ademir was the seven-goal leading scorer at the 1950 World Cup finals when he played centre-forward for Brazil. The inside-forward trio of Ademir, Zizinho and Jair da Rosa was considered one of the greatest in Brazil's history. Ademir scored 32 goals in 37 internationals after beginning his career as an outside-left. He had a powerful shot in both feet and was six times a Rio state league champion, five times with Vasco da Gama and once with Fluminense. It was said that Brazilian coaches created 4–2–4 because Ademir's ability forced opposing teams to play with an extra central defender.

José Pinto Carvalho dos Santos Aguas

Born: c. 1930, Portugal.
Clubs: Benfica (Port), FK Austria.

Aguas was captain and centre-forward of the Benfica side which succeeded Real Madrid as European champions in 1961. In his native Angola, legend has it, he was a famed local lion-hunter when Benfica persuaded him he could enjoy a more lucrative existence hunting goals. He flew to Portugal in 1950 and scored more than 250 goals for Benfica as well as finishing top league scorer five times. In 1960–61 he was also top scorer, with 11 goals, in the European Cup and collected the trophy as captain after the final victory over Barcelona. In 1963 he transferred to FK Austria but later returned to Portugal to work as a coach.

Florian Albert

Born: September 15, 1941, Hungary.
Club: Ferencvaros.

Albert was the first outstanding player to emerge in Hungary after the dissolution of the

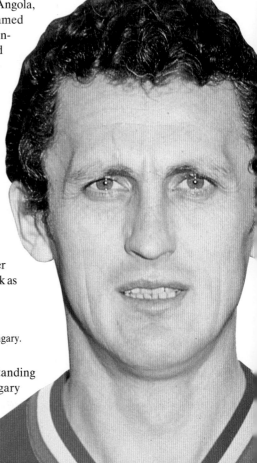

great team of the early 1950s. Albert was a farmer's son whose family moved to Budapest while he was still a boy. His talent was quickly recognized by the youth coaches of Ferencvaros, and he made his international debut at 17, in a 3–2 win over Sweden in Budapest, a few days after passing his major school examinations. Centre-forward Albert was three times the leading scorer in the Hungarian league and four times a league championship winner with Ferencvaros. His most memorable display was as the inspiration of Hungary's 3–1 win over Brazil at the 1966 World Cup finals, and he was voted European Footballer of the Year the following year.

Ivor Allchurch

Born: October 16, 1919, Wales.
Clubs: Swansea (Wales), Newcastle (Eng), Cardiff, Swansea (Wales).

Slim, elegant, creative and a natural scorer: Ivor the Golden Boy had just about everything an inside-forward needed in the first quarter-century after the Second World War, except luck. He was fated to play in mediocre club teams throughout his long career, and even his excellent work for his country went largely to waste, except in the 1958 World Cup. He won 68 caps, spread over 16 years, and scored 23 goals – records which stood until the 1990s. His 251 League goals in nearly 700 appearances emphasized his excellent finishing.

Luigi Allemandi

Born: November 18, 1903, Italy.
Clubs: Juventus, Internazionale, Roma.

Allemandi was a left-back and one of the outstanding personalities in *Calcio* in the inter-war years. He played 25 times for his country and would have made more appearances but for a match-fixing scandal. Allemandi was accused of having accepted a bribe from a director of Torino to fix a match while playing for Juventus in 1927. The matter did not emerge until a year later when Allemandi, despite reports identifying him as one of the best players on the field, was found guilty and suspended for life. By now he was playing for

Internazionale, who challenged the ban on his behalf and had it quashed. In 1929 Allemandi returned to Italy's team for a match against Czechoslovakia, and he went on to win a World Cup medal in 1934.

José Altafini

Born: August 27, 1938, Brazil.
Clubs: Palmeiras, São Paulo FC (Br), Milan, Napoli, Juventus (It), Chiasso (Swz).

Altafini was a subject of both confusion and admiration throughout his career. A direct, aggressive centre-forward, he began with Palmeiras of São Paulo, where he was known by the nickname of Mazzola because of his resemblance to the Italian star of the late 1940s. He played at the 1958 World Cup and was immediately signed by Milan. The Italians insisted on reverting to Altafini's own name and he played for his "new" country at the 1962 World Cup finals. A year later Altafini scored a record 14 goals in Milan's European Cup success, including two goals in the final victory over Benfica at Wembley. After falling out with Milan he joined Omar Sivori in inspiring a Napoli revival, then became a "super substitute" with Juventus. Altafini is now a TV soccer analyst in Italy.

AMANCIO *10 times a champion*

Amancio Amaro Varela

Born: October 12, 1939, Spain.
Clubs: La Coruña, Real Madrid.

In 1962 Real Madrid, seeking a replacement for Italy-bound Luis Del Sol, bought outside-right Amancio from his home-town club, Real Deportivo de La Coruña. Coach Miguel Muñoz switched him to inside-right, playing him first in midfield and then as a striker. His outstanding technique and acceleration brought him a string of honours. He played 42 times for Spain between 1964 and 1971, was 10 times a Spanish league champion with Madrid

and four times a cup-winner. In 1968 he was honoured with selection for a World XI against Brazil, but the highlight of his career was winning the European Nations Championship with Spain in 1964 on his home ground, the Estadio Bernabeu in Madrid.

Amarildo Tavaŕes Silveira

Born: June 29, 1939, Brazil.
Clubs: Botafogo (Br), Milan, Fiorentina (It).

Amarildo, an attacking inside-left whose slight appearance disguised a wiry frame, burst on to the international scene at the 1962 World Cup finals after Pele was injured. He had not expected to play when he was called in to deputize for O Rei in a decisive group match against Spain. Brazil recovered from a goal down to win 2–1 thanks to two late strikes from Amarildo, and in the Final against Czechoslovakia he proved decisive once more – scoring with a snapshot which deceived the goalkeeper on the near post. A year later Amarildo was bought by Milan, and he enjoyed a successful career in Italy with Milan and Fiorentina, with whom he won the championship in 1969. Amarildo stayed in Italy after retiring and joined Fiorentina's youth coaching staff.

Manuel Amoros

Born: February 1, 1961, France.
Clubs: Monaco, Marseille, Lyon.

Amoros played both right- and left-back in the outstanding French national team of the 1980s. Born in Nimes of Spanish parents, Amoros was an outstanding teenage exponent of both soccer and rugby. Monaco persuaded him to concentrate on soccer, and he played for France at youth and Under-21 levels before a surprise, and highly successful, promotion to the senior national team at the 1982 World Cup finals, in which France finished fourth. Amoros won a European Championship medal in 1984, despite missing most of the tournament after being sent off in the opening match against Denmark. During his career, most of which he spent with Monaco before joining Marseille, then Lyon, he set a French record of 82 caps.

(LEFT) ALBERT *National debut at 17*

AMOROS *Set a French record of 82 international caps*

José Leandro Andrade

Born: November 20, 1898, Uruguay.
Clubs: Bella Vista, Nacional.

Andrade was an old-fashioned wing-half in the 2–3–5 tactical system which served much of the world for the first half of the century. He was a stalwart of the great Uruguayan teams of the 1920s and 1930s, winning gold medals at the Olympic Games soccer tournaments of both 1924 and 1928. Injury then threatened to end his career but Andrade was recalled, because of his vast experience, for the inaugural World Cup finals which Uruguay won on home ground in 1930. He played 41 times for his country before retiring in 1933. Andrade's nephew, Victor Rodriguez Andrade, won the World Cup in 1950 and was never once booked or sent off.

Giancarlo Antognoni

Born: April 1, 1954, Italy.
Club: Fiorentina.

In the 1970s and early 1980s Antognoni was considered by Italian fans to be the successor to Milan's Gianni Rivera as their Golden Boy of Italian football. A graceful, wonderfully intuitive midfield general, Antognoni cost Fiorentina £750,000 as a teenager from Fourth Division Astimacombi in 1972. He went straight into the Fiorentina team and made the first of his 73 appearances for Italy in the autumn of 1974. Antognoni was a regular transfer target for Italy's richest clubs but remained faithful to Fiorentina until he eventually wound down his career in Switzerland. Sadly, Antognoni missed Italy's victory over West Germany in the 1982 World Cup Final after suffering a gashed ankle in the semi-final defeat of Poland.

Osvaldo Ardiles

Born: August 3, 1952, Argentina.
Clubs: Huracan (Arg), Tottenham (Eng), Paris S-G (Fr), Tottenham, Queen's Park Rangers (Eng).

Ardiles combined legal and soccer studies in the mid-1970s when he earned his initial reputation as midfield general of Argentina under manager Cesar Luis Menotti. Hardly had Ardiles collected his winners'

ANTOGNONI *Italian football's golden boy of the 1970s*

medal at the 1978 World Cup when he and national team-mate Ricardo Villa were together subjects of a remarkable transfer to Tottenham Hotspur. Ardiles cost Spurs £300,000, which made him one of the greatest bargains of modern soccer history. He completed his outstanding playing career which included Tottenham's FA Cup success of 1981 and their UEFA Cup triumph of 1984. He returned to White Hart Lane as manager in the summer of 1993, but lasted little more than a year.

ARDILES *success on two continents*

Luis Artime

Born: 1939, Argentina.
Clubs: Atlanta, River Plate, Independiente (Arg), Palmeiras (Br), Nacional (Uru), Fluminense (Br).

Artime was a centre-forward in the traditional Argentine mould: powerful, aggressive and prolific. He scored 47 goals in two teenage seasons with minor Buenos Aires club Atlanta to earn a move in 1961 to River Plate, with whom he will always be most closely linked. He climaxed

a three-year spell, including 66 league goals, by leading Argentina's attack at the 1966 World Cup finals. Artime then joined Independiente, scoring 44 goals in 18 months before moving on to Palmeiras and then to Nacional of Montevideo, with whom he was top Uruguayan league marksman three years in a row. He also scored 24 goals for Argentina.

Georgi Asparoukhov

Born: May 4, 1943, Bulgaria.
Clubs: Botev Plovdiv, Spartak Sofia, Levski Sofia.

"Gundi" Asparoukhov remains one of the most outstanding yet tragic players in Bulgaria's history. A tall, direct centre-forward, he had scored 19 goals in 49 internationals when he died in a car crash, aged 28, in 1971. Asparoukhov led Bulgaria's attack in the World Cup finals of 1962, 1966 and 1970 and scored 150 goals in 245 league games for his only senior club, Levski Sofia. Portuguese club Benfica tried to sign him in 1966 after he impressed in a European Cup tie. But Asparoukhov did not want to move because he had all he wanted in Bulgaria... including his favourite Alfa Romeo sports car which, ultimately, proved the death of him.

José Augusto

Born: April 13, 1937, Portugal.
Clubs: Barreirense, Benfica.

Augusto was originally a centre-forward, and had already made his debut for Portugal in this position when Benfica bought him from local

club Barreirense in 1959 on coach Bela Guttmann's recommendation. He then successfully converted him into an outside-right. Augusto was considered, after Frenchman Raymond Kopa, as the best "thinking" player in Europe and appeared in five European Cup finals. He was a winner in 1961 and 1962 and a loser in 1963, 1965 and finally in 1968 against Manchester United, by which time he was an attacking midfield player. Augusto was a key member of the Portugal side which finished third at the 1966 World Cup, and later coached both Benfica and Portugal.

Roberto Baggio

Born: February 18, 1967, Italy.
Clubs: Fiorentina, Juventus, Milan, Bologna, Internazionale.

Roberto Baggio became the world's most expensive footballer when Juventus bought him from Fiorentina on the eve of the 1990 World Cup finals for £8m. His transfer provoked three days of riots by angry fans in the streets of Florence but he proved his worth by scoring a glorious World Cup goal against Czechoslovakia. He then helped Juventus win the 1993 UEFA Cup and was voted World Player of the Year in 1994, despite missing a penalty in the World Cup final shoot-out against Brazil. He made up for that error in the 1998 finals, bravely volunteering to take a penalty against Chile and also scoring in a shoot-out against France. He won the league with Juventus in 1995 and with Milan in 1996 before moving to Bologna, where he rediscovered his best form.

Gordon Banks

Born: December 20, 1937, England.
Clubs: Leicester, Stoke.

A product of the prolific Chesterfield "goalkeeper academy", Banks went on to undying fame with England. He

ROBERTO BAGGIO *An inspiration to Italy in the 1994 World Cup finals*

126

BANKS *Saving England in the 1966 World Cup Final*

set all kinds of keeping records, including 73 caps, 23 consecutive internationals, and seven consecutive clean sheets, a run eventually ended by Eusebio's penalty in the 1966 World Cup semi-final. His late withdrawal from the 1970 quarter-final probably cost England the match from 2–0 up; he was a loser in two FA Cup finals with Leicester (at fault with two goals in the second); and, unluckiest of all, he lost an eye in a car crash when he still had years left to play. Only Shilton, perhaps, has equalled him as a goalkeeper for England.

Franceschino "Franco" Baresi

Born: May 8, 1960, Italy.
Club: Milan.

Baresi was perhaps the greatest in a long line of outstanding Italian sweepers. He began as an attacking midfielder with Milan in the late 1970s and was kept waiting for an international opportunity because of the dominance of Juventus's Gaetano Scirea. Finally, in 1987, Baresi secured a place in the national team, simultaneously providing the defensive foundation on which coach Arrigo Sacchi built Milan's all-conquering club team. While Dutchmen Ruud Gullit and Marco Van Basten were granted much of the glory, discerning observers recognized the enor-mous influence of Baresi. In the 1994 World Cup Final, Baresi shone like a beacon, despite having undergone knee surgery only two weeks earlier.

Bebeto (full name: Jose Roberto Gama de Oliveira)

Born: February 16, 1964, Brazil.
Clubs: Flamengo, Vasco da Gama (Br), Deportivo (Sp), Vitoria Bahia, Cruzeiro, Botafogo.

Bebeto could have made an international impact earlier in his career, but for weak temperament and injuries. He was outstanding for Flamengo when they won the Rio championship in 1986 and was the club's top scorer four years in a row. He was trans-

BARESI *Key to Milan's revival*

ferred to Rio rivals Vasco da Gama in 1989 but won Brazil fans over by scoring six goals in his country's 1989 South American Championship triumph. He then moved to Spain's La Coruña and hit three goals in Brazil's 1994 World Cup triumph and three on their way to the 1998 final in France.

Franz Beckenbauer

see Legends (pages 104–05).

Ferenc Bene

Born: December 17, 1944, Hungary
Clubs: Kaposzvar, Ujpest Dozsa.

Bene was a versatile attacker who played centre-forward for Ujpest Dozsa but usually outside-right for Hungary because of the presence of Florian Albert. Bene was first capped in 1962 but did not make much impact on the international scene until two years later when he top-scored with 12 goals in Hungary's victory at the Tokyo Olympics. Three times Bene was the Hungarian league's leading scorer and he won the championship four times with Ujpest. In the 1966 World Cup Bene was an outstanding member of the Hungarian team which scored a 3–1 victory over Brazil at Goodison Park, Liverpool. Hungary fell to the more organised Soviet Union side in the quarter-finals, but Bene's consolation was having scored in each of their four matches.

Dennis Bergkamp

Born: May 10, 1969, Holland.
Clubs: Ajax Amsterdam (Hol), Internazionale (It), Arsenal (Eng).

Bergkamp, a youth product of Ajax, was such a natural that he made his European club debut in a match against Malmö after sitting school examinations the previous afternoon. Bergkamp starred for Holland at the 1992 European Championship finals, and Inter beat Barcelona, Juventus and Milan to his £8 million signature the following spring. Bergkamp never settled in Italy, and in 1995 he was transferred to Arsenal for £7.5 million, inspiring the club to their league and cup double in 1998. He was one of the stars of France '98, scoring a glorious quarter-final winner against Argentina, and guiding Holland to fourth place.

Orvar Bergmark

Born: November 16, 1930, Sweden.
Clubs: Örebro, AIK Solna (Swe), Roma (It).

Bergmark's record of 94 international appearances stood for years as a Swedish record and established him as one of the great European full-backs of the 1950s and early 1960s. He began with Örebro in 1949 as a centre-forward but quickly switched to full-back and made his debut there for Sweden in 1951. He was voted best right-back at the 1958 World Cup finals, in which his steady play helped the hosts reach the Final against Brazil. Bergmark also had a spell in Italy with Roma before retiring. He was appointed manager of Sweden in 1966 and guided them to the 1970 World Cup finals. One of his players then was Tommy Svensson, who would emulate him as World Cup boss in 1994.

George Best

Born: May 22, 1946, Northern Ireland.
Clubs: Manchester United, Fulham (Eng), Hibernian (Scot), Tampa Bay Rowdies (US).

George Best was perhaps the outstanding British player of all time, despite a career much shorter than it could and should have been. "Wayward genius" is a cliché that cannot be bettered as a description of a player with so many incredible gifts packed into a slight frame: balance, two twinkling feet, a surprisingly high leap, a cold eye for the finishing chance ... everything. Best was twice a league championship winner with United, and won both the European Cup and the European Footballer of the Year award in 1968. Then fame and fortune and the temptations of the world beyond football all combined to force a sad finale scattered with retirements and comebacks.

Franz "Bimbo" Binder

Born: December 1, 1911, Austria.
Clubs: St Polten, Rapid Vienna (Aus).

Binder was a prolific marksman, either from centre-forward or inside-forward, and is popularly considered to have been the first European player to have topped 1,000 goals in his first-class career. When he retired in 1950 to become manager of his old club, Rapid, Binder claimed career

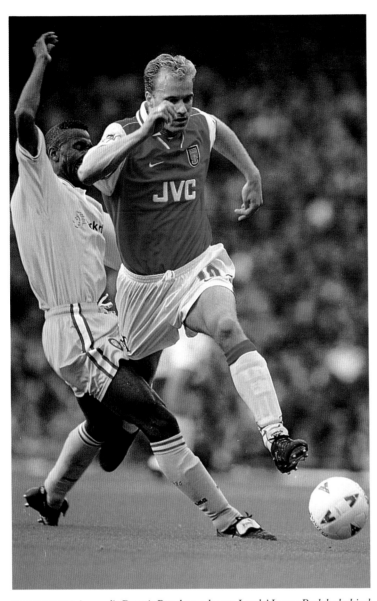

DIFFERENT CLASS *Arsenal's Dennis Bergkamp leaves Leeds' Lucas Radebe behind*

figures of 1,006 in 756 games. Binder was Rapid's greatest player in the 1930s, playing 20 times for Austria before being selected nine times for Greater Germany after the Anschluss of 1938. Binder's greatest achievement for Rapid was in the 1941 Greater German championship play-off, when he scored a hat-trick against Schalke

BEST *So appropriately named*

in Rapid's 4–3 victory. Later he coached not only Rapid but also the Austrian national team.

Danny Blanchflower

Born: February 10, 1926, Northern Ireland.
Clubs: Barnsley, Aston Villa, Tottenham (Eng).

A tactically astute play-maker, Danny Blanchflower was one of the major forces in Ireland's valiant 1958 World Cup side and Tottenham's excellent team of the early 1960s. The League and Cup "double" was followed by another Cup and the European Cup-winners' Cup, with Blanchflower's cerebral approach blending perfectly with the more robust forays of the other wing-half,

Dave Mackay. In the days when few sportsmen appeared on TV, the loquacious Blanchflower was a media darling, always entertaining and forthright in speech or in print. As so often with gifted players, his foray into management, with Chelsea, was an anti-climax. He died in 1993.

Oleg Blokhin

Born: November 5, 1952, Soviet Union.
Clubs: Kiev Dynamo (USSR), Vorwärts Steyr (Austria).

Blokhin was originally an outside-left, but, according to his friend, Olympic sprint champion Valeri Borzov, he could have been a star sprinter. Certainly he used his pace to electric effect, his key role in Kiev's European Cup-winners' Cup triumph of 1975 earning him the accolade of European Footballer of the Year. Blokhin played in the World Cup finals of 1982 and 1986, having by then become the first Soviet player to top a century of international appearances. By the time Blokhin, now a central striker, was "freed" to move west with Vorwärts Steyr of Austria, he had totalled a Soviet record 39 goals in a further record 109 internationals. After retiring he turned to coaching with the Greek champions, Olympiakos of Piraeus.

Steve Bloomer

Born: January 20, 1874, England.
Clubs: Derby, Middlesbrough, Derby.

England's most famous player before the First World War, Bloomer established long-lasting records: his 352 league goals were not exceeded until the 1930s; his 28 goals for his country, in only 23 games, were not surpassed until the 1950s. Bloomer was of medium height and slightly built, often the target for unscrupulous defenders with heavy boots and desperate intent. But he survived, thanks to agility and a sharp brain, through 22 years until the start of the First World War, when he was in his 41st year. Born at Cradley Heath in the West Midlands' "Black Country", he was, nevertheless, a Derby player throughout his career apart from a four-year spell with Middlesbrough. In later years he coached Derby players and did odd jobs at the ground.

Zvonimir Boban

Born: October 8, 1968
Clubs: Dinamo Zagreb (Yug/Cro), Bari, Milan (It)

Boban first made a name as a member of the former Yugoslavia team which won the 1987 World Youth Cup. He became Dinamo Zagreb's

BLOKHIN *Electrifying pace*

youngest-ever captain at 18 and was hailed a local hero after he came to the defence of Croat fans being man-handled by police at a high-tension match against Red Star Belgrade, for which he was given a six-month suspension. It cost him a place with Yugoslavia at the 1990 World Cup finals. His brilliant ball control, astute passing and explosive free kicks were noticed in Italy, however, and Milan snapped him up for £8m. At the San Siro he has won four championships and a European Cup, playing a major part in the 4-0 final victory over Barcelona in 1994. But the highlight of his career so far is captaining fledgling country Croatia to third place in the 1998 World Cup finals in France.

Zbigniew Boniek

Born: March 3, 1956, Poland.
Clubs: Zawisza Bydgoszcz, Widzew Lodz (Pol) Juventus (It) Roma (It)

Boniek must be considered the greatest Polish footballer of all time. He was the product of the next soccer generation after the outstanding side of the mid-1970s but his talents shone in World Cups and in European club competition with Juventus. Boniek made his name with Widzew Lodz and his hat-trick against Belgium in the 1982 World Cup finals persuaded Juventus to pay £1.1 million for him – then a record for a Polish player. Boniek scored Juve's winner in the 1984 European Cup-winners' Cup Final defeat of FC Porto and was a member of the side which won the

BONIEK *The greatest Polish player of all time thanks to his feats with Juventus*

earned him selection for Western Europe against Central Europe in 1938, and then for Europe against England that same year. He won 54 caps for Belgium.

Paul Breitner

Born: September 5, 1951, West Germany.
Clubs: Bayern Munich (W Ger), Real Madrid (Sp), Eintracht Braunschweig, Bayern Munich (W Ger).

Breitner was a flamboyant virtuoso of a left-back when Helmut Schön brought him into the West German national team in 1971–72. He was a key member of a the new, Bayern-dominated side which also featured Franz Beckenbauer, Sepp Maier, Uli Hoeness and Gerd Müller. Breitner demonstrated his big-match temperament by nervelessly converting the penalty which brought West Germany level in the 1974 World Cup Final against Holland. A footballing intellectual, he considered he was being stifled at Bayern and moved forward to midfield on transferring to Real Madrid. A falling-out with the German football authorities caused him to miss the 1978 World Cup, but he returned in 1982 and again scored in the Final — this time only the Germans' consolation goal in their defeat by Italy on his old home ground in Madrid. Only four players have scored in two World Cup Finals.

European Cup a year later, playing the Final against Liverpool in the shadow of the Heysel disaster. Boniek scored 24 goals in 80 internationals.

Giampiero Boniperti

Born: July 4, 1928, Italy.
Club: Juventus.

Boniperti was the original Golden Boy of Italian football. He enjoyed a meteoric rise: within a few months of being signed by Juventus from minor club Momo, in July 1946, he was promoted to the Italian national team and made his debut in a 5–1 defeat by Austria in Vienna. Originally a centre-forward, Boniperti later switched to inside-forward and played on the right wing for FIFA's World XI against England in 1953 (scoring twice in a 4–4 draw). Boniperti won five Italian league titles with Juventus, for whom he played a record 444 league games. He was a "father figure" in the Charles/Sivori team of the late 1950s and scored eight goals in 38 internationals. On retiring from

the game he took up a business career which eventually turned full circle when he became a hugely successful president of Juventus in the 1970s and early 1980s under the Agnelli family patronage.

Jozsef Bozsik

Born: September 28, 1929, Hungary.
Clubs: Kispest, Honved.

Bozsik will always be remembered as right-half of the wonderful Hungarian national team of the early 1950s. A team-mate of Ferenc Puskas with Kispest and then Honved, Bozsik was the midfield brains but could also score spectacular goals, including one from 30 yards in the historic 6–3 win over England at Wembley in 1953. Bozsik made his debut for Hungary against Bulgaria in 1947, returned home – unlike team-mates Puskas, Kocsis and Czibor – after the 1956 Revolution and combined a career as a footballer with that of an MP. In 1962 he scored a goal against Uruguay in a friendly to mark

his 100th and last game for his country. Bozsik had been a member of Hungary's victorious side at the 1952 Helsinki Olympics.

Raymond Braine

Born: April 28, 1907, Belgium.
Clubs: Beerschot (Bel), Sparta Prague (Cz), Beerschot (Bel).

Braine was considered the greatest Belgian footballer until the advent of Paul Van Himst in the 1960s. In 1922 he made his league debut for Beerschot at the age of 15 and was chosen, that same year, for a Belgian XI against Holland. Clapton Orient of London tried to sign Braine in 1928 but could not obtain a work permit for him to come to England, so instead he turned professional in Czechoslovakia with the great Sparta Prague club. The Czechs wanted him to take citizenship and play for them in the 1934 World Cup, but Braine preferred to represent Belgium – and did so at the 1938 World Cup after returning home to Beerschot. Braine's centre-forward talents

BREITNER *Football intellectual*

Billy Bremner

Born: December 9, 1942, Scotland.
Clubs: Leeds United, Hull, Doncaster (Eng).

Bremner made his debut for Leeds at 17, as a winger partnered by Don Revie, a man nearly twice his age. Later midfielder Bremner and manager Revie were outstanding figures as Leeds emerged from decades of mediocrity to be a force feared throughout the game. Bremner's fierce tackling, competitive spirit and selflessness made him a winner of various medals, though the list of second places was much longer. He was not a prolific scorer, but a useful one, providing the winner in each of three FA Cup semi-finals. He also won 55 caps, including three at the 1974 World Cup finals, when Scotland were eliminated, unbeaten, after three matches.

Tomas Brolin

Born: November 29, 1969, Sweden.
Clubs: GIF Sundsvall (Swe), Parma (It), Leeds (Eng), Parma (It), Zurich (Swz), Crystal Palace (Eng)

Brolin had long been considered one of Sweden's outstanding attacking prospects before proving the point by scoring twice on his debut for the senior team in the 4–2 win over Wales in 1990. He followed up with two more against Finland to earn a late call into Sweden's World Cup team. At Italia '90, Brolin's outstanding displays alerted Italian clubs and Parma immediately bought him. He starred for Sweden at the 1992 European Championship – scoring a marvellous solo goal against England – and then helped Parma to success in the 1993 European Cup-winners' Cup. A year later Brolin lead Sweden to third place at the World Cup Finals. But serious injury effectively wrecked his career. He was never the same again, despite stints in Switzerland, England (with Leeds and Crystal Palace) and Italy.

TOMAS BROLIN *Rocketed from nowhere to world star in six months in 1990*

C

Emilio Butragueño

Born: July 22, 1963, Spain
Clubs: Castilla, Real Madrid (Sp), Celaya (Mex).

Butragueño, nicknamed "the Vulture", was once considered not good enough by Real Madrid's youth coaches. Real's nursery club, Castilla, had second thoughts and Butragueño became "leader" of Madrid throughout the 1980s. His close control and talent as a marksman helped Madrid win the UEFA Cup in 1985 and 1986, and in both years Butragueño won the Prix Bravo as Europe's best young player. He made a scoring debut for Spain in 1984, and in 1986 became a World Cup sensation when he scored four times for Spain in a five-goal thrashing of the well-fancied Denmark in the second round of the finals in Mexico.

Rodion Camataru

Born: June 22, 1958, Romania.
Clubs: Universitatea Craiova, Dinamo Bucharest (Rom), Charleroi (Bel).

Camataru was a bluff, determined centre-forward who scored more than 300 goals in Romanian league football before transferring to Belgium towards the end of his career. In 1986–87 he won the Golden Boot awarded to Europe's top league marksman, albeit in controversial circumstances. Camataru totalled 44 goals but many of them were scored in a string of "easy" matches towards the end of the season and revelations after the collapse of the Communist regime cast doubt on the integrity of the matches. Not that this detracted from Camataru's abilities which were rewarded, even in the twilight of his career, with selection for the 1990 World Cup finals.

Claudio Paul Caniggia

Born: January 9, 1967, Argentina.
Clubs: River Plate (Arg), Verona, Atalanta, Roma (It), Benfica (Por), Boca Juniors (Arg).

Caniggia was one of the most intriguing stars of the 1994 World Cup, having only just completed a 13-month drugs suspension in Italy. He scored on his return to international duty in a 3–0 win over Israel, but was injured when Argentina lost to Romania in USA '94. Caniggia began with River Plate, moving to Italy in 1988. His play was one of Argentina's few redeeming features

CAMATARU *Golden Boot-winner*

at the 1990 World Cup, when he scored the quarter-final winner against Brazil and semi-final equalizer against Italy. Caniggia missed the Final through suspension and, without him, Argentina had nothing to offer in attack.

Eric Cantona

Born: May 24, 1966, France.
Clubs: Martigues, Auxerre, Marseille, Bordeaux, Montpellier (Fr), Leeds, Manchester United (Eng).

Eric Cantona's career was a mixture of glorious success and disciplinary muddle. Cantona, born in Marseille, was discovered by Auxerre and sold to Marseille for £2 million in 1988. Two months later he scored on his international debut against West Germany. Later he was banned for a year from the national team for insulting manager Henri Michel, then bounced controversially to Bordeaux, Montpellier and Nimes before quitting the game after a shouting match with a disciplinary panel. Cantona relaunched his career in England – winning the championship in 1992 with Leeds and four times in five years with Manchester United. A skirmish with a hooligan fan at Crystal Palace cost him a seven-month ban from football, but he returned to the field all the more hungry for success. He was voted as Footballer of the Year and then, as captain, sealed United's 1996 "double" by scoring the winning goal in the FA Cup Final against Liverpool. He retired, suddenly, a year later, much to the horror of his fans.

Antonio Carbajal

Born: June 7, 1929, Mexico.
Clubs: España, Leon.

Carbajal set a record, at the 1966 World Cup in England, as the only man then to have appeared in five finals tournaments. A tall, agile goalkeeper, he played for Mexico in Brazil in 1950, in Switzerland in 1954, in Sweden in 1958 and in Chile in 1962. The 1966 finals provided an appropriate retirement point, since Carbajal had made his international debut at the 1948 London Olympics. On his return to Mexico that year he turned professional with Leon and played for them until his retirement in 1966. Later he was presented with FIFA's gold award for services to the world game.

Careca

Born: October 5, 1960, Brazil.
Clubs: Guarani, São Paulo (Br), Napoli (It), Hitachi (Jap), Santos (Br).

Careca was one of the outstanding spearheads in the world game throughout the 1980s and early 1990s. Born in Brazil's Campinas state, he helped unrated Guarani win the 1987–88 national championship and was later sold to São Paulo. Careca missed the 1982 World Cup after being injured in training on the eve of the finals. He made superb amends with five goals in Mexico in 1986, was voted Brazil's Sportsman of the Year and was subsequently transferred to Italy's Napoli. His attacking partnership with Diego Maradona lifted Napoli to the 1989 UEFA Cup and 1990 Italian league titles.

Johnny Carey

Born: February 23, 1919, Rep. of Ireland.
Club: Manchester United (Eng).

Johnny Carey was one of the early all-purpose players, at home as full-back, wing-half, inside-forward, even as deputy goalkeeper. He was a calming influence, short on pace but long on perception. At £200 to a Dublin junior club he was one of the transfer bargains of all time. He captained Manchester United in the early post-war years, winning League and Cup once each and narrowly missing several more, earned 37 caps, and led the Rest of Europe selection against Great Britain in 1946. Carey later managed Black-

CAREY *One of the great captains*

burn (twice), Everton – until he was sacked in the back of a taxi when they were lying fifth in the table – Orient and Nottingham Forest.

Amadeo Carrizo

Born: June 12, 1926, Argentina.
Clubs: River Plate (Arg), Alianza (Peru), Millonarios (Col).

Carrizo set a string of longevity records in a goalkeeping career which lasted from the mid-1940s to the mid-1960s. A dominant character with great personality, Carrizo played 520 Argentine league matches over 21 seasons until he was 44. He won five league championships with River Plate in the early 1950s and played in the 1958 World Cup finals in Sweden. Carrizo was blamed for Argentina's

6–1 defeat by Czechoslovakia but was recalled two years later with great success when Argentina beat England and Brazil to win the 1960 "Little World Cup" in Brazil. After parting company with River Plate he played on in Peru and Colombia before returning home to coach youth teams.

Carlos Caszely

Born: July 5, 1950, Chile.
Clubs: Colo Colo (Chile), Levante (Sp), Colo Colo (Chile).

Caszely was outstanding as a goal-scoring inside-forward in the early 1970s when Colo Colo became the first Chilean club to reach a final of the South American club cup (Copa Libertadores). However, his loudly-proclaimed left-wing political beliefs placed him at risk after the revolution which overthrew President Allende in 1973, and he moved to Spain with Levante. Caszely played for Chile in the 1974 World Cup finals in West Germany and then again eight years later in Spain. By this time, the political situation had eased back home and he had returned to Colo Colo to end his playing days there.

Jan Ceulemans

Born: February 28, 1957, Belgium.
Clubs: Lierse, Club Brugge.

Ceulemans was the central pillar of Belgium's national team throughout the 1980s, first as a striker and then as a midfield general. He began with Lierse and cost Brugge a then record

JAN CEULEMANS *The pillar of Belgium's recent World Cup success*

STÉPHANE CHAPUISAT *Even more famous son of a famous father*

domestic fee of £250,000 in the summer of 1978. In 1980 he scored 29 of their 76 goals in a league title win and was voted Footballer of the Year for the first time. A year later Ceulemans was poised to join Milan but his mother persuaded him to stay in Belgium, a decision which he never regretted. Ceulemans played with distinction in the Belgian team which finished fourth at the 1986 World Cup finals in Mexico. In 96 internationals – a Belgian record – he scored 26 goals.

Cha Bum Kun

Born: May 21, 1953, South Korea.
Clubs: Darmstadt, Eintracht Frankfurt, Bayer Leverkusen (W Ger).

Thanks to his record at the peak of the European game in West Germany's Bundesliga, Cha ranks as South Korea's finest player. He was a popular fixture from 1978, when he arrived at Darmstadt, until his retirement in 1986 after appearing at his first and only World Cup finals. Cha, who won the UEFA Cup with both Eintracht Frankfurt (1980) and Bayer Leverkusen in 1988, when he scored one of the goals against Espanol, was mystifyingly ignored by his country after moving to Germany. But he used his time well to gain coaching qualifications and he subsequently managed South Korea at the 1998 World Cup Finals in France.

Stéphane Chapuisat

Born: June 28, 1969, Switzerland.
Clubs: FC Malley, Red Star Zurich, Lausanne (Swz), Bayer Uerdingen, Borussia Dortmund (Ger).

Chapuisat, the finest current Swiss striker, is son of a former international, Pierre-Albert Chapuisat, who earned notoriety in his day as a sharp-tempered defender. Son Stéphane, by contrast, not only plays his football at the other end of the pitch but has the most even temperament. Chapuisat moved to Germany in 1991 with Uerdingen and transferred to Dortmund a year later. His starring role at the 1994 World Cup finals led to a Footballer of the Year accolade. In 1997, after recovering from injury, he led Dortmund to both the European Champions Cup and World Club Cup.

John Charles

Born: December 27, 1931, Wales.
Clubs: Leeds (Eng), Juventus (It), Leeds (Eng), Roma (It), Cardiff (Wales).

Known as the Gentle Giant, John Charles allied great skill to an awesome physique, and was good enough to set a Leeds record of 42 goals in one season as a centre forward, while also playing as a dominant central defender for his country. He was one of the first British exports to Italy, in 1957, and probably the best. The £67,000 fee, a record for a British player, bought Juventus a man who became a legend and helped to win the Serie A title three times in five years, scoring 93 times in 155 games. After some unhappy final seasons he became a non-league manager, publican and shopkeeper.

Bobby Charlton

see Legends (pages 106–07)

Igor Chislenko

Born: January 4, 1939, Soviet Union.
Clubs: Moscow Torpedo, Moscow Dynamo.

Chislenko was one of Europe's most incisive outside- or inside-rights in the 1960s, despite standing only 5ft 7in. He began with the Moscow Torpedo youth section but transferred to Dynamo at 17 and played 300 league games, winning two league titles, with the club. Chislenko, also a good ice hockey player, appeared at the World Cups of 1962 and 1966 as well as in the European Nations Championship in between. He was the best Soviet forward in the 1966 World Cup, and their prospects of reaching the Final disappeared when he was sent off during the semi-final against West Germany.

Hector Chumpitaz

Born: April 12, 1944, Peru.
Club: Sporting Cristal.

Chumpitaz, a powerful, inspirational centre-back, starred for Peru in the World Cup finals of both 1970 and 1978. On the first occasion he was a promising youngster, on the second an experienced, resilient organizer of an otherwise fragile defence. Chumpitaz played all his senior career with Sporting Cristal of Lima and appeared around 100 times for his country between his debut in 1966 and the six-goal thrashing by Argentina which controversially ended Peru's 1978 World Cup campaign. Earlier claims that he played 147 full internationals have been discounted, Peru having played "only" 110 matches in that time.

Mario Esteves Coluna

Born: August 6, 1935, Mozambique.
Clubs: Deportivo Lourenço Marques (Mozambique), Benfica (Port).

Coluna was midfield general of Benfica's outstanding club side on the 1960s as well as commander of the Portuguese national team which reached the World Cup semi-finals in 1966. Born in Mozambique, Coluna was the local long-jump record-holder when he was lured away by Benfica to play football in 1954. Originally a centre-forward, he was converted to inside-left and then midfield by Benfica and won 73 caps for Portugal. In both of Benfica's European Cup Final victories of 1961 and 1962, he scored with typically spectacular long-range efforts. Coluna later turned to coaching and became Sports Minister in Mozambique.

Gianpiero Combi

Born: December 18, 1902, Italy.
Club: Juventus.

Combi was goalkeeper and captain of the Italian team which won the 1934 World Cup, thus pre-dating Dino

Zoff in that dual role by nearly 50 years. Combi was considered Italy's best goalkeeper until Zoff came along. He started unpromisingly, beaten seven times by Hungary in Budapest in his first international in 1924, and did not gain a regular place in Italy's team until the Paris Olympics of 1928. He was goalkeeper in Juventus's four consecutive league title successes of 1931 to 1934, the year when he retired – immediately after captaining Italy to victory over Czechoslovakia in the World Cup Final in Rome. That was Combi's 47th international.

Bruno Conti

Born: March 13, 1955, Italy.
Clubs: Roma, Genoa, Roma.

Wingers made a comeback on the tactical scene thanks to the displays of Bruno Conti at the 1982 World Cup. Italy's right-winger proved a crucial influence in increasing the momentum of their campaign, which took them past Argentina and Brazil and on via Poland to victory over West Germany in the Final. Conti had struggled to make an impression in the early years of his career but was rescued by Swedish coach Nils Liedholm, who brought Conti back from a loan spell with Genoa and turned him into one of the most consistently effective creative players in *Calcio*. Conti scored five goals in 47 internationals between his debut against Luxembourg in 1980 and the second round defeat by France at the 1986 World Cup.

Henri "Rik" Coppens

Born: April 29, 1930, Belgium.
Clubs: Beerschot, Charleroi, Crossing Molenbeek, Berchem, Tubantia.

Coppens was the *enfant terrible* of Belgian football in the 1950s: a centre-forward or occasional outside-left of great goal-scoring talent, but one who carried his aggression over into his dealings with team-mates, clubs and other officials. Coppens began with Beerschot as a 10-year-old, and on his debut at 16 in a crucial relegation match he scored twice and made Beerschot's two other goals. Three times he was the league's leading scorer and ended his career with a then

CONTI *Outwits West Germany's Uli Stielike in the 1982 World Cup Final*

record total of 217 goals. He once scored six goals in a game against Tilleur. Coppens altogether played 47 times for Belgium.

Alberto da Costa Pereira

Born: 1929, Portuguese East Africa.
Club: Benfica.

Costa Pereira was another of Portugal's great discoveries in the African colonies. He was born in Nacala, Portuguese East Africa, and joined Benfica in 1954. He was a tower of strength in their biggest triumphs, though prone to the odd unpredictable error when the pressure was off. Costa Pereira won seven league titles with Benfica and played in four European Cup finals – the victories of 1961 and 1962 and the defeats of 1963 and 1965. In the latter game, against Internazionale on a quagmire of a pitch in Milan, Costa Pereira was injured early in the game and had to leave the pitch. He retired soon after to take up coaching. Costa Pereira played 24 times for Portugal, but is not to be confused with the José Pereira who kept goal at the 1966 World Cup.

Johan Cruyff

see Legends (pages 108–09)

Teofilo Cubillas

Born: March 8, 1949, Peru.
Clubs: Alianza (Peru), Basel (Swz), FC Porto (Port), Alianza (Peru), Fort Lauderdale Strikers (US).

Cubillas was a key figure in Peru's greatest international successes, their appearances at the 1970 and 1978 World Cup finals, in which he scored a total of 10 goals. A powerfully-built inside left, he forged an ideal partnership with the more nimble Hugo Sotil in 1970 then, in 1978, emerged as an attacking director. Cubillas also packed a powerful shot, scoring

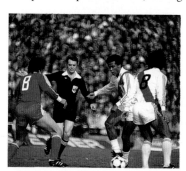

CUBILLAS *Attacking director*

a memorable goal against Scotland in the 1978 finals. He was not particularly successful in Europe, where he grew homesick. But in Peru he remained a legend after 38 goals in 88 internationals and an appearance for the World XI in a 1978 UNICEF charity match.

Zoltan Czibor

Born: 1929, Hungary.
Clubs: Ferencvaros, Csepel, Honved (Hun), Barcelona, Español (Sp).

Czibor was outside-left in the great Hungarian team of the early 1950s. He had pace and a powerful shot, which he used to great effect in 43 internationals before he moved to Spain following the Hungarian Revolution of 1956. Czibor and team-mate Sandor Kocsis were persuaded to sign for Barcelona by Ladislav Kubala and enjoyed five more years in the international spotlight, reaching a climax when Barcelona, most unluckily, lost to Benfica in the 1961 European Cup Final. Czibor had a short spell with neighbours Español before he retired and eventually returned home to live in Hungary.

D

Kenny Dalglish

Born: March 4, 1951, Scotland.
Clubs: Celtic (Scot), Liverpool (Eng).

Kenny Dalglish is the most "decorated" man in British soccer, having won 26 major trophies as player and manager, in addition to 102 caps (a record for Scotland) and 30 goals (another record, held jointly with Denis Law). Dalglish's signing for Celtic was their other coup – aside from their European Cup triumph – in 1967. He went on to inspire the club to more great deeds before joining Liverpool for £400,000 in 1977. Already a very good player, he became legendary at Anfield, thanks to initial pace, excellent control and an eye for a chance. He won many new friends for his dignified bearing after the disaster of Hillsborough. Those pressures contributed to Dalglish's surprise departure from Liverpool. He returned to manage Blackburn Rovers to the 1995 Premier League title then replaced Keegan as manager of Newcastle United, taking them to the 1998 FA Cup Final. He returned to Celtic as Director of Football in 1999.

Bill "Dixie" Dean

Born: January 22, 1907, England. n
Clubs: Tranmere, Everton, Notts Co.

Anybody who begins his international career by scoring 2, 3, 2, 2, 3 deserves a place in the Hall of Fame. Curly-topped Bill Dean was 20 at the time, and still only 21 when he scored his record 60 League goals in

DALGLISH *A winner as player and manager*

one season for Everton, finishing 2, 4, 3 to overhaul George Camsell's 59 for Middlesbrough. Overall, he scored 18 goals in 16 England appearances, 47 in 18 of the other representative matches which were so popular in pre-television days, 28 in 33 Cup ties (one in the 1933 Wembley win), and 379 in 438 League games. All this despite, as a teenager, fracturing his skull.

Luis Del Sol Miramontes

Born: 1938, Spain.
Clubs: Betis Seville, Real Madrid (Sp), Juventus (It).

Del Sol was inside-right in the legendary Real Madrid forward line which won the 1960 European Cup against Eintracht Frankfurt at Hampden. A neat, aggressive midfielder, he had been a wing-half at his hometown club, Betis of Seville, when the Madrid management decided that the great Brazilian, Didi, was not fitting in well enough alongside Alfredo Di Stefano. Del Sol was hurriedly bought in the middle of the 1959–60 season and ran his legs off in support of veterans Di Stefano and Puskas. In 1962 Madrid sold Del Sol to Juventus to raise the cash for a vain attempt to buy Pele from Santos. Del Sol was a pillar of the Italian league through eight seasons with Juventus and two with Roma, before his retirement and return to Spain in 1972.

Kazimierz Deyna

Born: October 23, 1947, Poland. *Clubs:* Starogard, Sportowy Lodz, Legia Warsaw (Pol), Manchester City (Eng), San Diego (US).

Poland's emergence as a world power in the early 1970s owed a huge debt to the skilled grace of Deyna, their midfield fulcrum. Deyna played centre midfield, supported by workers such as Maszczyk and Kasperczak, and was constantly creating openings for strikers Lato and Gadocha. He earned a domestic reputation in helping army club Legia win the league in 1969 and was promoted into the national squads when the Legia coach, Kazimierz Gorski, was appointed manager of Poland. Deyna won an Olympic gold medal with Poland in Munich in 1972 then returned to the Olympiastadion two years later to

DIDI *Making the ball "talk" in the 1958 World Cup finals*

celebrate Poland's best-ever third-place finish at the World Cup. He was never quite the same player after moving abroad, first to England and then to the United States, where he died in a car crash. Deyna scored 38 goals in 102 internationals.

Didi (full name: Waldyr Pereira)

Born: October 8, 1928, Brazil.
Clubs: FC Rio Branco, FC Lencoes, Madureiro, Fluminense, Botafogo (Br), Real Madrid, Valencia (Sp), Botafogo (Br).

The success of Brazil's 4–2–4 system, revealed in all its glory internationally at the 1958 World Cup, rested heavily on the creative talent of Didi, one of the greatest of midfield generals. Didi's technique was extraordinary. Team-mates said he could "make the ball talk", and drop it on a coin from any distance, any angle. Didi was the first to perfect the "dead leaf" free kick, with which he scored a dozen of his 31 goals in 85 appearances for Brazil. He won the World Cup in 1958 and 1962 and counted as the only failure of his career a spell in between with Real Madrid, where he failed to settle in alongside Di Stefano and Puskas.

Alfredo Di Stefano

see Legends (pages 110–11)

Domingos Antonio da Guia

Born: November 19, 1912, Brazil.
Clubs: Bangu, Vasco da Gama (Br), Nacional (Uru), Boca Juniors (Arg), Flamengo, Corinthians, Bangu (Br).

Domingos was a full-back of the old school, as much a pivoting central defender as a marker in the old-fashioned 2–3–5 formation. His talents earned him transfers all round South America, and he remains less of a legend in Uruguay and Argentina than he is in Brazil. The Uruguayans nicknamed him the Divine Master. Domingos made his debut for Brazil in 1931, was a key member of the team which reached the 1938 World Cup semi-finals, and did not retire until 1948. By this time he had returned to his original club, Bangu. His contemporary, centre-forward Leonidas da Silva, once said no defender ever "read a game" better than Domingos.

Dunga (full name: Carlos Bledorn Verri)

Born: October 31, 1963, Brazil.
Clubs: Vasco da Gama (Br), Pisa, Fiorentina, Pescara (It), Stuttgart (Ger), Jubilo Iwata (Jpn).

Dunga, one of the most controversial of modern Brazilian players, obtained the ultimate revenge over his critics when he lifted the World Cup after the victory over Italy in the 1994 Final. Dunga was criticized because, as a defensive midfield player, he was strong and keen in the tackle but slightly slow and relatively clumsy on the ball when comparised with his compatriots. But he possessed a strong shot in both feet and 1994 World Cup boss Carlos Alberto Parreira considered Dunga's tactical discipline vital to his strategy. He captained

his country at France '98, guiding them to the final, and was named in the team of the tournament before announcing his retirement from international football.

Dragan Dzajic

Born: May 30, 1956, Yugoslavia.
Clubs: Red Star Belgrade (Yug), Bastia (Fr), Red Star (Yug).

The British press baptized Dzajic the "magic Dragan" after his left-wing skills helped take England apart in the semi-finals of the 1968 European Nations Championship. Dzajic had pace, skill and intelligence and was perhaps the greatest football hero to have emerged in post-war Yugoslavia. He was five times a national champion, four times a cup-winner and earned selection for a variety of World and European XIs on five occasions. Dzajic remained an outside-left throughout a career which brought him 23 goals in 85 internationals, never needing to fade back into midfield like so many wingers who lose the edge of their talent. He retired in 1978 and became general manager of his original club, Red Star.

Duncan Edwards

Born: October 1, 1936, England.
Club: Manchester United.

Duncan Edwards was a giant who is still revered by generations who never saw him play. Comparatively few did, for his career was brief, but his awesome power and genuine all-round skill, as creator as well as destroyer, made him a man apart. At club level, Edwards was the outstanding discovery among Manchester United's Busby Babes. Sometimes he seemed to be a team in himself, as at Wembley in 1958, when 10 men fought bravely in a vain effort against an Aston Villa side set on depriving United of a merited cup and league "double". Having won 18 England caps, Edwards was looking forward to playing a starring role in the 1958 World Cup. His death in the Munich Air Disaster (see page 224) robbed England of one its finest ever players.

Arsenio Erico

Born: 1915, Paraguay.
Clubs: FC Asuncion (Par), Independiente, Huracan (Arg).

The quality of Erico as a centre-forward can best be illustrated by the fact that he was the boyhood hero of none other than Alfredo Di Stefano. Born in Paraguay, Erico went to Buenos Aires at 17 to play for a fund-raising team organized by the Paraguay Red Cross during the war with Bolivia. Directors of Independiente

EDWARDS *Epitome of the Busby Babes*

in the crowd were so impressed that immediately after the match they obtained his signature – in exchange for a donation to the Red Cross. Erico started badly, twice breaking an arm, but once he was fully fit he scored goals at a prolific rate and set a record with 47 goals in the 1936–37 league season. Several times he scored five goals in a game before going home to Paraguay in 1941 after squabbling over terms with Independiente. The club persuaded him to return, but knee cartilage trouble forced his premature retirement in 1944.

Eusebio

see Legends (pages 112–13)

F

Giacinto Facchetti

Born: July 18, 1942, Italy.
Clubs: Trevigliese, Internazionale.

Full-back was never a romantic role until the revolutionary emergence of Facchetti in the early 1960s. He had been a big, strapping centre-forward with his local club in Treviso when he was signed by Inter and converted into a left-back by master coach Helenio Herrera. The rigid man-to-man marking system perfected by Herrera permitted Facchetti the freedom, when Inter attacked, to stride upfield in support of his own forwards. Facchetti scored 60 league goals, a record for a full-back in Italy, including 10 in the 1965–66 season. But his most

FACCHETTI *Great attacking full-back*

TOM FINNEY *Preston plumber equally skilled at dismantling defences*

important goal was reserved for the 1965 European Cup semi-finals when he burst through in the inside-right position to score a decisive winning goal against Liverpool. Later Facchetti switched to sweeper, from which position he captained Italy against Brazil in the 1970 World Cup Final. He would surely have taken his total of 94 caps to 100 but for an injury before the 1978 World Cup finals.

Giovanni Ferrari

Born: December 6, 1907, Italy.
Clubs: Alessandria, Juventus, Internazionale, Bologna.

"Gioanin" Ferrari was inside-left of the Italian team who won the 1934 World Cup and was one of only two team members – the other was Giuseppe Meazza – retained for the 1938 triumph in France. Appropriately, both men made their international debut in the same game against Switzerland in Rome in 1930. Ferrari played then for Alessandria but soon moved to Juventus, with whom he won a record five consecutive league titles. He won further championship honours with Ambrosiana-Inter in 1940 and with Bologna in 1941. He scored 14 goals in 44 internationals and managed Italy at the 1962 World Cup finals in Chile.

Bernabe Ferreyra

Born: 1909, Argentina.
Clubs: Tigre, River Plate.

Nicknamed "the Mortar" for his ferocious shooting, Ferreyra was the

first great hero of Argentine football. He scored more than 200 goals for Tigre and then River Plate in the 1930s, having joined River for 45,000 pesos in one of the first formal transfers in Argentina after the establishment of professionalism. In his first season with River, 1932–33, Ferreyra scored a league record 43 goals and was such a regular feature of the weekly scoresheets that one Buenos Aires newspaper offered a gold medal to any goalkeeper who could defy him. Ferreyra played only four internationals before retiring in 1939 and going back to his home town of Rufino. In 1943 he returned to River's front office and in 1956 was honoured with a testimonial match in recognition of his loyalty and service to one of Argentina's great club institutions.

Tom Finney

Born: April 5, 1922, England.
Club: Preston.

Moderate in height, thin and fair, Finney was nondescript in appearance, but a player whose versatility was matched by his skill. "Grizzly strong" was the description applied to him by Bill Shankly, who played wing-half behind winger Finney at Preston – "Grizzly" in the sense of bear-like power rather than miserable attitude, for he always had a generous word for opponents as well as a rock-like solidity that belied his frame. Finney was genuinely two-footed, brave as they come, and in his later

years a deep-lying centre-forward on Hidegkuti lines. Lack of support left him bereft of honours at club level, but a 12-year England career, with 76 caps and a then-record 30 goals, earned him a belated knighthood.

Just Fontaine

Born: August 18, 1933, France.
Clubs: AC Marrakesh, USM Casablanca (Mor), Nice, Reims (Fr).

Fontaine secured a place in the history books when he scored a record 13 goals in the 1958 World Cup finals. Yet he was a surprising hero. Born in Morocco, he was a quick, direct centre-forward who had played only twice for France before 1958. He had been discovered by Nice, then bought by Reims as replacement for Raymond Kopa, who had joined Real Madrid in 1956. He expected to be reserve to Reims team-mate René

FONTAINE *World Cup record*

Bliard at the 1958 World Cup, but Bliard was injured on the eve of the finals and Fontaine took his opportunity in record-breaking style. He owed most of his goals to Kopa's creative work alongside him and the partnership was renewed when Kopa returned to Reims in 1959. Sadly Fontaine had to retire in 1961 owing to two double fractures of a leg. He was twice top league scorer and totalled 27 goals in 20 internationals. Later he was president of the French players' union and, briefly, national manager.

ENZO FRANCESCOLI *Sends Melgar of Bolivia (No. 7) the wrong way in a World Cup qualifier*

Enzo Francescoli

Born: November 12, 1961, Uruguay.
Clubs: Wanderers (Uru), River Plate (Arg), Matra Racing, Marseille (Fr), Cagliari, Torino (It), River Plate (Arg).

Francescoli followed in a long line of Uruguayan superstars, starting with the heroes of the 1920s and 1930s and continuing through Schiaffino, Goncalves and Rocha. He began with a small club, Wanderers, and then both Uruguayan giants, Penarol and Nacional, were outbid by River Plate of Argentina. Francescoli was top scorer in the Argentine league and voted South American Footballer of the Year before transferring to France with Racing in 1986. Even Francescoli's 32 goals in three seasons were not enough to save Racing from financial collapse. He scored 11 goals in Marseille's championship season of 1989–90 before moving, first, to Italy, then back to River Plate to wind down his career.

Arthur Friedenreich

Born: 1892, Brazil.
Clubs: Germania, Ipiranga, Americao, Paulistano, São Paulo FC, Flamengo.

Friedenreich was the first great Brazilian footballer and the first player officially credited with more than 1,000 goals. His overall total was 1,329. The son of a German father and a Brazilian mother, Friedenreich was also significant as the first black player to break through the early racial/cultural barriers in Brazilian soccer. Nicknamed "the Tiger", Friedenreich began playing senior football at 17 and did not retire until 1935, when he was 43. He scored eight goals in 17 internationals for Brazil between 1914 and 1930. His first representative appearance for Brazil was in a 2–0 win against the English club Exeter City on July 21, 1914, when he lost two teeth in a collision with a defender.

Paulo Futre

Born: February 28, 1966, Portugal.
Clubs: Sporting, FC Porto (Port), Atletico Madrid (Sp), Benfica (Port), Marseille (France), Reggiana, Milan (It), West Ham United (Eng), Athletico Madrid (Sp).

Futre was only 17 when he made his international debut and his star continued to shine brightly after FC Porto snatched him away from Sporting to inspire their European Cup victory of 1987. A few weeks later Futre was signed by Atletico Madrid as the first major coup in the controversial presidency of Jesus Gil. Futre

PAULO FUTRE *skipping over a tackle from Switzerland's Bregy*

survived all the tempests at Atletico until the start of 1993, when he forced his sale home to Benfica. However, financing the deal proved beyond even Benfica. They sold him to Marseille, who also had to sell him after only a few months to resolve their own cash crisis. Reggiana of Italy paid £8 million to become Futre's fourth club in a year – but he was never the same player after tearing knee ligaments in his first game.

Garrincha (full name: Manoel Francisco dos Santos)

Born: October 28, 1933, Brazil.
Clubs: Pau Grande, Botafogo, Corinthians (Br), AJ Barranquilla (Col), Flamengo (Br), Red Star Paris (Fr).

Garrincha was up there alongside Pele in Brazilian football in the 1960s. Born in poverty, childhood illness left his legs badly twisted and the surgeons who carried out corrective surgery thought he would do well merely to walk, let along turn out to be one of the quickest and most dangerous right-wingers of all time. Yet it took a players' deputation to persuade manager Vicente Feola to include him in the 1958 World Cup side in Sweden. Once in, Garrincha was there to stay and was the dominant personality at the 1962 finals after the early injury to Pele. Sadly, his private life was chaotic and he died prematurely of alcoholic poisoning.

Paul Gascoigne

Born: May 27, 1967, England.
Clubs: Newcastle, Spurs (Eng), Lazio (It), Rangers (Scot), Middlesbrough (Eng).

Gascoigne's career has been blighted by his own indiscipline and misfortune with injuries. A powerful midfielder, with a deft touch, he was England's star of the 1990 World Cup. He was memorably inconsolable when his second yellow card ruled him out of the third place game. Gascoigne left Newcastle for Spurs and led them to the 1991 FA Cup Final, where he suffered a bad knee injury making a rash

GARRINCHA *Team-mates' favourite*

tackle. After missing a year through injury he signed with Lazio but played only 42 games in three seasons. He moved to Rangers in 1995, where he won two league titles and was Scotland's Footballer of the Year in 1996, and then joined Middlesbrough in 1998, helping them to win promotion. But "Gazza's" England career looked over when he was sensationally omitted from the 1998 World Cup squad because of his lack of fitness.

Tommy Gemmell

Born: October 16, 1943, Scotland.
Clubs: Celtic (Scot), Nottingham Forest (Eng).

A big and sometimes clumsy fullback who became a folk hero because

of his goals. He scored eight in European matches for his club, a remarkable record for a defender, and two of them were in European Cup Finals. Gemmell crashed one past Internazionale to equalize when Celtic won in 1967, and also against Feyenoord when they lost in 1970. His extroverted style of play was well suited to upsetting foreign defences during Celtic's greatest years, but he also collected a large haul of domestic honours before a final fling at Forest.

Francisco Gento

Born: October 22, 1933, Spain.
Clubs: Santander, Real Madrid.

Real Madrid's great team of the 1950s and 1960s was more than "only" Di Stefano and Puskas. Tearing great holes in opposing defences was outside-left Gento, whose pace earned him the nickname of "El Supersonico". Gento began with Santander and was considered a player with pace but little else when Madrid signed him in 1953. Fortunately, he found a marvellous inside-left partner in José Hector Rial, who tutored Gento in the arts of the game. Gento is the only man to have won six European Cup medals. He scored 256 goals in 800 games for Madrid, with whom he won Spanish championship medals on 12 occasions. He played 43 times for Spain despite the challenging rivalry of Enrique Collar, an outstanding left-winger with Atletico Madrid.

Sergio Javier Goycochea

Born: October 17, 1963, Argentina.
Clubs: River Plate (Arg), Millonarios (Col), Racing (Arg), Brest (Fr), Cerro Porteno (Par), River Plate, Deportivo Mandiyu (Arg).

Goycochea earned fame at the 1990 World Cup finals when he stepped into the action during Argentina's match against the Soviet Union after Nery Pumpido had broken a leg. Goycochea's heroics in the penalty shootout victories over Yugoslavia and Italy subsequently took Argentina to the Final. Yet he had not played a competitive game over the previous six

GOYCOCHEA *Magic touch in World Cup penalty shoot-outs*

months because of the domestic unrest in Colombia, where he had been contracted to Millonarios of Bogota. After the 1990 World Cup finals Goycochea signed for the ambitious French provincial club, Brest. They soon went bankrupt, however, and he returned to Argentina.

Jimmy Greaves

Born: February 20, 1940, England.
Clubs: Chelsea (Eng), Milan (It), Tottenham, West Ham (Eng).

Greaves was an instinctive goalscorer, whose speed in thought and deed made up for lack of size and power. His 44 goals in 57 full internationals included two hauls of four goals and four threes, and his 357 in League games (all First Division) included three fives. An unhappy interlude in Italy did little to mar his scoring ability, and he gave wonderful value for

money until his closing chapter with West Ham. By then drink had taken a grip, and his overcoming that blight to become a popular television pundit set an inspiring example to others in the same position.

Harry Gregg

Born: October 25, 1932, Northern Ireland.
Clubs: Dundalk (Rep. of Ire.), Doncaster, Manchester United, Stoke (Eng).

Genial, popular Gregg won his first cap after only nine Football League games for Second Division Doncaster, and had established himself as Ireland's first choice before the fateful 1957–58 season. Hardly had he left Yorkshire for Manchester United when, as a survivor of the Munich air crash, he became a hero by helping to rescue some of the injured. Later that year he performed well in helping his club to the FA Cup Final, where they lost 2–0 to Bolton, and the Irish to the quarter-final of the World Cup in Sweden. Injury kept him out of United's FA Cup-winning side in 1963.

John Greig

Born: September 11, 1942, Scotland.
Club: Rangers.

A 16-year spell of hard labour in defence and midfield brought Greig a record 496 League appearances for Rangers and a considerable number of honours, although Celtic were the dominant team in Scotland for a large

TOMMY GEMMELL *Historic goal in the 1967 European Cup Final*

part of that time. He was Footballer of the Year in 1966, the season in which he scored a spectacular goal against Italy in a World Cup qualifier, and won 44 caps, often as skipper. Greig also played in two European Cup-winners' Cup finals, losing in 1967 and winning in 1972. Later, he had a spell as manager at Ibrox.

Gunnar Gren

Born: October 31, 1920, Sweden.
Clubs: IFK Gothenburg (Swe), Milan, Fiorentina (It), Orgryte, GAIS Gothenburg (Sw).

Gren, nicknamed "the Professor", claimed Italian attention when in the Olympic Games winning team in London in 1948. His nickname stemmed both from his premature baldness and his astute inside-forward play. Milan won the transfer race and Gren forged, with fellow Swedes Nordahl and Liedholm, the legendary "Grenoli" trio which took Italian football by storm. In 1955, after a spell with Fiorentina, he returned home to Sweden and, at 37, helped the hosts to the Final of the 1958 World Cup. That was the last of Gren's 57 internationals. Later he returned to IFK Gothenburg – with whom he had won the Swedish championship in 1942 – as manager of the souvenir shop.

Ruud Gullit

Born: September 1, 1962, Holland.
Clubs: Haarlem, Feyenoord, PSV Eindhoven (Hol), Milan, Sampdoria, Milan, Sampdoria (It), Chelsea (Eng).

Ruud Gullit was Europe's outstanding player in the late 1980s and early 1990s. He began his career as a sweeper, but at PSV he moved forward and after his world record £6.5 million sale to Milan in 1987 became an out-and-out attacker. A year later he led Holland to victory in the European Championship and won the European Cup with Milan. Serious knee injuries dogged him after that, but after one season at Chelsea in England he was made player-manager and won the FA Cup at the first attempt. His departure, over a wage dispute, in early 1998, rocked English football but he returned to lead Newcastle to the FA Cup final in 1999.

RUUD GULLIT *Showing off the 1988 European Championship trophy*

Gheorghe Hagi

Born: February 5, 1965, Romania.
Clubs: FC Constanta, Sportul Studentesc, Steaua Bucharest (Rom), Real Madrid (Sp), Brescia (It), Barcelona (Sp), Galatasaray (Tur).

Hagi was always destined for stardom. He played for Romania's youth team at 15, was a top-flight league player at 17, an international at 18, and a year later, in 1984, was taking part in the finals of the European Championship. In 1985 he hit 20 goals and in 1986 he 31, after scoring six in one match. Steaua Bucharest virtually kidnapped Hagi from neighbours Sportul without a transfer fee – an escapade approved by the ruling Ceaucescu family, who were Steaua supporters. After the 1990 World Cup Hagi played in Spain and Italy – returning, briefly, to Barcelona after inspiring Romania to reach the quarter-finals of the 1994 World Cup. He also played in the 1998 finals in France, guiding Romania to the second phase.

Helmut Haller

Born: July 21, 1939, Germany.
Clubs: BC Augsburg (W Ger), Bologna, Juventus (It), Augsburg (W Ger).

Haller earned a teenage reputation as an inside-forward in West Germany in the late 1950s, before the advent of full-time professionalism and the Bundesliga. Italian club Bologna gambled on his youth and were

HAGI *Accelerates away from Irish defender Paul McGrath*

superbly rewarded: in 1963 Haller's partnership with the Dane Harald Nielsen brought Bologna their first league title in more than 20 years. Later Haller played with further success for Juventus before returning to Augsburg. He will be remembered above all for his outstanding contribution to West Germany's 1966 World Cup campaign.

Kurt Hamrin

Born: November 19, 1934, Sweden.
Clubs: AIK Sola (Swe), Juventus, Padova, Fiorentina, Milan, Napoli, Caserta (It).

Hamrin ranks close behind Matthews and Garrincha among the great outside-rights of the modern game. He was a quick, darting attacker who was not only nimble and clever but one of the most successful goal-grabbers in the history of the Italian league. Hamrin disappointed Juventus and they sold him off after only one year. Once he had adjusted, however, Hamrin proved an irresistible one-man strike force with Fiorentina, with whom he scored 150 goals in nine seasons and won the European Cup-winners' Cup in 1961. At 34, while with Milan, he added a European Cup winners' medal to his collection.

Gerhard Hanappi

Born: July 9, 1929, Austria.
Clubs: Wacker, Rapid Vienna.

Hanappi was one of the most versatile footballers to be found anywhere

in the world in the 1950s. He played mainly wing-half or occasionally inside-forward for his long-time club, Rapid, but also lined up at centre-forward and at full-back in the course of winning 93 caps for Austria. He would have topped a century had it not been for a row with officialdom. Hanappi, an architect by profession, designed a new stadium for Rapid which was, after his premature death, named in honour of his memory. Hanappi was Austrian champion and a cup-winner once each with Wacker then national champion six times and cup-winner once again with Rapid. He played for FIFA's World XI against England in 1953.

Eddie Hapgood

Born: September 27, 1908, England.
Club: Arsenal.

Hapgood was small for a left-back, but as tough as teak. He was an inspiring captain who led England in 21 of his 30 games during the 1930s, with 13 more during the war. In his teens he was an amateur with Bristol Rovers, but was allowed to leave and was with non-league Kettering when Arsenal recruited him. He went on to earn five championship medals and played in three FA Cup finals, winning two. His first international was against Italy in Rome; his first as captain was also against Italy but on his club ground in the infamous "Battle of Highbury" – when he returned to play on after an opponent's elbow had smashed his nose.

HAMRIN (LEFT) *Goes for goal*

After retirement he managed Blackburn and Watford, but with little success.

Ernst Happel

Born: June 29, 1925, Austria.
Clubs: Rapid Vienna, 1st FC Vienna (Aus), Racing Club Paris (Fr).

Happel was a redoubtable centre-back with Rapid and Austria in the 1950s, his 51-cap playing career reaching a climax at the 1958 World Cup finals. He possessed a powerful shot and once scored a hat-trick, with free-kicks and a penalty, in an early European Cup tie against Real Madrid. After retiring, Happel became one of Europe's most successful coaches, taking Feyenoord to the World Club Cup and European Cup in 1970. In Argentina in 1978, he was manager of Holland when they reached the World Cup Final, and he had further success in the 1983 European Cup with Hamburg.

HURST *World Cup legend*

Johnny Haynes

Born: October 17, 1934, England.
Clubs: Fulham (Eng), Durban City (SA).

Like Tom Finney, Haynes won precisely nothing in nearly two decades with one club. However, he was the hub of many an England team in a 56-cap career, hitting long passes through a needle's eye and scoring a surprising number of goals with an incredibly powerful shot that belied his comparatively slight frame. As England's first £100-a-week player he often was unjustly criticized, but he earned every penny in the service of Fulham (generally struggling) and England (frequently rampant).

He was England captain from 1960 till a serious car accident in 1962, in a period when, in successive games, England won 5–2, 9–0, 4–2, 5–1, 9–3 and 8–0. The 9–3 result was a slaughter of Scotland, perhaps the best performance of his era. His career might have added up differently if Milan had persisted in their bid for him, or if, after his accident, a record-breaking bid from Tottenham Hotspur had succeeded. He ended his playing career in South Africa, winning a championship medal with Durban City.

Willie Henderson

Born: January 24, 1944, Scotland.
Clubs: Rangers (Scot), Sheffield Wednesday (Eng).

If "Wee Willie" had performed throughout his career as he did in his first few years, he would have been perhaps the best Scottish player ever. Despite persistent foot trouble and far from perfect eyesight, he had won all four domestic honours – league, cup, League Cup and cap – before his 20th birthday. By then Rangers had sold international winger Alex Scott to Everton in order to make room for the kid. Henderson went on to play in 29 internationals and captivate fans with his wizardry, but his career was marred by discontent, and gradually petered out in disappointment.

Geoff Hurst

Born: December 8, 1941, England.
Club: West Ham, Stoke.

A big man who was made for the big occasion, Hurst, strong and deceptively fast, was frequently mundane in West Ham's toils through their League programmes. But when needed in the big events, he was out of the traps like a greyhound. He scored the remarkable total of 46 goals in the League Cup, 23 in the FA Cup (including a fluke in the 1964 Final) and three in the 1966 World Cup Final, when he appeared virtually from nowhere to put the trophy on the nation's sideboard with his hat-trick against West Germany. Like so many big-name players, he became a mundane manager, at Chelsea. Memories of him as a player will last much longer.

JAIRZINHO *Unique World Cup feat*

Jairzinho (full name: Jair Ventura Filho)

Born: December 25, 1944, Brazil.
Clubs: Botafogo (Br), Marseilles (Fr), Cruzeiro (Br), Portuguesa (Ven).

Jairzinho was the heir to Garrincha's glory, both with Botafogo and with Brazil. He moved from his home town of Caxias to sign professional with Botafogo at 15, and played in the same Brazil squad as his hero at the 1966 World Cup. Four years later Jairzinho made history by scoring in every game in every round of the World Cup on the way to victory. He scored seven goals, including two in Brazil's opening win over Czechoslovakia and one in the defeat of Italy in the Final. He tried his luck in Europe with Marseille but returned home after disciplinary problems to win yet another trophy, the South American club cup, with Cruzeiro at the age of 32.

Alex James

Born: September 14, 1901, Scotland.
Clubs: Raith (Scot), Preston, Arsenal (Eng).

Eight caps were meagre reward for the outstanding inside-forward of the 1930s. James began as a fiery attacking player (sent off twice in successive matches at Raith) but changed his style to fit Arsenal manager Herbert Chapman's "W" formation. He scored only 26 League goals in eight years at Highbury, but made countless others with his astute passing from deep to the flying wingers or through the middle. Despite his superb display in the 5–1 rout of England by the "Wembley Wizards", James was often thought too clever by the selectors, though not by fans: at club level he won six major medals and undying fame.

Pat Jennings

Born: June 12, 1945, Northern Ireland.
Clubs: Newry Town (NI), Watford, Tottenham, Arsenal (Eng).

A goalkeeper with character and charm to match his size, Jennings even bowed out of football in a big way by winning his 119th cap on his 41st birthday – and in a World Cup, too. Only defeat, by Brazil, marred the occasion. By then Jennings had played well over 1,000 senior matches in a 24-year career, four of them in FA Cup finals. He won with Spurs

PAT JENNINGS *Veteran of more than 1,000 first-class matches*

in 1967 and Arsenal in 1979, lost with Arsenal in 1978 and 1980. Jennings also scored a goal with a clearance from hand during the 1967 Charity Shield against Manchester United. He remains one of the finest British goalkeepers ever seen.

Jimmy Johnstone

Born: September 30, 1944, Scotland.
Clubs: Celtic (Scot), San José (US), Sheffield United (Eng), Dundee (Scot), Shelbourne (Ire).

Johnstone was a remarkably talented winger, but infuriatingly inconsistent, as shown by the fact that his 23 caps were spread over 12 years. Small and nippy, he was an old-style "tanner-ball dribbler" and nicknamed The Flea. He won 16 medals with his club – one European Cup, eight league, three Scottish cup, four League Cup. Johnstone also earned a reputation for occasional wayward behaviour, on the field and off, but his courage was never in doubt, as many a far bigger opponent found to his cost. He was particularly effective in the 1966–67 season, when Celtic won every competition they entered, culminating in the European Cup Final defeat of Internazionale in Lisbon.

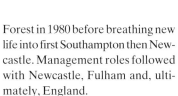

Kevin Keegan

Born: February 14, 1951, England.
Clubs: Scunthorpe, Liverpool (Eng), Hamburg (Ger), Southampton, Newcastle (Eng).

Keegan, the only British player to have won the European Footballer of the Year twice, cost Liverpool a bargain £35,000 when he signed from Scunthorpe United in 1971. He was an overnight success, first in his original position of outside-right, then as a free-ranging attacking raider. Keegan won two league titles with Liverpool, leaving for Hamburg after the European Cup victory of 1977. Keegan was a European Cup Final loser with Hamburg against Nottingham Forest in 1980 before breathing new life into first Southampton then Newcastle. Management roles followed with Newcastle, Fulham and, ultimately, England.

Jack Kelsey

Born: November 19, 1929, Wales.
Club: Arsenal (Eng).

Big Jack was beaten five times on his debut for Arsenal in 1951, but he went on to be first-choice keeper for 11 years until a spinal injury, sustained in a collision with Vava of Brazil, forced him to retire. He remained a familiar figure at Highbury as manager of the club shop. He was powerful enough to withstand the challenges of an age when keepers were not well protected, and agile enough to make many remarkable stops, helped by rubbing chewing gum into his palms. Kelsey won 43 caps for Wales and played for Britain against the Rest of Europe in 1955.

Mario Alberto Kempes

Born: July 15, 1952, Argentina.
Clubs: Instituto Cordoba, Rosario Central (Arg), Valencia (Sp), River Plate (Arg), Hercules (Sp), Vienna, Austria Salzburg (Austria).

Kempes, an aggressive young striker with legs like tree trunks, had a first

MARIO KEMPES
Argentina's World Cup hammer in 1978

taste of World Cup football in West Germany in 1974. He swiftly earned a transfer to Spain with Valencia, where he developed into such a devastating hammer of opposing defences that he was the only foreign-based player recalled to join the hosts' World Cup squad under Cesar Luis Menotti in 1978. His addition proved decisive: Kempes was the event's top scorer with six goals, including two in the 3–1 defeat of Holland in the Final. Strangely, he was never able to scale those heights again, despite playing once more for Argentina in the 1982 finals in Spain, where he should have felt at home.

Jürgen Klinsmann

Born: July 30, 1964, Germany.
Clubs: Stuttgart Kickers, VfB Stuttgart (Ger), Internazionale (It), Monaco (Fr), Tottenham (Eng), Bayern Munich (Ger), Sampdoria (It), Tottenham (Eng).

Jürgen Klinsmann needed little time before breaking through as the German league's top scorer and the country's Footballer of the Year during his first Bundesliga spell with VfB Stuttgart, whom he also led to the UEFA Cup Final in 1989. He then spent three successful years at Internazionale in Italy before moving to France with Monaco and then to England with Tottenham (where he spent two spells) before returning to Germany and Bayern Munich in July 1995. A year later Bayern won the UEFA Cup with Klinsmann contributing a European club competition record of 15 goals in a season. He won the World Cup with West Germany in 1990 and the European Championships in 1996 before announcing his international retirement after scoring three times at France '98.

Ronald Koeman

Born: March 21, 1963, Holland.
Clubs: Groningen, PSV Eindhoven (Hol), Barcelona (Sp), Feyenoord (Hol).

Despite lacking pace, Koeman turned himself into one of the world's best sweepers as well as becoming a free-kick expert. It was from a free kick that Koeman thundered the winner for Barcelona in the 1992 European Cup Final, a trophy he also won with PSV Eindhoven in 1988. Ronald and brother Erwin began with their father's old club, Groningen and were later members together of the Holland side which won the 1988 European Championship in Germany. Ronald won the treble of European Cup, Dutch league and cup in 1988 then moved to Barcelona in 1989, before returning to Holland and Feyenoord in 1995.

Ivan Kolev

Born: November 1, 1930, Bulgaria.
Club: CDNA/CSKA Sofia.

Kolev was the first great Bulgarian footballer, often compared for control and vision with Hungarian contemporary Ferenc Puskas. Kolev, who could play outside- or inside-left, spent all his career with the Bulgarian army club, variously known as CDNA and then CSKA Sofia. He scored 25 goals in 75 internationals and led Bulgaria on their first appearance at a major soccer tournament in

NICE WHILE IT LASTED *Jürgen Klinsmann was a hero in his first season at Spurs*

the 1952 Helsinki Olympic Games. With CDNA/CSKA he was champion of Bulgaria on 11 occasions and won the cup four times.

Sandor Kocsis

Born: September 30, 1929, Hungary.
Clubs: Ferencvaros, Honved (Hun), Young Fellows (Swz), Barcelona (Sp).

Kocsis was an attacking inside-right for Honved and Hungary in the early 1950s. He and fellow inside-forward Puskas pushed forward while the nominal centre-forward withdrew towards midfield, creating gaps for the others to exploit. Kocsis did so to the extent of 75 goals in 68 internationals. He was three times the Hungarian league's top scorer, as well as the leading marksman, with 11 goals, at the 1954 World Cup finals. After the Hungarian Revolution of 1956 Kocsis decided to stay abroad and joined Barcelona with further success,

winning the Fairs Cup in 1960. A year later Kocsis was on the losing side with Barcelona at the European Cup Final against Benfica in Bern.

Raymond Kopa

Born: October 13, 1931, France.
Clubs: Angers, Reims (Fr), Real Madrid (Sp), Reims (Fr).

Born Kopaszewski, the son of an emigrant Polish miner, Kopa gained an added incentive to escape from a mining future when he damaged a hand in a pit accident as a teenager. He was spotted by Angers and then sold on to Reims in 1950. Originally a right-winger, Kopa soon switched to a creative centre- or inside-forward role. He led Reims to the first European Cup Final in 1956, being transferred afterwards to their conquerors on the day, Real Madrid. Kopa starred in midfield for third-placed France at the 1958 World Cup, and

returned to Reims a year later as European Footballer of the Year. He played 45 times for France but his playing career ended amid controversy over his outspoken espousal of the cause of freedom of contract.

Johannes "Hans" Krankl

Born: February 14, 1953, Austria.
Clubs: Rapid Vienna (Austria), Barcelona (Sp), 1st FC Vienna (Austria), Barcelona (Sp), Rapid, Wiener Sportclub (Austria).

For Krankl everything happened in 1978. He scored 41 goals for Rapid Vienna, to win the Golden Boot as Euorpe's leading league marksman, and starred for Austria at the World Cup finals in Argentina. He joined Barcelona and inspired their victory in the 1979 European Cup-winners' Cup. Serious injury in a car crash interrupted Krankl's career in Spain and he went home to Austria briefly. Later he returned to Rapid, with whom he became general manager after retiring. Krankl scored 34 goals in 69 internationals and was top league scorer four times in Austria and once in Spain.

Ladislav Kubala

Born: June 10, 1927, Hungary.
Clubs: Ferencvaros (Hun), Bratislava (Cz), Vasas Budapest (Hun), Barcelona, Español (Sp), FC Zurich (Swz), Toronto Falcons (Can).

One of the ironies of 1950s football was that Hungary created a great team without one of their very greatest players. Centre- or inside-forward Kubala had escaped to the West after having played international football for both Czechoslovakia and Hungary in the late 1940s. In exile in Italy, Kubala formed a refugees' team called Pro Patria which played exhibition tours and provided him with the springboard to join Spain's Barcelona. There Kubala was Spanish champion five times and twice won the Fairs Cup. He also gained international recognition with a third country, winning 19 caps for Spain to add to his seven for Czechoslovakia and three for Hungary. He left Barcelona after the 1961 European Cup Final defeat by Benfica, but later returned to coach both Barcelona and the Spanish national team.

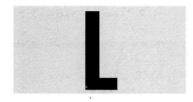

Angel Amadeo Labruna

Born: September 26, 1918, Argentina.
Clubs: River Plate, Platense (Arg), Green Cross (Chile), Rampla Juniors (Uru).

Labruna remains one of the greatest Argentine football personalities of all time. Not only was he a great inside-left, but he earned longevity records by playing with River Plate for 29 years and won a reputation as a South American Stanley Matthews by playing on until he was 41. At the 1958 World Cup finals in Sweden, Labruna was recalled at the age of 40 to complete an international career which brought him 17 goals in 36 games for Argentina. Labruna began with River Plate when he was 12 and won nine league championships. In the late 1940s he was a member of the legendary "Maquina", or "Machine", forward line. In 1986 Labruna was coach when River at last won the South American club cup.

Marius Lacatus

Born: April 5, 1964, Romania.
Clubs: Steaua Bucharest (Rom), Fiorentina (It), Oviedo (Sp), Steaua.

Tall, slim and sharp in front of goal, ·Lacatus was a key figure in the Romanian upsurge of the 1980s. Playing nominally as outside-right, he used his pace to great effect to help shoot his country to the 1990 World Cup finals. After the finals, he stayed on in Italy with Fiorentina, and the Romanian federation allocated much of the fee to the redevelopment of sports facilities in the country. Lacatus found it hard to adjust to Italian football and later moved on to Spain before returning home in the autumn of 1993.

LAUDRUP *Brilliant elder brother*

Grzegorz Lato

Born: April 8, 1950, Poland.
Clubs: Stal Mielec (Pol), Lokeren (Bel), Atlante (Mex).

Lato was a Polish phenomenon, an outstanding striker who later proved equally influential when he moved back into midfield. At the 1974 World Cup finals, Lato was top scorer with seven goals. He had made his debut for Poland against Spain in 1971 and was a member of the squad which won the Olympic gold medal in Munich a year later. Lato became a fixture in the senior national team in 1973, after impressing manager Kazimierz Gorski on a tour of the United States and Canada, and he went on to score 46 goals in 104 internationals, a Polish record. After leading Poland's attack at the 1978 World Cup finals in Argentina, Lato was permitted the "reward" of a transfer to Lokeren in Belgium, and he ended his career in Mexico with Atlante.

Michael Laudrup

Born: June 15, 1964, Denmark.
Clubs: Brondbyernes (Den), Lazio, Juventus (It), Barcelona, Real Madrid (Sp), Vissel Kobe (Jap), Ajax (Hol).

Michael and younger brother Brian are sons of a former Danish international, Finn Laudrup, who closely guided their early careers. Michael, as a teenager, attracted scouts from all Europe's top clubs but finally chose Juventus, who loaned him to Lazio before recalling him to replace Poland's Zbigniew Boniek. With Juventus Laudrup won the World Club Cup before moving on to win the European Cup with Barcelona. He starred at the 1986 World Cup finals before falling out with Denmark's national manager Richard Moller Nielsen and thus missing the 1992 European Championship triumph. But he was back for the 1998 World Cup finals in France and was named in the FIFA team of the tournament before retiring.

Denis Law

Born: February 22, 1940, Scotland.
Clubs: Huddersfield, Manchester City (Eng), Torino (It), Manchester United, Manchester City (Eng).

Denis Law and Jimmy Greaves were born within four days of each other, and spent several years as rival scorers and supreme entertainers. Law, of only medium height and slim in build, had a lion's heart and a salmon's leap, scoring many spectacular goals with headers and acrobatic shots. He was also an incisive passer of the ball, and a fierce competitor. Suspensions and injury cost him many more goals. He was European Footballer of the Year in 1964, won two league titles and the 1963 FA Cup, and scored 30 goals in 55 internationals, but missed United's European Cup victory in 1968 through knee trouble.

Tommy Lawton

Born: October 6, 1919, England.
Clubs: Burnley, Everton, Chelsea, Notts County, Brentford, Arsenal.

One of the first footballers to realize what his market value was, and to work at getting it. Lawton made frequent moves, at a time when there rarely was any percentage for a transferred player. Lawton was a star from his dubbin-smothered toe-caps to his glistening centre parting. He got a hat-trick on his senior debut aged 16, was the First Division top scorer two years in a row, won a title medal aged 19, scored 23 goals in 22 full internationals, and goals by the dozen

DENIS LAW *The promising youngster in Huddersfield days*

during the Second World War. Lawton was still frightening foes deep into his 30s and pulling in fans everywhere he went.

Leonidas da Silva

Born: November 11, 1910, Brazil.
Clubs: Havanesa, Barroso, Sul Americano, Sirio Libanes, Bomsucesso (Br), Nacional (Uru), Vasco da Gama, Botafogo, Flamengo, São Paulo (Br).

Leonidas was Brazil's 1930s superstar although he played only 23 times for his country. He was the inventor of the overhead bicycle kick, which was unveiled to the international game when he scored twice on his international debut against Uruguay in 1932. The Uruguayans were so impressed he was immediately signed by the top club, Nacional. Later he returned home with Vasco da Gama and was top scorer at the 1938 World Cup with eight goals, including four in a 6–5 victory over Poland. Unfortunately, an overconfident management rested Leonidas from the semi-final against Italy, wanting to keep him fresh for the Final . . . and they lost.

Billy Liddell

Born January 10, 1922, Scotland.
Club: Liverpool (Eng).

An accountant, Justice of the Peace and youth worker, Liddell allied all these activities to football. He is still revered as one of the greatest players in Liverpool's history, which is saying a great deal. Liddell missed six years on war service and spent all his career with one club. Apart from the championship in 1947 and a Cup Final defeat three years later, Liverpool achieved little during his 15 years, but he set club records with 492 league appearances and 216 goals, as well as representing Scotland 28 times and Great Britain in two games against the Rest of Europe.

Nils Liedholm

Born: October 8, 1922, Sweden.
Clubs: Norrköping (Swe), Milan (It).

Liedholm played originally at inside-forward, later moved back to wing-half and finally became one of the best of sweepers in his veteran years. He began with Norrköping, winning two championship medals and playing

LITTBARSKI *Testing the resolve of Italian defender Claudio Gentile*

18 times for his country. After helping Sweden win, from outside-left, the 1948 Olympic title, he moved to Italy. There Liedholm formed Milan's celebrated trio with Gunnar Gren and Gunnar Nordahl and he scored 60 goals in 367 league games. At the end of his career Liedholm captained hosts Sweden to runners-up spot at the 1958 World Cup finals. After retiring as a player, he stayed with Milan as a youth coach and later took charge of

the senior team in 1964. He also managed Fiorentina and Roma.

Gary Lineker

Born: November 30, 1960, England.
Clubs: Leicester, Everton (Eng), Barcelona (Sp), Tottenham (Eng), Nagoya Grampus 8 (Jap).

All sorts of records fell to this unassuming son of a market trader, who accepted good and bad with the smiling sincerity that, allied to his skill,

GARY LINEKER *Scoring, against the Irish Republic in the 1990 World Cup, one of his 48 international goals*

made him such a popular figure. This was never more evident than in the desperate days when serious illness struck his first-born son. He went within one goal of England's 49-goal scoring record, ten coming in World Cup final stages, led the First Division marksmen with three different clubs, scored a hat-trick for Barcelona against Real Madrid, and won the FA Cup despite missing a penalty. Lineker retired after two injury-plagued seasons in Japan, and immediately became a broadcaster.

Pierre Littbarski

Born: April 16, 1960, Germany.
Clubs: Hertha Zehlendorf, Köln (Ger), Racing Paris (Fr), Köln (Ger), JEF United (Japan).

Littbarski, an outside-right who later took his dribbling skills back into midfield, shot to prominence by hitting two goals on his debut for West Germany in a World Cup qualifier against Austria in 1981. He joined Köln, the club with which he is most associated, in 1978, played in the 1982 and 1986 World Cup Finals and finally achieved victory in Italy in 1990. Before heading out to Japan to wind down his career, Littbarski described his career ambition as "scoring a goal after beating all 10 outfield players, dribbling round the goalkeeper and putting the ball in the net with a back-heel".

Wlodzimierz Lubanski

Born: February 28, 1947, Poland.
Clubs: GKS Gliwice, Gornik Zabrze (Pol), Lokeren (Bel), Valenciennes, Quimper (Fr), Lokeren (Bel).

Lubanski ranks among Poland's finest players even though injuries were not kind to him. He emerged with the miners' club, Gornik, in the mid-1960s taking over the mantle of inspiration with both club and country from Ernest Pol. Lubanski was four times top league marksman in Poland and captained his country to the 1972 Olympic Games victory in Munich. The following year he suffered a serious thigh injury in a World Cup qualifier against England and missed the finals in which Poland finished third. He returned to national team duty at the 1978 finals in Argentina, before winding down his career in Belgium and France.

Ally McCoist

Born: September 24, 1962, Scotland.
Clubs: St. Johnstone (Scot), Sunderland (Eng), Rangers (Scot).

A powerful striker who survived a disastrous spell in England to become a hugely successful and popular player back in his homeland. McCoist started at St Johnstone, who earned a club record £400,000 when selling him to Sunderland in 1981. After 56 games and only eight goals, he was sold to Rangers, and began a decade of almost constant medal-collecting as the club dominated the Scottish game. He won the Golden Boot as Europe's leading league marksman and recovered from a broken leg to smash the legendary Bob McPhail's record of 233 league goals for Rangers. His one disappointment was being left out of Scotland's 1998 World Cup finals squad.

McCOIST *Crowned his goal-grabbing career with the Golden Boot*

Paul McGrath

Born: December 4, 1959, England.
Clubs: Man Utd, Aston Villa, Derby Co.

McGrath was a fine player whose career was dogged by ill-luck and – on occasions – lack of self-discipline. Born in Middlesex of Irish parentage, McGrath had a troubled progress through Manchester United's junior ranks and on into the senior squad, with injuries and authority combining to hinder him. But manager Ron Atkinson kept faith, and took McGrath with him when he moved to Villa. As a club player, one FA Cup win in 1985 – he performed heroically for ten-man United – was poor reward. As an international for the Republic of Ireland, his not inconsiderable skill and total commitment made him a folk hero among the Irish fans during European Championship and World Cup campaigns.

Jimmy McIlroy

Born: October 25, 1931, Northern Ireland.
Clubs: Glentoran (NI), Burnley, Stoke, Oldham (Eng).

If Blanchflower was the key man of

McGRATH *Defied knee injuries*

the Irish World Cup campaign in 1958, Jimmy McIlroy was only a little way behind him. His unhurried, elegant work at inside-forward proved ideal for the tactics devised by team manager Peter Doherty. Altogether McIlroy played 55 games for his country, to go with more than 600 at club level, earning a Championship medal with the attractive young Burnley squad in 1960, and a runners-up medal in the FA Cup two years later – against Blanchflower's Spurs. He later enjoyed a brief but brilliant combination with Stanley Matthews at Stoke.

Sammy McIlroy

Born: August 1, 1954, Northern Ireland.
Clubs: Manchester United, Stoke, Manchester City (Eng).

Another valuable midfielder, like his namesake, but of a totally different type. Sammy McIlroy's all-action style was in complete contrast to Jimmy's deliberate method, but was ideally suited to the hurly-burly of the modern game. It earned him 88 games for his country, spread over 15 years, but only five goals. He also played in three FA Cup Finals with United, losing to Southampton in 1976 and Arsenal in 1979, beating Liverpool in 1977. McIlroy's late equalizer in the 1979 Final seemed sure to take the game to extra time, but Arsenal went downfield to snatch the winner straight from the restart.

BILLY McNEILL *Celtic's captain in the glorious 1960s*

Billy McNeill

Born: March 2, 1940, Scotland.
Club: Celtic.

The nickname Caesar suited McNeill. In both size and style he was a big man, and was the hub of the Celtic defence during their great days of the 1960s. He won a host of domestic medals and, in 1967, became the first Briton to lift the European Cup, the most coveted prize in club football. He was a soldier's son and educated at a rugby-playing school, but made up for a late introduction to soccer with years of splendid service and a club record number of appearances. His international debut was in the 9–3 mauling by England in 1961, but he recovered to gain 28 more caps. McNeill was later manager of his old club (twice), as well as Aston Villa and Manchester City.

Paul McStay

Born: October 22, 1964, Scotland.
Club: Celtic.

This product of Hamilton played for his country as a schoolboy and at youth level before graduating to the Under-21 team and then to the full national squad. He made his senior debut against Uruguay in 1983 and has plied his creative midfield trade to such good effect that Kenny Dalglish's record of 102 caps might possibly be within his reach. McStay's loyalty to Celtic has been a welcome change in the modern climate of frequent transfers, and he has given good value for his high earnings in a period when his club have been very much overshadowed by Rangers. He sadly missed the 1996 European Championships through injury.

Josef "Sepp" Maier

Born: February 28, 1944, West Germany.
Clubs: TSV Haar, Bayern Munich.

Maier reached the pinnacle of his career in 1974 when he first won the European Cup with Bayern Munich and then, a few weeks later, the World Cup with West Germany on his home ground of the Olympic stadium in the Bavarian capital. He was noted, apart from his goalkeeping talent, for his trademark long shorts and his love of tennis. Maier even opened a tennis school thanks to the money he earned in a 19-year career with Bayern from 1960 to 1979. Maier played 473 league matches, including a run of 422 consecutive games. He made his international debut in 1966, when he was No. 3 goalkeeper in West Germany's World Cup squad in England, and was a member of the European Championship-winning side against the Soviet Union in Brussels in 1972. Maier won the European Cup three times with Bayern as well as the World Club Cup against Atletico Mineiro of Brazil in 1976.

Paolo Maldini

Born: June 26, 1968, Italy.
Club: Milan.

Football runs in the family for the fast raiding left-back of Italy and Milan. Paolo's father, Cesare, was a sweeper who captained Milan to their first European Cup success in 1963, played 16 times for his country and, after coaching Italy's Olympic and Under-21 teams, managed the national side at France '98. Paolo, who can play anywhere in defence, began with Milan's youth section and made his first-team debut at 17. He followed in father's footsteps by winning the European Cup in 1989, 1990 and 1994 and was soon acclaimed as one of the finest all-round footballers in the world when he helped Italy reach the 1994 World Cup Final, only losing to Brazil on penalties. He was voted 1994 World Player of the Year by *World Soccer* magazine and went on to captain his country, under the manament of his father, at the 1998 World Cup finals in France.

Diego Armando Maradona

see Legends (pages 114–15)

Silvio Marzolini

Born: 1940, Argentina.
Clubs: Ferro Carril Oeste, Boca Juniors.

To many experts, and not only Argentines, Marzolini is the finest full-back of the modern era. He was a left-back who could tackle and intercept with the best of them but also displayed the technique and virtuoso skill of a forward when he had the opportunity to go on attack. At only 13 Marzolini won the Buenos Aires youth title with Ferro Carril Oeste and became a first division regular at 19. In 1960 he was bought by Boca Juniors, winning the

MALDINI *Emulated his father*

league title in 1962, 1964 and 1965. He played in the World Cup finals of 1962 and 1966 – where he rose above all the unpleasant mayhem of the quarter-final defeat by England at Wembley. Marzolini, after retirement, enjoyed some success as a TV and film actor before he returned to Boca as coach and took them to the league title in 1981. He was forced to retire because of a heart condition.

Josef Masopust

Born: February 9, 1931, Czechoslovakia.
Clubs: Union Teplice, Dukla Prague (Cz), Crossing Molenbeek (Bel).

Masopust is the only Czechoslovak player to have won the European Footballer of the Year award, which he collected in 1962 after an outstanding World Cup campaign in Chile. Czechoslovakia finished runners-up to Brazil, and Masopust scored the opening goal in the Final, which they ultimately lost 3–1. Originally an inside-forward, Masopust made his name as a left-half but was, to all intents and purposes, more of an old-fashioned centre-half. He preferred to dominate games from a central position in midfield both for Czechoslovakia and the army club Dukla. His intuitive understanding with left-back Ladislav Novak and defensive wing-half Svatopluk Pluskal was renowned throughout the world.

Lothar Matthäus

Born: March 21, 1961, Germany.
Clubs: Borussia Mönchengladbach, Bayern Munich (Ger), Internazionale (It), Bayern Munich (Ger).

Matthäus has been Germany's outstanding leader from midfield – and, latterly, sweeper – since the early 1980s. His career reached its zenith in 1990 when he was not only West Germany's World Cup-winning captain in Rome, but was also voted Player of the Tournament by the world's media. Matthäus was a substitute for the West German side who won the 1980 European Championship and established himself only in 1986, when he scored a magnificent winner against Morocco in the World Cup second round on the way to defeat by Argentina in the Final. He began with Borussia, joined Bayern for £650,000 in 1984 and moved to Italy with Inter in

1988 for £2.4 million. Injury kept him out of the 1992 European Championship finals, but he won the 1996 UEFA Cup with Bayern Munich and the 1997 league title and then made a shock international return, aged 37, for the 1998 World Cup finals .

Stanley Matthews

see Legends (pages 116–17)

Alessandro "Sandro" Mazzola

Born: November 7, 1942, Italy.
Club: Internazionale.

Sandro is the son of Valentino, the skipper of Torino and Italy who was killed in the 1949 Superga air disaster when Sandro was six. To escape comparisons,

he launched his football career with Inter rather than Torino, and made his debut in a 9–1 defeat by Juventus – when Inter fielded their youth team in protest at the Italian federation's decision to order an earlier game to be replayed. In 1962–63 Mazzola, a striking inside-forward, scored 10 goals in 23 games as Inter won the league title. In both 1964 and 1965 he won the European Cup and World Club Cup, scoring in the victories over Real Madrid and Benfica. Mazzola reverted to midfield to help Italy win the 1968 European Championship and was outstanding when Italy reached the World Cup Final in Mexico in 1970.

Valentino Mazzola

Born: January 26, 1919, Italy.
Clubs: Venezia, Torino.

Mazzola was an inside-left who was born in Milan, where he played for Tresoldi and then the Alfa Romeo works side. In 1939 he was bought by Venezia, where he struck up a remarkable inside-forward partnership with Ezio Loik – with whom he moved to Torino in 1942. Mazzola captained and inspired Torino to five consecutive league championship victories in 1943 and 1946–49. Before he could celebrate the fifth title, however, Mazzola and 17 of his Torino colleagues had been killed in the 1949 Superga air disaster. Mazzola was the league's top scorer in 1947, and made his Italy debut against Croatia in Genoa in 1942. He scored four goals in 12 internationals and would almost certainly have captained Italy's World Cup defence in Brazil in 1950.

Giuseppe Meazza

Born: August 23, 1910, Italy.
Clubs: Internazionale, Milan, Juventus, Varese, Atalanta.

Only two Italian players won the World Cup in 1934 and 1938: Giovanni Ferrari was one, inside-forward partner Meazza was the other. Meazza was considered the most complete inside-forward of his generation, able both to score goals and create them. Born in Milan, Meazza made his debut with Inter at 17 and scored a then league record 33 goals in 1928–29. He spent a decade with Inter before switching to Milan in 1938, playing wartime football with Juventus and Varese and retiring in 1947 after two seasons with Atalanta. Meazza marked his international debut by scoring twice in a 4–2 win over Switzerland in Rome in 1930 and, later the same year, scored a hat-trick in a 5–0 defeat

MEAZZA *Double World Cup-winner*

of Hungary. In all, he scored 33 goals in 53 internationals.

Joe Mercer

Born: August 9, 1914, England.
Clubs: Everton, Arsenal.

"Your legs wouldn't last a postman his morning round" was Dixie Dean's description of Mercer's spindle shanks. But Joe played for a quarter of a century on his odd-shaped pins before breaking one of them and going into management. He won a league title with Everton and two with Arsenal after they had gambled on his durability when he was 32 and had two dodgy knees. He also won a cup final with the Gunners in 1950 and lost one two years later, when he captained a ten-man team (Arsenal had a player carried off injured and no substitutes were allowed at the time) to a narrow defeat. Mercer repeated his league and cup success as manager of Manchester City, and had a brief spell as England caretaker, manager between Alf Ramsey and Don Revie.

Billy Meredith

Born: July 30, 1874, Wales.
Clubs: Manchester City, Manchester United, Manchester City (Eng).

Meredith won his first medal, for a dribbling contest, at the age of ten, and played his last senior game – a losing FA Cup semi-final – when nearly 50. He was a rugged individual, originally a miner, and a strong union man, often involved in off-field rows with officialdom. On the field he was rarely in trouble, plying his trade down the right wing with enviable skill and consistency. He won 48 caps (scoring 11 goals) spread over 25 years, with five lost to the First World War, and played around 1,000 first-team matches, in spite of missing a complete season after being involved in a match-fixing scandal.

MATTHÄUS *Proud World Cup-winning skipper of West Germany in Italy in 1990*

MICHEL *Grounds Northern Ireland's Kingsley Black with his skill*

Michel (full name: José Miguel Gonzalez Maria del Campo)

Born: March 23, 1963, Spain.
Clubs: Castilla, Real Madrid (Sp), Celaya (Mex).

Michel was one of European football's classic midfield operators throughout the 1980s and early 1990s. He made his debut with Castilla, the nursery team of Real Madrid, and was promoted to the senior outfit in 1984. A year later he starred in the UEFA Cup Final defeat of Videoton, scoring Madrid's first goal and making the other two in their 3–0 win in the first leg in Hungary. Michel made his Spain debut in 1985. He was unlucky to be denied a goal at the 1986 World Cup finals when his shot was cleared from behind the line against Brazil, but in 1990 in Italy he claimed a hat-trick against South Korea.

Roger Milla

Born: May 20, 1952, Cameroon.
Clubs: Leopard Douala, Tonnerre Yaounde (Cam), Valenciennes, Monaco, Bastia, Saint-Etienne, Montpellier (Fr).

Centre-forward Milla – real name Miller – delighted crowds at the 1990 World Cup with his celebratory dances around the corner flags. His goals, especially the winner against Colombia, made him the first player to become African Footballer of the Year for a second time. Milla played most of his club football in France, winning the cup there in

1980 with Monaco and in 1981 with Bastia. He was first voted African Footballer of the Year in 1976. He became, at the age of 42, the oldest player ever to appear in the World Cup finals at USA '94.

Milos Milutinovic

Born: February 5, 1933, Yugoslavia.
Clubs: FK Bor, Partizan, OFK Belgrade (Yug), Bayern Munich (Ger), Racing Paris, Stade Français (Fr).

Milutinovic, a powerful, aggressive centre-forward, was head of a famous

dynasty of footballers which has included Bora Milutinovic, coach to the United States' 1994 World Cup side. Milos began with FK Bor, made his debut for Yugoslavia in 1951 and, the same year, transferred to Belgrade with army club Partizan. He scored 183 goals in 192 games before moving controversially to neighbours OFK, then to Germany with Bayern Munich and finally settling in France. Milutinovic proved a huge success with Racing Paris before injury forced his retirement in 1965. He scored 16 goals in 33 internationals between 1953 and 1958.

Severino Minelli

Born: September 6, 1909, Switzerland.
Clubs: Kussnacht, Servette, Grasshoppers.

Minelli was a steady, reliable right-back with great positional sense who played a then record 79 times for Switzerland during the inter-war years. In 1930 he made his national team debut while simultaneously winning his first league championship medal with Servette of Geneva. In the next 13 years he won another five league medals as well as eight cup finals with Grasshoppers of Zurich. Minelli was a key figure in the " *errou*" or "bolt" defence intro-

duced by fellow-countryman Karl Rappan, and played to great effect for Switzerland in the World Cups of both 1934 and 1938. One of his finest games was Switzerland's 2–1 defeat of England in Zurich in May 1938.

Luisito Monti

Born: January 15, 1901, Argentina.
Clubs: Boca Juniors (Arg), Juventus (It).

Monti was an old-style attacking centre-half in the late 1920s and early 1930s. He was notable for a rugged, ruthless style but was also one of the great achievers of the inter-war years. Monti won an Olympic Games silver medal in 1928 when Argentina lost to Uruguay in Amsterdam and was again on the losing side against the same opponents at the first World Cup Final two years later. In 1931 Juventus brought Monti to Italy. At first he looked slow and vastly over-weight, but a month's lone training brought him back to fitness and, little more than a year later, he made his debut for Italy in a 4–2 win over Hungary in Milan. Monti was not only a key figure in the Juventus side which won four successive league titles in the 1930s but he also played for Italy when they first won the World Cup, defeating Czechoslovakia in Rome in 1934.

MILLA *Runs away from Colombian goalkeeper Higuita to score the winner in the 1990 World Cup second round*

MOORE *Leadership by example*

Bobby Moore

Born: April 17, 1941, England.
Clubs: West Ham United, Fulham (Eng), San Antonio Thunder, Seattle Sounders (US).

Bobby Moore was the inspirational, ice-cool captain of England's victorious 1966 World Cup side. Yet an FA Cup, one European Cup-winners' Cup, the 1966 World Cup and 108 England caps (100 of them under Sir Alf Ramsey) represent only part of his value to West Ham and England. Even at 34 he went back to Wembley, for Fulham against his old club, but by then fate was no longer smiling on him. He is likely to remain the only English captain to receive the World Cup trophy. Cruelly he developed cancer, from which he died in 1993, but which he defied with the utmost bravery to the end.

Juan Manuel Moreno

Born: August 3, 1916, Argentina.
Clubs: River Plate (Arg), España (Mex), River Plate (Arg), Universidad Catolia (Chile), Boca Juniors (Arg), Defensor (Uru), FC Oeste (Arg), Medellin (Col).

Many Argentines consider Moreno to have been the greatest footballer of all time. An inside-right for most of his career, Moreno began with River Plate's youth teams and was a league championship winner in 1936. He won four league titles with River and was a member of the legendary forward line of the late 1940s, together with Muñoz, Pedernera, Labruna and Loustau. Moreno played for España in Mexico between 1944 and 1946, returned to River for two more years, then wandered off again to Chile, Uruguay and Colombia. He scored an impressive 20 goals in 33 internationals.

Stan Mortensen

Born: May 26, 1921, England.
Clubs: Blackpool, Hull, Southport.

As fast over ten yards as any English forward, with finishing skill to round off the openings his pace created, Mortensen scored four times in a 10–0 win over Portugal (away!) in his first international, and his goal in his last England game was his 23rd in 25 appearances. That was against the 1953 Hungarians, a few months after he had become the first man to score a hat-trick in a Wembley Cup Final: his third, after two defeats. Morty loved the FA Cup, scoring in each of Blackpool's first 12 post-war rounds in the tournament and finishing with 28 Cup goals as well as 225 in the league.

Alan Morton

Born: April 24, 1893, Scotland.
Clubs: Queen's Park, Rangers.

"The Wee Blue Devil" was a left-winger with elusive dribbling skill and a waspish shot who had a 20-year career and gained nine championship medals and three for the Scottish Cup. He was a mining engineer who spent several seasons with the amateurs at Queen's Park, before becoming the first signing for new Rangers manager, William Struth, who remained in charge for 34 years. Morton played well over 500 games for Rangers and is reputed never to have appeared in the reserves. He was always very much the gentleman, often appearing for matches in a bowler hat and carrying an umbrella.

Coen Moulijn

Born: February 15, 1937, Holland.
Clubs: Xerxes, Feyenoord.

Moulijn was perhaps Holland's first post-war superstar. A brilliant outside-left, he played 38 times for Holland between his debut in a 1–0 defeat by Belgium in Antwerp in 1956 and his last game, a 1–1 World Cup draw against Bulgaria, in October 1969. That may have been Moulijn's last international, but his final and greatest achievement came the following May when Feyenoord beat Celtic in the European Cup Final in 1970. Moulijn helped Feyenoord go on to beat Estudiantes de La Plata in the World Club Cup and retired in 1972 with five league championships to his name. At the insistence of the Dutch federation, Feyenoord had inserted a clause in Moulijn's contract that he should never be sold abroad.

Gerd Müller

Born: November 3, 1945, Germany.
Clubs: TSV Nordlingen, Bayern Munich, Fort Lauderdale (US).

Coach Tschik Cajkovski was not impressed when Bayern bought a stocky new centre-forward in 1964. "I can't put that little elephant in among my string of thoroughbreds," said Cajkovski. But once he had done so, Bayern never looked back. Müller not only had the opportunist's eye for goal, but he was a powerful header of the ball. His goals shot Bayern out of the regional league to victory in the European Cup-winners' Cup in little more than three years. He went on to score well over 600 goals, including a record 365 in the Bundesliga and an astonishing 68 in 62 internationals for West Germany. Müller once scored four goals in a victory over Switzerland, but his most famous goal was his last, the one with which the Germans beat Holland in the 1974 World Cup Final. Müller won the European Cup three times and was also a European Championship winner in 1972.

MÜLLER *Volleys the dramatic winner against England in 1970 in Leon*

N

José Nasazzi

Born: May 24, 1901, Uruguay.
Clubs: Lito, Roland Moor, Nacional, Bella Vista.

Nasazzi was one of the great captains in football history. He led Uruguay to their victories in the 1924 and 1928 Olympic Games and then to the 1930 World Cup. Nasazzi was nicknamed "The Marshall" for his organizational ability at the heart of defence from right-back, though he also played occasionally at centre-half and at inside-forward. Nasazzi was also a South American champion on four occasions in his 15-year, 64-game international career and was a key member of the Nacional team which so dominated the league championship in 1934 that it became nicknamed "The Machine".

Zdenek Nehoda

Born: May 9, 1952, Czechoslovakia.
Clubs: TJ Hulin, TJ Gottwaldov, Dukla Prague (Cz), SV Darmstadt (W Ger), Standard Liège (Bel), FC Grenoble (Swz).

Nehoda, a skilled, mobile general of a centre-forward was the first – and last – Czechoslovak player to go anywhere close to a century of caps. He scored 31 goals in 90 internationals, of which the highlight was the European Championship victory over West Germany in Belgrade in 1976. Nehoda was three times a champion of Czechoslovakia with the army club, Dukla Prague, twice a domestic cup-winner and was twice voted his country's Footballer of the Year, in 1978 and 1979. Nehoda's international reputation also earned him selection for a Europe XI against Italy in 1981.

Johan Neeskens

Born: September 15, 1951, Holland.
Clubs: Haarlem, Ajax (Hol), Barcelona (Sp), New York Cosmos (US).

Neeskens was an aggressive, sharp-tackling midfielder who fitted perfectly into the "total football" pattern set by Ajax and Holland in the early

NEESKENS *Goes past Argentina's Ardiles in the 1978 World Cup Final*

1970s. Neeskens provided the steel which supported the more technical gifts of team-mates Cruyff, Keizer and Van Hanegem. He scored 17 goals in 49 internationals and earned a place in history by converting the first-ever World Cup Final penalty against West Germany in Munich in 1974. With Ajax, Neeskens won hat-tricks of victories in the European Cup, the Dutch league and the Dutch cup. In 1974 he moved to Barcelona, with whom he won the Spanish cup in 1978 and the European Cup-winners' Cup in 1979. After a spell in the North American Soccer League he attempted a comeback, in vain, in Switzerland.

Oldrich Nejedly

Born: December 13, 1909, Czechoslovakia.
Clubs: Zebrak, Rakovnik, Sparta Prague.

Nejedly was inside-left for the Sparta club which dominated the Mitropa Cup for much of the 1930s and for the Czechoslovak national team which reached the 1934 World Cup Final. His skills were described as "pure as Bohemian crystal", and his partnership with outside-left Antonin Puc was one of the best of its kind in Europe in the inter-war years. Nejedly scored twice in the 3–1 defeat of Germany in the semi-finals but could make no headway against Italy in the Final. Nevertheless he was the World Cup's top scorer with five goals. A broken leg against Brazil in 1938 ended Nejedly's dream of revenge over Italy. He scored 28 goals in 44 internationals and was chosen for Central Europe against Western Europe in 1937.

Igor Netto

Born: September 4, 1930, Soviet Union.
Club: Moscow Spartak.

Netto was a left-half in the 1950s who captained the Soviet Union from 1954 to 1963, leading by example and winning what was then a record 57 caps with four goals. Netto led the Soviets to victory in the 1956 Olympic Games in Melbourne, but injury kept him out of all but one match at the 1958 World Cup finals. In 1962 he played in all four games when the Soviets reached the quarter-finals in Chile. Altogether he scored 37 goals in 367 league games for Spartak, with whom he stayed throughout his playing career, winning five Soviet championships.

Gunter Netzer

Born: September 14, 1944, West Germany.
Clubs: Borussia Mönchengladbach (Ger), Real Madrid (Sp), Grasshoppers (Swz).

In the late 1960s and 1970s, West Germany had a surfeit of outstanding midfield generals. Netzer was at his best in the West German side which won the 1972 European Championship, forging a marvellously refined partnership with sweeper Beckenbauer behind him. He lost his place in the national team to Wolfgang Overath after transferring to Spain with Real Madrid, and never regained it on a permanent basis, although he made an occasional appearance. He was twice West German champion with Borussia, twice Spanish champion with Real Madrid, and a cup-winner once in each country. Netzer was also once West German Footballer of the Year before, as manager, masterminding Hamburg's 1989 German championship.

Gunnar Nordahl

Born: October 19, 1921, Sweden.
Clubs: Degerfors, Norrköping (Swe), Milan, Roma (It).

Nordahl was the most famous of five first division brothers. He was born in Hornefors in northern Sweden and scored 77 goals in 58 games with local Degerfors. Next came 93 goals in 92 games which brought Norrköping four championships in a row. A fireman by training, Nordahl gave that up in 1948 when, after Sweden's Olympic Games victory in London, he was lured away to Milan. There Nordahl formed the central spearhead of the "Grenoli" trio (with Gunnar Gren and Nils Liedholm). Five times he was the Italian league's

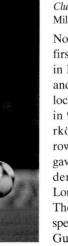

NEHODA *Provokes unorthodox attention from Italian defender Collovati*

leading scorer, and by the time he retired in 1957 he had totalled 225 goals in 257 Italian league matches.

Bjorn Nordqvist

Born: October 6, 1942, Sweden.
Clubs: IFK Hallsberg, Norrköping (Swe), PSV Eindhoven (Hol), IFK Gothenburg (Swe), Minnesota Kicks (US), Orgryte (Swe).

For some time in the mid-1980s, Nordqvist was the world's longest serving international with 115 caps. He played in three World Cups, in 1970, 1974 and 1978, and, with Norrköping, was twice champion of Sweden and once a cup-winner. Having taken the plunge to turn full-time professional in 1974, Nordqvist immediately won the Dutch league championship with PSV Eindhoven and later tried his luck briefly with Minnesota in the North American Soccer League. Surprisingly, considering his century of caps, Nordqvist had to wait a year between his first cap in 1963 and the second.

Ernst Ocwirk

Born: March 7, 1926, Austria.
Clubs: FK Austria (Austria), Sampdoria (It).

Ocwirk, nicknamed "Clockwork" by the British for his consistent creativity in midfield, was the last of the old-fashioned attacking centre-halves – a role for which he was ideally suited, with both technical and physical strengths. Ocwirk began with FK Austria of Vienna, made his debut for his country in 1947 and appeared at the 1948 Olympic Games in London. Three years later he was back at Wembley, captaining an Austrian side which thoroughly deserved a 2–2 draw against England. In 1953 the stopper centre-back had taken over throughout Europe and Ocwirk was selected at wing-half in the Rest of the World team which drew 4–4 with England in a match played to celebrate the 90th anniversary of the Football Associ-

ation. In 1956, at the advanced age of 30, he undertook the Italian adventure with Sampdoria with whom he spent five seasons before returning for one last campaign with FK Austria. Later he coached FKA to league titles in 1969 and 1970.

Raimundo Orsi

Born: December 2, 1901, Argentina.
Clubs: Independiente (Arg), Juventus (It).

Vittorio Pozzo, Italy's manager in the 1920s and 1930s, had no hesitation in picking imported South Americans such as Orsi for his team. "If they can die for Italy," said Pozzo, "they can play football for Italy." Orsi played outside-left for Argentina in the 1928 Olympic Final against Uruguay before switching, amid controversy, to Juventus. He spent six months kicking his heels before finally making his Juventus debut. Within four months he was playing for Italy and scoring twice on his debut in a 6–1 win over Portugal in November 1929. Orsi was one of the exceptional players who won five successive league titles with Juventus in the early 1930s. For good measure, he scored Italy's all-important equalizer on the way to an extra-time victory over Czechoslovakia in the 1934 World Cup Final.

Wolfgang Overath

Born: September 29, 1943, Germany.
Club: Köln.

Overath, an old-style inside-left and then a left-footed midfield general, was one of the most admired members of the West German

sides which featured in starring roles at the World Cups of 1966, 1970 and 1974. Overath played all his senior club career for Köln and scored 17 goals in 81 internationals between 1963 and 1974. He was a World Cup runner-up in 1966, scored the goal against Uruguay which earned West Germany third place in 1970, and won a personal duel to oust Gunter Netzer as midfield commander for the World Cup victory of 1974. Overath then retired from the national team, though he was selected for the World XI which played Brazil in Rio de Janeiro in 1968. The latter years of Overath's Köln career were sadly marred by disagreements with opinionated coach Hennes Weisweiler.

Antonin Panenka

Born: December 2, 1948, Czechoslovakia.
Clubs: Bohemians Prague (Cz), Rapid Vienna (Austria).

Panenka was a throw-back in style, a languid, skilled, dreamer of a midfield general who might have appeared more at home in the central European game of the 1930s than in the increasing hurly-burly of international football in the 1970s. He spent most of his career in the Czech shadows with Bohemians, from which the national manager, Vaclav Jezek, rescued him for the 1976 European Championship finals. Panenka was influential in midfield and struck the decisive blow in the Final when his penalty shot, stroked so deliberately past Sepp Maier, brought Czechoslovakia their shoot-out triumph. Later he spent several successful years in Austria with Rapid Vienna. Panenka's 65 caps including helping Czechoslovakia finish third, this time after a penalty shoot-out against Italy, in the 1980 European Championship.

Jean-Pierre Papin

Born: November 5, 1963, France. *Clubs:* Valenciennes, Club Brugge (Bel), Marseille, Milan (It), Bayern Munich (Ger), Bordeaux.

Papin was one of the outstanding strikers of the game. He began his career with

PAPIN *French goalscoring ace*

Valenciennes and played in Belgium with Brugge before returning to France to become captain and the attacking inspiration of Marseille. Papin was top scorer in the French league for four successive seasons before joining Milan in the summer of 1992. A year later he found himself appearing as a substitute for Milan against Marseille in the Final of the European Cup, which the French club won 1–0. That was Papin's second European Cup Final defeat, for he had been on the losing side in a penalty shoot-out when Red Star Belgrade beat Marseille in Bari in 1991. His consolation was in being voted European Footballer of the Year later that year. Injury upset his career after a 1994 transfer to Bayern Munich.

Daniel Passarella

Born: May 25, 1953, Argentina.
Clubs: Sarmiento, River Plate (Arg), Fiorentina, Internazionale (It).

Passarella belongs to that select band of heroes who can claim to have received the World Cup as winning captain. His moment of triumph came in the River Plate stadium – his own home club ground – in 1978. Passarella thoroughly deserved the honour of holding the cup aloft, since he had guided, controlled and commanded Argentina from central defence. Time and again Passarella powered up into midfield to serve Ardiles and Kempes, while his vicious free-kicks and strength in the air at

PASSARELLA *Argentina's inspiration*

corners added to the pressure on opposing defences. He ended his career as a goal-grabbing defender with Fiorentina and Inter in Italy, before returning to River Plate as coach. He later guided Argentina to the quarter-finals of France '98 after taking over the national side.

Adolfo Pedernera

Born: 1918, Argentina.
Clubs: River Plate, Atlanta, Huracan (Arg), Millonarios (Col).

Pedernera was a great centre-forward turned rebel. He made his debut for River Plate in 1936 and won five league championships in 11 years. In the late 1940s Pedernera led the legendary "Maquina", or "Machine", attack with Munoz, Moreno, Labruna and Loustau. River sold him, perhaps prematurely, to Atlanta and he joined Huracan just before the Argentine footballers' strike of 1948. Millonarios of Bogota, from the pirate Colombian league, signed up Pedernera not merely as a player but as "liaison officer" to lure away other top Argentines, including his centre-forward successor at River Plate, Alfredo Di Stefano. Later Pedernera returned to Argentina as coach of Gimnasia y Esgrima, Boca Juniors, Huracan and Independiente. He played 21 times for Argentina.

Pele

see Legends (pages 118–19)

Roger Piantoni

Born: December 26, 1931, France.
Clubs: Nancy, Reims.

Piantoni was one of the last great European inside-forwards, before the "old" positions were wiped out by the advent of the 4–2–4 and 4–3–3 formations, with their new roles and terminology. Piantoni, who was born at Etain, in the Meuse, built his reputation with Nancy and transferred to Reims in 1957. He played in the World Cup finals of 1958 – when France finished third – and in the European Cup Final of 1959 (which Reims lost to Real Madrid). Piantoni played 38 times for France, having made a scoring debut in a 1–1 draw against the Irish Republic in Dublin in 1952. He also scored in his last international, nine years later, against

Finland. Piantoni's left-wing partnership, for Reims and France, with outside-left Jean Vincent was famed throughout the continent.

Silvio Piola

Born: September 29, 1913, Italy.
Clubs: Pro Vercelli, Lazio, Torino, Juventus, Novara.

Piola was a tall, strong, athletic, aggressive centre-forward who scored 30 goals in 24 internationals between his debut against Austria in 1935 – when Piola scored both Italy's goals in a 2–0 win – and his last game, a 1–1 draw against England in 1952. Piola, a World Cup-winner in 1938 when he scored twice in the 4–2 Final defeat of Hungary, would have collected even more goals and won more caps

PIRRI *From striker to skipper to club doctor with Real Madrid*

had it not been for the war years. As it was he played on until he was 43 in a prolific career which included his fair share of controversy – such as the goal he later admitted he punched against England, nearly 50 years before Maradona's Hand of God repetition. Piola scored six goals in Pro Vercelli's 7–2 win over Fiorentina in 1933–34.

Pirri (full name: Jose Martinez Sanchez)

Born: March 11, 1945, Spain.
Club: Real Madrid.

Pirri epitomized the spirit of Spanish football during his 15 extraordinary years with Real Madrid between 1964 and 1979. He began as a goal-grabbing inside-forward, then shifted back successively to midfielder and central defender in a glittering career which brought honours flooding in – eight Spanish championships, three Spanish cups and the European Cup in 1966. Pirri played 44 times for Spain between 1966 and 1978 and was twice selected for Europe XIs, first against Benfica in 1970, then against South America in 1973. After retiring, Pirri completed his studies to qualify as a doctor and was appointed to the Real Madrid medical staff.

Frantisek Planicka

Born: June 2, 1904, Czechoslovakia.
Clubs: Slovan Prague, Bubenec, Slavia Prague.

Planicka was Central Europe's finest goalkeeper of the 1930s, a great personality as well as an outstanding and courageous player in the World Cups of both 1934 – when Czechoslovakia lost the Final 2–1 to Italy – and 1938. In the latter competition, long before the days of substitutes, Planicka played the last half of the quarter-final draw against Brazil despite the pain of a broken arm. Planicka won more honours than almost anyone in the history of the Czechoslovak game. He was a domestic league champion nine times with the great Slavia club, and won the cup six times and the Mitropa Cup – forerunner of today's European club competitions – in 1938. Planicka played 74 times for his country between 1925 and 1938.

Michel Platini

Born: June 21, 1955, France.
Clubs: Nancy-Lorraine, Saint-Etienne (Fr), Juventus (It).

Platini was the greatest achiever in world football in the early 1980s. He first appeared on the international stage at the 1976 Olympic Games in Montreal, and two years later, at his first World Cup in Argentina, gave an indication of the great things to come. In 1982 Platini inspired France to fourth place at the World Cup when he was man of the match in the dramatic semi-final defeat by West Germany in Seville. After the finals Platini was sold to Juventus, with whom he was three times the Italian league's top scorer. He also converted the penalty kick which brought "Juve" their long-awaited European Cup victory in 1985 (albeit overshadowed by the Heysel tragedy). After retiring, Platini concentrated on commercial interests and TV work until he was persuaded to become national manager and took France to the finals of the 1992 European Championship. France disappointed, and Platini left the job to become joint head of the team set up by the French federation to organize the 1998 World Cup.

Ernst Pol

Born: November 3, 1932, Poland.
Clubs: Legia Warsaw, Gornik Zabrze.

Pol was the first great Polish footballer of the post-war era. He played centre- or inside-forward and scored 40 goals in 49 internationals – then a Polish record – between 1950 and 1966. He was a complete player, with ball-control, good passing and tactical ability and an accurate shot. Pol won the Polish championship twice with the army club Legia, then five times with Gornik, the Silesian miners' club. He once scored five goals in an international against Tunisia in 1960, and had the consolation of scoring a marvellous individual strike for Gornik in their 8–1 thrashing by Tottenham in the European Cup in 1961. It was Pol's ill fortune that eastern European players were not allowed transfers to the professional west. His total of 186 Polish league goals stood as a record for 20 years.

Ferenc Puskas

see Legends (pages 120-1)

Helmut Rahn

Born: August 16, 1929, West Germany.
Clubs: Altenessen, Olde 09, Sportfreunde Katernberg, Rot-Weiss Essen, Köln (W Ger), Enschede (Hol), Meiderich SV Duisburg (W Ger).

Rahn was anything but a typical outside-right, being heavily built and tall, but his power carried him through many a defence and his right-foot shot was ferocious. Hungary discovered this to their cost in the 1954 World Cup Final, when Rahn struck the equalizer at 2–2 and then the winner with only eight minutes remaining. Yet Rahn, enfant terrible of the German game, might not have even been in Europe: shortly before the finals he had been on a South American tour with Rot-Weiss and was in negotiations with Nacional of Uruguay when national coach Sepp Herberger sent a telegram to summon him home. In 1958 Rahn was far from either his best form or his best playing weight, and could not repeat his World Cup feats. Altogether he scored 21 goals in 40 internationals.

Antonio Ubaldo Rattin

Born: May 16, 1937, Argentina.
Club: Boca Juniors.

Rattin was a midfield pillar with club and country in the 1950s and 1960s. He made his league debut in 1956 and played 14 inspiring seasons with Boca Juniors, setting a club record of 357 league appearances and winning five championships. Rattin was also a key figure in the Boca side – along with Silvio Marzolini and Angel Rojas – which lost narrowly to Pele's Santos in the final of the South American club cup in 1963. Born in the Tigre delta outside Buenos Aires, Rattin played 37 times for Argentina. His most unfortunate game is, however, the one for which he is best remembered. This was the 1966 World Cup quarter-final against England at Wembley, when Rattin's refusal to accept expulsion by German referee Kreitlein very nearly provoked a walk-off by the entire Argentine team. Rattin always insisted he was an innocent victim of dark circumstances.

Thomas Ravelli

Born: August 13, 1959, Sweden.
Clubs: Oster Vaxjo, IFK Gothenburg, Tampa Bay (US).

Ravelli and twin brother Andreas, a midfielder, are both internationals, but Thomas has been by far the most successful – with a world record number of 138 caps. Ravelli's parents emigrated to Sweden from Austria, and Thomas made his reputation with Oster Vaxjo. In 1989 he joined IFK Gothenburg, Sweden's leading club, as successor to Tottenham Hotspur-bound Erik Thorstvedt. Early in his career, Ravelli's temperament was considered suspect: for example, he was sent off for dissent during a 2–0 defeat in Mexico in November 1983. Ravelli learned his lesson to inspire Sweden to reach the semifinals of both the European Championship in 1992 and, two years later, the World Cup. In June 1995 he overtook Peter Shilton's record of 125 international caps, although he has failed to achieve his ambition of playing his club football outside Sweden.

MICHEL PLATINI *More successful as France's skipper than manager*

Frank Rijkaard

Born: September 30, 1962, Holland.
Clubs: Ajax (Hol), Sporting (Port), Zaragoza (Sp), Milan (It), Ajax (Hol).

Rijkaard has been one of the most universally-admired and versatile players over the past decade at both club and international level. He turned professional under Johan Cruyff at Ajax in 1979 and made his Holland debut at 19 despite Ajax protests that he was "too young". In 1987 Rijkaard fell out with Cruyff and had brief spells in Portugal and Spain before committing the key years of his career to Milan with whom he won the World Club Cup and the European Cup twice apiece. Rijkaard played in midfield for Milan, but usually in central defence for Holland, with whom he won the 1988 European Championship. Following Milan's defeat by Marseille in the 1993 European Cup Final he returned to Ajax, and was a vital member of their victorious 1995 European Cup and Dutch title-winning teams, after which he retired.

Luigi "Gigi" Riva

Born: November 7, 1944, Italy.
Club: Cagliari.

Riva is remembered as one of the finest strikers in Italian football history. Orphaned in early childhood, he made a teenage reputation with Third Division Legnano as a left-winger and was

RAVELLI *World record international*

signed by Second Division Sardinian club Cagliari in 1963. Riva's formidable left foot and nose for goal sent Cagliari rocketing out of the shadows to league championship success in 1970. Riva was top league marksman three times, including the 1969–70 season when he scored 21 goals in 28 games. His 35 goals in 42 internationals meant Riva bore much of the responsibility for Italy's World Cup challenge in 1970. He scored three times in the quarter- and semi-final defeats of Mexico and West Germany before Italy's defeat in the Final. Complications stemming from two broken legs ultimately enforced a premature retirement.

Roberto Rivelino

Born: January 1, 1946, Brazil.
Clubs: Corinthians, Fluminense.

Rivelino was originally the deep-lying left-winger who filled the Zagalo role in Brazil's 1970 World Cup-winning side. He was not particularly quick, but was possessed of a superb technique which made him a perpetual danger with his banana-bending of free-kicks and corners. Riv-

RIJKAARD *Great all-rounder*

BRYAN ROBSON *Manchester United and England's oft-injured captain*

elino later moved into centre midfield and was influential in the third-place finish of 1978. Rivelino is credited unofficially with the fastest goal in football history: scored in three seconds with a shot from the starting pass after he noticed the opposing goalkeeper still concentrating on his pre-match prayers.

Gianni Rivera

Born: August 18, 1943, Italy.
Clubs: Alessandria, Milan.

The "Bambino d'Oro", the Golden Boy: that was Rivera in the early 1960s. As a creative inside-forward, he had the lot: skill, pace and a deft shot, plus the rare natural gift of grace. Rivera in full flight was football poetry in motion. Milan paid Alessandria £65,000 for a half-share in the 15-year-old Rivera and signed him "for real" in 1960. In 16 years with the "Rossoneri" he was twice a winner of the World Club Cup, the European Cup and the Italian league, as well as three times an Italian cup-winner and once European Footballer of the Year, in 1969. Rivera became a controversial figure, however, as successive national managers struggled to build teams around him. Thus he played only the last six minutes of the 1970 World Cup Final – although his Italy career produced 14 goals in 60 games. On retiring Rivera turned to politics and became a member of the Italian parliament.

Bryan Robson

Born: January 11, 1957, England.

Clubs: West Bromwich, Manchester United, Middlesbrough.

A considerable part of English football in the 1980s was played to the accompaniment of breaking bones, many of them Bryan Robson's. Despite his season ticket to the surgery he won an impressive list of honours, with 90 caps (often as captain), three FA Cup medals, European Cup-winners' Cup in 1991, and inaugural Premier League championship in 1992–93. Robson was an inspiring, driving force in midfield and a believer in the value of an early strike: three of his England goals were in the first minute. He broke a leg twice as a teenager with West Bromwich, and then broke the transfer fee record when Manchester United bought him for £1.5 million. He moved into management in 1994, immediately leading Middlesbrough into the Premier League.

Pedro Rocha

Born: December 3, 1942, Uruguay.
Clubs: Penarol (Uru), São Paulo (Br).

Rocha was far removed from the typical image of angry, temperamental Uruguayans. A statuesque inside-left of great skill to match his height, he was surprisingly quick and soon became a local hero after joining mighty Penarol of Montevideo at 17. Seven times in the next nine seasons Rocha was a champion of Uruguay, and he inspired Penarol to victory both home and away over Real Madrid in the 1966 World Club Cup final. He captained Uruguay into the 1970 World Cup finals but was injured in the first match. Fit again, he moved to Brazil and led São Paulo to victory in the Paulista state championship in his debut season. Rocha won 62 caps for Uruguay.

Romario da Souza Faria

Born: 29 January, 1966, Brazil.
Clubs: Vasco da Gama (Br), PSV Eindhoven (Hol), Barcelona (Sp), Flamengo (Bra), Valencia (Sp), Flamengo (Bra).

Romario has been arguably the finest attacker in the world game in the 1990s. Discovered by Vasco da Gama, he was still a teenager when he began to establish a reputation for controversy after being banished from Brazil's World Youth Cup squad for flouting a hotel curfew. After starring at the 1988 Seoul Olympics, he transferred to PSV Eindhoven. There he clashed with coaches and team-mates, yet still totalled 98 league goals in five seasons to earn a £3 million sale to Barcelona in the summer of 1993. Simultaneously, he was recalled for USA'94 by Brazil after almost a year in the wilderness. Romario scored five crucial goals and followed Brazil's World Cup triumph by returning home to Flamengo.

Ronaldo (full name: Ronaldo Luiz Nazario da Lima)

Born: September 22, 1976, Brazil.
Clubs: Sao Cristovao, Cruzeiro (Br), PSV (Hol), Barcelona (Sp), Inter (Ita).

Ronaldo has been the most talked about footballer in Europe in the 1990s – a status underlined by his award as the 1996 and 1997 FIFA Player of the Year. He was compared favourably with Pele at his age by the likes of past Brazilian heroes as Zico and Tostao. Ronaldo grew up in a working class district of Rio. He failed a trial with Flamengo but was signed by minor club Sao Cristovao where his potential was discovered by 1970 World Cup star Jairzinho – who then sold Ronaldo on to Cruzeiro of Belo Horizonte. In his first year he scored 54 goals in 54 games. Ronaldo then moved to PSV Eindhoven and joined Barcelona in 1996 for £12.9 million. He ended his first season in Spain as the league's top scorer with 34 goals. He was on the bench when Brazil won the 1994 World Cup, but scored four goals in France '98 as Brazil reached the final, losing to France. But he was also the centre of controversy after playing in the final despite

PAOLO ROSSI *Stranger than fiction*

being unfit, having suffered a convulsive fit before the game.

Paolo Rossi

Born: September 23, 1956, Italy.
Clubs: Prato, Juventus, Como, Lanerossi Vicenza, Perugia, Juventus, Milan.

Paolo Rossi's story is more fantastic than fiction. As a teenager Juventus gave him away because of knee trouble. Later, when they tried to buy him back, they were outbid by provincial Perugia, who paid a world record £3.5 million. Rossi, a star already at the 1978 World Cup, was then banned for two years for alleged involvement in a betting-and-bribes scandal. Juventus finally got him back, but he was only three matches out of his ban when Italy took him to the 1982 World Cup finals, where he top-scored with six goals and collected a winner's medal from the Final victory over West Germany. Rossi was only 29 when he retired into legend.

Karl-Heinz Rummenigge

Born: September 25, 1955, West Germany.
Clubs: Lippstadt, Bayern Munich (W Ger), Internazionale (It), Servette (Swz).

Rummenigge was one of the great bargains of German football. Bayern Munich paid Lippstadt just £4,500 for their young, blond right-winger in 1974 and sold him to Italy a decade later for more than £2 million. In between Rummenigge had

RUMMENIGGE *Twice best in Europe*

won the World Club championship and the European Cup and had twice been hailed as European Footballer of the Year. The former bank clerk, who first impressed Internazionale officials with a World Cup hat-trick against Mexico in 1978, developed

into a central striker, as his career progressed. Injuries reduced his effectiveness in the early 1980s, and controversy lingered over whether national manager Jupp Derwall was right to play his injured captain from the start in the 1982 World Cup Final defeat by Italy.

Ian Rush

Born October 20, 1961, Wales.
Clubs: Chester, Liverpool (Eng), Juventus (It), Liverpool, Leeds, Newcastle

Rush was the goal-scorer supreme in modern British football, but he would have been a great player even if he had never hit a net. His off-the-ball running and excellent passing were bonuses to go with his acutely developed finishing ability. Rush was only 18 when Liverpool had to pay £300,000 to get him, but the fee was repaid many times over. In two spells at Anfield, interrupted by a none-too-happy Italian adventure, he broke scoring records for club, country and FA Cup Finals (five goals in three winning appearances), with medals for five league titles and four League Cups as well. Released on a free transfer in 1996, he was snapped up by Leeds and later Newcastle Utd.

IAN RUSH *One of the great bargains, at £300,000 from Chester*

Hugo Sanchez

Born: June 11, 1958, Mexico.
Clubs: UNAM (Mex), Atletico Madrid, Real Madrid (Sp), America (Mex), Rayo Vallecano (Sp).

Hugo Sanchez was top league goalscorer in Spain five seasons in a row in the late 1980s and early 1990s. His 230-plus goals in Spain left him second overall behind Bilbao's Telmo Zarra and underlined his claim to be considered one of the great strikers of the modern game. Each one of Sanchez's goals was followed by a celebratory somersault, taught him originally by a sister who was a gymnast in Mexico's team for the 1976 Olympics in Montreal – at which Hugo made his football debut on the international stage. Despite a World Cup finals debut as far back as 1978, Sanchez totalled only around 50 games for Mexico – his many absences caused either by club commitments in Spain or by disputes with Mexican soccer bureaucracy.

Leonel Sanchez

Born: April 25, 1936, Chile.
Club: Universidad de Chile.

Leonel Sanchez was the outstanding left-winger in South America in the late 1950s and early 1960s – perhaps not as fast as Pepe of Brazil or as intelligent a player as Zagalo of Brazil, but far more forceful when it came to making his presence felt in the penalty box. Sanchez was a star of the Chilean side which finished third as hosts in the 1962 World Cup, but he also featured in controversy: earlier in the tournament he somehow escaped punishment from the match referee for a punch which flattened Humberto Maschio in the so-called Battle of Santiago against Italy. Sanchez played 106 times for Chile, though only 62 of those appearances may be counted as full internationals. He was seven times national champion with "U", his only club.

José Emilio Santamaria

Born: July 31, 1929, Uruguay
Clubs: Nacional (Uru), Real Madrid (Sp).

Santamaria was a ruthless centre-back whose finest years were spent at Real Madrid in the 1950s and early 1960s, closing down the defensive gaps left by great attacking colleagues such as Di Stefano, Puskas and Gento. Santamaria was first called up at 20 by Uruguay but missed the 1950 World Cup finals because his club, Nacional, refused to let him accept the inside-forward spot allocated to him in the squad bound for Brazil. Four years later Santamaria was one of the stars of the 1954 World Cup, this time in his traditional place in the centre of defence. Madrid brought him to Europe in 1957 and, having played 35 times for Uruguay, he collected another 17 caps in the service of Spain, including the 1962 World Cup. He was a World Club championship and triple European Cup winner with Real Madrid and later managed hosts Spain at the 1982 World Cup finals.

Djalma Santos

Born: February 27, 1929, Brazil.
Clubs: Portuguesa, Palmeiras, Atletico Curitiba.

Djalma Santos is considered a cornerstone of the Brazil side which won the World Cup in 1958 and 1962 and lost it in 1966. Yet, in Sweden in 1958, he was brought in only for the

DJALMA SANTOS *A great survivor*

PETER SCHMEICHEL *In winning command of defence for Denmark*

GAETANO SCIREA *Skilled contrast to the rugged sweepers before him*

Final because manager Vicente Feola considered his acute football brain and positional sense would make him more effective against Swedish left-winger Skoglund than regular right-back Nilton Di Sordi. In due course he became the first Brazilian player to reach an official century of international appearances, though he was well past his best when – to his own surprise – he was recalled by Feola for the 1966 World Cup finals in England. He played for the World XI against England in 1963 in the match which celebrated the 100th anniversary of the FA.

Nilton Santos

Born: May 16, 1927, Brazil.
Club: Botafogo.

Nilton Santos was a left-back and, though no relation to Brazil partner Djalma Santos, equally outstanding. Nilton Santos played 83 times for his country between 1949 and 1963, having made his Brazil debut just a year after signing for his only club, Botafogo of Rio. He loved nothing more than powering forward in support of attack, a tactic which surprised the opposition and owed everything to the new free-dom afforded "wing backs" by the advent of 4–2–4. Santos was a World Cup-winner in 1958 and 1962 and was immensely respected by team-mates and officials. He led the player delegation which, in Sweden in 1958, crucially persuaded coach Vicente Feola to call up his Botafogo team-mate, the match-winning right-winger Garrincha.

Gyorgy Sarosi

Born: September 12, 1912, Hungary.
Club: Ferencvaros TC (Hun).

Sarosi, one of the world's greatest footballers between the wars, died in 1993 in his adopted home of Genoa, Italy, aged 81. Sarosi was born in Budapest, where he duly played both at centre-forward and centre-half for FTC (Ferencvaros), scoring 349 goals in 383 games. He won the Hungarian championship eight times, the cup once and the Mitropa Cup once. In internationals Sarosi scored 42 goals in 75 appearances, and captained Hungary to the 1938 World Cup Final. Doctor, lawyer and magistrate, he made his debut for Hungary in a 3–2 defeat by Italy in Turin in November, 1931. When the Communists took over in Hungary in 1947, Sarosi fled to Italy, where he coached Padova, Lucchese, Bari, Juventus (winners of the 1952 championship), Genoa, Roma, Bologna and Brescia. He also coached Lugano in Switzerland.

Hector Scarone

Born: June 21, 1898, Uruguay.
Clubs: Sportsman, Nacional (Uru), Barcelona(Sp), Ambrosiana-Internazionale, Palermo (It).

Scarone was Uruguay's inspiring inside-forward in their greatest era of the 1920s and early 1930s. He won the Olympic gold medals in Paris in 1924 and in Amsterdam in 1928 – in between playing in Spain for Barcelona – and was top scorer at both the 1926 and 1927 South American Championships. He then led Uruguay to victory at the inaugural World Cup finals on home soil in Montevideo in 1930. Inevitably, his talents drew more offers from Europe, but he insisted on waiting until after that World Cup before returning, this time to Italy with Ambrosiana-Inter. Later he went back to Spain in the early 1950s as coach to Real Madrid before making a playing comeback in Uruguay with Nacional and retiring finally at 55 – a South American and probably a world record.

Juan Alberto Schiaffino

Born: July 28, 1925, Uruguay.
Clubs: Penarol (Uru), Milan, Roma (It).

"Pepe" Schiaffino always wanted, as a boy, to play centre-forward, but youth coaches with Penarol of Montevideo, his first club, considered him too thin and fragile. They switched him to inside-forward and, at 20, he was playing for Uruguay at the South American Championship and top-scoring with 19 goals in Penarol's league-winning side. In World Cup terms, Schiaffino peaked in 1950 when he scored Uruguay's equalizer at 1–1 on the way to their shock victory over Brazil. After starring again at the finals in 1954, he was sold to Milan for a world record £72,000, and is regarded as one of the

DARTING IN *Two Uruguayans can't stop Uwe Seeler getting in a header*

ENZO SCIFO *A mixture of loyalties between football in Belgium, Italy and France*

greatest players ever to have graced *Calcio*. He wound down his career with Roma, after narrowly failing to lead Milan to victory over Real Madrid in the 1958 European Cup Final, when, despite Schiaffino's fine solo goal, they lost 3–2.

Peter Schmeichel

Born: November 18, 1963, Denmark.
Clubs: Hvidovre, Brondbyerenes (Den), Manchester United (Eng).

Schmeichel very nearly came to England in 1987, after Newcastle sent spies to watch him. Although he was then considered too inexperienced for the English First Division, Manchester United landed a bargain when they bought him for £800,000 in 1991. Later, he was one of the heroes in Denmark's astonishing triumph at the 1992 European Championship finals in Sweden. Schmeichel's saves at crucial moments against Holland in the semi-final and Germany in the Final helped secure him the accolade of the world's Best Goalkeeper. He won the English league and Cup "double" in 1994 and 1996 and the fabulous "treble" - adding European Cup glory in 1999.

Karl-Heinz Schnellinger

Born: March 31, 1939, West Germany.
Clubs: Duren, Köln (W Ger), Mantova, Roma, Milan (It).

Schnellinger, a left-back who later played in most other defensive positions, was to be found at the heart of the international action throughout the 1960s. He stood out not merely for his blond hair and bulky frame but for his power, pace and will to win. He made his World Cup finals debut at 19 in Sweden and was a key member of the West German sides which reached the quarter-finals (1962), the Final (1966) and third place (1970) over the next 12 years. His injury-time goal in the 1970 semi-final with Italy, which forced extra time, typified his fighting spirit. Roma took him to Italy but had to sell him to Milan to overcome a cash crisis. Their loss was Milan's gain as Schnellinger's steel lifted them to victory in the 1969 European Cup. This was the peak of a career which also earned success in the German and Italian championships and the Italian cup, three selections for World XIs and four for Europe Selects. He was West German Footballer of the Year in 1962.

Vincenzo "Enzo" Scifo

Born: February 19, 1966, Belgium.
Clubs: Anderlecht (Bel), Internazionale (It), Bordeaux, Auxerre (Fr), Torino (It), Monaco (Fr), Anderlecht (Bel).

Born in Belgium of Italian parents, Scifo joined Anderlecht as a teenager after scoring hatfuls of goals at junior level for La Louvière. In 1984 he chose to take up Belgian citizenship just in time to play for his country at the finals of the European Championship in France. His Latin technique and vision earned an almost instant transfer to Italy, but he was really too inexperienced to cope with the challenge of running Inter's midfield. A spell in France and appearances at the 1986 and 1990 World Cups (and later the 1998 finals, too) revived Italian interest and he joined Torino but, after Scifo schemed them to the 1992 UEFA Cup Final, he was sold to Monaco.

Gaetano Scirea

Born: May 25, 1953, Italy.
Clubs: Atalanta, Juventus.

Scirea was "the sweeper with charm", a skilled, graceful performer very different to the sort of ruthless "killers" employed by many Italian clubs in the 1960s and 1970s. Scirea began with Atalanta as an inside-forward and later became the defensive cornerstone of the all-conquering Juventus side of the 1980s. His central defensive partnership with Claudio Gentile was one of the most effective in the international game, as they proved at the heart of Italy's World Cup-winning defence in Spain in 1982. Scirea's sustained brilliance – he was seven times Italian champion with Juventus in 11 years – long thwarted the international ambitions of Milan's Franco Baresi. Sadly, soon after retiring, he was killed in a car crash in Poland while on a scouting mission for Juventus.

Uwe Seeler

Born: November 5, 1936, West Germany.
Club: Hamburg.

Seeler, son of a former Hamburg player, was so much the central figure in West German football in the 1960s and early 1970s that the fans used his name – "Uwe, Uwe" – as their chant at international matches. He made his full senior debut in a 3–1 defeat by England at Wembley in 1954 when still only 18. Seeler captained West Germany in their World Cup Final defeat at Wembley in 1966, but gained a measure of revenge by scoring a remarkable back-headed goal when Germany won 3–2 in extra time in the dramatic 1970 quarter-final. He scored 43 goals in 72 internationals: he and Pele are the only men to score in four World Cups. Seeler played for Hamburg throughout his career from 1952 to 1971, loyally rejecting a string of offers from Italy and Spain.

Alan Shearer

Born: August 13, 1970, England.
Clubs: Southampton, Blackburn Rovers, Newcastle United (Eng).

Shearer became the heir-apparent to Gary Lineker as England's top international marksman when he scored a record 13 goals in 11 matches for the under-21s and then collected a superb goal on his senior national team debut against France at Wembley in February 1992. Unfortunately, a serious knee injury cost Shearer a place alongside Lineker in England's attack at the European Championship finals in 1992. That same summer Blackburn signed Shearer for £3.3 million. He was their joint top scorer with 22 goals in his first season at Ewood Park. The top scorer at Euro 96 with five goals, Shearer was transferred to Newcastle in 1996 for £15 million. An horrific ankle injury disrupted much of 1997, but he captained England in the 1998 World Cup finals, scoring twice.

Peter Shilton

Born: September 18, 1949, England.
Clubs: Leicester, Stoke, Nottingham Forest, Southampton, Derby, Plymouth, Bolton Wanderers, West Ham United.

Shilton was only 20 when first capped, and nearly 41 when he made his 125th and last appearance for England, during the 1990 World Cup. That was his 17th game in such competitions, a record for a Briton. He conceded only 80 international goals, every one of them a dreadful blow to such a perfectionist. Shilton's awesome pursuit of personal fitness and elimination of error were renowned throughout the game. He played in an FA Cup Final with Leicester, who lost, when he was 19, but never appeared in another. Only with his move to Forest, and their brief dominance of England and Europe, did club honours flow. He played on well into his 40s, after entering management for a controversial spell with Plymouth.

Nikita Simonian

Born: October 12, 1926, Soviet Union.
Clubs: Kirilia Sovietov, Moscow Spartak.

Simonian, one of the few Armenian footballers to have succeeded in the Soviet game, was small for a centre-forward but skilful and quick – talents which brought him a then record 142 goals in 265 league matches in the 1950s. Three times he was leading scorer in the Soviet Supreme league, and his 1950 haul of 34 goals set a record that was not overtaken until the emergence of Oleg Protasov in the 1980s. Simonian began his career on Georgia's Black Sea coast, moved to Moscow with Kirilia Sovietov, or "Wings of the Soviet", and, three years later in 1949, joined Spartak. He won the league four times and the cup twice, and scored 12 goals in 23 internationals before retiring. Later he was coach to Spartak, then joint manager of the Soviet national team at the 1982 World Cup Finals in Spain.

SKUHRAVY *Outpaces Austrian defender Pecl in the 1990 World Cup*

Agne Simonsson

Born: October 19, 1935, Sweden.
Clubs: Orgryte (Swe), Real Madrid, Real Sociedad (Sp), Orgryte (Swe).

The Swedish team which reached the 1958 World Cup Final on home soil leaned heavily on foreign-based veterans but they, in turn, depended for the injection of a decisive attacking edge on Simonsson, the splendid centre-forward from the Gothenburg club of Orgryte. Simonsson enhanced his reputation by leading Sweden to victory over England at Wembley in 1959 and was signed the following summer by Real Madrid. They envisaged Simonsson becoming the successor to the ageing Alfredo Di Stefano, but Simonsson failed to adjust to life and football in Spain and, in any case, Di Stefano was not ready to go. After a spell with Real Sociedad, Simonsson returned to Orgryte and played again for Sweden, but never quite recovered his earlier spark.

Matthias Sindelar

Born: February 18, 1903, Austria.
Clubs: FC Hertha Vienna, FK Austria.

Nicknamed "the Man of Paper", for his slim build, Sindelar was the very spirit of the Austrian "Wunderteam" of the 1930s as well as their centre-forward and attacking leader. Born and brought up in Kozlau, in Czechoslovakia, he was discovered by a minor Viennese club, Hertha, in 1920, and joined neighbouring giants FK Austria a year later. Twice he won the Mitropa Cup – the interwar forerunner of the European Cup

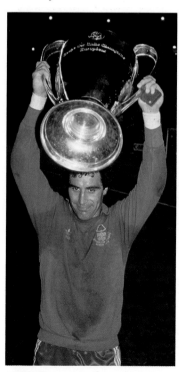

SHILTON *European Cup-winner*

– with FK Austria in the 1930s and added 27 goals in 43 internationals to his list of honours. Those 27 included two hat-tricks against old rivals Hungary in 1928 and the two goals which beat Italy in the newly-built Prater Stadium in Vienna in 1932. Sindelar scored in both Austria's classic matches against England in 1932 and 1936 and led Austria to the World Cup semi-finals of 1934. Depressed by the 1938 Anschluss, when Austria was swallowed up into Hilter's Greater Germany, he and his girlfriend committed suicide together in January, 1939.

Omar Enrique Sivori

Born: October 2, 1935, Argentina.
Clubs: River Plate (Arg), Juventus, Napoli (It).

Sivori was nicknamed "Cabezon" – Big Head – by his admirers in Argentina and Italy, because his technical virtuosity prompted him to humiliate and embarrass opposing defenders in the most outrageous ways. An inside-left with great talent and a quick temper, Sivori put fire into the Juventus attack of the late 1950s alongside the coolness of John Charles and the experience of veteran Giampiero Boniperti. He cost Juventus a world record £91,000 fee and repaid them with 144 goals in eight seasons before falling out with Paraguayan coach Heriberto Herrera and sulking off to Napoli, where his partnership with Milan outcast José Altafini produced the sort of fervour seen in the 1980s for Maradona. Sivori played 18 times for Argentina, as well as nine times for Italy, and was European Footballer of the Year in 1961.

Tomas Skuhravy

Born: September 7, 1965, Czechoslovakia.
Clubs: Sparta Prague (Cz), Genoa (It), Sporting Lisbon (Por), Genoa.

Tall, gangling Skuhravy earned instant acclaim when he opened up his 1990 World Cup finals campaign by scoring a hat-trick in the Czechoslovaks' 5–1 defeat of the United States. He finished the tournament as second-top scorer, with five goals, behind Toto Schillaci and with a lucrative new contract from Genoa in his pocket.

Skuhravy's partnership there with the Uruguayan, Carlos Aguilera, brought Genoa a measure of success in the league and the UEFA Cup before a succession of injuries took their toll. Skuhravy, who invested his money in an old prince's castle in Italy, always insisted that he would have preferred to star in Formula One motor racing rather than in football.

Graeme Souness

Born: May 6, 1953, Scotland.
Clubs: Tottenham, Middlesbrough, Liverpool (Eng), Sampdoria (It), Rangers (Scot).

Souness walked out of Spurs without playing in the first team in a League game, though he did appear for them in a European tie in Iceland. Even as a teenager, he was a player who knew his own value. He developed into a world-class midfielder, winning 54 caps and a string of honours with Liverpool, where he was an influential player and captain. Despite his abrasive style, he then became a great favourite with Sampdoria in Italy, but returned to become player-manager of Rangers. His huge spending ensured a string of titles for the club in the small arena of Scottish football, but he was less successful after his return to Anfield, where he succeeded his old friend Kenny Dalglish as Liverpool manager, and he lasted less than three seasons.

Neville Southall

Born: September 16, 1958, Wales.
Clubs: Bury, Everton, Port Vale (on loan), Everton (Eng).

A fiery character, Southall played Welsh League football at 14 and worked as a dish-washer, hod-carrier and dustman before joining Bury. He was then 21, and shortly afterwards was signed by Everton. A moderate start and a brief loan period were forgotten after his return, when he suddenly hit the form that established him as one of the world's top goalkeepers. He won two championship medals, two FA Cup, and one European Cup-winners' Cup medal, and was voted Footballer of the Year in 1985. After passing the Welsh record of 73 caps, ironically he made an expensive error in the defeat that prevented his country from qualifying for the 1994 World Cup.

STOICHKOV *Specially recommended to Barcelona by Johan Cruyff*

Jürgen Sparwasser

Born: June 14, 1948, East Germany.
Club: Magdeburg.

Sparwasser was one of the few outstanding footballers produced by East Germany in its 40 years of independent football existence. Sweeper Hans-Jürgen Dorner and centre-forward Joachim Streich both earned a century of caps, but the most memorable achievement fell to Sparwasser at the 1974 World Cup finals. An excellent attacking midfield player, Sparwasser scored the historic goal in Hamburg which beat World Cup hosts West Germany in the first and last meeting between the two states at international level. Sparwasser's career featured 15 goals in 77 internationals and a European Cup-winners' Cup medal after Magdeburg's victory over Milan in Rotterdam in 1974. Later he fled East Germany by taking advantage of his selection for a veterans' tournament in West Germany.

Pedro Alberto Spencer

Born: 1937, Ecuador.
Clubs: Everest (Ecu), Penarol (Uru), Barcelona Guayaquil (Ecu).

Spencer is probably the greatest Ecuadorian player of all time. He scored a record 50-plus goals in the South American club cup (Copa Libertadores), though all in the service of the Uruguayan club, Penarol, who dominated the event's early years in the 1960s. Spencer helped Penarol win the World Club Cup in 1961 and 1966 and earned such status on the field that, with his business interests, he was created Ecuadorian consul in Montevideo. Uruguayan officials so coveted Spencer's talents that he was called up to lead Uruguay's attack against England at Wembley in 1964, and scored their only goal in a 2–1 defeat. But protests from Ecuador and other South American nations ensured that this remained his one and only appearance for the "Celeste".

Hristo Stoichkov

Born: August 2, 1966, Bulgaria.
Clubs: CSKA Sofia (Bul), Barcelona (Sp), Parma (It), Barcelona (Sp), CSKA (Bul), Kawisa Reysol (Jpn).

Stoichkov built a reputation as one of Europe's finest marksmen since being reprieved from a six-month suspension after a controversial Bulgarian cup final between his army team, CSKA, and old Sofia rivals Levski-Spartak in 1985. Stoichkov then so impressed Barcelona they bought him for a Bulgarian record £2 million in 1990. Stoichkov rewarded coach Johan Cruyff's personal recommendation by scoring more than 60 goals in his first three seasons in league and European competition for the Catalan giants. He also led them to their long-awaited European Cup victory in 1992 and was the inspiration for Bulgaria's fourth place in the 1994 World Cup. He was European Footballer of the Year in 1994 and also played, with little impact, in the 1998 World Cup finals in France.

Luis Suarez

Born: May 2, 1935, Spain.
Clubs: Deportivo de La Coruna, Barcelona (Sp), Internazionale, Sampdoria (It).

Suarez was born and brought up in La Coruña, where he was discovered by Barcelona. The Catalans insisted on buying him immediately after he had earned a standing ovation in their own Nou Camp stadium, playing against them at 18 in 1953. Suarez was hailed as the greatest Spanish player of all time, a midfield general who was later the fulcrum of the Internazionale team which dominated world club football in the mid-1960s. Suarez's ability to turn defence into attack with one pinpoint pass suited Inter's hit-and-hold tactics admirably. Injury, significantly, prevented Suarez lining up against Celtic when Inter lost the 1967 European Cup Final in Lisbon. Later Suarez managed Spain at the 1990 World Cup finals.

Frank Swift

Born: December 26, 1913, England. *Club:* Manchester City.

Big Frank was a personality among goalkeepers, who enjoyed a joke with opponents and referees, but

SAFE KEEPING *Neville Southall, long-serving keeper for Everton and Wales*

was deadly serious at stopping shots. He stood in the crowd and watched Manchester City lose the 1933 FA Cup Final, then played for them when they won a year later, fainting at the finish as nervous exhaustion overcame him. During the war his entertainment value became even greater, and he won 19 caps while in his 30s – only twice on the losing side. After his retirement he became a journalist, and was one of those killed in the Munich air crash in 1958.

T

Marco Tardelli

Born: September 24, 1954, Italy.
Clubs: Pisa, Como, Juventus, Internazionale.

Tardelli was a utility defender or midfielder who was seen to best effect playing for Juventus and Italy in the first half of the 1980s. With both club and country Tardelli succeeded the more physical Romeo Benetti in midfield, though his Azzurri debut, against Portugal in Turin in 1976, was at right back. Tardelli is one of the very few players to have won every major prize in the modern domestic and European game, from the World Cup to the 1985 European Cup with Juventus. He scored six goals in 81 appearances for Italy and was voted official Man of the Match in the 1982 World Cup Final defeat of West Germany in Madrid.

Tostao (full name: Eduardo Goncalves Andrade)

Born: January 25, 1947, Brazil.
Clubs: Cruzeiro, Vasco da Gama.

Tostao, a small, nimble centre-forward, was already nicknamed "the White Pele" when he made his World Cup debut for Brazil at the 1966

MARCO TARDELLI
One of the elite few who have won a World Cup-winner's medal plus every major prize in European club football

finals in England. He scored Brazil's consolation goal in their 3–1 defeat by Hungary. It nearly became his only World Cup appearance when, in 1969, he suffered a detached retina during a South American cup tie against Millonarios in Bogota. Tostao underwent specialist surgery in Houston and recovered to become one of the heroes of Brazil's World Cup victory in Mexico a year later. However Tostao, a qualified doctor, recognized that the longer he played on, the greater the risk of permanent injury, and retired at 26 in 1973 … to become an eye specialist.

V

Jorge Valdano

Born: October 4, 1955, Argentina.
Clubs: Newell's Old Boys (Arg), Alaves, Zaragoza, Real Madrid (Sp).

Valdano has proved a rare personality in the world game: an author, poet, polemicist, coach and World Cup-winning player. Born in Las Parejas, he left Argentina for political reasons as a teenager and built his playing career in Spain. His success in winning the UEFA Cup twice in the mid-1980s with Real Madrid earned him selection for Argentina, and his positional and tactical skills were massive influences in the 1986 World Cup victory in Mexico. Originally an outside-left, Valdano was converted by Argentine coach Carlos Bilardo into a roving link between midfield and attack. He was later struck down by hepatitis, struggled in vain to make a World Cup comeback in 1990 and retired to become a journalist, an analyst and a successful coach with Tenerife before going back to Real as coach.

Carlos Valderrama

Born: September 2, 1961, Colombia.
Clubs: Santa Marta, Millonarios, Atletico Nacional (Col), Montpellier (Fr), Valladolid (Sp), Medellin, Atletico Junior Barranquilla (Col), Tampa Bay Mutiny (US), Miami Fusion (US).

Carlos Valderrama was voted South American Footballer of the Year in 1987 after guiding Colombia to a fine third place at the Copa America. The combination of frizzy hairstyle and all-round skill earned him the nickname of "the South American Gullit", and he shared South American Cup glory with Atletico Nacional before trying his luck in Europe with Montpellier of France and Valladolid

VALDERRAMA *Compared to Gullit for both hairstyle and talent, Valderrama dances past a Bolivian opponent*

of Spain. He failed to impress, but played well as Colombia reached the second round of the 1990 World Cup finals and rediscovered his touch after returning to Colombia in 1992. He was South American Footballer of the Year in 1994, after masterminded Colombia's sensational 1994 World Cup qualifying campaign (including a 5-0 win over Argentina). And, at the age of 36, he also played in the 1998 World Cup finals in France.

VAN BASTEN *Cruyff's protégé*

Marco Van Basten

Born: October 31, 1964, Holland.
Clubs: Ajax Amsterdam (Hol), Milan (It).

Marco Van Basten contributed one of the all-time great international goals when he volleyed home a long, looping cross in the 1988 European Championship Final in Munich. That was Van Basten just reaching his peak, one year after graduating from Ajax Amsterdam to Milan. Tall and angular, Van Basten made his international debut at the 1983 World Youth Cup and scored 128 league goals for Ajax before joining Milan for a mere £1.5 million in 1987. With Ajax he had won the European Golden Boot (37 goals in 1985–86) and the European Cup-winners' Cup, but with Milan he added even more honours – including FIFA, World and European Player of the Year awards plus World Club and European Cup medals. Sadly, ankle trouble wrecked the latter years of his career.

Paul Van Himst

Born: October 2, 1943, Belgium.
Clubs: Anderlecht, RWD Molenbeek, Eendracht Aalst.

Van Himst, the manager who guided Belgium to the 1994 World Cup finals, is still regarded as his country's greatest player. He joined the Brussels club Anderlecht at the age of nine and, at 16, was playing centre-forward in the first team. He was to be Belgian champion eight times, a cup-winner four times, league top scorer three times and was four times Footballer of the Year. Van Himst scored 31 goals in 81 internationals between 1960 and 1979, which included the 1970 World Cup finals and a third-place finish as hosts at the 1972 European Championship. Later he coached Anderlecht to victory in the UEFA Cup before being appointed manager of Belgium after the qualifying failure in the 1992 European Championship.

Odbulio Varela

Born: September 20, 1917, Uruguay.
Clubs: Wanderers, Penarol.

Varela was captain of the Uruguayan team which shocked Brazil by beating their hosts in Rio's Maracana stadium in the 1950 World Cup "Final" (the deciding match of the final pool). Varela was an old-style attacking centre-half and a captain who led by example. He had made his league debut with Wanderers at 21 and had already played for Uruguay before joining local giants Penarol in 1942. Twice he won the South American Championship with Uruguay but the 1950 World Cup saw him at his zenith, driving his team forward with every confidence even after Uruguay went 1–0 down early on. Varela was outstanding again, even at 37, in the 1954 World Cup finals in Switzerland. He retired immediately afterwards and was briefly coach to Penarol.

Vava (full name: Edvaldo Izidio Neto)

Born: November 12, 1934, Brazil.
Clubs: Recife, Vasco da Gama (Br), Atletico Madrid (Sp), Palmeiras, Botafogo (Br).

Vava may not have been one of the most refined centre-forwards in soccer history, but he was one of the most effective when it mattered. Originally an inside-left, Vava was switched to the centre of attack by Brazil at the 1958 World Cup to allow Pele into the line-up. He scored twice in the 5–2 Final victory over Sweden to earn a transfer to Spain with Atletico Madrid. The hawk-nosed Vava was successful and hugely popular in Spain, but his family grew homesick. Returning home in time to regain his Brazil place for the World Cup defence in Chile in 1962, he scored another of his typically vital goals in the 3–1 Final victory over Czechoslovakia. In all, Vava scored 15 goals in 22 internationals spread over 12 years between 1952 and 1964.

VALDANO *Sprinting into the clear*

Fritz Walter

Born: October 31, 1920, Germany.
Club: Kaiserslautern.

Fritz Walter and centre-forward brother Ottmar starred with Kaiserslautern in the late 1940s and early 1950s and were World Cup-winners together against hot favourites Hungary in the 1954 Final in Bern, Switzerland. Yet that triumph came late in a career which was cut in two by the war. Walter scored a hat-trick on his Germany debut in his favourite position of inside-left in a 9–2 thrashing of Romania in July 1940. After football was halted Walter was called up as a paratrooper, but his wartime flying experiences led him to refuse to fly to games in later, peacetime years. On the resumption of international football, Walter was restored as captain by long-time admirer and manager Sepp Herberger with success in the 1954 World Cup. Walter retired from the national team but was persuaded by Herberger to return in 1958 when, now 37, he led his team to the semi-finals. Walter, who scored 33 goals in his 61 internationals, later wrote successful football books.

Norman Whiteside

Born: May 7, 1965, Northern Ireland.
Clubs: Manchester United, Everton (Eng).

At the age of 17, Whiteside became the youngest World Cup player in history in 1982, when he made his debut after only two League appearances, one as a substitute. He later became the youngest-ever FA Cup Final and League Cup Final scorer, against Brighton (won) and Liverpool (lost), and curled a splendid winner into the Everton net to earn another FA Cup medal in 1985. By then his muscular work in attack had altered to a more painstaking approach through midfield, partially brought about by the amount of damage he had sustained up front. Everton bought him, but more injuries sadly ended his career before he was 30.

WALTER *1954 World Cup-winner*

Ernst Wilimowski

Born: June 23, 1916, Poland.
Clubs: Ruch Chorzow (Pol), PSV Chemnitz, TSV 1860 Munich, Hameln 07, BC Augsburg, Singen 04, VfR Kaiserslautern (Ger).

Wilimowski wrote his name into World Cup history when he scored four goals against Brazil in a first-round tie in France in 1938 – yet still finished on the losing side after a 6–5, extra-time defeat. He totalled 21 goals in 22 games for Poland, where he won five league titles with Ruch Chorzow. Yet, for years, his name was omitted from Polish sports records – because Wilimowski, after the German invasion, continued his career with German clubs and scored a further 13 goals in eight internationals for Greater Germany. In 1942 he scored 1860 Munich's first goal in their 2–0 defeat of Schalke in the Greater German cup final. After the war he played on in Germany with a string of regional league clubs before retiring at 37 in 1953. Ironically, Wilimowski, born in Katowice, made his Poland debut playing against Germany in 1934.

Billy Wright

Born: February 6, 1924, England.
Club: Wolverhampton Wanderers.

A lively wing-half who moved into the centre of defence and – by reading play superbly, timing tackles well and leaping to remarkable heights for a smallish man – he extended his career for years and years. Two League titles and one FA Cup went his way, plus the little matter of 105 caps (the majority as captain) in 13 seasons (out of a possible 108). He was the first in the world to reach a century of caps, and might have had more, even at 35, but for ending his career at virtually a moment's notice, in response to being left out of his club side for a lesser player. Later he managed Arsenal with little success, and then became a TV executive. He died in 1994.

BILLY WRIGHT *First Englishman to win 100 international caps*

Lev Yashin

see Legends (pages 122–3)

Rashidi Yekini

Born: October 23, 1963, Nigeria.
Club: Kaduna (Nga), Vitoria Setubal (Por), Olympiakos (Gr), Gijon (Sp), Zurich (Swz).

Yekini was, more than any other player, responsible for Nigeria's sensational first finals appearance at the 1994 World Cup. He had made his international debut 10 years earlier yet did not become a regular until the 1992 African Nations Cup when he scored four goals in a qualifier against Burkina Faso, then the winner in the third-place play-off against Cameroon. Yekini was eight-goal top scorer in the African qualifiers of the 1994 World Cup then top-scored again with five goals at the 1994 African Nations finals, and collected a winners' medal into the bargain. Yekini, the 1993 African Footballer of the Year, made history when he scored – against Bulgaria – Nigeria's first-ever goal in the World Cup finals. Following the finals, he then left Setubal for Olympiakos but ran out of luck, both losing form and suffering a serious knee injury.

Zico (full name: Artur Antunes Coimbra)

Born: March 3, 1953, Brazil.
Clubs: Flamengo (Br), Udinese (It), Flamengo (Br), Kashima Antlers (Jap).

The youngest of three professional football brothers, Zico was at first considered too lightweight by Flamengo. Special diets and weight training turned him into the wiry attacker who scored with one of what became his speciality free-kicks on his Brazil debut against Uruguay in 1975. Injury and disagreements over tactics

POWER PLAY *Rashidi Yekini inspired Nigeria's first World Cup finals appearance*

spoiled the 1978 and 1986 World Cups for Zico, and he was thus seen at his best only in Spain in 1982. At club level he inspired Flamengo's victory in the 1981 Copa Libertadores and their demolition of European champions Liverpool in Tokyo in the World Club Cup final. That was the start of Zico's mutual love affair with Japan which was resumed when, after a spell as Brazil's Minister of Sport, he joined Kashima Antlers to lead the launch of the professional J.League. He was assistant to Brazil coach Mario Zagallo for the 1998 World Cup finals in France.

Zinedine Zidane

Born: June 23, 1972, France
Clubs: Cannes, Bordeaux, Juventus (It)

Zidane proved himself to be one of the world's greatest midfielders when he scored twice in the 1998 World Cup final for France. He became a national hero as he masterminded a 3–0 victory over Brazil and lived up to his reputation as the new Platini.

The playmaker began his career at French club Cannes and made his name at Bordeaux (where he was named France's Player of the Year in 1996) before moving to Juventus.

Dino Zoff

Born: February 28, 1942, Italy
Clubs: Udinese, Mantova, Napoli, Juventus

Zoff is Italy's record international, with 112 appearances, of which the 106th was the World Cup final defeat of West Germany in Madrid in 1982. In 1973–74 he set a world record of 1,143 international minutes without conceding a goal. He won European trophies both as player and coach at Juventus.

Andoni Zubizarreta

Born: October 23, 1961, Spain.
Clubs: Bilbao, Barcelona, Valencia (Sp).

Zubizarreta was probably the finest product of the remarkable Basque school of goalkeeping which produced internationals such as Carmelo, Iribar, Artola, Arconada and Urruti. Zubizarreta was discovered by Bilbao in 1981, while playing for Alaves, and helped Bilbao win the league and cup double a year later. In 1986 he cost Barcelona a then world record fee for a goalkeeper of £1.2 million.

Zubizarreta overtook Jose Camacho's record of 81 caps for Spain in a 1993 World Cup qualifier against the Republic of Ireland in Dublin, and went on to top 100 appearances. He later left Barcelona for Valencia after a row with coach Johan Cruyff.

RECORD MAN *Andoni Zubizarreta defied opposition forwards – and Barcelona coach Johan Cruyff*

THE GREAT

Even before film, television and videos brought football to a much
certain matches became legendary. This section presents a number

April 28, 1923
THE WHITE HORSE FINAL

Wembley, London, FA Cup Final
Bolton Wanderers 2 (Jack 3, Smith, J.R., 55) West Ham United 0
HT: 1–0. Att: 126,047 (officially, though many thousands more forced their way in).
Ref: D. D. H. Asson (West Bromwich)
Bolton: Pym, Haworth, Finney, Nuttall, Seddon, Jennings, Butler, Jack, Smith, J.R., Smith, J., Vizard.
West Ham: Hufton, Henderson, Young, Bishop, Kay, Tresadern, Richards, Brown, Watson, Moore, Ruffell.

King George V was there, and somehow a match was laid on for him which, through good fortune and the crowd's good sense, was not the tragedy it might have turned out. Otherwise, the first event staged at the now historic Wembley Stadium might well have been the last. Such was the over-crowding that there could have been a disaster beyond even the awful proportions of Heysel or Hillsborough. Thanks to the self-discipline of the fans in a less impatient age, and to the police – led by Constable George Scorey on his leg-endary white horse, Billy – the Cup Final took place, starting almost an hour late. The match was not ticket-only, and nobody had anticipated such an enormous turn-out at the new stadium, built as part of the complex to house the Empire Exhibition. The ground was estimated to have a capacity of 125,000, but the combination of a fine spring day, the new arena and the appearance of a London club in the Final (even if a Second Division club) led to an estimated 250,000 trying to gain admittance – and mostly succeeding.

Many who had bought seats were unable to claim them in the crush. Some of the Bolton directors, travelling separately from the team, did not see a ball kicked, but the match went on and football entered the mass consciousness.

The first goal, by David Jack, came as an opponent was trying to climb back out of the crowd next to the touchline; and the second, by the Scot, J. R. Smith, was thought by some to have rebounded from a post: instead, it had hit spectators standing on the goal netting.

July 30, 1930
THE FIRST WORLD CHAMPIONS

Centenary Stadium, Montevideo
World Cup Final
Uruguay 4 (Dorado 12, Cea 57, Iriarte 68, Castro 90)
Argentina 2 (Peucelle 20, Stabile 37)
HT: 1–2. Att: 93,000. Ref: J. Langenus (Belgium)
Uruguay: Ballesteros, Nassazzi, Mascharoni, Andrade, Fernandez, Gestido, Dorado, Scarone, Castro, Cea, Iriarte.
Argentina: Botasso, Della Torre, Paternoster, Evaristo, Monti, Suarez, Peucelle, Varallo, Stabile, Ferreira, Evaristo.

Few papers outside South America and Central Europe bothered to report the match. The referee wore a tie and plus-fours, and several players covered their heads with handkerchiefs to keep the sun at bay. What film survives shows a near laughable standard of goalkeeping and defensive technique. Yet this game went into history simply because it could not be repeated. The first World Cup was over, and international football now had a standard to surpass.

Soccer statesmen Guérin from France and Hirschman from Holland had mooted the idea of a World Cup and brought it to fruition, even if only 13 nations turned up, including a mere four from Europe. Uruguay, celebrating 100 years of independence, guaranteed to refund all expenses to the visitors, just managed to get a new stadium built in time, and fittingly reached the Final. There were no seeds, just four groups, each of which sent one team to the semi-final, where Yugoslavia and the United States both lost 6–1. So the Final pitted hosts against neighbours, with thousands crossing the River Plate to play their part in a deafening climax to the fledgeling tournament.

The Uruguayans took the lead, fell behind, then went ahead again at 3–2 before Stabile, top scorer in the competition with eight goals, hit their bar. Castro, who had lost part of an arm in childhood, then headed the goal which clinched Uruguay's victory, to be greeted by a national holiday in his country . . . and bricks through the windows of the Uruguayan Embassy in Buenos Aires.

UNREPEATABLE *The first World Cup Final goal, by Uruguay's Dorado*

MATCHES

May 14, 1938
SHAMED ENGLAND HIT SIX

Olympic Stadium, Berlin
Friendly international
Germany 3 (Gauchel 20, Gellesch 42, Pesser 70)
England 6 (Bastin 12, Robinson 26, 50, Broome 36, Matthews 39, Goulden 72)
HT: 2–4. Att: 103,000. Ref: J. Langenus (Belgium)
Germany: Jakob, Janes, Muenzenberg, Kupfer, Goldbrunner, Kitzinger, Lehner, Gellesch, Gauchel, Szepan, Pesser.
England: Woodley, Sproston, Hapgood, Willingham, Young, Welsh, Matthews, Robinson, Broome, Goulden, Bastin.

One of England's most effective displays followed a shameful incident brought about by political pressures of the era. In an effort to placate Hitler, still furious at the way the majority of his athletes had been humbled in the same stadium at the 1936 Olympics, the England team were ordered to join the Germans in giving the Nazi salute as the German national anthem was played. The instruction came from the British Ambassador, Sir Neville Henderson,

MOMENT OF INFAMY *England salute*

supported by Stanley Rous (later Sir Stanley), then FA secretary. The players, unwilling to make a fuss, reluctantly got on with it, then showed their feelings by beating a very good German team out of sight. Don Welsh, one of two men making their England debut, was to say later: "You couldn't have asked for a greater team performance than this. Only when the heat got to us in the second half did we have to slow down a bit. I honestly thought we could have scored ten."

Jackie Robinson, only 20, was a perfect partner for Stan Matthews, and little Len Goulden hit a tremendous 30-yard goal to add to his all-round industry. The other debutant, Frank Broome, also scored.

July 16, 1950
BRAZIL FAIL AT THE FINISH

Maracana, Rio de Janeiro
World Cup final pool
Brazil 1 (Friaca 47)
Uruguay 2 (Schiaffino 66, Ghiggia 79)
HT: 0–0. Att: 199,000. Ref: G. Reader (England)
Brazil: Barbosa, Da Costa, Juvenal, Bauer, Alvim, Bigode, Friaca, Zizinho, Ademir, Jair, Chico.
Uruguay: Maspoli, Gonzales, Tejera, Gambetta, Varela, Andrade, Ghiggia, Perez, Miguez, Schiaffino, Moran.

Figures for the attendance vary from source to source, but this was certainly the highest at any soccer match since Wembley 1923. The first post-war World Cup, played without a knock-out final stage, provided what was in effect a final and established the tournament as the leading worldwide soccer competition. Even England were in it this time, having snubbed the three pre-war events. They failed miserably, however, struggling to beat Chile, then losing to the United States and to Spain. So the Spaniards went through to the final pool, with Brazil, Uruguay and Sweden, and the fixtures worked out perfectly.

Brazil, overwhelming favourites,

FOILED *Goalkeeper Maspoli stops a Brazilian attack*

won their first two games, scoring 13 goals to two. Uruguay trailed both Spain and Sweden 2–1, but drew the first game and won the second. So they had to beat Brazil at the enormous newly-built Maracana, while Brazil needed only to draw. Coach Flavio Costa seemed the only Brazilian unsure of victory, but his warnings about previous encounters in which Uruguay had disturbed Brazil went unheeded. Even after Friaca hit their 22nd goal in six games, Brazil kept pressing forward: Costa later protested that he had ordered men back into defence, but his words had gone either unheard or unheeded. Uruguay, remarkably calm amid the crescendo, equalized through Schiaffino. Then Ghiggia slipped through on the right and shot between Barbosa and his near, left-hand post: not a great goal, but an historic one.

EUPHORIC *Bill Perry (right) scores the seventh and last goal of Wembley's most dramatic Cup Final, as Ball lunges in vain*

May 2, 1953
STANLEY AND STANLEY

Wembley, London, FA Cup Final
Blackpool 4 (Mortensen 35, 68, 89, Perry 90)
Bolton 3 (Lofthouse 2, Moir 41, Bell 55)
HT: 1–2. Att: 100,000. Ref: M. Griffiths (Wales)
Blackpool: Farm, Shimwell, Garrett, Fenton, Johnston, Robinson, Matthews, Taylor, Mortensen, Mudie, Perry.
Bolton: Hanson, Ball, Banks, Wheeler, Barrass, Bell, Holden, Moir, Lofthouse, Hassall, Langton.

Stanley Matthews, at 38, stood football on its head. He gained a Cup-winners' medal after being on the losing side twice, he played a barely credible part in his team's rally from three down (the first of only two such recoveries in Wembley history) and he persuaded the hidebound FA to add him to their party to go to South America a few days later, after they had left him out on the grounds of his age. Blackpool's victory now seems to have been achieved by fate as much as by football: in Coronation Year, with Everest climbed, the Ashes regained and Gordon Richards winning his first Derby, how could unfancied, homespun Bolton have won the Cup?

But they very nearly did, in a game of remarkable drama, poor goalkeeping – goals 1, 3, 5 and 6 ought to have been stopped – and tactical naivety. In the last half-hour, with goalscorer Bell limping badly from a first-half injury and Banks limping not quite so badly, Bolton still kept both on their left (this was 13 years before substitutes). That was also Blackpool's right, the flank that Fenton and Taylor ensured was stuffed full of passes for the shuffling, mesmerizing genius named Matthews. In the incredible final moments, after the other Stanley, Mortensen, completed his hat-trick (still the only one in a Wembley FA Cup Final) with a free-kick, and Matthews had made the winner for Perry, the scoreboard momentarily showed the score as 4–4. Even today, when the talk is of Cup Finals, 1953 is usually No. 1.

November 25, 1953
THE MATCH THAT CHANGED THE GAME

Wembley, London
Friendly international
England 3 (Sewell 15, Mortensen 37, Ramsey 62 pen)
Hungary 6 (Hidegkuti 1, 20, 56, Puskas 22, 29, Bozsik 65)
HT: 2–4. Att: 100,000. Ref: L. Horn (Holland)
England: Merrick, Ramsey, Eckersley, Wright, Johnston, Dickinson, Matthews, Taylor, Mortensen, Sewell, Robb.
Hungary: Grosics (Geller 74), Buzansky, Lantos, Bozsik, Lorant, Zakarias, Budai, Kocsis, Hidegkuti, Puskas, Czibor.

Why were England so confident? Did they not know that Hungary went to Wembley having won 25 and drawn six of their previous 32 games, and having scored in every match they had played for six seasons? Yet England, fielding two debutants in a team averaging over 30 years of age, still looked on the match as something of a training spin, fooled by a xenophobic Press which had little or no direct knowledge of Ferenc Puskas and his colleagues. "This will be easy," said one England player as the teams walked out, "they've all got carpet slippers on." Indeed, Hungary's footwear did look like slippers compared with England's thunderous boots, but they could smack the ball pretty hard when they had to. As Hidegkuti did in the opening seconds, from 20 angled yards, arrow-straight past Gil Merrick. The Hungarians played in tight little triangles, then suddenly opened up with a raking pass of 30, 40, 50 yards or more to a sprinting colleague.

They gave the impression that they could always score a goal if they really needed one.

The defeat, clear and unequivocal, was England's first by a continental invader. That was not in itself important, but the manner and the margin of the massacre forced a furious tactical rethink in succeeding seasons. So great a rethink that it is fair to consider whether, without the shock treatment administered by Puskas and Co, England would have won the World Cup 13 years later.

HISTORIC *Ference Puskas (left) and Billy Wright lead the teams out*

June 27, 1954
THE BATTLE OF BERNE

Wankdorf Stadium, Berne
World Cup quarter-final
Brazil 2 (D. Santos 18 pen, Julinho 65)
Hungary 4 (Hidegkuti 4, Kocsis 7, 90, Lantos 55 pen)
HT: 1–2. Att: 40,000. Ref: A. Ellis (England)
Brazil: Castilho, Santos, D., Santos, N., Brandaozinho, Bauer, Pinheiro, Julino, Didi, Humberto, Indio, Maurinho.
Hungary: Grosics, Buzansky, Lantos, Bozsik, Lorant, Zakarias, Toth, M., Kocsis, Hidegkuti, Czibor, Toth, J.

This violent clash between two outstanding teams had a cleansing effect on soccer, for a time. The appalling scenes and continuing controversy

DISGRACE *Nilton Santos and Bozsik*

served to warn players and officials that football could go close to anarchy unless all concerned showed some respect for the traditions of the game as well as for its rules.

Hungary's part in this disgrace made a lot of people glad when they eventually lost the Final, although victory in the world championship would have been a fitting reward for a team of majestic power. Some of the blame must attach to referee Ellis, who sent off three players but never had the match under control.

Hungary, 2–0 up early on, showed unseemly arrogance, and a wild tackle cost them a penalty, halving their lead. When another penalty enabled them to go two up again, after most people felt that Kocsis had committed the foul, Brazil lost their heads. Offence followed offence on both sides of Julinho's goal, until Ellis at last sent off Bozsik (a Member of the Hungarian Parliament) and Nilton Santos for fighting, followed by Humberto for a deliberate kick. Kocsis headed a clinching goal in the last seconds, but the violence continued in the dressing-rooms, and Ellis needed an armed guard. FIFA abstained from punitive action, but the Hungarian authorities threatened all sorts of sanctions if there were any repetition. In the semi-final, three days later, Hungary – with nine of their quarter-finalists in action again – played superbly, and cleanly, to beat Uruguay 4–2. The lesson had been learned.

July 4, 1954
HUNGARY FAIL AT LAST

Wankdorf Stadium, Berne
World Cup Final
West Germany 3 (Morlock 10, Rahn 18, 82)
Hungary 2 (Puskas 6, Czibor 8)
HT: 2–2. Att: 60,000. Ref: W. Ling (England)
West Germany: Turek, Posipal, Kohlmeyer, Eckel, Liebrich, Mai, Rahn, Morlock, Walter, O., Walter, F., Schafer.
Hungary: Grosics, Buzansky, Lantos, Bozsik, Lorant, Zakarias, Czibor, Kocsis, Hidegkuti, Puskas, Toth, J.

German fortitude overtook Hungarian class in a thrilling final, played with great speed and skill despite steady rain. The match was perhaps the first major indication that West Germany's well-organized methods could prove too much for technically superior opposition. Germany have been a force in virtually every World Cup since, whereas Hungary have rarely approached the heights of the Puskas era.

The game also showed the benefit of tactical awareness. German coach Sepp Herberger had fielded only six of his eventual finalists in an earlier group game, which Hungary won 8–3, gambling on doing well in the play-off against Turkey that this defeat would bring. Sure enough, the Turks were beaten 7–2, and Germany went into the quarter-finals and then on to eventual victory. Ironically, Puskas could be held responsible for his team's defeat. He had been injured in the qualifying game against the Germans a fortnight earlier and had not played since. Although he said he was fit, and scored the first goal, he was nowhere near 100 per cent. The offside decision by linesman Mervyn Griffith that prevented what would have been his late equalizer was another decisive blow. Two early goals took Hungary's total for the tournament to 27, still the record for all finals, but two defensive errors enabled Germany to level with only 18 minutes gone. More than another hour passed before the powerful Rahn – a late addition to the squad after his international career had seemed over – shot Germany's third. Hungary had lost for the first time in 32 games, and the Germans had outsmarted the rest.

DELIGHT *Czibor (right) celebrates as Kohlmeyer and goalkeeper Turek are powerless to intervene*

May 13, 1956
REAL KINGS OF EUROPE

Parc des Princes, Paris
European Cup Final
Real Madrid 4 (Di Stefano 15, Rial 30, 80, Marquitos 72)
Reims 3 (Leblond 4, Templin 11, Hidalgo 63)
HT: 2–2. Att: 38,238. Ref: A. Ellis (England)
Real Madrid: Alonso, Atienza, Lesmes, Muñoz, Marquitos, Zarraga, Joseito, Marsal, Di Stefano, Rial, Gento.
Reims: Jacquet, Zimny, Giraudo, Leblond, Jonquet, Siatka, Hidalgo, Glovacki, Kopa, Bliard, Templin.

The European Champions Club Cup at last came struggling into life, having been conceived and forced through a difficult birth by a Frenchman, Gabriel Hanot, a former French international full-back and by now the editor of the influential daily newspaper, *L'Equipe*. Only 16 clubs were invited to compete – not all of them national champions: Hibernian, who reached the semi-finals, had finished only fifth in Scotland in the previous season.

England, still insular, did not take part, Chelsea meekly complying with a Football League ruling that a European tournament would complicate the fixture list. Now, of course, there are three of them, and many clubs would be destitute without the receipts these games bring in. Attack was the order of the day, or night, in those earlier, more innocent times. The 29 games contained 127 goals (an average of 4.37 per match), with Real Madrid scoring 20 and Reims 18, while attendances averaged 31,000. The tournament was a winner, beyond any shadow of doubt.

So too were Real, inspired off the field by far-seeing president Santiago Bernabeu and on it by Alfredo Di Stefano, arriving from Argentina via a brief stop in Colombia's rebel, unrecognized league. Real's exploits over this and the next few seasons established the club at the top of both the Spanish and European trees, proving the wisdom of Bernabeu's expenditure on a ground capable of holding 125,000. His team can seldom have rallied better than against Reims, who scored two easy early goals and under Raymond Kopa's direction – Real had already arranged to sign him immediately afterwards – looked capable of more. But Real, on a then massive bonus of £400 each, battled on to earn the first of their five successive European victories. A great team had arrived.

SUPERB *Pele (left) scores his first goal after a ball-juggling act that mesmerized the Swedish defence and the spectators*

June 29, 1958
FIRE IN THE FRIENDLY FINALS

Rasunda Stadium, Stockholm
World Cup Final
Brazil 5 (Vava 9, 30, Pele 55, 90, Zagalo 68)
Sweden 2 (Liedholm 4, Simonsson 80)
HT: 2–1. Att: 49,737. Ref: M. Guigue (France)
Brazil: Gilmar, Santos, D., Santos, N., Zito, Bellini, Orlando, Garrincha, Didi, Vava, Pele, Zagalo.
Sweden: Svensson, Bergmark, Axbom, Borjesson, Gustavsson, Parling, Hamrin, Gren, Simonsson, Liedholm, Skoglund.

Brazil's victory over the host nation in Stockholm proved to a vast audience – thanks to the spread of television – that South Americans can, after all, travel well. The team deservedly went into history as one of the greatest ever, after wonderful performances in the semi-final (5–2 against France) and the Final, when they overcame an early deficit with unstoppable power. Manager Vicente Feola had restored Didi, thought by some to be too old at 30, and preferred Vava to 19-year-old Mazzola as striker. These changes worked well, as did Feola's decision to bring back Djalma Santos in defence after Di Sordi had played all the previous games in the final stages. But perhaps the most crucial decision was made by the players, who demanded a place for Garrincha on the right wing. Feola, somewhat reluctantly agreed – and Garrincha, often tantalisingly inconsistent, responded superbly.

His speed left the Swedes for dead to make two goals for Vava, and Pele conjured a magical third, controlling a pass on one thigh, flicking the ball over his head, whirling and shooting, all in milliseconds. After adding the final goal, the boy dissolved in tears of joy. Pele, perhaps the greatest player ever, had made a world-wide mark.

May 18, 1960
GLASGOW SEES THE GREATEST

Hampden Park, Glasgow
European Cup Final
Real Madrid 7 (Di Stefano 27, 30, 73, Puskas 36, 48 pen, 58, 63)
Eintracht Frankfurt 3 (Kress 18, Stein 72, 80)
HT: 3–1. Att: 127,621. Ref: A. Mowat (Scotland)
Real Madrid: Dominguez, Marquitos, Pachin, Vidal, Santamaria, Zarraga, Canario, Del Sol, Di Stefano, Puskas, Gento.
Eintracht: Loy, Lutz, Hofer, Weilbacher, Eigenbrodt, Stinka, Kress, Lindner, Stein, Pfaff, Meier.

Real Madrid's fifth successive European Cup was achieved by their greatest performance in front of yet another great crowd. In their seven matches they scored 31 goals and were watched by 524,097 people – an average of nearly 75,000 per game. In the semi-final Real beat Barcelona

LAP OF HONOUR *Real players show off the European Cup after the Final*

3–1 home and away, after Barça had crushed Wolves, the English champions, 9–2 on aggregate. In the other semi-final, Eintracht performed the barely credible feat of twice scoring

six goals against Rangers, but in the Final they conceded hat-tricks to both Di Stefano and Puskas in a wonderful performance watched by a crowd so big that only one larger

attendance has been recorded in Britain since. Hardly any left early, even though the Germans were a beaten team well before the end. The fans stayed to bay a seemingly never-ending roar of tribute to one of the finest displays ever put on by any team, anywhere. The Scots were quick to appreciate their good fortune.

Real were now under their fourth coach in five years, wing-half Miguel Muñoz from their 1956 team having taken over. His two signings, Del Sol and Pachin, augmented an already illustrious squad, with the Uruguayan Santamaria a rock in defence, Gento a rapier on the left, and – towering above all – Di Stefano and Puskas, creators and finishers of a standard rarely seen before or since. Yet not even Real could win everything. Although they went on to beat Penarol 5–1 in the first (unofficial) club championship, they were runners-up in both their domestic league and cup.

May 31, 1961
BENFICA BETTER THAN BARÇA

Wankdorf Stadium, Berne
European Cup Final
Benfica 3 (Aguas 30, Ramallets 31 (o.g.), Coluna 55)
Barcelona 2 (Kocsis 20, Czibor 79)
HT: 2–1. Att: 33,000. Ref: G. Dienst (Switzerland)
Benfica: Costa Pereira, Mario Joao, Angelo, Neto, Germano, Cruz, José Augusto, Santana, Aguas, Coluna, Cavem.
Barcelona: Ramallets, Foncho, Gracia, Verges, Garay, Gensana, Kubala, Kocsis, Evaristo, Suarez, Czibor.

A curious match that showed a corporate rise and some individual falls. Benfica, little known outside Portugal and rank outsiders before the kick-off, took the European Cup and began a parade of domestic success that brought them 12 championships in the next 16 seasons, all in bunches of three: 1963–64–65, 1967–68–69, 1971–72–73 and 1975–76–77. And the Hungarian link with European Cup Finals was now almost severed. Kocsis and Czibor, who both scored for Barcelona, had been on the losing side – beaten by the same score on the same ground – in

the 1954 World Cup Final. They were virtually the last link with the marvellous Magyar team, although Puskas was to have the final word with a hat-trick for Real in the European Cup Final a year later. Another Hungarian, Kubala – who played for three countries – was a third key figure in the Barça side, but their downfall was due mainly to a home-bred player.

Their international keeper Ramallets missed a cross and let in Aguas for Benfica's equalizer. A minute later he fumbled a back-header by Gensana and allowed the ball to cross the line

before knocking it back again. Even Coluna's thunderous, long-range third might have been saved had Ramallets reacted more quickly.

Not surprisingly, these errors sapped a lot of Barca's confidence, but they kept battling. They hit the woodwork three times, four if Kubala's shot that came out after striking both posts is counted as doubly unlucky. Benfica, however fortunate with their goals, were a good, adventurous side. They held out calmly even after conceding a late second, and Kocsis and Czibor left the field in tears.

May 25, 1967
LISBON'S LIONS

National Stadium, Lisbon
European Cup Final
Celtic 2 (Gemmell 73, Chalmers 85)
Internazionale 1 (Mazzola 8 pen)
HT: 0–1. Att: 45,000.
Ref: H. Tschenscher (W Germany)
Celtic: Simpson, Craig, Gemmell, Murdoch, McNeill, Clark, Johnstone, Wallace, Chalmers, Auld, Lennox.
Internazionale: Sarti, Burgnich, Facchetti, Bedin, Guarneri, Picchi, Domenghini, Mazzola, Cappellini, Bicicli, Corso.

Celtic, one of Scotland's big two clubs, were minnows in the mainstream of Europe, despite frequent forays. Only two of their team on this balmy night in Portugal, before a frenzied crowd of adoring travellers, had any experience of the game outside their native land. Auld spent a none-too-productive spell at Birmingham, and Simpson had left Newcastle over a decade earlier (and now, at 37, was Scottish Footballer of the Year). The rest were a mixture of Glasgow lads and small-

fee bargains recruited by Jock Stein, a manager wondrously adept at making the whole much greater than the sum of the parts – nowadays he would have a degree in Human Resources.

Inter, European champions in 1965, returned to the Final with the help of a "deal" that would not now be allowed: after two draws with CSKA, Inter won the right to stage a vital home play-off in Bologna simply by promising the impoverished Bulgarians of CSKA 75 per cent of

the takings. When Inter won through by a lone goal, many neutrals turned against them: certainly Celtic had incredible support in a comparatively small crowd at Lisbon, where they won the right to be called Lions.

Even though they trailed for more than an hour, their faith in hard work and uncomplicated, attacking football paid off with two goals. So bargain-basement Celtic won every tournament they contested that season, while big-money Inter did not win a thing. Delightful irony!

May 29, 1968
BUSBY'S BELATED REWARD

Wembley, London
European Cup Final
Manchester United 4 (Charlton 53, 104, Best 91, Kidd 95)
Benfica 1 (Graça 85). After extra time.
HT: 0–0. 90 minutes: 1–1. Att: 100,000.
Ref: C. Lo Bello (Italy)
Manchester United: Stepney, Brennan, Dunne, Crerand, Foulkes, Stiles, Best, Kidd, Charlton, Sadler, Aston.
Benfica: Henrique, Adolfo, Cruz, Graça, Humberto, Jacinto, José Augusto, Eusebio, Torres, Coluna, Simoes.

One shot, one save . . . so much glorious English football history might never have happened. Eusebio, the mainspring of a fine Benfica side, had a chance to win the game, moments after Graça's late equalizer of a rare Bobby Charlton headed goal had sent United reeling. A thunderous right-foot shot from 18 yards after he had been put through the middle brought an instinctive save from Stepney and a rueful handclap from Eusebio: did he realize, even then, that a more delicate placing could have won the Cup for his own team?

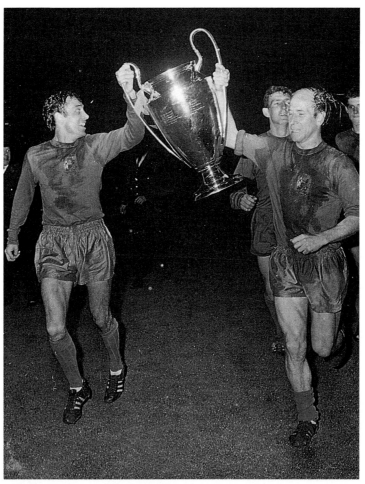

INSPIRED *Charlton (right) and Brennan lead the lap of honour*

In extra time, United regained their poise and power, with a glorious solo goal by Best being followed by two others, one from Kidd, on his 19th birthday, who headed the ball in on his second attempt after the goalkeeper had parried his first header, pushing it back out to him, and the other by skipper Charlton, one of the World Cup winners on the same pitch two years earlier.

So United, the third fine team assembled by manager Matt Busby in 20 years, became the first English club to annex Europe's leading trophy. The early postwar United were too soon for Europe: the mid-1950s Busby Babes reached the semifinals in 1957, losing to Real Madrid, and the patched-up, post-Munich side went down to inevitable defeat against Milan in 1958.

Thus a decade passed after Munich before Busby's third great team swept to their majestic triumph. Charlton and Foulkes were Munich survivors in the team. In so doing, they gave extra heart to other English clubs who had faltered on Europe's threshold: in the next decade, nine English clubs reached various finals on the Continent.

June 17, 1970
LOSERS AT THE LAST GASP

Azteca Stadium, Mexico City
World Cup semi-final
Italy 4 (Boninsegna 7, Burgnich 97, Riva 103, Rivera 111)
West Germany 3 (Schnellinger 90, Müller 95, 110). After extra time.
HT: 1–0. 90 minutes: 1–1. Att: 80,000.
Ref: A.Yamasaki (Mexico)
Italy: Albertosi, Burgnich, Cera, Bertini, Facchetti, Rosato (Poletti), Domenghini, Mazzola (Rivera), De Sisti, Boninsegna, Riva.
West Germany: Maier, Vogts, Beckenbauer, Schulz, Schnellinger, Grabowski, Patzke (Held), Overath, Seeler, Müller, Löhr (Libuda).

Six goals in 21 minutes made this one of the most exciting matches in the history of the World Cup or any other competition. Sadly, such are the demands of modern tournament structures, both teams ended up as losers. Three days earlier, in a thrilling quarter-final, Germany had played extra time before beating England 3–2, and coach Helmut Schön blamed defeat by Italy on the draining effects of that match. Four days later, an unchanged Italian side crashed 4–1 in the Final, and although there was no mistaking Brazil's right to the Jules Rimet Trophy, equally there was no doubting the fact that the Italians, in turn, had not fully recovered from their exertions against the Germans.

INSUFFICIENT *Gerd Müller scores, but the Italians rally to win*

Players, no matter how fit, need ample time to recuperate from two tense, testing hours in the Mexican sun. Schön, usually a master at tactical substitution, was caught out this time and forced to leave Beckenbauer on the field after dislocating a shoulder – bravery unquestioned but ability impaired. The gallant Beckenbauer played for an hour, including extra time, with the damaged shoulder strapped.

Germany could not afford such luxuries. Italy led for nearly all normal time, after Boninsegna's early snap shot, but Schnellinger, playing in his fourth World Cup, equalized for West Germany in injury time – only seconds from defeat. That began a remarkable scoring burst, with Germany leading 2–1, Italy levelling then leading 3–2, Germany getting level again – Müller's tenth goal of the tournament – and Rivera carefully rolling in what proved to be the decider, straight from the restart.

July 5, 1982
ROSSI'S TIMELY RETURN

Sarria Stadium, Barcelona
World Cup Group C
Italy 3 (Rossi 5, 25, 75)
Brazil 2 (Socrates 12, Falcao 68)
HT: 2–1. Att: 44,000. Ref: A. Klein (Israel)
Italy: Zoff, Gentile, Collovati (Bergomi), Scirea, Cabrini, Tardelli (Marini), Antognoni, Oriali, Graziani, Conti, Rossi.
Brazil: Waldir Peres, Leandro, Oscar, Luisinho, Junior, Toninho Cerezo, Socrates, Zico, Falcao, Serginho (Paulo Isidoro), Eder.

On the morning of April 29, 1982, Paolo Rossi returned from suspension, having been banned for three years – later reduced to two – for allegedly accepting a bribe and helping "fix" a match in the Italian league. Some 11 weeks later Rossi was the hero of all Italy. He scored three goals in this vital group qualifying match to eliminate the favourites, Brazil, two in the semi-final against Poland, and one in the Final, when Italy beat West Germany 3–1. His six goals made him the tournament's leading marksman and completed a remarkable comeback for one of the most effective strikers of his generation.

Rossi was still only 24, and Juven-

BRILLIANT *Rossi scores for Italy in Barcelona, and two great Brazilian goals are still two too few*

tus had such faith in him that they paid Perugia £600,000 to buy him while he had a year of the ban to run. He had always protested his innocence – and his demonic efforts to regain match fitness, plus his finishing, took

Italy to a merited success after they had managed only three draws in their initial qualifying group.

Brazil began against Italy needing only a draw to reach the semi-finals, and should have achieved it with

some ease. But their two brilliant goals encouraged them to keep on attacking and their over-stretched defence made too many errors against a forward in such inspired mood as Rossi, the man who came back.

July 8, 1982
THE MAN WHO STAYED ON

Sanchez Pizjuan Stadium, Seville
World Cup semi-final
West Germany 3 (Littbarski 18, Rummenigge 102, Fischer 107)
France 3 (Platini 27 pen, Trésor 92, Giresse 98). After extra time. West Germany won 5–4 on penalties
HT: 1–1. 90 minutes: 1–1. Att: 63,000.
Ref: C. Corver (Holland)
West Germany: Schumacher, Kaltz, Forster, K.-H., Stielike, Briegel (Rummenigge), Forster, B., Dremmler, Breitner, Littbarski, Magath (Hrubesch), Fischer.
France: Ettori, Amoros, Janvion, Bossis, Tigana, Trésor, Genghini (Battiston, Lopez), Giresse, Platini, Rocheteau, Six.

The first World Cup finals match to be decided on penalties was resolved because indomitable German spir-

it proved just too much for French skill. But West Germany were lucky to go through after an appalling foul by goalkeeper Harald Schumacher on French substitute Patrick Battiston. Schumacher's headlong charge left Battiston unconscious for several

BATTERED *For the semi-conscious Patrick Battiston, the semi-final is over*

minutes. A penalty? A sending-off? Not even a booking. The referee, in his wisdom, allowed Schumacher to remain, staring cold-eyed as Battiston was carried away.

France recovered so well after a poor opening that they might well have

won inside 90 minutes. Then two quick goals in extra time seemed to have made them safe, and delighted all neutrals. Yet the Germans, again showing remarkable spirit in adversity, pulled the game round. Rummenigge, the captain, went on as a substitute, although far from fit, and scored almost at once. Then an overhead hook from Fischer levelled the scores.

Even then France should have won. They were given the first penalty of the shoot-out, which usually proves a mental advantage, and when Stielike missed Germany's third attempt, France led 3–2. But Six failed with his and, after West Germany had levelled at 4–4, Schumacher made himself even less popular with the world at large by parrying a weak effort from Bossis. Hrubesch promptly hit the winner, deciding a made-for-TV soccer thriller.

June 21, 1986

THE CARNIVAL IS OVER

Jalisco Stadium, Guadalajara
World Cup quarter-final
France 1 (Platini 40)
Brazil 1 (Careca 18). After extra time.
France won 4–3 on penalties.
HT: 1–1. 90 minutes: 1–1. Att: 65,777.
Ref: I. Igna (Romania)
France: Bats, Battiston, Amoros, Bossis, Tousseau, Giresse (Ferreri), Tigana, Platini, Fernandez, Stopyra, Rocheteau (Bellone).
Brazil: Carlos, Josimar, Julio César, Edinho, Branco, Alemao, Socrates, Junior (Silas), Elzo, Muller (Zico), Careca.

Seven French survivors from Seville four years earlier had to go through another penalty shoot-out after a classic two-hour struggle ended in a draw. This time, French nerves held better than they had done in 1982, even though the captain and midfield inspiration, Michel Platini, failed with his shot when the score was 3–3. Julio César missed with the next Brazilian effort, and Luis Fernandez scored with his to put France into the semi-final . . . where West Germany, Schumacher included, were waiting to beat them 2–0.

Although the Brazil team could not compare with some of their predecessors, they were still a strongly-knit outfit, unusually so in defence. When Platini's shot from the brilliant Rocheteau's centre beat Carlos, this was the first goal the Brazilians had conceded for 401 minutes. More importantly, it wiped out the advantage Careca had given them with a typically fluent opening score. Manager Tele Santana kept half-fit Zico on the bench for most of the 90 minutes, before responding to the crowd's chants and sending him on. Almost at once goalkeeper Bats fouled Branco to concede a penalty, only to make amends by saving Zico's shot.

So France survived into extra time, when they looked slightly the better side as the midday heat drained the pace from tired legs. Eventually, a classic battle ended all square, and penalties were needed. The normally majestic Socrates missed the first shot, and France managed to stop the Brazilian carnival.

EQUAL *Tigana, Tousseau, the goal-scorer Platini and Fernandez (9) celebrate after the French had drawn level against Brazil*

June 24, 1990

A STRIKING SUCCESS

Stadio Meazza, Milan
World Cup second round
West Germany 2 (Klinsmann 50, Brehme 84)
Holland 1 (Koeman 86 pen)
HT: 0–0. Att: 74,559. Ref: J. C. Loustau (Argentina)
West Germany: Illgner, Reuter, Brehme, Kohler, Augenthaler, Buchwald, Berthold, Littbarski, Völler, Matthäus, Klinsmann (Reidle).
Holland: Van Breukelen, Van Aerle (Kieft), Rijkaard, Koeman, Van Tiggelen, Wouters, Witschge (Gillhaus), Winter, Van't Schip, Gullit, Van Basten.

Teamwork has become more and more important as soccer has developed. Organization, discipline and fitness now frequently obscure flair. But there is still no substitute for an outstanding individual, one who can win a game virtually single-handed.

SHADOWS *Van Basten and Kohler*

The audience in Milan and the millions watching on TV were privileged to see such a display in this match, when the German striker, Jurgen Klinsmann, played the game of his life to knock out the Dutch. Klinsmann was left as the only man up front after a disgusting incident in the 20th minute, when Voller was harshly sent off for a foul and Rijkaard went too after twice spitting at him. The versatile Holland team seemed better equipped to handle the loss but even their several outstanding defenders could not cope adequately with Klinsmann.

Helped by the tireless running of Matthäus and Littbarski, he kept up a remarkable degree of pressure on the Dutch, so that they were rarely able to launch their own renowned attacking force of Gullit and Van Basten. Early in the second half Klinsmann controlled an awkward pass, beat a marker and shot into the far side of the net to put Germany ahead. This led to the tightening of an already fierce grip, and a curling shot by Brehme left Holland with an impossible task. A controversial penalty after Van Basten went falling was too late. The night belonged to Germany, and especially Klinsmann, substituted near time to an ovation to end all ovations.

July 4, 1990
UNFORTUNATE END TO A CLASSIC

July 4, 1990. Stadio Delle Alpi, Turin
World Cup semi-final
West Germany 1 (Brehme 59)
England 1 (Lineker 80). After extra time.
Germany won 4–3 on penalties.
HT: 0–0. Att: 62,628. Ref: J. R. Wright
(Brazil).
West Germany: Illgner, Brehme, Kohler,
Augenthaler, Buchwald, Berthold,
Matthaus, Hässler (Reuter), Thom,
Völler (Riedle), Klinsmann.
England: Shilton, Wright, Parker, Butcher
(Steven), Walker, Peace, Beardsley,
Platt, Gascoigne, Waddle, Lineker.

FAILURE *Chris Waddle hits his penalty high and wide, so England go out of the World Cup*

Two of soccer's oldest rivals served up a magnificent match, sadly decided by what seems to be FIFA's only solution to draws after 120 minutes: penalties. England went so very, very close to reaching the Final for only the second time. Despite all the trials and tribulations besetting their manager, Bobby Robson, and despite the lack of class players – in the English game at large, let alone in the squad – there was only the merest fraction between the teams at the end. The splendid spirit in which the match was contested was another bonus. So, on a more personal level, was the flood of tears released by the England enigma, Paul Gascoigne, which made him a media and public darling overnight and earned him a wallet of gold to go with his later-revealed feet of clay.

This was a night with many heroes, perhaps none more so than the referee, José Roberto Wright, who let the game run without the nit-picking fussiness of so many other officials. The Germans, so often wanting to referee as well as to play, were none too keen on Wright's firm hand, but that suited England perfectly and helped them to play above themselves.

Only a freak goal by Brehme, deflected high over Shilton by Parker's attempted interception, put Germany in front. The indomitable Lineker pounced on a half-chance to level, and from then on penalties seemed the only solution. The Germans scored all the four they needed to take whereas Stuart Pearce and Chris Waddle missed England's last two. No arguing with that – only with the system.

June 26, 1992
HANS ANDERSEN FAIRY TALE

Ullevi Stadium, Gothenburg
European Championship Final
Denmark 2 (Jensen 18, Vilfort 78)
Germany 0
HT: 1–0. Att: 37,800. Ref: B. Galler
(Switzerland)
Denmark: Schmeichel, Piechnik, Olsen,
Nielsen, Sivebaek (Christiansen 68),
Vilfort, Jensen, Larsen, Christofte,
Laudrup, B., Povlsen.
Germany: Illgner, Reuter, Kohler,
Helmer, Buchwald, Brehme, Hässler,
Effenberg (Thom 80), Sammer (Doll 46),
Klinsmann, Riedle.

Germany or Holland seemed the likely winners of the ninth European Championship. France and perhaps even England looked likely to have a good run. As for Denmark, they had not even qualified for the final stages, and only got in when poor, war-ravaged Yugoslavia had to withdraw after topping their qualifying group, a point ahead of the Danes. When Denmark began by drawing with England and losing to Sweden, they seemed lost beyond retrieval. And why not? Many of the players had been on holiday and out of training when the call came for them to sweat off the pounds and make the short trip to neighbouring Sweden. The manager, Richard Moller Nielsen, was just about to start decorating his kitchen.

Apart from that, most of the fine team from the 1980s were no longer

SUCCESS *The Danish team celebrate their European Championship win*

in the reckoning, and several of the squad were injured as the tournament went on. But despite all that, the Danes showed remarkable spirit and considerable skill. A late goal against France made them second in their group and meant a semi-final against the Dutch, who snatched a late equalizer but then lost on penalties – the decisive kick being wasted by Marco Van Basten, of all people.

So Denmark went through to meet Germany in a what was expected to be a one-sided final, except that nobody had told the Danes. From Schmeichel to Povlsen, they all played their parts to perfection on an evening when little the Germans did went right. Vilfort, who scored the deciding goal (did he handle the ball first?) had just returned to the squad after going home because of his daughter's illness. Hans Christian Andersen could not have written a finer fairytale.

THE STADIUMS

The role of the stadium is simple: to organize spectators so that as many as possible can watch the action. Many grounds enjoy a fame which equals that of the clubs and individuals: permanent witnesses to the game's twin impostors of triumph and disaster.

NOU CAMP
BARCELONA, SPAIN

Capacity: 115,000
Opened: 1957
Club: FC Barcelona
Hosted: 1982 World Cup Opening Match (Belgium 1, Argentina 0); 1992 Olympic Final (Spain 3, Poland 2); 1989 European Cup Final (Milan 4, Steaua Bucharest 0); 1999 (Man. Utd 2, Bayern Munich 1);1982 European Cup-winners' Cup Final (Barcelona 2, Standard Liège 1)

PRIDE OF CATALONIA *Barcelona's 130,000 capacity Nou Camp stadium*

Higher and higher, bigger and better could be the motto of Barcelona's towering and breathtaking Nou Camp, "the new ground", which opened its doors on September 24, 1957 and was financed to the tune of 66 million pesetas by club members. Sport, it has been said, is the acceptable substitute for war, and Barcelona has always been a vehicle for the fervent nationalism of Catalonia. The rivalry with Madrid is intense, and the Nou Camp's continual improvements and expansion have much to do with the desire to outdo Real's Bernabeu stadium.

Barcelona, formed in 1899, outgrew their old Les Corts ground in the 1940s and moved to the new stadium, built in an area of gardens and allotments to the west, in 1957. When Nou Camp was inaugurated with a match against Legia Warsaw, plans had already been laid to extend facilities and increase capacity to 150,000.

An indoor sports hall, connected to Nou Camp by a concourse, was opened in 1971 and houses the club's basketball, handball and volleyball teams. Ice hockey is held in the adjacent Ice Palace. Even more remarkably, there is a walkway over a road leading to another football stadium, the 16,500 capacity Mini-Estad, opened in 1982 and used by Barcelona's nursery team in the Spanish Second Division as well as by the club's top amateur side.

The first major redevelopment of the main stadium was in the early 1980s, when the addition of a third tier increased capacity to 120,000 in time for Nou Camp to host the opening ceremony of the 1982 World Cup, after which a crowd of 85,000 saw Belgium upset the holders Argentina 1–0.

When the old Les Corts ground was opened in 1922, "Barca" had a membership of 5,000. When Pope John Paul II visited the Nou Camp in World Cup year he was enrolled as member No. 108,000. Since then membership has passed 110,000, making Barcelona the largest club in the world.

The work never stops. For the 1992 Olympic Games in Barcelona, two more tiers holding 10,000 seats were installed above the previous roof line, with a suspended cantilevered roof soaring overhead.

OLYMPIASTADION
BERLIN, GERMANY

Capacity: 76,006
Opened: 1936
Clubs: Hertha BSC, Blau-Weiss 90
Hosted: 1936 Olympic Final (Italy 2, Austria 1); 1974 World Cup group matches

LEGACY OF THE GREAT DICTATOR *Berlin's Olympiastadion was originally a stage for Adolf Hitler and his Nazis*

Berlin's historic – or notorious – stadium may be considered not so much a theatre of dreams, more a monument to the nightmarish world of Adolf Hitler and his national socialism. It was here that Hitler opened the 1936 Olympics, a giant propaganda exercise, to Wagnerian strains before an ecstatic 100,000 crowd. It was here, much to his chagrin, that the black American athlete Jesse Owens won four gold medals to challenge the myth of Aryan superiority. It was here two years later that the England team played Germany and avenged the politically-engineered demand that they give the Nazi salute by winning 6–3.

The Olympiapark, of which the Olympiastadion is the neo-classical centre-piece, had its origins before the First World War since Germany had been chosen to stage the Games in 1916. The unused facilities, adjacent to the Grunewald racecourse, were taken over when Hitler came to power in 1933. His grand plan involved the 86,000 capacity stadium on a 131-hectare sports field which also included hockey, riding and swimming stadia plus an open-air amphitheatre. These were all linked to the vast Maifeld, used by the Nazis for mass rallies.

The stadium suffered from Allied bombing but was repaired by the mid-1960s, when Hertha Berlin drew 70,000 crowds in the early years of the Bundesliga, the new national championship of West Germany. The stadium was renovated for the 1974 World Cup when it staged three group matches. The use of the Olympiastadion in the first place had caused political tension between East and West, and its incorporation in the World Cup programme at all was a triumph for German football chief Hermann Neuberger.

The unique political problems of Berlin meant that the stadium was underused for years. It was the home of both Hertha and Blau-Weiss Berlin but that meant mainly Second Division football. Now, since reunification, the Olympiastadion has regained its status as a focal point for German football and it is once again the permanent home of the German Cup Final.

HAMPDEN PARK
GLASGOW, SCOTLAND

Capacity: 52,000
Club: Queen's Park
Hosted: 1960 European Cup Final (Real Madrid 7, Eintracht Frankfurt 3), 1976 (Bayern Munich 1, Saint-Etienne 0); 1961 European Cup-winners' Cup (Fiorentina 2, Rangers 0), 1962 (Atletico Madrid 1, Fiorentina 1, replay in Stuttgart), 1966 (Borussia Dortmund 2, Liverpool 1); 1989 World Under-17 Championship Final (Saudi Arabia 1, Scotland 1 aet: Saudi Arabia 5–4 on pens).

As early as 1908, Glasgow had three of the largest grounds in the world:

GIANT OF THE PAST *In its heyday Hampden Park attracted record crowds*

Ibrox, home of protestant Rangers, Celtic Park, home of Catholic Celtic, and Hampden, owned by amateurs Queen's Park. Hampden was already the national stadium, never more vibrant than when hosting games against the old enemy England, whom Scotland had met in the first-ever international in 1872. It was the largest stadium in the world until the Maracana opened in 1950 and still holds several attendance records. In 1937, 149,415 paid to see the Scots beat England, a record for a match in Europe. A week later, 147,365 saw Celtic beat Aberdeen for the Scottish Cup, a European club record. In 1960, 135,000 watched Real Madrid trounce Eintracht Frankfurt 7–3 in the European Cup Final. That record was bettered five years later, when 136,505 saw Celtic's semi-final with Leeds. Since then there has been major redevelopment. First came a £3 million refurbishment in 1975 then a £12 million remodelling in the early 1990s. Hampden was shut again between 1996 and 1998 for the construction of an 18,000-capacity luxury South Stand.

ESTADIO DA LUZ
LISBON, PORTUGAL

Capacity: 130,000
Opened: 1954
Club: Benfica
Hosted: 1991 World Youth Cup Final (Portugal 0, Brazil 0: Portugal 4–2 on pens); 1967 European Cup Final (Celtic 2, Internazionale 1); 1992 European Cup-winners' Cup Final (Werder Bremen 2, Monaco 0)

Although the "Stadium of Light" is one of the most evocatively named arenas in the world, it takes its name not from the power of its floodlighting but from the nearby Lisbon district of Luz. Yet one of the most dazzling players in history, the "Black Pearl" Eusebio, led Benfica to unparalleled heights here during the 1960s and 1970s when 14 league titles, two European Cup wins (1960 and 1961) and three more final appearances established Benfica among the aristocracy of European football. In 1992, a statue of their greatest son was unveiled to celebrate his fiftieth birthday, before a match with old rivals Manchester United, and this now greets visitors as they arrive at the entrance.

Benfica, or Sport Lisboa e Benfica as they are officially named, were formed in 1908, and by the 1950s had long outgrown their fifth ground at Campo Grande. Plans for the 60,000 capacity Estadio da Luz were drawn up by a former Benfica athlete in 1951 and the two-tiered stadium was opened in 1954. Porto won the first game 3–0, and Portugal's first floodlit game, again won by Porto, took place four years later. By 1960 a third tier increased capacity to 75,000, and by the late 1970s the Estadio Da Luz, all white and bright, seated 130,000, and was a legend in Europe.

SANTIAGO BERNABEU
MADRID, SPAIN

Capacity: 105,000
Opened: 1947
Club: Real Madrid
Hosted: 1982 World Cup Final (Italy 3, West Germany 2); 1964 European Championship Final (Spain 2, Soviet Union 1); 1957 European Cup Final (Real Madrid 2, Fiorentina 0), 1969 (Milan 4, Ajax 1), 1980 (Nottingham Forest 1, Hamburg 0).

It is thanks to the visionary foresight of long-time president Santiago Bernabeu that Real Madrid boast an imposing edifice on Madrid's most prestigious street, the Castellana, housing one of the world's foremost clubs and a trophy room bulging with silverware and displaying more than 5,000 items. The ground, which began life as the Nuevo Chamartin Stadium in 1944 on five hectares of prime land, was Bernabeu's brainchild. He was a lawyer who had been, in turn, player, captain, club secretary, coach and then, from 1942, president. The old stadium had been ravaged during the Spanish Civil War and Bernabeu decided that a super new stadium was needed if the club were to raise the funds needed to build a super new team. Real, who now include the King and Queen of Spain and President of the International Olympic Committee Juan Antonio Samaranch among their members, raised an astonishing 41 million pesetas by public subscription to finance the land purchase and first stage of building. The stadium was opened, with a 75,000 capacity, for a testimonial match for veteran player Jesus

MONUMENT TO A VISIONARY *The Bernabeu stadium is a most exclusive venue*

Alonso against Belenenses of Lisbon in December, 1947.

In the 1950s the finance raised by Real's dominance of the fledgling European Cup enabled capacity within the distinctive white towers to be extended to 125,000. The name Estadio Santiago Bernabeu was adopted in 1955 and the floodlights were switched on in 1957 for the European Cup Final.

Bernabeu, who died in 1978, had plans for a new stadium north of the city but for once did not get his way and, instead, Spain's hosting of the 1982 World Cup led to more improvements. A total of 345,000 people watched three group matches and an outstanding Final in a stadium offering 30,200 seats and standing room for 60,000. Ten years on, the improvements continue. A third tier has been completed and further remodelling has increased the seating to 65,000 within a total capacity of 105,000.

STADIO GIUSEPPE MEAZZA
MILAN, ITALY

Capacity: 83,107
Opened: 1926
Clubs: Milan, Internazionale
Hosted: 1965 European Cup Final (Internazionale 1, Benfica 0), 1970 (Feyenoord 2, Celtic 1 aet); 1990 World Cup opening and group matches.

Fantastic is a much misused word but it seems appropriate to describe the home of two of Europe's leading clubs in the city which can claim to be the continent's premier soccer centre. The cylindrical towers which

allowed builders to construct a third tier and roof in advance of the 1992 World Cup have become just as much a trademark as the ramp system which gave access to the original two tiers of what used to be known as the San Siro. The cost of the remodelling came close to £50 million – even before the extra expense of sorting out problems with the pitch caused by shutting out both light and breeze.

San Siro, named after the suburb, was originally the home of Milan, formed in 1899 by the Englishman Alfred Edwards. They outgrew their original ground in the mid-1920s, and the site of their new stadium was bought by their wealthy president,

MAGNIFICO *Inter and Milan's home*

Piero Pirelli of tyre fame. It was Inter of all teams who ruined the opening party at the 35,000 capacity Stadio Calcistico San Siro by winning 6–3 in September 1926. The stadium was bought from Milan by the local council and was gradually enlarged until a 65,000 crowd were able to watch

Italy play their Axis partners Germany in 1940. Inter had outgrown their own Stadio Arena by 1947; but the proposed groundshare needed an even larger stadium. The San Siro reopened in 1955 with an increased capacity of 82,000 as the home ground for two teams who have been bettered in domestic football by Juventus and Torino but are second to none in European success. The San Siro was renamed Stadio Giuseppe Meazza in 1979 to honour the memory of one of the only two players to appear in both Italy's 1934 and 1938 World Cup-winning sides. The inside-forward had been hero-worshipped while playing for both Milan clubs.

LUZHNIKI STADIUM
MOSCOW, RUSSIA

Capacity: 100,000
Opened: 1956
Club: Spartak Moscow
Hosted: 1980 Olympic Final (Czechoslovakia 1, East Germany 0); 1999 UEFA Cup Final (Parma 3, Marseille 0).

A statue of Vladimir Ilyich Lenin, the now discredited father of the Russian Revolution, for years welcomed

the visitor to the Centralny Stadion Lenina on the banks of the Moscow River, which is the site of possibly the largest and most popular sports complex in the world. There are 140 separate sports centres, including a Palace of Sports, an open-air swimming centre, a multi-purpose hall, 22 smaller halls, 11 football pitches, four athletics tracks, three skating rinks and 55 tennis courts. The all-seater football stadium plays host to the capital's most popular club,

Spartak, and internationals. It is built on the site of the old Red Stadium where Spartak, then Moscow Sports Club, were founded in 1922. They adopted the present name in 1935 after affiliating to the trade unions for producers' co-operatives. The new stadium opened in 1956 with the first All Union Spartakia, which brought together 34,000 athletes to celebrate Communist sport. But the history of the Luzhinski is darkened by one of soccer's major disasters:

in 1982, Spartak were playing Haarlem of Holland in a UEFA Cup tie. Most of the crowd were leaving just before the end when Spartak scored a late goal. As fans tried to get back up the icy steps a fatal crush occurred in which 300 people died. The stadium was shut in the spring of 1996 for major refurbishment. It was reopened in 1999 to host the UEFA Cup Final, the first European single-match final to go behind the old Iron Curtain.

OLYMPIASTADION
MUNICH, GERMANY

Capacity: 74,000
Opened: 1972
Club: Bayern Munich
Hosted: 1972 Olympic Final (Poland 2, Hungary 1); 1974 World Cup Final (West Germany 2, Holland 1); 1988 European Championship Final (Holland 2, Soviet Union 0); 1979 European Cup Final (Nottingham Forest 1, Malmo 0), 1993 (Marseille 1, Milan 0), 1997 (Borussia Dortmund 3, Juventus 1)

Descriptions of the individualistic Olympiastadion vary from a futuristic Bedouin tent to a steel and glass spider's web – although the desert analogy can feel rather tenuous in the depths of a Bavarian winter on the site of the airfield to which Neville Chamberlain flew in 1938 for his infamous ("Peace in our time") meeting

NOTHING QUITE LIKE IT *Munich's futuristic Olympiastadion*

with Hitler. The tragic shadow of history fell across the stadium again at the end of the 1972 Olympics for which it had been built, when Arab terrorists took hostage and murdered Israeli athletes competing at the Games.

The bill for Behnisch and Otto's

staggering creation at the centre of the green and pleasant Olympiapark came to 137 million marks. It was money well spent. The Park has become Germany's leading tourist attraction and a stunning venue for major events.

Bayern Munich, about to establish themselves as European giants with players such as Franz Beckenbauer, Paul Breitner and Gerd Müller, moved into the new stadium in 1972, two seasons before they lifted the first of their three successive European Champions Cups. Müller had helped to celebrate the opening by scoring all four goals in West Germany's 4–1 win over the Soviet Union in 1972. Two years later the stocky striker's place in soccer's hall of fame was assured by his winning goal against Holland in the 1974 World Cup Final in front of his home fans.

The Dutch took happier memories away from the 1988 European Championship Final when they overcame the Soviets 2–0. Most recently Marseille became the first French club to win a European trophy by defeating Milan 1–0 there ... only to become embroiled in a major bribery scandal at home.

SAN PAOLO
NAPLES, ITALY

Capacity: 85,102
Opened: 1960
Club: Napoli
Hosted: 1968 European Championship semi-final (Italy 2, Soviet Union 1); 1980 European Championship finals venue; 1990 World Cup semi-final (Italy 1, Argentina 1: Argentina 4–3 on pens)

Regarded purely as a stadium, the concrete bowl of San Paolo, complete with roof since the 1992 World Cup, is unremarkable. But on match days it is transformed into a vibrant, uninhibited place by the local *tifosi*, some of the most colourful, eccentric and volatile fans (hence the moat and fences) in the world.

San Paolo represents the third home for Napoli, a club formed in 1904 with the help of English sailors and looked upon with some disdain by the more sophisticated clubs of Turin and Milan, though one of them, Juventus, deigned to come south to play the first match in the new stadium in the Olympic year of 1960.

Napoli, despite the largesse of millionaire president and shipping

UNRIVALLED ATMOSPHERE *Napoli's colourful fans turn a match in the San Paolo into an unforgettable experience*

owner Achille Lauro, had little success until the arrival of the Argentine superstar Diego Maradona in the mid-1980s. He filled San Paolo as it had never been filled before. The size of the stadium enabled Napoli to sell 70,000 season tickets, an Ital-

ian record, and thus not only pay Barcelona the then world record transfer fee of £5 million for Maradona but afford his wages and bring in other superstars, such as Brazil's Careca, into the bargain.

Sadly, the club has recently been

embroiled in controversy, first over links with the Camorra (the local version of the Mafia) and then over the misuse and misappropriation of funds set aside for development work in and around the stadium for the 1990 World Cup.

A THING OF BEAUTY *France's new national stadium*

STADE DE FRANCE
SAINT DENIS, PARIS, FRANCE

Capacity: 80,000
Opened: 1998
Clubs: none
Hosted: 1998 World Cup Final (France 3, Brazil 0) and eight other finals matches including opening ceremony. Due to host a quarter-final match in the 1999 Rugby World Cup

The award of the 1998 World Cup finals to France gave the government and the sports authorities the impetus to build a new national stadium. The original site was Melun Senart, to the south of Paris but complaints that this was too far from the city led to the eventual choice of Saint Denis north of Paris and a historic city in its own right.

The first national stadium had been the Stade Colombes which was used for the 1938 World Cup and was later succeeded for football, at

least by the Parc des Princes. But even after redevelopment in the early 1970s, the Parc was unsatisfactory as a major event venue. Placed in the south west corner of Paris in a residential area, it lacked parking facilities and with a 50,000 capacity was not big enough for a World Cup.

That accusation could not be levelled against the Stade de France, now one of the most majestic stadia in Europe. Built on the site of a disused gas works it can hold 80,000. Not that it was without teething troubles.

The stadium was opened in the spring of 1998 with a friendly between France and Spain but, to the embarassment of the authorities, the game remained in doubt until the last minute because of the freezing conditions since it had not been considered necessary to install under soil heating.

In due course, the stadium

proved a marvellous showcase for the 1998 World Cup. The opening game of the tournament between Brazil and Scotland took place at the stadium as did eight other World Cup games. It was fitting that the home nation should triumph so convincingly at their new home in the final against Brazil.

Major questions have remained over the long-term viability of the stadium. It had been hoped that Paris Saint-Germain would use it as home but they decided to stay at the Parc. Proposals to use the stadium to develop a second major capital club out of Red Star collapsed because of the lower division club's financial problems.

The French national rugby team are also using the stadium as their home ground and the stadium will be the venue for further World Cup action, this time in rugby, when a quarter-final tie will be played there.

OLIMPICO
ROME, ITALY

Capacity: 80,000
Opened: 1953
Clubs: Roma, Lazio
Hosted: 1960 Olympic Final (Yugoslavia 3, Denmark 1); 1990 World Cup Final (West Germany 1, Argentina 0); 1968 European Championship Final (Italy 1, Yugoslavia 1; replay, Italy 2, Yugoslavia 0), 1980 (West Germany 2, Belgium 1); 1977 European Cup Final (Liverpool 3, Borussia Mönchengladbach 1), 1984 (Liverpool 1, Roma 1: Liverpool 4–2 on pens) 1996 (Juventus 1, Ajax 1: Juventus 4–2 on pens)

Benito Mussolini was bad news for Italy. But allegedly he did make the trains run on time, and he also left the beautiful Foro Italico sports complex at the foot of Monte Mario as a legacy. His original plan was to stage the 1944 Olympics there, much as Hitler used Berlin for propaganda purposes in 1936. Then the Second World War intervened. The stadium was originally called Stadio dei Cipressi, but was inaugurated in 1953 as the Olimpico by the legendary Hungarian team who beat Italy 3–0 in front of an 80,000 crowd. The stadium became the focal point of the 1960 Olympic Games, a home to both Roma and Lazio, and the scene of a home triumph in the 1968 Euro-

pean Championship when Italy overcame Yugoslavia in a replay.

All roads led to Rome for Liverpool in 1977, when they turned the stadium into a sea of red celebrating the first of their four European Cup triumphs. They returned for the 1984 Final to beat Roma, playing on their own ground but unable to take

BELLA *Rome's Olympic Stadium*

advantage. Liverpool eventually won on penalties.

To allow the stadium to stage the 1990 World Cup, individual seating had to be increased to 80,000 and a roof added to give two-thirds cover. Only in Italy could the wrangling and talking have gone on until May 1988. A year later the roof design was ditched, costs had risen to £75 million, and the odds shifted against the stadium being ready.

FIFA's threat to move the final to Milan eventually saw to it that this beautiful venue was ready for West Germany's revenge over Argentina: a gracious setting for what proved to be an uninspiring contest.

ERNST-HAPPEL
VIENNA, AUSTRIA

Capacity: 62,958
Opened: 1931
Club: None as permanent
Hosted: 1964 European Cup Final (Internazionale 3, Real Madrid 1), 1987 (Porto 2, Bayern Munich 1), 1990 (Milan 1, Benfica 0), 1995 (Ajax 1, Milan 0); 1970 European Cup-winners' Cup Final (Manchester City 2, Gornik Zarbrze 1)

Long known as the Prater, the Ernst-

Happel stadion gained its new name in memory of the late Austrian international defender and coach. It overlooks the pleasure grounds forever associated with Orson Welles and *The Third Man*, but Austrian fans associate it more with the Hugo Meisl "Wunderteam" of the 1930s, who counted England among their victims in 1936. The Stadium has been transformed in recent years into one of Europe's leading venues, the original open two-tiered amphitheatre topped by a remarkable roof

which was erected in 10 months during 1985 at a cost of £17.5 million. The original 60,000-capacity stadium, a legacy of the socialist-controlled city administration, opened in July 1931 with a match appropriately between two workers' teams, and hosted athletics championships and the long-forgotten Workers Olympiad.

After the *Anschluss*, the stadium became an army barracks and, staged wartime internationals while serving as a staging post for Austrian Jews on their way to concentration

camps. Though badly damaged by Allied troops, the stadium was quickly restored after the war. Rapid played Real Madrid under floodlights in 1955 and a record 90,593 watched Austria play Spain in 1960. In the 1970s, the insertion of an all-weather track cut capacity to 72,000.

No club has used it permanently for league matches since FK Austria moved out in 1982. But Rapid, FK Austria and even Casino Salzburg have all used it intermittently for important European cup-ties.

WEMBLEY
LONDON, ENGLAND

Capacity: 80,000
Opened: 1923
Club: None
Hosted: 1948 Olympic Final (Sweden 3, Yugoslavia 1); 1966 World Cup Final (England 4, West Germany 2 aet); 1996 European Championship; 1963 European Cup Final (Milan 2, Benfica 1), 1968 (Manchester United 4, Benfica 1 aet), 1971 (Ajax 2, Panathinaikos 0), 1978 (Liverpool 1, Brugge 0), 1992 (Barcelona 1, Sampdoria 0 aet); 1965 Cup-Winners Cup Final (West Ham 2, Munich 1860 0); 1993 (Parma 3, Antwerp 1)

Wembley is the Mecca of world football, revered by players and fans throughout the world. The legend will not change even though the next few years will see the familiar old grand dame of the stadia demolished and replaced by a new structure to suit the 21st century. The financial terms

WEMBLEY *England's football home*

of the redevelopment will also bring change in commercial administration. But it will continue to play host to many more sporting events than just football – as in the past with the rugby league cup final, the Olympic Games (in 1948, greyhound racing, showjumping, speedway, rugby union and American football.

In the 1920s the green fields of Wembley Park were chosen as the site for the 1923 Empire Exhibition. The then Empire Stadium was built between January 22 and April 23.

Since a crowd of "only" 53,000 had

turned up for the 1922 FA Cup Final at Stamford Bridge, the authorities were concerned that Bolton and West Ham might not fill the new 126,000 capacity ground the following year. But on April 28 more than 200,000 people besieged Wembley, and that Bolton were eventually able to defeat West Ham 2–0 was due in no small part to the good nature of the crowd in the presence of King George V and a celebrated policeman on his white horse. The Wembley legend was born.

The watersheds of English football followed: the Cup was taken out of England for the only time by Cardiff in 1927; a year later Scotland destroyed England 5–1 with their famous forward line, dubbed the Wembley Wizards; Stanley Matthews had the 1953 Final "named" after him, when he inspired Blackpool to beat Bolton 4–3 from 3–1 down. Later that

year, Hungary changed world football by crushing England 6–3 there.

England held their heads high again in 1966, when they beat West Germany 4–2 and Geoff Hurst became the first player to score a hat-trick in a World Cup Final. And two years later Manchester United became the first English club to win the European Cup. Their triumph could not have come on a more appropriate turf.

Wembley has moved with the times. The surrounding exhibition centre was redeveloped while the stadium was remodelled in the 1980s at a cost of £60 million. Adapting to all-seater demands meant a capacity reduction from the historic 100,000. The addition of an Olympic Gallery beneath the roof edge kept an 80,000 level at which Wembley could take a pivotal role in England's hosting of the 1996 European Championship.

ROSE BOWL
PASADENA, CALIFORNIA, USA

Capacity: 102,083
*Opened:*1922
Hosted: 1984 Olympic Final (France 2, Brazil 0); 1994 World Cup Final (Brazil 0, Italy 0 – Brazil win 3–2 on penalties).

The Rose Bowl, synonymous with American football, came into its own as a soccer venue at the 1994 World Cup when it served as a home from home for the United States, then hosted second round matches, a semi-final, the third place match and the Final itself.

The rose-covered stadium, based in the leafy city of Pasadena seven miles north-west of downtown Los Angeles, cut its teeth on soccer in the 1984 Olympics, when the tournament drew massive crowds. Yugoslavia versus Italy drew 100,374, France's semi-final against Yugoslavia 97,451, and 101,799 watched France defeat Brazil in the Final. That topped the record attendance for gridiron football's Superbowl XVII in 1983, when 101,063 watched the Washington Redskins defeat the Miami Dolphins.

The Rose Bowl has hosted five Super Bowls but is best known as the home of UCLA and the annual Rose Bowl game on New Year's Day.

CALIFORNIA ROSE *The Rose Bowl rarely hosts professional sports events, but will forever be remembered as the venue for the 1994 World Cup Final*

NATIONAL OLYMPIC STADIUM
TOKYO, JAPAN

Capacity: 62,000
Opened: 1972
Club: None
Hosted: 1979 World Youth Cup Final (Argentina 3, Soviet Union 1); World Club Cup finals (every year since 1980)

Soccer is the 1990s growth sport in Japan, and it was natural that the stadium built to host the 1964 Olympics should serve as the home of the national team and launch the successful professional J-League in 1993. Japan's appetite for big-time soccer was whetted in 1980 when

Tokyo became the permanent home of the World Club Cup Final sponsored by Toyota. This previously two-leg affair between the European and South American Club Champions had become progressively discred-

GROWING PAINS *Surging crowds may make the Olympic stadium obsolete*

ited since its inception in 1960, often degenerating into violence. But the decision to change the format to a one-off game in front of an excitable but well-behaved Japanese crowd, beginning with Nacional of Uruguay's 1–0 defeat of Nottingham Forest in 1980, has transformed it into a popular fixture in the international calendar on the second Sunday each December. There is currently doubt about the stadium as a major venue following the Japanese bid to stage the 2002 World Cup. The capacity is well below the 80,000 required by FIFA, and the city of Tokyo and the Japanese government have yet to agree how a replacement venue should be funded. There is no room to expand the current stadium, and officials may decide to project the exciting new stadium in the port of Yokohama as a replacement to play prospective host to a Japanese World Cup Final in 2002.

GUILLERMO CANEDO
MEXICO CITY, MEXICO

Capacity: 110,000
Opened: 1960
Club: America (but others for big matches)
Hosted: 1968 Olympic Final (Hungary 4, Bulgaria 1); 1970 World Cup Final (Brazil 4, Italy 1); 1986 World Cup Final (Argentina 3, West Germany 2)

Formerly known as the Azteca, its name was changed in 1997 to the Estadio Guillermo Canedo, in memory of the late FIFA vice-president who had done so much to make Mexico the first nation to host two World Cups – those of 1970 and 1986. The 1970 finals are still revered as the greatest World Cup of all. The Azteca, as it then was, played host to the incredible semi-final in which Italy beat West Germany 4–3 and the Final itself, in which Pele's Brazil – probably the greatest-ever footballing side – crushed the Italians 4–1 on an unforgettable night

Some 16 years later Mexico stepped in at short notice as hosts after Colombia withdrew. This time

PRIDE AND JOY *Azteca stadium, home of two World Cup Finals, and an amazing experience for spectators*

Diego Maradona's Argentina defeated West Germany 3–2 in another thrilling final.

It is also one of the most enjoyable, passionate and colourful stadiums in which to watch a game since its lower tier is only thirty feet from the pitch, thus providing fans there

with a sense of immediacy while those in the upper tier benefit from the steep, cliff-like design.

The stadium, built on scrubland to the south-west of the sprawling mass which is Mexico City, required 100,000 tons of concrete, four times more than was used to build Wem-

bley. It was planned for the 1968 Olympics and opened in June 1966 with a match betweeen Mexico and Turin, but the first major internationals came during the 1968 Games. Since then, America, Atlante, Necaxa and Cruz Azul have all used the the three-tiered Azteca for important games.

MARIO FILHO/MARACANA
RIO DE JANEIRO, BRAZIL

Capacity: 120,000
Opened: 1950
Clubs: Botofago, Vasco da Gama, Flamengo, Fluminense
Hosted: 1950 World Cup Final (Uruguay 2, Brazil 1); 1989 South American Championship

What Wembley is to the old world, the Maracana is to the new. This architectural marvel is the largest stadium in the world and the spiritual home to Brazil's second religion, football. However, it has spent much of the last few years out of commission while work has been carried out to renovate a bowl which had started, literally, to fall apart.

The Maracana, which quite simply takes its name from the little river

that runs close by, was begun outside the city in 1948 in preparation for the 1950 World Cup, but was not completed until 1965. What has become Brazil's national stadium was originally intended to replace Vasco da Gama's club ground and was built and is still owned by the city, being formally named after the mayor, Mario Filho, who carried the project through. It was officially opened in June 1950 with a game beween Rio and São Paulo, the first goal being scored by Didi.

The first great matches were staged in the fourth World Cup, which culminated in the hosts losing to old rivals Uruguay before a world record crowd of 199,850. Like Hampden Park in Glasgow, the Maracana sets and holds attendance records. In 1963, 177,656 watched a league match between Flamengo and and Fluminense, a world club record attendance. Internationals have drawn crowds of 180,000, and league matches in the

1980s were watched regularly by 130,000. Santos even flew north to use Maracana for their World Club Cup Final ties against Benfica and Milan in 1962 and 1963.

The stadium is oval in shape and topped by a breathtaking cantilevered roof while a moat separates the fans from the pitch. Like Wembley

and the Olympiastadion in Munich, the Maracana has become a major tourist attraction and is held in such esteem that several smaller versions have been built throughout Brazil. Next to the stadium is the Maracanazinho, a scaled down indoor version which stages boxing, tennis, festivals and concerts.

A FADING GIANT *The Maracana still conjures up magic visions*

MONUMENTAL
BUENOS AIRES, ARGENTINA

Capacity: 76,000
Opened: 1938
Club: River Plate
Hosted: 1978 World Cup Final (Argentina 3, Holland 1 aet); 1946, 1959 and 1987 South American Championships

There were many misgivings about holding the 1978 World Cup in Argentina, not the least of which concerned the political climate. Ultimately, the ruling military junta invested huge sums in the renovation of the Monumental, which had been the home of the national side and of one of the world's great clubs, River Plate.

A MONUMENTAL VICTORY *Home advantage told for Argentina in 1978*

Several of River's own players – skipper Daniel Passarella, goalkeeper Ubaldo Fillol and forwards Leopoldo Luque and Oscar Ortiz – featured in the side which defeated The Netherlands 3–1 in the Final amid a paper snowstorm which tumbled down their "own" Monumental. Work had begun on the Monumental on September 27, 1936 and it was ready for River to move in by May 1938. The dressing-rooms and offices were of a standard then unique in South America, while

the three-sided horseshoe boasted an original capacity of 100,000, with the potential of a third tier which would lift it to 150,000. Needless to say, it was never needed.

The opening game, a 3–1 win over the Uruguayan champions Penarol, was watched by a crowd of 70,000. But the stadium itself was not completed, even in its initial phase, until 1957, when River invested much of the world record fee of £97,000 they had received from Italy's Juventus for inside-forward Omar Sivori.

Apart from the 1978 World Cup, the Monumental has played host to many internationals and South American club ties, as well as key games when Argentina have taken their turn to host the Copa America (the South American Championship).

CENTENARIO
MONTEVIDEO, URUGUAY

Capacity: 76,609)
Opened: 1930
Clubs: Penarol, Nacional
Hosted: 1930 World Cup Final (Uruguay 4, Argentina 2); 1942, 1956, 1967, 1983 and 1995 South American Championships

The Centenario holds a special place in football history, having been the stage for the first World Cup Final in 1930 when Uruguay, then Olympic champions and enjoying their golden age in international football, defeated Argentina, their old rivals from across the River Plate, by 4–2 after being 2–1 down at half-time. But it was a close call for Montevideo's magnificent new stadium, which was being built especially for the fledgeling world championship and to celebrate one hundred

HISTORY MAKER *The Centenario staged the first World Cup Final*

years of the country's independence. Work continued throughout the first days of the tournament to have it ready for the Final.

It has since become the regular venue for internationals, the South American Championship (the world's longest running international competition since the demise of the British Home Championship in 1984), the World Club Championship, the South American club championship (Copa Libertadores), Supercopa and Recopa. Uruguay's most recent international

success came in the 1995 South American Championship, when Brazil were beaten on penalties in the Centenario after a 1–1 draw.

Football in Uruguay is really all about football in Montevideo and the Centenario is home to two of the leading clubs, Penarol and Nacional, who dominated the Copa Libertadores, in its early years. From 1960, when Penarol defeated Olimpia of Paraguay 1–0 in the Centenario and 2–1 on aggregate, they and Nacional were involved in 10 of the first 11 finals, and in 1968 the stadium was full to see Estudiantes beat Palmeiras 2–0 in a final play-off. Penarol entertained Real Madrid in the first World Club Championship in 1960, but were held to a goalless draw and lost 5–0 away. They took their revenge by beating Benfica the next season in a play-off, and Real, by 2–0 both home and away, in 1966.

MORUMBI
SÃO PAULO, BRAZIL

Capacity: 150,000
Opened: 1978
Clubs: São Paulo FC, Corinthians
Hosted: 1992 Copa Libertadores (South American club championship)

Final 2nd leg (São Paulo 1, Newells Old Boys 0: agg 2–1)

The rivalry between Rio de Janeiro and São Paulo provides much of the dynamic which fires domestic football within Brazil. Fans from the respective cities consider "their" state championships – the Carioca and the Paulista – as the best and most important, and fail to understand why

players from the other city should ever be preferred to any of their favourites for the national team.

They are equally partisan about their stadia. Just as Rio de Janeiro boasts the Maracana, so São Paulo football centres on the magnificent Morumbi. The name, in fact, is that of the local suburb of São Paulo, and the stadium is formally entitled the

Estadio Cicero Pompeu de Toledo – explaining, perhaps, why it is generally known by the much shorter name "barrio".

São Paulo FC and Corinthians both play all their big games in the Morumbi, though Corinthians did have to move out briefly for a South American club tie in 1993 when the date clashed with a pop concert.

THE BUSINESS OF FOOTBALL

Professional football is a multi-million pound business in which 22 highly-trained, highly-paid, highly-valued athletes chase a ball around a potentially priceless development site. But it wasn't always so. . .

England are European champions when it comes to developing soccer's commercial opportunities. The financial and promotion innovations of the early 1990s drew observers from almost all the top clubs in Europe – including the giants of Italy, Spain and Germany.

This was all the more remarkable considering the fact, in many ways, British football's administration at national and club level remained steeped in an amateur tradition which owed more to the 19th century than the rapidly-approaching 21st.

Since organized football began in Britain in the middle of the nineteenth-century, the main source of income has come from gate receipts. From the 1970s on, however, other sources of revenue opened up. From advertising, sponsorship, TV income and controversial City-rich share flotations.

Gate money, although providing an ever-reducing percentage of overall income, remained the foundation of the average professional football club's balance sheet even after the advent of the Premier League.

BOOM TIME *Arsenal vs. Sunderland in 1937 attracted a massive crowd*

THE CLUBS

In 1991 Manchester United – one of the most famous clubs in world football – was floated on the London Stock Exchange. Net assets were estimated at £39.9 million, with each share offered at £3.85 with a guaranteed first dividend of 17.4 pence per share in the first year. All this is a far cry from the way United, in common with the rest of British football, used to be run. By 1991 gate receipts accounted for less than half United's income, with television, sponsorship, advertising and cater-

ing tipping the balance. This is a situation which is now becoming more and more common in world football.

One of the main sources of new revenue is sponsorship. Between 1976 and 1990 the sponsorship money spent in Britain rocketed from £2 million to £230 million. The High Street bank, Barclays, paid £11.5 million for the right to sponsor the Football League for six years from 1987; and brewers Bass took up sponsorship of the FA Premier League in 1993 – through its Carling brand – at a cost of £12 million over four years, to add to its patronage of the Scottish League and the Charity Shield. The attractions for the sponsors are obvious. Football is a huge market-place attracting all socio-economic groups. TV coverage provides nation-wide exposure, encourages brand loyalty and is a form of covert advertising.

Licensing the logos of clubs, national teams and competitions is another moneyspinner. The Football Association estimates that licens-

KITTED UP *England's strip 1998-style*

188

ON THE FRINGE *Perimeter advertising seen here at a ground during the 1993–94 European Champions League has become a lucrative business*

ing the logos of the England national team and the FA Cup alone could generate £35 million for the game. To this end, Littlewoods (the football pools company) became the first – discreet – FA Cup sponsors in 1994.

Merchandising is also an area of expansion – and controversy. Clubs have, for years, sold replica kits, but in recent times there has been an explosion of "official" club memorabilia. Tottenham Hotspur produce a lavish catalogue containing hundreds of items ranging from pens to pillow cases. But kit sales have attracted the most controversy. Many clubs have been accused of ripping off younger fans by constantly changing the design of their kit, knowing that fans will always want to wear the latest style. With junior kits costing anything up to £90, and with many clubs now having three kits – Manchester United in 1993–94 had four – there was a growing feeling that clubs were taking financial advantage of the loyalty of their supporters.

In the spring of 1994 Manchester United signed what was then the most lucrative kit deal in British football. The four-year deal negotiated with manufacturers Umbro guaranteed United £25 million, eclipsing the previous record – Umbro's £16 million four-year package with the England team.

Britain's pools companies also provide valuable income for the game, but without having any direct influence on it. It is thanks to the monies generated from pools revenue and channelled through the Football Trust that clubs were able to meet the capital costs incurred by redeveloping their grounds in the wake of the Taylor Report into the Hillsborough disaster.

More than 30 years earlier, the advent of floodlighting in the early 1950s had opened up another, perhaps less obvious, route to riches. The ability to play matches under lights in the evenings brought in mid-

190

week European competitive football and the switching of Football League Cup and even international matches from the weekend to midweek. Thus clubs – and national teams – were able to lure the paying public to more matches … and bind them still further and deeper into the commercial fabric of the game.

Closely allied to the development of sponsorship is advertising. Important income for many clubs comes from advertising on stadium perimeter boards around their pitches.

CHAMPIONS LEAGUE

The importance of and correlation between sponsorship, advertising and television is clear. By binding all three together to create a high-prestige "product", UEFA has effectively driven the cost of sponsorship up.

Originally, the Champions League had four sponsors who were guaranteed sole category rights covering all advertising within the stadia. Clubs taking part were not even allowed to display the name of their own domestic sponsors on their shirts – but that lasted two seasons. Nevertheless UEFA's thinking, it seems, is that exclusivity equals maximum returns.

The 1995–96 Champions League involved an entry of 24 clubs with the overspill of league title-winners being diverted into the UEFA Cup preliminaries. Further amendments were made for 1997–98 with the controversial decision to admit the eight runners-up from the domestic championship of Europe's top eight nations. That meant expanding the minileague section to six groups of four teams with the group winners and two "best" runners-up entering the traditional knock-out quarter-finals.

Further expansion from the 1999-2000 season meant clubs reaching the closing stages can earn £20million-plus from UEFA's appearance money and performance bonuses plus their own gate and catering revenues. No wonder Europe's big clubs all want a slice of the action and had imposed the creation of a European super league on UEFA.

Average attendances since the Premier League launch

Season	Average attendance
1992–93	21,125
1993–94	23,040
1994–95	24,271
1995–96	27,550
1996–97	28,434
1997–98	29,189
1998–99	30,581

THE PLAYERS

December 15, 1995, will go down in football history as the day the sky fell in on more than a century of financial and contractual tradition. That was the day when the European Court of Justice in Luxembourg ruled in favour of a restraint of trade complaint brought against the football authorities by Jean-Marc Bosman.

An ordinary, lower-division professional, Bosman had battled through the national and international courts after being denied the right to transfer from Belgian club FC Liege to French club Dunkerque.

The European Court ruled, after an exhausting five-year fight which cost Bosman not only his career, but his savings and his marriage too, that football's traditional transfer system and foreign player restrictions were illegal. It decreed that players whose contracts have expired are free to move to a club in another country without a transfer fee being due. It also ruled that no European Union country could restrict the number of EU citizens in any one team, on the grounds that this was a restraint of trade prohibited by the Treaty of Rome.

The judgement affected specifically only the 15 countries of the European Union. But since that means almost all western Europe (excluding Switzerland) it also meant the financial heart of the international game and thus football throughout the world. UEFA was virtually paralysed by shock and it was the national associations of western Europe, rather than their governing body, which initiated steps to resolve the immediate crisis.

Most quickly scrapped all restrictions on foreign players, or at least, those from other EU countries. Several – such as Holland, Germany and Italy – went further and extended the 'free transfer' concept for out-of-contract players into their domestic systems. Until then, players had been little more than personified banknotes in the game's financial structure.

A football club's most versatile and liquid assets are the players. For clubs everywhere, particularly those in the lower divisions, selling their best players to clubs further up the League is often the key to survival. One big sale can bring in more money than a season's gate receipts and help keep a struggling club afloat for another season.

The Bosman Judgement caused international consternation because it threatened the "trickle-down" financial value to minnow clubs of the transfer market, it wiped millions of pounds of playing assets off clubs' balance sheets, it opened up the prospect of the richest clubs buying perpetual control of competitive success … and it handed the top players the prospect of becoming multimillionaires, comparable to the superstars of American team sports, gridiron football, baseball and basketball.

But one basic value the Bosman Judgement could not undermine was the very existence of the transfer market.

For the clubs at the top end of the league, the need – some would say pressure – to buy players is twofold. First, clubs must have the best players available if they are to compete for survival in the FA Premiership – the top priority – and then for the prizes. Secondly, many clubs feel obliged to make big-name, big-money purchases during the summer months to help boost season ticket sales and maintain interest in the team. There are, after all, only three domestic trophies to be won, and with 20 teams in the Premiership, 17 are bound to go empty-handed each season – 18 if two trophies are won by the same club, as happened in 1993 when Arsenal won the FA Cup and the Coca-Cola-sponsored League Cup, and 1994, when Manchester United won the Premiership and the FA Cup. There are other, less obvious reasons for buying players. For example, if a club is coming to the end of its financial year and has too much cash sitting in the bank, the directors may well buy to reduce the tax liabilities.

Given that players are the most valuable asset, it follows that they are likely to be highly rewarded for agreeing to sign for a new club. A new player can add thousands to attendances and, with so many clubs competing for relatively few top-class players, transfer fees, signing-on fees and wages have spiralled much faster than the rate of inflation.

In Britain in the mid-1990s, the average weekly wage for a player in the Premiership was £3,000. In the First Division, the figure falls to £910; in the Second Division it is £456; in the Third Division £330. For those players at the top of their profession, the rewards are immense.

When Eric Cantona was on his best behaviour at Manchester United he was reputed to earn more than £10,000 a week. Even this seemingly unjustifiable wage is paltry compared with what players may earn in Italy. England's Paul Gascoigne was signed by Lazio in 1992 to a contract worth £18,000 a week; David Platt earned even more on transferring to Sampdoria in the summer of 1993; and Des Walker's season with Sampdoria in 1992–93 earned him a staggering £28,000 a week.

Even these vast figures pale into insignificance, however, when compared with the monumental sums lavished on top sportsmen in America. At his peak, Michael Jordan, of the Chicago Bulls basketball team, earned an estimated £24 million . . . £461,000 a week!

The wage gap between the Premiership and the First Division is widening – partly owing to Sky TV's

	Amount £	Player	Clubs involved	Year
WORLD RECORD TRANSFERS	1,000	Alf Common	Sunderland to Middlesbrough	1905
	10,890	David Jack	Bolton to Arsenal	1929
	23,000	Bernabe Ferreyra	Tigre BA to River Plate	1932
	52,000	Hans Jeppson	(amateur) to Napoli	1952
	72,000	Juan Alberto Schiaffino	Penarol to Milan	1954
	93,000	Enrique Omar Sivori	River Plate to Juventus	1957
	142,000	Luis Suarez	Barcelona to Internazionale	1961
	250,000	Angelo Sormani	Mantova to Roma	1963
	500,000	Pietro Anastasi	Varese to Juventus	1968
	922,000	Johan Cruyff	Ajax Amsterdam to Barcelona	1973
	1.20m	Giuseppe Savoldi	Bologna to Napoli	1975
	1.75m	Paolo Rossi	Juventus to L R Vicenza	1978
	3.00m	Diego Maradona	Boca Juniors to Barcelona	1982
	5.00m	Diego Maradona	Barcelona to Napoli	1984
	6.00m	Ruud Gullit	PSV Eindhoven to Milan	1987
	8.00m	Roberto Baggio	Fiorentina to Juventus	1990
	10.00m	Jean-Pierre Papin	Marseille to Milan	1992
	12.00m	Gianluca Vialli	Sampdoria to Juventus	1992
	13.00m	Gianluigi Lentini	Torino to Milan	1992
	15.00m	Alan Shearer	Blackburn Rovers to Newcastle United	1996
	19.50m	Ronaldo	Barcelona to Internazionale	1997
	23.00m	Denilson	Sao Paulo to Betis	1998
	31.00m	Christian Vieri	Lazio to Internazionale	1999

£304 million, five-year deal with the Premiership – and this in itself causes problems. Some reserves would rather be highly paid in the Premiership than move down to the First Division, where regular football would be accompanied by a wage cut. This denies other clubs and their supporters a "dead" pool of talent.

Another reason for the increase in players' wages, particularly in the top two divisions, is the activity of agents playing clubs in search of the most lucrative deals.

Arguments for and against agents raged for many years. Yet even the Football Association employed agents such as Harry Swales and then Jon Smith to try to ensure that the rulers of the domestic game were not trapped in a commercial minefield. In 1995 FIFA finally launched a system by which agents could be licensed for work in the transfer market and in match arrangement. Until Bosman, the English transfer market of the 1990s had turned over players to a value per season of up to £100 million. It was remarkably good business in a time of recession.

During the 1992–93 season in England £80 million changed hands in transfer fees, all during a time of

HE'S ALL DWIGHT *Alex Ferguson's big signing of 1998*

THE MEDIA

to the national associations. In this way, every football club in the world has access to FIFA through its league, national association and continental confederation.

From its modern headquarters overlooking Lake Zurich, FIFA controls everything in world soccer. Its statutes give it wide enforcement powers over 200 million players and more than one million teams worldwide. Recent crackdowns on doping and match-fixing serve to demonstrate the wide-ranging power within FIFA's mandate.

FIFA is not afraid to flex its muscles. After Marseille's 1993 European Champions Cup was tainted by match fixing allegations, FIFA forced its European affiliate, UEFA, to take sanctions against the French club even before a trial had been held. And when the club's owner – Bernard Tapie – threatened his own legal action, FIFA threatened to ban France from all competitions, so he was forced to back down.

Above all, FIFA's control of participation in the game's golden egg, the World Cup, provides it with the ultimate weapon for bringing wayward parties to heel. Chile were expelled from the 1990 World Cup when their goalkeeper Roberto Rojas faked an injury, claiming it came from a fire-cracker thrown from the crowd, and the team, losing to Brazil in a qualifying match, walked off.

Joao Havelange of Brazil, who was elected FIFA president in 1974, and who was replaced by Sepp Blatter in June 1998, proved a pragmatic visionary, and did much to spread the global commercialization of the game – not least by his politically-inspired expansions of the World Cup finals from 16 teams to 24 in 1982 and then to 32 in 1998.

Not that Havelange was without critics. European football leaders became increasingly disturbed by what they considered Havelange's autocratic approach. He stepped down after UEFA, led by president Lennart Johansson, began to agitate for changes in both FIFA's political structure and handling of World Cup finances.

MILAN MAN *Silvio Berlusconi*

The success of football around the world has generated massive interest in the professional game, a fact not lost on the world's media, which eagerly exploits the sport. The relationship, generally, is mutually beneficial, and in the case of television, particularly, the direct financial benefits are obvious. But while television could survive without soccer, it is becoming increasingly true that soccer in many countries could not survive without television and its huge investment in the game. The dangerous day ahead is the one on which TV moguls discover superior weapons in the ratings war.

To understand the relationship, it is necessary first to understand why television is so keen to show football. The entertainment value of football is not consistently high enough to merit its purchase alone, although televised football in Europe does attract large audiences. To the TV companies, the value of televised football comes not from the game itself, but from the access it provides advertisers to those who follow it. In televising football, they are not so much paying for the right to show the match, as they are buying the right to sell advertising space

during it. Football fans, and by logical extension, those who watch football on TV, are generally young males, with high disposable incomes. What better time, then, to advertise products such as cars, toiletries, hi-fi, alcohol and financial services than during a football match on TV?

Perhaps the best example of this intertwining of football and television comes from Italy. Silvio Berlusconi is owner of the Fininvest group which owns, among many other things, Milan football club, a string of local commercial TV stations including the flagship Canale 5, a supermarket chain and dozens of other non-related companies. Berlusconi has pumped millions of pounds into Milan to make them the best club side in Europe, if not the world. And, by showing football on his various TV channels, Berlusconi has a captive audience at which to aim his advertisements. It would seem to be the perfect relationship. Not only that, but Berlusconi hijacked Italy's football slogan – Forza Italia – for his political party when he won the General Election in March, 1994.

Press coverage of football varies. Italy, France, Portugal, Spain, Hungary, Poland, Slovakia, Romania and Bulgaria all sustain at least one daily sports newspaper. Yet Britain, such a sports-loving nation, is unable to do so. Or rather, it does not need to. In Britain the national press has always given far greater priority to football coverage than "general" daily newspapers on the continent – thus removing the need for a sports daily. Indeed the importance of football to the British newspaper industry can be gauged from the fact that the now-defunct *Today* newspaper sponsored the Football League during the 1986–87 season.

In Europe the situation is different, creating a need for daily newspapers such as the seven-day-a-week *Gazzetta dello Sport*, *Tuttosport* and *Corriere dello Sport/Stadio* (Italy), *A*

Bola (Portugal), *Marca* and *Mundo Deportivo* (Spain) and *L'Equipe* (France). These football papers devote wide coverage to the game and feature in-depth investigations, interviews and opinion as well as results and statistics. Britain does have many weekly and monthly football magazines, but a majority are aimed at the younger reader and are often little more than glorified posters. In Europe, football magazines tend to be aimed at older teenagers and adults, and there can be little doubt that *France Football*, *Kicker* (Germany), *Voetbal International* (Holland) and *Guerin Sportivo* (Italy) are "serious" football magazines.

Football is, it seems, an endless source of fascination to book publishers. Every year hundreds of football books are published worldwide, covering every conceivable angle. Many are straightforward statistical logs and yearbooks; others explore the wider influences of football on society. Britain has a tradition for the "kick and tell" book in which a famous player tells his life/career story in autobiographical terms with the help of a friendly journalist, who acts as "ghost" writer. Such books would not, generally, be commercially viable without a few controversial chapters which can be sold for serialization in one of the popular (usually Sunday) newspapers for a fee which helps to underwrite the book publisher's capital costs.

Radio has an important role to play too. In Britain, for example, BBC Radio 5 Live broadcasts live match commentaries as often as possible. The station also provides regular news bulletins and score checks – its output and style having been revolutionized in the 1990s to compete with the plethora of commercial stations which have sprung up around the country.

Managers and players can be notoriously sensitive to bad publicity. But, in commercial terms, no general business, no single company could afford to buy the acres of print and technological space being filled hour by hour, day by day, by football. All free publicity. The media, as ever, will always have the last word.

THE LAWS AND TACTICS

The first Laws of football were drawn up at Cambridge University in 1848, since when they have been considerably rewritten and amended. As the game changed, so tactics, too, have developed as teams try to outwit each other with bolts, liberos, 4–4–2 and the like.

THE LAWS OF FOOTBALL

The Laws (not the rules) of football have been honed down to 17 in number, with numerous sub-clauses. This evolutionary process began in the mid-nineteenth century and continued through to the 1930s, when Stanley Rous recodified the Laws. Recently the Laws were redrafted by FIFA. Law changes are made by the International Board, made up of eight members, four of them from the Home Countries of England, Scotland, Wales and Northern Ireland, and four from FIFA. It takes a three-quarter majority to alter a Law.

What follows is a summary of the Laws, as published by FIFA, simplified for general use.

THE OBJECT OF THE GAME

The game is played by two teams, each consisting of 11 players, one of whom must be a goalkeeper. The goalkeeper must wear clothing that distinguishes him from his team-mates and does not clash with the colours worn by his opponents or the referee. Substitutes are allowed to each team, but once a player has been replaced that player may not re-enter the game. Each competition has its own rules which dictate how many substitutes per side are permitted. In international soccer it is now usually three, selected from seven named before the match, but this does vary. Most domestic competitions allow either two or three, the third being a goalkeeper, all of whom have to be named beforehand.

On the pitch the game is regulated in senior football by a referee and two linesmen, whereas in junior football it is permitted simply to have a referee.

The object of the game is to propel a ball by foot or any part of the body other than the hands or arms into your opponents' goal. At each end of the field there is a goal consisting of two uprights placed eight yards (7.32m) apart (the inside measurement between the two posts), and joined at the top by a cross-bar eight feet in height (2.44m to the lower part of the bar) above the ground. The uprights and cross-bars should not exceed five inches (0.12m) in width and must be the same width. Normally these are made of wood or tubular steel. In senior football a net is is attached to the uprights and cross-bar or free-standing supports, to indicate clearly when a goal has been scored.

THE FIELD OF PLAY

The game is played on a pitch the surface of which is usually grass, although some competitions allow artificial surfaces of different types. The field of play is rectangular and measures between 100 to 130 yards (90–120m) in length and 50 to 100 yards (45–90m) in width. Under no circumstances can the pitch be square. The field of play is bounded by painted lines. Those down the longer side are known as the touch-lines, and those across the shorter side, on which the goals are positioned, as the goal-lines. All such boundary lines and other pitch markings, which should be no more than five inches (0.12m) wide, form part of the field of play.

Other pitch markings consist of a centre-line drawn across the pitch at a point midway between the two goal-lines. In the middle of this is

THE FIELD OF PLAY *The dimensions and appurtenances of a soccer field*

196

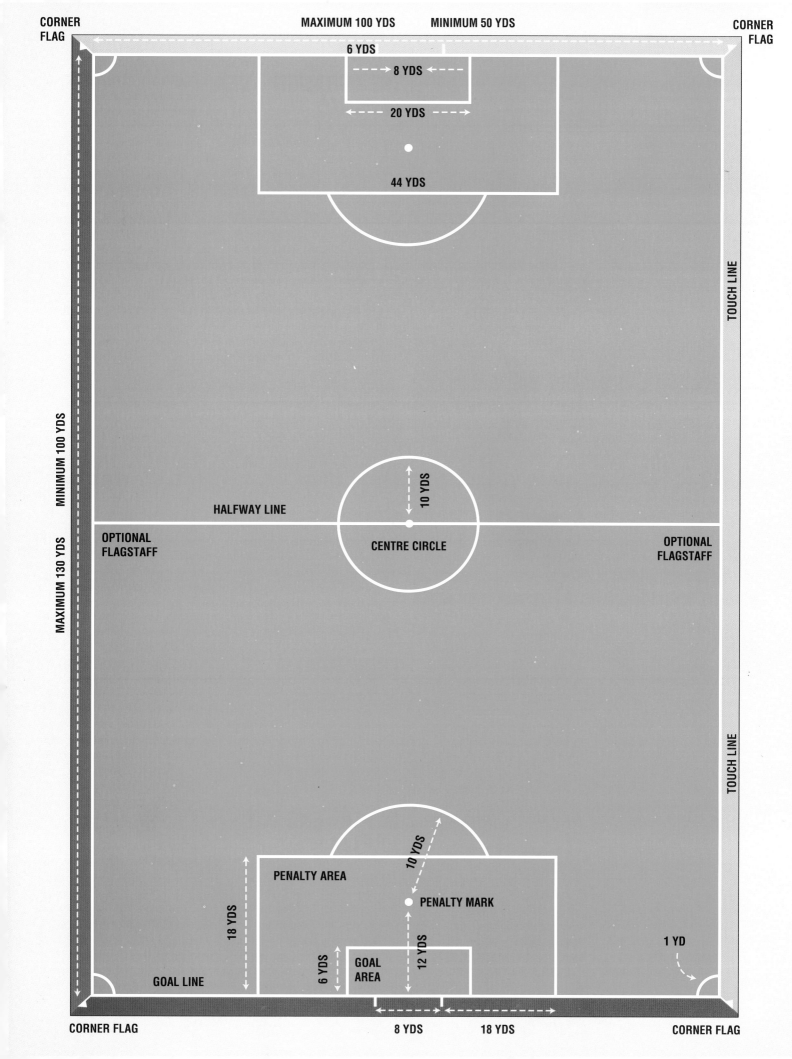

placed a centre spot, from which play commences at the start of each half and after a goal is scored. A circle is drawn, with a ten-yard (9.15m) radius from the centre spot, within which no opponent is allowed to encroach until the ball is kicked into play. In each corner of the field, where the goal-line and touch-line meet, is a corner flag with a minimum height of five feet (1.5m). A quadrant with a one-yard (1m) radius is drawn at each corner of the field. As an optional extra, flags may be placed opposite the centre-line but must be at least one yard (1m) behind the touch-lines.

The goals are placed at the centre of each goal-line, and two lines are drawn at right angles to the goal-line six yards (5.5m) from the goal-posts. They extend into the field of play for a distance of six yards (5.5m) and are joined by a line of 20 yards (18.3m) parallel to the goal-line. This section defines the goal area. The goal area is enclosed within the larger penalty area, which is created by drawing two lines at right angles to the goal-line, 18 yards (16.5m) from each goal-post, which extend into the field of play a distance of 18 yards (16.5m) and are joined by a line of 44 yards (40.3m) parallel to the goal-line.

The penalty mark from where penalty kicks must be taken is marked twelve yards (11m) from the goal-line and facing the mid point of the goal. The Laws decree that there must be no encroachment when a penalty kick is taken. In order to ensure that all players apart from the kicker stand 10 yards (9.15m) from the ball until such a kick is taken, an arc with a radius of ten yards (9.15m), using the penalty spot as its centre, is drawn outside the penalty area, and the players must stand outisde the penalty area and outside this arc.

The game is played with a ball which must be round and made of leather or any other approved material, its circumference being between 27 and 28 inches (0.68–0.71m) and its weight between 14 and 16 ounces (396–453gm).

The object of the game is to score more goals than the opposition. In order to score a goal the whole of the ball must pass between the goal posts, under the cross-bar and across the goal-line. The whole of the ball must cross the whole of the line. If no goals are scored, or the teams have an equal number of goals, the match is termed a draw.

THE PENALTY KICK

This is for the serious offences mentioned. Taken from the penalty mark, it can be awarded irrespective of where the ball is at the time the offence is committed, provided that the ball is in play and the offence takes place in the penalty area. A goal may be scored directly from a penalty and the only players allowed in the penalty area until the ball has been kicked are the one taking the penalty kick and the goalkeeper. If either team infringes these regulations, the kick will be retaken, except in the case of an infringement by the defending team where a goal has been scored. In that event the goal will normally be awarded, because to do otherwise would be to allow the offending team to gain an advantage from the infringement.

Examples of when a retake is ordered are: where the goalkeeper saves the ball or the kick is missed, but the goalkeeper moved forward from goal-line before the kick was taken or there is encroachment by the defending side; where a goal is scored and there is encroachment by the attacking side; and, finally, where the kick is taken, whether or not a goal is scored, and there is encroachment by both sides. A match shall be extended at half-time or full-time to allow the penalty kick to be taken or retaken, but the extension shall last only until the moment that the penalty kick has been completed, whether it results in a goal, a miss or a save. Different rules apply in cup competitions when the teams are level at full-time and the game is to be decided by the taking of an initial five penalties by each side.

THE DURATION OF PLAY

The match starts with a kick-off, with the ball placed on the centre spot and kicked forward by one of the attackers. Prior to that, the captains of the two teams meet the referee to spin a coin for choice of ends or kick-off. The winning captain generally makes the election for the first half, since the teams change ends to start the second half. The ball is in play once it has travelled its own circumference in the opponents' half of the pitch. The player taking the kick-off may not play the ball again until it has been touched by another player.

Play is divided into two equal halves, and in senior football a half lasts 45 minutes (although this can be reduced either by the rules of the competition or by agreement between the teams), and there is a half-time interval lasting a minimum of five minutes.

To decide cup matches which are drawn after 90 minutes, extra time, usually of 15 minutes each way, is played. Some competitions allow for a penalty kick decider to occur to ascertain the winner. A 'sudden death' system in extra-time, with the first goal deciding the outcome, will be used in the finals of the 1996 European Championship and 1998 World Cup.

EQUIPMENT

A player's equipment consists of a jersey or shirt, shorts, socks, shin-guards and footwear. The teams must wear colours that do not clash with each other or the referee. A player shall not wear anything that is dangerous to another player.

IN PLAY AND OUT OF PLAY

The ball is in play at all times from the start of the match to the finish, including where an infringement of the Laws occurs (until a decision is given and the game is stopped by the referee). It is still in play when it rebounds inside the boundaries of the field from a goal-post, cross-bar or cor-ner flag. The ball only goes out of play when it wholly crosses the boundaries of the field, whether on the ground or in the air.

When the ball leaves the field of play over the touch-line it re-enters the field by means of a throw-in. The throw is taken by a member of the team opposing that of the player who put it out of play. The throw must be taken from as close as possible to the point at which the ball left the field. If not taken from there it is described as a foul throw and the throw-in given to the other team. The thrower takes the ball in both hands and throws it from behind and over his head. He must face the pitch with both feet on the ground on or behind the touchline at the moment he delivers the throw.

When the ball leaves the field of play over the goal-line it is returned into play either by means of a goal-kick, if last touched by an attacker, or a corner kick, if last touched by a defender. At a goal-kick the defending side (usually the goalkeeper) restarts the game by kicking the ball from either half of his goal area, and the ball is not deemed to be in play until it has passed out of the penalty area. Any infringement of this procedure results in the kick being retaken.

At a corner-kick the ball is played from the quadrant, which is a quarter circle with a radius of one yard (1m) situated in the corner of the field. The ball must be within the quadrant, and the kick must be taken at the end of the defending side's goal-line nearest to where the ball went out of play. Again the player taking the corner-kick may not play the ball a second time until it has been touched by another player, and defenders must remain at a distance of ten yards (9.15m) until the ball has been kicked.

Where there is no other method of restarting the game, following an injury, interference by spectators or for any other accidental reason, the restart is achieved by dropping the ball at the point where it was when play was suspended. The ball is deemed to be in play the moment it touches the ground, and no player may kick or attempt to kick the ball until that moment. In the event of a breach of this procedure the drop is retaken.

OFFSIDE

Arguably the most complex of the 17 Laws is Law 11, relating to "offside". Even the wording is difficult, which pronounces that "a player is offside if he is nearer his opponents' goal-line than the ball and interfering with play or an opponent at the moment the ball is last played unless . . ." Then follow four exceptions: (1) from restarts, namely goal-kicks, corner-kicks and throw-ins, but not free-kicks; (2) if a player is in his own half of the field; (3) if the ball was last played to him by an opponent; (4) if he is not nearer to the goal-line than at least two defenders, even if one is the goalkeeper.

In these cases he is not offside. The main problems come in deciding when the ball was last "played", and whether or not an attacker is "interfering". If the referee considers that an attacking player, albeit in an "offside position", is not interfering with play or with an opponent or seeking to gain an advantage by being in that offside position, he shall refrain from penalizing him and stopping play. A player who is level with the penultimate defender is not in an offside position. In such cases, the attacking player must be given the benefit of any doubt. A player cannot be offside if he is behind the ball when it is played, even if there are no defenders between him and the goal.

INFRINGEMENTS OF THE LAWS

As football is a physical contact sport, infringements of the Laws will inevitably occur, giving rise to punishment by the referee in the form of "free-kicks". These free-kicks may be either "direct" or "indirect". The difference is that a goal may be scored directly from a direct free-kick but not from an indirect free-kick. At an indirect free-kick a second player must play the ball after the kicker before a goal can be scored.

A direct free-kick is awarded for more serious offences, and if these occur in the penalty area a penalty is awarded. All free-kicks (except penalties) are taken from the place

SEEING RED *Jonas Thern is sent off during Sweden's 1994 World Cup semi-final defeat by Brazil*

where the infringement occurred unless they take place in the goal area. Then the attacking side take this indirect free-kick from that place on the goal-area line which is parallel to the goal-line and is nearest the infringement. For the defending side, the free-kick can be taken from anywhere inside the goal area.

Although opponents must be at least 10 yards (9.15m) from the ball at the moment the free-kick is taken, the attacking side has the option of waiving this rule should they consider that they would obtain greater advantage from taking the kick quickly. The referee may play what is known as the "advantage clause" and not award a free-kick if he considers that to play on is advantageous to the attacking team.

The more serious offences, for which a direct free-kick can be award-ed, are intentional fouls or misconduct and are divided into nine categories, of which six are fouls against an opponent, two are against either an opponent or a team-mate, and one is technical. The six are: (a) tripping or throwing an opponent; (b) jumping at an opponent; (c) charging an opponent from behind (unless he is obstructing); (d) holding an opponent; (e) pushing an opponent; (f) charging an opponent in a violent or dangerous manner. The two more serious offences are kicking or attempting to kick another player and striking or attempting to strike or spit at another player – or indeed the referee. The final offence is deliberately handling the ball which is defined as "carrying, propelling or striking the ball with the hand or arm". If any of these nine offences is committed by

THE GOALKEEPER

The goalkeeper is the only player entitled to handle the ball, but he is only allowed to do this within his own penalty area. When he leaves his penalty area he becomes an ordinary player. He wears clothing which distinguishes him from all other members of his team, his opponents and the referee, and if he fails to do so he can be sent from the pitch until he complies with this ruling.

The goalkeeper is the only other player apart from the penalty-taker to be in the penalty area at the time a kick is taken. He has to stand on the goal-line though a recent Law change allows him to move his feet before the ball is struck.

The goalkeeper is king in his own goal area and may not be charged except when he is holding the ball or obstructing an opponent in that particular area.

However, he is capable of being penalized more than any other player on the pitch. He may be penalized for taking more than four steps in any direction while in possession of the ball, whether holding or bouncing the ball or throwing it in the air and catching it again without

releasing it into play; or if, having released the ball into play before, during or after the four steps, he touches it again with his hands before it has been touched or played by another player of the same team outside the penalty area, or by a player of the opposing team inside or outside the penalty area. Similarly, where a defending player deliberately kicks the ball to him, he is not permitted to touch it with his hands, and if he does he is penalized by the award of an indirect free-kick against him.

Finally, the goalkeeper is the only player to suffer the wrath of the Laws if he indulges in tactics which in the opinion of the referee are designed merely to hold up the game and thus waste time, giving an unfair advantage to his own team. These disadvantages are intended to balance out the advantage of being the only one who can legitimately handle the ball.

He is able to score a goal with a kick from his hands from his own penalty area, provided the ball is in play; and if he chooses to be just another player he can come out of his penalty area to score at the other end.

THE MAN IN CHARGE *The wisdom of Solomon and the patience of Job*

BLOWING THE WHISTLE *The appropriate punishment for a foul is administered*

the defending side in their own penalty area, the referee will award a penalty, which is taken from the penalty mark.

Indirect free-kicks are awarded for eight main offences, which are: (a) dangerous (rather than violent) play; (b) charging fairly but at a time when the opponent does not have the ball within playing distance; (c) obstruction; (d) charging the goalkeeper except when he is holding the ball or is obstructing an opponent or has passed outside his goal area; (e) time-wasting by the goalkeeper; (f) the goalkeeper taking more than four steps while in possession of the ball; (g) any occasion when a player deliberately kicks the ball to his goalkeeper and the goalkeeper then touches it with his hand or hands, or when the goalkeeper deliberately handles the ball twice without an opponent touching it if he is not attempting to save the ball; (h) indulging in anything which the referee considers to be ungentlemanly conduct, including trying to circumvent the Laws – particularly the deliberate kick to the goalkeeper rule. In addition, an indirect free-kick is also awarded for the technical offence of offside.

The referee has power to punish these offences further if they are considered serious enough. A play-er shall be cautioned and shown the yellow card by the referee if he (a) enters or leaves the field of play without receiving a signal from the referee to do so; (b) persistently infringes the Laws of the Game; (c) shows, by word or actions, dissent from any decision given by the referee, or (d) is guilty of any act of ungentlemanly conduct, with particular reference to kicking the ball away after the award of a free-kick, encroaching from a "defensive wall" or standing in front of the ball to stop a free-kick being taken.

For even more serious offences a player shall be shown the red card and sent off the field if (a) in the opinion of the referee a defending player impedes an opponent through unlawful means when that opponent has an obvious goalscoring opportunity; (b) any player is guilty of violent conduct or serious foul play, such as a violent tackle from behind with little or no attempt to play the ball, but also including spitting; (c) a defending player other than the goalkeeper in his own penalty area intentionally handles the ball to deny a goal or goalscoring opportunity; (d) any player uses foul or abusive language to anyone on the field of play; (e) a player after already having received a caution persists in misconduct.

THE OFFICIALS

Originally soccer was played with an umpire and a referee rather like the game of tennis. Gradually it was necessary to introduce touch judges with the umpire's role transformed into that of the modern day referee who has two assistants, better known as linesmen, The assistant referees are qualified officials who specifically indicate ball in and out of play at throw-ins, corner kicks and goal kicks; who mainly are given the responsibility of deciding offside; who are required to attract the attention of the referee at substitutions and are generally there to aid and assist the referee.

The referee is the sole time-keeper and enforcer of the Laws. He therefore in order to carry these obligations into effect takes on to the field with him a stop watch, a whistle to start and stop the game, a pencil so as to write in all weather conditions, a note book or paper and a red and yellow card to administer punishment. In senior football he is usually entrusted with one match ball to take on to the pitch although he is required to inspect all match balls before the match starts to ensure they comply with the Laws.

The referee must report all misconduct to the appropriate body governing the game; he may refrain from punishing to play the advantage in favour of the attacking team

and he can reverse his decision so long as the game has not been re-started. He should only accept the intervention of a linesman if the linesman is better placed to see the incident.

Referees are encouraged to absorb and administer the unwritten eighteenth Law shortly known as "common sense" and therefore he should indicate by means of approved signals various decisions. The referee will decide how to administer the game with his referee's assistants (formerly known as linesmen) and advise them where to stand. The usual system is known as the "diagonal system" and involves the referee being in the middle with each of the assistants being on either the right or left diagonal so that they are always in vision of each other. He will also discuss with them what positions to take up at penalties and corners. In addition, the three officials all compare watches before the start of the game.

Over a period of years the referees' outfit evolved from a jacket top and plus-fours trousers into a blazer and shorts, followed by a tunic top, which ultimately became an all-black outfit with white trimmings and socks to match. In recent years experiments have taken place with different colour outfits but FIFA generally requires referees to wear predominantly black in international competitions of all varieties.

THREE WISE MEN *A referee flanked by two assistants before the kick-off*

THE HISTORY OF TACTICS

Tactics can be divided into three main categories:

(1) Team formations
(2) Team tactics involving the whole or part of the team, whether for (a) attack or (b) defence
(3) Re-starts or set-pieces

For coaches and players it is important to identify the roles of the players within the team framework and how they dovetail to achieve the object of the game – which is to score goals and to prevent your opponents from scoring (i.e. score more goals than the opposition). The objective here is to deal with tactics under the three categories mentioned above, and to follow the evolution of the game as a whole.

TEAM FORMATIONS

Team formations basically set out where players are positioned on the field, on the general principle of keeping to a "shape". Although all football should ideally be free-flowing and full of innovation, none the less all successful teams have had in common a large measure of discipline, enabling the players to maintain the formation devised by the manager or coach.

As time has gone on, more and more systems have evolved since the game was first organized in the nineteenth century. In those days there was little or no method employed to bring players into the game in intricate playing formations because there were no clearly defined positions. Just as children who are not conditioned to play "small-sided" games, or to stick to positions, will follow the ball all over the field in great

numbers, so the game was played in its earliest days. Individual skills, particularly the art of dribbling, tended to predominate.

Gradually, as the game became more sophisticated, greater use was made of the offside Law. This was borrowed from rugby football and stemmed from the influence of the Public Schools, where most football was played. At that time the offside provision applied whenever the ball was passed to a player who was in front of the ball, irrespective of how many opponents he had in front of him. It was not uncommon for eight of the team to attack the opposition goal, leaving the goalkeeper with two down field, one of whom would be a defender and the other a "half-back", so named because he was half attacker, half defender. At that point the first real formation was created – in effect 1–1–1–8 – but within a short space of time one of the forwards was pulled back to a wing-half position, thus making it 1–1–2–7.

Soon, however, the influence of Scottish football started to make itself felt. Because their game had a set of Laws which were commonly adhered to, they were able to vary their methods of play and evolve a system of passing to supplement the dribbling. Their leading club, Queens Park, promoted the passing game to such an extent that instead of the mad scramble upfield, the ball was spread across and along the whole of the pitch.

Owing to this new method of play it was necessary to pull another attacker back and spread the game a little wider, thus creating a 1–2–2–6 formation; and once it was established that the ball could be moved across field and from one side to

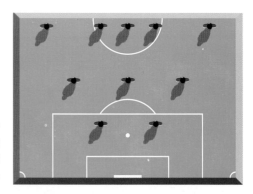

The "2–3–5" formation, used at the turn of the century.

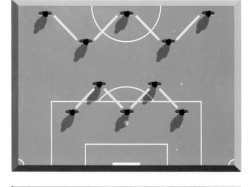

The "WM" formation, which developed out of the 1925 change in the offside law.

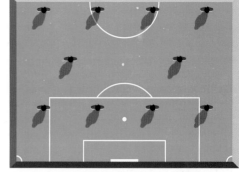

Brazil's 1958 World Cup winning "4–2–4" system.

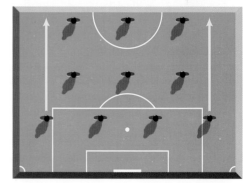

The "4–3–3" stystem, used by Brazil in the 1970 World Cup.

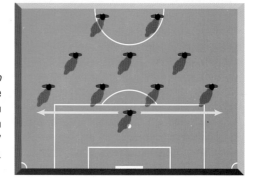

Italy's *catenaccio* defensive formation with the introduction of the "sweeper" or *libero*.

another, radical changes took place until eventually the "WM" formation was evolved, as hereafter mentioned.

In 1866 the offside law was modified to stipulate that a player was now onside if he had at least three opponents (one of whom could be the goalkeeper) between himself and the opposing goal-line at the time the ball was passed. Thus it was now possible to pass the ball forward instead of always worrying about trying to pass it back. The use of a system based loosely on a 1–2–3–5 formation, with a combination of dribbling and passing, brought a spate of goals. However, in the early twentieth century the Newcastle defender Bill McCracken organized his defence in such a way that everyone moved up at his given signal to create a trap into which the opposition attackers readily fell. Attacks were therefore killed off at the half way line and some games were even stopped as often as every two minutes. Like every successful tactic it was copied slavishly by other teams, and as a result pressure grew for a change in the Laws to stop the game being destroyed as a spectacle.

In 1925 the law-making International Board put forward and passed proposals to change the offside law so that the number of opponents required to be between the attacker and the goal line was reduced from three to two. The effect was dramatic: whereas in the previous season a total of 4,700 goals had been scored across the board in the Football League, the total now rose to 6,373. By judicious use of the attacking centre-half and astute wing play with crosses for the striking centre-forward, goals abounded. In the 1926–27 season George Camsell scored 59, which was then a record, bettered immediately the following season by Dixie Dean, who scored 60 goals (a record which incidentally still stands). The ability of the centre-forwards in the air and the massive number of goals they were scoring soon caused consternation amongst defenders, but it was not long before the best combination of captain and manager found a remedy.

Charlie Buchan, once the most expensive player in football, got together with his Arsenal manager, Herbert Chapman, to devise a system whereby the centre-half, who had previously lined up alongside the other two half-backs, was taken out of that midfield line and put into the back line between the full-backs. Although initially Jack Butler was drafted into the position, it was not until Herbie Roberts became the regular centre-half (or really centre-back) that the "stopper" position was cemented into place. Having achieved that success, Chapman then withdrew two of his attackers into more midfield positions and, with a system of 1–3–2–2–3, the "WM" formation was now complete. It was so named because if you looked from the back it formed a W and if you looked from the front it formed an M. That was a system adopted not only in Britain but in much of Europe. This owed much to Arsenal's achievements, as they rapidly became the most successful side in English football, winning five First Division titles and two FA Cups during the 1930s. Additionally, with English coaches and English teams travelling abroad, the system became universally recognized, although in a number of European countries it was not adopted. Hungary, Austria and Switzerland had other ideas.

TEAM TACTICS

In Austria, led by Hugo Meisl, the national side continued to play with the attacking centre-half. In Italy Vittorio Pozzo encouraged his teams to attack with mobility, using long passing and an adaptation of the attacking centre-half. Switzerland developed a system known as "Le Verrou", meaning "the bolt". This was based on the attacking centre-half and the full-backs defending the centre, and the wing-halves defending the wings. One of the inside-forwards was pulled back to play alongside the centre-half, but one of the full-backs played behind the other in a role similar to that of the sweeper, as we know it today. Because centre-forwards were so revered, the aim was to double mark the opposition's No. 9. As with many sweeper systems, utilized correctly it enabled other members of the team to attack more readily and with freedom.

Just prior to a spate of innovations, the Italians moved from their attacking centre-half system to a similar but more restrictive bolt system. Coaches such as Alfredo Foni, Nereo Rocco and – above all – Helenio Herrera perfected a catenaccio system in which the sweeper was placed behind the line of three or four defenders, with no serious attacking pretensions. His job was merely to stop anyone who got through the line of defenders in front of him. Whereas the Swiss bolt system lined up 1–1–3–2–4, the Italian system's line-up was 1–1–3–3–3 or 1–1–3–4–2 or 1–1–4–3–2.

One of the coaches who had left England and created enormous changes abroad was Jimmy Hogan. As time went on, he moved his footballing bandwagon from Austria through Italy to Hungary, and in the 1950s the Hungarian side were vastly effective. They became the first foreign side to win on English soil and in the process revolutionized football in Britain. Whereas with the cult of the centre-forward the man in the No.9 shirt was regarded as the all-important striker, the Hungarians changed the system completely. They withdrew their No.9, Nandor Hidegkuti, towards the midfield, and played with two wingers and two strikers wearing traditional inside-forward numbers. In addition, they withdrew one of the wing-halves to a central defensive position and created a 1–4–2–4 system.

Although the Hungarians' only international prize was the 1952 Olympic gold medal, they dominated European playing and thinking. Meanwhile, their "4–2–4" system was being simultaneously – and independently – refined by the magnificent Brazilians, who won three out of four World Cups between 1958 and 1970. Later they cautiously revised it by pulling left-winger Mario Zagalo back into midfield, thus creating a 1–4–3–3 formation.

In between the Brazilians' successes in the World Cup Sir Alf Ramsey devised a new English system which relied heavily on strong midfield running, with "over-lapping" by the full-backs since the wingers had been subsumed into midfield. While most sides in England, after the revolutionary examples of Hungary and Brazil, played a 4–2–4 system, Ramsey withdrew his wingers into a tactical formation that read 1–4–4–2. His club side Ipswich won the First Division title and subsequently England went on to win the World Cup. Ever since, English sides and a good many Continental teams have adopted his 4–4–2 system, and wing play has suffered as a result, almost to the point of extinction. There have been calls for the return of the WM formation, which effectively was a 3–3–4 system, but many sides are unwilling to attempt it, preferring to restrict themselves to 4–3–3 or 4–4–2.

One country who almost won the World Cup twice with what they termed "total football" were Holland. They attempted to attack from all departments of the field. When their defenders were attacking it was the job of the attackers to defend. Unfortunately this, more than any other system, relies upon having a squad of exceptionally intelligent and technically gifted players who can both attack and defend. It could be said that Holland's ultimate failure resulted not from any weakness of their defenders in attack but from their attackers' weakness in defence. As a result very few club teams or countries have ever dared follow the spectacular Dutch experiment.

In modern football, the English fan may see any number of combinations. While 4–4–2 still predominates, several clubs and their managers have finally caught up with the economically effective system pioneered most successfully by Argentina at the 1986 World Cup finals.

Coach Carlos Bilardo, appreciating that opponents used only two full-time central strikers, reasoned that defensive security could be maintained by the use of two central man-markers plus a sweeper. That left his fullbacks free to push up into what then became a five-man midfield – stifling the opposition's creative efforts.

Of course, few teams have a Diego Maradona or Jorge Valdano to add the world-class cutting edge in attack.

But, throughout the 1990s, the logic of a three-man defence has proved irresistible and has been adopted wholesale in Germany before infiltrating the tactically conservative English league game.

Experiments with other modern formations have included the Soviet, then Russian, national sides in the late 1980s and 1990s. Valeri Lobanovsky, their scientifically studious coach in the 1980s, employed a sweeper behind a four-man defence and a four-man midfield. Few opponents could ever break them down; on the other hand, a defence-heavy system meant the Soviets depended to an almost unfair extent on the lone striker – be it Oleg Blokhin or Oleg Protasov – to capitalize on the few counter-attacks which opened his way to goal.

Such a method was adapted by Tottenham in England under David Pleat, for whom Clive Allen scored 40 goals in one season as a lone raider. Later, under Osvaldo Ardiles, Spurs followed the 'diamond formation' fashion which was designed to assist the four midfield men in creating more space for each other in which to work.

Clearly managers can go on altering all the systems, but it is obviously much easier to produce defensive tactics than attacking ones, and every attempt to score goals by a new formula provokes new methods to defeat it.

The stopper centre-back in England produced a defensive formation of a diagonal/dogleg system. This involved the three backs always keeping in a line, so that, if the right-back went to meet the left-winger, the centre-back – or pivot – tucked in directly behind him and the far full-back tucked in behind him, but slightly straighter to form a shape like a dog's hind leg. When teams played four at the back and the flat back four became prevalent, this encouraged the use of the offside trap, with defenders squeezing up to the halfway line to compress the play into their opponents' half. In this way anyone getting in behind them too quickly would be offside. Modifications of this have seen the two central defenders drop slightly

behind the two full-backs, while in the defensive sweeper system one player will line up behind four others and will then try to pick up the pieces of any ball or player getting through that line of four.

Frequently the defensive choice is between, on the one hand, playing with a sweeper and adopting a man-for-man approach (catenaccio, in which each defender is allocated an attacker, whom he follows all over the pitch) and, on the other, the "zonal" system. In the latter, a player is allocated an area of the pitch and marks anyone who comes into that area. This technique requires a high degree of teamwork, which in turn requires defenders to "pass on" opponents to one another.

RE-STARTS OR SET-PIECES:
CORNERS

Corners are one of three basic set-pieces, the others being free-kicks and throw-ins. It is estimated that more than 50 per cent of all goals come from such dead-ball situations.

Corners fall into three types. The one hit to the far post; the one swung into the near post; and the short corner. For many years the English game favoured the long ball to the far post, where an attacker would attempt to head home – a somewhat basic ploy. In the 1960s, Spurs dominated with the short corner, with Danny Blanchflower passing to Tommy Harmer, who would run forward and either draw defenders or chip the ball long or short. Finally there was the in-swinging corner kick adopted by Wimbledon in their rise from non-League football to the Premier League. Arsenal have also used this tactic, particularly in their 1989 Championship success. Brian Marwood would swing the ball into the near-post area, where Steve Bould would flick it on, and again a team-mate coming in late would score from directly in front of goal or at the far post. This tactic can also be used without the flick-on, as when Jackie Milburn headed home for Newcastle against Manchester City in the 1955 FA Cup Final.

The near-post corner is one of the hardest of set plays to defend against. Here, in the 1994 European Cup-winners' Cup semi-final, the Paris St. Germain corner-taker (1) is aiming at David Ginola (2). Two Arsenal defenders, Paul Merson (in front) and Lee Dixon (formerly guarding post) are trying to cut off the danger. However, Merson goes to the edge of the goal area and the ball is hit over him to Ginola, now unmarked. Dixon rushes out to cover the danger, but is not quick enough. Ginola heads the ball just inside the near post as goalkeeper David Seaman, trying to cover the spot Dixon left, helps the ball over the line and PSG score their equalizer.

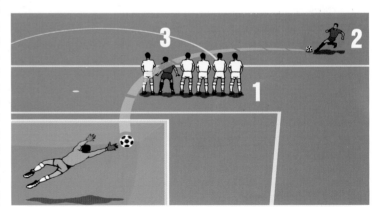

As was proved at the 1990 World Cup in Italy, direct free-kicks around the edge of the opponents' penalty area always pose a threat. Michel's second goal in his hat-trick for Spain against South Korea was a fine example of the dead-ball kicker's art. Faced with a free-kick 20 metres out, just to the left of the goal, the South Koreans lined up the wall (1). With a swerving shot, Michel (2) curved the ball over the wall – aided by a ducking team-mate (3) – into the top corner of the net.

FREE-KICKS

The opportunity of scoring from free-kicks depends on their distance from goal and whether they are direct or indirect. West Ham, in particular, developed the near-post free-kick, and it worked with great success in the 1966 World Cup Final, when Bobby Moore curled a near-post kick for Geoff Hurst to head the equaliser against West Germany. The Brazilians have always been noted for their long-range shooting and deliberate attempts at goal from free-kicks. Pele, Garrincha and Rivileno used them to score spectacular goals in the 1966 and 1970 World Cup competitions. Lately Ronald Koeman scored for Holland against England in a World Cup qualifier with a clever chip from a twice-taken free-kick from just outside the area, and has scored regularly with tremendous long-range efforts for the Spanish club, Barcelona, including the winner in the 1992 European Cup Final.

THROW-INS

Throw-ins which carry into the penalty area can be designed either to create a "flick-on" or a direct header or shot at goal. A move used by the 1961 "double"-winning Spurs side involved Dave Mackay throwing the ball to the head of Bobby Smith, who stood on the goal-line. Smith would then head sideways for a colleague to score. If a defender reached the ball first, Spurs usually won at least a corner, but quite often they created a goal. Some of the most spectacular long throws involved Cliff Holton of Arsenal throwing the ball almost to the penalty spot for Doug Lishman to head past keeper Bobby Brown in a prestigious friendly match in 1951, Simon Stainrod throwing to Bob Hazell for Terry Fenwick's equalizer for Queen's Park Rangers against Tottenham in the 1982 FA Cup Final, and Ian Hutchinson's long throw, inadvertently headed on by Jack Charlton, which led to David Webb's 1970 FA Cup winning goal for Chelsea in their replay against Leeds United.

This diagram, of the only goal in the Cameroon vs. Argentina 1990 World Cup game, illustrates the importance of heading the ball downwards. Argentina concede a free-kick on Cameroon's left wing and the kick (1) is driven hard across goal. Makanaky (2) sticks out a boot and deflects the ball high towards the far post. François Omam Biyik (3a), covered by two defenders sprints to the far post and leaps brilliantly to actually get his header at goal (3b). The defender at the far post plays Omam Bikik onside and makes no attempt to go for the ball, it being too high for him. Omam Biyik's header is not particularly powerful, but because he heads the ball down Nery Pumpido in the Argentina goal is surprised and cannot make the easy save.

England's goal after 27 seconds of their 1982 World Cup match with France came as a result of three important factors. First, the throw-in taken by Steve Coppell (1) is long. Second, Terry Butcher rises above the two French defenders and team-mate Paul Mariner all contesting the ball level with the goal area seven metres from goal (2) and he heads the ball behind him. Third, and most important, Bryan Robson (3A, 3B and 3C) makes a late run into the penalty area. Robson gambles that Butcher (who is a little taller than the three players with whom he is jumping) will win the ball, and it pays off as he is alone (3C) when the flick-on reaches him four metres from goal. Robson acrobatically scores with the goalkeeper coming off his line too late to stop the shot. The defender just inside the penalty area starts to follow Robson's run (3a), but stops as he does not think Robson will reach the ball, so the England captain's chance is easier than it should have been.

EQUIPMENT

When football first took root in England during the 1870s, it was a game for the upper classes, played by gentlemen to a strict amateur code. Early photographs of teams such as Old Harrovians and Hampstead Heathens show players dressed more like Little Lord Fauntleroy than serious sportsmen. But with the advent of professionalism a decade or so later, working-

class teams from the north of England soon started to dominate the game, bringing with them a demand for cheap, basic clothing. Even in today's highly commercialized game, a complete football strip remains relatively inexpensive when compared to other sports, explaining the huge appeal and rapid growth of football in Third World countries.

Today, well over a hundred years after the beginning of professional football, many aspects of the football kit still look remarkably familiar in basic design. The materials may have changed, but the function remains the same — as the following pages will demonstrate.

1994

The shirt worn by modern Swedish internationals demonstrates the influence of commercialism on design. The three stripes have little to do with aesthetics, nothing to do with tradition and everything to do with the manufacturers' branding.

One of football's greatest appeals is its simplicity. Law IV of the Laws of the Game merely states: "the basic compulsory equipment of a player shall consist of a jersey or shirt, shorts, stockings, shinguards and footwear. A player shall not wear anything which is dangerous to another player. The goalkeeper shall wear colours which will distinguish him from the other players and the referee."

1909

The first football shirts were made of thick wool, but cotton soon proved to be cheaper and more practical. This shirt, worn by Manchester United right-back George Stacey in the FA Cup Final, shows the original lace-up collar design which briefly resurfaced in recent seasons.

1911

Two years on and buttons have replaced laces in this England trialist's shirt. The original England kit for the 1872 game against Scotland was white jerseys, dark blue caps and white knickerbockers.

1948

The shirt worn by Charlie Mitten for Manchester United against Blackpool in the FA Cup Final bears a remarkable resemblance to modern day rugby shirts, with thick cuffs and button-up collars.

1960

Thick woollen goalkeeper's jersey as worn by Dominguez of Real Madrid. It wasn't until 1913 that goalkeepers had to wear distinctive colours. Until then they wore the same shirt as their teammates and were distinguished by a cap.

1982

The development of synthetics from the 1960s signalled the end of cotton. This Brazilian shirt of light nylon is specially designed for maximum ventilation to cope with the heat and altitude of South American football.

1992

Multi-coloured, synthetic goalkeeper's shirt, worn by Denmark's Peter Schmeichel in the 1992 European Championship Final. Less than ten years previously the rules stated that goalkeepers could wear only green, yellow or white. How times change!

Equipment

1958

(Top right) *The arrival of
the modern football boot.
Superior quality leather
was used in a design cut
under the ankles in these
boots belonging to Man-
chester United's David
Pegg. The specially
designed leather soles
allowed for screw-in
moulded nylon studs.*

1936

(Below) *Arsenal socks,
made of thick wool and
weighing a couple of
pounds each when wet!
During the Second World
War, in Britain such items
of football equipment
were available only with
clothing coupons allocat-
ed by the Board of Trade.*

1994

(Bottom right) *Millions
are spent on the research
and manufacture of boots,
and the results are plain to
see. Today's top quality
boots are usually made of
kangaroo leather with
aluminium studs and
moulded plastic soles.*

208

The changing face of football is demonstrated by the way boots have developed. Manufacturing is now a huge industry, generating millions of pounds on the back of improved scientific and technical developments.

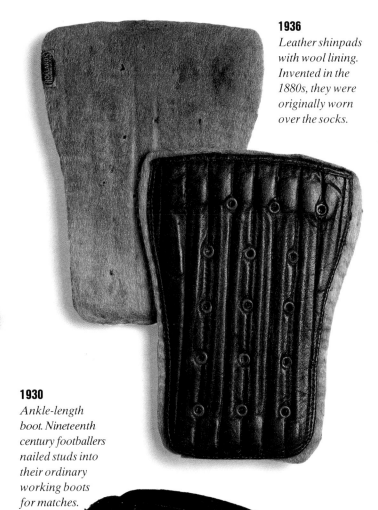

1936
Leather shinpads with wool lining. Invented in the 1880s, they were originally worn over the socks.

1972
Stylo Matchmaker boots as worn by George Best. Possibly seeking to reflect the image of the wearer rather than provide solid protection, these look more like a pair of slippers than football boots.

1930
Ankle-length boot. Nineteenth century footballers nailed studs into their ordinary working boots for matches.

1936
Stud-making kit. Using the hand stamp, three circles were removed from a 5 mm thick strip of leather and nailed together to make one stud.

Even ordinary items like footballs and goalkeeper's gloves have changed over the years. Medals and caps change, too, though only the lucky few who win them would know...

1992

Modern day goalkeeper's gloves. Like so many other areas of football kit, these now represent a lucrative market for the manufacturers. Until the mid-1970s, keepers were more than happy with simple cotton gloves.

1968

Captain's armband, as worn by Manchester United's Bobby Charlton during his side's European Cup campaign. They were once worn only in European ties to help the referees identify captains.

1990

Official World Cup ball. Modern balls actually weigh an ounce more than pre-War footballs but seem lighter due to the plastic coating and superior manufacturing techniques that mean virtually no water retention.

1948

FA Cup Final ball with laces. During the previous two finals the ball had burst due to the inferior quality leather that was used shortly after the Second World War.

1961
This cap was won by Dennis Viollet, in a 4–1 victory.

1963
A pennant presented to Manchester United in a friendly played at Old Trafford. It is customary for teams to exchange favours before international matches.

1930
FA Cup winner's medal, won by Arsenal's Jack Lambert in the 2–0 defeat of Huddersfield Town.

1913
One of the seven England caps awarded to Manchester United's George Wall. This earlier cap is a different colour and lacks the embroidery and tassel.

1958
Although the white ball had come into official use in 1951, the brown ball continued to dominate for another 20 years. The lacing had now been replaced by stitched panels, saving dedicated headers of the ball too many headaches.

1931
Championship winners' medal awarded to Arsenal forward Jack Lambert. Players no longer have to appear in a specific number of games to win one.

SOCCER CULTURE

Football supporters are as much a part of football as the players themselves. Without them, there would be no professional game. It would cease to exist. Football needs its supporters in order to survive.

Soccer still looks for its largest single source of revenue to the fans who flood into the stadia – though how long this may continue is open to question in an age of multi-million TV contracts, sponsorship, corporate hospitality, merchandising and advertising.

But even those commercial undertakings depend on one common denominator: that ever since the second half of the 19th century, people have been prepared to pay to watch soccer. The devotion to soccer is universal. It is – by far – the biggest spectator sport in the world, uniting men, women and children from all walks of life, and from nations whose social and political ideologies may conflict most harshly.

This chapter examines the culture of football supporters and considers how the game has catered for them over the years. From the early days of standing on vast open terraces to the modern game, with executive boxes and satellite television, football has held a unique appeal.

Vast crowds now travel long distances to watch their teams in action and, belatedly, clubs are starting to appreciate their importance. In the United Kingdom, facilities are being improved, and watching is now becoming a more pleasant experience. This is because fans will no longer accept second-rate conditions while being asked to pay ever larger sums of money for the privilege of watching their side.

The authorities' slow awakening of the supporters' value is leading to a better relationship between the corridors of power and the stadium gangways. Only while that relationship improves can the game expect to continue to grow and prosper.

A WORKING-CLASS GAME

Football, for much of the century, was considered the game of the working classes. Once the game had been codified by the universities and public schools in the middle of the last century it was quickly popularized among the common man because it did not discriminate between the haves and have-nots. It was a recreational and spectator pursuit which was readily accessible to all, not merely the well-off. And it was that welcoming outlook which attracted so many people.

As the game grew in the early 1900s, men would spend all week working in blue-collar jobs, and then either play themselves or congregate on the terraces on a Saturday afternoon. The development of Wednesday half-day closing in the

SAMBA SOCCER *Brazilian fans celebrate a victory during the 1986 World Cup*

High Street led to the proliferation of many popular Wednesday league competitions for amateurs to contest and support at amateur levels up and down the country.

Soon Saturday on the terraces became the traditional meeting place where men could lose themselves for 90 minutes and escape the pressures of everyday life. Football was a man's game then, both on and off the pitch.

But what was it really like for the football supporter of those times? Not for those hardy souls the luxury of all-seater, covered stadiums with excellent toilet and refreshment facilities. Times were hard and the conditions reflected those times. Huge wide open terraces were the norm and biting winds and rain often made watching decidedly unpleasant. There was none of the protection that fans today take for granted, but the public still turned up in their thousands as the game developed into the biggest spectator sport in the world.

For a few old pence, a man could enjoy an afternoon's entertainment with his friends and they flocked into grounds all over the country.

It is estimated that 250,000 people crammed into Wembley to try to watch the 1923 FA Cup Final between Bolton and West Ham. Perhaps it was unfortunate for the FA, who had switched the game from Stamford Bridge when the construction of Wembley finished a year earlier than planned, that West Ham were one of the finalists. The authorities, used to the smaller crowds who had attended finals at Chelsea's home, clearly felt that Wembley's capacity would be sufficient. But the Hammers – as events would prove – were one of the biggest draws of those times and practically the whole of the East End wanted to see the game.

Huge attendances were not unusual in the years between the wars. On February 12, 1938, 75,031 people crammed into The Valley to watch Charlton take on Aston Villa in an FA Cup fifth-round tie. Never again will British football see a crowd like that at a domestic game, other than for cup finals at Wembley.

Indeed, when The Valley re-opened in December 1991 after being closed for nearly seven years, it was with a capacity of just 7,600 all-seated, which will eventually rise to around 16,000.

Not only were the grounds different, so were the people. It was common to see fathers entering grounds with their young sons, a feature that is now, thankfully, beginning to return. But it was easy, then. Football stadiums were considered safe places, far removed from the ugly violence which beset the British and European game in the 1970s and 1980s. Fans supported their local teams and that was all. Fighting for its own sake would not have occurred to them and the sights and sounds of the stadiums were far removed from those we know today.

Community singing, brass bands and rattles were once the norm where now crude chanting reflects a change in society which has left football the poorer. Clubs had their "wags" on the terraces – jokers who were the forerunners of today's fanzine wits. The humour was sharp but not malicious, and visiting teams were treated sportingly.

Perhaps the best time to be a football fan was in the 1960s. Certainly those who grew up in those times speak fondly of the era. Britain as a whole was on the up and the mood of the people reflected that. Nowhere was it more evident than on Merseyside. The area boasted The Beatles, the biggest thing ever to hit the music scene, and it also boasted Liverpool, about to be the biggest thing ever to hit domestic football. Liverpool Football Club, under the management of Bill Shankly, was set for a period of unprecedented success and there was no better place to watch football than on the Kop.

Television pictures of the day have captured forever the unique atmosphere that was generated by those fans on that particular block of concrete. Tens of thousands of fans singing as one was truly a sight and sound to behold . . . and which the arrival of all-seater stadiums denied the game's next generation.

THE KOP *A last glance at the Anfield terrace stronghold demolished in May 1994*

INVADERS *England fans earned a reputation for violence at home and abroad, but they were also a soft target for hooligans of other nations*

SOCCER TRIBES

Supporters may be the lifeblood of the game but their presence and involvement brings problems of their own. And those problems in recent years have threatened to tear the game apart.

As a competitive sport played between two teams, football will always generate rival opinions and loyalties. And rival opinions and loyalties can lead to trouble.

Football will always create that special kind of rivalry because it is a tribalistic game. Not in a malevolent or evil way, but by its very nature. Supporters of one particular team become their own tribe, with their own identity, and repel anyone who threatens it. When supporters travel away to watch their team, they are bonded together even more closely. It's as simple as that. There's no

malice intended – or at least, not usually, not among the real fans.

Most of the time the banter between rival fans is good-natured and limited to exchanging chants from opposing ends of the ground. Sadly though, particularly during the 1970s and 1980s, this rivalry occasionally spilled over into mindless violence. There was no excuse for some of the sickening behaviour witnessed at grounds around the world, but it took a long time for the authorities to bring the problem under control.

The disease has been seen worldwide but English fans developed the worst hooligan reputation for the manner in which they exported their terrace and street violence. Partly this was because the culture of the travelling fan is much more widely accepted in a comparatively small country

such as England than in, say, Spain, Italy or France.

When European football arrived with increasingly easy foreign travel facilities, so the disease travelled too and the problem has not been confined to English football followers alone. The 1988 European Championship finals in Germany, and those in Sweden in 1992, were marred by violent clashes between rival supporters. English fans were sometimes caught in the middle and there was a feeling that they had become victims of their own reputation. Certainly gangs among the Dutch and Germans took great delight in trying to prove that they had the "hardest fans in football".

Sadly the disease has sometimes led to tragedy. The 1985 European Cup Final in Brussels will always be

remembered as the Heysel Disaster, the night 39 Juventus fans lost their lives trying to escape a terrace charge by Liverpool supporters. No one who was present or saw those pictures will ever forget the terror that was wreaked on that fateful night in Belgium. No sporting event can be worth such a price and the scenes shocked and sickened the world.

As a result of that shameful night, English teams spent five years in European exile, first withdrawn and then banned from international club competition – as much to protect innocent citizens in continental towns and cities as punishment.

The situation provoked calls in Parliament for drastic measures of control. The Government threatened to ban the England national team and moves were made to introduce an ID card scheme which would make it easy to spot – and do something about – the hooligans. The proposal caused uproar among genuine fans who considered it an infringement of civil liberties.

The move eventually proved unworkable and was quietly forgotten though many clubs did undertake tighter control of membership and season ticket arrangements in an effort to combat hooliganism.

The result was the turning of a corner: the game is no longer blighted in such measure by the terrace thugs and, for the first time, football is beginning to think in terms of full-family entertainment – catering for female as well as male spectators. But the game never dare lapse into complacency. Tighter crowd security does not mean hooligan violence has been eradicated. A chilling reminder was witnessed in Dublin in 1995, when the Ireland v England "friendly" had to be abandoned after less than half an hour because of trouble fomented by England followers.

PROGRAMMES AND FANZINES

One of the biggest changes down the years has been in the development of club programmes. In dim and distant days gone by, they consisted of nothing more than a single sheet of paper containing the team line-ups and a few advertisements. At the turn of the century, they would sell at around one old penny. Now, they are glossy brochures which retail at £1.50 or more just for a normal League fixture. As for the "brochures" which accompany major internationals and Cup finals, the cost goes spiralling up to £6. That was how much supporters of Chelsea and Middlesbrough were asked to pay for the programme at the 1997 FA Cup Final.

As programmes became, more and more, vehicles for the football establishment's commercial, promotional face, so the arrival of the fanzine became inevitable. Fans had become increasingly disillusioned by the "everything in the garden is rosy" outlook of club programmes and their growing demand for their own voice within the game led to a nationwide movement to secure outlets for independent comment. Generally witty and irreverent, the fanzines became a vehicle in which the fans could express their honest – frequently caustic – opinions of the people running "their" clubs and "their" game. The days of supporters accepting everything their clubs told them are long gone and fanzines have played an important role in the mobilisation of terrace opinion on issues such as bond schemes and the redevelopment of stadia.

TERRACE SOUNDS

Viewing the old newsreel television pictures of supporters in the 1930s and 1940s, it is hard to associate them with today's modern game. Cloth caps and overcoats as far as the eye could see with wooden rattles providing the most distinguishable sounds of the games gone by. Wooden and heavy, they would be twirled around the air to make that distinctive, ratchet sound that was unique to football grounds. There are modern equivalents, such as the klaxon horn, but the daddy of all football instruments was that old wooden rattle.

Not that the boys and men who twirled them would recognize today's terrace sounds as a development of the same culture. The community singing, which now lives on only through the moving relic of "Abide With Me" before the FA Cup Final, has been replaced by repetitive chants with no more stirring lyrics than "Here we go! Here we go! Here we go!"

Some clubs' fans have kept their link with past traditions alive. Bristol Rovers fans sing "Goodnight, Irene," Birmingham City supporters still persist with "Keep right on to the end of the road", but the street culture of the 1960s and 1970s led to many clubs replacing their traditional songs with pop-led creations, few of which lasted more than a season or two.

Of course, "You'll never walk alone", has surged and inspired several generations of players at Liverpool and served the community anew in sad circumstances in 1989, when a new recording by the Merseyside singer, Gerry Marsden, raised thousands of pounds for the Hillsborough disaster fund.

Many of the other modern terrace sounds, however, have done the game a disservice. "Industrial language" echoed through the traditional shouts of encouragement and criticism and the increasing influence of black players met volleys of racial abuse, often quite illogically aimed by fans whose own teams included black players.

In the 1990s, as part of English football's drive to clean up its act and raise the class profile of the game, stringent attempts were launched to police bad language and eject the louts whose foul-mouth abuse hindered the drive to attract a family audience.

The message for the 21st century is that attending a match should be an enjoyment and that the traditional humour can still flourish.

SCARVES AND COLOURS

Wearing your club colours is a trait which is, largely, unique to football. It's become a tradition to go to games wearing replica shirts, scarves and badges to let everyone know who you support.

A down side has been the criticism heaped upon sportswear manufacturers and clubs – Manchester United having been a prime target of consumer groups. Both sides of the industry have been accused of exploiting young fans (and their parents) with frequent changes of colours and styles. Nor has the Football Association, responsible for the England strip, been exempt from criticism.

ROLIGANS *Danish fans, so-called because of the derivation from a word meaning "peace"*

FACE IN THE CROWD *Courtesy of a giant screen, video technology brings the teams to the fans at Arsenal's Highbury stadium*

CHANGING FACE OF FOOTBALL

In the approach to the year 2000, professional football is changing radically. Money talks. Football is big business which needs to generate serious income and is targeting the "middle class" as a more lucrative audience.

That shift in emphasis has brought increasing demands on the game; people want better value for their money. Thus clubs are learning to listen to supporters' views and act on them – particularly now that many more leisure interests are competing for the public's support and cash.

For too long, football's rulers remained oblivious to the reasons why the public might prefer to spend its time and money watching other sports in a civilized atmosphere rather than huddling together on a cold terrace in the pouring rain. Clubs now realize that their facilities must be improved if they expect to continue to attract the crowds their budgets demand.

Europe has led the way – proof is to be seen in the superb stadiums in Italy, Germany and Spain – but it took the pressure of disaster and legislation before English football finally got the message.

After the Hillsborough Disaster in 1989, in which 95 Liverpool fans died at an FA Cup semi-final against Nottingham Forest, the Taylor Report deemed that all higher-division clubs must make their grounds all-seater.

This was obviously going to take time, as well as vast sums of money, but it was a development which was long overdue – despite many fans' initial opposition that the removal of terraces would take something away from the game and lead to a more muted atmosphere.

A significant by-product is that, with so many all-seater stadiums available, England could once more compete to host major international events – starting in 1996 with the European Championship finals whose successful staging was followed by an application to host the World Cup finals in 2006.

Indeed, after an pre-event inspection of the eight stadiums designated for use at the 1996 European Championship, UEFA's stadium chief, Ernie Walker, said: "City for city, England now has the best football stadiums in the world."

EXECUTIVE BOXES

Despite initial terrace resistance, executive boxes generate huge revenue to help keep prices down elsewhere within grounds. Perhaps the image of supporters in pin-stripe suits smoking cigars behind glass panels is alien to the football tradition, but football today is a branch of the entertainment industry and needs its high-income supporters. Corporate entertainment is a thriving business and companies are prepared to pay substantial sums of money to wine and dine potential clients at top sporting events.

INDOOR STADIUMS

When England played Germany in the Pontiac Silverdome near Detroit in the US Cup in June 1992, it represented a revolutionary new move in world soccer. For the first time, a major international was being played on artificially-grown grass in an indoor stadium. With science and technology becoming more and more advanced in the cause of sport, the numbers of fully-covered stadiums will increase. If it is possible to recreate the same playing conditions as outdoors, then it must be a logical step forward. The indoor stadiums would mean no more games falling victim to extreme weather conditions, and no more tedious midfield battles played out on mud-bath pitches in the middle of winter. So-called "plastic pitches" were tried, without conspicuous success, but the fully-covered stadium is something the elements cannot touch.

VIDEO SCREENS

For years, clubs have been seeking ways to encourage supporters to arrive early for matches and one solution is the "entertainment package". Pre-match entertainment, in various guises, has been tried by just about everybody, with varying degrees of success. What better way to keep fans happy before kick-off than by showing action on giant video screens? Arsenal were the first club in Britain to get in on the act and such huge screens have proved popular with fans. Attitudes still vary from country to country, however, on the replaying of important match incidents.

FAMILY AUDIENCES

Clubs are now beginning to cater for the whole family on match-days. With ideas ranging from family stands to the introduction of crèches, the English game is doing its best to appeal to a brand new audience. Clubs have realized – not before time – that if a father can sit with his wife and son or daughter in an area just for them, then he is more likely to take them along.

Family stands boast a two-fold attraction: they offer reduced admission prices compared with other areas of the ground, and they are safe places from where to watch. The youngsters who now take their place in those stands are the fans of tomorrow. Clubs should do everything possible to keep them.

POMPOM PAGEANTRY *Brazilian fans were as colourful as the nation they followed at World Cup '94*

SAMBA SOCCER

Pele once described football as "the beautiful game". And that sums up Samba Soccer. The Brazilians are the best exponents of it, both on the pitch and off it. The fans who play their part in Samba Soccer certainly know how to enjoy themselves.

Whether their team is winning or losing, you can rely on the Brazilians to give you a show. The Samba beat of the lone drummer is always heard from the terraces, where the fans treat the event as a carnival. Brightly coloured clothing and frantic dance routines are all part of the culture of Samba Soccer.

That culture has been adapted by the rest of the world as fans seek to reap maximum enjoyment from sporting events. A world away from the snarling and intimidating attitude of the hooligans, it's a practice which should be encouraged. Thus Spain's national team was accompanied all over the world in the 1980s and 1990s by the familiar figure of the

drummer known only as Manolo; thus Holland's total football was played out to the vibrant, strident tones of a brass band; and the medium of television allowed fans of different countries to swap their favourite tune chants.

The Danish fans added to the fun not only with their enthusiasm for their nation's cause but by introducing the practice of face-painting. Now the sight is commonplace at football grounds around the world, even in the exciting new J. League in Japan.

It seems that everyone, from the youngest fan to the oldest, has been caught up in the craze of decorating themselves in the colours of club and country. The World Cup and European Championship have now become a pageant of facial colour as thousands of fans take their places proudly coloured in their country's flag for the whole world to see. Some have even gone as far as to dye their hair in the appropriate colours in

order to demonstrate their allegiance.

"Football watching" around the world can be very different to watching in Britain. Even the English love of the game pales in comparison with the demonstrations of passion to be seen in, say, Italy.

In Italy, football is a religion. Everyone it seems is a supporter, right across the social and financial divides, and that has helped establish the Italian league championship as the world's No 1. Supporters of the top Italian clubs have the best of everything. The stadiums are magnificent and so are the facilities. So, too, are the prices. That is why the Italian clubs compete regularly to sign the game's greatest players: they learned long ago that their passionate fans demand value for money. The fact that Italy, until recently, boasted the highest average top division attendances in the world – around 30,000-plus on average – proves that such a philosophy works.

SCANDALS & DISASTERS

Football has always had its seamy side and its tragic side. With so much money involved there was bound to be financial crookedness, and with such large and passionate crowds there were bound to be disasters.

SOCCER BABYLON

Ever since professionalism transformed an English public school pastime towards the end of the last century, the game's underworld has been hard at work refining its activities. For years, the little tax-free extras or inducements took the form of "boot money" – a few notes left surreptitiously in a player's boot – but in the era of the multi-million pound transfer, corruption, feeding on ambition and greed, has embroiled leading chairmen, players and referees, and the new breed of shadowy middlemen, the agents, have devised ever more sophisticated ways of keeping a cut for themselves and their clients, even to the extent of using off-shore tax havens.

In 1993–94 alone European champions Marseille, Italian giants Torino, and leading English clubs Tottenham Hotspur and Arsenal were tainted by the seamy side of the game. At the same time, the growing curse of drug-taking reduced Diego Maradona, one of the greatest players the game has ever seen, to a pathetic figure in the twilight of his career.

Even in the Edwardian era, however, with the Football League in its infancy, the leading lights of the game were already being brought to book for bribery, illegal payments, and match-fixing, either to ensure league placings or to make profit from betting.

Billy Meredith, Manchester City captain and the Wales outside-right, a figure as famous in his day as Matthews, Best or Maradona, was at the heart of British football's first major scandal in 1905 when he was suspended for a season for attempting to bribe the Aston Villa captain with £10 to lose a game as City challenged for the title.

A year earlier, ambitious City had been found guilty of illegal payments to players, but the Meredith case eventually proved catastrophic for the club when he fell out with his employers and informed the FA of widespread financial corruption in the club's affairs. In 1906, seventeen current or former City players were fined, suspended for a year and forbidden to play for the club again because

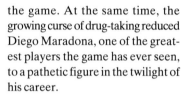

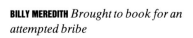
BILLY MEREDITH *Brought to book for an attempted bribe*

MARADONA *His football was sublime but drugs were his downfall and he was arrested for possession in Argentina*

CASH AND CORRUPTION

1891 Maximum £10 signing-on fee introduced.

1900 Maximum wage of £4 introduced in England, but not Scotland.

1900 Burnley goalkeeper Jack Hillman banned for one year for trying to bribe Nottingham Forest to lose. Forest won 4–0, Burnley were relegated.

1904 Second Division Glossop fined £250 for wholesale mismanagement and deception. Four directors suspended for three seasons, secretary censured, six players suspended for three months.

1904 Sunderland fined £250 and directors and secretary suspended for one to three seasons for illegal payments.

1904 Manchester City found to have broken transfer rules involving Glossop players Irvine Thornley and Frank Norgrove. Clubs fined £250, Hyde Road ground shut for two games, five directors suspended and Thornley banned for a season.

1905 Billy Meredith, Manchester City's captain and Welsh international outside-right, banned for a season after attempting to bribe Aston Villa captain Alec Leake towards end of 1904–05 season when City were making a challenge for the championship.

1905 Middlesbrough, who had just paid the first £1,000 transfer fee for Alf Common from Sunderland (three times the previous record), fined £250, 11 of 12 directors suspended until 1908 for illegal payments.

1906 Seventeen current and former Manchester City players fined a total of £900, suspended for six months and banned from playing for the club again after accepting illegal payments. Chairman W. Forrest and manager Tom Maley banned sine die, directors suspended. Players later auctioned by League for £2,600.

1909 George Parsonage of Fulham banned for life after requesting £50 signing-on fee from Chesterfield.

1911 Middlesbrough's respected manager Andy Walker and chairman Thomas Gibson Poole, a prospective MP, banned from football for

---

they had accepted illegal payments.

The whole issue of these payments stemmed from the attempt by the English football authorities to impose limits on wages and signing-on fees. In Meredith's day wages were £4, and the maximum wage, rising to £20, survived until 1961. Within months of its abolition, Fulham were paying England international Johnny Haynes £100 per week. Incredibly, the £10 signing-on fee was abolished in Britain only in 1958, a year after John Charles is reputed to have received £10,000 for joining Juventus.

The system was abused by the majority for years, involving even such famous names as Herbert Chapman, manager of Leeds City when they were thrown out of the League in 1919, and Stanley Matthews, manager of Port Vale when they were expelled, then re-elected in the 1960s.

Meredith exposed the hypocrisy which still survives when he said: "Clubs are not punished for breaking the laws. They are punished for being found out." But the end of the maximum wage did not bring an end to under-the-counter payments in England, which are still widespread and have become an integral part of the transfer system.

Today it is not just the football mandarins clubs and officials have to fear, but an increasingly vigilant taxman. The English can of worms was

opened when Swindon Town were raided in 1990 and manager Lou Macari, the former Scotland and Manchester United player, and chairman Brian Hillier were arrested. The inquiry uncovered illegal payments, petty cash being paid to club officials as perks, and the understating of gate receipts. Macari was acquitted, Hillier jailed for tax fraud.

In 1994 Tottenham were punished with a 12-point deduction, heavy fine and ban from the FA Cup for financial irregularities which had come to light during a power struggle between chairman Alan Sugar and dismissed manager Terry Venables. The punishments were later quashed in the law courts, but the image of the club and game had been seriously damaged.

But the tip of an English iceberg

pales into insignificance beside the bribery and match-fixing scandals affecting Italy and France, as the European club competitions have grown in stature since the 1950s and begun to attract television deals capable of financing some Third World countries. Italy, a country where corruption in public life is little short of endemic, has suffered post-war match-fixing and bribery scandals involving Lazio, Milan, Roma and now Torino, while France's league boom in the 1980s led to problems with the taxman over illegal payments. In 1993 French football was rocked to the core when their first European champions, Marseille, were found to have bought a match to ensure they retained the championship.

MADNESS *Eric Cantona's infamous kung-fu assault on a Crystal Palace fan*

trying to fix home game against local rivals Sunderland. Boro won 1–0.

1919 An example is made. Leeds City expelled from League for making illegal payments.

1924 John Browning, former Scotland player, and Archibald Kyle of Rangers, Blackburn and Airdrie, given 60 days' hard labour for offering Bo'Ness players £30 to fix Second Division match with Lochgelly.

1932 Former Montrose captain Gavin Hamilton given 60 days' jail for offering £40–£50 to Montrose player David Mooney to fix home match against Edinburgh City.

1957 Sunderland fined record £5,000 by Football League for illegal payments to players.

1958 Leyton Orient fined £2,000 for irregularities in accounts.

1965 Everton alleged to have been involved in match-fixing during their 1962–63 championship. No proof.

1965 England's most sensational match-fixing scandal. Ten League professionals found guilty at Nottingham Assizes of match-fixing. Jimmy Gauld, an inside-forward for Charlton, Everton, Plymouth, Swindon and Mansfield between 1955 and 1960, was jailed for four years, the others for terms between four and 15 months. After years of rumours, Gauld had told all for £7,000. Although Gauld was the ringleader, the three most celebrated players among the ten were England players Peter Swan (Sheffield Wednesday) and Tony Kay (Everton, but previously with Wednesday) and their Sheffield Wednesday colleague David Layne.

1965 Kay, Layne and Swan banned from football for life, although after many campaigns the bans were lifted in 1972.

1967 Peterborough United fined £500 and demoted from Third to Fourth Division for illegal payments.

1967 Millwall fined £1,000 for attack on referee by spectators at The Den.

1968 Port Vale fined £4,000 and expelled from League for illegal payments, but re-elected for following season.

1969 Manchester United fined £7,000 for administrative irregularities.

1970 Derby fined £10,000 and barred from Fairs Cup for a year for administrative irregularities.

CLOUD OVER TORINO *A bribery scandal erupted over Torino's (in white vs. Aberdeen) 1991–92 UEFA Cup campaign*

1971 Officials of Arminia Bielefeld found guilty of putting up £90,000 to fix four West German League games.

1973 Wolverhampton Wanderers player Bernard Shaw alleged he was approached to sell a championship deciding game against Leeds in 1972.

1974 The Solti-Lobo Case. Juventus accused of using a go-between, Deszo Solti, to try to bribe Portuguese referee Francisco Marques Lobo, the official for their European Cup semi-final against Derby in 1973.

1974 Italian players accused by Polish opponents of offering money to them on the field to lose a World Cup match in Stuttgart. Italy, needing a draw to stay in the finals, lose 2–1.

1978 Millwall fined £1,500 and have their ground closed for two weeks after crowd trouble during FA Cup tie against Ipswich. Millwall's notorious fans had also caused The Den to be closed in 1934, 1947 and 1950.

1978 Fulham fined £15,000 for illegal payments.

1978 Scotland's top referee John Gordon and linesmen Rollo Kyle and David McCartney suspended by Scottish FA after admitting they accepted presents worth £1,000 from Milan before a UEFA Cup match with Levski Spartak. Milan, fined £8,000 by UEFA, had drawn 1–1 in Bulgaria and won 3–0 at home.

1980 The world's highest paid player, Italian striker Paolo Rossi, is one of more than 30 banned for their part in widespread Italian match-fixing on behalf of an illegal betting ring. Milan and Lazio relegated. Rossi's ban ended just in time for him to lead Italy to their 1982 World Cup victory in Spain.

1983 Derby fined £10,000 by the Football League for poaching manager Roy McFarland from Bradford City.

1983 Tottenham fined £8,000 for illegal payments to Argentine World Cup stars Osvaldo Ardiles and Ricky Villa.

1985 Celtic fined £17,000 by UEFA for crowd trouble at a European Cup-winners' Cup replay against Rapid Vienna at Old Trafford.

1986 UEFA bar Roma from their competitions for a season and president Dino Viola from UEFA activities for four years after he tried to bribe a European Cup referee in a

FALLEN IDOLS *Peter Swan (left) and Tony Kay were gaoled for match-fixing*

semi-final game against Dundee United in 1982. Roma won 3–0, and 3–2 on aggregate, before losing to Liverpool in the Final.

1988 Peterborough fined £2,500 for transfer irregularity.

1988 Hungarian full-back Sandor Sallai and former national team manager Kalman Meszoly are among more than 40 players and officials arrested in match-fixing investigation.

1988 Chelsea fined record £75,000 by FA for serious crowd trouble in play-off against Middlesbrough.

1989 Nottingham Forest manager, Brian Clough, fined £5,000 by FA and banned from touchline for a season for striking a spectator at League Cup tie against QPR.

1989 Wimbledon fined £10,000 for making unauthorized loans to their players.

1989 Bradford City fined £10,000 for poaching manager Terry Yorath from Swansea.

1990 Swindon Town fined £7,500 by FA, former manager Lou Macari £1,000 and censured, chairman Brian Hillier suspended from football for three years after breaching rules by betting on Newcastle vs. Swindon FA Cup tie in January 1988.

1990 Swindon, having been promoted to Division One via play-offs, demoted to Division Three (Division Two on appeal), for irregular payments to players over four years.

1990 FA deduct two points from Arsenal, one from Manchester United and fine both clubs £50,000 after players involved in mass brawl.

1991 League fine Chelsea record £105,000 for illegal payments to three players. A company linked to Chelsea was found to have paid £100,000 over market price for the Scottish home of England defender Graham Roberts, who signed from Rangers.

1991 Diego Maradona arrested in Argentina for possession of drugs. He had just left Italy where he was banned from playing for 15 months after taking cocaine before a Napoli match. He is also given a 14-month suspended sentence by a Naples court for possessing cocaine.

1992 FA fines Vinnie Jones of Wimbledon £20,000 – a record for an individual – for bringing game into disrepute by narrating the Soccer Hard Men video.

1993 League newcomers Barnet fined £25,000 for making irregular payments and warned that any further indiscretion could cost them their League status.

1993 Jean-Jacques Eydelie, Marseille midfielder, arrested and accused of trying to bribe three Valenciennes players to lose league match, six days before the French champions beat Milan to win the European Cup. General manager Jean-Pierre Bernes also charged. An envelope containing £30,000 is dug up in the garden of the mother-in-law of Valenciennes player Christophe Robert.

1993: In the High Court battle over Tottenham Hotspur between Terry Venables and Alan Sugar, evidence is offered suggesting that some managers accept cash "bungs" as part of transfer deals.

1993 UEFA bar Marseille from defending the European Cup over the Valenciennes bribery scandal.

1994 Four directors and five referees accused by federal police of fraud for their alleged involvement in Brazilian match-fixing. The directors included Eduardo Viana, president of the Rio de Janeiro federation, and Eurico Miranda, a director of leading club Vasco da Gama. Former referee Reginaldo Mathias claims match-fixing had been common since 1985.

1994 Bernard Tapie is charged with corruption and ordered to quit as president of Marseille. He is later sentenced to two years in jail, with one suspended, for match-fixing.

1994 Torino are placed under investigation by the Italian fraud squad after being accused of providing prostitutes for match officials in their attempt to win the 1992 UEFA Cup. The club are also alleged to have siphoned off under-the-counter cash from transfers, including £465,000 for the "phantom transfer" of Alessandro Palestro, son of a club secretary and not registered with the club but studying at university.

1995 Malaysian football embroiled in huge bribery scandal in 1994 league season. Dozens of players are arrested, some are sent into internal exile. Australian-born Singapore international Abbas Saad is first to be convicted and fined $36,000.

SEASON OF SLEAZE

The 1994–95 season has gone down in English football history as the "Season of Sleaze" when the game reeled from one unsavoury incident to another.

• *The Sun* newspaper alleged that Southampton and former Liverpool goalkeeper Bruce Grobbelaar took bribes to fix matches. The FA charged him with misconduct. Grobbelaar denied any wrongdoing – as did Wimbledon goalkeeper Hans Segers and Aston Villa forward John Fashanu, who were also questioned by police.

• Arsenal and England striker Paul Merson spent six weeks in a rehabilitation clinic after admitting to cocaine, alcohol and gambling addiction.

• Chelsea fans invaded the pitch after losing to London rivals Millwall in the FA Cup at Stamford Bridge. Mounted police separated brawling fans

• England's friendly international against the Republic of Ireland was abandoned after English hooligans tore up their seats and threw them at spectators below. Wimbledon's Vinnie Jones, a spectator at the match in Dublin was dropped by his club for three matches after biting a reporter's nose in a city hotel bar.

• George Graham was dismissed as Arsenal manager after a Premier League inquiry alleged he received £425,000 in under-the-table transfer payments. He denied any wrongdoing and initiated legal proceedings for wrongful dismissal.

• Chelsea captain Dennis Wise was sentenced to three months in jail after a being found guilty of assaulting a taxi driver. He was released on bail pending an appeal, when the conviction was overturned.

CRYSTAL PALACE v MANCHESTER UNITED

Manchester United's French striker Eric Cantona launched a two-footed, kung-fu-style assault on a taunting Crystal Palace fan – after he had been sent off – at Selhurst Park. He was later suspended by the FA until the end of September 1995 and sentenced by a court to a 120 hours of community service. Upon leaving the court, he said, "When seagulls follow the trawler, it is because they think sardines will be thrown into the sea."

In the aftermath of Cantona's attack, team-mate Paul Ince was charged with common assault by police for attacking another Crystal Palace fan. He was found not guilty at a trial in May 1995.

A Crystal Palace fan died after an incident at a bar five miles from the ground which was hosting the FA Cup semi-final tie between the two teams.

In the FA Cup semi-final replay Darren Patterson (Palace) and Roy Keane (Man Utd) were sent off for fighting – despite public pleas from their managers before the game for the match to be an example of peace and sportsmanship.

SOCCER DISASTERS

Drama and excitement have attracted huge crowds to soccer stadiums around the world, just as ambition and the explosion of international competition have kept the world's airlines busy with teams criss-crossing the oceans and continents. Sadly, but inevitably, the game could not avoid the accompanying disasters which turned sporting events into national and international tragedies. From the Superga air disaster of 1949 to the Zambian air crash in 1993; from the first Ibrox Park disaster in 1902 to the Corsica tragedy more than 90 years later ... sad shadows have been cast over the game.

STADIUM DISASTERS AND PLANE CRASHES

1902: Scotland play out a 1–1 draw with England, largely unaware that 25 fans have been killed and hundreds more injured after wooden planking, 40 feet above the ground, collapses in Ibrox Park's new 20,000-capacity West Stand.

1946: The Burnden Park gates are closed on 65,000 fans before Bolton meet Stoke in a sixth round FA Cup tie, but another 20,000 are milling around outside. Many force their way in and two crush barriers collapse under sheer weight of numbers. Thirty-three die from crush injuries and more than 500 are injured. The match is eventually completed, scoreless and without an interval, Bolton winning 2–0 over the two legs.

1949: The cream of Italian football is wiped out when the plane carrying the Torino team back from a match in Portugal crashes into a hillside at Superga just outside Turin. Eighteen players die, including the bulk of Italy's team led by captain Valentino Mazzola. Journalists, officials and English coach Leslie Lievesley raise the death toll to 31. Torino had won four successive League

BUSBY'S TRAGIC BABES *Manchester United's team in 1957; in February 1958 seven of this team perished at Munich*

titles and were four points clear at the top on the day of the crash. The Torino youth team complete the season and receive the championship trophy.

1958: Manchester United's plane crashes on take-off at snowy Munich airport, killing eight of the famous Busby Babes, three club officials and eight journalists. United are returning from a 3–3 draw with Red Star Belgrade which had earned them a place in the European Cup semi-finals.

1961: A plane crashes into the Las Lastimas mountain, killing 24 members of the Green Cross team on their way from Santiago to Osorno for the Chile Cup play-offs.

1962: In Libreville, Gabon, an international between Congo-Brazzaville and Gabon is halted when a landslide hits the stadium. Nine spectators die and 30 are injured.

1964: The world's worst soccer disaster. In Lima, Peru, 318 people die and another 500 are injured during rioting sparked by a last-minute

Peruvian goal being disallowed in an Olympic tie against Argentina. The goal would have sent Peru to the Tokyo Games. Martial law was in force for 30 days after the game.

1967: Another disallowed goal sparks rioting during a Turkish championship game, and 41 people die with a further 600 injured, many being trampled as they flee the stadium.

Jun 23, 1968: In Buenos Aires at the Monumental Stadium, venue ten years later for the World Cup Final, 74 people die and another 113 are injured

1931 JOHN THOMPSON

Tragedy struck in the Old Firm derby between Rangers and Celtic on September 5, 1931 when Celtic's 23-year-old goalkeeper John Thomson dived at the feet of Rangers' Sam English.

Thomson, who had joined Celtic as a 17-year-old and had already established himself in the Scotland team, was renowned for his dashes off the line to thwart opposing forwards. This time, Thomson did not get up, having fractured his skull. He died five hours later in the local hospital.

Such was his popularity that 30,000 mourners saw his coffin off at Glasgow's Queen Street Station, and 3,000 attended his funeral.

1934 HERBERT CHAPMAN

If ever a man died in harness, it was the great Arsenal manager Herbert Chapman. On New Year's Day, 1934, Arsenal were dominating English football and the envy of the world. They had won the League twice and the Cup once in the previous four seasons under the innovative and tactically astute Chapman, and were top of the League again.

Chapman caught a chill watching a game at Bury, but still decided to go and watch Arsenal's next opponents Sheffield Wednesday the following day. Against doctor's advice, he also travelled to Guildford to see Arsenal's reserves. When he eventually took to his bed it was too late, pneumonia had set in, and he died at 3 a.m. on Saturday, January 6.

Stunned Arsenal fans learned the news from newspaper billboards on their way to Highbury for the game against Wednesday.

when Boca Juniors supporters drop lighted torches on their arch rivals from River Plate and panic ensues.

1969: Nineteen players and officials of The Strongest, Bolivia's most popular team, die when their plane crashes in the Andes, 72 miles from their destination La Paz.

1969: El Salvador and Honduras go to war over a World Cup tie played in Mexico and won 3–2 by the Salvadorians. Hundreds of Hondurans launch attacks on Salvadorians living in their country, causing deaths, and the Salvadorian government retaliates with an armed attack lasting a week. The conflict is stopped eventually by the intervention of the Organization of American States.

1971: Sixty-six people die and 150 are injured when they tumble down a stairway while leaving a Rangers vs. Celtic match. A last-minute Rangers equalizer has led to departing fans attempting to get back in the ground, with horrific results.

1979: Seventeen players of Pakhtakor Tashkent of the Soviet Union are killed in a plane crash on their way to a league match.

1981: Eighteen fans die and a further 45 are injured when a wall collapses during a match between Deportes Tolima and Deportivo Cali in Ibague, Colombia.

1982: In Cali, Colombia, drunken youths urinate from the upper deck of the Pascual Geurrero stadium, causing a stampede in which 22 die and more than 100 are injured.

1982: More than 300 Soviet fans die at a UEFA Cup match between Spar-

STEPS TO DISASTER *66 died at Ibrox Park when fans tried to return to the terraces*

tak Moscow and Haarlem of Holland. As revealed seven years later by the authorities, a last-minute Spartak goal sent departing fans surging back into the Lenin Stadium, causing an horrific crush.

1985: A day of celebration turns to tragedy. Fifty-six people are burned to death and more than 200 taken to hospital when Bradford City's 77-year-old wooden main stand is engulfed by flames within five minutes just before half-time in the last match of the season against Lincoln City.

Before the game City had been presented with the Third Division championship.

1985: Thirty-nine people die and more than 400 are injured when a wall collapses during rioting started by English fans an hour before the European Cup Final between Liverpool and Juventus in the the Heysel Stadium, Brussels. Live TV pictures relay the tragedy around the world. The game is eventually played, Juventus winning 1–0, but as a result English club teams are banned from European competition.

1987: Forty-three players, officials' wives and supporters of Alianza Lima die while returning from a league game, their plane crashing into the sea six miles north of the Peruvian capital.

1988: A stand collapses just before half-time at an international between Libya and Malta in Tripoli, causing 30 deaths and many injuries. A man runs amok brandishing a gun among the 65,000 crowd, causing a stampede for the exits, and the weight of numbers breaks a retaining wall.

1988: Between 70 and 100 fans die in Katmandu when a violent hailstorm

causes a stampede among the 25,000 fans at a game between Janakpur of Nepal and Mukti Jodha of Bangladesh.

1989: In Britain's worst sports disaster, 95 Liverpool supporters are crushed to death and almost 200 injured at Hillsborough, Sheffield, before an FA Cup semi-final against Nottingham Forest. Crowds anxious to see the start surge into the Leppings Lane End and pin fans against the security fences designed to keep people off the pitch. The tragedy leads to the dismantling of security fences and to requirements for all-seater stadiums.

1989: Twelve people in Lagos, Nigeria, are trampled to death, and a player dies on the field during a World Cup qualifier between Nigeria and Angola. Nigerian winger Sam Okwaraji collapses with exhaustion in the 82nd minute and cannot be revived.

1991: Forty people are killed and more than 50 injured in South Africa's worst sports disaster at a match in the gold mining town of Orkney, 80 miles from Johannesburg. Most of the victims are trampled as they try to escape fighting between fans, following the referee's decision to allow Kaizer Chiefs a disputed goal against arch rivals Orlando Pirates.

1992: Disaster strikes before a French Cup semi-final in the Corsican town of Bastia, whose team are due to play Marseille. Fifteen spectators die and 1,300 are injured when a temporary metal stand collapses. The whole competition is cancelled by the authorities at the insistence of the clubs.

1993: Eighteen members of the Zambian national team are killed when their plane crashes into the sea off Gabon after a refuelling stop on their way to a World Cup qualifying tie against Senegal.

1995: A 21-year-old Genoa fan is stabbed to death when he is set upon by a group of Milan fans.

1996: Incompetent crowd control measures bring disaster in the national Mateo Flores stadium in Guatemala City when 82 fans are crushed to death and more than 150 are injured before a World Cup qualifying tie against Costa Rica.

1953 DEREK DOOLEY

Derek Dooley was 23 and on the brink of a great career as a prolific goalscorer with Sheffield Wednesday. The big centre-forward had earned a reputation for scoring from apparently impossible situations, with 46 goals in 30 games as Wednesday won promotion, and 16 in 29 First Division games up to St Valentine's Day, 1953.

On that day, he broke his right leg challenging the Preston goalkeeper for a 50–50 ball. A few days later, when he was about to be discharged from hospital, it was discovered that gangrene had set in and there was no alternative but to have it amputated.

Dooley stayed in football, eventually managing Wednesday and being sacked by them, and later joining rivals Sheffield United as commercial manager.

FOOTBALL IN GREAT BRITAIN AND IRELAND

Association football has flourished in the British Isles for well over 100 years. The game has distinct origins in the four "home countries" and has developed along separate lines at club and international level. The Republic of Ireland, too, has a long soccer-playing history, nurtured in the 1990s by World Cup success.

ENGLAND

Association football is a game of speed, strength, colour, excitement and passion. These may not all be qualities one instantly associates with the English, but football is also a structured recreation, dependent on formal rules and regulations and a spirit of sportsmanship which are particular to what might be termed "the English way".

Although football was probably played in its earliest forms in China and in medieval Italy, it was in the context of English society that the tradition of kicking a ball around was developed – right through to the days in the nineteenth century when the universities and public schools sought to codify the game.

The FA Makes the Rules

The most significant day is a matter of record: October 26, 1863, when captains and other representatives from metropolitan and suburban clubs met at the Freemasons Tavern in London to set up the Football Association, which was to become one of the world's greatest sporting institutions.

Agreement, however, was not easily reached. The 11 founders soon fell out over the question of "hacking", the unpleasant practice of kicking opponents on the shin. Supporters of the handling game wanted hacking to remain in the rules. When it came to the vote, which they lost 13–4 on December 1, they withdrew from the Football Association.

Significant advances were made when the Sheffield Association – the Sheffield club being the oldest on record – threw in their lot in with the FA; when C.W. Alcock was installed as secretary in 1870; and through the appointments of Major Marindin as president and the Hon. A.F. (later Lord) Kinnaird as treasurer.

Alcock's inspiration was the FA Cup, which was instituted in 1871–72, and international competition, which he introduced a year later. The first official England vs. Scotland clash was staged in Glasgow on November 30, 1872. Alcock was the driving force behind the FA for a quarter of a century, holding the reins of administration during the game's rapid evolution.

The FA is the ultimate governing body in English football, its primacy expressed in its title as simply the Football Association without need of "English".

Football's administrative development has not been without conflict. In the formative world of the late nineteenth century the first crisis was produced by the encroachment of professionalism, which the FA did not legalize until 1885.

The other major body in England, only 25 years younger, is the Football League. The prime instigator was a Scot, William McGregor of Aston Villa, who became known as "the father of the League", and who had become frustrated by teams failing to arrive to fulfil fixtures or cry-ing off at short notice. McGregor, together with the representatives of Bolton Wanderers, Derby County, Everton, Accrington Stanley, Preston North End, Burnley, Stoke City, Blackburn Rovers, Notts County, West Brom-wich Albion and Wolverhampton Wanderers, formed a separate competition on April 17, 1888. It remained unchallenged as the major unifying competition in English football for more than a century, until the pressures of a changing commercial world led to the historic breakaway now formalized as the Premier League.

The Football League was launched on September 8, 1888, Preston North End becoming the first champions. Undefeated with 18 wins and four draws, they finished a clear 11 points above second-placed Aston Villa. Preston became known as the "Old Invincibles" as they completed the League and Cup "double" with a 3–0 win over Wolverhampton Wanderers in the FA Cup Final that year. They did not concede a single goal in the cup competition.

Preston retained their League title in 1890 and were close to winning it again in 1891. But it was Huddersfield Town who made history in 1926 by clinching their third successive League Championship. In 1924 they pipped Cardiff City on goal average; in 1925 they finished two points ahead of West Bromwich; and they completed their hat-trick of titles with a five-point margin over Arsenal.

Showing the Foreigners

Huddersfield's manager, Herbert Chapman, was later to take charge at Highbury, where he repeated the three-championship trick with Arsenal in 1933, 1934 and 1935. These were the founding years of an awesome tradition and reputation which saw Arsenal's fame spin around the world. Today clubs of the same name may be found as far afield as Chile, Uruguay and Argentina. The credit all belongs to that era in the 1930s during which, inspired by Chapman, the Gunners secured five championships in eight years.

Success in soccer always attracts its critics. In Chapman's case the carping was focused on his revolutionary

tactic of the stopper centre-half. To many at the time this was a negative step which undermined the quality of domestic football. Not that 100-plus goals in three seasons out of five (as Arsenal managed in 1930–31, 1932–33 and 1934–35) would be considered negative by later standards. But the stopper centre-half was a step down a long road which did eventually lead to the *catenaccio* system of defence.

The years immediately after the Second World War saw a one-off resurgence in support, with many clubs setting attendance records which will never be beaten. England – and the other three home associations – had only rejoined FIFA in 1946, having left it in 1928 following what now appears a ludicrous row over broken-time payments for amateurs. Significantly, one clause of the agreement by which England, Scotland, Wales and Northern Ireland returned to FIFA was a guarantee within FIFA statutes that the separate, historical identity of the four home associations should remain inviolate within the international game.

A product of returning to FIFA was entry into the 1950 World Cup, where a 1–0 defeat by the United States in Belo Horizonte, Brazil, was shrugged off as the sort of embarrassment at international level to which the great clubs are occasionally subjected by the giant-killers of the FA Cup.

English football remained supremely confident of its superiority over the rest of the world right through into the early 1950s, when Stan Cullis's Wolves swept aside the likes of Hungary's Honved and Moscow Spartak with a long-ball style which was the epitome of the English game. Billy Wright, at wing-half and then centre-half, was their inspirational skipper; Johnny Hancocks and Jimmy Mullen provided the devastating wing-to-wing passes which left opponents breathless. Wolves blasted more than 100 goals in four successive First Division campaigns from 1957–58 to 1960–61.

But the days of English self-sufficiency and complacency were coming to an end. Continental superiority

in tactics and technique was never better illustrated than at Wembley on Wednesday, November 25, 1953. On that grey afternoon England's best, including goalkeeper Gil Merrick, right back Alf Ramsey, Wright, fellow wing-half Jimmy Dickinson, Stan Mortensen and Stanley Matthews, were humiliated by Hungary 6–3. Apart from a 2–0 defeat by the Irish Republic at Goodison Park, Liverpool, in 1949, it was the first home defeat ever inflicted on England by a foreign side. On that day Hungary's captain, Ferenc Puskas, inscribed his name indelibly on the pages of English football history. The scoreline in the return match in Budapest the following year was an even more emphatic 7–1.

Wolves' success in those early floodlit friendlies prompted such trumpeted fuss in the English newspapers as to provoke the launch of the European Cup. Here, the true worth of the English club game was exposed as successive League champions were put to the test and, for a decade, found wanting. Only Manchester United's Busby Babes could hold their heads high alongside clubs such as Real Madrid, Milan and Reims. In 1957 Manchester United won the League Championship for a second successive year and just missed out on the "double" when they lost in controversial circumstances to Aston Villa in the FA Cup Final. Alas, they were cut down in their prime, eight players being killed when their plane crashed on the runway at Munich on February 6, 1958.

Not until ten yeras later did United become the first English club to win the European Cup.

Many greats teams had entranced and entertained over the years in their varied ways, including Arthur Rowe's "push and run" Tottenham Hotspur side of the early 1950s and Bill Nicholson's double-winning wonders of the early 1960s. Perhaps none have matched the precision and sheer artistry of that 1960–61 Tottenham side, yet none matched the consistency of Liverpool, the Mersey Reds, who dominated the 1970s and 1980s in a manner which had always been considered impossible under the phys-

ical pressures of the English game.

The foundations laid by their own legendary Scottish manager, Bill Shankly, produced achievements which no English club can match: a record 18 League Championships; five FA Cup triumphs; plus successes in the League Cup, the European Champions Cup, the UEFA Cup and the European Supercup.

Increasingly, however, the advent of sponsorship and a realization of football's value as a weapon in the television ratings wars were changing the face of the game. The big clubs were slowly growing away from the traditional roots of what was now a 92-club, four-division Football League. In the autumn of 1991 the First Division, virtually en masse, signalled their joint intention to resign from the Football League and set up a new competitive structure, the Premier League, under the auspices of the Football Association.

In a strange way, this return to the FA fold had brought English football full circle. Manchester United won the first Premier League championship, their first league title for 26 years. Alex Ferguson's team not only retained the title in 1994 but secured the League and Cup "double" with a 4–0 win over Chelsea in the FA Cup Final. The Reds from Manchester thus emulated the achievements of Preston North End (1889), Aston Villa (1897), Tottenham Hotspur (1961), Arsenal (1971) and Liverpool (1986).

Even better, in 1996, United created history by becoming the first club to win the "double" twice beating Liverpool 1–0 in the FA Cup Final with Eric Cantona not only scoring the winning goal but collecting the Cup as captain on the day. Two years later, Arsenal emulated that "Double-double", the Arsène Wenger's 1998 side following on from their 1971 predecessors.

But the greatest club achievement was saved until the last season of the century when United not only achieved the "double" for a record third time– but made it a unique treble by winning the European Champions League.

FOOTBALL LEAGUE

Season	Champions	Pts	Runners-up	Pts
1888–89	Preston NE	40	Aston Villa	29
1889–90	Preston NE	33	Everton	31
1890–91	Everton	29	Preston NE	27
1891–92	Sunderland	42	Preston NE	37

FIRST DIVISION

1892–93	Sunderland	48	Preston NE	37
1893–94	Aston Villa	44	Sunderland	38
1894–95	Sunderland	47	Everton	42
1895–96	Aston Villa	45	Derby County	41
1896–97	Aston Villa	47	Sheffield Utd	36
1897–98	Sheffield Utd	42	Sunderland	37
1898–99	Aston Villa	45	Liverpool	43
1899–1900	Aston Villa	50	Sheffield Utd	48
1900–01	Liverpool	45	Sunderland	43
1901–02	Sunderland	44	Everton	41
1902–03	Sheffield Wed	42	Aston Villa	41
1903–04	Sheffield Wed	47	Manchester C	44
1904–05	Newcastle Utd	48	Everton	47
1905–06	Liverpool	51	Preston NE	47
1906–07	Newcastle Utd	51	Bristol City	48
1907–08	Manchester Utd	52	Aston Villa*	43
1908–09	Newcastle Utd	53	Everton	46
1909–10	Aston Villa	53	Liverpool	48
1910–11	Manchester Utd	52	Aston Villa	51
1911–12	Blackburn R	49	Everton	46
1912–13	Sunderland	54	Aston Villa	50
1913–14	Blackburn R	51	Aston Villa	44
1914–15	Everton	46	Oldham Ath	45
1919–20	WBA	60	Burnley	51
1920–21	Burnley	59	Manchester C	54
1921–22	Liverpool	57	Tottenham H	51
1922–23	Liverpool	60	Sunderland	54
1923–24	Huddersfield T*	57	Cardiff C	57
1924–25	Huddersfield T	58	WBA	56
1925–26	Huddersfield T	57	Arsenal	52
1926–27	Newcastle Utd	56	Huddersfield T	51
1927–28	Everton	53	Huddersfield T	51
1928–29	Sheffield Wed	52	Leicester C	51
1929–30	Sheffield Wed	60	Derby County	50
1930–31	Arsenal	66	Aston Villa	59
1931–32	Everton	56	Arsenal	54
1932–33	Arsenal	58	Aston Villa	54
1933–34	Arsenal	59	Huddersfield T	56
1934–35	Arsenal	58	Sunderland	54
1935–36	Sunderland	56	Derby County	48
1936–37	Manchester C	57	Charlton Ath	54
1937–38	Arsenal	52	Wolves	51
1938–39	Everton	59	Wolves	55
1946–47	Liverpool	57	Manchester Utd*	56
1947–48	Arsenal	59	Manchester Utd*	52
1948–49	Portsmouth	58	Manchester Utd*	53
1949–50	Portsmouth*	53	Wolves	53
1950–51	Tottenham H	60	Manchester Utd	56
1951–52	Manchester Utd	57	Tottenham H	53
1952–53	Arsenal*	54	Preston NE	54
1953–54	Wolves	57	WBA	53
1954–55	Chelsea	52	Wolves	48
1955–56	Manchester Utd	60	Blackpool*	49
1956–57	Manchester Utd	64	Tottenham H*	56
1957–58	Wolves	64	Preston NE	59
1958–59	Wolves	61	Manchester Utd	55
1959–60	Burnley	55	Wolves	54
1960–61	Tottenham H	66	Sheffield Wed	58
1961–62	Ipswich T	56	Burnley	53
1962–63	Everton	61	Tottenham H	55
1963–64	Liverpool	57	Manchester Utd	53
1964–65	Manchester Utd*	61	Leeds Utd	61
1965–66	Liverpool	61	Leeds Utd*	55
1966–67	Manchester Utd	60	Nottm Forest*	56
1967–68	Manchester C	58	Manchester Utd	56
1968–69	Leeds Utd	67	Liverpool	61
1969–70	Everton	66	Leeds Utd	57
1970–71	Arsenal	65	Leeds Utd	64
1971–72	Derby County	58	Leeds Utd*	57
1972–73	Liverpool	60	Arsenal	57
1973–74	Leeds Utd	62	Liverpool	57
1974–75	Derby County	53	Liverpool*	51
1975–76	Liverpool	60	QPR	59
1976–77	Liverpool	57	Manchester C	56
1977–78	Nottm Forest	64	Liverpool	57
1978–79	Liverpool	68	Nottm Forest	60
1979–80	Liverpool	60	Manchester Utd	58
1980–81	Aston Villa	60	Ipswich T	56
1981–82	Liverpool	87	Ipswich T	83
1982–83	Liverpool	82	Watford	71
1983–84	Liverpool	80	Southampton	77
1984–85	Everton	90	Liverpool*	77
1985–86	Liverpool	88	Everton	86
1986–87	Everton	86	Liverpool	77
1987–88	Liverpool	90	Manchester Utd	81
1988–89	Arsenal*	76	Liverpool	76
1989–90	Liverpool	79	Aston Villa	70
1990–91	Arsenal+	83	Liverpool	76
1991–92	Leeds Ud	82	Manchester Utd	78

Notes: * Position decided by goal average or goal difference, + 2 points deducted

FA PREMIER LEAGUE

1992–93	Manchester Utd	84	Aston Villa	74
1993–94	Manchester Utd	92	Blackburn R	84
1994–95	Blackburn R	89	Manchester Utd	88
1995–96	Manchester Utd	82	Newcastle Utd	78
1996–97	Manchester Utd	75	Newcastle Utd	68
1997–98	Arsenal	78	Manchester Utd	77
1998–99	Manchester Utd	79	Arsenal	78

FOOTBALL LEAGUE CUP

Year	Winners	Runners-up	Result
1961	Aston Villa	Rotherham Utd	0–2,3–0*
1962	Norwich C	Rochdale	3–0, 1–0
1963	Birmingham C	Aston Villa	3–1, 0–0
1964	Leicester C	Stoke C	1–1, 3–2
1965	Chelsea	Leicester C	3–2, 0–0
1966	WBA	West Ham Utd	1–2, 4–1
1967+	QPR	WBA	3–2
1968	Leeds Utd	Arsenal	1–0
1969	Swindon T	Arsenal	3–1*
1970	Manchester C	WBA	2–1*
1971	Tottenham H	Aston Villa	2–0
1972	Stoke C	Chelsea	2–1
1973	Tottenham H	Norwich C	1–0
1974	Wolves	Manchester C	2–1
1975	Aston Villa	Norwich C	1–0
1976	Manchester C	Newcastle Utd	2–1
1977	Aston Villa	Everton 0–0*, 1–1*, 3–2*	
1978	Nottm Forest	Liverpool	0–0*, 1–0
1979	Nottm Forest	Southampton	3–2
1980	Wolves	Nottm Forest	1–0
1981	Liverpool	West Ham Utd	1–1*, 2–1
1982	Liverpool	Tottenham H	3–1*
1983	Liverpool	Manchester Utd	2–1*
1984	Liverpool	Everton	0–0*, 1–0
1985	Norwich C	Sunderland	1–0
1986	Oxford Utd	QPR	3–0
1987	Arsenal	Liverpool	2–1
1988	Luton Town	Arsenal	3–2
1989	Nottm Forest	Luton Town	3–1
1990	Nottm Forest	Oldham Ath	1–0
1991	Sheffield Wed	Manchester Utd	1–0
1992	Manchester Utd	Nottm Forest	1–0
1993	Arsenal	Sheffield Wed	2–1
1994	Aston Villa	Manchester Utd	3–1
1995	Liverpool	Bolton Wanderers	2–1
1996	Aston Villa	Leeds Utd	3–0
1997	Leicester City	Middlesbrough	1–1*, 1–0*
1998	Chelsea	Middlesbrough	2–0
1999	Tottenham	Leicester City	1–0

Notes: * After extra time, + One-leg Final from this year

FA CUP

Year	Winners	Runners-up	Result
1872	Wanderers	Royal Engineers	1–0
1873	Wanderers	Oxford University	2–0
1874	Oxford University	Royal Engineers	2–0
1875	Royal Engineers	Old Etonians	1–1*, 2–0
1876	Wanderers	Old Etonians	0–0*, 3–0
1877	Wanderers	Oxford University	2–0*
1878	+Wanderers	Royal Engineers	3–1
1879	Old Etonians	Clapham Rovers	1–0
1880	Clapham Rovers	Oxford University	1–0
1881	Old Carthusians	Old Etonians	3–0
1882	Old Etonians	Blackburn R	1–0
1883	Blackburn Olympic	Old Etonians	2–1*
1884	Blackburn R	Queens Park Glasgow	2–1
1885	Blackburn R	Queens Park Glasgow	2–0
1886	Blackburn R	WBA	0–0*, 2–0
1887	Aston Villa	WBA	2–0
1888	WBA	Preston NE	2–1
1889	Preston NE	Wolves	3–0
1890	Blackburn R	Sheffield Wed	6–1
1891	Blackburn R	Notts County	3–1
1892	WBA	Aston Villa	3–0
1893	Wolves	Everton	1–0
1894	Notts County	Bolton W	4–1
1895	Aston Villa	WBA	1–0
1896	Sheffield Wed	Wolves	2–1
1897	Aston Villa	Everton	3–2
1898	Nottm Forest	Derby County	3–1
1899	Sheffield Utd	Derby County	4–1
1900	Bury	Southampton	4–0
1901	Tottenham H	Sheffield Utd	2–2*, 3–1
1902	Sheffield Utd	Southampton	1–1*, 2–1
1903	Bury	Derby County	6–0
1904	Manchester C	Bolton W	1–0
1905	Aston Villa	Newcastle Utd	2–0
1906	Everton	Newcastle Utd	1–0
1907	Sheffield Wed	Everton	2–1
1908	Wolves	Newcastle Utd	3–1
1909	Manchester Utd	Bristol C	1–0
1910	Newcastle Utd	Barnsley	1–1*, 2–0
1911	Bradford C	Newcastle Utd	0–0*, 1–0
1912	Barnsley	WBA	0–0*, 1–0
1913	Aston Villa	Sunderland	1–0
1914	Burnley	Liverpool	1–0
1915	Sheffield Utd	Chelsea	3–0
1920	Aston Villa	Huddersfield T	1–0*
1921	Tottenham H	Wolves	1–0
1922	Huddersfield T	Preston NE	1–0
1923	Bolton W	West Ham Utd	2–0
1924	Newcastle Utd	Aston Villa	2–0
1925	Sheffield Utd	Cardiff C	1–0
1926	Bolton W	Manchester C	1–0
1927	Cardiff C	Arsenal	1–0
1928	Blackburn R	Huddersfield T	3–1
1929	Bolton W	Portsmouth	2–0
1930	Arsenal	Huddersfield T	2–0
1931	WBA	Birmingham C	2–1
1932	Newcastle Utd	Arsenal	2–1
1933	Everton	Manchester C	3–0
1934	Manchester C	Portsmouth	2–1
1935	Sheffield Wed	WBA	4–2
1936	Arsenal	Sheffield Utd	1–0
1937	Sunderland	Preston NE	3–1
1938	Preston NE	Huddersfield T	1–0*
1939	Portsmouth	Wolves	4–1
1946	Derby County	Charlton Ath	4–1*
1947	Charlton Ath	Burnley	1–0*
1948	Manchester Utd	Blackpool	4–2
1949	Wolves	Leicester C	3–1
1950	Arsenal	Liverpool	2–0
1951	Newcastle Utd	Blackpool	2–0
1952	Newcastle Utd	Arsenal	1–0
1953	Blackpool	Bolton W	4–3
1954	WBA	Preston NE	3–2
1955	Newcastle Utd	Manchester C	3–1
1956	Manchester C	Birmingham C	3–1
1957	Aston Villa	Manchester Utd	2–1
1958	Bolton W	Manchester Utd	2–0
1959	Nottm Forest	Luton T	2–1
1960	Wolves	Blackburn R	3–0
1961	Tottenham H	Leicester C	2–0
1962	Tottenham H	Burnley	3–1
1963	Manchester Utd	Leicester C	3–1
1964	West Ham Utd	Preston NE	3–2
1965	Liverpool	Leeds Utd	2–1*
1966	Everton	Sheffield Wed	3–2
1967	Tottenham H	Chelsea	2–1
1968	WBA	Everton	1–0*
1969	Manchester C	Leicester C	1–0
1970	Chelsea	Leeds Utd	2–2*, 2–1*
1971	Arsenal	Liverpool	2–1*
1972	Leeds Utd	Arsenal	1–0
1973	Sunderland	Leeds Utd	1–0
1974	Liverpool	Newcastle Utd	3–0
1975	West Ham Utd	Fulham	2–0
1976	Southampton	Manchester Utd	1–0
1977	Manchester Utd	Liverpool	2–1
1978	Ipswich T	Arsenal	1–0
1979	Arsenal	Manchester Utd	3–2
1980	West Ham Utd	Arsenal	1–0
1981	Tottenham H	Manchester C	1–1*, 3–2
1982	Tottenham H	QPR	1–1*, 1–0
1983	Manchester Utd	Brighton & HA	2–2*, 4–0
1984	Everton	Watford	2–0
1985	Manchester Utd	Everton	1–0*
1986	Liverpool	Everton	3–1
1987	Coventry C	Tottenham H	3–2*
1988	Wimbledon	Liverpool	1–0
1989	Liverpool	Everton	3–2*
1990	Manchester Utd	Crystal Palace	3–3*, 1–0
1991	Tottenham H	Nottm Forest	2–1*
1992	Liverpool	Sunderland	2–0
1993	Arsenal	Sheffield Wed	1–1*, 2–1*
1994	Manchester Utd	Chelsea	4–0
1995	Everton	Manchester Utd	1–0
1996	Manchester Utd	Liverpool	1–0
1997	Chelsea	Middlesbrough	2–0
1998	Arsenal	Newcastle Utd	2–0
1999	Manchester Utd	Newcastle Utd	2–0

Notes: * After extra time; + Cup won outright but restored to the FA;

INTERNATIONAL RESULTS

1872–1929

Date	Opponents	Venue	Score
30/11/72	Scotland	Glasgow	0–0
8/3/73	Scotland	Kennington Oval	4–2
7/3/74	Scotland	Glasgow	1–2
6/3/75	Scotland	Kennington Oval	2–2
4/3/76	Scotland	Glasgow	0–3
3/3/77	Scotland	Kennington Oval	1–3
2/3/78	Scotland	Glasgow	2–7
18/1/79	Wales	Kennington Oval	2–1
5/4/79	Scotland	Kennington Oval	5–4
13/3/80	Scotland	Glasgow	4–5
15/3/80	Wales	Wrexham	3–2
26/2/81	Wales	Blackburn	0–1
12/3/81	Scotland	Kennington Oval	1–6
18/2/82	Ireland	Belfast	13–0
11/3/82	Scotland	Glasgow	1–5
13/3/82	Wales	Wrexham	3–5
3/2/83	Wales	Kennington Oval	5–0
24/2/83	Ireland	Liverpool	7–0
10/3/83	Scotland	Sheffield	2–3
25/2/84	Ireland	Belfast	8–1
15/3/84	Scotland	Glasgow	0–1
17/3/84	Wales	Wrexham	4–0
28/2/85	Ireland	Manchester	4–0
14/3/85	Wales	Blackburn	1–1
21/3/85	Scotland	Kennington Oval	1–1
13/3/86	Ireland	Belfast	6–1
29/3/86	Wales	Wrexham	3–1
31/3/86	Scotland	Glasgow	1–1
5/2/87	Ireland	Sheffield	7–0
26/2/87	Wales	Kennington Oval	4–0
19/3/87	Scotland	Blackburn	2–3
4/2/88	Wales	Crewe	5–1
17/3/88	Scotland	Glasgow	5–0
31/3/88	Ireland	Belfast	5–1
23/2/89	Wales	Stoke	4–1

2/3/89	Ireland	Everton	6–1
13/4/89	Scotland	Kennington Oval	2–3
15/3/90	Wales	Wrexham	3–1
15/3/90	Ireland	Belfast	9–1
5/4/90	Scotland	Glasgow	1–1
7/3/91	Wales	Sunderland	4–1
7/3/91	Ireland	Wolverhampton	6–1
6/4/91	Scotland	Blackburn	2–1
5/3/92	Wales	Wrexham	2–0
5/3/92	Ireland	Belfast	2–0
2/4/92	Scotland	Glasgow	4–1
25/2/93	Ireland	Birmingham	6–1
13/3/93	Wales	Stoke	6–0
1/4/93	Scotland	Richmond	5–2
1/3/94	Ireland	Belfast	2–2
12/3/94	Wales	Wrexham	5–1
7/4/94	Scotland	Glasgow	2–2
9/3/95	Ireland	Derby	9–0
18/3/95	Wales	Queen's Club, London	1–1
6/4/95	Scotland	Goodison Park	3–0
7/3/96	Ireland	Belfast	2–0
16/3/96	Wales	Cardiff	9–1
4/4/96	Scotland	Glasgow	1–2
20/2/97	Ireland	Nottingham	6–0
29/3/97	Wales	Sheffield	4–0
3/4/97	Scotland	Crystal Palace	1–2
5/3/98	Ireland	Belfast	3–2
28/3/98	Wales	Wrexham	3–0
2/4/98	Scotland	Glasgow	3–1
18/2/99	Ireland	Sunderland	13–2
20/3/99	Wales	Bristol	4–0
8/4/99	Scotland	Birmingham	2–1
17/3/00	Ireland	Dublin	2–0
26/3/00	Wales	Cardiff	1–1
7/4/00	Scotland	Glasgow	1–4
9/3/01	Ireland	Southampton	3–0
18/3/01	Wales	Newcastle	6–0
30/3/01	Scotland	Crystal Palace	2–2
3/3/02	Wales	Wrexham	0–0
22/3/02	Ireland	Belfast	1–0
3/5/02	Scotland	Birmingham	2–2
14/2/03	Ireland	Wolverhampton	4–0
2/3/03	Wales	Portsmouth	2–1
4/4/03	Scotland	Sheffield	1–2
29/2/04	Wales	Wrexham	2–2
12/3/04	Ireland	Belfast	3–1
9/4/04	Scotland	Glasgow	1–0
25/2/05	Ireland	Middlesbrough	1–1
27/3/05	Wales	Liverpool	3–1
1/4/05	Scotland	Crystal Palace	1–0
17/2/06	Ireland	Belfast	5–0
19/3/06	Wales	Cardiff	1–0
7/4/06	Scotland	Glasgow	1–2
16/2/07	Ireland	Goodison Park	1–0
18/3/07	Wales	Fulham	1–1
6/4/07	Scotland	Newcastle	1–1
15/2/08	Ireland	Belfast	3–1
16/3/08	Wales	Wrexham	7–1
4/4/08	Scotland	Glasgow	1–1
6/6/08	Austria	Vienna	6–1
8/6/08	Austria	Vienna	11–1
10/6/08	Hungary	Budapest	7–0
13/6/08	Bohemia	Prague	4–0
13/2/09	Ireland	Bradford	4–0
15/3/09	Wales	Nottingham	2–0
3/4/09	Scotland	Crystal Palace	2–0
29/5/09	Hungary	Budapest	4–2
31/5/09	Hungary	Budapest	8–2
1/6/09	Austria	Vienna	8–1
12/2/10	Ireland	Belfast	1–1
14/3/10	Wales	Cardiff	1–0
2/4/10	Scotland	Glasgow	0–2
11/2/11	Ireland	Derby	2–1
13/3/11	Wales	Millwall	3–0
1/4/11	Scotland	Goodison Park	1–1
10/2/12	Ireland	Dublin	6–1
11/3/12	Wales	Wrexham	2–0
23/3/12	Scotland	Glasgow	1–1
15/2/13	Ireland	Belfast	1–2
17/3/13	Wales	Bristol	4–3
5/4/13	Scotland	Stamford Bridge	1–0
14/2/14	Ireland	Middlesbrough	0–3
16/3/14	Wales	Cardiff	2–0
4/4/14	Scotland	Glasgow	1–3
25/10/19	Ireland	Belfast	1–1
15/3/20	Wales	Highbury	1–2
10/4/20	Scotland	Sheffield	5–4
23/10/20	Ireland	Sunderland	2–0
14/3/21	Wales	Cardiff	0–0
9/4/21	Scotland	Glasgow	0–3
21/5/21	Belgium	Brussels	2–0
22/10/21	Ireland	Belfast	1–1
13/3/22	Wales	Anfield	1–0
8/4/22	Scotland	Birmingham	0–1
21/10/22	Ireland	West Bromwich	2–0
5/3/23	Wales	Cardiff	2–2
19/3/23	Belgium	Highbury	6–1
14/4/23	Scotland	Glasgow	2–2
10/5/23	France	Paris	4–1
21/5/23	Sweden	Stockholm	4–2
24/5/23	Sweden	Stockholm	3–1
20/10/23	Ireland	Belfast	1–2
1/11/23	Belgium	Antwerp	2–2
3/3/24	Wales	Blackburn	1–2
12/4/24	Scotland	Wembley	1–1
17/5/24	France	Paris	3–1
22/10/24	Ireland	Anfield	3–1
8/12/24	Belgium	West Bromwich	4–0
28/2/25	Wales	Swansea	2–1
4/4/25	Scotland	Glasgow	0–2
21/5/25	France	Paris	3–2
24/10/25	Ireland	Belfast	0–0
1/3/26	Wales	Selhurst Park	1–3
17/4/26	Scotland	Manchester	0–1
24/4/26	Belgium	Antwerp	5–3
20/10/26	Ireland	Anfield	3–3
12/2/27	Wales	Wrexham	3–3
2/4/27	Scotland	Glasgow	2–1
11/5/27	Belgium	Brussels	9–1
21/5/27	Luxembourg	Luxembourg	5–2
26/5/27	France	Paris	6–0
22/10/27	Ireland	Belfast	0–2
28/11/27	Wales	Burnley	1–2
31/3/28	Scotland	Wembley	1–5
17/5/28	France	Paris	5–1
19/5/28	Belgium	Antwerp	3–1
22/10/28	Ireland	Anfield	2–1
17/11/28	Wales	Swansea	3–2
13/4/29	Scotland	Glasgow	0–1
9/5/29	France	Paris	4–1
11/5/29	Belgium	Brussels	5–1
15/5/29	Spain	Madrid	3–4
19/10/29	Ireland	Belfast	3–0
20/11/29	Wales	Stamford Bridge	6–0

1930–1939

5/4/30	Scotland	Wembley	5–2
10/5/30	Germany	Berlin	3–3
14/5/30	Austria	Vienna	0–0
20/10/30	Ireland	Sheffield	5–1
22/11/30	Wales	Wrexham	4–0
28/3/31	Scotland	Glasgow	0–2
14/5/31	France	Paris	2–5
16/5/31	Belgium	Brussels	4–1
17/10/31	Ireland	Belfast	6–2
18/11/31	Wales	Anfield	3–1
9/12/31	Spain	Highbury	7–1
9/4/32	Scotland	Wembley	3–0
17/10/32	Ireland	Blackpool	1–0
16/11/32	Wales	Wrexham	0–0
7/12/32	Austria	Stamford Bridge	4–3
1/4/33	Scotland	Glasgow	1–2
13/5/33	Italy	Rome	1–1
20/5/33	Switzerland	Berne	4–0
14/10/33	Ireland	Belfast	3–0
15/11/33	Wales	Newcastle	1–2
6/12/33	France	White Hart Lane	4–1
14/4/34	Scotland	Wembley	3–0
10/5/34	Hungary	Budapest	1–2
16/5/34	Czechoslovakia	Prague	1–2
29/9/34	Wales	Cardiff	4–0
14/11/34	Italy	Highbury	3–2
6/2/35	Ireland	Goodison Park	2–1
6/4/35	Scotland	Glasgow	0–2
18/5/35	Holland	Amsterdam	1–0
19/10/35	Ireland	Belfast	3–1
4/12/35	Germany	White Hart Lane	3–0
5/2/36	Wales	Wolverhampton	1–2
4/4/36	Scotland	Wembley	1–1
6/5/36	Austria	Vienna	1–2
9/5/36	Belgium	Brussels	2–3
17/10/36	Wales	Cardiff	1–2
18/11/36	Ireland	Stoke	3–1
2/12/36	Hungary	Highbury	6–2
17/4/37	Scotland	Glasgow	1–3
14/5/37	Norway	Oslo	6–0
17/5/37	Sweden	Stockholm	4–0
20/5/37	Finland	Helsinki	8–0
23/10/37	Ireland	Belfast	5–1
17/11/37	Wales	Middlesbrough	2–1
1/12/37	Czechoslovakia	White Hart Lane	5–4
9/4/38	Scotland	Wembley	0–1
14/5/38	Germany	Berlin	6–3
21/5/38	Switzerland	Zurich	1–2
26/5/38	France	Paris	4–2
22/10/38	Wales	Cardiff	2–4
26/10/38	FIFA	Highbury	3–0
9/11/38	Norway	Newcastle	4–0
16/11/38	Ireland	Manchester	7–0
15/4/39	Scotland	Glasgow	2–1
13/5/39	Italy	Milan	2–2
18/5/39	Yugoslavia	Belgrade	1–2
24/5/39	Romania	Bucharest	2–0

1940–49

28/9/46	N Ireland	Belfast	7–2
30/9/46	Rep of Ireland	Dublin	1–0
19/10/46	Wales	Maine Road	3–0
27/11/46	Holland	Huddersfield	8–2
12/4/47	Scotland	Wembley	1–1
3/5/47	France	Highbury	3–0
18/5/47	Switzerland	Zurich	0–1
27/5/47	Portugal	Lisbon	10–0
21/9/47	Belgium	Brussels	5–2
18/10/47	Wales	Cardiff	3–0
5/11/47	N Ireland	Goodison Park	2–2
19/11/47	Sweden	Highbury	4–2
10/4/48	Scotland	Glasgow	2–0
16/5/48	Italy	Turin	4–0
26/9/48	Denmark	Copenhagen	0–0
9/10/48	N Ireland	Belfast	6–2
10/11/48	Wales	Villa Park	1–0
1/12/48	Switzerland	Highbury	6–0
9/4/48	Scotland	Wembley	1–3
13/5/49	Sweden	Stockholm	1–3
18/5/49	Norway	Oslo	4–1
22/5/49	France	Paris	3–1
21/9/49	Rep of Ireland	Goodison Park	0–2
15/10/49	Wales	Cardiff	4–1 (WCQ)
16/11/49	N Ireland	Maine Road	9–2 (WCQ)
30/11/49	Italy	White Hart Lane	2–0

1950–59

15/4/50	Scotland	Glasgow	1–0 (WCQ)
14/5/50	Portugal	Lisbon	5–3
18/5/50	Belgium	Brussels	4–1
15/6/50	Chile	Rio de Janeiro	2–0 (WCF)
29/6/50	USA	Belo Horizonte	0–1 (WCF)
2/7/50	Spain	Rio de Janeiro	0–1 (WCF)
7/10/50	N Ireland	Belfast	4–1
15/11/50	Wales	Sunderland	4–2
22/11/50	Yugoslavia	Highbury	2–2
14/4/51	Scotland	Wembley	2–3
9/5/51	Argentina	Wembley	2–1
9/5/51	Portugal	Goodison Park	5–2
3/10/51	France	Highbury	2–2
20/10/51	Wales	Cardiff	1–1
14/11/51	N Ireland	Villa Park	2–0
28/11/51	Austria	Wembley	2–2
5/4/52	Scotland	Glasgow	2–1
18/5/52	Italy	Florence	1–1
25/5/52	Austria	Vienna	3–2
28/5/52	Switzerland	Zurich	3–0
4/10/52	N Ireland	Belfast	2–2
12/11/52	Wales	Wembley	5–2
26/11/52	Belgium	Wembley	5–0
18/4/53	Scotland	Wembley	2–2
17/5/53	Argentina	Buenos Aires	0–0
	(abandoned after 21 minutes)		
24/5/53	Chile	Santiago	2–1
31/5/53	Uruguay	Montevideo	1–2
8/6/53	USA	New York	6–3
10/10/53	Wales	Cardiff	4–1 (WCQ)
21/10/53	Rest of Europe	Wembley	4–4
11/11/53	N Ireland	Goodison Pk	3–1 (WCQ)
25/11/53	Hungary	Wembley	3–6
3/4/54	Scotland	Glasgow	4–2 (WCQ)
16/5/54	Yugoslavia	Belgrade	0–1
23/5/54	Hungary	Budapest	1–7
17/6/54	Belgium	Basle	4–4* (WCF)
20/6/54	Switzerland	Berne	2–0 (WCF)
26/6/54	Uruguay	Basle	2–4 (WCF)
2/10/54	N Ireland	Belfast	2–0
10/11/54	Wales	Wembley	3–2
1/12/54	W Germany	Wembley	3–1
2/4/55	Scotland	Wembley	7–2
18/5/55	France	Paris	0–1
18/5/55	Spain	Madrid	1–1
22/5/55	Portugal	Oporto	1–3
2/10/55	Denmark	Copenhagen	5–1
22/10/55	Wales	Cardiff	1–1
2/11/55	N Ireland	Wembley	3–0
30/11/55	Spain	Wembley	4–1
14/4/56	Scotland	Glasgow	1–1
9/5/56	Brazil	Wembley	4–2
16/5/56	Sweden	Stockholm	0–0
20/5/56	Finland	Helsinki	5–1
26/5/56	West Germany	Berlin	3–1
6/10/56	N Ireland	Belfast	1–1
14/11/56	Wales	Wembley	3–1
28/11/56	Yugoslavia	Wembley	3–0
5/12/56	Denmark	Wolverhampton	5–2 (WCQ)
6/4/57	Scotland	Wembley	2–1
8/5/57	Rep of Ireland	Wembley	5–1 (WCQ)
15/5/57	Denmark	Copenhagen	4–1 (WCQ)
19/5/57	Rep of Ireland	Dublin	1–1 (WCQ)
19/10/57	Wales	Cardiff	4–0
6/11/57	N Ireland	Wembley	2–3
27/11/57	France	Wembley	4–0
19/4/58	Scotland	Glasgow	4–0
7/5/58	Portugal	Wembley	2–1
11/5/58	Yugoslavia	Belgrade	0–5
18/5/58	USSR	Moscow	1–1
8/6/58	USSR	Gothenburg	2–2 (WCF)
11/6/58	Brazil	Gothenburg	0–0 (WCF)
15/6/58	Austria	Boras	2–2 (WCF)
17/6/58	USSR	Gothenburg	0–1 (WCF)
4/10/58	N Ireland	Belfast	3–3
22/10/58	USSR	Wembley	5–0
26/11/58	Wales	Villa Park	2–2
11/4/59	Scotland	Wembley	1–0
6/5/59	Italy	Wembley	2–2
13/5/59	Brazil	Rio de Janeiro	0–2
17/5/59	Peru	Lima	1–4
24/5/59	Mexico	Mexico C	1–2
28/5/59	USA	Los Angeles	8–1
17/10/59	Wales	Cardiff	1–1
28/10/59	Sweden	Wembley	2–3
18/11/59	N Ireland	Wembley	2–1

1960–69

19/4/60	Scotland	Glasgow	1–1
11/5/60	Yugoslavia	Wembley	3–3
15/5/60	Spain	Madrid	0–3
22/5/60	Hungary	Budapest	0–2
8/10/60	N Ireland	Belfast	5–2
19/10/60	Luxembourg	Luxembourg	9-0 (WCQ)
26/10/60	Spain	Wembley	4–2
23/11/60	Wales	Wembley	5–1
15/4/61	Scotland	Wembley	9–3

10/5/61	Mexico	Wembley	8–0
21/5/61	Portugal	Lisbon	1–1 (WCQ)
24/5/61	Italy	Rome	3–2
27/5/61	Austria	Vienna	1–3
28/9/61	Luxembourg	Highbury	4–1 (WCQ)
14/10/61	Wales	Cardiff	1–1
25/10/61	Portugal	Wembley	2–0 (WCQ)
22/11/61	N Ireland	Wembley	1–1
4/4/62	Austria	Wembley	3–1
14/4/62	Scotland	Glasgow	0–2
9/5/62	Switzerland	Wembley	3–1
20/5/62	Peru	Lima	4–0
31/5/62	Hungary	Rancagua	1–2 (WCF)
2/6/62	Argentina	Rancagua	3–1 (WCF)
7/6/62	Bulgaria	Rancagua	0–0 (WCF)
10/6/62	Brazil	Vina del Mar	1–3 (WCF)
3/10/62	France	Hillsborough	1–1 (ECQ)
20/10/62	N Ireland	Belfast	3–1
21/11/62	Wales	Wembley	4–0
27/2/63	France	Paris	2–5 (ECQ)
6/4/63	Scotland	Wembley	1–2
8/5/63	Brazil	Wembley	1–1
20/5/63	Czechoslovakia	Bratislava	4–2
2/6/63	East Germany	Leipzig	2–1
5/6/63	Switzerland	Basle	8–1
12/10/63	Wales	Cardiff	4–0
23/10/63	Rest of World	Wembley	2–1
20/11/63	N Ireland	Wembley	8–3
11/4/64	Scotland	Glasgow	0–1
6/5/64	Uruguay	Wembley	2–1
17/5/64	Portugal	Lisbon	4–3
24/5/64	Rep of Ireland	Dublin	3–1
27/5/64	USA	New York	10–0
30/5/64	Brazil	Rio de Janeiro	1–5 (BJT)
4/6/64	Portugal	São Paulo	1–1 (BJT)
6/6/64	Argentina	Rio de Janeiro	0–1 (BJT)
3/10/64	N Ireland	Belfast	4–3
21/10/64	Belgium	Wembley	2–2
18/11/64	Wales	Wembley	2–1
9/12/64	Holland	Amsterdam	1–1
10/4/65	Scotland	Wembley	2–2
5/5/65	Hungary	Wembley	1–0
9/5/65	Yugoslavia	Belgrade	1–1
12/5/65	W Germany	Nuremberg	1–0
16/5/65	Sweden	Gothenburg	2–1
2/10/65	Wales	Cardiff	0–0
20/10/65	Austria	Wembley	2–3
10/11/65	N Ireland	Wembley	2–1
8/12/65	Spain	Madrid	2–0
5/1/66	Poland	Anfield	1–1
23/2/66	W Germany	Wembley	1–0
2/4/66	Scotland	Glasgow	4–3
4/5/66	Yugoslavia	Wembley	2–0
26/6/66	Finland	Helsinki	3–0
29/6/66	Norway	Oslo	6–1
3/7/66	Denmark	Copenhagen	2–0
5/7/66	Poland	Chorzow	1–0
11/7/66	Uruguay	Wembley	0–0 (WCF)
16/7/66	Mexico	Wembley	2–0 (WCF)
20/7/66	France	Wembley	2–0 (WCF)
23/7/66	Argentina	Wembley	1–0 (WCF)
26/7/66	Portugal	Wembley	2–1 (WCF)
30/7/66	W Germany	Wembley	4–2* (WCF)
22/10/66	N Ireland	Belfast	2–0 (ECQ)
2/11/66	Czechoslovakia	Wembley	0–0
16/11/66	Wales	Wembley	5–1 (ECQ)
15/4/67	Scotland	Wembley	2–3 (ECQ)
24/5/67	Spain	Wembley	2–0
27/5/67	Austria	Vienna	1–0
21/10/67	Wales	Cardiff	3–0 (ECQ)
22/11/67	N Ireland	Wembley	2–0 (ECQ)
6/12/67	USSR	Wembley	2–2
24/2/68	Scotland	Glasgow	1–1 (ECQ)
3/4/68	Spain	Wembley	1–0 (ECQ)
8/5/68	Spain	Madrid	2–1 (ECQ)
22/5/68	Sweden	Wembley	3–1
1/6/68	W Germany	Hanover	0–1
5/6/68	Yugoslavia	Florence	0–1 (ECF)
8/6/68	USSR	Rome	2–0 (ECF)
6/11/68	Romania	Bucharest	0–0
11/12/68	Bulgaria	Wembley	1–1
15/1/69	Romania	Wembley	1–1
12/3/69	France	Wembley	5–0
3/5/69	N Ireland	Belfast	3–1
7/5/69	Wales	Wembley	2–1
10/5/69	Scotland	Wembley	4–1
1/6/69	Mexico	Mexico C	0–0
8/6/69	Uruguay	Montevideo	2–1
12/6/69	Brazil	Rio de Janeiro	1–2
5/11/69	Holland	Amsterdam	1–0
10/12/69	Portugal	Wembley	1–0

1970

14/1	Holland	Wembley	0–0
25/2	Belgium	Brussels	3–1
18/4	Wales	Cardiff	1–1
21/4	N Ireland	Wembley	3–1
25/4	Scotland	Glasgow	0–0
20/5	Colombia	Bogota	4–0
24/5	Ecuador	Quito	2–0
2/6	Romania	Guadalajara	1–0 (WCF)
7/6	Brazil	Guadalajara	0–1 (WCF)
11/6	Czechoslovakia	Guadalajara	1–0 (WCF)
14/6	W Germany	Leon	2–3* (WCF)
25/11	E Germany	Wembley	3–1

1971

3/2	Malta	Valletta	1–0 (ECQ)
21/4	Greece	Wembley	4–0 (ECQ)
12/5	Malta	Wembley	5–0 (ECQ)
15/5	N Ireland	Belfast	1–0
19/5	Wales	Wembley	0–0
22/5	Scotland	Wembley	3–1
13/10	Switzerland	Basle	3–2 (ECQ)
10/11	Switzerland	Wembley	1–1 (ECQ)
1/12	Greece	Athens	2–0 (ECQ)

1972

29/4	W Germany	Wembley	1–3 (ECQ)
13/5	W Germany	Berlin	0–0 (ECQ)
20/5	Wales	Cardiff	3–0
23/5	N Ireland	Wembley	0–1
27/5	Scotland	Glasgow	1–0
11/10	Yugoslavia	Wembley	1–1
15/11	Wales	Cardiff	1–0 (WCQ)

1973

24/1	Wales	Wembley	1–1 (WCQ)
14/2	Scotland	Glasgow	5–0
12/5	N Ireland	Anfield	2–1
15/5	Wales	Wembley	3–0
19/5	Scotland	Wembley	1–0
27/5	Czechoslovakia	Prague	1–1
6/6	Poland	Chorzow	0–2 (WCQ)
10/6	USSR	Moscow	2–1
14/6	Italy	Turin	0–2
26/9	Austria	Wembley	7–0
17/10	Poland	Wembley	1–1 (WCQ)
14/11	Italy	Wembley	0–1

1974

3/4	Portugal	Lisbon	0–0
11/5	Wales	Cardiff	2–0
15/5	N Ireland	Wembley	1–0
18/5	Scotland	Glasgow	0–2
22/5	Argentina	Wembley	2–2
29/5	East Germany	Leipzig	1–1
1/6	Bulgaria	Sofia	1–0
5/6	Yugoslavia	Belgrade	2–2
30/10	Czechoslovakia	Wembley	3–0 (ECQ)
20/11	Portugal	Wembley	0–0 (ECQ)

1975

12/3	W Germany	Wembley	2–0
16/4	Cyprus	Wembley	5–0 (ECQ)
11/5	Cyprus	Limassol	1–0 (ECQ)
17/5	N Ireland	Belfast	0–0
21/5	Wales	Wembley	2–2
24/5	Scotland	Wembley	5–1
3/9	Switzerland	Basle	2–1
30/10	Czechoslovakia	Bratislava	1–2 (ECQ)
19/11	Portugal	Lisbon	1–1 (ECQ)

1976

24/3	Wales	Wrexham	2–1
8/5	Wales	Cardiff	1–0
11/5	N Ireland	Wembley	4–0
15/5	Scotland	Glasgow	1–2
23/5	Brazil	Los Angeles	0–1 (USBT)
28/5	Italy	New York	3–2 (USBT)
13/6	Finland	Helsinki	4–1 (WCQ)
8/9	Rep of Ireland	Wembley	1–1
13/10	Finland	Wembley	2–1 (WCQ)
17/11	Italy	Rome	0–2 (WCQ)

1977

9/2	Holland	Wembley	0–2
30/3	Luxembourg	Wembley	5–0 (WCQ)
28/5	N Ireland	Belfast	2–1
31/5	Wales	Wembley	0–1
4/6	Scotland	Wembley	1–2
8/6	Brazil	Rio de Janeiro	0–0
12/6	Argentina	Buenos Aires	1–1
15/6	Uruguay	Montevideo	0–0
7/9	Switzerland	Wembley	0–0
12/10	Luxembourg	Luxembourg	2–0 (WCQ)
16/11	Italy	Wembley	2–0 (WCQ)

1978

22/2	W Germany	Munich	1–2
19/4	Brazil	Wembley	1–1
13/5	Wales	Cardiff	3–1
16/5	N Ireland	Wembley	1–0
20/5	Scotland	Glasgow	1–0
24/5	Hungary	Wembley	4–1
20/9	Denmark	Copenhagen	4–3 (ECQ)
25/10	Rep of Ireland	Dublin	1–1 (ECQ)
29/11	Czechoslovakia	Wembley	1–0

1979

7/2	N Ireland	Wembley	4–0 (ECQ)
19/5	N Ireland	Belfast	2–0
23/5	Wales	Wembley	0–0
26/5	Scotland	Wembley	3–1
6/6	Bulgaria	Sofia	3–0 (ECQ)
10/6	Sweden	Stockholm	0–0
13/6	Austria	Vienna	3–4
12/9	Denmark	Wembley	1–0 (ECQ)
17/10	N Ireland	Belfast	5–1 (ECQ)
22/11	Bulgaria	Wembley	2–0 (ECQ)

1980

6/2	Rep of Ireland	Wembley	2–0 (ECQ)
26/3	Spain	Barcelona	2–0
13/5	Argentina	Wembley	3–1
17/5	Wales	Wrexham	1–4
20/5	N Ireland	Wembley	1–1
24/5	Scotland	Glasgow	2–0
31/5	Australia	Sydney	2–1
12/6	Belgium	Turin	1–1 (ECF)
15/6	Italy	Turin	0–1 (ECF)
18/6	Spain	Naples	2–1 (ECF)
10/9	Norway	Wembley	4–0 (WCQ)
15/10	Romania	Bucharest	1–2 (WCQ)
19/11	Switzerland	Wembley	2–1 (WCQ)

1981

25/3	Spain	Wembley	1–2
29/4	Romania	Wembley	0–0 (WCQ)
12/5	Brazil	Wembley	0–1
20/5	Wales	Wembley	0–0
23/5	Scotland	Wembley	0–1
30/5	Switzerland	Basle	1–2 (WCQ)
6/6	Hungary	Budapest	3–1 (WCQ)
9/9	Norway	Oslo	1–2 (WCQ)
18/11	Hungary	Wembley	1–0 (WCQ)

1982

23/2	N Ireland	Wembley	4–0
25/5	Holland	Wembley	2–0
29/5	Scotland	Glasgow	1–0
2/6	Iceland	Reykjavik	1–1
3/6	Finland	Helsinki	4–1
16/6	France	Bilbao	3–1 (WCF)
20/6	Czechoslovakia	Bilbao	2–0 (WCF)
25/6	Kuwait	Bilbao	1–0 (WCF)
29/6	W Germany	Madrid	0–0 (WCF)
5/7	Spain	Madrid	0–0 (WCF)
22/9	Denmark	Copenhagen	2–2 (ECQ)
13/10	W Germany	Wembley	1–2
17/11	Greece	Salonika	3–0 (ECQ)
15/12	Luxembourg	Wembley	9–0 (ECQ)

1983

23/2	Wales	Wembley	2–1
30/3	Greece	Wembley	0–0 (ECQ)
27/4	Hungary	Wembley	2–0 (ECQ)
28/5	N Ireland	Belfast	0–0
1/6	Scotland	Wembley	2–0
12/6	Australia	Sydney	0–0
15/6	Australia	Brisbane	1–0
19/6	Australia	Melbourne	1–1
21/9	Denmark	Wembley	0–1 (ECQ)
12/10	Hungary	Budapest	3–0 (ECQ)
16/11	Luxembourg	Luxembourg	4–0 (ECQ)

1984

29/2	France	Paris	0–2
4/4	N Ireland	Wembley	1–0
2/5	Wales	Wrexham	0–1
26/5	Scotland	Glasgow	1–1
2/6	USSR	Wembley	0–2
10/6	Brazil	Rio de Janeiro	2–0
13/6	Uruguay	Montevideo	0–2
17/6	Chile	Santiago	0–0
12/9	E Germany	Wembley	1–0
17/10	Finland	Wembley	5–0 (WCQ)
14/11	Turkey	Istanbul	8–0 (WCQ)

1985

27/2	N Ireland	Belfast	1–0 (WCQ)
26/3	Rep of Ireland	Wembley	2–1
1/5	Romania	Bucharest	0–0 (WCQ)
22/5	Finland	Helsinki	1–1 (WCQ)
25/5	Scotland	Glasgow	0–1
6/6	Italy	Mexico C	1–2
9/6	Mexico	Mexico C	0–1
12/6	W Germany	Mexico C	3–0
16/6	USA	Los Angeles	5–0
11/9	Romania	Wembley	1–1 (WCQ)
16/10	Turkey	Wembley	5–0 (WCQ)
13/11	N Ireland	Wembley	0–0 (WCQ)

1986

29/1	Egypt	Cairo	4–0
26/2	Israel	Ramat Gan	2–1
26/3	USSR	Tblisi	1–0
23/4	Scotland	Wembley	2–1
17/5	Mexico	Los Angeles	3–0
24/5	Canada	Burnaby	1–0
3/6	Portugal	Monterrey	0–1 (WCF)
6/6	Morocco	Monterrey	0–0 (WCF)
11/6	Poland	Monterrey	3–0 (WCF)
18/6	Paraguay	Mexico C	3–0 (WCF)
22/6	Argentina	Mexico C	1–2 (WCF)
10/9	Sweden	Stockholm	0–1
15/10	N Ireland	Wembley	3–0 (ECQ)
12/11	Yugoslavia	Wembley	2–0 (ECQ)

1987

10/2	Spain	Madrid	4–2
1/4	N Ireland	Belfast	2–0 (ECQ)
29/4	Turkey	Izmir	0–0 (ECQ)
19/5	Brazil	Wembley	1–1
23/5	Scotland	Glasgow	0–0
9/9	W Germany	Düsseldorf	1–3
14/10	Turkey	Wembley	8–0 (ECQ)
11/11	Yugoslavia	Belgrade	4–1 (ECQ)

1988			
17/2	Israel	Tel Aviv	0–0
23/3	Holland	Wembley	2–2
27/4	Hungary	Budapest	0–0
21/5	Scotland	Wembley	1–0
24/5	Colombia	Wembley	1–1
28/5	Switzerland	Lausanne	1–0
12/6	Rep of Ireland	Stuttgart	0–1 (ECF)
15/6	Holland	Düsseldorf	1–3 (ECF)
18/6	USSR	Frankfurt	1–3 (ECF)
14/9	Denmark	Wembley	1–0
19/10	Sweden	Wembley	0–0 (WCQ)
16/11	Saudi Arabia	Riyadh	1–1

1989			
8/2	Greece	Athens	2–1
8/3	Albania	Tirana	2–0 (WCQ)
26/4	Albania	Wembley	5–0 (WCQ)
23/5	Chile	Wembley	0–0
27/5	Scotland	Glasgow	2–0
3/6	Poland	Wembley	3–0 (WCQ)
7/6	Denmark	Copenhagen	1–1
6/9	Sweden	Stockholm	0–0 (WCQ)
11/10	Poland	Katowice	0–0 (WCQ)
15/11	Italy	Wembley	0–0
13/12	Yugoslavia	Wembley	2–1

1990			
28/3	Brazil	Wembley	1–0
25/4	Czechoslovakia	Wembley	4–2
15/5	Denmark	Wembley	1–0
22/5	Uruguay	Wembley	1–2
2/6	Tunisia	Tunis	1–1
11/6	Rep of Ireland	Cagliari	1–1 (WCF)
16/6	Holland	Cagliari	0–0 (WCF)
21/6	Egypt	Cagliari	1–0 (WCF)
26/6	Belgium	Bologna	1–0 (WCF)
1/7	Cameroon	Naples	3–2 (WCF)
4/7	W Germany	Turin	1–1* (WCF)
	(England lost 3–4 on penalties)		
7/7	Italy	Bari	1–2 (WCF)
12/9	Hungary	Wembley	1–0
17/10	Poland	Wembley	2–0 (ECQ)
14/11	Rep of Ireland	Dublin	1–1 (ECQ)

1991			
6/2	Cameroon	Wembley	2–0
27/3	Rep of Ireland	Wembley	1–1 (ECQ)
1/5	Turkey	Izmir	1–0 (ECQ)
21/5	USSR	Wembley	3–1
25/5	Argentina	Wembley	2–2
1/6	Australia	Sydney	1–0
3/6	New Zealand	Auckland	1–0
8/6	New Zealand	Wellington	2–0
12/6	Malaysia	Kuala Lumpur	4–2
11/9	Germany	Wembley	0–1
16/10	Turkey	Wembley	1–0 (ECQ)
13/11	Poland	Poznan	1–1 (ECQ)

1992			
19/2	France	Wembley	2–0
25/3	Czechoslovakia	Prague	2–2
29/4	CIS	Moscow	2–2
12/5	Hungary	Budapest	1–0
17/5	Brazil	Wembley	1–1
3/6	Finland	Helsinki	2–1
11/6	Denmark	Malmö	0–0 (ECF)
14/6	France	Malmö	0–0 (ECF)
17/6	Sweden	Stockholm	1–2 (ECF)
9/9	Spain	Santander	0–1
14/10	Norway	Wembley	1–1 (WCQ)
18/11	Turkey	Wembley	4–0 (WCQ)

1993			
17/2	San Marino	Wembley	6–0 (WCQ)
31/3	Turkey	Izmir	2–0 (WCQ)
28/4	Holland	Wembley	2–2 (WCQ)
29/5	Poland	Katowice	1–1 (WCQ)
2/6	Norway	Oslo	0–2 (WCQ)
9/6	USA	Boston	0–2 (USC)

1993 (cont.)			
13/6	Brazil	Washington	1–1 (USC)
19/6	Germany	Detroit	1–2 (USC)
8/9	Poland	Wembley	3–0 (WCQ)
13/10	Holland	Rotterdam	0–2 (WCQ)
17/11	San Marino	Bologna	7–1 (WCQ)

1994			
9/3	Denmark	Wembley	1–0
17/5	Greece	Wembley	5–0
22/5	Norway	Wembley	0–0
7/9	United States	Wembley	2–0
16/11	Nigeria	Wembley	1–0

1995			
15/2	Rep of Ireland	Dublin	0–1
	(abandoned after 21 minutes)		
29/3	Uruguay	Wembley	0–0
3/6	Japan	Wembley	2–1 (UT)
8/6	Sweden	Leeds	3–3 (UT)
11/6	Brazil	Wembley	1–3 (UT)
6/9	Colombia	Wembley	0–0
11/10	Norway	Oslo	0–0
15/11	Switzerland	Wembley	3–1
12/12	Portugal	Wembley	1–1

1996			
27/3	Bulgaria	Wembley	1–0
24/4	Croatia	Wembley	0–0
18/5	Hungary	Wembley	3–0
23/5	China	Beijing	3–0
8/6	Switzerland	Wembley	1–1 (ECF)
15/6	Scotland	Wembley	2–0 (ECF)
18/6	Holland	Wembley	4–1 (ECF)
22/6	Spain	Wembley	0–0 (ECF)
	(England won 4–2 on penalties)		
26/6	Germany	Wembley	1–1 (ECF)
	(England lost 5–6 on penalties)		
1/9	Moldova	Chisinau	3–0 (WCQ)
9/10	Poland	Wembley	2–1 (WCQ)
9/11	Georgia	Tbilisi	2–0 (WCQ)

1997			
12/2	Italy	Wembley	0–1 (WCQ)
29/3	Mexico	Wembley	2–0
30/4	Georgia	Wembley	2–0 (WCQ)
24/5	South Africa	Old Trafford	2–1
31/5	Poland	Chorzow	2–0 (WCQ)
4/6	Italy	Nantes	2–0 (TDF)
7/6	France	Montpellier	1–0 (TDF)
10/6	Brazil	Paris	0–1 (TDF)
10/9	Moldova	Wembley	4–0 (WCQ)
11/10	Italy	Rome	0–0 (WCQ)
15/11	Cameroon	Wembley	2–0

1998			
11/2	Chile	Wembley	0–2
25/3	Switzerland	Berne	1–1
22/4	Portugal	Wembley	3–0
23/5	Saudi Arabia	Wembley	0–0
27/5	Morocco	Casablanca	2–0 (KHT)
29/5	Belgium	Casablanca	0–0 (KHT)
	(Belgium won 4–3 on penalties)		
15/6	Tunisia	Marseilles	2–0 (WCF)
22/6	Romania	Toulouse	1–2 (WCF)
26/6	Columbia	St. Etienne	2–0 (WCF)
30/6	Argentina	Lens	2–2 (WCF)
	(Argentina won 4–3 on penalties)		
5/9	Sweden	Stockholm	1–2 (ECQ)
10/10	Bulgaria	Wembley	0–0 (ECQ)
14/10	Luxembourg	Luxembourg	3–0 (ECQ)
18/11	Czech Republic	Wembley	3–0

1999			
10/2	France	Wembley	0–2
27/3	Poland	Wembley	3–1 (ECQ)
28/4	Hungary	Budapest	1–1
5/6	Sweden	Wembley	0–0 (ECQ)
9/6	Bulgaria	Sofia	1–1 (ECQ)

SCOTLAND

Nobody knows just when football was introduced to Scotland. There is reference to it being played there in the early seventeenth century, but no further record of it until a report of a challenge match staged between a team of Highlanders and the YMCA on the Queen's Park Recreation Ground (with 20 men a side) in 1867.

That game so caught the participants' imagination that on July 9, 1867, a meeting was organized at 3 Eglinton Terrace, Glasgow, for the purpose of forming a football club. Thus the famous Queen's Park club came into existence. They did not concede a single goal in their first five years, and they represented Scotland in the very first official international against England in 1872.

Before that Queen's Park had enrolled in the (English) Football Association and participated in the inaugural FA Cup competition, gaining a bye to the semi-final. Here they met the Wanderers in London and surprised everyone south of the border by forcing a goalless draw. Unfortunately funds did not stretch to a replay and Queen's Park were forced to scratch.

The visit to London nevertheless stimulated Scottish enthusiasm, and early in 1873 a move to form their own Association was set in progress. Seven clubs attended this historic gathering in Glasgow on March 13, and the Queen's Park officials had little difficulty persuading their colleagues of the good sense of the proposition on the table.

The founder members alongside Queen's Park were Third Lanark, Vale of Leven, Clydesdale, Eastern, Dumbreck and Granville. All were eventually persuaded to adopt the FA rules, but only after considerable argument over the offside rule.

The initial Scottish Cup competition was patronized by 16 clubs. Predictably, Queen's Park won it without conceding a goal, beating Clydesdale 2–0 in the final.

Religion and Rivalry

Having maintained their dominance in this competition for two more years, Queen's Park then found their pre-eminence in Scottish football gradually fading. Other names began to appear on the silverware: the Vale of Leven, Dumbarton, Renton – and then Hibernian, a club run by Roman Catholics and based in Edinburgh.

Hibs' SFA Cup Final win over Dumbarton in 1887 was considered sensational and created such a wave of enthusiasm among fellow religionists in Glasgow that the Celtic club was born. Celtic's success was immediate. Their first official game was a friendly with Rangers in May 1888. It was the first of the "Old Firm" clashes which have been the centre-piece of the Scottish domestic calendar ever since, and the beginning of a rivalry, both sporting and religious, which has been exploited to the full.

Rangers, as Queen's Park had done, entered the English FA Cup and in 1886–87 were eliminated by Aston Villa at the semi-final stage at Crewe. This was the last time a Scottish team competed in the English Cup. The Scottish FA disapproved and at their annual meeting on May 10, 1887, decreed that all Scottish clubs must withdraw their memberships of the FA. They were compensated for the loss of games by the popularity of the Glasgow Cup.

A League of Their Own

Scottish football, however, was losing ground. The administrators, still strongly influenced by amateur Queen's Park, repeatedly refused to accept professionalism and many of the best players were tempted to English clubs.

The practice of illegal payments through "boot money" became an open secret, but clubs needed revenue to finance their subterfuge. The success of the Football League in England had not gone unnoticed, and in 1890–91 Rangers, Celtic, Third Lanark, Hearts, St Mirren, Dumbarton, Renton, Cowlairs, Cambuslang, Vale of Leven and Abercorn formed the Scottish League. Three years later the SFA reluctantly bowed to professionalism and this coincided with Rangers winning the Scottish Cup for the first time. Their opponents? Celtic, who were beaten 3–1.

Scottish football entered the twentieth century on a firm footing. Their national side had won 15 and drawn six of the 29 games against England, and it was widely accepted that the Scots had applied a more scientific mind to their game.

In contrast with England, where the early protaganists on the field were mainly drawn from the gentry, the majority of players north of the border were recruited from working-class backgrounds. Their concept of the game was totally different.

The English persisted in a dribbling game, with individuals taking on opponents one after the other until they lost possession. The Scots, on the other hand, developed the passing game, attacking in groups and moving the ball one to the other. The slightly built inside-forward who could throw an opponent with a shrug of the shoulders, the flick of a hip, the precise pass, became symbolic of the artistry of Scottish football.

Over the years the Scottish game produced a galaxy of great individualists who never lost sight of their role in the team pattern.

From players of this type, it was said, most of Scotland's greatness in the game was measured. These included Bobby Walker of Hearts and later Jimmy Mason, Jimmy Williamson, Willie Buchan and Tommy Walker; then came "Slim" Jim Baxter in the 1960s; the impish brilliance of Denis Law and Gordon Strachan.

The "Old Firm"

In the 32 years from 1900 the dominance of Rangers and Celtic became almost suffocating. Third Lanark had won the Championship flag in 1904, but after that the "Old Firm" left the rest in their wake. Celtic reeled off six successive titles, and Rangers

responded with three. So it went on, Rangers stringing five more Championships together in consecutive seasons before Motherwell intervened to disturb the pattern in 1932. The game had overcome its blackest day: April 5, 1902, the day of the Ibrox disaster. A terrace of wooden steps supported by pillars collapsed during an international with England, plunging hundreds of fans into a chasm; 25 died and more than 500 were injured, yet the game continued – the players, officials, and indeed majority of fans, unaware of the tragedy in their midst.

The alteration to the offside law in 1925 significantly altered the Scottish style of play. The stopper centre-half was introduced, a more cautious approach leading to negative play. Even the new defensive formula, however, could not contain Jimmy McCrory, the Celtic centre-forward, who in January 1928 set a Scottish First Division record when he scored eight goals in one match against Dunfermline Athletic.

The Scottish League Cup was born in 1946 out of the wartime Southern Cup competition, and following the war there was also an attempt to reorganize the League itself. The concept was very similar to the Premiership, introduced in England in 1992. The idea was for the more powerful clubs to break away and invite others to join them in a 16-club competition under the banner of the "Super-League".

It was all about the distribution of wealth. The big clubs did not want to continue to support the smaller clubs. However, at a special meeting Clyde, opponents of such a split, received backing from a most unexpected source when both Celtic and Rangers supported them.

The Super-League was dead

On the playing front Hibernian were to emerge as one of the most attractive and effective combinations since the mid-thirties. They won three Championships in 1948, 1951 and 1952. Aberdeen, Hearts, Dundee and Kilmarnock also enjoyed League success before Celtic set a record with nine successive League Championship wins between 1966 and

1974.

Billy McNeill and company also gained universal acclaim as Celtic became the first British side to win the European Cup. A 2–1 win over Internazionale in Lisbon on 25 May, 1967, provided the Parkhead faithful's greatest hour-and-a-half.

In 1975 the Premier Division was introduced and Rangers ran away with the honours, finishing a clear six points ahead of Celtic. The Ibrox Park club established yet another record in 1993, claiming their fifth Premiership title in a row after never looking like being caught.

The Rangers revival was instigated by manager Graeme Souness, who set a new trend by looking to England for players. He took England goalkeeper Chris Woods, centre-forward Mark Hateley, midfielder Ray Wilkins, right-back Gary Stevens and many more.

Dundee United, winners in 1983, and Aberdeen, winners in 1984 and 1985, under manager Alex Ferguson, had stimulated public interest by breaking the "Old Firm" monopoly. But it was only a brief interruption.

Dundee United won the 109th Cup Final in 1994, to end Rangers' dream of landing successive trebles for the first time in Scottish history. It was United's first victory in seven Final appearances.

Scots on the World Stage

At international level Scotland had remained an enigma. Capable of beating the best, they have usually tripped up against "easy" opponents. Scotland remained unbeaten against foreign opposition until 1931 when, lacking the players of Rangers and Celtic, they were heavily beaten in Vienna and Rome. Austria did manage a 2–2 draw in Glasgow in 1933, but had to wait till 1950 before they could shatter Scotland's proud home record.

The withdrawal of the British Associations from FIFA in 1928 no doubt hampered the Scots' development at international level, but there were no hints of this on March 31 of that year at Wembley.

Scotland took England apart with football as delightful as any which had been seen. Their slick combina-

tion play, speed of thought and precision passing were all too much for England, and the 5–1 scoreline emphasized the gulf between the two teams. This team were hailed as the "Wembley Wizards": Harkness in goal, full-backs Nelson and Law, half-backs Gibson, Bradshaw and McMullen and forwards Jackson, Dunn, Gallacher, James and Morton. In 1950 Scotland qualified for the World Cup Finals in Brazil by finishing second to England in the Home Championship. But the SFA had declared they would go only if they finished first, and a golden opportunity to test the world waters was wasted – to their cost, as Scotland discovered four years later. They did compete in the finals in Switzerland but had a disastrous time, losing 1–0 to Austria and 7–0 to Uruguay and it was not until 1958 that Scotland qualified again for the World Cup Finals. This was an achievement they were to repeat for the next four competitions – with consequent nightmares which included winger Willie Johnston failing a dope test in Argentina in 1978 and defeat by the minnows of Costa Rica in Italia' 1990.

Failure to qualify for the 1994 finals was a bitter blow at a turbulent time in Scotland, with the competitive structure under permanent review. At least they qualified for the finals of the 1992 and 1996 European Championship, but at club level, none have made an impression.

This was not for a lack of investment. The Rangers hierarchy spent heavily on international superstars including Denmark's Brian Laudrup and England's Paul Gascoigne. Each man, in turn, inspired Rangers to maintain their dominance of the league championship to the continuing disappointment of Celtic. In 1997 Rangers emulated Celtic's feat of the 1960s and 1970s by winning their ninth consecutive league title.

Celtic's revival to win the league in 1997–98 also marked the end of an era as the top Scottish clubs followed England's example by forming a breakaway championship of their own. A compensatory financial package secured the reluctant assent of the rump of the Scottish Football League.

SCOTTISH LEAGUE CHAMPIONS

FIRST DIVISION

Season	Champions	Pts	Runners-up	Pts
1890–91	Dumbarton	29	Rangers	29 +
1891–92	Dumbarton	37	Celtic	35
1892–93	Celtic	29	Rangers	28
1893–94	Celtic	29	Hearts	26
1894–95	Hearts	31	Celtic	26
1895–96	Celtic	30	Rangers	26
1896–97	Hearts	28	Hibernian	26
1897–98	Celtic	33	Rangers	29
1898–99	Rangers	36	Hearts	26
1899–1900	Rangers	32	Celtic	25
1900–01	Rangers	35	Celtic	29
1901–02	Rangers	28	Celtic	26
1902–03	Hibernian	37	Dundee	31
1903–04	Third Lanark	43	Hearts	39
1904–05	Celtic	41	Rangers	41+
1905–06	Celtic	49	Hearts	43
1906–07	Celtic	55	Dundee	48
1907–08	Celtic	55	Falkirk	51
1908–09	Celtic	51	Dundee	50
1909–10	Celtic	54	Falkirk	52
1910–11	Rangers	52	Aberdeen	48
1911–12	Rangers	51	Celtic	45
1912–13	Rangers	53	Celtic	49
1913–14	Celtic	65	Rangers	59
1914–15	Celtic	65	Hearts	61
1915–16	Celtic	67	Rangers	56
1916–17	Celtic	64	Morton	54
1917–18	Rangers	56	Celtic	55
1918–19	Celtic	58	Rangers	57
1919–20	Rangers	71	Celtic	68
1920–21	Rangers	76	Celtic	66
1921–22	Celtic	67	Rangers	66
1922–23	Rangers	55	Airdrieonians	50
1923–24	Rangers	59	Airdrieonians	50
1924–25	Rangers	60	Airdrieonians	57
1925–26	Celtic	58	Airdrieonians*	50
1926–27	Rangers	56	Motherwell	51
1927–28	Rangers	60	Celtic*	55
1928–29	Rangers	67	Celtic	51
1929–30	Rangers	60	Motherwell	55
1930–31	Rangers	60	Celtic	58
1931–32	Motherwell	66	Rangers	61
1932–33	Rangers	62	Motherwell	59
1933–34	Rangers	66	Motherwell	62
1934–35	Rangers	55	Celtic	52
1935–36	Celtic	66	Rangers*	61
1936–37	Rangers	61	Aberdeen	54
1937–38	Celtic	61	Hearts	58
1938–39	Rangers	59	Celtic	48
1946–47	Rangers	46	Hibernian	44
1947–48	Hibernian	48	Rangers	46
1948–49	Rangers	46	Dundee	45
1949–50	Rangers	50	Hibernian	49
1950–51	Hibernian	48	Rangers*	38
1951–52	Hibernian	45	Rangers	41
1952–53	Rangers*	43	Hibernian	43
1953–54	Celtic	43	Hearts	38
1954–55	Aberdeen	49	Celtic	46
1955–56	Rangers	52	Aberdeen	46
1956–57	Rangers	55	Hearts	53
1957–58	Hearts	62	Rangers	49
1958–59	Rangers	50	Hearts	48
1959–60	Hearts	54	Kilmarnock	50
1960–61	Rangers	51	Kilmarnock	50
1961–62	Dundee	54	Rangers	51
1962–63	Rangers	57	Kilmarnock	48
1963–64	Rangers	55	Kilmarnock	49
1964–65	Kilmarnock*	50	Hearts	50
1965–66	Celtic	57	Rangers	55
1966–67	Celtic	58	Rangers	55
1967–68	Celtic	63	Rangers	61
1968–69	Celtic	54	Rangers	49
1969–70	Celtic	57	Rangers	45
1970–71	Celtic	56	Aberdeen	54
1971–72	Celtic	60	Aberdeen	50
1972–73	Celtic	57	Rangers	56
1973–74	Celtic	53	Hibernian	49
1974–75	Rangers	56	Hibernian	49

PREMIER DIVISION

1975–76	Rangers	54	Celtic	48
1976–77	Celtic	55	Rangers	46
1977–78	Rangers	55	Aberdeen	53
1978–79	Celtic	48	Rangers	45
1979–80	Aberdeen	48	Celtic	47
1980–81	Celtic	56	Aberdeen	49
1981–82	Celtic	55	Aberdeen	53
1982–83	Dundee Utd	56	Celtic*	55
1983–84	Aberdeen	57	Celtic	50
1984–85	Aberdeen	59	Celtic	52
1985–86	Celtic*	50	Hearts	50
1986–87	Rangers	69	Celtic	63
1987–88	Celtic	72	Hearts	62
1988–89	Rangers	56	Aberdeen	50
1989–90	Rangers	51	Aberdeen*	44
1990–91	Rangers	55	Aberdeen	53
1991–92	Rangers	72	Hearts	63
1992–93	Rangers	73	Aberdeen	64
1993–94	Rangers	58	Aberdeen	55
1994–95	Rangers	69	Motherwell	54
1995–96	Rangers	87	Celtic	83
1996–97	Rangers	80	Celtic	75
1997–98	Celtic	74	Rangers	72
1998–99	Rangers	77	Celtic	71

Notes:* On goal average/difference; + Championship held jointly

SCOTTISH LEAGUE CUP

Season	Winners	Runners-up	Score
1946–47	Rangers	Aberdeen	4–0
1947–48	East Fife	Falkirk	0–0, 4–1
1948–49	Rangers	Raith Rovers	2–0
1949–50	East Fife	Dunfermline Ath	3–0
1950–51	Motherwell	Hibernian	3–0
1951–52	Dundee	Rangers	3–2
1952–53	Dundee	Kilmarnock	2–0
1953–54	East Fife	Partick T	3–2
1954–55	Hearts	Motherwell	4–2
1955–56	Aberdeen	St Mirren	2–1
1956–57	Celtic	Partick T	0–0, 3–0
1957–58	Celtic	Rangers	7–1
1958–59	Hearts	Partick T	5–1
1959–60	Hearts	Third Lanark	2–1
1960–61	Rangers	Kilmarnock	2–0
1961–62	Rangers	Hearts	1–1, 3–1
1962–63	Hearts	Kilmarnock	1–0
1963–64	Rangers	Morton	5–0
1964–65	Rangers	Celtic	2–1
1965–66	Celtic	Rangers	2–1
1966–67	Celtic	Rangers	1–0
1967–68	Celtic	Dundee	5–3
1968–69	Celtic	Hibernian	6–2
1969–70	Celtic	St Johnstone	1–0
1970–71	Rangers	Celtic	1–0
1971–72	Partick T	Celtic	4–1
1972–73	Hibernian	Celtic	2–1
1973–74	Dundee	Celtic	1–0
1974–75	Celtic	Hibernian	6–3
1975–76	Rangers	Celtic	1–0
1976–77	Aberdeen	Celtic	2–1
1977–78	Rangers	Celtic	2–1
1978–79	Rangers	Aberdeen	2–1
1979–80	Dundee Utd	Aberdeen	0–0, 3–0
1980–81	Dundee Utd	Dundee	3–0
1981–82	Rangers	Dundee Utd	2–1
1982–83	Celtic	Rangers	2–1
1983–84	Rangers	Celtic	3–2
1984–85	Rangers	Dundee Utd	1–0
1985–86	Aberdeen	Hibernian	3–0
1986–87	Rangers	Celtic	2–1
1987–88	Rangers	Aberdeen	3–3
	Rangers won 5–3 on penalties		
1988–89	Rangers	Aberdeen	3–2
1989–90	Aberdeen	Rangers	2–1
1990–91	Rangers	Celtic	2–1
1991–92	Hibernian	Dunfermline A	2–0
1992–93	Rangers	Aberdeen	2–1
1993–94	Rangers	Hibernian	2–1
1994–95	Raith Rovers	Celtic	0–0
	(Raith Rovers won 6–5 on penalties)		
1995–96	Aberdeen	Dundee	2–0
1996–97	Rangers	Hearts	4–3
1997–98	Celtic	Dundee Utd	3–0
1998–99	Rangers	St Johnstone	2–1

SCOTTISH FA CUP

Year	Winners	Runners-up	Score
1874	Queen's Park	Clydesdale	2–0
1875	Queen's Park	Renton	3–0
1876	Queen's Park	Third Lanark	1–1, 2–0
1877	Vale of Leven	Rangers	0–0, 1–1, 3–2
1878	Vale of Leven	Third Lanark	1–0
1879	Vale of Leven	Rangers	
	Rangers failed to appear for replay after 1–1 draw. Vale awarded Cup		
1880	Queen's Park	Thornlibank	3–0
1881	Queen's Park	Dumbarton	3–1
1882	Queen's Park	Dumbarton	2–2, 4–1
1883	Dumbarton	Vale of Leven	2–2, 2–1
1884	Queen's Park	Vale of Leven	
	Vale of Leven failed to appear. Queen's Park awarded Cup		
1885	Renton	Vale of Leven	0–0, 3–1
1886	Queen's Park	Renton	3–1
1887	Hibernian	Dumbarton	2–1
1888	Renton	Cambuslang	6–1
1889	Third Lanark	Celtic	3–0+, 2–1
	+Replay ordered because of playing conditions in the first game		
1890	Queen's Park	Vale of Leven	1–1, 2–1
1891	Hearts	Dumbarton	1–0
1892	Celtic	Queen's Park	5–1
	After mutually protested game which Celtic won 1–0		
1893	Queen's Park	Celtic	2–1
1894	Rangers	Celtic	3–1
1895	St Bernard's	Renton	2–1
1896	Hearts	Hibernian	3–1
1897	Rangers	Dumbarton	5–1
1898	Rangers	Kilmarnock	2–0
1899	Celtic	Rangers	2–0
1900	Celtic	Queen's Park	4–3
1901	Hearts	Celtic	4–3
1902	Hibernian	Celtic	1–0
1903	Rangers	Hearts	1–1, 0–0, 2–0
1904	Celtic	Rangers	3–2
1905	Third Lanark	Rangers	0–0, 3–1
1906	Hearts	Third Lanark	1–0
1907	Celtic	Hearts	3–0
1908	Celtic	St Mirren	5–1
1909	Owing to riot, the cup was withheld after two drawn games		
	Celtic vs. Rangers		2–2, 1–1
1910	Dundee	Clyde	2–2, 0–0, 2–1
1911	Celtic	Hamilton A	0–0, 2–0
1912	Celtic	Clyde	2–0
1913	Falkirk	Raith R	2–0
1914	Celtic	Hibernian	0–0, 4–1
1920	Kilmarnock	Albion R	3–2
1921	Partick T	Rangers	1–0
1922	Morton	Rangers	1–0
1923	Celtic	Hibernian	1–0
1924	Airdrieonians	Hibernian	2–0
1925	Celtic	Dundee	2–1
1926	St Mirren	Celtic	2–0
1927	Celtic	East Fife	3–1
1928	Rangers	Celtic	4–0
1929	Kilmarnock	Rangers	2–0
1930	Rangers	Partick T	0–0, 2–1
1931	Celtic	Motherwell	2–2, 4–2
1932	Rangers	Kilmarnock	1–1, 3–0
1933	Celtic	Motherwell	1–0
1934	Rangers	St Mirren	5–0
1935	Rangers	Hamilton A	2–1
1936	Rangers	Third Lanark	1–0
1937	Celtic	Aberdeen	2–1
1938	East Fife	Kilmarnock	1–1, 4–2
1939	Clyde	Motherwell	4–0
1947	Aberdeen	Hibernian	2–1
1948	Rangers	Morton	1–1, 1–0
1949	Rangers	Clyde	4–1
1950	Rangers	East Fife	3–0
1951	Celtic	Motherwell	1–0
1952	Motherwell	Dundee	4–0
1953	Rangers	Aberdeen	1–1, 1–0
1954	Celtic	Aberdeen	2–1
1955	Clyde	Celtic	1–1, 1–0
1956	Hearts	Celtic	3–1
1957	Falkirk	Kilmarnock	1–1, 2–1
1958	Clyde	Hibernian	1–0
1959	St Mirren	Aberdeen	3–1
1960	Rangers	Kilmarnock	2–0
1961	Dunfermline A	Celtic	0–0, 2–0
1962	Rangers	St Mirren	2–0
1963	Rangers	Celtic	1–1, 3–0
1964	Rangers	Dundee	3–1
1965	Celtic	Dunfermline A	3–2
1966	Rangers	Celtic	0–0, 1–0
1967	Celtic	Aberdeen	2–0
1968	Dunfermline A	Hearts	3–1
1969	Celtic	Rangers	4–0
1970	Aberdeen	Celtic	3–1
1971	Celtic	Rangers	1–1, 2–1
1972	Celtic	Hibernian	6–1
1973	Rangers	Celtic	3–2
1974	Celtic	Dundee Utd	3–0
1975	Celtic	Airdrieonians	3–1
1976	Rangers	Hearts	3–1
1977	Celtic	Rangers	1–0
1978	Rangers	Aberdeen	2–1
1979	Rangers	Hibernian	0–0, 0–0, 3–2
1980	Celtic	Rangers	1–0
1981	Rangers	Dundee Utd	0–0, 4–1
1982	Aberdeen	Rangers	4–1*
1983	Aberdeen	Rangers	1–0*
1984	Aberdeen	Celtic	2–1*
1985	Celtic	Dundee Utd	2–1
1986	Aberdeen	Hearts	3–0
1987	St Mirren	Dundee Utd	1–0 *
1988	Celtic	Dundee Utd	2–1
1989	Celtic	Rangers	1–0
1990	Aberdeen	Celtic	0–0*
	(Aberdeen won 9–8 on penalties)		
1991	Motherwell	Dundee Utd	4–3*
1992	Rangers	Airdrieonians	2–1
1993	Rangers	Aberdeen	2–1
1994	Dundee Utd	Rangers	1–0
1995	Celtic	Airdrieonians	1–0
1996	Rangers	Hearts	5–1
1997	Kilmarnock	Falkirk	1–0
1998	Hearts	Rangers	2–1
1999	Rangers	Celtic	1–0

INTERNATIONAL RESULTS 1872–1899

Date	Opponents	Venue	F–A
30/11/72	England	Glasgow	0–0
8/3/73	England	London	2–4
7/3/74	England	Glasgow	2–1
6/3/75	England	London	2–2
4/3/76	England	Glasgow	3–0
25/3/76	Wales	Glasgow	4–0
3/3/77	England	London	3–1
5/3/77	Wales	Wrexham	2–0
2/3/78	England	Glasgow	7–2
23/3/78	Wales	Glasgow	9–0
7/4/79	Wales	Wrexham	3–0

5/4/79	England	London	4–5
13/3/80	England	Glasgow	5–4
27/3/80	Wales	Glasgow	5–1
12/3/81	England	London	6–1
14/3/81	Wales	Wrexham	5–1
11/3/82	England	Glasgow	5–1
25/3/82	Wales	Glasgow	5–0
10/3/83	England	Sheffield	3–2
12/3/83	Wales	Wrexham	3–0
26/1/84	Ireland	Belfast	5–0
15/3/84	England	Glasgow	1–0
29/3/84	Wales	Glasgow	4–1
14/3/85	Ireland	Glasgow	8–2
21/3/85	England	London	1–1
23/3/85	Wales	Wrexham	8–1
20/3/86	Ireland	Belfast	7–2
31/3/86	England	Glasgow	1–1
10/4/86	Wales	Glasgow	4–4
19/2/87	Ireland	Glasgow	4–1
19/3/87	England	Blackburn	3–2
21/3/87	Wales	Wrexham	2–0
10/3/88	Wales	Edinburgh	5–1
17/3/88	England	Glasgow	0–5
24/3/88	Ireland	Belfast	10–2
9/3/89	Ireland	Glasgow	7–0
13/4/89	England	London	3–2
15/4/89	Wales	Wrexham	0–0
22/3/90	Wales	Glasgow	5–0
29/3/90	Ireland	Belfast	4–1
5/4/90	England	Glasgow	1–1
21/3/91	Wales	Wrexham	4–3
28/3/91	Ireland	Glasgow	2–1
6/4/91	England	Blackburn	1–2
19/3/92	Ireland	Belfast	3–2
26/3/92	Wales	Edinburgh	6–1
2/4/92	England	Glasgow	1–4
18/3/93	Wales	Wrexham	8–0
25/3/93	Ireland	Glasgow	6–1
1/4/93	England	Richmond	2–5
24/3/94	Wales	Kilmarnock	5–2
31/3/94	Ireland	Belfast	2–1
7/4/94	England	Glasgow	2–2
23/3/95	Wales	Wrexham	2–2
30/3/95	Ireland	Glasgow	3–1
6/4/95	England	Liverpool	0–3
21/3/96	Wales	Dundee	4–0
28/3/96	Ireland	Belfast	3–3
4/4/96	England	Glasgow	2–1
20/3/97	Wales	Wrexham	2–2
27/3/97	Ireland	Glasgow	5–1
3/4/97	England	London	2–1
19/3/98	Wales	Motherwell	5–2
26/3/98	Ireland	Belfast	3–0
2/4/98	England	Glasgow	1–3
18/3/99	Wales	Wrexham	6–0
25/3/99	Ireland	Glasgow	9–1
8/4/99	England	Birmingham	1–2

1900–1909

3/2/00	Wales	Aberdeen	5–2
3/3/00	Ireland	Belfast	3–0
7/4/00	England	Glasgow	4–1
23/2/01	Ireland	Glasgow	11–0
2/3/01	Wales	Wrexham	1–1
30/3/01	England	London	2–2
1/3/02	Ireland	Belfast	5–1
15/3/02	Wales	Greenock	5–1
3/5/02	England	Birmingham	2–2
9/3/03	Wales	Cardiff	1–0
21/3/03	Ireland	Glasgow	0–2
4/4/03	England	Sheffield	2–1
12/3/04	Wales	Dundee	1–1
26/3/04	Ireland	Dublin	1–1
9/4/04	England	Glasgow	0–1
6/3/05	Wales	Wrexham	1–3
18/3/05	Ireland	Glasgow	4–0
1/4/05	England	London	0–1
3/3/06	Wales	Edinburgh	0–2
17/3/06	Ireland	Dublin	1–0
7/4/06	England	Glasgow	2–1
4/3/07	Wales	Wrexham	0–1
16/3/07	Ireland	Glasgow	3–0
6/4/07	England	Newcastle	1–1
7/3/08	Wales	Dundee	2–1
14/3/08	Ireland	Dublin	5–0
4/4/08	England	Glasgow	1–1
1/3/09	Wales	Wrexham	2–3
15/3/09	Ireland	Glasgow	5–0
3/4/09	England	London	0–2

1910–1914

5/3/10	Wales	Kilmarnock	1–0
19/3/10	Ireland	Belfast	0–1
2/4/10	England	Glasgow	2–0
6/3/11	Wales	Cardiff	2–2
18/3/11	Ireland	Glasgow	2–0
1/4/11	England	Liverpool	1–1
2/3/12	Wales	Edinburgh	1–0
16/3/12	Ireland	Belfast	4–1
23/3/12	England	Glasgow	1–1
3/3/13	Wales	Wrexham	0–0
15/3/13	Ireland	Dublin	2–1
5/4/13	England	Stamford Bridge	0–1
28/2/14	Wales	Glasgow	0–0
14/3/14	Ireland	Belfast	1–1
4/4/14	England	Glasgow	3–1

1920–1929

26/2/20	Wales	Cardiff	1–1
13/3/20	Ireland	Glasgow	3–0
10/4/20	England	Sheffield	4–5
12/2/21	Wales	Aberdeen	2–1
26/2/21	Ireland	Belfast	2–0
9/4/21	England	Glasgow	3–0
4/2/22	Wales	Wrexham	1–2
4/3/22	Ireland	Glasgow	2–1
8/4/22	England	Birmingham	1–0
3/3/23	Ireland	Belfast	1–0
17/3/23	Wales	Glasgow	2–0
14/4/23	England	Glasgow	2–2
16/2/24	Wales	Cardiff	0–2
1/3/24	Ireland	Glasgow	2–0
12/4/24	England	Wembley	1–1
14/2/25	Wales	Edinburgh	3–1
28/2/25	Ireland	Belfast	3–0
4/4/25	England	Glasgow	2–0
31/10/25	Wales	Cardiff	3–0
27/2/26	Ireland	Glasgow	4–0
17/4/26	England	Manchester	1–0
30/10/26	Wales	Glasgow	3–0
26/2/27	Ireland	Belfast	2–0
2/4/27	England	Glasgow	1–2
29/10/27	Wales	Wrexham	2–2
25/2/28	Ireland	Glasgow	0–1
31/3/28	England	Wembley	5–1
27/10/28	Wales	Glasgow	4–2
23/2/29	Ireland	Belfast	7–3
13/4/29	England	Glasgow	1–0
26/5/29	Norway	Bergen	7–3
1/6/29	Germany	Berlin	1–1
4/6/29	Holland	Amsterdam	2–0
26/10/29	Wales	Cardiff	4–2

1930–1939

22/2/30	Ireland	Glasgow	3–1
5/4/30	England	Wembley	2–5
18/5/30	France	Paris	2–0
25/10/30	Wales	Glasgow	1–1
21/2/31	Ireland	Belfast	0–0
28/3/31	England	Glasgow	2–0
16/5/31	Austria	Vienna	0–5
20/5/31	Italy	Rome	0–3
24/5/31	Switzerland	Geneva	3–2
19/9/31	Ireland	Glasgow	3–1
31/10/31	Wales	Wrexham	3–2
9/4/32	England	Wembley	0–3
8/5/32	France	Paris	3–1
19/9/32	Ireland	Belfast	4–0
26/10/32	Wales	Edinburgh	2–5
1/4/33	England	Glasgow	2–1
16/9/33	Ireland	Glasgow	1–2
4/10/33	Wales	Cardiff	2–3
29/11/33	Austria	Glasgow	2–2
14/4/34	England	Wembley	0–3
20/10/34	Ireland	Belfast	1–2
21/11/34	Wales	Aberdeen	3–2
6/4/35	England	Glasgow	2–0
5/10/35	Wales	Cardiff	1–1
13/11/35	Ireland	Edinburgh	2–1
4/4/36	England	Wembley	1–1
14/10/36	Germany	Glasgow	2–0
31/10/36	Ireland	Belfast	3–1
2/12/36	Wales	Dundee	1–2
17/4/37	England	Glasgow	3–1
9/5/37	Austria	Vienna	1–1
22/5/37	Czechoslovakia	Prague	3–1
30/10/37	Wales	Cardiff	1–2
10/11/37	Ireland	Aberdeen	1–1
8/12/37	Czechoslovakia	Glasgow	5–0
9/4/38	England	Wembley	1–0
21/5/38	Holland	Amsterdam	3–1
8/10/38	Ireland	Belfast	2–0
9/11/38	Wales	Edinburgh	3–2
7/12/38	Hungary	Glasgow	3–1
15/4/39	England	Glasgow	1–2

1940–1949

19/10/46	Wales	Wrexham	1–3
27/11/46	N Ireland	Glasgow	0–0
12/4/47	England	Wembley	1–1
18/5/47	Belgium	Brussels	1–2
24/5/47	Luxembourg	Luxembourg	6–0
4/10/47	N Ireland	Belfast	0–2
12/11/47	Wales	Glasgow	1–2
10/4/48	England	Glasgow	0–2
28/4/48	Belgium	Glasgow	2–0
17/5/48	Switzerland	Berne	1–2
23/5/48	France	Paris	0–3
23/10/48	Wales	Cardiff	3–1
17/11/48	N Ireland	Glasgow	3–2
9/4/49	England	Wembley	3–1
27/4/49	France	Glasgow	2–0
1/10/49	N Ireland	Belfast	8–2 (WCQ)
9/11/49	Wales	Glasgow	2–0 (WCQ)

1950–1959

15/4/50	England	Glasgow	0–1 (WCQ)
26/4/50	Switzerland	Glasgow	3–1
25/5/50	Portugal	Lisbon	2–2
27/5/50	France	Paris	1–0
21/10/50	Wales	Cardiff	3–1
1/11/50	N Ireland	Glasgow	6–1
13/12/50	Austria	Glasgow	0–1
14/4/51	England	Wembley	3–2
12/5/51	Denmark	Glasgow	3–1
16/5/51	France	Glasgow	1–0
20/5/51	Belgium	Brussels	5–0
27/5/51	Austria	Vienna	0–4
6/10/51	N Ireland	Belfast	3–0
28/11/51	Wales	Glasgow	0–1
5/4/52	England	Glasgow	1–2
30/4/52	USA	Glasgow	6–0
25/5/52	Denmark	Copenhagen	2–1
30/5/52	Sweden	Stockholm	1–3
15/10/52	Wales	Cardiff	2–1
5/11/52	N Ireland	Glasgow	1–1
18/4/53	England	Wembley	2–2
6/5/53	Sweden	Glasgow	1–2
3/10/53	N Ireland	Belfast	3–1 (WCQ)
4/11/53	Wales	Glasgow	3–3 (WCQ)
3/4/54	England	Glasgow	2–4 (WCQ)
5/5/54	Norway	Glasgow	1–0
19/5/54	Norway	Oslo	1–1
25/5/54	Finland	Helsinki	2–1
16/6/54	Austria	Zurich	0–1 (WCF)
19/6/54	Uruguay	Basle	0–7 (WCF)
16/10/54	Wales	Cardiff	1–0
3/11/54	N Ireland	Glasgow	2–2
8/12/54	Hungary	Glasgow	2–4
2/4/55	England	Wembley	2–7
16/5/55	Portugal	Glasgow	3–0
15/5/55	Yugoslavia	Belgrade	2–2
19/5/55	Austria	Vienna	4–1
29/5/55	Hungary	Budapest	1–3
8/10/55	N Ireland	Belfast	1–2
9/11/55	Wales	Glasgow	2–0
14/4/56	England	Glasgow	1–1
2/5/56	Austria	Glasgow	1–1
20/10/56	Wales	Cardiff	2–2
7/11/56	N Ireland	Glasgow	1–0
21/11/56	Yugoslavia	Glasgow	2–0
6/4/57	England	Wembley	1–2
8/5/57	Spain	Glasgow	4–2 (WCQ)
19/5/57	Switzerland	Basle	2–1 (WCQ)
22/5/57	W Germany	Stuttgart	3–1
26/5/57	Spain	Madrid	1–4 (WCQ)
5/10/57	N Ireland	Belfast	1–1
6/11/57	Switzerland	Glasgow	3–2 (WCQ)
13/11/57	Wales	Glasgow	1–1
19/4/58	England	Glasgow	0–4
7/5/58	Hungary	Glasgow	1–1
1/6/58	Poland	Warsaw	2–1
8/6/58	Yugoslavia	Vasteras	1–1 (WCF)
11/6/58	Paraguay	Norrköping	2–3 (WCF)
15/6/58	France	Örebro	1–2 (WCF)
18/10/58	Wales	Cardiff	3–0
5/11/58	N Ireland	Glasgow	2–2
11/4/59	England	Wembley	0–1
6/5/59	W Germany	Glasgow	3–2
27/5/59	Holland	Amsterdam	2–1
3/6/59	Portugal	Lisbon	0–1
3/10/59	N Ireland	Belfast	4–0
14/11/59	Wales	Glasgow	1–1

1960–69

9/4/60	England	Glasgow	1–1
4/5/60	Poland	Glasgow	2–3
29/5/60	Austria	Vienna	1–4
5/6/60	Hungary	Budapest	3–3
8/6/60	Turkey	Ankara	2–4
22/10/60	Wales	Cardiff	0–2
9/11/60	N Ireland	Glasgow	5–2
15/4/61	England	Wembley	3–9
3/5/61	Rep of Ireland	Glasgow	4–1 (WCQ)
7/5/61	Rep of Ireland	Dublin	3–0 (WCQ)
14/5/61	Czechoslovakia	Bratislava	0–4 (WCQ)
26/9/61	Czechoslovakia	Glasgow	3–2 (WCQ)
7/10/61	N Ireland	Belfast	6–1
8/11/61	Wales	Glasgow	2–0
29/11/61	Czechoslovakia	Brussels	2–4 (WCQ)
14/4/62	England	Glasgow	2–0
2/5/62	Uruguay	Glasgow	2–3
20/10/62	Wales	Cardiff	3–2
7/11/62	N Ireland	Glasgow	5–1
6/4/63	England	Wembley	2–1
8/5/63	Austria	Glasgow	4–1
4/6/63	Norway	Bergen	3–4
9/6/63	Rep of Ireland	Dublin	0–1
13/6/63	Spain	Madrid	6–2
12/10/63	N Ireland	Belfast	1–2
7/11/63	Norway	Glasgow	6–1
20/11/63	Wales	Glasgow	2–1
11/4/64	England	Glasgow	1–0
12/5/64	W Germany	Hanover	2–2
3/10/64	Wales	Cardiff	2–3
21/10/64	Finland	Glasgow	3–1 (WCQ)
25/11/64	N Ireland	Glasgow	3–2
10/4/65	England	Wembley	2–2
8/5/65	Spain	Glasgow	0–0
23/5/65	Poland	Chorzow	1–1 (WCQ)
27/5/65	Finland	Helsinki	2–1 (WCQ)
2/10/65	N Ireland	Belfast	2–3
13/10/65	Poland	Glasgow	1–2 (WCQ)
9/11/65	Italy	Glasgow	1–0 (WCQ)
24/11/65	Wales	Glasgow	4–1
7/12/65	Italy	Naples	0–3 (WCQ)
2/4/66	England	Glasgow	3–4
11/5/66	Holland	Glasgow	0–3
18/6/66	Portugal	Glasgow	0–1
25/6/66	Brazil	Glasgow	1–1

22/10/66	Wales	Cardiff	1–1 (ECQ)
16/11/66	N Ireland	Glasgow	2–1 (ECQ)
15/4/67	England	Wembley	3–2 (ECQ)
10/5/67	USSR	Glasgow	0–2
21/10/67	N Ireland	Belfast	0–1 (ECQ)
22/11/67	Wales	Glasgow	3–2 (ECQ)
24/2/68	England	Glasgow	1–1 (ECQ)
30/5/68	Holland	Amsterdam	0–0
16/10/68	Denmark	Copenhagen	1–0
6/11/68	Austria	Glasgow	2–1 (WCQ)
11/12/68	Cyprus	Nicosia	5–0 (WCQ)
16/4/69	W Germany	Glasgow	1–1 (WCQ)
3/5/69	Wales	Wrexham	5–3
6/5/69	N Ireland	Glasgow	1–1
10/6/69	England	Wembley	1–4
12/5/69	Cyprus	Glasgow	8–0 (WCQ)
21/9/69	Rep of Ireland	Dublin	1–1
22/10/69	W Germany	Hamburg	2–3 (WCQ)
5/11/69	Austria	Vienna	0–2 (WCQ)

1970–79

18/4/70	N Ireland	Belfast	1–0
22/4/70	Wales	Glasgow	0–0
25/4/70	England	Glasgow	0–0
11/11/70	Denmark	Glasgow	1–0 (ECQ)
3/2/71	Belgium	Liège	0–3 (ECQ)
21/4/71	Portugal	Lisbon	0–2 (ECQ)
15/5/71	Wales	Cardiff	0–0
18/5/71	N Ireland	Glasgow	0–1
22/5/71	England	Wembley	1–3
9/6/71	Denmark	Copenhagen	0–1 (ECQ)
14/6/71	USSR	Moscow	0–1
13/10/71	Portugal	Glasgow	2–1 (ECQ)
10/11/71	Belgium	Aberdeen	1–0 (ECQ)
1/12/71	Holland	Rotterdam	1–2
26/4/72	Peru	Glasgow	2–0
20/5/72	N Ireland	Glasgow	2–0
24/5/72	Wales	Glasgow	1–0
27/5/72	England	Glasgow	0–1
29/6/72	Yugoslavia	Belo Horizonte	2–2
2/7/72	Czechoslovakia	Porto Alegre	0–0
5/7/72	Brazil	Rio de Janeiro	0–1
18/10/72	Denmark	Copenhagen	4–1 (WCQ)
15/11/72	Denmark	Glasgow	2–0 (WCQ)
14/2/73	England	Glasgow	0–5
12/5/73	Wales	Wrexham	2–0
16/5/73	N Ireland	Glasgow	1–2
19/5/73	England	Wembley	0–1
22/6/73	Switzerland	Berne	0–1
30/6/73	Brazil	Glasgow	0–1
26/9/73	Czechoslovakia	Glasgow	2–1 (WCQ)
17/10/73	Czechoslovakia	Bratislava	0–1 (WCQ)
14/11/73	W Germany	Glasgow	1–1
27/3/74	W Germany	Frankfurt	1–2
11/5/74	N Ireland	Glasgow	0–1
14/5/74	Wales	Glasgow	2–0
18/5/74	England	Glasgow	2–0
2/6/74	Belgium	Brussels	1–2
6/6/74	Norway	Oslo	2–1
14/6/74	Zaïre	Dortmund	2–0 (WCF)
18/6/74	Brazil	Frankfurt	0–0 (WCF)
22/6/74	Yugoslavia	Frankfurt	1–1 (WCF)
30/10/74	E Germany	Glasgow	3–0
20/11/74	Spain	Glasgow	1–2 (ECQ)
5/2/75	Spain	Valencia	1–1 (ECQ)
16/4/75	Sweden	Gothenburg	1–1
13/5/75	Portugal	Glasgow	1–0
17/5/75	Wales	Cardiff	2–2
20/5/75	N Ireland	Glasgow	3–0
24/5/75	England	Wembley	1–5
1/6/75	Romania	Bucharest	1–1 (ECQ)
3/9/75	Denmark	Copenhagen	1–0 (ECQ)
29/10/75	Denmark	Glasgow	3–1 (ECQ)
17/12/75	Romania	Glasgow	1–1 (ECQ)
7/4/76	Switzerland	Glasgow	1–0
6/5/76	Wales	Glasgow	3–1
8/5/76	N Ireland	Glasgow	3–0
15/5/76	England	Glasgow	2–1
8/9/76	Finland	Glasgow	6–0
13/10/76	Czechoslovakia	Prague	0–2 (WCQ)
17/11/76	Wales	Glasgow	1–0 (WCQ)
27/4/77	Sweden	Glasgow	3–1
28/5/77	Wales	Wrexham	0–0
1/6/77	N Ireland	Glasgow	3–0
4/6/77	England	Wembley	2–0
15/6/77	Chile	Santiago	4–2
18/6/77	Argentina	Buenos Aires	1–1
23/6/77	Brazil	Rio de Janeiro	0–2
7/9/77	E Germany	E Berlin	0–1
21/9/77	Czechoslovakia	Glasgow	3–1 (WCQ)
12/10/77	Wales	Liverpool	2–0 (WCQ)
22/2//78	Bulgaria	Glasgow	2–1
13/5/78	N Ireland	Glasgow	1–1
17/5/78	Wales	Glasgow	1–1
20/5/78	England	Glasgow	0–1
3/6/78	Peru	Cordoba	1–3 (WCF)
7/6/78	Iran	Cordoba	1–1 (WCF)
11/6/78	Holland	Mendoza	3–2 (WCF)
20/9/78	Austria	Vienna	2–3 (ECQ)
25/10/78	Norway	Glasgow	3–2 (ECQ)
29/11/78	Portugal	Lisbon	0–1 (ECQ)
19/5/79	Wales	Cardiff	0–3
22/5/79	N Ireland	Glasgow	1–0
26/5/79	England	Wembley	1–3
2/6/79	Argentina	Glasgow	1–3
7/6/79	Norway	Oslo	4–0 (ECQ)
12/9/79	Peru	Glasgow	1–1
17/10/79	Austria	Glasgow	1–1 (ECQ)
21/11/79	Belgium	Brussels	0–2 (ECQ)
19/12/79	Belgium	Glasgow	1–3 (ECQ)

1980–84

26/3/80	Portugal	Glasgow	4–1 (ECQ)
16/5/80	N Ireland	Belfast	0–1
21/5/80	Wales	Glasgow	1–0
24/5/80	England	Glasgow	0–2
28/5/80	Poland	Poznan	0–1
31/5/80	Hungary	Budapest	1–3
10/9/80	Sweden	Stockholm	1–0 (WCQ)
15/10/80	Portugal	Glasgow	0–0 (WCQ0
25/2/81	Israel	Tel Aviv	1–0 (WCQ)
25/3/81	N Ireland	Glasgow	1–1 (WCQ)
28/4/81	Israel	Glasgow	3–1 (WCQ)
16/5/81	Wales	Swansea	0–2
19/5/81	N Ireland	Glasgow	2–0
23/5/81	England	Wembley	1–0
9/9/81	Sweden	Glasgow	2–0 (WCQ)
14/10/81	N Ireland	Belfast	0–0 (WCQ)
18/11/81	Portugal	Lisbon	1–2 (WCQ)
24/2/82	Spain	Valencia	0–3
23/3/82	Holland	Glasgow	2–1
28/4/82	N Ireland	Belfast	1–1
24/5/82	Wales	Glasgow	1–0
29/5/82	England	Glasgow	0–1
15/6/82	New Zealand	Malaga	5–2 (WCF)
18/6/82	Brazil	Seville	1–4 (WCF)
22/6/82	USSR	Malaga	2–2 (WCF)
13/10/82	E Germany	Glasgow	2–0 (ECQ)
17/11/82	Switzerland	Berne	0–2 (ECQ)
15/12/82	Belgium	Brussels	2–3 (ECQ)
30/3/83	Switzerland	Glasgow	2–2 (ECQ)
24/5/83	N Ireland	Glasgow	0–0
28/5/83	Wales	Cardiff	2–0
1/6/83	England	Wembley	0–2
12/6/83	Canada	Vancouver	2–0
16/6/83	Canada	Edmonton	3–0
20/6/83	Canada	Toronto	2–0
21/9/83	Uruguay	Glasgow	2–0
12/10/83	Belgium	Glasgow	1–1 (ECQ)
16/11/83	E Germany	Halle	1–2 (ECQ)
13/12/83	N Ireland	Belfast	0–2
28/2/84	Wales	Glasgow	2–1
26/5/84	England	Glasgow	1–1
1/6/84	France	Marseille	0–2
12/9/84	Yugoslavia	Glasgow	6–1
17/10/84	Iceland	Glasgow	3–0 (WCQ)
14/11/84	Spain	Glasgow	3–1 (WCQ)

1985

27/2	Spain	Seville	0–1 (WCQ)
27/3	Wales	Glasgow	0–1 (WCQ)
25/5	England	Glasgow	1–0
28/5	Iceland	Reykjavik	1–0 (WCQ)
10/9	Wales	Cardiff	1–1 (WCQ)
16/10	E Germany	Glasgow	0–0
20/11	Australia	Glasgow	2–0 (WCQ)
4/12	Australia	Melbourne	0–0 (WCQ)

1986

28/1	Israel	Tel Aviv	1–0
26/3	Romania	Glasgow	3–0
23/4	England	Wembley	1–2
29/4	Holland	Eindhoven	0–0
4/6	Denmark	Nezahualcoyot	0–1 (WCF)
8/6	W Germany	Queretaro	1–2 (WCF)
13/6	Uruguay	Nezahualcoyot	0–0 (WCF)
10/9	Bulgaria	Glasgow	0–0 (ECQ)
15/10	Rep of Ireland	Dublin	0–0 (ECQ)
12/11	Luxembourg	Glasgow	3–0 (ECQ)

1987

18/2	Rep of Ireland	Glasgow	0–1 (ECQ)
1/4	Belgium	Brussels	1–4 (ECQ)
6/5	Brazil	Glasgow	0–2
23/5	England	Glasgow	0–0
9/9	Hungary	Glasgow	2–0
14/10	Belgium	Glasgow	2–0 (ECQ)
11/11	Bulgaria	Sofia	1–0 (ECQ)
2/12	Luxembourg	Esch	0–0 (ECQ)

1988

17/2	Saudi Arabia	Riyadh	2–2
22/3	Malta	Valletta	1–1
27/4	Spain	Madrid	0–0
17/5	Colombia	Glasgow	0–0
21/5	England	Wembley	0–1
14/9	Norway	Oslo	2–1 (WCQ)
19/10	Yugoslavia	Glasgow	1–1 (WCQ)
22/12	Italy	Perugia	0–2

1989

8/2	Cyprus	Limassol	3–2 (WCQ)
8/3	France	Glasgow	2–0 (WCQ)
26/4	Cyprus	Glasgow	2–1 (WCQ)
27/5	England	Glasgow	0–2
30/5	Chile	Glasgow	2–0
6/9	Yugoslavia	Zagreb	1–3 (WCQ)
11/10	France	Paris	0–3 (WCQ)
15/11	Norway	Glasgow	1–1 (WCQ)

1990

28/3	Argentina	Glasgow	1–0
25/4	E Germany	Glasgow	0–1
19/5	Poland	Glasgow	1–1
28/5	Malta	Valletta	2–1
11/6	Costa Rica	Genoa	0–1 (WCF)
16/6	Sweden	Genoa	2–1 (WCF)
20/6	Brazil	Turin	0–1 (WCF)
12/9	Romania	Glasgow	2–1 (ECQ)
17/10	Switzerland	Glasgow	2–1 (ECQ)
14/11	Bulgaria	Sofia	1–1 (ECQ)

1991

6/2	USSR	Glasgow	0–1
27/3	Bulgaria	Glasgow	1–1 (ECQ)
1/5	San Marino	Serravalle	2–0 (ECQ)
11/9	Switzerland	Berne	2–2 (ECQ)
16/10	Romania	Bucharest	0–1 (ECQ)
13/11	San Marino	Glasgow	4–0 (ECQ)

1992

25/3	Finland	Glasgow	1–1
17/5	USA	Denver	1–0
21/5	Canada	Toronto	3–1
3/6	Norway	Oslo	0–0
12/6	Holland	Gothenburg	0–1 (ECF)
15/6	Germany	Gothenburg	0–2 (ECF)
18/6	CIS	Norrkoping	3–0 (ECF)
9/9	Switzerland	Berne	1–3 (WCQ)
14/10	Portugal	Glasgow	0–0 (WCQ)
18/11	Italy	Glasgow	0–0 (WCQ)

1993

17/2	Malta	Glasgow	3–0 (WCQ)
24/3	Germany	Glasgow	0–1
28/4	Portugal	Lisbon	0–5 (WCQ)
19/5	Estonia	Tallinn	3–0 (WCQ)
2/6	Estonia	Aberdeen	3–1 (WCQ)
8/9	Switzerland	Glasgow	1–1 (WCQ)
13/10	Italy	Rome	1–3 (WCQ)
17/11	Malta	Sliema	2–0 (WCQ)

1994

23/3	Holland	Glasgow	0–1
20/4	Austria	Vienna	2–1
27/5	Holland	Utrecht	1–3
7/9	Finland	Helsinki	2–0 (ECQ)
12/10	Faroe Islands	Glasgow	5–1 (ECQ)
16/11	Russia	Glasgow	1–1 (ECQ)
19/12	Greece	Athens	0–1 (ECQ)

1995

29/3	Russia	Moscow	0–0 (ECQ)
26/4	San Marino	Serravalle	2–0 (ECQ)
21/5	Japan	Hiroshima	0–0
24/5	Ecuador	Toyama, Japan	2–1
7/6	Faroe Islands	Toftir	2–0 (ECQ)
16/8	Greece	Glasgow	1–0 (ECQ)
6/9	Finland	Glasgow	1–0 (ECQ)
11/10	Sweden	Stockholm	0–2
15/11	San Marino	Glasgow	5–0 (ECQ)

1996

27/3	Australia	Glasgow	1–0
24/4	Denmark	Copenhagen	0–2
26/5	United States	New Britain, Conn	1–2
29/5	Colombia	Miami	0–1
10/6	Holland	Birmingham	0–0 (ECF)
15/6	England	Wembley	0–2 (ECF)
18/6	Switzerland	Birmingham	1–0 (ECF)
31/8	Austria	Vienna	0–0 (WCQ)
5/10	Latvia	Riga	2–0 (WCQ)
9/10	Estonia	Tallinn	0–0 (WCQ)
10/11	Sweden	Glasgow	1–0 (WCQ)

1997

11/2	Estonia	Monaco	0–0 (WCQ)
29/3	Estonia	Kilmarnock	2–0 (WCQ)
2/4	Austria	Glasgow	2–0 (WCQ)
30/4	Sweden	Gothenburg	1–2 (WCQ)
27/5	Wales	Kilmarnock	0–1
1/6	Malta	Valletta	3–2
8/6	Belarus	Minsk	1–0 (WCQ)
7/9	Belarus	Aberdeen	4–1 (WCQ)
11/10	Latvia	Glasgow	2–0 (WCQ)
12/11	France	Saint-Etienne	1–2

1998

25/3	Denmark	Glasgow	0–1
22/4	Finland	Edinburgh	1–1
23/5	Colombia	New Jersey	2–2
30/5	United States	Washington	0–0
10/6	Brazil	Paris	1–2 (WCF)
16/6	Norway	Bordeaux	1–1 (WCF)
23/6	Morocco	St. Etienne	0–3 (WCF)
5/9	Lithuania	Vilnius	0–0 (ECQ)
10/10	Estonia	Edinburgh	3–2 (ECQ)
14/10	Faroe Islands	Aberdeen	2–1 (ECQ)

1999

31/3	Czech Republic	Glasgow, Cel	1–2 (ECQ)
28/4	Germany	Bremen	1–0
5/6	Faroe Islands	Toftir	1–1 (ECQ)
9/6	Czech Republic	Prague	2–3 (ECQ)

WALES

At the close of the 1992–93 season Cwmbran became the first Konica-sponsored League of Wales champions, finishing four points ahead of Inter Cardiff.

Until then the participation of the principality's senior clubs, Cardiff City, Swansea City, Newport County and Wrexham, in the Football League meant that the senior tournament under the auspices of the FA of Wales was always the Welsh Cup.

This competition celebrated its 100th anniversary in 1977, the first Cup tie between Newtown and Druids having kicked-off on October 30, 1877 with Wrexham winning 1–0. Druids were captained by Llewelyn Kenrick, the founder of the FA of Wales, and Wrexham played with three half-backs. This was the first occasion such a formation was adopted.

The Village That Grew Footballers

In the formative years of the Welsh Cup the little village of Chirk figured prominently. Chirk was the home club of the great Billy Meredith, Charlie Morris of Derby, Lot Jones of Manchester City, Dai Jones of Bolton and many others. Not surprising then that between 1886 and 1894 Chirk appeared in six finals, winning five. Meredith played in two finals, against Wrexham and Westminster Rovers, and it was then that he was snapped up by Manchester City. Consequently Meredith became the first Welsh player to win Welsh Cup and FA Cup medals.

In modern times the competition has gained more significance with entry into the European Cup-Winners Cup as the prize for the winners. Entry into European competition has also been granted to to the champions of the new league.

The FA of Wales was formed in 1876 and on March 25 the national team lost 4–0 to Scotland in their first international. In 1907 they won the British Championship for the first time and they qualified for the World Cup Finals in 1958, when they surprised everyone by reaching the quarter-finals, losing 1–0 to Brazil – by a deflected goal from Pele.

LEAGUE OF WALES

Year	Winners
1993	Cwmbran Town
1994	Bangor C
1995	Bangor C
1996	Barry T
1997	Barry T
1998	Barry T
1999	Barry T

LEAGUE OF WALES CUP

Year	Winners	Runners-up	Score
1993	Caersws	Afan Lido	Penalties
1994	Afan Lido	Bangor	1–0
1995	Llansantffraid	Ton Pentre	2–1
1996	Connah's Quay	Ebbw Vale	1–0
1997	Barry Town	Bangor City	2–2
	(Barry Town won 4–2 on penalties)		
1998	Barry Town	Bangor City	1–1
1999	Barry Town	Caernarfon Town	3–0

WELSH CUP FINALS

Year	Winners	Runners-up	Score
1878	Wrexham	Druids	1–0
1879	Newtown	Wrexham	1–0
1880	Druids	Ruthin	2–1
1881	Druids	Newtown White Stars	2–0
1882	Druids	Northwich	2–1
1883	Wrexham	Druids	1–0
1884	Oswestry	Druids	3–2
1885	Druids	Oswestry	2–0
1886	Druids	Newtown	5–0
1887	Chirk	Davenham	4–2
1888	Chirk	Newtown	5–0
1889	Bangor	Northwich	2–1
1890	Chirk	Wrexham	1–0
1891	Shrewsbury T	Wrexham	5–2
1892	Chirk	Westminster R	2–1
1893	Wrexham	Chirk	2–1
1894	Chirk	Westminster R	2–0
1895	Newtown	Wrexham	3–2
1896	Bangor	Wrexham	3–1
1897	Wrexham	Newtown	2–0
1898	Druids	Wrexham	1–1, 2–1
1899	Druids	Wrexham	2–2, 1–0
1900	Aberystwyth	Druids	3–0
1901	Oswestry	Druids	1–0
1902	Wellington	Wrexham	1–0
1903	Wrexham	Aberaman	8–0
1904	Druids	Aberdare	3–2
1905	Wrexham	Aberdare	3–0
1906	Wellington	Whitchurch	3–2
1907	Oswestry	Whitchurch	2–0
1908	Chester	Connah's Quay	3–1
1909	Wrexham	Chester	1–0
1910	Wrexham	Chester	2–1
1911	Wrexham	Connah's Quay	6–1
1912	Cardiff C	Pontypridd	0–0, 3–0
1913	Swansea	Pontypridd	0–0, 1–0
1914	Wrexham	Llanelly	1–1, 3–0
1915	Wrexham	Swansea	0–0, 1–0
1920	Cardiff C	Wrexham	2–1
1921	Wrexham	Pontypridd	1–1, 3–1
1922	Cardiff C	Ton Pentre	2–0
1923	Cardiff C	Aberdare	3–2
1924	Wrexham	Merthyr	2–2, 1–0
1925	Wrexham	Flint	3–1
1926	Ebbw Vale	Swansea	3–2
1927	Cardiff C	Rhyl	0–0, 4–2
1928	Cardiff C	Bangor	2–0
1929	Connah's Quay	Cardiff C	3–0
1930	Cardiff C	Rhyl	0–0, 4–2
1931	Wrexham	Shrewsbury	7–0
1932	Swansea	Wrexham	1–1, 2–0
1933	Chester	Wrexham	2–0
1934	Bristol C	Tranmere R	1–1, 3–0
1935	Tranmere R	Chester	1–0
1936	Crewe	Chester	2–0
1937	Crewe	Rhyl	1–1, 3–1
1938	Shrewsbury	Swansea	2–1
1939	S Liverpool	Cardiff C	2–1
1940	Welling T	Swansea	4–0
1947	Chester	Merthyr Tydfil	0–0, 5–1
1948	Lovells Ath	Shrewsbury T	3–0
1949	Merthyr Tydfil	Swansea T	2–0
1950	Swansea T	Wrexham	4–1
1951	Merthyr Tydfil	Cardiff C	1–1, 3–2
1952	Rhyl	Merthyr Tydfil	4–3
1953	Rhyl	Chester	2–1
1954	Flint T Utd	Chester	2–0
1955	Barry T	Chester	1–1, 4–3
1956	Cardiff C	Swansea T	3–2
1957	Wrexham	Swansea T	2–1
1958	Wrexham	Chester	1–1, 2–0
1959	Cardiff C	Lovells Ath	2–0
1960	Wrexham	Cardiff C	0–0, 1–0
1961	Swansea T	Bangor C	3–1
1962	Bangor C	Wrexham	3–1
1963	Borough Utd	Newport Co	2–1 *
1964	Cardiff C	Bangor C	5–3 *
1965	Cardiff C	Wrexham	8–2 *
1966	Swansea T	Chester	2–1
1967	Cardiff C	Wrexham	2–1 *
1968	Cardiff C	Hereford Utd	6–1 *
1969	Cardiff C	Swansea T	5–1 *
1970	Cardiff C	Chester	5–0
1971	Cardiff C	Wrexham	4–1 *
1972	Wrexham	Cardiff C	3–2 *
1973	Cardiff C	Bangor C	5–1 *
1974	Cardiff C	Stourbridge	2–0 *
1975	Wrexham	Cardiff C	5–2 *
1976	Cardiff C	Hereford Utd	6–5 *
1977	Shrewsbury T	Cardiff C	4–2 *
1978	Wrexham	Bangor C	3–1 *
1979	Shrewsbury T	Wrexham	2–1 *
1980	Newport Co	Shrewsbury T	5–1 *
1981	Swansea C	Hereford Utd	2–1 *
1982	Swansea C	Cardiff C	2–1 *
1983	Swansea C	Wrexham	4–1 *
1984	Shrewsbury T	Wrexham	2–0 *
1985	Shrewsbury T	Bangor C	5–1 *
1986	Kidderminster H	Wrexham	1–1, 2–1
1987	Merthyr Tydfil	Newport Co	2–2, 1–0
1988	Cardiff C	Wrexham	1–0
1989	Swansea C	Kidderminster H	5–0
1990	Hereford Utd	Wrexham	2–1
1991	Swansea C	Wrexham	2–0
1992	Cardiff C	Hednesford T	1–0
1993	Cardiff C	Rhyl	5–0
1994	Barry T	Cardiff C	2–1
1995	Wrexham	Cardiff C	2–1
1996	Llansantffraid	Barry T	3–3
	(Llansantffraid won 3–2 on penalties)		
1997	Barry T	Cwmbran T	2–1
1998	Bangor City	Connah's Quay	1–1
	(Bangor City won 4–2 on penalties)		
1999	Inter CableTel	Carmarthen	1–1
	(Inter CableTel won 4–2 on penalties)		

* Aggregate score

INTERNATIONAL RESULTS 1876–1899

Date	Opponents	Venue	F–A
25/3/76	Scotland	Glasgow	0–4
5/3/77	Scotland	Wrexham	0–2
23/3/78	Scotland	Glasgow	0–9
18/1/79	England	London	1–2
7/4/79	Scotland	Wrexham	0–3
15/3/80	England	Wrexham	2–3
27/3/80	Scotland	Glasgow	1–5
26/2/81	England	Blackburn	1–0
14/3/81	Scotland	Wrexham	1–5
25/2/82	Ireland	Wrexham	7–1
13/3/82	England	Wrexham	5–3
25/3/82	Scotland	Glasgow	0–5
3/2/83	England	London	0–5
12/3/83	Scotland	Wrexham	0–3
17/3/83	Ireland	Belfast	1–1
9/2/84	Ireland	Wrexham	6–0
17/3/84	England	Wrexham	0–4
29/3/84	Scotland	Glasgow	1–4
14/3/85	Ireland	Blackburn	1–1
23/3/85	Scotland	Wrexham	1–8
11/4/85	Ireland	Belfast	8–2
27/2/86	Ireland	Wrexham	5–0
29/3/86	England	Wrexham	1–3
10/4/86	Scotland	Glasgow	1–4
26/2/87	England	London	0–4
12/3/87	Ireland	Belfast	1–4
21/3/87	Scotland	Wrexham	0–2
4/2/88	England	Crewe	1–5
3/3/88	Ireland	Wrexham	11–0
10/3/88	Scotland	Edinburgh	1–5
23/2/89	England	Stoke	1–4
15/4/89	Scotland	Wrexham	0–0
27/4/89	Ireland	Belfast	3–1
8/2/90	Ireland	Shrewsbury	5–2
15/3/90	England	Wrexham	1–3
22/3/90	Scotland	Glasgow	0–5
7/2/91	Ireland	Belfast	2–7
7/3/91	England	Sunderland	1–4
21/3/91	Scotland	Wrexham	3–4
27/2/92	Ireland	Bangor	1–1
5/3/92	England	Wrexham	0–2
26/3/92	Scotland	Edinburgh	1–6
13/3/93	England	Stoke-on-Trent	0–6
18/3/93	Scotland	Wrexham	0–8
5/4/93	Ireland	Belfast	3–4
24/2/94	Ireland	Swansea	4–1
12/3/94	England	Wrexham	1–5
24/3/94	Scotland	Kilmarnock	2–5
16/3/95	Ireland	Belfast	2–2
18/3/95	England	London	1–1
23/3/95	Scotland	Wrexham	2–2
29/2/96	Ireland	Wrexham	6–1
16/3/96	England	Cardiff	1–9
21/3/96	Scotland	Dundee	0–4
6/3/97	Ireland	Belfast	3–4
20/3/97	Scotland	Wrexham	2–2
29/3/97	England	Sheffield	0–4
19/2/98	Ireland	Llandudno	0–1
19/3/98	Scotland	Motherwell	2–5

28/3/98	England	Wrexham	0–3
4/3/99	Ireland	Belfast	0–1
18/3/99	Scotland	Wrexham	0–6
20/3/99	England	Bristol	0–4

1900–1919

3/2/00	Scotland	Aberdeen	2–5
24/2/00	Ireland	Llandudno	2–0
26/3/00	England	Cardiff	1–1
2/3/01	Scotland	Wrexham	1–1
18/3/01	England	Newcastle	0–6
23/3/01	Ireland	Belfast	1–0
22/2/02	Ireland	Cardiff	0–3
3/3/02	England	Wrexham	0–0
15/3/02	Scotland	Greenock	1–5
2/3/03	England	Portsmouth	1–2
9/3/03	Scotland	Cardiff	0–1
28/3/03	Ireland	Belfast	0–2
29/2/04	England	Wrexham	2–2
12/3/04	Scotland	Dundee	1–1
21/3/04	Ireland	Bangor	0–1
6/3/05	Scotland	Wrexham	3–1
27/3/05	England	Liverpool	1–5
8/4/05	Ireland	Belfast	2–2
3/3/06	Scotland	Edinburgh	2–0
19/3/06	England	Cardiff	0–1
2/4/06	Ireland	Wrexham	4–4
23/2/07	Ireland	Belfast	3–2
4/3/07	Scotland	Wrexham	1–0
18/3/07	England	Fulham	1–1
7/3/08	Scotland	Dundee	1–2
16/3/08	England	Wrexham	1–7
11/4/08	Ireland	Aberdare	0–1
1/3/09	Scotland	Wrexham	3–2
15/3/09	England	Nottingham	0–2
20/3/09	Ireland	Belfast	3–2
5/3/10	Scotland	Kilmarnock	0–1
14/3/10	England	Cardiff	0–1
11/4/10	Ireland	Wrexham	4–1
28/1/11	Ireland	Belfast	2–1
6/3/11	Scotland	Cardiff	2–2
13/3/11	England	London	0–3
2/3/12	Scotland	Edinburgh	0–1
11/3/12	England	Wrexham	0–2
13/4/12	Ireland	Cardiff	2–3
18/1/13	Ireland	Belfast	1–0
3/3/13	Scotland	Wrexham	0–0
17/3/13	England	Bristol	3–4
19/1/14	Ireland	Wrexham	1–2
28/2/14	Scotland	Glasgow	0–0
16/3/14	England	Cardiff	0–2

1920–1929

14/2/20	Ireland	Belfast	2–2
26/2/20	Scotland	Cardiff	1–1
15/3/20	England	London	2–1
12/2/21	Scotland	Aberdeen	1–2
16/3/21	England	Cardiff	0–0
9/4/21	Ireland	Swansea	2–1
4/2/22	Scotland	Wrexham	2–1
13/3/22	England	Liverpool	0–1
1/4/22	Ireland	Belfast	1–1
5/3/23	England	Cardiff	2–2
17/3/23	Scotland	Glasgow	0–2
14/4/23	Ireland	Wrexham	0–3
16/2/24	Scotland	Cardiff	2–0
3/3/24	England	Blackburn	2–1
15/3/24	Ireland	Belfast	1–0
14/2/25	Scotland	Edinburgh	1–3
28/2/25	England	Swansea	1–2
18/4/25	Ireland	Wrexham	0–0
31/10/25	Scotland	Cardiff	0–3
13/2/26	Ireland	Belfast	0–3
1/3/26	England	London	3–1
30/10/26	Scotland	Glasgow	0–3
14/2/27	England	Wrexham	3–3
9/4/27	Ireland	Cardiff	2–2
29/10/27	Scotland	Wrexham	2–2
28/11/27	England	Burnley	2–1
4/2/28	Ireland	Belfast	2–1
27/10/28	Scotland	Glasgow	2–4
17/11/28	England	Swansea	2–3
2/2/29	Ireland	Wrexham	2–2
26/10/29	Scotland	Cardiff	2–4
20/11/29	England	London	0–6

1930–1939

1/2/30	Ireland	Belfast	0–7
25/10/30	Scotland	Glasgow	1–1
22/11/30	England	Wrexham	0–4
22/4/31	Ireland	Wrexham	3–2
31/10/31	Scotland	Wrexham	2–3
18/11/31	England	Liverpool	1–3
5/12/31	Ireland	Belfast	0–4
26/10/32	Scotland	Edinburgh	5–2
16/11/32	England	Wrexham	0–0
7/12/32	Ireland	Wrexham	4–1
25/5/33	France	Paris	1–1
4/10/33	Scotland	Cardiff	3–2
4/11/33	Ireland	Belfast	1–1
15/11/33	England	Newcastle	2–1
29/9/34	England	Cardiff	0–4
21/11/34	Scotland	Aberdeen	2–3
27/3/35	Ireland	Wrexham	3–1
5/10/35	Scotland	Cardiff	1–1
5/2/36	England	Wolverhampton	2–1
11/3/36	Ireland	Belfast	2–3
17/10/36	England	Cardiff	2–1
2/12/36	Scotland	Dundee	2–1
17/3/37	Ireland	Wrexham	4–1
30/10/37	Scotland	Cardiff	2–1
17/11/37	England	Middlesbrough	1–2
16/3/38	Ireland	Belfast	0–1
22/10/38	England	Cardiff	4–2
9/11/38	Scotland	Edinburgh	2–3
15/3/39	Ireland	Wrexham	3–1
20/5/39	France	Paris	1–2

1940–1949

19/10/46	Scotland	Wrexham	3–1
13/11/46	England	Manchester	0–3
16/4/47	N Ireland	Belfast	1–2
18/10/47	England	Cardiff	0–3
12/11/47	Scotland	Glasgow	2–1
10/3/48	N Ireland	Wrexham	2–0
23/10/48	Scotland	Cardiff	1–3
10/11/48	England	Villa Park	0–1
9/3/49	N Ireland	Belfast	2–0
15/5/49	Portugal	Lisbon	2–3
23/5/49	Belgium	Liege	1–3
26/5/49	Switzerland	Berne	0–4
15/10/49	England	Cardiff	1–4 (WCQ)
9/11/49	Scotland	Glasgow	0–2 (WCQ)
23/11/49	Belgium	Cardiff	5–1

1950–1959

8/3/50	N Ireland	Wrexham	0–0 (WCQ)
21/10/50	Scotland	Cardiff	1–3
15/11/50	England	Sunderland	2–4
7/3/51	N Ireland	Belfast	2–1
12/5/51	Portugal	Cardiff	2–1
16/5/51	Switzerland	Wrexham	3–2
20/10/51	England	Cardiff	1–1
20/11/51	Scotland	Glasgow	1–0
5/12/51	Rest of UK	Cardiff	3–2
19/3/52	N Ireland	Swansea	3–0
18/10/52	Scotland	Cardiff	1–2
12/11/52	England	Wembley	2–5
15/4/53	N Ireland	Belfast	3–2
14/5/53	France	Paris	1–6
21/5/53	Yugoslavia	Belgrade	2–5
10/10/53	England	Cardiff	1–4 (WCQ)
4/11/53	Scotland	Glasgow	3–3 (WCQ)
31/3/54	N Ireland	Wrexham	1–2 (WCQ)
9/5/54	Austria	Vienna	0–2 (ECQ)
22/9/54	Yugoslavia	Cardiff	1–3
16/10/54	Scotland	Cardiff	0–1
10/11/54	England	Wembley	2–3
20/4/55	N Ireland	Belfast	3–2
22/10/55	England	Cardiff	2–1
9/11/55	Scotland	Glasgow	0–2
23/11/55	Austria	Wrexham	1–2 (ECQ)
11/4/56	N Ireland	Cardiff	1–1
20/10/56	Scotland	Cardiff	2–2
14/11/56	England	Wembley	1–3
10/4/57	N Ireland	Belfast	0–0
1/5/57	Czechoslovakia	Cardiff	1–0 (WCQ)
19/5/57	E Germany	Leipzig	1–2 (WCQ)
26/5/57	Czechoslovakia	Prague	0–2 (W
25/9/57	E Germany	Cardiff	4–1 (WCQ)
19/10/57	England	Cardiff	0–4
13/11/57	Scotland	Glasgow	1–1
15/1/58	Israel	Tel Aviv	2–0 (WCQ)
5/2/58	Israel	Cardiff	2–0 (WCQ)
16/4/58	N Ireland	Cardiff	1–1
8/6/58	Hungary	Sandviken	1–1 (WCF)
11/6/58	Mexico	Stockholm	1–1 (WCF)
15/6/58	Sweden	Stockholm	0–0 (WCF)
17/6/58	Hungary	Stockholm	2–1 (WCF)
19/6/58	Brazil	Gothenburg	0–1 (WCF)
18/10/58	Scotland	Cardiff	0–3
26/11/58	England	Villa Park	2–2
22/4/59	N Ireland	Belfast	1–4
17/10/59	England	Cardiff	1–1
4/11/59	Scotland	Glasgow	1–1

1960–69

6/4/60	N Ireland	Wrexham	3–2
28/9/60	Rep of Ireland	Dublin	3–2
22/10/60	Scotland	Cardiff	2–0
23/11/60	England	Wembley	1–5
12/4/61	N Ireland	Belfast	5–1
19/4/61	Spain	Cardiff	1–2 (WCQ)
18/5/61	Spain	Madrid	1–1 (WCQ)
28/5/61	Hungary	Budapest	2–3
14/10/61	England	Cardiff	1–1
8/11/61	Scotland	Glasgow	0–2
11/4/62	N Ireland	Cardiff	4–0
12/5/62	Brazil	Rio de Janeiro	1–3
16/5/62	Brazil	São Paulo	1–3
22/5/62	Mexico	Mexico City	1–2
20/10/62	Scotland	Cardiff	2–3
7/11/62	Hungary	Budapest	1–3 (ECQ)
21/11/62	England	Wembley	0–4
20/3/63	Hungary	Cardiff	1–1 (ECQ)
3/4/63	N Ireland	Belfast	4–1
12/10/63	England	Cardiff	0–4
20/11/63	Scotland	Glasgow	1–2
15/4/64	N Ireland	Swansea	2–3
3/10/64	Scotland	Cardiff	3–2
21/10/64	Denmark	Copenhagen	0–1 (WCQ)
18/11/64	England	Wembley	1–2
9/12/64	Greece	Athens	0–2 (WCQ)
17/2/65	Greece	Cardiff	4–1 (WCQ)
31/3/65	N Ireland	Belfast	5–0
1/5/65	Italy	Florence	1–4
30/5/65	USSR	Moscow	1–2 (WCQ)
2/10/65	England	Cardiff	0–0
27/10/65	USSR	Cardiff	2–1 (WCQ)
24/11/65	Scotland	Glasgow	1–4 (ECQ)
1/12/65	Denmark	Wrexham	4–2 (WCQ)
30/3/66	N Ireland	Cardiff	1–4
14/5/66	Brazil	Rio de Janeiro	1–3
18/5/66	Brazil	Belo Horizonte	0–1
22/5/66	Chile	Santiago	0–2
22/10/66	Scotland	Cardiff	1–1 (ECQ)
16/11/66	England	Wembley	1–5 (ECQ)
12/4/67	N Ireland	Belfast	0–0 (ECQ)
21/10/67	England	Cardiff	0–3 (ECQ)
22/11/67	Scotland	Glasgow	2–3
28/2/68	N Ireland	Wrexham	2–0 (ECQ)
8/5/68	W Germany	Cardiff	1–1
23/10/68	Italy	Cardiff	0–1 (WCQ)
26/3/69	W Germany	Frankfurt	1–1
16/4/69	E Germany	Dresden	1–2 (WCQ)
3/5/69	Scotland	Wrexham	3–5
7/5/69	England	Wembley	1–2
10/5/69	N Ireland	Belfast	0–0
28/7/69	Rest of UK	Cardiff	0–1
22/10/69	E Germany	Cardiff	1–3 (WCQ)
4/11/69	Italy	Rome	1–4 (WCQ)

1970–79

18/4/70	England	Cardiff	1–1
22/4/70	Scotland	Glasgow	0–0
25/4/70	N Ireland	Swansea	1–0
11/11/70	Romania	Cardiff	0–0 (ECQ)
21/4/71	Czechoslovakia	Swansea	1–3 (ECQ)
15/5/71	Scotland	Cardiff	0–0
18/5/71	England	Wembley	0–0
22/5/71	N Ireland	Belfast	0–1
26/5/71	Finland	Helsinki	1–0 (ECQ)
13/10/71	Finland	Swansea	3–0 (ECQ)
27/10/71	Czechoslovakia	Prague	0–1 (ECQ)
24/11/71	Romania	Bucharest	0–2 (ECQ)
20/5/72	England	Cardiff	0–3
24/5/72	Scotland	Glasgow	0–1
27/5/72	N Ireland	Wrexham	0–0
15/11/72	England	Cardiff	0–1 (WCQ)
24/1/73	England	Wembley	1–1 (WCQ)
28/3/73	Poland	Cardiff	2–0 (WCQ)
12/5/73	Scotland	Wrexham	0–2
15/5/73	England	Wembley	0–3
19/5/73	N Ireland	Liverpool	0–1
26/9/73	Poland	Chorzow	0–3 (WCQ)
11/5/74	England	Cardiff	0–2
14/5/74	Scotland	Glasgow	0–2
18/5/74	N Ireland	Wrexham	1–0
4/9/74	Austria	Vienna	1–2 (ECQ)
30/10/74	Hungary	Cardiff	2–0 (ECQ)
20/11/74	Luxembourg	Swansea	5–0 (ECQ)
16/4/75	Hungary	Budapest	2–1 (ECQ)
1/5/75	Luxembourg	Luxembourg	3–1 (ECQ)
17/5/75	Scotland	Cardiff	2–2
21/5/75	England	Wembley	2–2
23/5/75	N Ireland	Belfast	0–1
19/11/75	Austria	Wrexham	1–0 (ECQ)
24/3/76	England	Wrexham	1–2
24/4/76	Yugoslavia	Zagreb	0–2 (ECQ)
6/5/76	Scotland	Glasgow	1–3
8/5/76	England	Cardiff	0–1
14/5/76	N Ireland	Swansea	1–0
22/5/76	Yugoslavia	Cardiff	1–1 (ECQ)
6/10/76	W Germany	Cardiff	0–2
17/11/76	Scotland	Glasgow	0–1 (WCQ)
30/3/77	Czechoslovakia	Wrexham	3–0 (WCQ)
28/5/77	Scotland	Wrexham	0–0
31/5/77	England	Wembley	1–0
3/6/77	N Ireland	Belfast	1–1
6/9/77	Kuwait	Wrexham	0–0
20/9/77	Kuwait	Kuwait	0–0
12/10/77	Scotland	Liverpool	0–2 (WCQ)
16/11/77	Czechoslovakia	Prague	0–1 (WCQ)
14/12/77	W Germany	Dortmund	1–1
18/4/78	Iran	Teheran	1–0
13/5/78	England	Cardiff	1–3
17/5/78	Scotland	Glasgow	1–1
19/5/78	N Ireland	Wrexham	1–0
25/10/78	Malta	Wrexham	7–0 (ECQ)
29/11/78	Turkey	Wrexham	1–0 (ECQ)
2/5/79	W Germany	Wrexham	0–2 (ECQ)
19/5/79	Scotland	Cardiff	3–0
23/5/79	England	Wembley	0–0
25/5/79	N Ireland	Belfast	1–1
2/6/79	Malta	Valetta	2–0 (ECQ)
11/9/79	Rep of Ireland	Swansea	2–1
17/10/79	W Germany	Cologne	1–5 (ECQ)
21/11/79	Turkey	Izmir	0–1 (ECQ)

1980-87

17/5/80	England	Wrexham	4–1
21/5/80	Scotland	Glasgow	0–1
23/5/80	N Ireland	Cardiff	0–1
2/6/80	Iceland	Reykjavic	4–0 (WCQ)
15/10/80	Turkey	Cardiff	4–0 (WCQ)
19/11/80	Czechoslovakia	Cardiff	1–0 (WCQ)
24/2/81	Rep of Ireland	Dublin	3–1

25/3/81	Turkey	Ankara	1–0 (WCQ)
16/5/81	Scotland	Swansea	2–0
20/5/81	England	Wembley	0–0
30/5/81	USSR	Wrexham	0–0 (WCQ)
9/9/81	Czechoslovakia	Prague	0–2 (WCQ)
14/10/81	Iceland	Swansea	2–2 (WCQ)
18/11/81	USSR	Tbilisi	0–3 (WCQ)
24/3/82	Spain	Valencia	1–1
27/4/82	England	Cardiff	0–1
24/5/82	Scotland	Glasgow	0–1
27/5/82	N Ireland	Wrexham	3–0
2/6/82	France	Toulouse	1–0
22/9/82	Norway	Swansea	1–0 (ECQ)
15/12/82	Yugoslavia	Titograd	4–4 (ECQ)
23/2/83	England	Wembley	1–2
27/4/83	Bulgaria	Wrexham	1–0 (ECQ)
28/5/83	Scotland	Cardiff	0–2
31/5/83	N Ireland	Belfast	1–0
12/6/83	Brazil	Cardiff	1–1
21/9/83	Norway	Oslo	0–0 (ECQ)
12/10/83	Romania	Wrexham	5–0
16/11/83	Bulgaria	Sofia	0–1 (ECQ)
14/12/83	Yugoslavia	Cardiff	1–1 (ECQ)
28/2/84	Scotland	Glasgow	1–2
2/5/84	England	Wrexham	1–0
22/5/84	N Ireland	Swansea	1–1
6/6/84	Norway	Trondheim	0–1
10/6/84	Israel	Tel Aviv	0–0
12/9/84	Iceland	Reykjavik	0–1 (WCQ)
17/10/84	Spain	Seville	0–3 (WCQ)
14/11/84	Iceland	Cardiff	2–1 (WCQ)
26/2/85	Norway	Wrexham	1–1
27/3/85	Scotland	Glasgow	1–0 (WCQ)
30/4/85	Spain	Wrexham	3–0 (WCQ)
5/6/85	Norway	Bergen	2–4
10/9/85	Scotland	Cardiff	1–1 (WCQ)
16/10/85	Hungary	Cardiff	0–3
25/2/86	Saudi Arabia	Dhahran	2–1
26/3/86	Rep of Ireland	Dublin	1–0
21/4/86	Uruguay	Cardiff	0–0
10/5/86	Canada	Toronto	0–2
20/5/86	Canada	Vancouver	3–0
10/9/86	Finland	Helsinki	1–1 (ECQ)
18/2/87	USSR	Swansea	0–0
1/4/87	Finland	Wrexham	4–0 (ECQ)
29/4/87	Czechoslovakia	Wrexham	1–1 (ECQ)
9/9/87	Denmark	Cardiff	1–0 (ECQ)
14/10/87	Denmark	Copenhagen	0–1 (ECQ)
11/11/87	Czechoslovakia	Prague	0–2 (ECQ)

1988

23/3	Yugoslavia	Swansea	1–2
27/4	Sweden	Stockholm	1–4
1/6	Malta	Valletta	3–2
4/6	Italy	Brescia	1–0
14/9	Holland	Amsterdam	0–1 (WCQ)
19/10	Finland	Swansea	2–2 (WCQ)

1989

8/2	Israel	Tel Aviv	3–3
26/4	Sweden	Wrexham	0–2
31/5	W Germany	Cardiff	0–0 (WCQ)
6/9	Finland	Helsinki	0–1 (WCQ)
11/10	Holland	Wrexham	1–2 (WCQ)
15/11	W Germany	Cologne	1–2 (WCQ)

1990

28/3	Rep of Ireland	Dublin	0–1
25/4	Sweden	Stockholm	2–4
20/5	Costa Rica	Cardiff	1–0
1/9	Denmark	Copenhagen	0–1
17/10	Belgium	Cardiff	3–1 (ECQ)
14/11	Luxembourg	Luxembourg	1–0 (ECQ)

1991

6/2	Rep of Ireland	Wrexham	0–3
27/3	Belgium	Brussels	1–1 (ECQ)
1/5	Iceland	Cardiff	1–0
29/5	Poland	Radom	0–0
5/6	W Germany	Cardiff	1–0 (ECQ)

11/9	Brazil	Cardiff	1–0
16/10	W Germany	Nüremberg	1–4 (ECQ)
13/11	Luxembourg	Cardiff	1–0 (ECQ)

1992

19/2	Rep of Ireland	Dublin	1–0
29/4	Austria	Vienna	1–1
20/5	Romania	Bucharest	1–5 (WCQ)
30/5	Holland	Utrecht	0–4
3/6	Argentina	Tokyo	0–1
7/6	Japan	Matsuyama	1–0
9/9	Faeroes	Cardiff	6–0 (WCQ)
14/10	Cyprus	Limassol	1–0 (WCQ)
18/11	Belgium	Brussels	0–2 (WCQ)

1993

17/2	Rep of Ireland	Dublin	1–2
31/3	Belgium	Cardiff	2–0 (WCQ)
28/4	Czechoslovakia	Ostrava	1–1 (WCQ)
6/6	Faeroes	Toftir	3–0 (WCQ)
8/9	RCS*	Cardiff	2–2 (WCQ)
13/10	Cyprus	Cardiff	2–0 (WCQ)
17/11	Romania	Cardiff	1–2 (WCQ)

* Representation of Czechs & Slovaks (was Czechoslovakia).

1994

9/3	Norway	Cardiff	1–3
20/4	Sweden	Wrexham	0–2
23/5	Estonia	Tallinn	2–1
7/9	Albania	Cardiff	2–0 (ECQ)
12/10	Moldova	Chislau	2–3 (ECQ)
16/11	Georgia	Tbilisi	0–5 (ECQ)
14/12	Bulgaria	Cardiff	0–3 (ECQ)
7/9	Albania	Cardiff	2–0 (ECQ)

1995

29/3	Bulgaria	Sofia	1–3 (ECQ)
26/4	Germany	Düsseldorf	1–1 (ECQ)
7/6	Georgia	Cardiff	0–1 (ECQ)
6/9	Moldova	Cardiff	1–0 (ECQ)
11/10	Germany	Cardiff	1–2 (ECQ)
15/11	Albania	Tirana	1–1 (ECQ)

1996

24/1	Italy	Terni	0–3
24/4	Switzerland	Lugano	0–2
2/6	San Marino	Sarravalle	5–0 (WCQ)
31/8	San Marino	Cardiff	6–0 (WCQ)
5/10	Holland	Cardiff	1–3 (WCQ)
9/11	Holland	Eindhoven	1–7 (WCQ)
14/12	Turkey	Cardiff	0–0 (WCQ)

1997

11/2	Rep of Ireland	Cardiff	0–0
29/3	Belgium	Cardiff	1–2 (WCQ)
27/5	Scotland	Kilmarnock	1–0
20/8	Turkey	Istanbul	4–6 (WCQ)
11/10	Belgium	Brussels	2–3 (WCQ)
11/11	Brazil	Brasilia	0–3

1998

25/3	Jamaica	Cardiff	0–0
5/9	Italy	Liverpool	0–2 (ECQ)
10/10	Denmark	Copenhagen	2–1 (ECQ)
14/10	Belarus	Cardiff	3–2 (ECQ)

1999

31/3/99	Switzerland	Zurich	0–2 (ECQ)
5/6/99	Italy	Bologna	0–4 (ECQ)
9/6/99	Denmark	Liverpool	0–2 (ECQ)

NORTHERN IRELAND

The story of Irish football runs parallel to that of mainland Britain. The start is familiar ground, with the founding of the Irish Football Association on November 18, 1880, and the launching of the Irish Cup by the pioneering J. M. McAlery. Entry cost seven participants ten shillings each, and though Knock beat Distillery 11–0 in the opening round, it was Cliftonville – the first club formed in Ireland in 1879 – who took on the Castledawson team Moyola Park in the inaugural final.

That Moyola Park, the underdogs, should become the winners amply demonstrated the magic of the knock out competition. A single goal from outside-left Morrow was the decisive strike.

Thirteen clubs figured in the Cup in its second season, Queen's Island proving successful with a 2–1 final victory over Cliftonville. At last, Cliftonville won the trophy at their third successive attempt, convincingly disposing of Ulster by 5–0.

Distillery became the first club to win the Cup three years in a row. Their initial success in 1883–84, when they thrashed Wellington Park 5–0, followed by victories over Limavady (2–0) in 1895 and by 1–0 a year later.

Alas, a protest lodged by Limavady on the conduct of some Distillery players who, they claimed, had intimidated them, was upheld by the Association, who decreed "that the Cup and medals be witheld for the year owing to the conduct of players of both teams". Such were the trials and tribulations of those formative years.

Regiments of British troops were then stationed throughout Ireland, and military sides entered the Irish Cup from time to time. Only one won it, however, the Gordon Highlanders in 1890, a season in which the Black Watch and the East Lancashire Regiment also participated.

An important change was made in the rules allowing players from Great Britain to play if they had three months' residence in Ireland. Linfield reached the final for the fifth year in succession in 1895, celebrating with a 10–1 win over Bohemians, who opened the scoring.

By the turn of the century Dublin was hosting the finals. The first, in 1903, between Distillery and Bohemians, attracted 6,000 spectators to Dalymount Park. In 1905 Shelbourne became the first Dublin side to win the trophy, but in the season of 1911–12 a serious split parted the Dubliners from Belfast. The Belfast clubs withdrew their support and organized a new Irish Cup, with a trophy made of gold. Belfast Celtic beat Glentoran 2–0 in the final, but the rift was healed before the start of the next season.

Another oddity occurred in 1920, when Shelbourne were awarded the trophy without kicking a ball in the final. Unprecedented scenes at the semi-final between Glentoran and Belfast Celtic resulted in both teams being expelled from the competition.

Meanwhile Ireland was heading for political division, and that was formalized in football by a split within the game's administration. The Irish Football Association continued to run the game in the North while the new Football Association of Ireland controlled soccer in the Irish Free State, now the Republic of Ireland.

Domestic football in the North has been dominated by Linfield, who first made headlines in 1958 by signing England centre-forward Jackie Milburn from Newcastle United. He gained only a runners-up medal in the Irish Cup that year, being not fully fit after injuring a knee while playing for the Irish League against the League of Ireland at Cliftonville. But "Wor Jackie", now player-coach, steered Linfield to another League title in 1959.

Overseas Campaigns

On the international front, Northern Ireland's most memorable year was 1957, when they beat England 3–2 at Wembley for the first time and qualified, also for the first time, for the World Cup Finals in Italy – beating Italy, of all people, on the way with a fine team inspired by Harry Gregg in goal, Danny Blanchflower and Jimmy McIlroy in midfield, and Billy Bingham and Peter McParland.

Little Wilbur Cush scored the goal which defeated Czechoslovakia in Northern Ireland's opening game at the finals in Sweden, but a 3–1 defeat by Argentina and a 2–2 draw with Germany left Irish hopes resting on a play-off, again against Czechoslovakia. Two goals from McParland clinched a brilliant 2–1 win in Malmo. Northern Ireland were through to the quarter-finals, but the fatigue and injuries carried over from the first round play-off proved too much and they went down 4–0 to the France of Raymond Kopa and Just Fontaine.

Bingham was to enjoy more World Cup glory in 1982 and 1986 as manager. In 1982, in Spain, Norman Whiteside became the youngest player ever to appear in the finals (at 17 years and 42 days). His youthful talent, mixed with the experience of Martin O'Neill and Pat Jennings, saw Northern Ireland create a sensation by defeating hosts Spain 1–0 through a goal by Gerry Armstrong. In the second round, however, it was France – orchestrated by Platini – who again ended Irish dreams, this time 4–1. In 1986 Bingham, undaunted, brought Northern Ireland again to the finals in Mexico, where goalkeeper Jennings played, in the game lost to Brazil, his 119th and last international – then a world record – on his 41st birthday. It was, of course, a British goalkeeping colleague in Peter Shilton who broke the Jennings record four years later in the 1990 World Cup finals in Italy.

Bingham retired at 62, waving farewell to Windsor Park in the final World Cup qualifying tie against the Republic of Ireland in November 1993. In charge for 14 years, he was by far his country's most successful manager. His highlights were winning the 1980 British Championship, and beating West Germany in Hamburg in 1983 – standards which proved beyond successors Bryan Hamilton and Lawrie McMenemy.

LEAGUE CHAMPIONS

1891–1899

1891	Linfield	1892	Linfield
1893	Linfield	1894	Glentoran
1895	Linfield	1896	Distillery
1897	Glentoran	1898	Glenfield
1899	Distillery		

1900–1909

1900	Belfast Celtic	1901	Distillery
1902	Linfield	1903	Distillery
1904	Linfield	1905	Glentoran
1906	Cliftonville/Distillery	1907	Linfield
1908	Linfield	1909	Linfield

1910–1915

1910	Cliftonville	1911	Linfield
1912	Glentoran	1913	Glentoran
1914	Linfield	1915	Belfast Celtic

1920–1929

1920	Belfast Celtic	1921	Glentoran
1922	Linfield	1923	Linfield
1924	Queen's Island	1925	Glentoran
1926	Belfast Celtic	1927	Belfast Celtic
1928	Belfast Celtic	1929	Belfast Celtic

1930–1939

1930	Linfield	1931	Glentoran
1932	Linfield	1933	Belfast Celtic
1934	Linfield	1935	Linfield
1936	Belfast Celtic	1937	Belfast Celtic
1938	Belfast Celtic	1939	Belfast Celtic

1940–1949

1940	Belfast Celtic	1948	Belfast Celtic
1949	Linfield		

1950–1959

1950	Linfield	1951	Glentoran
1952	Glentoran	1953	Glentoran
1954	Linfield	1955	Linfield
1956	Linfield	1957	Glentoran
1958	Ards	1959	Linfield

1960–1969

1960	Glenavon	1961	Linfield
1962	Linfield	1963	Distillery
1964	Glentoran	1965	Derry City
1966	Linfield	1967	Glentoran
1968	Glentoran	1969	Linfield

1970–1979

1970	Glentoran	1971	Linfield
1972	Glentoran	1973	Crusaders
1974	Coleraine	1975	Linfield
1976	Crusaders	1977	Glentoran
1978	Linfield	1979	Linfield

1980–1989

1980	Linfield	1981	Linfield
1982	Linfield	1983	Linfield
1984	Linfield	1985	Linfield
1986	Linfield	1987	Linfield
1988	Glentoran	1989	Linfield

1990–1999

1990	Portadown	1991	Portadown
1992	Glentoran	1993	Linfield
1994	Linfield	1995	Crusaders
1996	Portadown	1997	Crusaders
1998	Cliftonville	1999	Glentorran

IRISH CUP FINALS

Year	Winners	Runners-up	Result
1881	Moyola Park	Cliftonville	1–0
1882	Queen's Island	Cliftonville	2–1
1883	Cliftonville	Ulster	5–0
1884	Distillery	Ulster	5–0
1885	Distillery	Limavady	2–0
1886	Distillery	Limavady	1–0
1887	Ulster	Cliftonville	3–1
1888	Cliftonville	Distillery	2–1
1889	Distillery	YMCA	5–4
1890	Gordon Highlanders	Cliftonville	2–2, 3–0
1891	Linfield	Ulster	4–2
1892	Linfield	The Black Watch	7–0
1893	Linfield	Cliftonville	5–1
1894	Distillery	Linfield	2–2, 3–2
1895	Linfield	Bohemians	10–1
1896	Distillery	Glentoran	3–1
1897	Cliftonville	Sherwood Foresters Curragh	3–1
1898	Linfield	St Columbs Hall Celtic Derry	2–0
1899	Linfield	Glentoran	1–0
1900	Cliftonville	Bohemians	2–1
1901	Cliftonville	Freebooters, Dublin	1–0
1902	Linfield	Distillery	5–1
1903	Distillery	Bohemians	3–1
1904	Linfield	Derry Celtic	5–0
1905	Distillery	Shelbourne	3–0
1906	Shelbourne	Belfast Celtic	2–0
1907	Cliftonville	Shelbourne	0–0, 1–0
1908	Bohemians	Shelbourne	1–1, 3–1
1909	Cliftonville	Bohemians	0–0, 2–1
1910	Distillery	Cliftonville	1–0
1911	Shelbourne	Bohemians	0–0, 2–1
1912	Not played: Linfield awarded cup		
1913	Linfield	Glentoran	2–0
1914	Glentoran	Linfield	3–1
1915	Linfield	Belfast Celtic	1–0
1916	Linfield	Glentoran	1–0
1917	Glentoran	Belfast Celtic	2–0
1918	Belfast Celtic	Linfield	0–0, 0–0, 2–0
1919	Linfield	Glentoran	1–1, 0–0, 2–1
1920	Not played: Shelbourne awarded cup		
1921	Glentoran	Glenavon	2–0
1922	Linfield	Glenavon	2–0
1923	Linfield	Glentoran	2–0
1924	Queen's Island	Willowfield	1–0
1925	Distillery	Glentoran	2–1
1926	Belfast Celtic	Linfield	3–2
1927	Ards	Cliftonville	3–2
1928	Willowfield	Larne	1–0
1929	Ballymena Utd	Belfast Celtic	2–1
1930	Linfield	Ballymena United	4–3
1931	Linfield	Ballymena United	3–0
1932	Glentoran	Linfield	2–1
1933	Glentoran	Distillery	1–1, 1–1, 3–1
1934	Linfield	Cliftonville	5–0
1935	Glentoran	Larne	0–0, 0–0, 1–0
1936	Linfield	Derry City	0–0, 2–1
1937	Belfast Celtic	Linfield	3–0
1938	Belfast Celtic	Bangor	0–0, 2–0
1939	Linfield	Ballymena Utd	2–0
1940	Ballymena Utd	Glenavon	2–0
1941	Belfast Celtic	Linfield	1–0
1942	Linfield	Glentoran	3–1
1943	Belfast Celtic	Glentoran	1–0
1944	Belfast Celtic	Linfield	3–1
1945	Linfield	Glentoran	4–2
1946	Linfield	Distillery	3–0
1947	Belfast Celtic	Glentoran	1–0
1948	Linfield	Coleraine	3–0
1949	Derry City	Glentoran	3–1
1950	Linfield	Distillery	2–1
1951	Glentoran	Ballymena Utd	3–1
1952	Ards	Glentoran	1–0
1953	Linfield	Coleraine	5–0
1954	Derry City	Glentoran	1–0
1955	Dundela	Glenavon	3–0
1956	Distillery	Glentoran	1–0
1957	Glenavon	Derry City	2–0
1958	Ballymena Utd	Linfield	2–0
1959	Glenavon	Ballymena Utd	2–0
1960	Linfield	Ards	5–1
1961	Glenavon	Linfield	5–1
1962	Linfield	Portadown	4–0
1963	Linfield	Distillery	2–1
1964	Derry City	Glentoran	2–0
1965	Coleraine	Glenavon	2–1
1966	Glentoran	Linfield	2–0
1967	Crusaders	Glentoran	3–1
1968	Crusaders	Linfield	2–0
1969	Ards	Distillery	4–2
1970	Linfield	Ballymena Utd	2–1
1971	Distillery	Derry City	3–0
1972	Coleraine	Portadown	2–1
1973	Glentoran	Linfield	3–2
1974	Ards	Ballymena Utd	2–1
1975	Coleraine	Linfield	1–1, 0–0, 1–0
1976	Carrick Rangers	Linfield	2–1
1977	Coleraine	Linfield	4–1
1978	Linfield	Ballymena Utd	3–1
1979	Cliftonville	Portadown	3–2
1980	Linfield	Crusaders	2–0
1981	Ballymena Utd	Glenavon	1–0
1982	Linfield	Coleraine	2–1
1983	Glentoran	Linfield	1–1, 2–1
1984	Ballymena Utd	Garrick Rangers	4–1
1985	Glentoran	Linfield	1–1, 1–0
1986	Glentoran	Coleraine	2–1
1987	Glentoran	Larne	1–0
1988	Glentoran	Glenavon	1–0
1989	Ballymena Utd	Larne	1–0
1990	Glentoran	Portadown	3–0
1991	Portadown	Glenavon	2–1
1992	Glenavon	Linfield	2–1
1993	Bangor	Ards	1–1, 1–1, 1–0
1994	Linfield	Bangor	2–0
1995	Linfield	Carrick Rangers	3–1
1996	Glentoran	Glenavon	1–0
1997	Glenavon	Cliftonville	1–0
1998	Glentoran	Glenavon	1–0
1999	Not played: Portadown awarded cup		

INTERNATIONAL RESULTS

1882–89

Date	Opponents	Venue	F–A
18/2/82	England	Belfast	0–13
25/2/82	Wales	Wrexham	1–7
24/2/83	England	Liverpool	0–7
17/3/83	Wales	Belfast	1–1
26/1/84	Scotland	Belfast	0–5
9/2/84	Wales	Wrexham	0–6
23/2/84	England	Belfast	1–8
28/2/85	England	Manchester	0–4
14/3/85	Scotland	Glasgow	2–8
11/4/85	Wales	Belfast	2–8
27/2/86	Wales	Wrexham	0–5
13/3/86	England	Belfast	1–6
20/3/86	Scotland	Belfast	2–7
5/2/87	England	Sheffield	0–7
19/2/87	Scotland	Glasgow	1–4
12/3/87	Wales	Belfast	4–1
3/3/88	Wales	Wrexham	0–11
24/3/88	Scotland	Belfast	2–10
7/4/88	England	Belfast	1–5
2/3/89	England	Liverpool	1–6
9/3/89	Scotland	Glasgow	0–7
27/4/89	Wales	Belfast	1–3

1890

8/2	Wales	Shrewsbury	2–5
15/3	England	Belfast	1–9
29/3	Scotland	Belfast	1–4

1891

7/2	Wales	Belfast	7–2
7/3	England	Wolverhampton	1–6
28/3	Scotland	Glasgow	1–2

1892
27/2	Wales	Bangor	1–1
5/3	England	Belfast	0–2
19/3	Scotland	Belfast	2–3

1893
25/2	England	Birmingham	1–6
25/3	Scotland	Glasgow	1–6
5/4	Wales	Belfast	4–3

1894
24/2	Wales	Swansea	1–4
3/3	England	Belfast	2–2
31/3	Scotland	Belfast	1–2

1895
9/3	England	Derby	0–9
16/3	Wales	Belfast	2–2
30/3	Scotland	Glasgow	1–3

1896
29/2	Wales	Wrexham	1–6
7/3	England	Belfast	0–2
28/3	Scotland	Belfast	3–3

1897
20/2	England	Nottingham	0–6
6/3	Wales	Belfast	4–3
27/3	Scotland	Glasgow	1–5

1898
19/2	Wales	Llandudno	1–0
5/3	England	Belfast	2–3
26/3	Scotland	Belfast	0–3

1899
18/2	England	Sunderland	2–13
4/3	Wales	Belfast	1–0
25/3	Scotland	Glasgow	1–9

1900
24/2	Wales	Llandudno	0–2
3/3	Scotland	Belfast	0–3
17/3	England	Dublin	0–2

1901
23/2	Scotland	Glasgow	0–11
9/3	England	Southampton	0–3
23/3	Wales	Belfast	0–1

1902
22/2	Wales	Cardiff	3–0
1/3	Scotland	Belfast	1–3
22/3	England	Belfast	0–1

1903
14/2	England	Wolverhampton	0–4
21/3	Scotland	Glasgow	2–0
28/3	Wales	Belfast	2–0

1904
12/3	England	Belfast	1–3
21/3	Wales	Bangor	1–0
26/3	Scotland	Dublin	1–1

1905
25/2	England	Middlesbrough	1–1
18/3	Scotland	Glasgow	0–4
8/4	Wales	Belfast	2–2

1906
17/2	England	Belfast	0–5
17/3	Scotland	Dublin	0–1
2/4	Wales	Wrexham	4–4

1907
16/2	England	Liverpool	0–1
23/2	Wales	Belfast	2
16/3	Scotland	Glasgow	0–3

1908
15/2	England	Belfast	1–3
14/3	Scotland	Dublin	0–5
11/4	Wales	Aberdare	1–0

1909
13/2	England	Bradford	0–4
15/3	Scotland	Glasgow	0–5
20/3	Wales	Belfast	2–3

1910
12/2	England	Belfast	1–1
19/3	Scotland	Belfast	1–0
11/4	Wales	Wrexham	1–4

1911
28/1	Wales	Belfast	1–2
11/2	England	Derby	1–2
18/3	Scotland	Glasgow	0–2

1912
10/2	England	Dublin	1–6
16/3	Scotland	Belfast	1–4
13/4	Wales	Cardiff	3–2

1913
18/1	Wales	Belfast	0–1
15/2	England	Belfast	2–1
15/3	Scotland	Dublin	1–2

1914
19/1	Wales	Wrexham	2–1
14/2	England	Middlesbrough	3–0
14/3	Scotland	Belfast	1–1

1919
25/10	England	Belfast	1–1

1920
14/2	Wales	Belfast	2–2
13/3	Scotland	Glasgow	0–3
23/10	England	Sunderland	0–2

1921
26/2	Scotland	Belfast	0–2
9/4	Wales	Swansea	1–2
22/10	England	Belfast	1–1

1922
4/3	Scotland	Glasgow	1–2
1/4	Wales	Belfast	1–1
21/10	England	West Bromwich	0–2

1923
3/3	Scotland	Belfast	0–1
14/4	Wales	Wrexham	3–0
20/10	England	Belfast	2–1

1924
1/3	Scotland	Glasgow	0–2
15/3	Wales	Belfast	0–1
22/10	England	Liverpool	1–3

1925
28/2	Scotland	Belfast	0–3
18/4	Wales	Wrexham	0–0
24/10	England	Belfast	0–0

1926
13/2	Wales	Belfast	3–0
27/2	Scotland	Glasgow	0–4
20/10	England	Liverpool	3–3

1927
26/2	Scotland	Belfast	0–2
19/4	Wales	Cardiff	2–2
22/10	England	Belfast	2–0

1928
4/2	Wales	Belfast	1–2
25/2	Scotland	Glasgow	1–0
22/10	England	Liverpool	1–2

1929
2/2	Wales	Wrexham	2–2
23/2	Scotland	Belfast	3–7
19/10	England	Belfast	0–3

1930
1/2	Wales	Belfast	0–7
22/2	Scotland	Glagow	1–3
20/10	England	Sheffield	1–5

1931
21/2	Scotland	Belfast	0–0
22/4	Wales	Wrexham	2–3
19/9	Scotland	Glasgow	1–3
17/10	England	Belfast	2–6
5/12	Wales	Belfast	4–0

1932
12/9	Scotland	Belfast	0–4
17/10	England	Blackpool	0–1
7/12	Wales	Wrexham	1–4

1933
16/9	Scotland	Glasgow	2–1
14/10	England	Belfast	0–3
4/11	Wales	Belfast	1–1

1934
20/10	Scotland	Belfast	2–1

1935
6/2	England	Liverpool	1–2
27/3	Wales	Wrexham	1–3
19/10	England	Belfast	1–3
13/11	Scotland	Edinburgh	1–2

1936
11/3	Wales	Belfast	3–2
31/10	Scotland	Belfast	1–3
18/11	England	Stoke-on-Trent	1–3

1937
17/3	Wales	Wrexham	1–4
23/10	England	Belfast	1–5
10/11	Scotland	Aberdeen	1–1

1938
16/3	Wales	Belfast	1–0
8/11	Scotland	Belfast	0–2
16/11	England	Manchester	0–7

1939
15/3	Wales	Wrexham	1–3

1940
28/9	England	Belfast	2–7
27/11	Scotland	Glasgow	0–0

1947
16/4	Wales	Belfast	2–1
4/10	Scotland	Belfast	2–0
5/11	England	Everton	2–2

1948
10/3	Wales	Wrexham	0–2
9/10	England	Belfast	2–6
17/11	Scotland	Glasgow	2–3

1949
9/3	Wales	Belfast	0–2
1/10	Scotland	Belfast	2–8 (WCQ)
6/11	England	Manchester	2–9 (WCQ)

1950
8/3	Wales	Wrexham	0–0 (WCQ)
7/10	England	Belfast	1–4
1/11	Scotland	Glasgow	1–6

1951
7/3	Wales	Belfast	1–2
12/5	France	Belfast	2–2
6/10	Scotland	Belfast	0–3
20/11	England	Villa Park	0–2

1952
19/3	Wales	Swansea	0–3
4/10	England	Belfast	2–2
5/11	Scotland	Glasgow	1–1
11/11	France	Paris	1–3

1953
15/4	Wales	Belfast	2–3
3/10	Scotland	Belfast	1–3 (WCQ)
11/11	England	Everton	1–3 (WCQ)

1954
31/3	Wales	Wrexham	2–1 (WCQ)
2/10	England	Belfast	0–2
3/11	Scotland	Glasgow	2–2

1955
20/4	Wales	Belfast	2–3
8/10	Scotland	Belfast	2–1
2/11	England	Wembley	0–3

1956
11/4	Wales	Cardiff	1–1
6/10	England	Belfast	1–1
7/11	Scotland	Glasgow	0–1

1957
16/1	Portugal	Lisbon	1–1 (WCQ)
10/4	Wales	Belfast	0–0
25/4	Italy	Rome	0–1 (WCQ)
1/5	Portugal	Belfast	3–0 (WCQ)
5/10	Scotland	Belfast	1–1
6/11	England	Wembley	3–2
4/12	Italy	Belfast	2–2

1958
15/1	Italy	Belfast	2–1 (WCQ)
16/4	Wales	Cardiff	1–1
8/10	Czechoslovakia	Halmstad	1–0 (WCF)
11/6	Argentina	Halmstad	1–3 (WCF)
15/6	West Germany	Malmo	2–2 (WCF)
17/6	Czechoslovakia	Malmo	2–1 (WCF)
19/6	France	Norrkoping	0–4 (WCF)
4/10	England	Belfast	3–3
15/10	Spain	Madrid	2–6
5/11	Scotland	Glasgow	2–2

1959
22/4	Wales	Belfast	4–1
3/10	Scotland	Belfast	0–4
18/11	England	Wembley	1–2

1960
6/4	Wales	Wrexham	2–3
8/10	England	Belfast	2–5
26/10	W Germany	Belfast	3–4 (WCQ)
9/11	Scotland	Glasgow	2–5

1961
12/4	Wales	Belfast	1–5
25/4	Italy	Bologna	2–3
3/5	Greece	Athens	1–2 (WCQ)
10/5	W Germany	Berlin	1–2 (WCQ)
7/10	Scotland	Belfast	1–6
17/10	Greece	Belfast	2–0 (WCQ)
22/11	England	Wembley	1–1

1962
11/4	Wales	Cardiff	0–4

Date	Opponent	Venue	Result
9/5	Holland	Rotterdam	0–4
10/10	Poland	Katowice	2–0 (ECQ)
20/10	England	Belfast	1–3
7/11	Scotland	Glasgow	1–5
28/11	Poland	Belfast	2–0 (ECQ)

1963
Date	Opponent	Venue	Result
3/4	Wales	Belfast	1–4
30/5	Spain	Bilbao	1–1
12/10	Scotland	Belfast	2–1
30/10	Spain	Belfast	0–1
20/11	England	Wembley	3–8

1964
Date	Opponent	Venue	Result
15/4	Wales	Swansea	3–2
29/4	Uruguay	Belfast	3–0
3/10	England	Belfast	3–4
14/10	Switzerland	Belfast	1–0 (WCQ)
14/11	Switzerland	Lausanne	1–2 (WCQ)
25/11	Scotland	Glasgow	2–3

1965
Date	Opponent	Venue	Result
17/3	Holland	Belfast	2–1 (WCQ)
31/3	Wales	Belfast	0–5
7/4	Holland	Rotterdam	0–0 (WCQ)
7/5	Albania	Belfast	4–1 (WCQ)
2/10	Scotland	Belfast	3–2
10/11	England	Wembley	1–2
24/11	Albania	Tirana	1–1 (WCQ)

1966
Date	Opponent	Venue	Result
30/3	Wales	Cardiff	4–1
7/5	W Germany	Belfast	0–2
22/6	Mexico	Belfast	4–1
22/10	England	Belfast	0–2 (ECQ)
16/11	Scotland	Glasgow	1–2

1967
Date	Opponent	Venue	Result
12/4	Wales	Belfast	0–0 (ECQ)
21/10	Scotland	Belfast	1–0
22/11	England	Wembley	0–2 (ECQ)

1968
Date	Opponent	Venue	Result
28/2	Wales	Wrexham	0–2 (ECQ)
10/9	Israel	Jaffa	3–2
23/10	Turkey	Belfast	4–1 (WCQ)
11/12	Turkey	Istanbul	3–0 (WCQ)

1969
Date	Opponent	Venue	Result
3/5	England	Belfast	1–3
6/5	Scotland	Glasgow	1–1
10/5	Wales	Belfast	0–0
10/9	USSR	Belfast	0–0 (WCQ)
22/10	USSR	Moscow	0–2 (WCQ)

1970
Date	Opponent	Venue	Result
18/4	Scotland	Belfast	0–1
21/4	England	Wembley	1–3
25/4	Wales	Swansea	0–1
11/11	Spain	Seville	0–3 (ECQ)

1971
Date	Opponent	Venue	Result
3/2	Cyprus	Nicosia	3–0 (ECQ)
21/4	Cyprus	Belfast	5–0 (ECQ)
15/5	England	Belfast	0–1
18/5	Scotland	Glasgow	1–0
22/5	Wales	Belfast	1–0
22/9	USSR	Moscow	0–1 (ECQ)
13/10	USSR	Belfast	1–1 (ECQ)

1972
Date	Opponent	Venue	Result
16/2	Spain	Hull	1–1 (ECQ)
20/5	Scotland	Glasgow	0–2
23/5	England	Wembley	1–0
27/5	Wales	Wrexham	0–0
18/10	Bulgaria	Sofia	0–3 (WCQ)

1973
Date	Opponent	Venue	Result
14/2	Cyprus	Nicosia	0–1 (WCQ)
28/3	Portugal	Coventry	1–1 (WCQ)
8/5	Cyprus	London	3–0 (WCQ)
12/5	England	Liverpool	1–2
16/5	Scotland	Glasgow	2–1
19/5	Wales	Liverpool	1–0
26/9	Bulgaria	Hillsborough	0–0 (WCQ)
14/11	Portugal	Lisbon	1–1 (WCQ)

1974
Date	Opponent	Venue	Result
11/5	Scotland	Glasgow	1–0
15/5	England	Wembley	0–1
18/5	Wales	Wrexham	0–1
4/9	Norway	Oslo	1–2 (ECQ)
30/10	Sweden	Solna	2–0 (ECQ)

1975
Date	Opponent	Venue	Result
16/3	Yugoslavia	Belfast	1–0 (ECQ)
17/5	England	Belfast	0–0
20/5	Scotland	Glasgow	0–3
23/5	Wales	Belfast	1–0
3/9	Sweden	Belfast	1–2 (ECQ)
29/10	Norway	Belfast	3–0 (ECQ)
19/11	Yugoslavia	Belgrade	0–1 (ECQ)

1976
Date	Opponent	Venue	Result
24/3	Israel	Tel Aviv	1–1
8/5	Scotland	Glasgow	0–3
11/5	England	Wembley	0–4
14/5	Wales	Swansea	0–1
13/10	Holland	Rotterdam	2–2 (WCQ)
10/11	Belgium	Liège	0–2 (WCQ)

1977
Date	Opponent	Venue	Result
27/4	W Germany	Cologne	0–5
28/5	England	Belfast	1–2
1/6	Scotland	Glasgow	0–2
3/6	Wales	Belfast	1–1
11/6	Iceland	Reykjavik	0–1 (WCQ)
21/9	Iceland	Belfast	2–0 (WCQ)
12/10	Holland	Belfast	0–1 (WCQ)
16/11	Belgium	Belfast	3–0 (WCQ)

1978
Date	Opponent	Venue	Result
13/5	Scotland	Glasgow	1–1
16/5	England	Wembley	0–1
19/5	Wales	Wrexham	0–1
20/9	Rep of Ireland	Dublin	0–0 (ECQ)
25/10	Denmark	Belfast	2–1 (ECQ)
29/11	Bulgaria	Sofia	2–0 (ECQ)

1979
Date	Opponent	Venue	Result
7/2	England	Wembley	0–4 (ECQ)
2/5	Bulgaria	Belfast	2–0 (ECQ)
19/5	England	Belfast	0–2
22/5	Scotland	Glasgow	0–1
25/5	Wales	Belfast	1–1
6/6	Denmark	Copenhagen	0–4 (ECQ)
17/10	England	Belfast	1–5 (ECQ)
21/11	Rep of Ireland	Belfast	1–0 (ECQ)

1980
Date	Opponent	Venue	Result
26/3	Israel	Tel Aviv	0–0 (WCQ)
16/5	Scotland	Belfast	1–0
20/5	England	Wembley	1–1
23/5	Wales	Cardiff	1–0
11/6	Australia	Sydney	2–1
15/6	Australia	Melbourne	1–1
18/6	Australia	Adelaide	2–1
15/10	Sweden	Belfast	3–0 (WCQ)
19/11	Portugal	Lisbon	0–1 (WCQ)

1981
Date	Opponent	Venue	Result
25/3	Scotland	Glasgow	1–1 (WCQ)
29/4	Portugal	Belfast	1–0 (WCQ)
19/5	Scotland	Glasgow	0–2
3/6	Sweden	Stockholm	0–1 (WCQ)
14/10	Scotland	Belfast	0–0
18/11	Israel	Belfast	1–0 (WCQ)

1982
Date	Opponent	Venue	Result
23/2	England	Wembley	0–4
24/3	France	Paris	0–4
28/4	Scotland	Belfast	1–1
27/5	Wales	Wrexham	0–3
17/6	Yugoslavia	Zaragoza	0–0 (WCF)
21/6	Honduras	Zaragoza	1–1 (WCF)
25/6	Spain	Valencia	1–0 (WCF)
1/7	Austria	Madrid	2–2 (WCF)
4/7	France	Madrid	1–4 (WCF)
13/10	Austria	Vienna	0–2 (ECQ)
17/11	W Germany	Belfast	1–0 (ECQ)
15/12	Albania	Tirana	0–0 (ECQ)

1983
Date	Opponent	Venue	Result
30/3	Turkey	Belfast	2–1 (ECQ)
27/4	Albania	Belfast	1–0 (ECQ)
24/5	Scotland	Glasgow	0–0
28/5	England	Belfast	0–0
31/5	Wales	Belfast	0–1
21/9	Austria	Belfast	3–1 (ECQ)
12/10	Turkey	Ankara	0–1 (ECQ)
16/11	W Germany	Hamburg	1–0 (ECQ)
13/12	Scotland	Belfast	2–0

1984
Date	Opponent	Venue	Result
4/4	England	Wembley	0–1
22/5	Wales	Swansea	1–1
27/5	Finland	Pori	0–1 (WCQ)
12/9	Romania	Belfast	3–2 (WCQ)
16/10	Israel	Belfast	3–0
14/11	Finland	Belfast	2–1 (WCQ)

1985
Date	Opponent	Venue	Result
27/2	England	Belfast	0–1 (WCQ)
27/3	Spain	Palma	0–0
1/5	Turkey	Belfast	2–0 (WCQ)
11/9	Turkey	Izmir	0–0 (WCQ)
16/10	Romania	Bucharest	1–0 (WCQ)
13/11	England	Wembley	0–0 (WCQ)

1986
Date	Opponent	Venue	Result
26/2	France	Paris	0–0
26/3	Denmark	Belfast	1–1
23/4	Morocco	Belfast	2–1
3/6	Algeria	Guadalajara	1–1 (WCF)
7/6	Spain	Guadalajara	1–2 (WCF)
12/6	Brazil	Guadalajara	0–3 (WCF)
15/10	England	Wembley	0–3 (ECQ)
12/11	Turkey	Izmir	0–0 (ECQ)

1987
Date	Opponent	Venue	Result
18/2	Israel	Tel Aviv	1–1
1/4	England	Belfast	0–2 (ECQ)
29/4	Yugoslavia	Belfast	1–2 (ECQ)
14/10	Yugoslavia	Sarajevo	0–3 (ECQ)
11/11	Turkey	Belfast	1–0 (ECQ)

1988
Date	Opponent	Venue	Result
17/2	Greece	Athens	2–3
23/3	Poland	Belfast	1–1
27/4	France	Belfast	0–0
21/5	Malta	Belfast	3–0 (WCQ)
14/9	Rep of Ireland	Belfast	0–0 (WCQ)
19/10	Hungary	Budapest	0–1 (WCQ)
21/12	Spain	Seville	0–4 (WCQ)

1989
Date	Opponent	Venue	Result
8/2	Spain	Belfast	0–2 (WCQ)
26/4	Malta	Valletta	2–0 (WCQ)
26/5	Chile	Belfast	0–1
6/9	Hungary	Belfast	1–2 (WCQ)
11/10	Rep of Ireland	Dublin	0–3 (WCQ)

1990
Date	Opponent	Venue	Result
27/3	Norway	Belfast	2–3
18/5	Uruguay	Belfast	1–0
12/9	Yugoslavia	Belfast	0–2 (ECQ)
17/10	Denmark	Belfast	1–1 (ECQ)
14/11	Austria	Vienna	0–0 (ECQ)

1991
Date	Opponent	Venue	Result
5/2	Poland	Belfast	3–1
27/3	Yugoslavia	Belgrade	1–4 (ECQ)
1/5	Faeroes	Belfast	1–1 (ECQ)
11/9	Faeroes	Landsrona	5–0 (ECQ)
16/10	Austria	Belfast	2–1 (ECQ)
13/11	Denmark	Odense	1–2 (ECQ)

1992
Date	Opponent	Venue	Result
28/4	Lithuania	Belfast	2–2 (WCQ)
2/6	Germany	Bremen	1–1
9/9	Albania	Belfast	3–0 (WCQ)
14/10	Spain	Belfast	0–0 (WCQ)
18/11	Denmark	Belfast	0–1 (WCQ)

1993
Date	Opponent	Venue	Result
17/2	Albania	Tirana	2–1 (WCQ)
31/3	Rep of Ireland	Dublin	0–3 (WCQ)
28/4	Spain	Seville	1–3 (WCQ)
25/5	Lithuania	Vilnius	1–0 (WCQ)
2/6	Latvia	Riga	2–1 (WCQ)
8/9	Latvia	Belfast	2–0 (WCQ)
13/10	Denmark	Copenhagen	0–1 (WCQ)
17/11	Rep of Ireland	Belfast	1–1 (WCQ)

1994
Date	Opponent	Venue	Result
20/4	Liechtenstein	Belfast	4–1 (ECQ)
3/6	Colombia	Boston	0–2
12/6	Mexico	Miami	0–3
7/9	Portugal	Belfast	1–2 (ECQ)
12/10	Austria	Vienna	2–1 (ECQ)
16/11	Rep of Ireland	Belfast	0–4 (ECQ)

1995
Date	Opponent	Venue	Result
29/3	Rep of Ireland	Dublin	1–1 (ECQ)
26/4	Latvia	Riga	1–0 (ECQ)
22/5	Canada	Edmonton	0–2
25/5	Chile	Edmonton	1–2
7/6	Latvia	Belfast	1–2 (ECQ)
26/4	Latvia	Riga	1–0 (ECQ)
3/9	Portugal	Lisbon	1–1 (ECQ)
11/10	Liechtenstein	Eschen	4–0 (ECQ)
15/11	Austria	Belfast	5–3 (ECQ)

1996
Date	Opponent	Venue	Result
27/3	Norway	Belfast	0–2
24/4	Sweden	Belfast	1–2
29/5	Germany	Belfast	1–1
31/8	Ukraine	Belfast	0–1 (WCQ)
5/10	Armenia	Belfast	1–1 (WCQ)
9/11	Germany	Nüremburg	1–1 (WCQ)
14/12	Albania	Belfast	2–0 (WCQ)

1997
Date	Opponent	Venue	Result
29/3	Portugal	Belfast	0–0 (WCQ)
2/4	Ukraine	Kiev	1–2 (WCQ)
30/4	Armenia	Yerevan	0–0 (WCQ)
21/5	Thailand	Bangkok	0–0
20/8	Germany	Belfast	1–3 (WCQ)
10/9	Albania	Zurich	0–1 (WCQ)
11/10	Portugal	Lisbon	0–1 (WCQ)

1998
Date	Opponent	Venue	Result
25/3	Slovakia	Belfast	1–0
22/4	Switzerland	Belfast	1–0
5/9	Turkey	Istanbul	0–3 (ECQ)
10/10	Finland	Belfast	1–0 (ECQ)
18/11	Moldova	Belfast	2–2 (ECQ)

1999
Date	Opponent	Venue	Result
27/3/99	Germany	Belfast	0–3 (ECQ)
31/3/99	Moldova	Chisinau	0–0 (ECQ)
27/4/99	Canada	Belfast	1–1
29/5/99	Ireland	Dublin	1–0

REPUBLIC OF IRELAND

The Irish Republic developed as an independent international soccer entity after partition and the creation of the Irish Free State in the early 1920s. They competed in the World Cup qualifiers of 1934 and 1938, and the clubs founded before partition lived on and gained new strength.

However, many old links survived. Several players appeared for both Irelands, and an interesting fact of which few are aware is that the first foreign nation to beat England in England was the Irish Republic – who won 2–0 at Goodison Park, Liverpool in September 1949. England, that day, included the likes of Wright, Franklin, Finney and Mannion.

The Republic Comes Into Its Own

Almost all the best players raised in the Republic were quickly sold to English and Scottish clubs. Ironically, it was not until the advent of an Englishman, Jack Charlton, as a national manager prepared to take full advantage of the parental qualification loophole, that the Irish Republic eventually gained international prestige. Equally importantly, Charlton brought organization and discipline to the Irish play, and by 1988 had proved his worth by leading them to their first appearance in the European Championship Finals. Better still, they beat England 1–0 in their opening game.

Two years later the Irish were experiencing their first World Cup Finals. Again they were to face England, this time forcing a 1–1 draw in Cagliari. A second round victory on penalties over Romania took the Irish into the quarter-finals where hosts Italy proved too strong.

Charlton's men were back at the finals in 1994 and beat Italy 1–0 in their opening game at Giants Stadium in New Jersey, before falling to Holland in the second round. Holland repeated their 2–0 victory in the qualifying play-off for the 1996 European Championship. This defeat at Anfield proved the end of the road for Charlton. His former defensive mainstay, Mick McCarthy, succeeded him as manager.

FAI LEAGUE CHAMPIONS

Year	Champions	Runners-up
1922	St James's Gate	Bohemians
1923	Shamrock R	Shelbourne
1924	Bohemians	Shelbourne
1925	Shamrock R	Bohemians
1926	Shelbourne	Shamrock R
1927	Shamrock R	Shelbourne
1928	Bohemians	Shelbourne
1929	Shelbourne	Bohemians
1930	Bohemians	Shelbourne
1931	Shelbourne	Dundalk
1932	Shamrock R	Cork
1933	Dundalk	Shamrock R
1934	Bohemians	Cork
1935	Dolphin	St James's Gate
1936	Bohemians	Dolphin
1937	Sligo R	Dundalk
1938	Shamrock R	Waterford
1939	Shamrock R	Sligo R
1940	St James's Gate	Shamrock R
1941	Cork Utd	Waterford
1942	Cork Utd	Shamrock R
1943	Cork Utd	Dundalk
1944	Shelbourne	Limerick
1945	Cork Utd	Limerick
1946	Cork Utd	Drumcondra
1947	Shelbourne	Drumcondra
1948	Drumcondra	Dundalk
1949	Drumcondra	Shelbourne
1950	Cork Ath	Drumcondra
1951	Cork Ath	Shelbourne
1952	St Patrick's Ath	Sligo R
1953	Shelbourne	Evergreen Utd
1954	Shamrock R	Drumcondra
1955	St Patrick's Ath	Waterford
1956	St Patrick's Ath	Shamrock R
1957	Shamrock R	Drumcondra
1958	Drumcondra	Shamrock R
1959	Shamrock R	Evergreen Utd
1960	Limerick	Cork Celtic
1961	Drumcondra	St Patrick's Ath
1962	Shelbourne	Cork Celtic
1963	Dundalk	Waterford
1964	Shamrock R	Dundalk
1965	Drumcondra	Shamrock R
1966	Waterford	Shamrock R
1967	Dundalk	Bohemians
1968	Waterford	Dundalk
1969	Waterford	Shamrock R
1970	Waterford	Shamrock R
1971	Cork Hibs	Shamrock R
1972	Waterford	Cork Hibs
1973	Waterford	Finn Harps
1974	Cork Celtic	Bohemians
1975	Bohemians	Athlone T
1976	Dundalk	Finn Harps
1977	Sligo R	Bohemians
1978	Bohemians	Finn Harps
1979	Dundalk	Bohemians
1980	Limerick	Dundalk
1981	Athlone T	Dundalk
1982	Dundalk	Shamrock R
1983	Athlone T	Drogheda Utd
1984	Shamrock R	Bohemians
1985	Shamrock R	Bohemians
1986	Shamrock R	Galway Utd
1987	Shamrock R	Dundalk
1988	Dundalk	St Patrick's Ath
1989	Derry City	Dundalk
1990	St Patrick's Ath	Derry City
1991	Dundalk	Cork City
1992	Shelbourne	Derry City
1993	Cork City	Bohemians
1994	Shamrock R	Cork City
1995	Dundalk	Shelbourne
1996	St Patrick's Ath	Bohemians
1997	Derry City	Bohemians
1998	St Patrick's Ath	Shelbourne
1999	St Patrick's Ath	Cork City

FAI SENIOR CHALLENGE CUP

Year	Winners	Runners-up	Score
1922	St James's Gate	Shamrock R	1–1, 1–0
1923	Alton Utd	Shelbourne	1–0
1924	Athlone T	Fordsons	1–0
1925	Shamrock R	Shelbourne	2–1
1926	Fordsons	Shamrock R	3–2
1927	Drumcondra	Brideville	1–1, 1–0
1928	Bohemians	Drumcondra	1–0
1929	Shamrock R	Bohemians	0–0, 3–0
1930	Shamrock R	Brideville	1–0
1931	Shamrock R	Dundalk	1–1, 1–0
1932	Shamrock R	Dolphin	1–0
1933	Shamrock R	Dolphin	3–3, 3–0
1934	Cork	St James's Gate	2–1
1935	Bohemians	Dundalk	4–3
1936	Shamrock R	Cork	2–1
1937	Waterford	St James's Gate	2–1
1938	St James's Gate	Dundalk	2–1
1939	Shelbourne	Sligo R	1–1, 1–0
1940	Shamrock R	Sligo R	3–0
1941	Cork Utd	Waterford	2–2, 3–1
1942	Dundalk	Cork Utd	3–1
1943	Drumcondra	Cork Utd	2–1
1944	Shamrock R	Shelbourne	3–2
1945	Shamrock R	Bohemians	1–0
1946	Drumcondra	Shamrock R	2–1
1947	Cork Utd	Bohemians	2–2, 2–0
1948	Shamrock R	Drumcondra	2–1
1949	Dundalk	Shelbourne	3–0
1950	Transport	Cork Ath	2–2, 2–2, 3–1
1951	Cork Ath	Shelbourne	1–0
1952	Dundalk	Cork Ath	1–1, 3–0
1953	Cork Ath	Evergreen Utd	2–2, 2–1
1954	Drumcondra	St Patrick's Ath	1–0
1955	Shamrock R	Drumcondra	1–0
1956	Shamrock R	Cork Ath	3–2
1957	Drumcondra	Shamrock R	2–0
1958	Dundalk	Shamrock R	1–0
1959	St Patrick's Ath	Waterford	2–2, 2–1
1960	Shelbourne	Cork Hibs	2–0
1961	St Patrick's Ath	Drumcondra	2–1
1962	Shamrock R	Shelbourne	4–1
1963	Shelbourne	Cork Hibs	2–0
1964	Shamrock R	Cork Celtic	1–1, 2–1
1965	Shamrock R	Limerick	1–1, 1–0
1966	Shamrock R	Limerick	2–0
1967	Shamrock R	St Patrick's Ath	3–2
1968	Shamrock R	Waterford	3–0
1969	Shamrock R	Cork Celtic	1–1, 4–1
1970	Bohemians	Sligo R	0–0, 0–0, 2–1
1971	Limerick	Drogheda	0–0, 3–0
1972	Cork Hibs	Waterford	3–0
1973	Cork Hibs	Shelbourne	0–0, 1–0
1974	Finn Harps	St Patrick's Ath	3–1
1975	Home Farm	Shelbourne	1–0
1976	Bohemians	Drogheda Utd	1–0
1977	Dundalk	Limerick	2–0
1978	Shamrock R	Sligo R	1–0
1979	Dundalk	Waterford	2–0
1980	Waterford	St Patrick's Ath	1–0
1981	Dundalk	Sligo R	2–0
1982	Limerick Utd	Bohemians	1–0
1983	Sligo R	Bohemians	2–1
1984	University College	Shamrock R	2–1
1985	Shamrock R	Galway Utd	1–0
1986	Shamrock R	Waterford Utd	2–0
1987	Shamrock R	Dundalk	3–0
1988	Dundalk	Derry City	1–0
1989	Derry City	Cork City	0–0, 1–0
1990	Bray W	St Francis	3–0
1991	Galway Utd	Shamrock R	1–0
1992	Bohemians	Cork City	1–0
1993	Shelbourne	Dundalk	1–0
1994	Sligo R	Derry City	1–0
1995	Derry City	Shelbourne	1–0
1996	Shelbourne	St Patrick's Ath	1–1, 2–1
1997	Shelbourne	Derry City	2–0
1998	Cork City (after replay)	Shelbourne	0–0, 1–0
1999	Bray Wanderers	Finn Harps	0–0, 2–2, 2–1

INTERNATIONAL RESULTS 1920–1959

Date	Opponents	Venue	F–A
21/3/26	Italy	Turin	0–3
23/4/27	Italy	Dublin	1–2
12/2/28	Belgium	Liège	4–2
30/4/29	Belgium	Dublin	4–0
11/5/30	Belgium	Brussels	3–1
26/4/31	Spain	Barcelona	1–1
13/12/31	Spain	Dublin	0–5
8/5/32	Holland	Amsterdam	2–0
25/2/34	Belgium	Dublin	4–4 (WCQ)
8/4/34	Holland	Amsterdam	2–5 (WCQ)
15/12/34	Hungary	Dublin	2–4
5/5/35	Switzerland	Basle	0–1
8/5/35	Germany	Dortmund	1–3
8/12/35	Holland	Dublin	3–5
17/3/36	Switzerland	Dublin	1–0
3/5/36	Hungary	Budapest	3–3
9/5/36	Luxembourg	Luxembourg	5–1
17/10/36	Germany	Dublin	5–2
6/12/36	Hungary	Dublin	2–3
17/5/37	Switzerland	Berne	1–0
23/5/37	France	Paris	2–0
10/10/37	Norway	Oslo	2–3 (WCQ)
7/11/37	Norway	Dublin	3–3 (WCQ)
18/5/38	Czechoslovakia	Prague	2–2
22/5/38	Poland	Warsaw	0–6
18/9/38	Switzerland	Dublin	4–0
13/11/38	Poland	Dublin	3–2
19/3/39	Hungary	Cork	2–2
18/5/39	Hungary	Budapest	2–2
23/5/39	Germany	Bremen	1–1
16/6/46	Portugal	Lisbon	1–3

23/6/46	Spain	Madrid	1–0
30/9/46	England	Dublin	0–1
2/3/47	Spain	Dublin	3–2
4/5/47	Portugal	Dublin	0–2
23/5/48	Portugal	Lisbon	0–2
30/5/48	Spain	Barcelona	1–2
5/12/48	Switzerland	Dublin	0–1
24/4/49	Belgium	Dublin	0–2
22/5/49	Portugal	Dublin	1–0
2/6/49	Sweden	Stockholm	1–3 (WCQ)
12/6/49	Spain	Dublin	1–4
8/9/49	Finland	Dublin	3–0 (WCQ)
21/9/49	England	Everton	2–0
9/10/49	Finland	Helsinki	1–1 (WCQ)
13/11/49	Sweden	Dublin	1–3 (WCQ)
10/5/50	Belgium	Brussels	1–5
26/11/50	Norway	Dublin	2–2
13/5/51	Argentina	Dublin	0–1
30/5/51	Norway	Oslo	3–2
17/10/51	W Germany	Dublin	3–2
4/5/52	W Germany	Cologne	0–3
7/5/52	Austria	Vienna	0–6
1/6/52	Spain	Madrid	0–6
25/3/53	Austria	Dublin	4–0
4/10/53	France	Dublin	3–5 (WCQ)
28/10/53	Luxembourg	Dublin	4–0 (WCQ)
25/11/53	France	Paris	0–1 (WCQ)
7/3/54	Luxembourg	Luxembourg	1–0 (WCQ)
8/11/54	Norway	Dublin	2–1
1/5/55	Holland	Dublin	1–0
25/5/55	Norway	Oslo	3–1
28/5/55	W Germany	Hamburg	1–2
19/9/55	Yugoslavia	Dublin	1–4
27/11/55	Spain	Dublin	2–2
10/5/56	Holland	Rotterdam	4–1
3/10/56	Denmark	Dublin	2–1 (WCQ)
25/11/56	W Germany	Dublin	3–0
8/5/57	England	Wembley	1–5 (WCQ)
19/5/57	England	Dublin	1–1 (WCQ)
2/10/57	Denmark	Copenhagen	2–0 (WCQ)
14/3/58	Austria	Vienna	1–3
11/5/58	Poland	Katowice	2–2
5/10/58	Poland	Dublin	2–2
5/4/59	Czechoslovakia	Dublin	2–0 (ECQ)
10/5/59	Czechoslovakia	Bratislava	0–4 (ECQ)
1/11/59	Sweden	Dublin	3–2

1960–1995

30/3/60	Chile	Dublin	2–0
11/5/60	W Germany	Düsseldorf	1–0
18/5/60	Sweden	Malmö	1–4
28/9/60	Wales	Dublin	2–3
6/11/60	Norway	Dublin	3–1
3/5/61	Scotland	Glasgow	1–4 (WCQ)
7/5/61	Scotland	Dublin	0–3 (WCQ)
8/10/61	Czechoslovakia	Dublin	1–3 (WCQ)
29/10/61	Czechoslovakia	Prague	1–7 (WCQ)
8/4/62	Austria	Dublin	2–3
12/8/62	Iceland	Dublin	4–2 (ECQ)
2/9/62	Iceland	Reykjavik	1–1 (ECQ)
9/6/63	Scotland	Dublin	1–0
25/9/63	Austria	Vienna	0–0 (ECQ)
13/10/63	Austria	Dublin	3–2 (ECQ)
11/3/64	Spain	Seville	1–5 (ECQ)
8/4/64	Spain	Dublin	0–2 (ECQ)
10/5/64	Poland	Cracow	1–3
13/5/64	Norway	Oslo	4–1
24/5/64	England	Dublin	1–3
25/10/64	Poland	Dublin	3–2
24/3/65	Belgium	Dublin	0–2
5/5/65	Spain	Dublin	1–0 (WCQ)
27/10/65	Spain	Seville	1–4 (WCQ)
10/11/65	Spain	Paris	0–1 (WCQ)
4/5/66	W Germany	Dublin	0–4
22/5/66	Austria	Vienna	0–1
25/5/66	Belgium	Liège	3–2
23/10/66	Spain	Dublin	0–0 (ECQ)
16/11/66	Turkey	Dublin	2–1 (ECQ)
7/12/66	Spain	Valencia	0–2 (ECQ)
22/2/67	Turkey	Ankara	1–2 (ECQ)
21/5/67	Czechoslovakia	Dublin	0–2 (ECQ)
22/11/67	Czechoslovakia	Prague	2–1 (ECQ)
15/5/68	Poland	Dublin	2–2
30/10/68	Poland	Katowice	0–1
10/11/68	Austria	Dublin	2–2
4/12/68	Denmark	Dublin	1–1 (WCQ)
	(abandoned after 51 minutes)		
4/5/69	Czechoslovakia	Dublin	1–2 (WCQ)
27/5/69	Denmark	Copenhagen	0–2 (WCQ)
8/6/69	Hungary	Dublin	1–2 (WCQ)
21/9/69	Scotland	Dublin	1–1
7/10/69	Czechoslovakia	Prague	0–3 (WCQ)
15/10/69	Denmark	Dublin	1–1 (WCQ)
5/11/69	Hungary	Budapest	0–4 (WCQ)
6/5/70	Poland	Dublin	1–2
9/5/70	W Germany	Berlin	1–2
23/9/70	Poland	Dublin	0–2
14/10/70	Sweden	Dublin	1–1 (ECQ)
28/10/70	Sweden	Malmö	0–1 (ECQ)
8/12/71	Italy	Rome	0–3 (ECQ)
10/5/71	Italy	Dublin	1–2 (ECQ)
30/5/71	Austria	Dublin	1–4 (ECQ)
10/10/71	Austria	Linz	0–6 (ECQ)
18/6/72	Iran	Recife	2–1
19/6/72	Ecuador	Natal	3–2
21/6/72	Chile	Recife	1–2
25/6/72	Portugal	Recife	1–2
18/10/72	USSR	Dublin	1–2 (WCQ)
15/11/72	France	Dublin	2–1 (WCQ)
13/5/73	USSR	Moscow	0–1 (WCQ)
16/5/73	Poland	Wroclaw	0–2
19/5/73	France	Paris	1–1 (WCQ)
6/6/73	Norway	Oslo	1–1
21/10/73	Poland	Dublin	1–0
8/5/74	Uruguay	Montevideo	0–2
12/5/74	Chile	Santiago	2–1
30/10/74	USSR	Dublin	3–0 (ECQ)
20/11/74	Turkey	Izmir	1–1 (ECQ)
1/3/75	W Germany B	Dublin	1–0 +
11/5/75	Switzerland	Dublin	2–1 (ECQ)
18/5/75	USSR	Kiev	1–2 (ECQ)
29/10/75	Turkey	Dublin	4–0 (ECQ)
24/3/76	Norway	Dublin	3–0
26/5/76	Poland	Prosjan	2–0
8/9/76	England	Wembley	1–1
13/10/76	Turkey	Ankara	3–3
17/11/76	France	Paris	0–2 (WCQ)
9/2/77	Spain	Dublin	0–1
30/3/77	France	Dublin	1–0 (WCQ)
24/4/77	Poland	Dublin	0–0
1/6/77	Bulgaria	Sofia	1–2 (WCQ)
12/10/77	Bulgaria	Dublin	0–0 (WCQ)
5/4/78	Turkey	Dublin	4–2
12/4/78	Poland	Lodz	0–3
21/5/78	Norway	Oslo	0–0
24/5/78	Denmark	Copenhagen	3–3 (ECQ)
20/9/78	N Ireland	Dublin	0–0 (ECQ)
25/10/78	England	Dublin	1–1 (ECQ)
2/5/79	Denmark	Dublin	2–0 (ECQ)
19/5/79	Bulgaria	Sofia	0–1 (ECQ)
22/5/79	W Germany	Dublin	1–3
11/9/79	Wales	Swansea	1–2
26/9/79	Czechoslovakia	Prague	1–4
17/10/79	Bulgaria	Dublin	3–0 (ECQ)
29/10/79	USA	Dublin	3–2
21/11/79	N Ireland	Belfast	0–1 (ECQ)
6/2/80	England	Wembley	0–2 (ECQ)
26/3/80	Cyprus	Nicosia	3–2 (WCQ)
30/4/80	Switzerland	Dublin	2–0
16/5/80	Argentina	Dublin	0–1
10/9/80	Holland	Dublin	2–1 (WCQ)
15/10/80	Belgium	Dublin	1–1 (WCQ)
28/10/80	France	Paris	0–2 (WCQ)
19/11/80	Cyprus	Dublin	6–0 (WCQ)
24/2/81	Wales	Dublin	1–3
25/3/81	Belgium	Brussels	0–1 (WCQ)
29/4/81	Czechoslovakia	Dublin	3–1
21/5/81	W Germany	Bremen	0–3
	(W Germany 'B' side)		
23/5/81	Poland	Bydgoszcz	0–3
9/9/81	Holland	Rotterdam	2–2 (WCQ)
14/10/81	France	Dublin	3–2 (WCQ)
22/5/82	Chile	Santiago	0–1
27/5/82	Brazil	Vberlandia	0–7
30/5/82	Trinidad & Tobago	Port Of Spain	1–2
22/9/82	Holland	Rotterdam	1–2 (ECQ)
17/11/82	Spain	Dublin	3–3 (ECQ)
30/3/83	Malta	Valletta	1–0 (ECQ)
27/4/83	Spain	Zaragoza	0–2 (ECQ)
12/10/83	Holland	Dublin	2–3 (ECQ)
16/11/83	Malta	Dublin	8–0 (ECQ)
4/4/84	Israel	Tel Aviv	0–3
23/5/84	Poland	Dublin	0–0
3/6/84	China	Sapporo	1–0
8/8/84	Mexico	Dublin	0–0
12/9/84	USSR	Dublin	1–0 (WCQ)
17/10/84	Norway	Oslo	0–1 (WCQ)
14/11/84	Denmark	Copenhagen	0–3
5/2/85	Italy	Dublin	1–2
26/3/85	England	Wembley	1–2
1/5/85	Norway	Dublin	0–0 (WCQ)
21/5/85	Israel	Tel Aviv	0–0
26/5/85	Spain	Cork	0–0 (WCQ)
2/6/85	Switzerland	Dublin	3–0 (WCQ)
11/9/85	Switzerland	Berne	0–0 (WCQ)
16/10/85	USSR	Moscow	0–2 (WCQ)
13/11/85	Denmark	Dublin	1–4 (WCQ)
26/3/86	Wales	Dublin	0–1
23/4/86	Uruguay	Dublin	1–1
25/5/86	Iceland	Reykjvik	2–1
27/5/86	Czechoslovakia	Reykjvik	1–0
10/9/86	Belgium	Brussels	2–2 (ECQ)
15/10/86	Scotland	Dublin	0–0 (ECQ)
12/11/86	Poland	Warsaw	0–1
18/2/87	Scotland	Glasgow	1–0 (ECQ)
1/4/87	Bulgaria	Sofia	1–2 (ECQ)
29/4/87	Belgium	Dublin	0–0 (ECQ)
23/5/87	Brazil	Dublin	1–0
28/5/87	Luxembourg	Luxembourg	2–0 (ECQ)
9/9/87	Luxembourg	Dublin	2–1 (ECQ)
14/10/87	Bulgaria	Dublin	2–0 (ECQ)
10/11/87	Israel	Dublin	5–0
23/3/88	Romania	Dublin	2–0
27/4/88	Yugoslavia	Dublin	2–0
22/5/88	Poland	Dublin	3–1
1/6/88	Norway	Oslo	0–0
12/6/88	England	Stuggart	1–0 (ECF)
15/6/88	USSR	Hanover	1–1 (ECF)
18/6/88	Holland	Gelsenkirchen	0–1 (ECF)
14/9/88	N Ireland	Belfast	0–0 (WCQ)
19/10/88	Tunisia	Dublin	4–0
16/11/88	Spain	Seville	0–2 (WCQ)
7/2/89	France	Dublin	0–0
8/3/89	Hungary	Budapest	0–0 (WCQ)
26/4/89	Spain	Dublin	1–0 (WCQ)
28/5/89	Malta	Dublin	2–0 (WCQ)
4/6/89	Hungary	Dublin	2–0 (WCQ)
6/9/89	W Germany	Dublin	1–1
11/10/89	N Ireland	Dublin	3–0 (WCQ)
15/11/89	Malta	Valetta	2–0 (WCQ)
12/1/90	Morocco	Dublin	1–0
28/3/90	Wales	Dublin	1–0
25/4/90	USSR	Dublin	1–0
16/5/90	Finland	Dublin	1–1
27/5/90	Turkey	Izmir	0–0
3/6/90	Malta	Valetta	3–0
11/6/90	England	Cagliari	1–1 (WCF)
17/6/90	Egypt	Palermo	0–0 (WCF)
21/6/90	Holland	Palermo	1–1 (WCF)
25/6/90	Romania	Genoa	0–0 (WCF)
	(Rep of Ireland won on penalties: 5–4)		
30/6/90	Italy	Rome	0–1 (WCF)
17/10/90	Turkey	Dublin	5–0 (ECQ)
14/11/90	England	Dublin	1–1 (ECQ)
6/2/91	Wales	Wrexham	3–0
27/3/91	England	Wembley	1–1 (ECQ)
1/5/91	Poland	Dublin	0–0 (ECQ)
22/5/91	Chile	Dublin	1–1
2/6/91	USA	Foxboro	1–1
11/9/91	Hungary	Gyor	2–1
16/10/91	Poland	Poznan	3–3 (ECQ)
13/11/91	Turkey	Istanbul	3–1 (ECQ)
19/2/92	Wales	Dublin	0–1
25/3/92	Switzerland	Dublin	2–1
29/4/92	USA	Dublin	4–1
26/5/92	Albania	Dublin	2–0 (WCQ)
30/5/92	USA	Washington	1–3
4/6/92	Italy	Foxboro	0–2
7/6/92	Portugal	Foxboro	2–0
9/9/92	Latvia	Dublin	4–0 (WCQ)
14/10/92	Denmark	Copenhagen	0–0 (WCQ)
18/11/92	Spain	Seville	0–0 (WCQ)
17/2/93	Wales	Dublin	2–1
31/3/93	N Ireland	Dublin	3–0 (WCQ)
28/4/93	Denmark	Dublin	1–1 (WCQ)
26/5/93	Albania	Tirana	2–1 (WCQ)
2/6/93	Latvia	Riga	2–1 (WCQ)
16/6/93	Lithuania	Vilnius	1–0 (WCQ)
8/9/93	Lithuania	Dublin	2–0 (WCQ)
13/10/93	Spain	Dublin	1–3 (WCQ)
17/11/93	N Ireland	Belfast	1–1 (WCQ)
23/3/94	Russia	Dublin	0–0
20/4/94	Holland	Tilburg	1–0
24/5/94	Bolivia	Dublin	1–0
29/5/94	Germany	Hannover	2–0
4/6/94	Czech Republic	Dublin	1–3
18/6/94	Italy	New York	1–0 (WCF)
24/6/94	Mexico	Orlando	1–2 (WCF)
28/6/94	Norway	New York	0–0 (WCF)
4/7/94	Holland	Orlando	0–2 (WCF)
7/9/94	Latvia	Riga	3–0 (ECQ)
12/10/94	Liechtenstein	Dublin	4–0 (ECQ)
16/11/94	N Ireland	Belfast	4–0 (ECQ)
15/2/95	England	Dublin	1–0
	(abandoned after 21 minutes)		
29/3/95	N Ireland	Dublin	1–1 (ECQ)
26/4/95	Portugal	Dublin	1–0 (ECQ)
3/6/95	Liechtenstein	Vaduz	0–0 (ECQ)
11/6/95	Austria	Dublin	1–3 (ECQ)
6/9/95	Austria	Vienna	1–3 (ECQ)
11/10/95	Latvia	Dublin	2–1 (ECQ)
15/11/95	Portugal	Lisbon	0–3 (ECQ)
13/12/95	Holland	Liverpool	0–2 (ECQ)

1996

27/3	Russia	Dublin	0–2
24/4	Czech Republic	Prague	0–2
29/5	Portugal	Dublin	0–1
31/8	Liechtenstein	Vaduz	5–0 (WCQ)
9/10	FYR Macedonia	Dublin	3–0 (WCQ)
10/11	Iceland	Dublin	0–0 (WCQ)

1997

11/2	Wales	Cardiff	0–0
2/4	FYR Macedonia	Skopje	2–3 (WCQ)
30/4	Romania	Bucharest	0–1 (WCQ)
21/5	Liechtenstein	Dublin	5–0 (WCQ)
20/8	Lithuania	Dublin	0–0 (WCQ)
10/9	Lithuania	Vilnius	2–1 (WCQ)
11/10	Romania	Dublin	1–1 (WCQ)
29/10	Belgium	Dublin	1–1 (WCQ)
15/11	Belgium	Brussels	1–2 (WCQ)

1998

25/3	Czech Rep.	Olomouc	1–2
22/4	Argentina	Dublin	0–2
23/5	Mexico	Dublin	0–0
5/9	Croatia	Dublin	2–0 (ECQ)
14/10	Malta	Dublin	5–0 (ECQ)
18/11	Yugoslavia	Belgrade	0–1 (ECQ)

1999

10/2	Paraguay	Dublin	2–0
28/4	Sweden	Dublin	2–0
29/5	Northern Ireland	Dublin	0–1
9/6	Macedonia	Dublin	1–0 (ECQ)

SOCCER CHRONOLOGY

1848: First code of rules compiled at Cambridge University

1855: Sheffield FC, world's oldest club, formed

1862: Notts County, world's oldest league club, formed

1863: FA formed, Oct 26

1871: FA Cup inaugurated

1872: Size of ball fixed

1872: Scotland draw 0–0 with England in first official international at West of Scotland cricket ground

1873: Scottish FA and Cup launched

1874: Shinguards introduced by Sam Weller Widdowson of Nottingham Forest and England

1875: Crossbar replaces tape

1876: FA of Wales formed

1878: Referee's whistle used for first time at Nottingham Forest's ground

1878: Almost 20,000 people watch first floodlit match, between two Sheffield teams, with lighting provided by four lamps on 30ft wooden towers

1882: International Board formed

1883: Two-handed throw-in introduced

1885: Professionalism legalized

1888: Football League, brainchild of Aston Villa director, William McGregor, founded, and first matches played on Sept 8

1888: Scottish Cup winners Renton beat English FA Cup winners West Bromwich for the "Championship of the World"

1889: Unbeaten Preston, "The Invincibles", become first club to win League and Cup double

1890: Scottish and Irish Leagues formed

1891: Goal nets and penalties introduced

1891: Referees and linesman replace umpires and referees

1892: Football League Second Division formed

1893: Genoa, oldest Italian League club, formed

1895: FA Cup, held by Aston Villa, stolen from Birmingham shop window and never seen again

1897: Players' Union formed

1897: Juventus formed

1898: Promotion and relegation introduced

1899: Barcelona formed

1901: Maximum wage rule in force

1901: Southern League Tottenham Hotspur become first professional club to take FA Cup south

1901: First 100,000 attendance (110,802) at Cup Final, venue Crystal Palace

1901: Argentina beat Uruguay 3–2 in first international between South American countries

1902: Ibrox Park disaster: 25 killed when part of new wooden stand collapses at Scotland vs. England match

1902: Real Madrid formed

1902: Austria beat Hungary 5–0 in Vienna, the first international between teams outside the home countries

1904: FIFA formed with seven members

1905: England join FIFA

1905: Goalkeepers ordered to stay on goal-line at penalties

1905: First £1,000 transfer: Alf Common, from Sunderland to Middlesbrough

1908: Transfer limit of £350 introduced in January, withdrawn in April

1908: UK beat Denmark to win first Olympic title at Shepherds Bush

1908: England travel to Vienna to beat Austria 6–1 in their first international on foreign soil

1910: Argentina win the first South American Championship

1919: League extended to 44 clubs

1920: Third Division South formed

1921: Third Division North formed

1923: Football pools introduced

1923: First Wembley FA Cup final: Bolton 2 West Ham 0

1924: First Wembley international: England 1 Scotland 1

1924: Goal can be scored direct from corner kick

1925: Offside rule change: a player needs two, not three, players between him and goal to stay onside

1926: Huddersfield complete first hat-trick of championships

1927: Hughie Ferguson's goal against

Arsenal makes Cardiff first club to take FA Cup out of England

1928: The four home countries withdraw from FIFA

1928: Bill "Dixie" Dean scores 60 First Division goals, still a record

1929: Goalkeepers ordered to stay on goal-line until penalty is kicked

1930: Uruguay win first World Cup

1933: Numbered shirts worn in the FA cup final for first time, winners Everton wearing 1–11, Manchester City 12–22

1934: Sudden death of Arsenal manager Herbert Chapman on Jan 6

1936: Joe Payne's 10-goal record (Luton 12 Bristol Rovers 0)

1938: First live TV transmission of Cup Final (Preston 1 Huddersfield 0)

1939: Compulsory numbering of players in Football League

1939: All normal competitions suspended because of war

1946: British Associations rejoin FIFA

1946: 33 killed and 500 injured as wall and crowd barriers collapse at Bolton vs. Stoke FA Cup tie

1947: First £20,000 transfer: Tommy Lawton, from Chelsea to Notts Co.

1949: England's first home defeat by a non-Home nation (0–2 vs. Republic of Ireland at Goodison Park, Liverpool)

1949: Entire Torino team wiped out when aircraft taking them home from Lisbon crashes near Turin

1950: League extended from 88 to 92 clubs

1950: England humbled 1–0 by US in World Cup group match, and world

GOAL GLUT

Arbroath beat Bon-Accord 36–0 on September 5, 1885 in the first round of the Scottish FA Cup, which is still a record score for a British first-class match. But it was little wonder the visitors went down by a cricket score, for the Aberdonians from 30 miles up the coast were actually cricketers, playing in their working clothes and not possessing a pair of boots between them. Their goalkeeper, who had never played football before, was injured and replaced at half-time by a half-back. The Arbroath goalkeeper was not called upon to touch the ball, and winger John Petrie scored 13 goals – a record for an individual. It was not a good day for Aberdeen: Dundee Harp beat Aberdeen Rovers 35–0.

record crowd (203,500) see Uruguay beat Brazil 2–1 in the Final in Rio

1950: Scotland first beaten at home by foreign team (Austria, 1–0)

1951: White ball comes into use

1951: First official match under flood-lights played at Highbury: between Arsenal and Hapoel Tel Aviv

1952: Newcastle become first to win successive FA Cup finals at Wembley

1953: Hungary beat England 6–3 at Wembley

1954: Hungary beat England 7–1 in Budapest

1955: First floodlit FA Cup tie (replay): Kidderminster vs. Brierley Hill Alliance

1956: First floodlit League match: Portsmouth vs. Newcastle

1956: Real Madrid, from an entry of 16 teams, win first European Cup

1956: South Korea defeat Israel to win first Asian Cup

1957: First African Nations Cup final: Egypt 4 Ethiopia 1

1958: Electrified pitch used by Everton to beat frost

1958: Munich air disaster kills 19, including eight Manchester United players

1958: English League restructured into four divisions

1958: Barcelona beat a London Select team 8–2 over two games to win first Inter City Fairs Cup

1959: Billy Wright of Wolves, first man to reach 100 caps for England, retires on 105

1960: FA recognizes Sunday football

1960: Football League Cup introduced

1960: European champions Real Madrid win first World Club Championship, beating South American champions Penarol over two legs

1960: Soviet Union win the first European Championship

1960: Penarol of Uruguay win first Copa Libertadores

1961 Tottenham complete first League and Cup double this century

1961: Maximum wage (£20) abolished

1961: First British £100-a-week wage paid to Johnny Haynes by Fulham

1961: First £100,000 British transfer: Denis Law, from Manchester City to Torino

1961: Fiorentina beat Rangers 4–2 over two games to win first European Cup-winners' Cup

1961: Hapoel Tel Aviv defeat Selangor

of Malaysia 2–1 to win first Asian Champions Cup

1963: Tottenham beat Atletico Madrid 5–1 in Cup-winners' Cup Final to become first British club to win European trophy

1963: First Pools Panel

1964: First televised Match of the Day (BBC 2, Liverpool 3 Arsenal 2, August 22)

1964: 318 die and 500 injured in riot over disallowed goal during Peru vs. Argentina Olympic tie in Lima

1964: Oryx Douala of Cameroon defeat Stade Malien of Mali 2–1 to win first African Champions Club Cup

1965: Ten Football League players jailed and banned for life for match-fixing

1965: Stanley Matthews knighted

1965: Substitutes allowed for injured players in League matches

1966: England win World Cup, beating West Germany 4–2 after extra time at Wembley

1967: Alf Ramsey, England manager, knighted

1967: Celtic beat Internazionale 2–1 to become first British winners of European Cup and complete unprecedented grand slam: European Cup, Scottish League, League Cup, Scottish Cup and Glasgow Cup

1967: First substitutes in Cup final (Chelsea vs. Tottenham), but neither is used

1968: 74 die at Nunez, Buenos Aires, when panic breaks out during River Plate vs. Boca Juniors match

1968: Alan Mullery becomes first England player sent off, vs. Yugoslavia in European Championship

1968: Manchester United become first English winners of European Cup beating Benfica 4–1 after extra time

1970: Brazil beat Italy 4–1 to capture World Cup for third time and win Jules Rimet trophy outright

1971: 66 fans trampled to death and 100 injured in second Ibrox disaster, as they tumbled down stairway just before end of Rangers vs. Celtic New Year's Day game

1972: Fairs Cup becomes UEFA Cup and is won by Tottenham, who defeat Wolves 3–2 over two games

1974: League football played on Sunday for first time

1974: Last FA Amateur Cup Final

1974: Joao Havelange succeeds Sir Stanley Rous as FIFA president

1977: Liverpool win League Championship and European Cup

1978: Freedom of contract accepted for League players

1978: Liverpool first English club to win successive European Cups

1978: Ban on foreign players in English football lifted

1979: First all-British £500,000 transfer: David Mills, from Middlesbrough to West Bromwich

1979: First £1m British transfer: Trevor Francis, from Birmingham City to Nottingham Forest

1981: Tottenham win 100th Cup Final

1981: Liverpool win European Cup, becoming first British side to hold it three times

1981: Three points for a win introduced in Football League

1981: Record British transfer: Bryan Robson, from WBA to Manchester United for £1.5m

1981: QPR install first artificial pitch in English football

1982: 340 fans crushed to death during Spartak Moscow vs. Haarlem UEFA Cup tie at Lenin Stadium

1982: Aston Villa become sixth consecutive English winners of European Cup

1982: Tottenham retain FA Cup, first time since Spurs in 1961–62

1982 League Cup becomes Milk Cup

1982: Italy defeat West Germany 3–1 in Madrid to complete third World Cup triumph

1983: Football League sponsored by Canon for three years

1984: Aberdeen take Scottish Cup for third successive season and win championship

1984: Liverpool win European Cup in penalty shoot-out and complete unique treble for an English club, with Milk Cup and League title

1984: Northern Ireland win last British Home Championship

1984: France win their first honour – the European Championship

1984: Britain's biggest score this century: Stirling Albion beat Selkirk 20–0 in Scottish Cup

1985: Bradford City fire disaster kills 56

1985: Kevin Moran (Manchester United) is first player sent off in Cup Final

1985: Heysel disaster: 39 die as a result of rioting at Liverpool vs. Juventus European Cup Final in Brussels. UEFA ban English clubs indefi-

nitely from European competition

1986: Sir Stanley Rous dies, aged 91

1986: Wales FA move HQ from Wrexham to Cardiff after 110 years

1987: Play-offs introduced for last promotion place; re-election abolished; automatic promotion for winners of Conference

1987: The 18-strong squad plus youth players and officials of Alianza Lima die in plane crash

1989: Hillsborough disaster: 95 crushed to death at Liverpool vs. Notting-ham Forest FA Cup semi-final

1990: International Board amends off-side law (player level no longer off-side); FIFA make professional foul a sending-off offence

1990: English clubs (Manchester United and Aston Villa) restored to European competition

1990 Guiseppe Lorenzo of Bologna cre-ates world record by being sent off after 10 seconds for striking Parma opponent

1991: End of artificial pitches in Division One (Oldham and Luton)

1992: Premier League of 22 clubs launched; Football League reduced to 71 clubs in three divisions

1992: 15 killed and 1,300 injured when temporary stand collapses at Bastia, Corsica, during Bastia vs. Marseille in French Cup semi-final

1993: Marseille are the first French team to win European Cup, but cannot defend their trophy following bribery scandal

1994: Manchester United win "double"

1994: Brazil become first country to win the World Cup on penalties.

1995: Jean-Marc Bosman wins landmark European Court judgement against European Union player transfer restrictions.

1996: Manchester United become first club to win English "double" twice.

1996: Germany beat the Czech Republic to win the first European Champi-onships hosted in England.

1997: Eric Cantona announces his retire-ment from football.

1998: Arsenal remain unbeaten in the League for last five months of sea-son to win the "double-double".

1998: France defeat Brazil 3–0 to win the World Cup for the first time.

1999: Manchester United win historic treble of Premiership, FA Cup, and European Cup.

MAJOR SOCCER AWARDS

FOOTBALLER OF THE YEAR

FIFA WORLD FOOBALLER OF THE YEAR

1991 Lothar Matthäus (Germany)
1992 Marco Van Basten (Holland)
1993 Roberto Baggio (Italy)
1994 Romario (Brazil)
1995 George Weah (Liberia)
1996 Ronaldo (Brazil)
1997 Ronaldo (Brazil)
1998 Zinedine Zidane (France)

WORLD FOOTBALLER OF THE YEAR (WORLD SOCCER MAGAZINE)

1982 Paolo Rossi (Juventus & Italy)
1983 Zico (Udinese & Brazil)
1984 Michel Platini (Juventus & France)
1985 Michel Platini (Juventus & France)
1986 Diego Maradona (Napoli & Argentina)
1987 Ruud Gullit (Milan & Holland)
1988 Marco Van Basten (Milan & Holland)
1989 Ruud Gullit (Milan & Holland)
1990 Lothar Matthäus (Internazionale & West Germany)
1991 Jean-Pierre Papin (Marseille & France)
1992 Marco Van Basten (Milan & Holland)
1993 Roberto Baggio (Juventus & Italy)
1994 Paolo Maldini (Milan & Italy)
1995 Gianluca Vialli (Juventus & Italy)
1996 Ronaldo (Barcelona & Brazil)
1997 Ronaldo (Internazionale & Brazil)
1998 Zinedine Zidane (Juventus & France)

EUROPEAN FOOTBALLER OF THE YEAR (FRANCE FOOTBALL MAGAZINE)

1956 Stanley Matthews (Blackpool)
1957 Alfredo Di Stefano (Real Madrid)
1958 Raymond Kopa (Real Madrid)
1959 Alfredo Di Stefano (Real Madrid)
1960 Luis Suarez (Barcelona)
1961 Omar Sivori (Juventus)
1962 Josef Masopust (Dukla Prague)
1963 Lev Yashin (Moscow Dynamo)
1964 Denis Law (Manchester Utd)
1965 Eusebio (Benfica)
1966 Bobby Charlton (Manchester U)
1967 Florian Albert (Ferencvaros)
1968 George Best (Manchester U)
1969 Gianni Rivera (Milan)
1970 Gerd Müller (Bayern Munich)
1971 Johan Cruyff (Ajax)
1972 Franz Beckenbauer (B Munich)
1973 Johan Cruyff (Barcelona)
1974 Johan Cruyff (Barcelona)
1975 Oleg Blokhin (Dynamo Kiev)
1976 Franz Beckenbauer (B Munich)
1977 Allan Simonsen (Borussia MG)
1978 Kevin Keegan (Hamburg)
1979 Kevin Keegan (Hamburg)
1980 Karl-Heinz Rumenigge (B Munich)
1981 Karl-Heinz Rumenigge (B Munich)
1982 Paolo Rossi (Juventus)
1983 Michel Platini (Juventus)
1984 Michel Platini (Juventus)
1985 Michel Platini (Juventus)
1986 Igor Belanov (Dynamo Kiev)
1987 Ruud Gullit (Milan)
1988 Marco Van Basten (Milan)
1989 Marco Van Basten (Milan)
1990 Lothar Matthäus (Inter)
1991 Jean-Pierre Papin (Marseilles)
1992 Marco Van Basten (Milan)
1993 Roberto Baggio (Juventus)
1994 Hristo Stoichkov (Barcelona)
1995 George Weah (Milan)
1996 Matthias Sammer (B Dortmund)
1997 Ronaldo (Internazionale)
1998 Zinedine Zidane (Juventus)

SOUTH AMERICAN FOOTBALLER OF THE YEAR

1971 Tostao (Brazil)
1972 Teofilio Cubillas (Peru)
1973 Pele (Brazil)
1974 Elias Figueroa (Chile)
1975 Elias Figueroa (Chile)
1976 Elias Figueroa (Chile)
1977 Zico (Brazil)
1978 Mario Kempes (Argentina)
1979 Diego Maradona (Argentina)
1980 Diego Maradona (Argentina)
1981 Zico (Brazil)
1982 Zico (Brazil)
1983 Socrates (Brazil)
1984 Enzo Francescoli (Uruguay)
1985 Romero (Brazil)
1986 Alzamendi (Uruguay)
1987 Carlos Valderrama (Colombia)
1988 Ruben Paz (Uruguay)
1989 Bebeto (Brazil)
1990 Raul Amarilla (Paraguay)
1991 Oscar Ruggeri (Argentina)
1992 Rai (Brazil)
1993 Carlos Valderrama (Colombia)
1994 Cafu (Brazil)
1995 Enzo Francescoli (Uruguay)
1996 Jose Luis Chilavert (Paraguay)
1997 Carlos Valveirama (Colombia)
1998 Martin Palermo (Argentina)

AFRICAN FOOTBALLER OF THE YEAR (FRANCE FOOTBALL MAGAZINE)

1970 Salif Keita (Mali)
1971 Ibrahim Sunday (Ghana)
1972 Cherif Souleymane (Guinea)
1973 Tshimen Bwanga (Zaïre)
1974 Paul Moukila (Congo)
1975 Ahmed Faras (Morocco)
1976 Roger Milla (Cameroon)
1977 Tarak Dhiab (Tunisia)
1978 Karim Abdoul Razak (Ghana)
1979 Thomas N'Kono (Cameroon)
1980 Manga Onguene (Cameroon)
1981 Lakhdar Belloumi (Algeria)
1982 Thomas N'Kono (Cameroon)
1983 Mahmoud Al Khatib (Egypt)
1984 Theophile Abega (Cameroon)
1985 Mohamed Timoumi (Morocco)
1986 Badou Zaki (Morocco)
1987 Rabah Madjer (Algeria)
1988 Kalusha Bwalya (Zambia)
1989 George Weah (Liberia)
1990 Roger Milla (Cameroon)
1991 Abedi Pele (Ghana)
1992 Abedi Pele (Ghana)
1993 Abedi Pele (Ghana)
1994 George Weah (Liberia)
1995 George Weah (Liberia)
1996 Nwankwo Kanu (Nigeria)

The African Confederation player of the year award has been awarded to:

1993 Rashidi Yekini (Nigeria)
1994 Emanuel Amunike (Nigeria)
1995 George Weah (Liberia)
1996 Nwankwo Kanu (Nigeria)
1997 Victor Ikpeba (Nigeria)
1998 Mustapha Hadji (Morocco)

ASIAN FOOTBALLER OF THE YEAR

1990 Kim Joo-sung (South Korea)
1991 Kim Joo-sung (South Korea)
1992 *no award*
1993 Kazu Miura (Japan)
1994 Said Al-Owairan (Saudi Arabia)
1995 Masami Ihara (Japan)
1996 Kholdad Azizi (Iran)
1997 Hidoteshi Nakata (Japan)
1998 Hidetoshi Nakata (Japan)

OCEANIA FOOTBALLER OF THE YEAR

1990 Robby Slater (Australia)
1991 Wynton Rufer (New Zealand)
1992 Wynton Rufer (New Zealand)
1993 Robby Slater (Australia)
1994 Aurelio Vidmar (Australia)
1995 Christian Karembeu (New Caledonia & France)
1996 No award
1997 Mark Bosnich (Australia)
1998 Christian Karembeu (New Caledonia & France)

ENGLISH FOOTBALLER OF THE YEAR FOOTBALL WRITERS' ASSOCIATION)

1948 Stanley Matthews (Blackpool)
1949 Johnny Carey (Manchester U)
1950 Joe Mercer (Arsenal)
1951 Harry Johnston (Blackpool)
1952 Billy Wright (Wolves)
1953 Nat Lofthouse (Bolton W)
1954 Tom Finney (Preston North End)
1955 Don Revie (Manchester C)
1956 Bert Trautmann (Manchester C)
1957 Tom Finney (Preston North End)
1958 Danny Blanchflower (Tottenham H)
1959 Syd Owen (Luton Town)
1960 Bill Slater (Wolverhampton W)
1961 Danny Blanchflower (Tottenham H)
1962 Jimmy Adamson (Burnley)
1963 Stanley Matthews (Stoke City)
1964 Bobby Moore (West Ham United)
1965 Bobby Collins (Leeds United)
1966 Bobby Charlton (Manchester U)
1967 Jackie Charlton (Leeds United)
1968 George Best (Manchester United)
1969 Dave Mackay (Derby County) *and* Tony Book (Manchester City)
1970 Billy Bremner (Leeds United)
1971 Frank McLintock (Arsenal)
1972 Gordon Banks (Stoke City)
1973 Pat Jennings (Tottenham H)
1974 Ian Callaghan (Liverpool)
1975 Alan Mullery (Fulham)
1976 Kevin Keegan (Liverpool)
1977 Emlyn Hughes (Liverpool)
1978 Kenny Burns (Nottingham Forest)
1979 Kenny Dalglish (Liverpool)
1980 Terry McDermott (Liverpool)
1981 Frans Thijssen (Ipswich Town)
1982 Steve Perryman (Tottenham H)
1983 Kenny Dalglish (Liverpool)
1984 Ian Rush (Liverpool)
1985 Neville Southall (Everton)
1986 Gary Lineker (Everton)
1987 Clive Allen (Tottenham H)
1988 John Barnes (Liverpool)
1989 Steve Nicol (Liverpool)
1990 John Barnes (Liverpool)
1991 Gordon Strachan (Leeds United)
1992 Gary Lineker (Tottenham H)
1993 Chris Waddle (Sheffield W)
1994 Alan Shearer (Blackburn Rovers)
1995 Jürgen Klinsmann (Tottenham H)
1996 Eric Cantona (Manchester U)
1997 Gianfranco Zola (Chelsea)
1998 Dennis Bergkamp (Arsenal)
1999 David Ginola (Tottenham)

SCOTTISH FOOTBALLER OF THE YEAR

1966 John Greig (Rangers)
1967 Ronnie Simpson (Celtic)
1968 Gordon Wallace (Raith Rovers)
1969 Bobby Murdoch (Celtic)
1970 Pat Stanton (Hibernian)
1971 Martin Buchan (Aberdeen)
1972 Dave Smith (Rangers)
1973 George Connelly (Celtic)
1974 Scotland World Cup squad
1975 Sandy Jardine (Rangers)
1976 John Greig (Rangers)
1977 Danny McGrain (Celtic)
1978 Derek Johnstone (Rangers)
1979 Andy Ritchie (Morton)
1980 Gordon Strachan (Aberdeen)
1981 Alan Rough (Partick Thistle)
1982 Paul Sturrock (Dundee United)
1983 Charlie Nicholas (Celtic)
1984 Willie Miller (Aberdeen)
1985 Hamish McAlpine (Dundee United)
1986 Sandy Jardine (Hearts)
1987 Brian McClair (Celtic)
1988 Paul McStay (Celtic)
1989 Richard Gough (Rangers)
1990 Alex McLeish (Aberdeen)
1991 Maurice Malpas (Dundee United)
1992 Ally McCoist (Rangers)
1993 Andy Goram (Rangers)
1994 Mark Hateley (Rangers)
1995 Brian Laudrup (Rangers)
1996 Paul Gascoigne (Rangers)
1997 Brian Laudrup (Rangers)
1998 Craig Burley (Celtic)
1999 Henrik Larsson (Celtic)

LEADING GOAL SCORERS IN EUROPE — EUROPEAN GOLDEN BOOT

Year	Player	Club	Goals
1968	Eusebio	Benfica	42
1969	Petar Jekov	CSKA Sofia	36
1970	Gerd Müller	Bayern Munich	38
1971	Josip Skoblar	Olympique Marseille	44
1972	Gerd Müller	Bayern Munich	40
1973	Eusebio	Benfica	40
1974	Hector Yazalde	Sporting Lisbon	46
1975	Dudu Georgescu	Dinamo Bucharest	33
1976	Sotiris Kaiafas	Omonia Nicosia	39
1977	Dudu Georgescu	Dinamo Bucharest	47
1978	Hans Krankl	Rapid Vienna	41
1979	Kees Kist	AZ Alkmaar	34
1980	Erwin Vandenburgh	Lierse	39
1981	Georgi Slavkov	Trakia Plovdiv	31
1982	Wim Kieft	Ajax	32
1983	Fernando Gomes	Porto	36
1984	Ian Rush	Liverpool	32
1985	Fernando Gomes	Porto	39
1986	Marco Van Basten	Ajax	37
1987	Rodion Camataru	Dinamo Bucharest	44
1988	Tanju Colak	Galatasaray	39
1989	Dorin Mateut	Dinamo Bucharest	43
1990	Hugo Sanchez	Real Madrid	38
	Hristo Stoichkov	CSKA Sofia	38
1991	Darko Pancev	Red Star Belgrade	34
1992–96	Not organized		
1997	Ronaldo	Barcelona	34
1998	Nikos Machlas	Vitesse Arnhem	34
1999	Mario Jardel	FC Porto	36

INDEX
& ACKNOWLEDGEMENTS

A

Abega, Theophile 73
Abegglen, André 65, 124
Abegglen, Max 65, 124
Aberdeen **43**, 45, 48, 63, 181, **222**
Ademir 124
Afghanistan 77
Africa 73–6
African Champions Cup 49, 73
African Cup-winners' Cup 49
African Footballer of the Year 73, 74, 150, 167
African Nations Cup 34–5, **34–5**, 73, 75, 76
Aguas, José 61, 85, 112, 124
Aguilera, Carlos 163
AIK Stockholm 64
Ajax 57, 80–2, 128
    European Cup 41, 43
    European Cup-winners' Cup 46, 48
    players 108–9, 152, 156, 165
    UEFA Cup 46
    World Club Cup 37
Akers-Stahl, Michelle 30
Al Ahly 74
Al Khatib, Mahmoud 74
Albania 50
Albert, Florian 58, 124–5, **124**, 128
Alberto, Carlos 67
Alcock, C.W. **11**, 12, 226
Aldair **67**
Algeria 23, 34, 35, 73, **73**
Alianza Lima 225
All Union Spartakia 182

Allchurch, Ivor 65, 125
Allemandi, Luigi 125
Allen, Clive 204
Allison, Malcolm 102
Allofs, Klaus 48, 56
Alonso, Jesus 181
Alonso, Norberto 99
Altafini, José 45, 94, 125, 162
Amancio 125, **125**
Amarildo 125
Ambrosiana-Internazionale 160
American Samoa 72
Amoros, Manuel 125, **125**
Anderlecht 45, 48, 82, 161, 165
Andorra 50
Andrade, Jose 126
Andrade, Victor Rodriguez 96, 126
Andreolo, Michele 95
Anfield **214–15**
Angers 144
Angola 73, 225
Antigua and Barbuda 70
Antognoni, Giancarlo 126, **126**
Antwerp 48
Aragones, Luis 83
Archibald, Steve 84
Ardiles, Osvaldo 126, **126**, **152**, 154, 222
Argentina 12, 13, 70, **70**
    Ardiles 126
    Copa America 32, **32**
    Maradona 115
    players 128, 131, 132, 139, 145, 150, 153, 154, 155, 162, 164
    World Cup **22**, **143**, 154
        1930-34 16, 168
        1960-66 19, 20
        1974-78 21, 22–3, 143, 154
        1986/94 24, 25, 26–7, 139, **205**
Argentinos Juniors 115
Armah, Adolf 74

Armani, Gino 89
Armenia 50
Arminia Bielefeld 222
Armstrong, Chris 223
Arsenal 82, 129, **129**, **188**, **208**, 223, 224, 227
    European Cup-winners' Cup 48
    FA Cup 1993 192
    players 141, 142, 143, 149, 166
    transfers 193
    UEFA Cup 47
    video screens **218**, 219
Artime, Luis 95, 126
Aruba 70
Asante Kotoko 74
Asian Championship 58, 77–8, 79
Asian Confederation 62
Asian Cup 35
Asian Games 35, 78
Asparoukhov, Georgi 52, 126
Asprilla, Faustino **68**
Assad **73**
Assistant referees 201, **201**
Aston Villa **12**, 42, 147, 148, 215, 227
Atalanta 149
Athletic Bilbao 45, 63
Atkinson, Ron 147
Atlante 145
Atletico Madrid 37, 45, 47, 48, 64, 83, **83**, 138, 165
Atletico Nacional Medellin 83, 164
Augsburg 141
Augusto, José 61, **61**, 126
Auld, Bertie 86
Australia 72
Austria 13, 50–2
    players 129, 141, 142, 144, 153
    World Cup 16, 18, 22
    'Wunderteam' 52, 87–8, 98, 162
Auxerre 132

Awards 246–7
Ayala, Ruben Hugo 83
AZ Alkmaar 45
Azerbaijan 52
Azeris 52
Aznar, Emmanuel 93
Azteca Stadium, Mexico City 174, 186, **186**

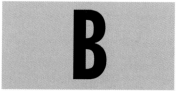

B

Baggio, Roberto 27, 59, 91, 126
Baggio, Dino 46
Bahamas 70
Bahrain 77
Ball, Alan 20
Balls **210**
Bangladesh 77
Bangor City 236
Banks, Gordon 21, 55, 126, 128, **128**
Barbados 70
Barcelona 63–4, 83–4
    Cruyff, Johan 109
    De Stefano, Alfredo 111
    European Cup 40, 42, 144, 173
    European Cup-winners' Cup 44, **45**, 180
    Maradona 115
    Olympic Games 1992 180
    players 134, 141, 144, 145, 147, 152, 157, 160, 163, 167
    UEFA Cup 45, 43, 44, 47, 48
    World Cup, 1982 180
Barek, Larbi Ben 75

Baresi, Franco 27, **27**, 94, 128, **128**, 148
Barnet 223
Basle 44
Bastia 45, 150, 225
Bats, Joel 176
Battiston, Patrick 175, **175**
'Battle of Highbury' 141
Batty, David 28, 29
Baxter, Jim 232
Bayer Leverkeusen 46
Bayern Munich 47, 56, 84–5, **84**, 91, 182
   European Cup **40**, 41, 43
   European Cup-winners' Cup 43
   players 105, 130, 144, 148, 149, 150, 151, 158
Beara, Vladimir 99
Bebeto 102, 128
Beckenbauer, Franz 103, 104–5, **105**, 122
   Bayern Munich 84–5
   NASL 71–2
   West Germany 56, 152, 174, 182
Beckham, David 28, 55
Beerschot 130, 134
Belanov, Igor 91, **91**
Belarus 52
Belenenses 61
Belfast Celtic 238
Belgium 52
   European Championship 33, 38
   Olympic Games 31
   players 130, 132–3, 134, 161, 165
   World Cup 16, 17, 18, 24, 25, 26, 180
Belize 70
Bell, Charlie 93
Bell, Eric 170
Bellini, Luiz 102
Belloumi, Lakhdar 73
Bene, Ferenc 58, 128
Benetti, Romeo 164
Benfica 61, 85, 181
   European Cup 40, 173, 174
   players 112–13, 124, 126, 133, 134, 138
   World Club Cup 36
Benin 73
Bergkamp, Dennis 29, 57, 128, **129**
Bergmark, Orvar 128
Berlusconi, Silvio 93, 94, 195, **195**
Bermuda 70
Bernabeu, Santiago 99, 172, 181, **181**
Bernes, Jean-Pierre 223
Bertoni **22**
Beschastnikh, Mikhail 95
Besiktas 65
Beskov, Constantin 94, 95
Best, George 41, 60, 92, 128–9, **129**, 174, **174**, **209**
Betis Seville 135
Bhutan 77
Bierhoff, Oliver 33
Bielik, Julius 102
Bilardo, Carlos 164
Bilbao 167
Bilek, Michal 102
Bilic, Slaven 29, 53
Binder, Franz 98
Bingham, Billy 60, 239

Birmingham City 43, 44, 45, 217
Bishovets, Anatoli 91
Black, Kingsley **150**
Black Watch 238
Blackburn Rovers 132, 135, 142, 161–2, 193
Blackpool 117, 151, 170
Blanchflower, Danny 60, 129, 204
Blanc, Laurent 28
Blanco, Cuauhtemoc 28, 71
Blatter, Sepp 193
Blau-Weiss, Berlin 180
Blaut, Bernard 79
Bliard, René 137
Blokhin, Oleg 48, 62, 91, 129, **129**, 204
Bloomer, Steve 129
Boban, Zvonimir 129
Bobek, Stejan 65
Boca Juniors 38–9, 66, 85, 115, 148, 155, 224–5
Bochini, Ricardo 89
Bodola, Iuliu 61
Bohemians 153, 238
Boli, Basile **93**
Bolivia 17, 32, 66, **138**
Bologna 137, 141
Bolton Wanderers 168, 170, 215
Boniek, Zbigniew 60, 129–30, **130**, 145
Boninsegna, Roberto 174
Boniperti, Giampiero 130, 162
Bonner, Pat 26, **61**
Boots **208**, 209, **209**
Bordeaux 46, 153
Borussia Dortmund **5**, 43, 44, 46, 47
Borussia Mönchengladbach 45, 46, 148, 152
Borzov, Valeri 129
Bosman Judgement 191
Bosnia-Herzegovina 52
Boston Minutemen 113
Botafogo 67, 142, 160
Botswana 73
Bouderbala, Aziz 75
Bould, Steve 204
Bozsik, Jozsef 121, 130, **171**
Bradford City 223, 225
Brady, Liam 61
Braine, Raymond 130
Brazil 13, **34**, 66–7
   Copa America 32
   Copa Libertadores 39, 40
   players 125, 132, 136, 138, 142, 157, 158–9, 160, 164, 165, 167
   World Cup 22–3, 124, 183, **213**, **219**
      1930-38 16, 17, 136
      1950-58 17, 18, 18–19, 119, 136, 138, 158–9, 169, 171, 172, **202**
      1962-66 19, 20, 119, 125, 136, 142, 158–9
      1970-78 21, 22–3, 119, 142, **202**
      1982-94 26–7, 136, 175, 176, **199**, **213**, **219**
Brehme, Andy 84, 177
Breitner, Paul 64, 84, 130, **130**, 182
Bremner, Billy **63**, 131
Brennan, Shay **174**

Brest 139
Bribery 220–3
Bristol Rovers 141, 217
British Championship 14, 54
Brolin, Tomas 131, **131**
Brondby 54
Broome, Frank 169
Brown, Bobby 205
Browning, John 222
Brugge 45, 132–3, 154
Brunei 77
Buchan, Charlie 82, 203
Buchan, Willie 232
Bulgaria 52–3, **52**, 144, 163
   World Cup 20, 26, 27, 126
Bundesliga 84, 86, 89, 133, 141, 144, 151
Burgnich, Tarcisio 89
Burkina Faso 73
Burma *see* Myanmar
Burnden Park disaster 224
Burnley 147
Burruchaga, Jorge 115
Burundi 73
Bury 163
Busby, Matt **41**, 63, 92, 107, 147, 174
Butcher, Terry **46**
Butler, Jack 203
Butragueño, Emilio 99, 131
Byrne, Roger 92

Cabrini, Antonio 91
CAF Cup 49
Cafu 67, 101
Cagliari 156
Cajkovski, Tschik 105, 151
Cali 225
Camacho, Jose 167
Camataru, Rodion 131, **132**
Cambodia 77
Cambridge Rules 11
Cameroon 25, 34, 35, 73, 195, **205**
Camsell, George 135, 203
Canada 70, **70**
Caniggia, Claudio Paul 131–2
Cantona, Eric 56, 132, 192, **221**, 223, 227
Cape Verde 73
Carbajal, Antonio 70, 132
Cardiff City 236
Careca 132
Carey, Johnny 132, **132**
Carl Zeiss Jena 44
Carlos, José 102
Carol, King 61
Carreiro 88
Carrizo, Amadeo 132
Carvalho, Paulo Machado de 101
Castilla 131, 150

Castro, Hector 69, 168
Caszely, Carlos 86, 132
Catenaccio 45, 59, 89, **202**, 227
Cayman Islands 70
CDNA Sofia *see* CSKA Sofia
Celso 96
Celtic 63, 85–6, **85**, 222, 224, 225
   European Cup 41, 173
   history 231, 232
   players 135, 139, 143, 148, **148**
   World Club Cup 36, 37
Celtic Park Stadium, Glasgow 181
Centenario Stadium, Montevideo 187, **187**
Central African Republic 73
César, Julio 176
Cesar, Paulo 93
Ceulemans, Jan 52, 132–3, **132**
Cha Bum Kun 79, 133
Chad 73
Chalmers, Steve 86
Champions League 40, 43, 92, 96, 227
Chapman, Herbert 82, 142, 203, 221, 224, 227
Chapuisat, Pierre-Albert 133
Chapuisat, Stéphane 133, **133**
Charles, John 65, 91, 99, 133, 162, 221
Charlton Athletic 215
Charlton, Bobby 103, 106–7, **107**
   European Cup 41, 174, **174**
   Manchester United 92
   World Cup 20, 55
   World Cup Club 37
Charlton, Jack 55, 61, 205, 242
Chelsea 44, 45, 47, **48**, 141, 142, 172, 223
Cherenyshev, Arkady 122–3
Chilavert, Jose 68
Chile 67, 68, **73**, 132, 158
   Copa America 32
   World Cup 17, 19, 169
China 77
Chirk, Wales 236
Chislenko, Igor 133
Chronology 244–5
Chumpitaz, Hector 133
Cintra, José Sousa 102
Clapton Orient 130
Cliftonville 238
Clothes, laws 198, 207
Clough, Brian 223
Cobreola, Copa Libertadores 39
Cocu, Philip **87**
Collar, Enrique 83, 139
Collovati **152**
Colman, Eddie 107
Colo Colo 39, 67, 86, 132
Cologne 44
Colombia 19, 25, 26, 39, 68, **68**, **150**, 164
Colours 217
Coluna, Mario 61, 113, 133, 173
Combi, Gianpiero 91, 133–4, 167
Common, Alf 221
Commonwealth of Independent States 62, 95
CONCACAF 35, 49, 69, 70, 72
Confédération Africaine de Football 74

Congo 34, 73
CONMEBOL 32
Conti, Bruno 134, **134**
Cook Islands 72
Copa America 32, **32**
Copa Libertadores 38–40, 68, 69, 83, 85, 88, 95, 101, 145
Copenhagen 44
Coppens, Henri 134
Corners 198, 204–5
Corporate entertainment 218
La Coruña 128
Corver, Wiel 82
Costa, Flavio 169
Costa Pereira, Alberto 61, 134
Costa Rica 35, 70
Costacurta, Alessandro **93**
Coutinho, Claudio 88, 100
Cox, Arthur 88
Cozzi, Julio 94
Croatia 53, **53**
Cruyff, Johan 64, 103, 108–9, **108**, **109**
    Ajax 80, 152
    Barcelona 84, 163, 167
    European Cup 41
    NASL 71–2
    World Cup 21, **21**, 22, 57
Cruzeiro 142
Crystal Palace 223
CSKA Sofia 144
Cuba 16, 70
Cubilla, Luis 83
Cubillas, Teofilo 69, **69**, 134, **134**
Cush, Wilbur 239
Cwmbran 236
Cyprus 53
Czech Republic 53–4
Czechoslovakia
    European Championship 33
    Olympic Games 29
    players 144, 152, 153, 155
    World Cup 16, 17, 18, 19, 148, 162
Czibor, Zoltan 44, 58, 64, 83, 134, 171

Da Rosa, Jair 124
Da Silva, Carlos Alberto 96
Da Silva, Leonidas 88, 136, 146
Dahlin, Martin **26**
Dalglish, Kenny 41, 63, 92, 135, **135**, 148, 161, 163, 193
Damiao, Cosme 85
Davids, Edgar 28, 57
Darmstadt 133
Dean, Bill 135
Dean, Dixie 149, 203
De Boer, Frank 57
De Boer, Ronald 57
Decker, Karl 98
Del Piero, Alessandro 59
Del Sol, Luis 91, 111, 135, 173
Delaunay, Henri 33, 36
Denmark 13, 54, **54**, **159**, 161
    European Championship 33, 177, **177**
    Olympic Games 30, 31, 30
Deportes Tolima 225
Deportivo Cali 225
Deportivo La Coruna 48
Deportivo Mandiyu 115
Deportivo Saprissa 70
Derby County 129, 193, 222
Derwall, Jupp 105, 158
Deschamps, Didier **15**
Deyna, Kazimierz 60, 135–6
Di Canio, Paolo 85
Di Sordi, Nilton 160
Di Stefano, Alfredo 89, 110–11, **110**, **111**, 117, 121, 123, 172, 173
    Millionarios 94
    Real Madrid 64, 99, 135, 136, 158, 162
Dickinson, Jimmy 227
Didi 67, 88, 99, 135, 136, **136**, 172
Dinamo Bucharest 61
Disasters 223–5
Distillery 238
Dixon, Lee **204**
Djibouti 73
Docherty, Tommy 107
Doherty, Peter 147
Domingos da Guia, Antonio 85, 88, 136
Dominguez **41**
Dominica 70
Dominican Republic 70
Doncaster 139
Dooley, Derek 225
Dorado **168**
Dorner, Hans-Jürgen 163
Dortmund 133
Dorval 100
Drugs 115
Dukla Prague 53–4, 148, 152
Dumbarton 231
Dumitrescu, Ilie 27
Dundee United **46**, 63, 193, 232
Dunga 27, **27**, 136
Duration of play, rules 198
Durban City 142
Durrant, Iain **85**
Dutch East Indies 16, 17
Dynamo Tbilisi 44–5
Dyson, Terry 43, 47
Dzajic, Dragan 65, 99, 136

East Germany 31, 163
East Lancashire Regiment 238
Ecuador 32, 68, 163
Edward II 10, **10**
Edward III 10
Edwards, Duncan 92, 107, 136, **136**
Edwards, Leslie 117
Effenberg, Stefan 26
Egypt 34, 73–4, **74**
Eintracht Frankfurt 44, 45, 86, 121, 133, 173, 181
El Kass **74**
El Salvador 70–1, 225
Elkjaer, Preben 54
Elyot, Sir Thomas 10
England 54–5, 226–31
    European Championship 33
    Friendly international 169, 170
    Olympic Games 30
    players 129, 135, 141–2, 143, 151, 157, 161
    strip **189**
    World Cup 17, 55, 117
        1950-54 17, 18, 169
        1962-70 19, 20, 21, 174
        1982-90 23, 24, 25, 177, **205**
English, Sam 224
Equatorial Guinea 74
Equipment 206–11
Erico, Arsenio 89, 111, 136–7
Ernst-Happel Stadium, Vienna 184
ES Setif 73
Escobar, Andres 26, 68
Escobar, Pablo 83
España 151
Espanol 43, 46
Estadio Cicero Pompeu de Toledo *see* Morumbi Stadium
Estadio da Luz, Lisbon 181
Esteghal SC 78
Estonia 55, 58
Estudiantes de la Plata 37, 38, 66
Ethiopia 34, 74
European Champions League 190, 191
European Championship 33, **33**, 216
    1960-72 62, 64, 149, 152
    1976-88 33, **33**, 54, 62, 141, 153, 242
    1992-96 **54**, 55, 65, 128, 131, 218
    1996 32–3, **32**, **33**, **50**, 233
European Cup 40–3, **40**, 44, 45, 46, 64, 80, 85, 161, 191, 227 *see also* European Champions League
    1956-60 86, 92, 96, 111, 121, 135, 172, 173
    1961-65 89, 94, 124, 137, 144, 149, 173
    1967-69 85, 92, 94, 113, **139**, 149, 173, 174
    1970-79 57, 83, 86, 99, 109, 151, 222
    1980-89 91, 96, 155
    1990-97 56, 83, 93, **93**, **94**, 99, 144, 149, 154
European Cup-winners' Cup 43–5, **44**, 151
    1962-68 83, 84, 94, 102
    1972-77 89, 91, 94, 96
    1984-97 91, 96, 98, **98**, 131
European Footballer of the Year 94, 105, 109, 143, 158, 163, 247
    1959-65 113, 123, 144, 148, 162
    1967-77 54, 125, 129, 157
1986-97 91, 126, 154
European Golden Boot 247
European Super Cup 48
European Under-21 Championship 34
European Youth Championship 34
Eusebio 79, 103, 112–13, **112–13**, 122, 123, 128
    Benfica 61, 85, 181
    European Cup 40, 174
    World Club Cup 36
    World Cup 20
Evans, Roy 92
Everton 48, 98, **98**, 222, 223
    European Cup-winners' Cup 45
    players 132, 135, 149, 163, 166
Exeter City 138
Eydelie, Jean-Jacques **93**, 223

FA Cup **12**, 43, 44, 117, 138–9, 215, 217, 231
Facchetti, Giacinto 89, 137, **137**
Fagan, Joe 92
Fairs Cup *see* UEFA Cup
Falcao 67
Family stands 219
Fanzines 217
FAR Rabat 75
Farmer, Peter **93**
Faroe Islands 52, 55
Fashanu, John 223
FC Magdeburg 44
FC Porto 42, 61, 96, **96**, 138
Fédération Internationale de Football Association *see* FIFA
Fenerbahce 65
Fenton 170
Fenwick, Terry 205
Feola, Vicente 119, 138, 160, 172
Ferencvaros 45, 46, 48, 125, 160
Ferguson, Alex 63, 92, 227
Fernandez, Luis 176, **176**
Ferrar, Albert **31**
Ferrari, Giovanni 137, 149
Ferreyra, Bernabe 99, 137
Ferro Carril Oeste 148
Feyenoord 57, 86–7, **87**
    European Cup 41
    players 142, 144, 151
    UEFA Cup 45
    World Club Cup 37
FIFA 14, 50, 74, 193–5, 227
FIFA Under-17 World Championship 30
FIFA Under-20 World Championship 30
Figo, Luis **84**
Fiji 72
Fillol, Ubaldo 99, 187
Finland 55
Finney, Tom 137, **137**

Fiorentina 46, 47, 125, 126, 128, 141, 145
FK Austria 87–8, 124, 153, 162
FK Bor 150
Flamengo 67, 88, 128, 157, 167
Flo, Tore Andre 60
Floriana 47
Fluminense 67, 88, **88**, 124
Foni, Alfredo 89
Fontaine, Just 55–6, 137, **137**
Football Association (FA) 11–12, 54, 55, 226, 227
Football Association of Ireland 238
Football Association of Wales 236
Football League 54, 226–7
Footballer of the Year 132, 139, 141, 144, 162, 163, 165
Formations 21, 202–3
    4-2-4 18, 124, 136
    4-3-3 19
    catenaccio 59, 89, **202**, 227
    WM **202**
Forrest, W. 221
Fortuna Dusseldorf 48
Foulkes, Bill 92
Fouls, rules 200
France 55–6
    European Championship 33
    Olympic Games 31
    players 125, 144, 154, 155
    World Cup 15–16, 17, 18–19, 23, 24, **55**, 175, 176, 183, **205**
Francescoli, Enzo 138, **138**
Francis, Trevor 41
Free transfers 191
Free-kicks 199–201, **204**, 205
Friaca 169
Friedenreich, Arthur 67, 138
Fruhwirth, Edi 98
Fulham 142, 143, 151, 221, 222
Futre, Paulo 83, **83**, 96, 138, **138**

Gabon 74, 224
Gadocha, Robert 60, 135
Gaetjens, Joe 71
GAIS Gothenburg 64
Galatasaray 65
Galic, Milan 65
Gallacher, Hughie 63
Gallego **57**
Gambia 74
Garcia, Atilio 95
Garger, Kurt **98**
Garrincha 67, 138, **139**, 160, 172, 205
Gascoigne, Paul 138–9, 177, 192
Gauld, Jimmy 222
Gemmell, Tommy 86, 139, **139**
Genoa 134, 162–3, 225
Gensana, 173

Gentile, Claudio 91, **146**
Gento, Francisco 139, 158, 173
George V, King 168, 184
Georgia 56
Gerets, Eric 52
German Cup 98
Germany 13, 56, 166, 169
    see also East Germany; West Germany
    European Championship 177
    World Cup 16, 26, 27, 105
Gerson 67
Gestar, Dariusz **31**
Ghana 30, 34, 35, 74
Ghiggia, Alcide 96, 169
Gibson, Victor 93
Giggs, Ryan 65, 92
Gil, Jesus **83**, 138
Giles, John 45
Gillespie, Robert 232
Gilmar 100
Ginola, David **204**
Giudice, Manuel 89
Glasgow Cup 231
Glossop 221
Goalkeepers 200, **200**
Goalposts 196
Goethals, Raymond 82
Golden Boot 131, 144, 147, **147**, 165
Goncalves, Nestor 96, 138
Gordon Highlanders 238
Gordon, John 222
Gorgon, Jerzy 60
Gornik, Zabrze 47, 60, 147, 155
Gorski, Kazimierz 135, 145
Goulden, Len 169
Goycochea, Sergio Javier 139, **139**
Graça 174
Graham, George 63, 82, **112**, 223
Grasshoppers 64, 124, 150
Great Britain, Olympics 54
Greaves, Jimmy 47, 123, 139, 145
Greece 57
Green Cross 224
Greenwood, Ron 23
Gregg, Harry 139
Greig, John 139, 141
Gren, Gunnar 59, 64, 93, 141, 146, 152
Grenada 71
Griffith, Mervyn 171
Grobbelaar, Bruce 76, **76**, 223
Groningen 144
Grosics, Gyula 121
Guadalajara, Jalisco Stadium 176
Guarani 132
Guarneri, Aristide 89
Guatemala 71
Gudjohnson, Arnor 58
Guinea 74
Guinea-Bissau 74
Gullit, Ruud **33**, 57, 86, 94, 96, 128, 141
Guttmann, Bela 85, 112, 126
Guyana 71

Haan, Arie 57
Haarlem 182, 225
Hacking 226
Hadgi, Mustapha 75
Hagi, Gheorghe 26, 61, 141, **141**
Haiti 21, 71
Haller, Helmut 141
Hamburg 45, 88–9, **89**, 143, 161
Hamilton, Gavin 222
Hampden Park Stadium 173, 181, **181**
Hamrin, Kurt 47, 141, **141**
Hanappi, Gerhard 52, 98, 141
Hancocks, Johnny 227
Hanot, Gabriel 40, 172
Hansen, Alan 92
Hansen, John 91
Hansen, Karl 91
Hapgood, Eddie 141–2
Happel, Ernst 86, 98, 142
Harmer, Tommy 204
Harpastum 8
Hasek, Ivan 102
Hässler, Thomas 56
Havelenge, Joao **193**, 195
Haynes, Johnny 142, 221
Hazell, Bob 205
Hellers, Guy 59
Henderson, Sir Neville 169
Henderson, Willie 142
Herberger, Sepp 56, 155, 166, 171
Heredia, Ramon 83
Hernandez, Luis 71
Herrera, Helenio 84, 89, 137
Herrera, Heriberto 162
Hertha BSC, Berlin 180
Heynckes, Jupp 45, 86
Heysel Stadium 41, 92, 168, 216, 225
Hibernian 44, 172, 231, 232
Hidegkuti, Nandor 58, **58**, 121, 170, 203
Higuita **150**
Hilario 102
Hillier, Brian 221, 223
Hillman, Jack 221
Hillsborough Stadium 168, 218, 225
History 8–13, **9**
Hoddle, Glenn 55
Hodgson, Roy 65
Hoeness, Uli 130
Hogan, Jimmy 87, 203
Holland 13, 57, 182
    European Championship 33, 177
    players 128, 144, 151, 152, 156
    World Cup 21–3, 26, 109, 142, 176
Holton, Cliff 205
Hölzenbein, Bernd 86
Honduras 23, 71, 225
Hong Kong 77

Honved 121, 130, 144
Hooligans 216
Hrubesch, Horst 175
Huddersfield Town **145**, 227
Hughes, Emlyn 92
Hughes, Mark **46**, 48, 65
Humberto 171
Hungary 13, 55, 57–8, 227
    Friendly international 1953 170
    'Magic Magyars' 55, 56, 57–8, **58**, 67, 121
    Olympic Games 31
    players 130, 134, 144, 160
    World Cup 16, 17, 18, 19, 20, 22, 24, 125, 128, 171
Hunt, Roger 92
Huracan 154
Hurst, Geoff 20, **54**, 142, **142**, 205
Hutchinson, Ian 205
Hutton, Alexander 66

Ibrox Park 141, 181, 232
    disaster (1902) 224, 232
    disaster (1971) 96, 225, **225**
Iceland 58
IFK Gothenburg 45, **46**, 64, 141, 155
In play, rules 198
Ince, Paul 223
Independiente 37, **38**, 89, 126, 136–7
India 77
Indonesia 77
Inter-American Cup 49
Inter-Toto Cup 46, 49
Intercontinental Cup *see* World Club Cup
Internazionale 89–91
    European Cup 41, 173
    players 109, 125, 137, 144, 149, 154, 158, 163
    UEFA Cup 44, 46,
    World Club Cup 36
Iordanescu, Anghel 61
Ipswich Town 45, 55
Iran 22, 77–8, **77**
Iraq **77**, 78
Ireland 61, **74**, 139, 147, 242–3
    see also Northern Ireland
    European Championship 33
    World Cup 25, 26, 129
Irish Football Association 238
Israel 58
Italy 13, 58–9, 182
    European Championship 33
    players 130, 131, 133–4, 149, 154, 156, 157, 164, 167
    World Cup 126, 137
        1934-38 16, **16**, 17
        1950-66 17, 19, 20

1970-82 21, 22, 23–4, **23**, 174, 175
1990-94 25, 26–7
Ivanauskas, Valdas 59
Ivanov, Valentin 62
Ivory Coast 35, 74

Jack, David 168
Jackson, Alex 63
Jacquet, Aime **15**, 28
Jairzinho 21, 67, 93, 142, **142**
Jamaica 71
James, Alex 63, 82, 142, 147
Jansen, Wim 57, 87
Japan 30, 37, 78, **78**
Jennings, Pat 60, 142–3, **142**, 239
Jeunesse Esch 59
Jezek, Vaclav 153
Johnston, Mo 96
Johnston, Willie 232
Johnstone, Jimmy **63**, 143
Jones, Vinnie 223
Jordan 78
Jorge, Artur 96
JS Kabylie 73
Juanito 99
Juary 96
Jules Rimet Trophy *see* World Cup
Julinho 171
Juventus 37, 41, 43, 44, 45, 48, 91, **91**
Junior 67
Juventus 91, 175, 216, 222
    European Cup 41, 43, 45
    UEFA Cup 47, 48

Kaiserslautern 166
Kaltz, Manni 89
Kanchelskis, Andrei **62**
Kashima Antlers 167
Kasperczak 135
Katmandu 225
Kay, Tony 222, **222**
Kazakhstan 78
Keane, Roy 223
Keegan, Kevin 41, 45, 89, **89**, 92, 135, 143
Keizer, Piet 152
Kelsey, Jack 143
Kempes, Mario 66, 99, 143, **143**, 154
Kenari 8
Kenrick, Llewelyn 236
Kenya 76

Kettering 141
Khomich, Alexei 94, 122
Kidd, Brian 41, 174
Kieboom, C.R.J. 86
Kiev, Dynamo 62, 91, 129
Kindvall, Ove 86
Kinnaird, A.F. 226
Kirilia Sovietov 162
Kirkwood, Billy **46**
Kispest 130
Klaasens, Jan 86
Klinsmann, Jürgen 28, **33**, 46, 56, 143–4, **144**, 176
Kluivert, Patrick 29
Knock 238
Kobylanski, Andrzej **31**
Kocsis, Sandor 44, 58, 64, 83, 121, 134, 144, 171
Koeman, Ronald 57, 64, 84,144, 205
Kohler, Jurgen 84, **176**
Kohlmeyer **171**
Kolev, Ivan 144
Köln 45, 147, 153
Kop, the **214–15**
Kopa, Raymond 40, 55, 99, 126, 137, 144, 172
Köpke, Andy 33
Korea, World Cup 18
Kostadinov, Emil 52
Kostic, Bora 65, 99, 161
Kotkov, Nikola 52
Kovacs, Stefan 109
Kraay, Hans 86
Krankl, Hans 48, 98, 144
Kress, Richard 86
Kreyermaat, Reinier 86
Krol, Ruud 57
Kubala, Ladislav 44, 64, 83, 123, 134, 144, 173
Kulkov, Vasili 95
Kuwait 23, 78
Kvasnak, Andrzej 101
Kyle, Archibald 222
Kyle, Rollo 222
Kyrgyzstan 78

Labruna, Angel 99, 145, 154
Lacatus, Marius 145
Lambert, Jack **210**, **211**
Lamptey, Nii 74
Laos 78
Las Vegas Quicksilver 113
Latin Cup 49
Lato, Grzegorz 60, 135, 145
Latvia 59
Laudrup, Brian 96, **96**, 145
Laudrup, Michael **36**, 54, 84, 145, **145**
Lauro, Achille 183

Lausanne 44
Law, Denis 63, 92, 135, 145, **145**, 232
Laws 196–201
Lawton, Tommy 145–6
Layne, David 222
Lazio 46, 48, 139, 145, 167
LD Alajeulense 69
Leake, Alec 221
Lebanon 78
Lechkov, Iordan 27
Lediakhov, Igor 95
Leeds City 222
Leeds United 41, 45, 47, 131, 132, 133
Legia Warsaw 135, 155, 180
Leicester 128
Leipzig 44, 48
Lenin Stadium 225
Leon 132
Lerby, Soren 54
Lesotho 74
Levante 132
Levski Sofia 126
Leyton Orient 222
Liberia 75
Libertadores Cup *see* Copa Libertadores
Libya 35, 75, 225
Liddell, Billy 146
Liechtenstein 59
Liedholm, Nils 59, 64, **64**, 93, 134, 141, 146, 152
Lierse 132
Lievesley, Leslie 224
Limavady 238
Lindner, Jurgen 86
Lineker, Gary 24, 64, 146–7, **146**, 161, 177
Linesmen 196, 201
Linfield 238
Lisbon Eagles 41
Lisbon National Stadium 173
Lishman, Doug 205
Lithuania 59
Littbarski, Pierre **146**, 147
Littlewoods 190
Liverpool 92, **214–15**, 215, 216, 227
    European Cup 41
    European Cup-winners' Cup 47
    players 130, 135, 143, 146, 158, 163
    UEFA Cup 45
    World Club Cup **38**
Lobanovsky, Valeri 91
Lodz, Widzew 129
Loik, Ezio 149
Lokeren 145
London, UEFA Cup 45
Lorenzo, Juan Carlos 85
Los Angeles Aztecs 109
Loustau 99, 154
Lubanski, Wlodzimierz 60, 147
Luque, Leopoldo 99, 187
Luxembourg 59
Luzern 46
Luzhnike Stadion, Moscow 182
Lyon 125

McAlery, J.M. 238
Macao 78
Macari, Lou 221, 223
Maccabi Haifa 58
Macedonia (FYR) 59
McCarthy, Mick 61, 242
MacCarthy, Patrick 85
McCartney, David 222
McCoist, Ally 147, **147**
McCracken, Bill 203
McCrory, Jimmy 232
McFarland, Roy 222
McGrath, Paul **141**, 147, **147**
McGregor, William 226–7
McIlroy, Jimmy 147
McIlroy, Sammy 147
Mackay, Dave 129, 205
McMenemy, Lawrie 239
McNeill, Billy 148, **148**
McParland, Peter 239
McPhail, Bob 96
McStay, Paul **85**, 148
Madagascar 75
Madjer, Rabah 73, 96
Magallanes FC 86
Magath, Felix 89
Magdeburg 163
Magnusson, Roger 93
Mahdavikia, Mehdi 78
Maier, Sepp 56, 84, 130, 148, 153
Malawi 75
Malaysia 78
Maldini, Cesare 148
Maldini, Paolo 148, **148**
Maldives 78
Maley, Tom 221
Mali 34, 75
Malmo 64
Malta 60, 225
Manchester City 47, 148, 149, 164, 220, 221
Manchester United 92, 99, 188, 190, **192**, **211**, 222, 223
    'Busby Babes' 92, 99, 107, 136, **224**, 227
    European Cup 41, 43, 174
    European Cup-winners' Cup 43, **44**, 45, 47, 48
    FA Cup 1994 192
    players 107, 132, 139, 145, 147, 157, 161
    Premier League 227
    transfers 192
    UEFA Cup 45, 46
    World Club Cup 37
Mantova 167
'Maquina, La' *see* River Plate
Maracana Stadium 169, 186, **186**
Maradona, Diego 64, 66, 85, 103, 114–15, **115**, 220, **221**, 223
    Naples 183

UEFA Cup **44**, 48
World Cup 24, 26, 186
Marcelino 45
Marindin, Major 226
Mario Filho Stadium *see* Maracana
Stadium
Marlboro, Lawrence 96
Marsden, Gerry 217
Marseille 56, 93, **93**, 182, 221
European Cup 42
players 125, 132, 138, 142, 154
Martinez, William 96
Marwood, Brian 204
Marzolini, Silvio 148, 155
Maschio, Humberto 158
Mason, Jimmy 232
Masopust, Josef 53, 54, 123, 148
Maspoli, Roque 96, **169**
Massaro 101
Maszczyk 135
Match fixing 56, 93, 125, 149, 221, 222
Mathias, Reginaldo 223
Matthäus, Lothar **25**, 27, 56, 84, **89**,
148–9, **149**
Matthews, Stanley 103, 116–17, **117**,
123, 147, 170, 184, 221, 227
Maturana, Francisco 68, 83
Mauritania 75
Mauritius 75
Mauro 100
Mazzola, Sandro 149
Mazzola, Valentino 149, 224
MC Algiers 73
Meazza, Giuseppe 59, 137, 149, **149**
Mechelen 48
Mee, Bertie 82
Meisl, Hugo 13, 16, 48, 52, 184, 203
Meisl, Willi 80, 108
Melgar **138**
Mengalvio 100
Menotti, César Luis 83, 115, 126, 143
Mercer, Joe 149
Meredith, Billy 65, 149, 220–1, **220**, 236
Merrick, Gil 170, 227
Merson, Paul **204**, 223
Meszoly, Kalman 223
Mexico 71, 158
CONCACAF Championship 35
Copa America 32
World Cup 15–16, 19, 21, 24, 26, 132
Michel (del Campo) 150, **150**, 204
Michel, Henri 132
Michels, Rinus 57, 80
Middelboe, Nils 54
Middlesborough 157, 221
Miguez, Oscar 96
Mihajlovic, Sinisa **65**
Milan 93–4, **93**, **94**, 138, 182, 222, 225
European Cup 41, 42, 180
European Cup-winners' Cup 47, 48
players 125, 128, 141, 146, 148, 149,
152, 154, 156, 157, 160, 161, 165
Milburn, Jackie 107, 204, 238
Milla, Roger 34, 73, 150, **150**
Miller, Charles 13
Millonarios 83, 94, 111, 139, 154

Millwall 217, 222
Milutinovic, Bora 69, 150
Milutinovic, Milos 150
Minelli, Severino 150
Minotti, Lorenzo **48**
Miranda, Eurico 223
Mitropa Cup 13, 14, 48–9, 50, 58, 87,
89, 91, 98, 102, 152, 160, 162
Mitten, Charles **207**
Miura, Kazu **78**
Mlynarczyk 96
Mohammedan Sporting 77
Mohun Bagan 77
Moldova 60
Möller, Andy 33, 86
Monaco 48, 125, 144, 150
Montayo, Camacho 94
Montevideo Centenary Stadium 168
Monti, Luisito 59, 150
Montpellier 164
Montrose 222
Monumental Stadium, Buenos Aires
187, **187**
Mooney, David 222
Moore, Bobby 20, **20**, 55, 117, **119**,
151, **151**, 205
Morais 102
Moran **74**
Morena, Fernando 96
Moreno, Juan Manuel 99, 151, 154
Morlock **18**
Morocco 24, 34, 35, 75, **75**, 195
Mortensen, Stanley 151, 170
Morton, Alan 96, 151
Morumbi Stadium, São Paulo 187
Moscow Dynamo 94, 122, 123, 133
Moscow Spartak 94–5, **95**, 152, 162,
182, 225
Moscow Torpedo 133
Mostovoi, Alexander 95
Motherwell 232
Moulijn, Coen 86, 151
Moyola Park 238
Mozambique 75
MTK Budapest 58
Mullen, Jimmy 227
Müller, Gerd 22, 33, 44, 47, 56, 84,
130, 174, **174**, 182
Munich air crash 41, 92, 99, 107, 136,
139, 164, 224
Muñoz, Miguel 99, 111, 154, 173
Murphy, Jimmy 107
Murray, David 96
Myanmar (Burma) 78

Namibia 75
Nancy 154
Napoli 46, 115, 125, 132, 162, 167, 193
Narbekovas, Arminas 59
Nasazzi, José 152
NASL Soccer Bowl 105
National Olympic Stadium, Tokyo
185, **185**
Nations Cup 13
Neeskens, Johan 57, 64, 152, **152**
Nehoda, Zdenek 54, 152, **152**
Nehru Cup 77
Nejedly, Oldrich 53, 101, 152
Nepal 78
Netherlands Antilles 71
Netto, Igor 62, 95, 152
Netzer, Gunter 64, 152, 153
Neuberger, Hermann 180
Nevis (and Saint Kitts) 71
New Caledonia 72
New York Cosmos 105
New Zealand 72
Newcastle United 47, 138, 141, 143,
193
Newport County 48, 236
Nicaragua 71
Nice 137
Nicholson, Bill 47
Nielsen, Harald 141
Nielsen, Richard Moller 145, 177
Nigeria 26, 27, 29, 34, 75, 167, 195, 225
Nilis, Luc 52
Nkongo **26**
N'Kono, Thomas 73
Nordahl, Gunnar 59, 64, 93, 141, 146,
152–3
Nordqvist, Bjorn 64, 153
Norgrove, Frank 221
Norrköping 146, 152, 153
North American Soccer League
(NASL) 70, 71, 119, 152, 153
North Korea 20, 78–9
Northern Ireland 60, **150**, 238–41
World Cup 18, 23
Norway 17, 26, 60
World Championship 30
Nou Camp 45, 47, 48
Norwich City 193
Nottingham Forest 41–2, 132, 162
Nou Camp Stadium, Barcelona 180, **180**
Novak, Ladislav 148

Okwaraji 225
Olimpia 39, 70
Olimpico Stadium, Rome 184, **184**
Olsen, Jesper 54
Olsen, Morten 54
Olympiakos 129, 167
Olympiastadion, Berlin 169, 180, **180**
Olympiastadion, Munich 182
Olympic Games 12, 30–30, 54, 57
1908-12 **13**, 30, 62
1924-36 59, 60, 64, 150
1948-52 64, 130, 132, 141, 144, 146,
153
1956-60 65, 77, 152
1972-76 60, 135, 145, 147, 155
1984-96 30–9, **30**, **31**, **39**, 64, 157
Oman 79
Ondrus, Anton 54
Onguene, Jean 73
Onopko, Viktor 95, **95**
Orellano, David 86
Orgryte 64, 162
Orient 132 *see also* Leyton Orient
Orsi, Raimundo 89, 153
Ortega, Ariel 66
Ortiz, Oscar 187
Oster Vaxjo 155
Out of play, rules 198
Overath, Wolfgang 152, 153
Owen, Michael 28, 55

Pachin 173
Padros, Carlos 98
Paisley, Bob 92
Pak Do Ik 78
Pakhtakor Tashkent 225
Pakistan 79
Palestine 79
Palestro, Alessandro 223
Pallo **9**
Palmeiras 125, 126
Palmer **60**
Panagoulias, Alketas **57**
Panama 71
Panathinaikos 37–8, 57, 121
Pancev, Darko 99
Panenka, Antonin 54, 153
Papin, Jean-Pierre 56, 93, 153–4, **153**
Papua New Guinea 72
Paraguay 32, 68
Paramithiotti, Giovanni 89
Parc des Princes Stadium, Paris 46,
172, 183
Paris St Germain 48, 183
Parma 48, **48**, 59, 131, 182
Parreira, Carlos Alberto 26, 136
Parsonage, George 221
Partizan 150

Nacional 38, 40, 95, 126, 146, 152, 158,
160
Nacional Medellin 68

Oceania 72
Ocwirk, Ernst 52, 153
Odense 54
Offside law 199, 232
Ohms, Matthias 86
Okocha, Jay Jay 75

Passarella, Daniel **57**, 99, 154, **154**, 187
Patterson, Darren 223
Pearce, Stuart 177
Pecl **162**
Pedernera, Adolfo 94, 99, 111, 154
Pedroto, José Maria 96
Pegg, David 107, **208**
Peiro, Joaquin 83
Pele **19**, 67, 72, 100, **100**, 103, 113, 118–19, **119**, 125, 135, 161, 165
   Copa Libertadores 38
   free-kicks 205
   World Club Cup 37
   World Cup 18–19, 21, 172, **172**
Pele, Abedi 74
Penalty kick, rules 198
Penarol 95–6
   Copa Libertadores 38, 40
   players 157, 160, 163, 165
   World Club Cup 36
Pepe 100
Pereira, Costa 112
Pereira, José 134
Pereira, Waldyr *see* Didi
Perry, Bill 170, **170**
Peru 22, 32, 69, **69**, 133, 134, 224
Perugia 157, 175
Peterborough United 222, 223
Peters, Martin 20
Petit, Emmanuel 29
Petrescu, Dan 28
Pfaff, Alfred 86
Pfaff, Jean-Marie 52
Phelan, Terry 26
Philippines 79
Philips SV *see* PSV Eindhoven
Piantoni, Roger 154
Picchi, Armando 89
Pieters-Graafland, Eddie 86
Pinto, Jair da Rosa **96**, 100
Piola, Silvio 154
Pirelli, Piero 182
Pirri 99, 154–5, **154**
Pitches, laws 196–8, **197**
Planicka, Frantisek 53, 155
Platini, Michel 33, 56, 59, 91, 126, 155, **155**, 176, **176**, 183
Platko, Ferenc 86
Platt, David 25, 192
Pluskal, Svatopluk 148
Plymouth 162
Pol, Ernst 147, 155
Poland 60
   Olympic Games 31, 180
   players 135–6, 145, 147, 155, 166
   World Cup 16, 17, 21, 22–3, 23, 24
Polo, Mohamed Ahmed 74
Poole, Thomas Gibson 221
Porkuyan, Valeri 91
Port Vale 117, 221, 222
Porto, Portugal 48, 180
Portugal 20, 24, 60–1, 113, 126, 133
Pospichal, Tomas 101
Povlsen, Flemming 133
Pozzo, Vittorio **17**, 58, 153, 203
Premier Division 232

Premier League 157, 227
Preston North End 227
Preud'homme, Michel 52, **52**
Prix Bravo 131
Pro Patria 144
Pro Vercelli 154
Professionalism 12, 50, 54, 226, 231–2
Programmes 217
Prohaska, Herbert 87
Prohibition 10
Prosinecki, Robert 99, **99**
Protasov, Oleg 162, 204
PSV Eindhoven 45, 57, 96, 141, 153, 157
   European Cup 42, 144
   UEFA Cup 45
Puc, Antonin 53, 152
Puerto Rico 71
Pumpido, Nery 99, 139
Puskas, Ferenc 58, 103, 120–1, **121**, 123, 130, 135, 144, 158, 227
   Friendly international 1953 170, **170**
   Real Madrid 64, 99, 173
   World Cup 171

Qatar 79
Queens Park, Glasgow 181, 202, 231
Queens Park Rangers 181
Queiros, Carlos 102

Racing Avellaneda 115
Racing Club 36, 38, 138
Racing Paris 150
Radebe, Lucas **129**
Radhi, Ahmed 78
Rahn, Helmut 155, 171
Rai **36**, 101
Raith Rovers 142
Raja Casablanca 75
Ramallets 173
Ramsey, Sir Alf 55, 149, 151, 203, 227
Rangers 48, 63, **85**, 96, 181, 225, 231, 232
   European Cup Final 1960 173
   European Cup-winners' Cup 47
   players 139, 142, 147, 151, 163
   transfers 193
Rapid Vienna 48, 96, 98, 129, 141, 142, 144, 153
Rappan, Karl 65, 98, 150
Rasunda Stadium, Stockholm 172
Rattin, Antonio Ubaldo 155

Rattles 217
Ravelli, Thomas 155, **156**
Real Madrid 63, 64, 98–9, **98**, 181
   European Champions Club Cup 1956 172
   European Cup 40–1, **41**, 173, **173**, 181
   UEFA Cup 45, 47, 48
   World Club Cup 36
Real Mallorca 46, 48
Real Sociedad 162
Real Zaragoza 45, **47**, 48, 64
Reasdale, William 95
Red card 201
Red Star Belgrade 37, 42, 99, **99**, 136, 161
Referees 196, 201, **201**
Reggiana 138
Reims 137, 144, 154, 172
Rep, Johnny **57**, 64
Reunion 75
Reuter, Stefan 84
Revie, Don 131, 149
Rial, José Hector 139
Ricken, Lars 43
Riedle, Karlheinz **42**, 43
Rijkaard, Frank 57, 94, 156, **157**, 176
Rimet, Jules 14
Riva, Luigi 156
Rivaldo 29, 67
Rivelino, Roberto 67, 156–7, 205
River Plate 41, 66, 99, 224–5
   Copa Libertadores 38
   'La Maquina' 66, 111, 145, 154
   players 110, 111, 126, 131, 132, 137, 138, 145, 151, 154
Rivera, Gianni 94, 157, 174
Rix, Graham 48
Roberto Carlos, 67
Roberts, Graham 223
Roberts, Herbie 203
Robinson, Jackie 169
Robles, Carlos 38
Robson, Bobby 96, 102, 177
Robson, Bryan 23, 92, 157, **157**
Rocha, Pedro 138, 157
Rocha, Ricardo 101
Rojas, Angel 155
Rojas, Roberto 195
Roligans **217**
Roma 44, 45, 161, 222–3
Romania 26, 27, 61, 141, 145
Romantsev, Oleg 95
Romario **15**, 26, **27**, 88, 157
Romero, Julio César 88, **88**
Romeu 88
Ronaldo 29, **43**, 48, 67, **157**
Rose Bowl Stadium, Pasadena 185, **185**
Rossi, Nestor 94
Rossi, Paolo 23, **59**, 91, 157, **157**, 175, **175**, 222
Rot-Weiss 155
Rous, Sir Stanley 195, 196
Rowe, Arthur 227
Ruch Chorzow 166
Ruggeri, Oscar **24**, **32**, 99
Rules 10, 11–12
Rummenigge, Karl-Heinz 24, **24**, 56,

   84, 158, **158**, 175
Rush, Ian 65, 158, **158**
Russia 13, 62 (*see also* Soviet Union)
Rwanda 75

Sa, Pedro **108**
Sabo, Iosif 91
Sacchi, Arrigo 59, 94, 128
St John, Ian 92
St Johnstone 147
Saint Kitts and Nevis 71
Saint Lucia 71
Saint Vincent and the Grenadines 71
Salas, Marcelo 28, 67
Saldanha, Joao 119
Salenko, Oleg **26**, 62
Sallai, Sandor 223
Samaranch, Juan Antonio 181
Samba Soccer 219, **219**
Samoa, American 72
Sampdoria 48, 141, 153, 163
San Marino 63
Sanchez, Hugo 64, 71, 99, 158
Sanchez, Leonel 158
Sanfilippo, José 85
Santamaria, José 99, 158, 173
Santana, Joaquim 113
Santana, Tele 37, 101, 176
Santander 139
Santiago Bernabeu Stadium, Madrid 181
Santillana 99
Santos 37, 38, 100–1, 119, 135
Santos, Djalma 158, **158**, 160, 172
Santos, Nilton 160, 171, **171**
Sao Paolo Stadium, Naples **183**
São Paulo 39, 40, 101, 132, 157
São Tome and Principe 75
Sarosi, Gyorgy 58, 160
Sarria Stadium, Barcelona 175
Sarti, Giuliano 89
Sastre, Antonio 101
Saudi Arabia 26, 79
Saunders, Dean 65
Scandals 220–3
Scandinavian Championship 60
Scarone, Hector 160
Scarves 217
Schalke **48**
Schiaffino, Juan 93, 96, 138, 160–1
Schillaci, Toto 25, 162
Schmeichel, Peter **159**, 161, **207**
Schnellinger, Karl-Heinz 161, 174
Schön, Helmut 56, 130, 174
Schulz, Willi 105
Schumacher, Harald "Toni" 23, 175
Schuster, Bernd 64
Scifo, Enzo 82, **82**, 161, **161**
Scirea, Gaetano 91, 128, **160**, 161

Scotland 55, 63, 143, 148, 231–5
    European Championship 33
    Footballer of the Year 139
    World Cup 18, 21, 22, 25, 131, 183
Scott, Alex 142
Scottish Cup 231
Scottish FA 231
Scottish League 232
Scunthorpe United 143
Sealey, Tony 43–4, 47
Sebes, Gusztav 58
Seeler, Uwe 89, **160**, 161
Segers, Hans 223
Sekularac, Dragoslav 65, 99
Senegal **35**, 76
Senior, Alfonso 94
Serebryanikov, Viktor 91
Servette 64, 150
Sevilla 115
Seychelles 76
Shalimov, Igor 95
Shankly, Bill 63, 92, 137, 143, 215, 227
Sharp, Graeme **98**
Shaw, Bernard 222
Shearer, Alan **5**, 32, 33, **32**, 161–2, 192
Sheffield Association 226
Shelbourne 238
Sheringham, Teddy 43
Shilton, Peter 24, 115, 162, **162**, 177, 239
Shinpads **209**
Shirts 207, **207**
Shrove Tuesday 8–9, **10**
Sierra Leone 76
Sigurvinsson, Asegir 58
Silva, Leonidas de 67
Simoes, Antonio 71
Simoes, Rene 113
Simonian, Nikita 95, 162
Simonsen, Allan 45, 54
Simonsson, Agne 162
Simonyan, Nikita 62
Simpson, Ronnie 86
Sindelar, Matthias 52, 87, 162
Singapore 79
Singing 217
Sinibaldi, Pierre 82
Sivori, Omar 91, 99, 125, 162
Skoblar, Josip 93
Skoglund, Nacka 64, 160
Skuhravy, Tomas 54, 102, 162–3, **162**
Sky Sports **194**
Sky TV contract 55
Slavia 155
Slovakia 63
Slovenia 63
Smistik, Pepe 98
Smith, Bobby 205
Smith, J.R. 168
Smith, Ted 85
Soares, Mario 113
Socrates 67, 176
Solskjaer, Ole Gunnar 43
Solomon Islands 72
Solti, Deszo 222
Somalia 76
Sordi, Di 172

Sotil, Hugo 134
Souness, Graeme 92, 96, 163, 232
South Africa 34, 76, 225
South America 66–9
South American Championship 14, 32, 68
    see also Copa America
South American Club Cup *see* Copa Libertadores
South American Footballer of the Year 88, 138, 164, 165
South American Recopa 40
South American Super Cup 40
South Korea 79, **79**, 133
Southgate, Gareth 33
Southall, Neville 163, **163**
Southampton 143
Southern Cup 232
Soviet Union 152, 162, 182
    see also Russia
    European Championship 33
    Olympic Games 31
    World Cup 19, 20, 21, 24, 123, **123**, 133
Spain 63–4, **63**
    Copa America 31
    European Championship 33
    Olympic Games 31, **31**, 180
    players 125, 131, 144, 154–5, 167
    World Cup 16, 17, 24, 26, 150, 169
Sparta Prague 98, 101–2, **101**, 130, 152
Sparwasser, Jürgen 163
Spencer, Alberto 38, 96, 163
Sport Lisboa e Benfica *see* Benfica
Sporting Cristal 38, 133
Sporting Lisbon 47, 61, 102, 112
Sri Lanka 79
Stade de France 182
Stabile, Guillermo 16
Stacey, George **207**
Stade de Reims 55
Stadio Calcistico San Siro 182
Stadio Giuseppe Meazza, Milan 176, 182
Stadio Giuseppe Meazza, Naples 183
Stadiums 178–87, 218–19
Stainrod, Simon 205
Stamford Bridge 44
Standard Liege 180
Starostin, Nikolai 95
Steaua Bucharest 42, 61, 141, 180
Stein, Jock 86, 173
Stejskal, Jan **101**, 102
Stepanovic, Dragoslav 86
Stepney, Alex 113
Stevenson, Billy 92
Stielike, Uli 45, **134**
Stiles, Nobby 37
Stinka, Dieter 86
Stock, Constant Vanden 82
Stoichkov, Hristo 52, 53, 84, 163, **163**
Stojkovic, Dragan 99
Stoke City 117, 147

Strachan, Gordon 232
Streich, Joachim 163
Strongest, The 225
Struth, William 151
Stuttgart 46, 48, 136, 144
Suarez, Luis 44, 64, 83, 91, 163
Sudan 34, 76
Sugar, Alan 223
Suker, Davor 28, 53, **53**
Sukur, Hakan 65
Sunderland 147, **188**, 221, 222
Super-League 232
Superga air crash 149, 224
Supporters 212–19, **216**, **217**
Surinam 71
Sutton, Chris 193
Suurbier, Wim 57
Svensson, Tommy **64**, 128
Swan, Peter 222, **222**
Swansea City 236
Swansea Town 47
Swaziland 76
Sweden 64, **199**
    European Championship 33, 177
    players 128, 131, 146, 152, 153, 155, 162
    shirt **206**
    World Cup 16, 17, 18–19, 21, 26, 27, 169, 172
Swift, Frank 163–4
Swindon Town 221, 223
'Swiss Bolt' 65
Switzerland 44, 64–5, **64**, **68**, 124, 150
    World Cup 17, 18, 20, 26
Syria 79
Szarmach, Andrzej 60

Tactics 196–201, 202–5, 203–4
Tahiti 72
Taillibert, Roger 183
Taiwan 79
Taj Club 78
Tanzania 76
Tapie, Bernard 42, 93, 193, **193**, 223
Tardelli, Marco **23**, 91, 164, **164**
Taument, Gaston **87**
Taylor Report 218
Tbilisi, Dynamo 44, 62
Terrace sounds 217
Thailand 79
Thern, Jonas **199**
Third Lanark 231, 232
Thommen, Ernst 43
Thompson, John 224
Thompson, Peter 92
Thornley, Irvine 221
Thornton, Willie 96
Thorstvedt, Erik 155
Thring, J. C. 11

Throw-ins 205
Thuram, Lilian 29
Tigana, Jean **176**
Tigre 137
Timoumi, Mohammed 75
Togo 76
Tomaszewski, Jan 60
Tonga 72
Torino 46, 59, 125, 149, 161, 182, **222**, 223, 224
Toronto Metros-Croatia 113
Torres, Carlos Alberto 88
Toshack, John 92
Tostao 67, 164
'Total Football' 21, 41, 57, 80, 108, 152
Toth, Jozsef 58
Tottenham Hotspur 227
    European Cup-winners' Cup 45
    players 126, 129, 138–9, 142, 144, **144**, 163
    transfers 193
    UEFA Cup 47, 48
Tousseau **176**
Transfer payments 192–3
Trapattoni, Giovanni 91
Trinidad and Tobago 71
TSV Munich 47
Tunisia 22, 34, 76
Turek **171**
Turkey 18, 65, 171, 224
Turkmenistan 79
Twente Enschede 45

Udinese 167
UEFA 191
UEFA Cup 45–8, **43**, **48**, 64, 86, 96, 99, 144, 182, **222**
Uerdingen 133
Uganda 76
Ujpest Dozsa 47, 128
Ukraine 65
Ullevi Stadium, Gothenburg 177
United Arab Emirates 79
United States 16, 17, 26, 57, 71–2, 150, 168, 169
Uruguay 69
    Copa America 32
    Olympic Games 31
    players 126, 152, 157, 158, 160, 163
    South American Championship 187
    World Cup 165
        1930 16–17, 168
        1950 17, 169
        1954 18, 171
        1962 19, 20
        1970 21
Uzbekistan 79

V

Valdano, Jorge 45, 164, **165**
Valderrama, Carlos 25, 68, 164–5, **165**
Valencia 45, 48, 64, 143, 167
Valenciennes 154, 223
Valladolid 164
Valley, the 215
Van Basten, Marco 33, 48, 57, 82, **93**, 94, 128, 165, **165, 176**, 177
Van Gaal, Louis 82
Van Hanegem, Wim 57, 86, 152
Van Heel, Puck 86
Van Himst, Paul 82, 130, 165
Vanuatu 72
Varela, Obdulio 96, 165
Varese 149
Vasco da Gama 39, 102, 124, 128, 146, 157
Vava 67, 102, 165, 172
Venables, Terry 42, 84, 223
Venezia 149
Venezuela 69
Verri, Carlos Bledorn *see* Dunga
Vialli, Gianluca 48, 91
Viana, Eduardo 223
Victorino, Waldemar 95
Video screens **218**, 219
Videoton 45
"Vienna School" 87
Vieri, Christian 28
Vietnam 79
Viktor, Ivo 54
Vilfort, Kim 177
Villa, Ricardo 126, 222
Villa Park 46
Vincent, Jean 154
Viola, Dino 223
Viollet, Dennis **211**
Vitoria Setubal 167
Vogts, Berti 109
Völler, Rudi 26, 56, 176
Vorwärts Steyr 129
Vitoria Setubal 167

Vogts, Berti 109
Völler, Rudi 26, 56, 176
Vorwärts Steyr 129

W

Waddell, Willie 96
Waddle, Chris 93, 177, **177**
Wales 18, 65, 143, 163, 236–8
Walker, Andy 221
Walker, Bobby 232
Walker, Des 192
Walker, Mike 223
Walker, Tommy 232
Wall, George **211**
Walter, Fritz 166, **166**
Wankdorf Stadium, Berne 171, 173
Wark, John 45
Washington Diplomats 109
Watford 142
Weah, George 166
Webb, Daivd 205
Weisweiler, Hennes 153
Welsh Cup 236
Welsh, Don 169
Wembley Stadium 47, 168, 170, 184, **184**
Wenger, Arsene 82
Werder Bremen 48
Wernersson, Thomas **46**
West Bromwich Albion 157
West Germany 182
  European Championship 33
  players 147, 148, **149**, 151, 152, 153, 155, 161
  World Cup 130, 141, 161
    1954–66 18–19, 20, 171, 183, 205
    1970–82 21–2, 23–4, 174, 175
    1986–90 24, 25, **25**, 176, 177
West Ham 47, 48, 139, 151, 168, 205, 215
Western Samoa 72
Whiteside, Norman 23–4

Wilimowski, Ernst 166
Williamson, Jimmy 232
Wimbledon 223
Winton, H. de 11
Wise, Dennis 223
Wojcicki, Roman **167**
Wolverhampton Wanderers 45, 46, 173, 193, 222, 227
Women's World Championship 30
Woodward, Vivian 30
World Club Cup 36–8, 95–6, 119, 149, 151, 163
  1966–76 83, 89, 95, 148, 157
  1984–93 101
World Cup 14–27, 67, 70, 151
World Cup 1962 67
World Cup
  1930 14, 16, 52, 66, 67, 71, 95, 160
  1934 16, **16**, 52, 64, 73, 98, 133–4, 153
  1938 16–17, **17**, 160
  1950 17, 55, 71, 95–6, 117, 124, 160, 165, 227
  1954 18, **18**, 52, 65, 121, 155, 166, **166**
  1958 18–19, **19**, 56, 58, 64, 137–8, 141, 162, 236
  1962 19, 68, **68**, 119, 125, 148
  1970 21, 55, 119, 149, 156, 174
  1974 21–2, **21**, 60, **108**, 109, 130–1, 145, 151, 163, 232
  1978 22–3, **143, 152**, 154
  1982 23–4, **23**, 56, **59**, 60, 71, 73, 91, 134, **134**, 157, 167, **167**, 175
  1986 24, **24**, 52, **52**, **55**, **66**, **68**, **79**, 115, **167**, 176, **213**
  1990 195
  1994 26–7, **26**, **27**, 67, 72, **199**
  1998 56
  2002 74, 77, 78
  2006 218
World Cup War 225
World Footballer of the Year 126
World Player of the Year 148
World Youth Championship 30
World Youth Cup 115
Worns, Christian 29
Wrexham 236
Wright, Billy 117, 121, 166, **166, 170**, 227

Wright, José Roberto 88, 177

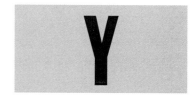

Y

Yashin, Lev 62, 94, 103, **113**, 117, 122–3, **122–3**
Yeats, Ron 47, 92
Yeboah, Anthony 86
Yekini, Rashidi 167, **167**
Yellow card 201
Yemen 79
Yorath, Terry 223
Young Boys, Bern 64
Yugoslavia 65, **65**, 136, 150
  European Championship 33, 177
  World Cup 16, 18, 19, 21, 168

Z

Zabrz, Gornik 60
Zagallo, Mario 67, 79, 203
Zaire 21, 34, 76
Zaki 75
Zalgris Vilnius 59
Zambia 35, 76, 225
Zamora, Ricardo 64, 98
Zarra, Telmo 158
Zico 67, 78, 88, 167, 176
Zidane, Zinedine **3**, 28, 29, **29**, 56, 167
Zimbabwe 76, **76**
Zizinho 124
Zmuda, Wladyslaw 60
Zoff, Dino **23**, 59, 91, 133–4, 167
Zola, Gianfranco 48
Zsengeller, Gyula 58
Zubeldia, Osvaldo 83
Zubizarreta, Andoni 28, 167, **167**

PHOTO CREDITS

The Publishers would like to thank the following sources for their kind permission to reproduce the pictures used in this publication:

Allsport/Shaun Botterill, Clive Brunskill, Simon Bruty, David Cannon, Chris Cole, Stu Forster, Mike Hewitt, David Leah, Gray Mortimore, Ben Radford; NS Barrett; Colorsport/Gadoffre, Rick Rickman, David Rogers, Norbert Rzepka, SIPA, Mark Thompson, Varley, Zabci; Empics; Mary Evans Picture Library; Hulton Deutsch Collection; Illustrated London News; Mirror Syndication International; Popperfoto Russell Boyce/Reuters; Sporting Pictures (UK) Ltd; Bob Thomas/Shaun Botterill, Clive Brunskill, Tony Feeder, Stuart Forster, Gamma-Barrault, David Joyner, Dave Rogers, Tempsport, Mark Thompson.

Thanks are also due to Matthew Impey at Colorsport and Andrew Wrighting at Bob Thomas. In addition a number of individuals very kindly loaned their memorabilia from their collections for special photography:
  p.207 tl P. Stacey – 1909 FA Cup Final shirt
  p.207 cl Charlie Mitten – 1948 FA Cup Final shirt
  p.207 bl Frank Stapleton – Brazil shirt
  p.207 tr Mrs I. Beevers – 1911 England Trials shirt
  p.207 cr Harry Gregg – 1960 Real Madrid goalkeeper's shirt
  p.208 t   Mrs I. Beevers – boots
  p.208 cl Alf Kirchen – 1936 socks
  p.209 tr Alf Kirchen – 1936 shin pads
  p.211 bl Mrs M. Whittaker – ball, 1958 FA Cup game
  p.211 tr Dennis Viollet – 1961 England cap
  p.211 cr George Wall – 1910 England cap
  p.211 br Tony Hurley – 1930 FA Cup-winner's medal

040–863